THE NORTH AMERICAN
FREE TRADE AGREEMENT

THE
NORTH AMERICAN
FREE TRADE AGREEMENT

A Comprehensive Guide

The Law Firm of
GOODMAN & GOODMAN
(*internationally* GOODMAN PHILLIPS & VINEBERG)

Jon R. Johnson
B.A., LL.B., LL.M.
of the Ontario Bar

Canada Law Book Inc.
240 Edward Street, Aurora, Ontario

Canadian Cataloguing in Publication Data

Johnson, Jon R. (Jon Ragnar), 1942

   The North American Free Trade Agreement

Includes index.

ISBN 0-88804-176-4

1. Canada. Treaties, etc. 1992 Oct. 7.
2. Free trade — United States. 3. Free trade — Canada.
4. Free trade — Mexico. I. Title.

KDZ944.A41992J6 1994   341.7′543   C94-932536-8

To

Patricia and Marion

PREFACE

When I wrote *The Free Trade Agreement: A Comprehensive Guide* with Joel Schachter in 1988, neither or us had any idea that the then-new Free Trade Agreement (FTA) would be superseded in five years by a more comprehensive agreement that included Mexico. However, the *North American Free Trade Agreement* (NAFTA) came into effect on January 1, 1994, and the FTA became history.

This book is based on the same two principles as its predecessor. First, understanding an agreement begins with the text of the agreement itself. Conclusions respecting the effect of an international agreement, whether by a lawyer, an economist, a political scientist, a business person or a journalist that are not based on an accurate understanding of the text of the agreement will be flawed. This book is primarily a guide to the NAFTA text and is intended as a starting point for anyone wishing to draw conclusions about NAFTA. Second, trade agreements such as the FTA and NAFTA do not exist in a vacuum. This is particularly true for NAFTA. Like the FTA, NAFTA is in many respects an extension of the *General Agreement on Tariffs and Trade* (GATT). However, the drafters of NAFTA adapted many provisions incorporated in the agreements arising from the Uruguay Round of GATT negotiations and the NAFTA text relies much more than the FTA on other international agreements, such as the intellectual property conventions referred to in NAFTA's intellectual property chapter and the international agreements respecting arbitration upon which the NAFTA investor/state dispute settlement procedures are based. This book attempts to place NAFTA in the context of the other international agreements to which it refers, upon which it is based and which affect its interpretation.

I would be remiss not to thank my publishers, Canada Law Book Inc., for their infinite patience in awaiting the completion of this book and their unfailing support while it was being written. I particularly thank Fran Cudlipp, Geralyn Christmas, Cheryl McPherson and Julia Raeside. Special thanks go to my partners at Goodman & Goodman for their encouragement. My thanks also to Dianne Haist and Mary Saulig of Goodman & Goodman's library for their assistance in research, Francis O'Connell and Colleen Robinson for the word processing and the formatting, and my secretary, Bonnie Parr, for her support. I would like also to thank the following people for their assistance: Bruce Oddson, David Zitzerman, Carrie Smit, John Loukidelis, Paul Collins, Jayne Kirton and Phil Taylor. Finally, I thank my wife, Patricia, and my mother, Marion, for their consistent encouragement and support.

The views expressed in this book are my own and are not in any way to be attributed to the Government of Canada. This book is intended to act as a guide to understanding NAFTA and should not be construed as legal advice of Goodman & Goodman.

Jon R. Johnson

NOTES TO THE READER

REFERENCES TO NAFTA AND THE FTA

The following system of reference to NAFTA and FTA provisions has been adopted in this book:

Reference	*Example*
Chapter of NAFTA or the FTA	NAFTA Chapter One or FTA Chapter One
Article of NAFTA or the FTA	NAFTA 101 or FTA 101
Paragraph of an Article of NAFTA or the FTA	NAFTA 104(1) or FTA 104(1)
Subparagraph of an Article of NAFTA or the FTA	NAFTA 104(1)(a) or FTA 301(3)(a)
Annex of NAFTA or the FTA	NAFTA Annex 104.1 or FTA Annex 301.2

References to the parts of each Annex conform generally to the reference system in that Annex.

REFERENCES TO THE GATT

The following system of reference to the GATT has been adopted:

Reference	*Example*
Article of the GATT	GATT Article XI
Paragraph of an Article of the GATT	GATT Article XI:2 or GATT Article XX(g)
Subparagraph of an Article of the GATT	GATT Article XXIV:8(b)

INTERNAL REFERENCES

Cross-references within this book are indicated by the symbol § followed by the relevant heading or subheading number.

GLOSSARY

Abbreviations and other terms and expressions used in this book are set out in the glossary.

DEFINITIONS IN NAFTA

As in the FTA, terms used in NAFTA are defined in a number of places and care must be taken when reading the NAFTA text to determine which terms are defined terms. NAFTA 201 contains seventeen defined terms and expressions used throughout NAFTA and NAFTA Annex 201.1 contains several country-specific definitions. Separate definitions, applicable only within a particular chapter, are found in the last article of the chapter. NAFTA makes extensive use of annexes and appendices to annexes and these include their own sets of definitions.

It is the practice in drafting commercial legal documents to capitalize defined expressions and to list all defined expressions in a definition section. NAFTA is not drafted in this manner and defined terms are not readily apparent. When analyzing any provision of NAFTA, reference must be made to NAFTA 201 and NAFTA Annex 201.1 and to the last article of the particular chapter or annex or appendix in which the provision appears to determine whether any of the words or phrases in the provision have a defined meaning as opposed to their plain meaning. Throughout this book, defined terms and expressions are explained as they are encountered. However, not all terms and expressions are covered and the reader is advised to review NAFTA 201, NAFTA Annex 201.1 and the definition section in the relevant chapter, annex or appendix before reaching a conclusion as to the meaning of any particular NAFTA provision.

TEXTS USED

Comments on NAFTA are based on the *North American Free Trade Agreement between the Government of Canada, the Government of the United Mexican States and the Government of the United States of America* published by the Minister of Supply and Services Canada, Ottawa, 1993. References to pages of Annexes I through to VII are based on the pagination set out in this NAFTA text. Comments on the Uruguay Round agreements are based on the Marrakesh text of April 15, 1994, unless otherwise indicated. Comments on the Environmental Cooperation Agreement in §6.9 and the Labour Cooperation Agreement in §6.10 are based on the text of those agreements set out in the *NAFTA Text including Supplemental agreements* published in 1994 by CCH Incorporated.

TABLE OF CONTENTS

CHAPTER 1

INTRODUCTION

1.1 INTRODUCTORY COMMENTS

The *Free Trade Agreement between Canada and the United States of America* (the "FTA") came into effect on January 1, 1989. The FTA was barely two years' old when Canada, the United States and Mexico began negotiating a trilateral free trade agreement which came to be known as the *North American Free Trade Agreement* ("NAFTA"). NAFTA was signed on December 17, 1992, by Prime Minister Brian Mulroney, President George Bush and President Carlos Salinas. The Bush administration was defeated in the presidential election of 1992. During the campaign, President Bill Clinton made his support of NAFTA contingent on improving several areas, most notably labour standards and the environment. These concerns resulted in the negotiation of side agreements, which were signed by the three NAFTA countries in September, 1993.

While the side agreements satisfied the concerns of the administration, they did not satisfy many Democratic members of Congress. The acrimonious national debate over NAFTA in the United States in some ways resembled the even more acrimonious national debate over the FTA that took place in Canada in 1988. The House of Representatives and the Senate approved the NAFTA implementing legislation in November, 1993, with the majority of Democrats in the House of Representatives voting against it.

The Canadian government enacted its implementing legislation in June, 1993. A federal election was held on October 25, 1993, and the ruling Progressive Conservative party was defeated by the Liberal party. The Liberals bitterly opposed the FTA in 1988 but had substantially modified their position by 1993. Unemployment and deficit reduction dominated the 1993 election campaign, and NAFTA was not a significant issue. During the campaign, the Liberal leader, Jean Chrétien, made his support of NAFTA contingent on improvements, including completing the FTA process of negotiating substitute antidumping and countervailing duty rules that NAFTA had dropped.[1] The NAFTA countries agreed to establish a Working Group to address antidumping and subsidy issues. The Canadian government proclaimed the implementing legislation into force in December, 1993.

Unlike the other two NAFTA countries, Mexico did not experience a change in government between the time that NAFTA was signed and its sched-

1

uled entry into effect. The Mexican Senate gave the required approval, and with the completion of approval procedures in all three NAFTA countries being complete, NAFTA became effective on January 1, 1994.

Like the FTA, NAFTA is a multi-faceted agreement that is inter-connected with other international agreements and cannot be read in a vacuum. However, NAFTA is much more complex than the FTA for a number of reasons. NAFTA has three parties rather than two, and while NAFTA is comprised largely of trilateral rules that apply equally to all three countries, in some sectors NAFTA breaks down into separate sets of bilateral arrangements. At the time that NAFTA became effective, Canada and the United States were already part way through their transition to free trade. Mexico's transition will proceed on a separate track. The inclusion of Mexico required the NAFTA negotiators to create provisions that tied into complex regulatory structures, such as the Mexican Automotive Decree, the U.S. sugar import rules and the international rules respecting textile and apparel restraint agreements.

NAFTA had to take into account future international trading rules that were in a state of flux because when NAFTA was signed the Uruguay Round negotiations were largely complete but still ongoing. The draft agreements arising from the *General Agreement on Tariffs and Trade* ("GATT") Uruguay Round covered areas never before addressed by GATT agreements. Like the FTA, NAFTA builds on GATT principles, and the draft Uruguay Round agreements established more principles from which to build. Drawing in part from these agreements and in part from concepts developed in other international arrangements, NAFTA covers areas such as investment, services and financial services more comprehensively than the FTA. Following the Uruguay Round lead, NAFTA extends into areas such as intellectual property which were untouched by the FTA.

The purpose of this book is to explain the provisions of NAFTA by fitting them into the overall structure of the agreement, explaining their origins and purpose, and describing their impact on existing laws and policy options open to government.

1.2   CANADA, THE UNITED STATES AND MEXICO

The United States is the focal point in the NAFTA relationship. Each of Canada and Mexico is bound by geography and trading relationships to the United States. The United States is overwhelmingly the largest trading partner of each of Canada and Mexico. Canada and Mexico are respectively the largest and third largest trading partners of the United States. However, Canada and Mexico are insignificant trading partners of each other.

There are significant disparities in the size of the three NAFTA countries.

The United States is the world's sole remaining superpower and is a very large country, both in terms of its population and its economy. Canada is the smallest NAFTA country in terms of population, with one tenth that of the United States and one third that of Mexico. Mexico is the smallest in terms of its economy. Measured in terms of gross domestic product, the Mexican economy is about half that of the Canadian, which in turn is about one tenth of that of the United States.

While Canada and the United States differ in size, their economies are at similar stages of development. Mexico, on the other hand, is a developing country, with wage and salary scales significantly below those in Canada and the United States. The real disparity in wages together with the perception of some in Canada and the United States that Mexico is a pollution haven have caused tension and will continue to be a source of tension among the NAFTA countries.

The historical relationships between the United States and the other two NAFTA countries have not been without difficulties. Canada and the United States have had a peaceful relationship for a long time and have many common interests. However, Canadian views on matters such as social policy differ significantly from American views, and many Canadians favour the "good fences make good neighbours" approach to Canada-U.S. relations. Mexico-U.S. relations have been less neighbourly. Much of the southwestern United States was at one time Mexican territory. Actions by Mexican governments, such as nationalizing the petroleum industry in the 1930s, have run directly contrary to American interests. Recent Mexican administrations have adopted much more market-oriented approaches to economic matters. Mexico became a party to the *General Agreement on Tariffs and Trade* in 1986. The Mexican government has unilaterally reduced trade barriers, deregulated large parts of its economy and embarked on an extensive privatization program. These steps have significantly improved Mexico-U.S. relations. However, significant problems continue along the Mexico-U.S. border in terms of illegal immigration, environmental degradation and drug trafficking. Canada-Mexico relations have been minimal. One positive effect of NAFTA has been to increase Canadians' and Mexicans' awareness of each other.

Canada and the United States are both democracies, although very different in structure. Canadians never cease to be baffled at the relationship between the U.S. President and his own party in Congress, which is in stark contrast to Canada's system of strict party discipline that confers near dictatorial powers on a Prime Minister with a parliamentary majority. Mexico has been ruled by the same political party for the last seventy years, but has a multi-party system and is moving towards democracy. Canadian and American legal systems are similar in that both are based on English common law principles.[2] Mexico's legal system is based on civil law principles. Canada and the United States have well-developed judicial systems and sophisticated regulatory structures covering such areas as taxation, securities, competition, trade remedies and the environment, with extensive cross-border communication between regulators and practitioners. The Mexican judicial system is not as well developed as its Canadian and American counterparts, and its regulatory structures are not as sophisticated. Many Mexicans see NAFTA as an impetus to upgrade Mexican political, judicial and regulatory structures.

While there are good reasons for the three NAFTA countries to develop closer economic relations, there is not the compelling need for co-operation among them that existed in post-war Europe and drove the countries of the European Union to create a common market. For various historical reasons, the governments of Canada, the United States and Mexico all have strong views on sovereignty and place a high priority on preserving it.

These relationships among the NAFTA countries have shaped the form of NAFTA and its substantive provisions.

1.3 INTERNATIONAL AGREEMENTS

Nations entering into international agreements subordinate their ability to pursue national objectives to governance by principles and, in some instances, by supranational institutions. In deciding whether to enter any international agreement, a nation must balance the surrender of sovereignty against the benefits of having the other countries that are party to the agreement adhere to the norms or institutional structure that the agreement establishes.

(1) Principles of Non-discrimination

The most-favoured-nation ("MFN") principle and the principle of national treatment are the two fundamental principles of non-discrimination that form the basis of many international agreements. The MFN principle requires that if a member state extends an advantage to another member state, it must extend the same advantage to all member states. The principle of national treatment requires that a member state treat goods or service providers or investors or nationals of other member states no less favourably than its own.

(2) Norms, Harmonization and Reciprocity

International agreements can also establish standards or norms to be followed by member states in their laws and regulations. Agreeing to standards entails a greater surrender of sovereignty than adhering to principles of non-discrimination. National treatment requires a member state to apply its laws in a non-discriminatory manner but it remains free to craft its laws as it sees fit. A member state agreeing to a standard must adjust its laws so that persons from other member states are treated according to that standard, even if that state has not applied that standard to its own nationals.

Harmonization goes a step beyond establishing standards. An agreement imposing standards leaves each member state free to determine how they are carried forward. An agreement to harmonize requires each member state to have identical laws or regulations in the areas covered by the agreement.

Reciprocity is a principle of mutual recognition. Each member state recognizes the regulatory actions of other member states as producing an acceptable result, even though the procedures followed may differ. Reciprocity is frequently coupled with the acceptance of standards. In the period following the adoption in 1985 by the European Union of the Single European Act (which formally commenced the 1992 initiative), considerable effort was made to harmonize regulations in a wide range of areas. This was a very difficult process because regulators in each member state had different ideas as to how the minutiae of regulatory detail was to be worded. Therefore, the European Commission adopted the practice of combining basic standards with a concept of mutual recognition so long as those standards were adhered to.

(3) Supranational Institutions

Many international agreements have no institutional structure. Others such as the treaties creating the European Union create elaborate institutional structures with power both to adjudicate and to legislate.

An institutional structure can make an international agreement much more effective. Disputes inevitably arise as to interpretation. Disputes can be left to be resolved through negotiations between the member states involved. Alternatively, the agreement can establish a means of resolving disputes, either through the creation of panels on an *ad hoc* basis, as under the GATT and the FTA, or through a formal institutional structure, as in the European Union. The adjudication can be treated as non-binding or binding. Dispute resolution is most effective through a permanent judicial body with the power to make binding decisions. However, effective dispute resolution of this sort entails a substantial surrender of sovereignty.

An international agreement can also be made more effective through the creation of a legislative body. Broad principles are stated in the agreement or treaty, and the legislative body fills in the details with regulations. The European Commission, the European Council of Ministers and the European Parliament collectively fulfil these functions. The advantage in creating supranational institutions with legislative power is that general principles set forth in a treaty can be effected through detailed regulations. Also, changes in circumstances can be accommodated without going through the difficult process of amending the treaty. Without a legislative body, general principles remain general and detailed provisions can become obsolete. Changes can be effected only through a formal amendment of the treaty. However, perhaps even more than with binding dispute resolution, creation of a supranational body with legislative powers entails a significant surrender of sovereignty.

(4) Arbitrary or Unjustifiable Discrimination and Disguised Restriction

Several NAFTA provisions are subject to the requirement that they not constitute "arbitrary or unjustifiable discrimination" or a "disguised restriction". As discussed in §4.3(5), the GATT Article XX exceptions to GATT obligations that are incorporated into NAFTA are subject to these qualifications. NAFTA 2101(2) applies identical qualifications to a rule of construction respecting the adoption by a NAFTA country of measures to enforce laws, including laws respecting health, safety and consumer protection, that are not inconsistent with NAFTA. NAFTA 712(4) and 712(6) require that sanitary and phytosanitary measures not "arbitrarily or unjustifiably discriminate" between the goods of the NAFTA country adopting the measure and goods of other NAFTA countries, or constitute a "disguised restriction on trade". NAFTA 907(2)(a) and 907(2)(b) use similar language respecting risk assessments.

In *World Trade and the Law of GATT*, published in 1969, Professor John Jackson stated that these qualifications were "so nebulous as to make exact definition impossible" and observed that there were few GATT decisions that considered the meaning of the language.[3] Several subsequent GATT decisions analyzed in a 1992 article by Jan Klabbers[4] have considered these expressions. Klabbers points out that no distinction is made between "arbitrary discrimination" and "unjustifiable discrimination", and that implicit in the concept of "arbitrary or unjustifiable discrimination" is the notion that some degree of discrimination is permitted, so long as it is not "arbitrary or unjustifiable".[5] Steve Charnovitz pointed out in a 1991 article that no measure has ever been found in breach of the "arbitrary or unjustifiable discrimination" condition.[6] Both Klabbers and Charnovitz report that the decisions involving "disguised restriction" have emphasized "disguised" rather that "restriction" with the result, which Klabbers views as illogical, that transparent restrictions are not caught by the language.[7]

Exact definition is still impossible. However, as "arbitrary or unjustifiable discrimination" and "disguised restriction" are GATT concepts, the meaning of these expressions will be guided by such GATT jurisprudence as is available.

1.4   THE GATT AND THE FTA

Like the FTA, NAFTA builds on the principles established under the GATT. Apart from tariff elimination, rules of origin, the elimination of duty drawback and provisions affecting areas of specific concern, the NAFTA trade in goods provisions are largely elaborations of principles to which Canada, the United States and Mexico are already bound under the GATT. However, unlike the FTA, NAFTA has been strongly influenced by concepts developed during the Uruguay Round of GATT negotiations.

(1) The GATT, the GATT Codes and the Uruguay Round

The history of the GATT is briefly set forth in §1.2 of *The Free Trade Agreement: A Comprehensive Guide* (*"Comprehensive Guide"*).[8] The GATT covers only trade in goods and is based primarily on the MFN and national treatment principles. The GATT itself does not eliminate tariffs, but successive rounds of GATT negotiations have resulted in the substantial reduction of tariffs on goods traded among GATT member states. The GATT does not create any formal institutional structure because at the time it was signed it was contemplated that the institutional structure would be provided through the International Trade Organization ("ITO"). However, the ITO never came into existence and an *ad hoc* structure developed under the GATT for the resolution of disputes.

The GATT itself has been amended very infrequently. However, during the Tokyo Round, which concluded in 1979, a major effort was made to address various non-tariff barriers to trade. As a consequence of the Tokyo Round, a number of separate codes were entered into by many GATT member states, covering such areas as government procurement, technical standards, valuation of goods for customs purposes, antidumping and subsidies.

The Uruguay Round of GATT negotiations, which commenced in 1986, was even more ambitious than the Tokyo Round. For the first time, areas such as services, investment and intellectual property became the subject-matter of a round of GATT negotiations. The Uruguay Round negotiators wished to develop a subsidies code that distinguished in a meaningful way those subsidies which are properly the target of countervailing duties from those which are not and, for the first time, to develop a formal institutional structure. The Uruguay Round negotiators also addressed difficult areas such as the trade in textiles, which is not subject to GATT disciplines, and agricultural subsidies. The text of these agreements that was available to the NAFTA negotiators is commonly referred to as the "Dunkel Text".[9]

At the time that the governments of Canada, the United States and Mexico agreed to negotiate NAFTA, it was anticipated that the Uruguay Round would be concluded before the NAFTA came into effect. However, the

Uruguay Round negotiations broke down in late 1991 over the intractable subject of agricultural subsidies. Negotiations continued for another two years and final agreement was reached in December, 1993. The GATT member countries will ratify the Uruguay Round agreements over the course of 1994 and these agreements are scheduled to take effect in 1995. The principal agreement resulting from the Uruguay Round negotiations is the *Agreement Establishing the World Trade Organization* ("WTO Agreement"). All the other Uruguay Round agreements are set out in annexes to the WTO Agreement. Unlike the Tokyo Round codes, the "Multilateral Trade Agreements" set out in Annexes 1A, 1B and 1C of the WTO Agreement are binding on all member countries. Four additional agreements set out in Annex 4 of the WTO Agreement are characterized as "Plurilateral Trade Agreements" and are binding only on those member countries that accept them. The WTO Agreement establishes the World Trade Organization ("WTO"), an entirely new institutional structure through which the Multilateral and Plurilateral Trade Agreements will be implemented and administered. The WTO will also serve as a forum for further negotiations and for the settlement of disputes. Annex 2 of the WTO Agreement sets out an understanding on rules and procedures governing the settlement of disputes and Annex 3 sets out a trade policy review mechanism.

The first Multilateral Trade Agreement in Annex 1A of the WTO Agreement is the "General Agreement on Tariffs and Trade 1994", or "GATT 1994". GATT 1994 is comprised of the provisions of the original GATT (referred to in the Uruguay Round agreements as "GATT 1947") as "rectified, amended or otherwise modified" by legal instruments which entered into force before the WTO Agreement.[10] The effect is to include in GATT 1994 the GATT jurisprudence developed since 1947. Some GATT provisions are modified or clarified in GATT 1994 by understandings.[11] GATT 1994 includes the protocols and certifications relating to tariff concessions negotiated in the successive rounds of GATT negotiations and the protocols under which various countries like Mexico that were not original signatories have become GATT members. However, GATT 1994 does not include the Protocol of Provisional Application discussed in §4.3(7)(b) or provisions in protocols of accession providing for provisional application of GATT obligations.[12] GATT 1994 also incorporates the waivers granted to GATT member countries under GATT Article XXV.[13]

The remaining Multilateral Trade Agreements set out in Annex 1A of the WTO Agreement are the *Agreement on Agriculture*, the *Agreement on Sanitary and Phytosanitary Measures*, the *Agreement on Textiles and Clothing*, the *Agreement on Technical Barriers to Trade*, the *Agreement on Trade-Related Investment Measures*, the *Agreement on the Implementation of Article VI* (antidumping duties), the *Agreement on the Implementation of Article VII* (customs valuation), the *Agreement on Preshipment Inspection*, the

Agreement on Rules of Origin, the *Agreement on Import Licensing Procedures*, the *Agreement on Subsidies and Countervailing Duties* and the *Agreement on Safeguards*. The two remaining Multilateral Trade Agreements set out in Annexes 1B and 1C are the *General Agreement on Trade in Services* and the *Agreement on Trade-Related Aspects of Intellectual Property, Including Trade in Counterfeit Goods*. The Plurilateral Agreements set out in Annex 4 are the *Agreement on Civil Aircraft*, the *Agreement on Government Procurement*, *International Dairy Arrangement* and the *Arrangement Regarding Bovine Meat*.

(2) Preferential Trading Arrangements

Both the FTA and NAFTA create preferential trading arrangements. Preferential trading arrangements are contrary to the MFN principle which requires that an advantage or preference given to one member state be extended to all member states. However, notwithstanding the MFN principle, the GATT permits two or more member states to form a customs union or a free trade area within the GATT. Both structures involve the elimination of tariffs on goods traded among the member states, but on different principles. The distinction between the two is significant because a number of the fundamental characteristics and consequent limitations of NAFTA flow from the fact that NAFTA, like the FTA, creates a free trade area and not a customs union.

A customs union is a preferential trading arrangement in which internal tariffs are eliminated and the member states form a single customs territory with a common external tariff. Once a good enters a member state and the common tariff is paid, the good is, theoretically at least, free to circulate from member state to member-state. One of the four freedoms that stand at the core of the European Union is the free movement of goods from member state to member state.[14] An objective of the 1992 initiative was to remove remaining impediments to the free movement of goods, such as border controls.

Tariffs are also eliminated on goods traded among the member states of a free trade area. However, a free trade area is a much less intrusive arrangement than a customs union because each member state retains its own tariff policy. A common tariff policy entails coordinated administration of a number of important areas of government policy. Rates of duties on and border measures applied to goods from all countries must be the same and policies respecting the application of trade remedies (antidumping and countervailing duties, safeguards) must be harmonized. Consider, for example, how Canada and the United States treat goods from the Peoples Republic of China ("PRC"). The United States allows goods from the PRC conditional MFN treatment. The PRC's MFN status must be renewed each year and since June

1989 the renewal has been contentious. Canada, on the other hand, allows PRC goods the unconditional benefit of Canada's General Preferential Tariff. A free trade area such as that created by the FTA permits these divergent policies. However, if Canada and the United States were members of a customs union, their policies respecting goods from countries such as the PRC, Cuba and Vietnam would have to be harmonized.

However, the free movement of goods from member state to member state, an achievable objective in a customs ur:on, is not possible in a free trade area because of the need to ascertain the origin of goods. The origin of a good imported from one member state to another must be determined because each member state applies its own rules to goods from non-member states ("third countries"). While it will not matter in which member state an imported good is produced or whether it is the combined product of several member states, customs officials of the importing member state will have to be satisfied that the good has not been produced in a third country and merely trans-shipped through the exporting member state. If the good is a material produced in a third country but used in the exporting member state in the production of a finished good, customs officials will have to be satisfied that the finished good is sufficiently different from the imported material so as to be considered a good of the exporting member state.

To answer questions such as this, an agreement creating a free trade area establishes rules of origin. For a good imported from one member state into another to receive preferential treatment, it must be "originating" under the rules of origin established for the free trade area. While goods traded among the member states in a free trade area may be free from tariffs, they are subject to origin determinations which impede the free movement of goods by imposing additional burdens on producers. The rules of origin created by the NAFTA are discussed in Chapter 3.

(3) The FTA

While NAFTA draws upon ideas developed in agreements developed in the negotiation of the Uruguay Round, the prime model for NAFTA is the FTA. The basic format of NAFTA closely follows that of the FTA and a number of the provisions of NAFTA have been designed to rectify difficulties experienced under the FTA.

The FTA created a free trade area comprised of Canada and the United States. Tariffs were to have been eliminated on all goods by January 1, 1998.[15] Typical of agreements creating free trade areas, the FTA established rules of origin for determining whether goods were "originating" and entitled to FTA benefits. While the FTA rules of origin were for the most part well conceived, they became the source of a number of acrimonious disputes between Canada and the United States, particularly in the contentious area of automotive goods. Duty drawback was to have been eliminated by January 1, 1994. The trade in goods provisions of the FTA incorporated certain GATT provisions (such as the national treatment provision in GATT Article III) and modified the use of others (such as the use of export controls). The FTA also addressed some areas of specific contention between the United States and Canada, both generally, such as Canada's duty remission programs, and in specific areas such as automotive goods, energy, agriculture and wine and distilled spirits. GATT rights were specifically reserved respecting a number of goods, including beer. Apart from antidumping and countervailing duty actions, the most intractable trade dispute that arose between Canada and the United States since the FTA came into effect has involved U.S. GATT rights respecting beer marketing practices in Ontario and several other provinces.

Emulating the Tokyo Round, the FTA took tentative steps in the area of technical barriers and government procurement. The FTA also addressed the application of the GATT safeguard provisions to Canada-U.S. trade and established a special safeguard remedy for import surges resulting from tariff elimination under the FTA.

The FTA was heralded as ground breaking in imposing disciplines respecting services and investment. In GATT terms the FTA was venturesome. However, in European Union terms and its concepts of the free movement of services, capital and people, the FTA services and investment provisions are very modest. The FTA services and investment chapters both relied heavily on the principle of national treatment but made no mention of the MFN principle. In the FTA investment chapter, norms were established in respect of certain matters such as minimum equity requirements, performance requirements and expropriation. However, other than requiring certain amendments to Canada's *Investment Canada Act*, the FTA grandfathered all non-conforming measures so long as they were not made more non-conforming. Moreover, only certain services were covered under the FTA services chapter and there were important exemptions from the requirements of the FTA investment chapter. To complement the services and investment chapters, the FTA liberalized rules for temporary entry for Canadian and American citizens into each others' countries. These rules fell far short of the European Union principle of free movement of people. The FTA addressed financial services, but merely by way of the exchange of certain specific concessions, and not by way of non-discrimination principles or setting standards.

One objective of the Canadian FTA negotiations was the negotiation of a subsidies code which would identify those subsidies against which countervailing duties could be levied. This objective was not achieved. However, the FTA created a unique binational panel process for resolving disputes arising out of antidumping and countervailing duty actions. These so called Chapter Nineteen provisions have been much more effective than anyone at the time ever expected.

The FTA did not create any institutional structure. For resolution of disputes not arising out of antidumping or countervailing duty actions, the FTA established *ad hoc* panel procedures. At the time of writing, only five matters had been resolved by these Chapter Eighteen panels.

The NAFTA negotiators used the FTA as their basic model. The FTA was also looked at by the NAFTA negotiators as the source of problems to be solved and agendas to be completed.

1.5 OVERVIEW OF NAFTA

Part One of NAFTA creates a free trade area comprised of Canada, the United States and Mexico, and sets forth matters of general application.

Part Two of NAFTA covers trade in goods. Tariffs on virtually all goods traded among Canada, the United States and Mexico will be eliminated within fifteen years. NAFTA creates new rules of origin modelled on the FTA rules, with modifications designed to rectify perceived deficiencies in the FTA rules and, for some goods, to narrow the concept of origin. Elimination of duty drawback and duty deferral will commence January 1, 1996, for goods traded between Canada and the United States and January 1, 2001, for goods traded with Mexico. FTA provisions respecting duty waivers are carried forward and, unlike the FTA, NAFTA establishes rules covering temporary entry of goods. NAFTA incorporates GATT Article III, prohibits export taxes and carries forward (subject to an exemption for Mexico) the FTA export control regime. Specific provisions are made for automotive goods, textile and apparel goods, agricultural goods, energy and basic petrochemical goods, and wine and distilled spirits. NAFTA contains safeguard provisions similar to those in the FTA, as well as special safeguards for textile and apparel goods.

Part Three of NAFTA covers technical barriers to trade. NAFTA sets forth more comprehensive standards provisions than the FTA. Part Two of NAFTA also sets out provisions respecting sanitary and phytosanitary measures that are largely based on the Dunkel Text.

Part Four of NAFTA covers government procurement. Unlike the FTA government procurement provisions, which covered only small procurements and left larger procurements to be governed by the GATT Government Procurement Code, the NAFTA government procurement provisions comprise a complete code.

Part Five of NAFTA covers investment, services and related matters. The NAFTA provisions respecting investment, services and financial services are more comprehensive than those of the FTA. The NAFTA investment provisions benefit a much wider range of investments than the FTA and entitle a broader range of persons to these benefits. The NAFTA investment chapter also incorporates investor/state dispute procedures which enable investors to recover damages and other limited forms of relief against governments of NAFTA countries that do not fulfil their NAFTA obligations. Unlike the FTA, the NAFTA services provisions are general in application and the NAFTA financial services provisions are principle-based rather than concession-based. The NAFTA investment, services and financial services do not contain general grandfathering provisions. Instead, NAFTA incorporates the General Agreement on Trade in Services ("GATS")[16] concept of reservations. Each Party must list those non-conforming measures that it will retain following NAFTA becoming effective. Some reservations contain timetables for phasing out non-conforming measures or making them less non-conforming. Part Five also contains an amended version of the FTA monopolies provision and new provisions respecting state enterprises and competition law.

Part Six of NAFTA covers intellectual property. Like the WTO Agreement and unlike the FTA, NAFTA contains a comprehensive code respecting intellectual property. The NAFTA intellectual property provisions prescribe minimum standards that must be carried forward in the domestic law of each NAFTA country.

Part Seven of NAFTA covers administrative and institutional provisions. Like the FTA, NAFTA does not create supranational institutions. Disputes in antidumping and countervailing duty actions will be handled in much the same way as under the FTA. Other disputes arising under NAFTA will be settled under NAFTA Chapter Twenty, which provides for an *ad hoc* panel procedure similar to that in FTA Chapter Eighteen.

Part Eight of NAFTA sets forth miscellaneous other provisions, which include exceptions for such matters as national security, taxation, balance of payments and cultural industries. Unlike the FTA, NAFTA contains an accession clause which provides for other countries to become signatories to NAFTA.

1.6 RELATION OF NAFTA WITH OTHER AGREEMENTS

Canada, the United States and Mexico are all parties to various bilateral and multilateral agreements which must co-exist with NAFTA. As under the FTA, there is the question as to which agreement applies in case of an inconsistency. Like the FTA, NAFTA establishes a basic rule of prevalence that is reversed in certain circumstances. However, the relationship of NAFTA with other agreements is more complex than that of the FTA because NAFTA relies upon other agreements for standard setting and procedural purposes.

(1) Basic Rule of Prevalence

NAFTA 103 sets forth the basic rule governing the relationship between NAFTA and other agreements. In NAFTA 103(1), the Parties affirm their existing rights and obligations under the GATT and other agreements. NAFTA 103(2) provides that if there is an inconsistency between NAFTA and another agreement, NAFTA prevails to the extent of the inconsistency, unless otherwise provided. The rights and obligations covered by this rule are those in effect when NAFTA became effective on January 1, 1994.

(2) Incorporation of GATT and FTA Provisions by Reference

NAFTA incorporates many provisions of both the GATT and the FTA by reference. Provisions of agreements incorporated by reference become part of the NAFTA text and are not subject to the rule of prevalence in NAFTA 103.

NAFTA 301 incorporates GATT Article III (the GATT national treatment provision) and its interpretative notes. NAFTA 309 incorporates GATT Article XI (import and export restrictions) and its interpretative notes. The FTA merely affirmed this GATT provision but did not incorporate it. NAFTA 603(1) incorporates the GATT provisions respecting prohibitions or restrictions on trade in energy and basic petrochemical goods. Article 2101 incorporates GATT Article XX (exceptions) and its interpretative notes. The application of these incorporated provisions is sometimes modified by NAFTA. For example, NAFTA 710 provides that incorporated GATT Articles III, XI and XX do not apply to sanitary or phytosanitary measures. NAFTA 315 restricts the application of GATT Articles XI:2(a), XX(g), XX(i) and XX(j), but NAFTA 2101 expands the meaning of the exceptions contained in GATT Articles XX(b) and (g).

Unlike the FTA, NAFTA does not incorporate the *GATT Agreement on Government Procurement* because of the enlarged scope of the NAFTA government procurement chapter.

As between Canada and the United States, NAFTA incorporates many FTA provisions. NAFTA Annex 302.2 incorporates the FTA Tariff Schedules of Canada and the United States for tariff elimination purposes. NAFTA Annex 302.2 also incorporates FTA 401(7) and 401(8) (concessionary rates and temporary reductions). NAFTA Annex 304.2 incorporates FTA 405 (duty waivers). Section A of NAFTA Annex 312.2 incorporates the FTA provisions respecting wine and distilled spirits. NAFTA Appendix 300-A.1 incorporates certain provisions of FTA Chapter Ten (automotive goods). Appendix 5.1 of NAFTA Annex 300-B incorporates FTA 407 (import and export restrictions) solely in respect of certain safeguard procedures respecting textile and apparel goods. NAFTA Annex 608.2 incorporates FTA Annexes 902.5 and

905.2 (import, export and certain regulatory measures respecting energy goods). NAFTA Annex 702.1 incorporates FTA 701, 702, 704, 705, 706, 707, 710 and 711 respecting agricultural goods. NAFTA Annex 801.1 incorporates FTA 1101 (safeguards). NAFTA Annex 1401.4 incorporates FTA 1702(1) and (2) (commitments of the United States respecting financial services). NAFTA Annex 2106 incorporates the entire FTA regime respecting cultural industries.

The technique of incorporating FTA provisions by reference can be convoluted. For example, NAFTA Appendix 300-A.1 states that notwithstanding the incorporation of certain FTA automotive provisions, the NAFTA rules of origin apply. NAFTA Annex 801.1, incorporating the safeguard provision in FTA 1101, also contains a clarification respecting origin. However, NAFTA Annex 702.1 incorporates virtually the entire FTA chapter on trade in agricultural goods but is silent as to whether the expression "originating" used in the incorporated provisions means "originating" under the FTA or NAFTA rules of origin.[17] NAFTA Annex 801.1 is unclear as to whether the procedures set forth in NAFTA 803 to be followed in safeguard actions are to apply to safeguard actions to which the incorporated FTA 1101 applies.

NAFTA makes no specific reference to FTA 2006 (retransmission rights) or to FTA 2007 (print-in-Canada requirements). However, as discussed in §10.1, the effect of the cultural exemption set forth in NAFTA Annex 2106 is to incorporate these FTA provisions.

(3) Use by NAFTA of Other Agreements

Like the FTA, NAFTA 1902(2)(d)(i) requires that amendments to antidumping or countervailing duty laws not be inconsistent with the GATT, the *Agreement on Implementation of Article VI of the General Agreement on Tariffs and Trade* ("Antidumping Code") or the *Agreement on the Interpretation and Application of Articles VI, XVI and XXIII of the General Agreement on Tariffs and Trade* ("Subsidies Code").[18] Also like the FTA, but with greater precision, NAFTA requires that measures respecting balance of payments difficulties taken pursuant to the exception in NAFTA 2104 be consistent with the *Articles of Agreement of the International Monetary Fund* ("IMF Agreement").[19]

However, NAFTA relies more than the FTA on other international agreements for its meaning and substance. Certain definitions in NAFTA depend for their meaning on other international agreements or the activities of international organizations. For example, the meaning of "nationals of another Party" in NAFTA 1721 depends upon a number of international intellectual property conventions. The definition of "international standard, guideline or recommendation" in NAFTA 724 means standards, guidelines or recommendations adopted by specifically identified international organizations.

NAFTA uses procedural rules and institutional structures established in other international agreements. The investor state dispute settlement procedures set forth in Section B of NAFTA Chapter Eleven are based upon the *Convention on the Settlement of Investment Disputes between States and nationals of other States* ("ICSID Convention"), the *Inter-American Convention on International Commercial Arbitration* ("Inter-American Convention"), the *United Nations Convention on the Recognition and Enforcement of Foreign Arbitral Awards* ("New York Convention") and the arbitration rules of the United Nations Commission on International Trade Law ("UNCITRAL Arbitration Rules").

NAFTA requires that the NAFTA countries give effect to certain international agreements. For example, NAFTA 1701.2 requires the Parties to give effect to certain international conventions respecting intellectual property rights. NAFTA 1710 requires the Parties to protect integrated circuits in accordance with certain articles of the *Treaty on Intellectual Property in Respect of Integrated Circuits.*

None of these agreements is incorporated into the NAFTA and the NAFTA rule of prevalence is not reversed in respect of any of them. Accordingly, if any of these agreements is inconsistent with NAFTA, NAFTA prevails to the extent of the inconsistency.

(4) The Fate of the FTA

The governments of Canada and the United States have agreed that upon NAFTA becoming effective, the FTA will be suspended. If NAFTA is terminated or if one of Canada or the United States withdraws, the FTA will resume. With the FTA suspended, there will be no question as to which of the FTA and NAFTA prevails. For all practical purposes, the FTA, except as incorporated into NAFTA or as continued by collateral agreement by Canada and the United States, will cease to exist.

There are some curious omissions from the FTA provisions incorporated into NAFTA. For example, while FTA 401(7) and 401(8) (concessionary rates and temporary reductions) are incorporated, FTA 401(6), which allows U.S. goods the continuing benefit of treatment under Canada's Machinery Program, is not. NAFTA does not incorporate FTA 2008 (plywood standards). Presumably it is intended that, as between Canada and the United States these provisions continue and the agreement between Canada and the United States suspending the FTA will so provide.

(5) Specific Affirmation of Certain GATT Provisions

Like the FTA, NAFTA 903 affirms the rights and obligations of the Parties under the *GATT Agreement on Technical Barriers to Trade.* Affirmation is not incorporation by reference. This Tokyo Round GATT code does not become part of NAFTA and, because the rule of prevalence is not reversed, NAFTA prevails if there is an inconsistency.[20]

(6) Subsequent Agreements

(a) Covered by specific NAFTA provisions

NAFTA recognizes that the GATT and certain other international agreements may be amended as a result of the Uruguay Round and takes into account some of these future changes. For example, NAFTA 301, NAFTA 309 and NAFTA 2101, which respectively incorporate GATT Articles III, IX and XX and their interpretative notes, also incorporate "any equivalent provision of a successor agreement to which all Parties are party". NAFTA 1902(2)(d) discussed in §11.4 makes specific reference to successor agreements to the Antidumping Code and the Subsidies Code which are the *Agreement on the Implementation of Article VI* and the *Agreement on Subsidies and Countervailing Duties* mentioned in §1.4(1). NAFTA Annex 300-B, Section 1(2) provides that NAFTA prevails if there is an inconsistency between NAFTA and the *Arrangement Regarding International Trade in Textiles* ("Multifibre Arrangement") discussed in §5.2(3)(a). However, NAFTA Annex 300-B, Section 3(2) requires the NAFTA countries to eliminate any restriction respecting textile and apparel goods permitted by NAFTA, but required to be eliminated under any successor agreement to the Multifibre Arrangement.[21] The Uruguay Round successor agreement to the Multifibre Arrangement is the *Agreement on Textiles and Clothing* mentioned in §1.4(1). As discussed in §4.7(4), NAFTA 802 sets out rules respecting the application among the NAFTA countries of "any safeguard agreement" pursuant to GATT Article XIX. When the Uruguay Round agreements become effective, the safeguard agreement referred to in NAFTA 802 will be the *Agreement on Safeguards* mentioned in §1.4(1). NAFTA 2005 sets out rules governing the relationship between the dispute settlement procedures in NAFTA Chapter Twenty and those under the GATT and its successor agreements, which will include the WTO Agreement and the *Understanding on Rules and Procedures Governing the Settlement of Disputes* when the Uruguay Round agreements become effective. The relationship between NAFTA and these Uruguay Round agreements will be governed by these NAFTA provisions.

(b) Rule in the Vienna Convention

As mentioned in §1.6(1), the basic rule of prevalence in NAFTA 103(2) applies to rights and obligations existing on January 1, 1994. There is no general rule of prevalence covering rights and obligations under agreements becoming effective after January 1, 1994. The rights and obligations under the Uruguay Round agreements mentioned in §1.4(1) will not become effective until some time in 1995. Accordingly, none of these is affected by the basic rule of prevalence in NAFTA 103(2). Article 30 of the *Vienna Convention on the Law of Treaties*[22] provides that an earlier treaty applies only to the extent that its provisions are compatible with those of a later treaty to which all the parties to the earlier treaty are party. This rule will apply to agreements among the NAFTA countries that become effective after January 1, 1994, including those Uruguay Round agreements that are not incorporated into NAFTA or whose relationship with NAFTA is not specifically covered by a NAFTA provision.

Issues of incompatibility are most likely to occur with NAFTA provisions such as those respecting sanitary and phytosanitary measures, standards-related measures and intellectual property that have parallel but somewhat different counterparts in Uruguay Round agreements. It should be kept in mind, however, that differently worded provisions are not necessarily incompatible. While a more onerous provision in a later agreement is clearly incompatible with a less onerous provision in an earlier agreement, it does not follow that a more onerous provision in an earlier agreement is incompatible with a less onerous provision in a later one, particularly when the later agreement involves more parties than the earlier one. In this latter case, it would not be unreasonable to conclude that the more onerous provision of the earlier agreement continues to apply as among the parties to it and the less onerous provision applies as between each of those parties and the parties to the later agreement who were not parties to the earlier one. In any event, the question as to whether a NAFTA provision or a provision of Uruguay Round agreement applies in a dispute between NAFTA countries will largely depend on the forum for dispute resolution chosen or otherwise determined under NAFTA 2005.

(7) Retention of Rights

Like the FTA, NAFTA identifies certain GATT rights retained by the Parties. Following FTA 1102, NAFTA 802 provides that the Parties retain their rights and obligations under GATT Article XIX (safeguards). The retention of GATT rights in FTA 710 (agriculture) is incorporated by reference by NAFTA Annex 702.1. The retention of rights in FTA 807 (wine and distilled spirits) is incorporated by NAFTA Annex 312.2, and NAFTA Annex 312.2(6) contains a similar retention of rights as between Canada and Mexico. As under the FTA, these retentions are all qualified by NAFTA requirements or to FTA requirements incorporated into NAFTA.

The FTA retained without qualification the Parties' GATT rights in respect of raw logs, unprocessed fish and beer.[23] NAFTA carries forward the exceptions for raw logs and unprocessed fish but GATT rights are not retained.

The FTA exception for beer and malt containing beverage does not appear in NAFTA.

(8) Exceptions to the Basic Rule of Prevalence

NAFTA reverses the basic rule of prevalence in some cases. NAFTA 104 provides that certain international conventions respecting the environment prevail over NAFTA. Like the FTA, NAFTA Annex 608.2(2) provides that if NAFTA is inconsistent with the *Agreement on an International Energy Program* ("IEP"), the IEP prevails. NAFTA 2103 provides that if there is an inconsistency between NAFTA and a tax convention, the tax convention prevails. The reversal of the rule of prevalence in FTA 405(4) is carried forward into NAFTA as between Canada and the United States because of its incorporation under NAFTA Annex 304.2.

There is no NAFTA equivalent to FTA 1608(3) which provides that nothing in the FTA investment chapter affects the Parties' rights under the GATT or other agreements. In fact, in incorporating the GATT Article XX exceptions, NAFTA 2101 has the opposite effect by providing that they do not apply to services or investment.

1.7 NAFTA AND STATE AND PROVINCIAL GOVERNMENTS

Canada, the United States and Mexico are all federal states. Canada has ten provinces, each with its own legislature and exclusive areas of jurisdiction. The United States has fifty states and Mexico has thirty-one states. Each one of these states has its own government. NAFTA is an agreement among the federal governments of Canada, the United States and Mexico. No province or state is a party to it.

NAFTA 105 requires each of Canada, the United States and Mexico to ensure that all necessary measures are taken by provincial and state governments to ensure compliance with NAFTA. This is a stronger obligation than that contained in GATT Article XXIV:12. Provincial measures have been the subject of several GATT panels. Canada has never been successful in persuading a panel that it had satisfied GATT Article XXIV:12 in respect of the measure.

Provinces and states are exempt from some provisions of NAFTA, such as government procurement. In other instances, provinces and states are subject to a more lenient rule than their federal counterparts. For example, states and provinces have a period of time to list their reservations to the obligations under the investment, services and financial services chapters. In yet other instances, the federal government obligation to "ensure compliance" is replaced with the somewhat less onerous obligation to "seek, through appropriate measures, to ensure observance".[24] The NAFTA text must be read carefully to determine whether an exemption for provinces and states applies or whether the obligation in NAFTA 105 has been modified.

ENDNOTES

[1] See FTA 1906 and compare it to NAFTA 1907(2). See also *Creating Opportunity: The Liberal Plan for Canada* (Ottawa, Liberal Party of Canada, 1993), at p. 24. Besides antidumping and subsidies codes, the list of matters to be renegotiated includes "a more effective dispute resolution mechanism" and "the same energy protection as Mexico".

[2] The laws of the Province of Quebec and the State of Louisiana are based on civil law principles.

[3] John H. Jackson, *World Trade and the Law of GATT* (Indianapolis, Bobbs-Merrill Co., 1969), at p. 744.

[4] Jan Klabbers, "Jurisprudence in International Trade: Article XX of GATT", 26 *Journal of World Trade* 63 (April 1992).

[5] *Ibid.*, pp. 89-90.

[6] Steve Charnovitz, "Exploring the Environmental Exceptions in GATT Article XX", 25 *Journal of World Trade* 37 (October 1991), at p. 47.

[7] Klabbers, *op. cit.*, note 4, at p. 91; Charnovitz, *op. cit.*, note 6, at p. 38.

[8] Jon R. Johnson and Joel S. Schachter, *The Free Trade Agreement: A Comprehensive Guide* (Aurora, Canada Law Book Inc., 1988), at p. 2.

[9] After Arthur Dunkel, the Director General of GATT during the Uruguay Round of negotiations. See *"The Dunkel Draft" from the GATT Secretariat*, collected and edited by The Institute for International Legal Information (Buffalo, N.Y., Wm. S. Hein & Co., Inc., 1992).

[10] References to the "GATT" in this book are to the original *General Agreement on Tariffs and Trade* and not to GATT 1994.

[11] These are: Article II:1(b) respecting "other duties or charges" in connection with schedules of tariff concessions; Article XVII respecting state trading enterprises; Articles XII and XVIII:B respecting balance of payments; Article XXIV respecting the creation of customs unions and free trade areas; Article XXVIII respecting the modification or withdrawal of concessions; and Article XXXV respecting non-application between particular contracting parties. There is also an understanding respecting the granting of waivers.

[12] Paragraph 1(e) of the general interpretative note to Annex 1A of the WTO Agreement provides that the provisions of Part II of GATT 1994 do not apply to measures taken under mandatory legislation prior to the time that a member became a contracting party to GATT 1947 in respect of foreign-built reconstructed vessels.

[13] The waivers are listed in Note 7 referred to in paragraph 1(b)(iii) of the general interpretative note to Annex 1A of the WTO Agreement. The waiver granted to the United States in respect of s. 22 of the Agricultural Adjustment Act, 3d Supp. BISD 32 (1955), is not included on the list.

[14] The other three freedoms are the free movement of services, the free movement of capital and the free movement of people.

[15] Subject only to the "snapback" provisions for certain fresh fruits and vegetables set forth in FTA 702. Under these provisions, if certain conditions are met, temporary duties may be imposed on these goods. This right expires on December 31, 2008.

[16] See The Dunkel Draft, *op. cit.*, note 9, at Annex II, pp. 1-56.

[17] This issue is discussed in §5.3(4)(c).

[18] *Comprehensive Guide* includes FTA 1902(2)(d)(i) under the exceptions to the basic rule of prevalence. FTA 1902(2)(d)(i) and its virtually identical NAFTA counterpart, NAFTA 1902(2)(d)(i), do not reverse the rule of prevalence. Rather, they use the Antidumping and Subsidies Codes to set standards to which amendments of AD/CVD laws must conform.

[19] The balance of payments provision in FTA 2002 also refers to the *1961 OECD Code of Liberalization of Capital Movements*. NAFTA 2104 does not refer to this agreement.

[20] This Tokyo Round GATT code will be replaced by the *Agreement on Technical Barriers to*

Trade mentioned in §1.4(1) when the Uruguay Round agreements become effective. As discussed in §6.7, the rule of prevalence in NAFTA 103 does not apply to this Uruguay Round agreement.

[21] This provision is discussed in §5.2(3)(d).

[22] *Vienna Convention on the Law of Treaties*, May 23, 1969, 8 I.L.M. 679. As discussed in note 2 of Chapter 4, the United States is not a signatory to the Vienna Convention but recognizes its principles.

[23] See FTA 1205 for the retention of GATT rights. See NAFTA Annex 301.3 for the exceptions for raw logs and unprocessed fish.

[24] For example, see NAFTA 606(2) respecting energy regulatory measures and NAFTA 902(2) respecting standards-related measures. As noted in §6.6(2), "seek" means to "try to bring about or effect" and has been interpreted in an FTA Chapter 18 binational panel decision as imposing a "best efforts" obligation.

CHAPTER 2

TRADE IN GOODS: TARIFF MEASURES

Chapters 2 to 5 of this book deal with Part Two of NAFTA, "Trade in Goods". This chapter covers tariffs, duty drawback, duty waivers, temporary entry of goods and various other border measures. Chapter 3 covers the NAFTA rules of origin, country of origin rules and customs procedures. Chapter 4 covers national treatment, import and export measures and safeguard procedures. Chapter 5 covers special provisions respecting automotive goods, textiles and apparel, agriculture, energy and basic petrochemicals, and wine, beer and distilled spirits.

2.1 TARIFF STRUCTURES OF CANADA, THE UNITED STATES AND MEXICO

The tariff schedules of each of Canada, the United States and Mexico are based on the Harmonized Commodity Description and Coding System ("Harmonized System" or "HS"). The Harmonized System has been adopted by many countries under the *International Convention on the Harmonized Commodity Description and Coding System* and is now used for classifying goods in schedules of GATT tariff concessions. The draft agreements resulting from the Uruguay Round negotiations refer to goods in terms of the Harmonized System.

The Harmonized System is divided into sections covering broad categories of goods. Each section is broken down into chapters, which in turn are further broken down into headings and subheadings. The numbering system in the Harmonized System is based on the chapter (first two digits), heading (first four digits) and subheading (first six headings) within which a good falls. The tariff schedule of a country applying the Harmonized System classifies each good under a tariff item. A tariff item is a number with eight or more digits, the first six of which correspond to the six digit number of the HS subheading under which the good falls. The classification of goods by all countries that have adopted the Harmonized System is identical down to the six digit subheading level. Harmonization ceases below the subheading level and each country develops its own tariff items. The Harmonized System contains general rules of interpretation, as well as additional rules that appear at the beginning of sections and chapters. Individual countries supplement these with their own rules of interpretation.

Consider the classification of caviar in the Harmonized Systems in each of Canada, the United States and Mexico. In the Canadian Harmonized System, caviar and caviar substitutes all fall under tariff item 1604.30.00. The first two digits indicate Chapter 16, which is "Preparations of Meat, of Fish or of Crustaceans, Molluscs or Other Aquatic Invertebrates". The first four digits indicate heading 16.04, which is "Prepared or preserved fish; caviar and caviar substitutes prepared from fish eggs". The first six digits indicate subheading 1604.30, which is "Caviar and caviar substitutes". The Canadian Harmonized System has only one tariff item under this subheading, and does not break it down further. In the U.S. Harmonized System, this subheading is broken down into three tariff items, 1604.30.20 (caviar), 1604.30.30 (caviar substitutes, boiled and in airtight containers), and 1604.30.40 (caviar substitutes, other). In the Mexican Harmonized System, this subheading is broken down into two tariff items, 1604.30.01 (caviar) and 1604.30.99 (other).

Like the FTA, many provisions of NAFTA are based on the Harmonized System. Unlike the FTA, NAFTA makes frequent reference to individual tariff items as well as Harmonized System chapters, headings and subheadings. References in this book to "headings" and "subheadings" are to headings and subheadings of the Harmonized System. These references are not country specific because HS headings and subheadings are the same in all three countries. References to tariff items are country specific because they differ among the NAFTA countries.

(1) The Canadian Tariff Structure

Before NAFTA became effective, the *Customs Tariff* set out four different rates of duty. The MFN Tariff applies to all GATT members. The British Preferential Tariff applies to certain goods imported from Commonwealth countries other than the United Kingdom. The General Preferential Tariff ("GPT") applies to goods imported from many developing countries, including Mexico. When the FTA came into effect, Canada created the United States Tariff ("UST") for goods from the United States. The General Tariff, set at a flat rate of 35%, applies to goods imported from a few non-GATT countries with which Canada does not have special trading arrangements. Canada also admits goods duty free from certain Caribbean countries and from the least developed developing countries.

(2) The United States Tariff Schedule

The United States adopted the Harmonized System on January 1, 1989, and the U.S. tariff schedule is now called the Harmonized Tariff System of the United States ("HTSUS"). The HTSUS provides for a variety of tariff treatments. The MFN rate, which appears in the HTSUS subcolumn headed

"General", applies to all GATT members and a number of non-GATT members to which MFN status has been accorded. Special HTSUS tariff treatments are identified in the HTSUS subcolumn marked "Special". The Generalized System of Preferences ("GSP") applies to most developing countries, and applied to Mexican goods until NAFTA became effective.[1] Goods imported from developing countries designated as "least developed developing countries" receive duty free treatment. The Caribbean Basin Initiative applies to most Caribbean countries. The United States-Canada Free Trade Agreement designation identifies the rate applicable to goods from Canada under the U.S. FTA schedule. The United States-Israel Free Trade Agreement applies to goods from Israel. The Andean Trade Preference Act applies to goods from Bolivia and Columbia. The HTSUS Column 2 rate applies to countries not entitled to the MFN rate or any of the special rates. The HTSUS Column 2 rates vary from good to good, but most are very high.[2]

HTSUS Chapter 98 sets out special classification provisions, including in particular the outward processing rules set out in tariff items 9802.00.60 and 9802.00.80 that are discussed in §2.3(1)(b)(ii). HTSUS Chapter 99 sets out certain temporary measures and import restrictions. Subchapter II sets forth temporary reductions in rates of duty. While most of these have expired, the reductions continue for a number of specified goods originating in Canada.[3] The U.S. temporary reductions are discussed under §2.8. Subchapter III sets forth temporary modifications pursuant to trade legislation. Most notable is tariff item 9903.87.00 that imposes a 25% duty on most trucks. Trucks originating in Canada under the FTA rules of origin enter duty free and are not subject to this duty.[4] Subchapter IV sets out the import fees and quantitative restrictions established under Section 22 of the Agricultural Adjustment Act. These are discussed in §5.3(2)(b)(i).

(3) The Mexican Tariff Schedule

Like the tariff schedules of Canada and the United States, the tariff schedule of Mexico is based on the Harmonized System. The Mexican tariff schedule corresponds to that of Canada and the United States down to the six digit subheading level. As with the other two schedules, the Mexican tariff schedule sets out its own individual tariff items.

The Mexican MFN rate applies to goods from both Canada and the United States. While Mexican duty rates have been significantly reduced in recent years, they are on average significantly higher than those in Canada or the United States.

2.2   TARIFF ELIMINATION

As under the FTA, the NAFTA tariff elimination provisions apply to "customs duties". NAFTA 318 defines this expression in much the same manner as FTA 410. Customs duties include customs or import duties imposed on the importation of goods, including surcharges but not including internal taxes, such as Canada's goods and services tax, antidumping and countervailing duties, importation fees commensurate with the cost of service and certain fees applied under the U.S. Agricultural Adjustment Act ("AAA"). [5]

(1) Elimination of Duties

By the year 2008 NAFTA will eliminate duties on virtually all goods traded among the three NAFTA countries.[6] Elimination of duties will apply only to goods that are "originating" under the NAFTA rules of origin (described in Chapter 3).[7]

Elimination of duties under NAFTA is complicated by the fact that Canada and the United States have partially completed eliminating duties under the FTA. For trade between Canada and the United States, the elimination of duties will continue as under the FTA while for Mexican trade with each of Canada and the United States, NAFTA creates entirely new schedules for the elimination of duties. As under the FTA, the NAFTA rules of origin do not identify the country of origin of goods. However, until duties for a good are "free" under all schedules, it will be necessary to determine whether that good is "Canadian", "American" or Mexican" to ascertain which schedule applies. The general rules for determining country of origin are described in §3.3. The determination of the country of origin of textile and apparel goods is described in §5.2(4) and of agricultural goods in §5.3(4).

There are some special bilateral arrangements respecting the elimination of duties on agricultural goods that will be described in §5.3.

(2) The FTA Schedules

NAFTA incorporates the Schedules of Canada and the United States set out in FTA Annex 401.2 ("FTA Schedules").[8] Under the FTA Schedules, the only goods still subject to duties are those in FTA staging category C. Duties on these goods were reduced to one-half[9] their pre-FTA levels at the beginning of 1993, and duties will be completely eliminated by January 1, 1998. Duties on all other goods have been eliminated.

Under NAFTA, tariff elimination as between Canada and the United States continues on the FTA Schedules. However, goods will have to satisfy the NAFTA rules of origin to be eligible, and the FTA rules will no longer apply. Canada will apply the FTA Schedule of Canada to originating goods that are "American" and such goods will be eligible for Canada's UST rate. The United States will apply the FTA Schedule of the United States to originating goods that are "Canadian".

(3) The NAFTA Schedules

NAFTA Annex 302.2 sets forth a Schedule of Canada, a Schedule of the United States and a Schedule of Mexico ("NAFTA Schedules"). These schedules apply to Mexican trade with each of Canada and the United States. As under the FTA Schedules, for goods for which elimination of duties is not immediate, the NAFTA Schedules combine a base rate with a staging category to arrive at a rate of duty that will apply for each year during which the duty is being phased out. The base rate establishes the starting point for duty elimination and the staging category sets forth the annual stages over which the base rate is to be reduced and ultimately eliminated. With a few exceptions, the rate resulting from the application of a staging category to a base rate is rounded down to the nearest tenth of a percentage point, or for duties expressed as currency units, to the nearest .001 of the applicable currency unit.

The NAFTA provides four basic staging categories that apply to the vast majority of goods in all three schedules. Following the FTA format, these are:

Category A: Duties on goods in staging category A will be eliminated immediately upon NAFTA becoming effective.

Category B: Duties on goods in staging category B will be eliminated in five equal stages, with complete elimination on January 1, 1998.

Category C: Duties on goods designated in staging category C will be eliminated in ten equal stages, with complete elimination on January 1, 2003.

Category D: Goods designated in staging category D are goods that were previously duty free and will continue to be duty free.[10]

(4) The NAFTA Schedule of Canada

Canada will apply the NAFTA Schedule of Canada to originating goods that are not "American".

For goods other than agricultural goods[11] and textile and apparel goods,[12] the NAFTA Schedule of Canada is split into Columns I and II. If a good is "Mexican", duties are eliminated under Column I and the resulting tariff is the "Mexico Tariff". If it is neither "American" nor "Mexican" (such as a good of mixed origin produced from U.S. materials and assembled in a Mexican maquiladora plant) duties are eliminated under Column II and the resulting tariff is the "Mexico-United States Tariff".[13] Column II does not apply to agricultural, textile or apparel goods. These goods are either "American" and entitled to FTA treatment or "Mexican" and entitled to Column I treatment. The *Customs Tariff* has been amended to include these two additional tariffs.

(a) Base rates

The base rate under Column I for each good is the Canadian GPT rate in effect on July 1, 1991, if there was one, and the Canadian MFN rate if there was not.[14]

For many goods, the Column II rate for each year is the higher of the GPT rate in effect on July 1, 1991, reduced in accordance with the applicable staging category and the applicable UST rate.[15] For most of these goods, the July 1991 GPT rate exceeded the UST applicable in 1993, so the base rate is the GPT rate. For these goods the base rate is the same as the Column I base rate and the tariff treatment under each column is the same. However, there are some goods for which the 1993 UST rate exceeded the GPT rate. For these goods, the commencing Column II rate corresponds to the UST rate.

For the remaining goods to which Column II applies, the base rate is the MFN rate in effect on July 1, 1991.[16]

(b) Staging categories

The staging categories for most goods in the NAFTA Schedule of Canada are categories A, B, C and D described above. However, some additional staging categories have been created.

(i) Textile and apparel goods

In addition to the staging categories described above, NAFTA Annex 300-B (Textile and Apparel Goods) sets out two special staging categories that apply to most originating textile and apparel goods imported from Mexico into Canada. These categories are:

Category B*l*: Duties on goods designated in staging category B*l* will be eliminated in six equal annual stages, with complete elimination of duty on January 1, 1999.[17]

Category B+ : Duties on goods designated in staging category B+ will be eliminated in seven stages. On NAFTA becoming effective, the rate is reduced to eight-tenths of the base rate. On January 1st of each of 1996 to 1999, the rate will be reduced by one-tenth of the base rate, and on January 1, 2000, by a further two-tenths of the base rate. Duty will be completely eliminated on January 1, 2001.[18]

(ii) Staging for motor vehicles

The NAFTA Schedule of Canada provides special staging for some motor vehicles. For passenger vehicles[19] and trucks with a gross vehicle weight of less than 5 tonnes,[20] duties are reduced immediately upon NAFTA becoming effective by 50%, from 6% to 3%. Remaining duties are phased out in nine equal stages for the passenger vehicles, with complete elimination of duties on January 1, 2003, and four equal stages for the trucks, with complete elimination of duties on January 1, 1998. Most other motor vehicles are in staging category C.[21]

(iii) Cross over from Column II to Column I

While the staging categories for Columns I and II are the same, for goods in staging category C for which the commencing Column II rate is the UST rate, there is a cross-over effect as the UST drops below its GPT counterpart.[22] For these goods, the UST rate is used only so long as it exceeds the Column I rate. Thereafter, the Column I and Column II rates are the same. Consider, for example, tariff item 8210.00.00 (hand-operated mechanical appliances, weighing 10 kg or less, used in the preparation, conditioning or serving of food or drink). The MFN rate is 9.2%. The GPT rate is 2.5%. The UST rate is 4.6%. The Column I (Mexico Tariff) and Column II (Mexico-United States Tariff) rates are as follows:

	Column I	Column II
Base or commencing rate:	2.5%	4.6%
On NAFTA becoming effective:	2.2%	3.6%
From January 1, 1995	2.0%	2.7%
From January 1, 1996	1.7%	1.8%
From January 1, 1997	1.5%	1.5%
From January 1, 1998	1.2%	1.2%
From January 1, 1999	1.0%	1.0%
From January 1, 2000	0.7%	0.7%
From January 1, 2001	0.5%	0.5%
From January 1, 2002	0.2%	0.2%
On and after January 1, 2003	Free	Free

All goods for which tariff elimination is provided[23] under Canada's NAFTA schedules will be duty free at the latest by January 1, 2003.

(iv) Agricultural goods

The special circumstances that apply to agricultural goods are described in §5.3.

(5) The U.S. and Mexican NAFTA Schedules

Unlike the NAFTA Schedule of Canada, the NAFTA Schedules of the United States and Mexico do not provide for separate treatment for goods of mixed origin. U.S. Customs will distinguish between goods that are "Canadian" and those that are "Mexican", and duties on originating goods that are "Mexican" will be eliminated in accordance with the NAFTA Schedule of the United States.

Similarly, Mexican Customs will distinguish between originating goods that are "American" and "Canadian". Goods that are "American" fall under Column I[24] of the NAFTA Schedule of Mexico and goods that are "Canadian" fall under Column II.[25] For most goods, this distinction will not matter because "American" and "Canadian" goods receive the same treatment. However, the distinction will be relevant for agricultural goods, textile and apparel goods, goods subject to tariff rate quotas,[26] some categories of brandy, footwear, glassware, fibre glass goods, upholstered seats, furniture, typewriters and mattresses, and goods subject to bilateral agreements to accelerate elimination of duties.[27]

(a) Base rates

The base rate for each good in the U.S. NAFTA Schedule is the U.S. GSP rate that applied on July 1, 1991, if there was one and the MFN rate if there was not.[28] The base rate for each good in the Mexican NAFTA Schedule is the MFN rate for that good in effect on July 1, 1991.[29]

(b) Staging categories

The staging categories for the vast majority of goods in both the U.S. and the Mexican NAFTA schedules are staging categories A, B, C and D described above. However, there a number of other special staging categories.

(i) Textile and apparel goods

Tariffs on textile and apparel goods traded between the United States and Mexico will be eliminated under staging categories A and C and new category B6. Under category B6, the existing duty was reduced to the designated base rate when NAFTA became effective. Duties are eliminated in five equal stages, beginning on January 1, 1995, with complete elimination by January 1, 1999.[30]

NAFTA establishes five additional staging categories for specified textile goods traded between the United States and Mexico. These categories specify annual rates of duty to be in effect from 1994 through to 1998 and completely eliminate duties in 1999. Two categories are incorporated into the NAFTA Schedule of the United States and start from a rate of 25%. One applies to various wool fabrics[31] and the other applies to other wool fabrics and various fabrics of man-made filaments and staple fibres.[32] Three categories are incorporated into the NAFTA Schedule of Mexico. Two of these apply to goods in the same tariff subheadings as the two U.S. categories just described,[33] and each of these starts from 15%. The third special category in the NAFTA Schedule of Mexico starts from a rate of 20% and applies to certain sizes of carpets made from certain man-made textile materials.[34]

(ii) Motor vehicles

The NAFTA Schedule of the United States establishes a special staging category for trucks with a gross vehicle rate of less than 5 tonnes. Duties are reduced from 25% to 10% upon NAFTA becoming effective and will be reduced to 7.5%, 5.0% and 2.5% on January 1, 1995, January 1, 1996 and January 1, 1997 respectively, with full elimination on January 1, 1998.[35] Other trucks are in staging category C and passenger vehicles are in staging category A.

Tariff elimination for motor vehicles in the NAFTA Schedule of Mexico closely parallels that of Canada. With passenger vehicles,[36] the base rate of 20% is reduced to 10% in the first stage and the balance is eliminated in nine stages with complete elimination on January 1, 2003.[37] With trucks with a gross vehicle rate less than 5 tonnes,[38] the base rate of 20% is reduced to 10% in the first stage and the balance is eliminated in four stages with complete elimination on January 1, 1998.[39]

(iii) Agricultural goods

The special tariff elimination rules that apply to agricultural goods are described in §5.3.

(iv) Other special staging categories

The NAFTA Schedules of the United States and Mexico set out a number of other staging categories to cover a variety of goods. Staging categories C+ and C10 described below are set out, respectively, in the NAFTA Annex 302.2(1)(d) and Note 3 of the general notes to the NAFTA Schedule of the United States. All the other special staging categories are set out in chapter notes in each of these NAFTA Schedules.

Staging category C+ provides for elimination of duties by January 1, 2008, in fifteen equal annual stages and applies to tuna products, some footwear, certain ceramic goods,[40] various glass products and battery-powered wrist watches in the NAFTA Schedule of the United States and to tuna products in the NAFTA Schedule of Mexico.

Staging category C10 in the NAFTA Schedule of the United States and comparable staging in the NAFTA Schedule of Mexico apply to various dyes and certain categories of footwear and certain ceramic goods.[41] These staging categories are identical to staging category C except that the reduction when NAFTA became effective was 20% rather than 10% of the base rate and there is no reduction on January 1, 1995.

A special staging category applies to non-wired float glass in the NAFTA Schedules of each of the United States and Mexico. Duties on these goods are reduced by an amount equal to one-tenth of the base rate when NAFTA became effective and on January 1st in each of the years 1995 to 2000. Remaining duty will be eliminated on January 1, 2001.[42]

In the NAFTA Schedule of the United States, a special staging category applies to brooms other than whisk brooms. Duties on these goods were reduced by 30% of the base rate when NAFTA became effective, with a further reduction on January 1, 2000, equal to 20% of the base rate. Remaining duty will be eliminated on January 1, 2005.[43]

In the NAFTA Schedule of Mexico, a special staging category applies to various paper products. Duties on these goods are reduced to 80% of the base rate on January 1, 1997, 70% of the base rate on January 1, 1998, with full duty elimination on January 1, 1999.[44] A special staging category eliminating tariffs by January 1, 2001, in seven stages applies to some polypropylene and glass products and certain boilers.[45] A special staging category eliminating tariffs by January 1, 2001, in two stages applies to cartons. Duties on these goods will be reduced to 50% of the base rate on January 1, 1998, and will be completely eliminated on January 1, 2001.[46] A special category applies to upholstered seats and certain categories of wooden furniture from the United States. Duties on these goods were reduced by 40% of the base rate when NAFTA became effective, with a further reduction on January 1, 1998, equal to 20% of the base rate. Remaining duty will be eliminated on January 1, 2003.[47] Tariff rate quotas, described in §2.2(8), are established for certain types of wood.[48]

(6) Mexico, the GPT and the GSP

Goods imported into Canada from Mexico continue to be eligible for GPT treatment if they meet the prescribed rule of origin and satisfy other Canadian requirements. Goods imported into the United States from Mexico are no longer eligible for GSP treatment.

(7) Acceleration of Elimination of Duties

Like the FTA, NAFTA provides for the acceleration of duty elimination.[49] Acceleration may be by way of agreement between any two or more of the Parties. The elimination of duties on a number of goods was accelerated under the corresponding FTA provision.

(8) Tariff Rate Quotas and Allocation of In-quota Imports

NAFTA 302(4) permits NAFTA countries to allocate "in-quota" imports respecting tariff rate quotas set out in the NAFTA tariff schedules. A tariff rate quota is a quantity of imports (usually annual) below which a certain rate of duty will apply and above which a higher rate will apply. Consider Mexican tariff item 4401.21.01, which is coniferous wood chips. The NAFTA Schedule of Mexico provides that in each calendar year, 66,500 tonnes from the United States and 3,500 tonnes from Canada shall enter Mexico duty free, and duties on imports over these "in-quota quantities" will be eliminated under staging category C from a base rate of 10%. Imports within these quantities are "in-quota" imports. The NAFTA Schedules of each of the United States and Mexico make extensive use of tariff rate quotas in respect of agricultural goods. These are described in §5.3(7).

A tariff rate quota can be administered by collecting the higher duty once total imports in a year exceed the in-quota quantity. Alternatively, the quota can be allocated to specified importers. NAFTA 302(4) permits allocation provided that it does not have trade restrictive effects additional to those resulting from the tariff rate quota. A Party may request consultations to review the administration of an allocation system.[50]

2.3 RESTRICTION ON DRAWBACK AND DUTY DEFERRAL PROGRAMS

Drawback is the refund of duty paid on imported goods if the goods are subsequently exported, either in the same condition or after being used as materials in producing other goods that are exported. Drawback includes refunds of duty paid on imported goods when identical or similar goods are used in manufacturing goods that are subsequently exported.[51] Canadian, American and Mexican customs law all provide for drawback.

Duty deferral is the postponement of duty on imported goods until the good enters the commerce of the importing country. If the good never enters the commerce of the importing country but is exported, either in the same condition or as a material used in producing an exported good, the duty is never paid. Each NAFTA country has its unique duty deferral programs.

Drawback and duty deferral programs are consistent with the notion that customs duties, like other commodity taxes, are taxes on domestic and not foreign consumers. It makes little sense for a country to penalize its exports by not refunding or waiving duties paid on imported materials or domestic commodity taxes paid on any materials. These programs are also important industrial policy tools used by many countries to reduce material costs of exported goods and thereby encourage exports.[52] While use of domestic materials may be preferable from a job creation viewpoint, this option may not be viable if domestic materials are uncompetitive. In assisting manufacturers through drawback or duty deferral, a country retains manufacturing activity that might otherwise locate in the countries from which materials are sourced. Duty deferral programs are also used actively to promote the development of export-based industries.

Drawback and duty deferral programs create distortions within preferential trading blocs. Consider a free trade area comprised of Canada and the United States. A Canadian and American producer produce identical products at the same cost. The Canadian producer exports its product to the United States and the American producer sells its product into the domestic U.S. market. Suppose that each imports the same component from a third country and pays duty of $10. Assume that the Canadian product enters the United States duty free. If Canada allows drawback, the Canadian producer receives a refund of $10. Its U.S. counterpart does not receive a comparable refund because its product is not exported. Unless drawback is eliminated, the Canadian product will have a $10 advantage in the U.S. domestic market over the American product. As one writer expressed it, one secures "the double benefit of (a) evading one's own national tariffs (through drawback), and (b) evading the tariffs of other Member States (through Area Tariff Treatment)".[53]

(1) Duty Deferral Programs

(a) United States — Foreign trade zones

Of the three NAFTA countries, only the United States uses the foreign trade zone ("FTZ") form of duty deferral. FTZs were first authorized in the United States by the Foreign Trade Zone Act in 1934. Zones or subzones are used for both manufacturing and distribution. Some zones are general purpose zones and many companies have access to them. Others are used by single companies for specific manufacturing operations. Imported materials can be combined with domestic materials within a zone. FTZs are widely used in the United States and result in considerable savings to U.S. manufacturers. Most U.S. automotive production takes place in FTZs.

An FTZ is not part of the United States for customs purposes. An import entering an FTZ, which can be a factory or a warehouse, is not subject to U.S. customs laws and duty is not paid. The import can be a material processed within the FTZ into a finished good. The import does not enter the U.S. customs territory until the finished good is sold into the U.S. market. The duty charged is the lower of the duty applicable to the finished good and the duty that would have applied to the import in the form in which it was imported. Under the HTSUS, duties on parts and components are frequently higher than those on the finished goods. If the finished good is exported, the imported material never enters the U.S. customs territory and no duty is paid. Also, duty is not paid if the imported material becomes scrap.

(b) Mexico — Maquiladoras, PITEX and ALTEX

(i) Maquiladoras

The Mexican maquiladora program has combined duty deferral and export-based performance requirements to create a separate export-based industry.

The maquiladora program was first established in 1965 to increase foreign investment and provide employment opportunities in Mexico's border regions with the United States.[54] Maquiladoras were originally confined to border zones but after 1972 they could be established anywhere in Mexico. By March, 1991, there were over 1,900 maquiladora plants in operation, employing more than 470,000 people.[55]

Maquiladoras are in-bond manufacturing plants. To operate as a maquiladora, a company must receive authorization from Mexico's Secretariat of Commerce and Industrial Development ("SECOFI").[56] Maquiladoras may be 100% foreign owned and may be established in any industry not reserved to the Mexican government or Mexican nationals. A maquiladora may import materials for periods of up to six months (which can be renewed) and machinery and equipment, work manuals and industrial plans on a duty-free basis.[57] However, a maquiladora is not a foreign trade zone, and items imported by the maquiladora enter the customs territory of Mexico. Owners of maquiladoras must guarantee payment of duties by posting security.[58] No duties are paid if the finished goods are exported. There are special rules covering imported materials that become waste. The waste must be destroyed, donated to social or educational institutions or returned abroad.[59]

Duties are paid on the imported materials if the maquiladora sells its products into Mexico's national market. Maquiladoras are restricted in their ability to sell goods into the national market. A maquiladora must receive SECOFI authorization and sales into the national market cannot exceed 55% of annual exports.[60] As a result of this export requirement, maquiladoras stand largely apart from the rest of Mexican industry.

(ii) HTSUS tariff items 9802.00.60 and 9802.00.80

Mexico's maquiladora program is complemented by HTSUS tariff items 9802.00.60 and 9802.00.80, which limit U.S. duty on goods assembled abroad from U.S. components to the value added abroad. Under these provisions, a U.S. manufacturer can produce components in the United States and export them to a maquiladora for assembly into a finished good. No duty is paid on the components when they enter Mexico. When the finished good re-enters the United States, the manufacturer only pays duty on the value of the value added in the maquiladora. Many U.S. companies have taken advantage of these favourable tariff provisions and most foreign-owned maquiladoras are owned by U.S. companies. There are no comparable provisions in Canada's customs law.

(iii) PITEX and ALTEX

Mexico operates two other duty deferral programs in conjunction with export promotions. Under the PITEX Decree,[61] a company can import machinery, equipment and tooling duty free on a temporary basis provided that it exports 30% or more of its total production. A company can also import duty free on a temporary basis raw materials, parts and components, packages and various containers, fuel, lubricants, tools and equipment used for exported goods provided that it exports 10% of its total production or $500,000 (US). Under the ALTEX Decree,[62] companies can import certain items duty free provided that prescribed percentages of their total sales are exported.

(c) Canada — Inward processing

Foreign trade zones or in-bond manufacturing plants along the maquiladora model do not exist in Canada. However, Canada's inward processing rules constitute a duty deferral program. The program applies to imported goods "used in, wrought into or attached to" goods processed in Canada and subsequently exported or imported materials "directly consumed or expended" in the processing in Canada of goods subsequently exported.[63] The manufacturer must apply for duty relief before the goods or materials are imported and produce either evidence of an agreement for the sale and exportation of the goods to be processed or pattern of past sales which, if continued, would result in the processed goods being exported. Security is required in some instances.

(2) Provisions of the FTA

The FTA provided for the elimination of drawback and duty deferral on goods traded between Canada and the United States. The elimination was scheduled to commence on January 1, 1994, although the FTA contemplated that the Parties might agree on a later date. There were exceptions for goods entered under bond, same condition drawback, duty-free shops, stores or supplies for ships and aircraft, goods used in joint undertakings of the Parties, goods imported from a Party and subsequently exported to that Party, goods failing to conform to specification, citrus fruits and certain fabrics.[64]

The FTA made no general exception for non-originating goods. Generally, elimination of drawback or duty deferral was to apply regardless of whether the exported goods were subject to the other Party's duty.

(3) Provisions of NAFTA — Basic Rules

(a) Drawback or deferral restricted

NAFTA restricts refunding duty paid or waiving or reducing duty owed on imported goods exported to another NAFTA country or used as materials in goods exported to another NAFTA country or substituted by identical or similar goods that are used as materials in goods exported to another NAFTA country. Unlike the FTA, NAFTA allows a NAFTA country to refund, waive or reduce duty in an amount equal to the lesser of the duty paid or owed to it and the duty paid to the other NAFTA country on the exportation of the goods.[65]

Suppose a Canadian producer imports a material valued at $60 subject to Canadian duty of 10%. The producer pays $6 in Canadian duty. The producer processes the material into a finished good which is exported to the United States. The Canadian dollar equivalent of the value of the finished good is $100. If the good is non-originating and the U.S. MFN duty rate is 5%, the U.S. importer pays $5 of U.S. duty. The Canadian government may refund to the producer the lesser of the $6 of Canadian duty or the $5 of U.S. duty. NAFTA permits a $5 refund to the producer while under the FTA, the producer would not receive any refund.

Following January 1, 1996, the drawback and duty deferral restriction will apply to goods exported from Canada to the United States and to goods exported from the United States to Canada. Following January 1, 2001, this restriction will apply to goods exported from Mexico to either the United States or Canada and to goods exported from either the United States or Canada to Mexico. It is important to remember that the event to which these cut-off dates relate is the date that the goods are exported. Thus the restriction will apply to a material imported into Canada on December 1, 1995, that is processed into a good exported to the United States on January 15, 1996.

(b) Drawback or deferral prohibited

NAFTA prohibits refunding, waiving or reducing antidumping and countervailing duties, premiums arising out of quota allocation systems and, for the United States, fees applied pursuant to s. 22 of the AAA on condition of export. These prohibitions apply as of the dates mentioned in §2.3(3)(a).

NAFTA also prohibits refunding, waiving or reducing customs duties on imported goods that are substituted by identical or similar goods that are exported.[66] This is called "same-condition substitution duty drawback", and the prohibition applies as soon as NAFTA becomes effective. This is a different situation from that described above where a good that is identical or similar to the imported good is used as a material in the production of a good that is exported.

The bilateral rules respecting agricultural goods between the United States and Mexico repeat the prohibition on same-condition substitution duty drawback.[67] Thus, upon NAFTA becoming effective, duty paid on tomatoes imported into Mexico from Honduras cannot be refunded upon identical or similar tomatoes being exported from Mexico to the United States. If the identical or similar tomatoes are processed into salsa, the rules described in §2.3(3)(a) apply and this rule does not.

The rule described in §2.3(3)(a) that permits a refund or waiver of duties up to the amount of duty paid to another NAFTA country on the exported good does not apply in any of these situations.

(c) Rules respecting duty deferral programs

Under NAFTA 303(3), a good imported under a duty deferral program and exported to another NAFTA country or used as a material or substituted by an identical or similar good used as a material in a good exported to another NAFTA country will be treated the same as if the good had been withdrawn for domestic consumption. Duties must be assessed to the extent that they exceed duties paid to the other NAFTA country on the exported good.[68] If satisfactory evidence of the payment of the duties to the other NAFTA country is not presented within sixty days of the date of exportation, the Party shall collect the duties as if the good had been withdrawn for domestic consumption, and may refund such duties to the extent permitted when the evidence is produced.[69]

(4) Colour Cathode-Ray Picture Tubes

NAFTA prohibits refunding or reducing customs duties paid or owed on non-originating colour cathode-ray picture tubes with diagonals exceeding 14 inches.[70] This prohibition took effect when NAFTA came into force and is not subject to any of the exceptions described below. The rule permitting refund or waiver of duty up to the amount of duty paid to another NAFTA country on the exported good does not apply. NAFTA Annex 303.8 contains an exception to the prohibition for Mexico respecting any person who imported at least 20,000 tubes[71] between July 1, 1991 and June 30, 1992. The exception limits drawback or duty deferral to an aggregate of 1,200,000 units exported to the United States in 1994. This amount diminishes by 200,000 each year to zero in the year 2000 and the years following. The corresponding limitation for exports to Canada is 75,000 units in 1994, 50,000 units in 1995 and zero units in 1996 and years following.

(5) Exceptions

As under the FTA, there are a number of exceptions to the NAFTA restrictions on drawback and duty deferral.

(a) Goods under bond and same-condition drawback

The restrictions do not apply to goods entered under bond for transportation and exportation to another NAFTA country. The restrictions also do not apply to goods exported in the same condition as when imported. Testing, cleaning, repacking or inspecting a good or preserving it are not considered to change its condition. Similar exceptions appeared in the FTA.

Imported goods may be commingled with fungible goods and exports from the stock of commingled fungible goods tracked through inventory methods provided for in the Uniform Regulations[72] will be considered as falling within this exception. However, this commingling rule will not apply to the restriction referred to in §2.3(3)(b) respecting agricultural goods as between the United States and Mexico. If a Mexican exporter imports tomatoes from Honduras and commingles them with fungible Mexican tomatoes, the exporter will not be entitled to same-condition drawback when exports from the commingled supply of goods are made to the United States. However, the exporter would be entitled to the benefit of the commingling rule if the exports go to Canada.[73]

(b) Duty-free shops, vessels, aircraft and joint undertakings

NAFTA contains exceptions for goods deemed to be exported by reason of delivery to a duty-free shop, for ship's stores or aircraft or for use in joint undertakings of two or more of the Parties similar to those exceptions in the FTA.[74]

(c) Goods failing to conform

As under the FTA, the NAFTA restrictions do not apply to a refund of duty on a good exported to another NAFTA country because the good fails to conform to sample or specification requirements or because the good has been shipped without the consent of a consignee.

(d) Originating goods

As under the FTA, the NAFTA restrictions do not apply to refunds or waivers of duty on imports of originating goods that are exported or used as materials or substituted by identical or similar materials used as materials in goods that are exported to another NAFTA country.[75] If a U.S. producer imports a material from Mexico that is originating under the rules of origin but still subject to duty because duty elimination is not complete and uses it to produce a good that is exported to Canada, the duty on the material can be refunded or waived. This exception will become increasingly irrelevant as duty elimination progresses to completion. This exception will also be irrelevant for materials imported into the United States from Canada, or vice versa, and incorporated into goods exported to Mexico, because duty elimination between Canada and the United States will be complete by January 1, 1998, but the restriction on drawback and duty deferral will not apply to trade with Mexico until January 1, 2001.

The restriction will not apply to goods temporarily imported from another NAFTA country for repair or alteration, regardless of the goods' origin.

(e) Exceptions as between Canada and the United States

NAFTA Annex 303.6, paragraph 2 sets forth several exceptions that apply only as between Canada and the United States.

(i) Citrus fruits

As under the FTA, the NAFTA restrictions on drawback and duty deferral do not apply to imported citrus products.[76]

(ii) Apparel and certain piece goods

The NAFTA restrictions do not apply to an imported good used as a material or substituted by an identical good used as a material in the production of apparel that is subject to the MFN rate of duty when exported to another NAFTA country.[77] The corresponding FTA exception applied only to fabric. The NAFTA exception also applies to yarn or any other material that could be used in producing apparel. Presumably this is part of the *quid pro quo* for tightening the rules of origin as applied to apparel goods.

Unlike the FTA, which does not contain any comparable exception for textiles, NAFTA contains a specific exception for quilted cotton piece goods, quilted man-made piece goods and furniture moving pads.[78]

(f) Refined sugar exported from the United States

NAFTA Annex 303.6, paragraph 1 contains an exception from the NAFTA restrictions for imports into the United States of raw sugar cane[79] that is used or substituted by an identical or similar good that is used in producing refined sugar that is exported to Canada or Mexico.[80] There is no corresponding exception for refined sugar exported from Canada or Mexico.

(6) Uniform Regulations

Article X of the Uniform Regulations described in §3.4(1) sets out technical clarifications respecting the application of certain provisions of NAFTA 303.

(7) Concluding Remarks

Restriction of drawback and duty deferral is a casualty of "free trade". Producers gain duty free access to the other member countries of the free trade area but lose their right to refund of duty paid or waiver of duty owed on goods imported from non-member countries.

Given the theoretical basis for restricting or prohibiting drawback or duty deferral described above, the restriction or prohibition should apply only to goods on which duties are eliminated because of the creation of the free trade area. However, the FTA prohibition of drawback and duty deferral would have applied whether or not the exported goods were subject to duty. Under the FTA, producers of non-originating goods exported from Canada to the United States or vice versa would clearly be worse off as a result of "free trade". The FTA drawback and duty deferral provision was intended to change sourcing practices and not just correct a trade distortion. The drafters of the FTA must have been uneasy with the provision because they contemplated that Canada and the United States may wish to delay its implementation.[81]

Many producers in both the United States and Canada were unhappy with the prospect of the FTA provision coming into effect. This discontent is reflected in the NAFTA provision which delays the implementation of the restriction on drawback and duty deferral as between Canada and the United States for two years beyond the FTA date. NAFTA also allows the refund or waiver of duty up to the amount of duty paid to another NAFTA country on the exported goods. A producer of a non-originating good will not be worse off under NAFTA unless the rate of duty on its imported material is substantially higher than on its exported good. While this aspect of the NAFTA drawback and duty deferral provisions may reduce the incentive for certain producers to maintain sufficient levels of North American content in their goods so that they are originating,[82] the NAFTA approach is more equitable than that under the FTA.

Unlike the FTA, the NAFTA drafters did not contemplate a delay in the implementation of NAFTA drawback and deferral restrictions beyond the dates specified.

One important factor that the theoretical basis described above for the restrictions of drawback and duty deferral does not take into account is differences in external rates of duty between the member states in a free trade area. So long as a member state can refund or waive duty on imported goods that are exported, the differences in external rates of duty do not matter. However, once the member state can no long maintain these programs, the differences in the rates prejudice producers located in the member states with the higher external rates. The only practical course of action open to the member states with the higher external rates of duty is to harmonize them with those of the member state with the lowest external rates. The NAFTA country with the lowest external rates is the United States. Once the NAFTA restriction on drawback and duty deferral become effective, both Canada and Mexico will be under considerable pressure to harmonize their external rates of duty with those of the United States.

2.4 WAIVERS OF CUSTOMS DUTIES

Like the FTA, NAFTA 304 restricts the use of measures that waive customs duties on goods imported from any country, including NAFTA countries, on the condition that the recipient meet performance requirements. As under the FTA, "performance requirements" are requirements that a given level of goods be exported, or domestic goods or services be substituted for imported goods or services, or the recipient purchase other goods or services or accord preference to domestic goods or services or the recipient produce goods or provide services with given levels of domestic content. Because of Mexican programs imposing trade balancing requirements, NAFTA adds to the definition requirements that relate import volumes or values with those of exports or to foreign exchange inflows.

As between Canada and the United States, the provisions of FTA 405 continue in effect and are incorporated into NAFTA. Under FTA 405(1), Canada and the United States agreed not to introduce new programs or extend existing programs that waive duties based on performance requirements being fulfilled. Existing programs must be eliminated by January 1, 1998. As between Canada and Mexico, Canada may continue the programs that existed on January 1, 1989 until January 1, 1998. There is no similar provision as between the United States and Mexico. However, the United States customs law does not provide for these sorts of programs.

Canada's duty remission programs for automotive goods and textile and apparel goods are waivers of customs duties that are conditional upon fulfilment of performance requirements. Canada's duty remission programs for automotive goods are subject to special rules described in §5.1(4). Canada's textile and apparel duty remission program currently consists of six duty remission orders enacted in 1988. Some were new and others replaced earlier programs. The orders cover women's and girl's blouses and shirts, denim apparel fabrics, outerwear fabrics and outerwear,[83] outerwear greige[84] fabrics, shirting fabrics and tailored shirt collars.[85] These orders employ various performance requirements. For example, the blouses and shirts order provides for duty remission for imported blouses and shirts based on the net factory value of domestically manufactured shirts and blouses. None of these duty remission orders by its own terms extends beyond the end of 1997.[86]

Mexico may continue programs in effect on January 1, 1991 until January 1, 2001.[87] Notwithstanding the general prohibition to the contrary, Mexico may expand or extend to new recipients the application of conditional duty waiver programs existing when NAFTA became effective.[88] However, Mexico may not increase the ratio of duties waived to duties owed relative to performance required or apply the program to an imported good not qualifying on July 1, 1991.

Like the FTA, NAFTA 304(3) requires waivers of customs duties granted with respect to goods for commercial use by a designated person to be discontinued or made generally available if they have adverse impact on the commercial interests of a national or enterprise constituted under the laws of another NAFTA country, or a subsidiary of such an enterprise located within the NAFTA country granting the waiver. Thus, if Canada granted a company specific duty remission order to a Canadian company and a subsidiary of a U.S. enterprise was placed at a competitive disadvantage, Canada could be required to discontinue the remission order or make it generally available. Waivers of customs duties affected by this provision need not be conditional upon fulfilment of performance requirements. While the NAFTA 304 does not affect drawback or duty deferral programs covered by NAFTA 303, NAFTA 304(3) will have to be taken into account if a NAFTA country wishes to assist companies adversely affected by the restriction of drawback or duty deferral through company-specific duty remission orders rather than a general lowering of tariffs.

2.5 TEMPORARY ADMISSION OF GOODS AND SAMPLES

(1) Temporary Entry of Goods

The FTA provided for the temporary entry of persons but had no complementary provisions for the temporary duty-free entry of goods. An American or Canadian national could be granted temporary entry to Canada or the United States to pursue a business activity, but the FTA provided no assurance that equipment necessary for carrying on that business activity would be admitted duty free. In Canada, the circumstances under which temporary entry of goods on a duty-free basis is granted are very specific and duty-free entry will not be granted unless the facts fit the circumstances.[89]

NAFTA 305 rectifies this deficiency. Each NAFTA country must grant duty-free admission for professional equipment, equipment for the press or for sound or television broadcasting, cinematographic equipment, goods imported for sports purposes and goods for display or demonstration, and commercial samples and advertising films. The professional equipment must be necessary for carrying out the business activity of a business person who qualifies for temporary entry under the NAFTA temporary entry provisions.[90] The origin of the imported goods and the domestic availability of directly competitive or substitutable goods are irrelevant to determining eligibility for temporary entry.

The only conditions that may be imposed are that the good be imported by a national or resident of another NAFTA country seeking temporary entry, used solely by or under the supervision of such person, accompanied by a bond not exceeding 110% of charges that would otherwise be owed,[91] capable of identification when exported and exported on the departure of such person or within a time period reasonably related to the purpose of the temporary entry, and not be leased or imported in greater quantity than is reasonable for the intended use. Temporary entry of commercial samples and advertising films may be conditional on the goods being imported solely for the solicitation of orders for goods or services provided from other NAFTA or non-NAFTA countries.

The NAFTA provisions require that "duty free" entry be granted to these goods. This expression means free of "customs duties", which do not include excise taxes or the Canadian goods and services tax ("GST"). The NAFTA does not require the NAFTA countries to grant relief from these sorts of commodity taxes for goods entered on a temporary basis.

(2) Samples

Consistent with facilitating the temporary entry of business persons, NAFTA requires each NAFTA country to grant duty-free entry to commercial samples of negligible value and to printed advertising materials imported from other NAFTA countries.[92] A NAFTA country may require that samples be solely for solicitation of orders for goods and services and that advertising materials be imported in packets containing no more than one copy of each such material.

(3) Transportation Equipment

The NAFTA temporary entry of goods provisions set forth special rules respecting transportation equipment. NAFTA requires that vehicles or containers used in international traffic that enter a NAFTA country be allowed to depart on any route reasonably related to its economic and prompt departure. No bond may be required or penalty or charge imposed by reason of a difference between the port of entry and the port of exit. No NAFTA country may require that containers leave for another NAFTA country on the same vehicle or carrier that brought them in. These provisions, which are subject to the NAFTA provisions respecting cross-border trade in services, are directed at practices followed along the U.S.-Mexico border.

(4) Goods Re-entered After Repair or Alteration

No NAFTA country may apply a customs duty to a good, regardless of origin, imported from another NAFTA country for repair or alteration. NAFTA countries may impose duties on the value of repairs or alterations to goods only in the circumstances in NAFTA Annex 307.1. Section D of NAFTA Annex 307.1 lists various types of ships, boats and other vessels.

Canada may impose duty on the value of repairs or alterations to Section D goods returned from Mexico at the rate for the goods repaired or altered provided in the NAFTA Schedule of Canada,[93] and to Section D goods returned from the United States and to any other good (except a good repaired or altered pursuant to a warranty) returned from either the United States or Mexico at the rate for the goods repaired or altered set forth in Canada's FTA Schedule.

The United States may impose duty on the value of the repairs or alterations to goods (other than a good not in Section D repaired or altered pursuant to a warranty) returned from Canada at the rate for the goods repaired or altered provided in the U.S. FTA Schedule. The United States may impose duty on the value of the repairs or alterations to Section D goods returned from Mexico at a rate of 40% in 1994, 30% in 1995, 20% in 1996, 10% in 1997 and nil in 1998 and years following.

Mexico may impose duty on the value of the repairs or alterations to Section D goods returned from either Canada or the United States at the rate that would apply if the goods were in staging category B in the NAFTA schedule of Mexico.

These limitations apply regardless of the origin of the goods.

2.6 CUSTOMS USER FEES

Like the FTA, NAFTA prohibits customs user fees on originating goods. The United States shall eliminate its merchandise processing fee on originating goods that are Canadian according to the schedule in FTA 403. Under this schedule, fees were eliminated completely by January 1, 1994. The United States may maintain these fees for originating goods that are Mexican until June 30, 1999. There is no phasing out process as under the FTA. The determination of the status of a good as Canadian or Mexican is described in §3.3. Mexico shall not increase its customs processing fee and shall eliminate it for originating goods by June 30, 1999.

2.7 MOST-FAVOURED-NATION RATES ON CERTAIN GOODS

(1) Certain Automatic Data Processing Equipment and Their Parts

NAFTA creates a mini-customs union with respect to certain categories of computer goods, including automatic data processing machines, digital processing units, input or output units, storage units, other units of automatic data processing machines, computer parts and computer power supplies.[94] Printers and cathode-ray tube computer monitors are not included.

Canada, the United States and Mexico will move towards a common MFN rate for these goods. The common rate for each good will be the lower of the rate specified in NAFTA Annex 308.1 or the lowest rate for the good agreed to by a NAFTA country in the Uruguay Round, or such lower rate as may be agreed. Each NAFTA country shall reduce its MFN rate (which does not include concessionary rates) in five equal stages commencing January 1, 1999, so that the rates of all three countries correspond to the common rate for each good by January 1, 2003. With a few exceptions, Canadian and U.S. rates are at or near the target rates set forth in NAFTA Table 308.1.1.[95] Mexican rates for these goods are generally in the 10% to 20% range, which is considerably higher than the 3.9%, 3.7% or Free rates provided for in the table.

Once this process is complete (which will occur for all these goods by January 1, 2004), any of these goods crossing from one NAFTA country to another will be deemed to be originating, and rules of origin for these goods will be dispensed with. After several years of working with the NAFTA rules of origin, other industries may wish to adopt this innovative approach.

(2) Semiconductors and Related Devices and Local Area Networks

When NAFTA became effective, Canada, the United States and Mexico reduced to "free" their MFN rates on metal oxide varistors, various semiconductor devices, light emitting diodes, mounted plezo-electric crystals, and electronic integrated circuits and microassemblies.[96] Mexican MFN rates on all these items ranged from 10% to 15%. The Canadian MFN rates on metal oxide varistors was 10.3% and the U.S. MFN rate was 6%. The Canadian MFN rate on the remaining items was Free. U.S. MFN rates were Free or low, with a few items being 4.2%.

As with the automatic data processing machines and related items, the effect will be to create a mini-customs union for semiconductors and related devices. There is no deeming provision respecting origin, but the originating status of these goods under NAFTA will not be relevant because MFN rates for all three countries are free. These goods will have to satisfy requirements for MFN treatment to be free of duty and could be subject to any trade sanctions that apply to their country of origin. This is quite different from the effect of the provision described in §2.7(2) respecting automatic data processing equipment that deems goods imported from another NAFTA country to be originating. This deeming provision has the effect of making them "goods of a Party" and subject to NAFTA obligations,[97] so that MFN requirements need not be satisfied and trade sanctions against third country goods would not apply.

The approach to local area network apparatus is the same as with semiconductors and related devices. Upon NAFTA becoming effective, each

NAFTA country is required to accord MFN duty-free treatment to any of these goods imported into its territory.[98]

(3) Colour Cathode-Ray Television Picture Tubes

NAFTA adopts a completely different approach respecting colour cathode-ray television picture tubes. If a NAFTA country wishes to reduce its MFN rate on tubes (including those for high definition television) with a diagonal exceeding fourteen inches during the first ten years of NAFTA being effective, it must first consult with the other NAFTA countries. Unless the reduction is required as a result of the conclusion of the Uruguay Round of negotiations, a NAFTA country that objects to the reduction can raise its rate for originating goods under the corresponding tariff item in its NAFTA schedule to the rate that would have applied if the item had been in NAFTA staging category C. As between Canada and the United States, the relevant schedules would be the NAFTA schedules and not the FTA schedules.

These goods are in staging category A in the NAFTA schedules for each of Canada, the United States and Mexico. United States and Mexican MFN rates of duty are 15% and the Canadian MFN rate is 9.3%. If staging category C applied, rather than being duty-free, duty would not be eliminated until January 1, 2003.

These provisions complement the special restriction on drawback and duty deferral for these goods described in §2.3(4).

2.8 OTHER DUTY RELIEF PROGRAMS

NAFTA Annex 302.2(9) incorporates FTA 401(7) and 401(8). Under FTA 401(7), Canada agreed not to increase rates of duties set forth in Canada's Schedule of Statutory and Temporary Concessionary Provisions on goods originating in the United States. Section 68(2) of the *Customs Tariff* provides that duties be reduced as set forth in Schedule II of that legislation. These are the statutory provisions referred to in FTA Article 401(7). Section 68(1) of the *Customs Tariff* authorizes the Governor in Council to reduce duties on goods used as materials in Canadian manufactures and certain goods specifically identified in the legislation. The reductions made pursuant to s. 68(1) are the Temporary Concessionary Provisions referred to in FTA 401(7). The reductions in the Statutory and Temporary Concessionary Provisions are almost invariably tied to the end use of the good.[99] If the good is imported for the use specified, the reduction applies. There are some exceptions set forth in FTA Annex 401.7.

FTA 401(8) contains a similar provision that applies to goods that were subject to a temporary suspension of duty on October 3, 1987, and which are listed with a base rate of "free" in subchapter II of chapter 99 of the U.S. Tariff Schedule. The goods listed are mainly products of the chemical industry. There are a few exceptions listed in FTA Annex 407.7.

These provisions apply to "originating goods". NAFTA Annex 302.2, paragraph 9 makes it clear that origin for the purposes of these incorporated provisions is to be determined in accordance with the NAFTA rules of origin, and not those of the FTA.

NAFTA Annex 302.2 does not incorporate FTA 401(6), which provided that Canada continue to exempt from duty machinery and equipment originating from the United States that, at the time that the FTA became effective, was listed as "not available" in Canada and entitled to duty-free treatment under Canada's machinery program. However, the agreement between Canada and the United States suspending the operation of the FTA will continue this provision as between Canada and the United States.

These provisions are only relevant until January 1, 1998. After that time, all originating goods affected by these provisions imported from the United States will enter Canada duty-free because duty elimination as between Canada and the United States will have been completed.

ENDNOTES

[1] The U.S. GSP program is the U.S. version of the GATT generalized system of preferences.
[2] The HTSUS also identifies the Automotive Products Trade Act ("APTA") and the Agreement on Trade in Civil Aircraft as special tariff treatments. APTA relates to the Auto Pact which is described under §5.1(1) and §5.1(5). The Agreement on the Trade in Civil Aircraft provides for duty-free treatment for specified articles imported for use in civil aircraft.
[3] See HTSUS Subchapter II, Note 8 for the list of tariff items that are to be free if imported from Canada, even if the period for the temporary reduction has expired.
[4] The HTSUS tariff items are 8704.10.50, 8704.21, 8704.22.50, 8704.23, 8704.31, 8704.32 and 8704.90. These include virtually all types of trucks. The MFN rate for these items is 8.5%. The Column 2 rate is 25%. Under Note 1 to Subchapter III, the temporary rate of 25% applies in lieu of the rate under HTSUS Chapter 87.
[5] For further discussion of s. 22 of the AAA, see §5.3(2)(b)(i) and §5.3(5)(b).
[6] Duties will not be eliminated on some agricultural goods imported into Canada from Mexico. See §5.3(9). There are few items, such as ceramic tableware, drinking glasses and certain categories of footwear imported into Mexico for which tariffs are not being eliminated.
[7] With one exception. NAFTA Annex 300B(6) and Appendix 6 establish tariff preference levels for certain non-originating textile and apparel goods, described in §5.2(2)(d).
[8] NAFTA Annex 302.2, paragraphs 4 and 12.
[9] Subject to rounding.
[10] NAFTA Annex 302.2, paragraph 1.
[11] As defined in NAFTA 708.
[12] Identified in Appendix 1.1 of NAFTA Annex 300-B.
[13] The terms, "Mexico Tariff" and "Mexico-United States Tariff" are taken from the amendments to the *Customs Tariff* set forth in ss. 109 to 145 of Bill C-115 [S.C. 1993, c. 44]. They do not appear in the NAFTA text.
[14] See NAFTA Annex 302.2, paragraph 2. However, for a few goods, Canada's MFN rate is used as the base rate, even though there is a GPT rate for the goods in question. Consider,

for example, the various items of rubber footwear under subheadings 6401.10.10, 6401.91.10, 6401.92.91, 6401.99.10, 6402.20.10. The GPT for these items is Free. Upon the NAFTA becoming effective, the base rate for originating goods that are Mexican entering Canada under these subheadings will be based on Canada's MFN rate. This duty will be phased out in ten equal stages.

[15] NAFTA Annex 302.2, subparagraph 6(a).

[16] See NAFTA Annex 302.2, subparagraph 6(b). Note that the base rates in Column I correspond to those set forth in the column headed "Mexico Tariff" in Schedule I to Part A of the *North American Free Trade Agreement Implementation Act*, S.C. 1993, c. 44, and the base rates in Column II correspond to those set forth in the column headed "Mexico-United States Tariff" in that schedule.

[17] NAFTA Annex 300-B, Appendix 2.1.C(b).

[18] NAFTA Annex 300-B, Appendix 2.1.C(c). This description is taken from the Canadian implementing legislation and varies slightly from staging category B+ as set out in Appendix 2.1.C(c).

[19] Tariff subheadings 8703.21 to 8703.91.

[20] Tariff subheadings 8704.21 and 8704.31.

[21] All-terrain vehicles are in staging category A. For all motor vehicles, the Column I and Column II rates are the same.

[22] See NAFTA Annex 302.2, subparagraph 6(a). The goods affected are Canadian tariff items 4010.99.90, 7324.90.10, 8210.00.00, 8302.41.10, 8414.51.00, 8416.10.99, 8416.20.99, 8416.30.99, 8418.30.00, 8418.40.00, 8450.20.90, 8501.52.10, 8509.40.90, 8536.30.11, 8536.50.21, 8536.50.80, 9028.20.10, 9028.90.91, 9030.89.99, 9030.90.24, 9030.90.94 and 9032.89.80.

[23] As will be discussed in §5.3, the Canadian NAFTA tariff schedules do not provide for tariff elimination on dairy, poultry or egg goods. The goods affected are set forth in NAFTA Annex 703.2, Appendix 703.2.B.7, Dairy, Poultry and Egg Goods, Schedule of Canada.

[24] NAFTA Annex 302.2, paragraph 10.

[25] NAFTA Annex 302.2, paragraph 11.

[26] A number of agricultural goods are subject to tariff rate quotas in the NAFTA Schedule of Mexico. See §5.3(7) and §5.3(10). A few other goods are also subject to tariff rate quotas. See, for example, Mexican tariff item 4401.21.01, coniferous wood chips or particles.

[27] See NAFTA 302(3).

[28] Subject to any temporary modification under HTSUS Chapter 99, Subchapter III, that imposes a higher rate, in which case the higher rate applies. The most notable example is the trucks covered by HTSUS tariff item 9903.87.00 referred to above, for which the base rate is 25%.

[29] Base rates for goods subject to tariffication, described below in §5.3(7), are not determined in this manner.

[30] NAFTA Annex 300-B, Appendix 2.1.B(b).

[31] See NAFTA Annex 300-B, Appendix 2.1, Schedule 2.1.B, paragraph 1, which appears as Note 1 to Chapter 51 of the NAFTA Schedule of the United States.

[32] See NAFTA Annex 300-B, Appendix 2.1, Schedule 2.1.B, paragraph 3, which appears as Note 2 to Chapter 51 and Note 1 to each of Chapters 54 and 55 of the NAFTA Schedule of the United States.

[33] See NAFTA Annex 300-B, Appendix 2.1, Schedule 2.1.B, paragraph 2, which applies to various fabrics in the same tariff subheadings as the U.S. staging category in paragraph 1 of Schedule 2.1.B. This category appears as Note 1 to Chapter 51 of the NAFTA Schedule of Mexico. See also paragraph 4 of Schedule 2.1.B, which applies to the other wool fabrics and fabrics of man-made fibres and staple fibres in the subheadings as the U.S. staging category in paragraph 3 of Schedule 2.1.B. This category appears as Note 2 to Chapter 51, Note 4 to Chapter 51 and Note 1 to Chapter 55 of the NAFTA Schedule of Mexico.

[34] See NAFTA Annex 300-B, Appendix 2.1, Schedule 2.1.B, paragraph 5, which appears as Note 1 to Chapter 57 of the NAFTA Schedule of Mexico.

[35] See Note 1, Chapter 87, NAFTA Schedule of the United States.

[36] Tariff subheadings 8703.21 to 8703.91.

[37] See Note 1 to Chapter 87 of the NAFTA Schedule of Mexico.

[38] HS subheadings 8704.21 and 8704.31. See Mexican tariff items 8704.21.99 and 8704.31.99,

to which this staging applies. The staging category for vehicles under tariff items 8704.21.01 and 8704.31.01, described as "acarreadores de escoria", is "A".

[39] See Note 2 to Chapter 87 of the NAFTA Schedule of Mexico.

[40] These goods are certain categories of glazed and unglazed ceramic products (such as tiles) falling under headings 69.07 and 69.08. Staging category C+ is modified for these goods by Notes 1 and 2 to Chapter 69 of the NAFTA Schedule of the United States.

[41] See, for example, goods under U.S. tariff item 6912.00.20, ceramic hotel or restaurant ware and other ware not household ware. Goods from the United States falling under subheading 6912.00 (ceramic tableware, etc.) for these uses of the NAFTA Schedule of Mexico receive comparable tariff treatment. See Note 2 to Chapter 69. Tariffs on U.S. goods for other uses and all Canadian goods under this subheading are removed under staging category B.

[42] See Notes 1 and 2 to Chapter 70 of the NAFTA Schedule of the United States, and U.S. tariff items 7005.29.05 and 7005.29.15. See Note 2 to Chapter 70 of the NAFTA Schedule of Mexico and Mexican tariff item 7005.29.03. The Mexican staging applies to goods of both the United States and Canada. Staging category C applies to goods in Mexican tariff item 7005.29.02, except that tariffs are eliminated on January 1, 2001.

[43] See Note 1 to Chapter 96 of the NAFTA Schedule of the United States and tariff item 9603.10.60, which are brooms wholly or in part of broom corn valued at over 96 cents. Under tariff item 9603.10.60.A, the first 100,000 dozen originating from Mexico are admitted duty free. Tariff item 9603.10.60.B, which provides for the staging in Note 1, cover brooms above this quantity.

[44] See Notes 1 and 2 to Chapter 48 of the NAFTA Schedule of Mexico. The goods affected are identified by reference to Note 1 or Note 2, depending on the base rate, in Columns I and II.

[45] See Note 1 to Chapter 39, Note 2 to Chapter 70 and Note 1 to Chapter 84. This staging applies to the goods in these chapters identified by reference to these notes in Columns I and II.

[46] See Note 3 to Chapter 48 of the NAFTA Schedule of Mexico. The products affected are those under subheadings 4819.10 and 4819.20.

[47] See Note 1 to Chapter 94 of the NAFTA Schedule of Mexico. The goods affected are identified by reference to the note in Column I. Tariffs on these goods from Canada are eliminated under staging category C.

[48] Notes 1 and 2 set out the in-quota quantities for goods from the United States and Canada respectively, imported under specified Mexican tariff items.

[49] NAFTA 302(3). The corresponding FTA provision is FTA 401(5).

[50] NAFTA 302(4) and (5). As discussed in §5.2(2), the concept of the tariff rate quota is used in respect of textile and apparel goods, except that the expression used is "tariff preference level". The tariff preference levels for textile and apparel goods are not set out in NAFTA Annex 302.2 and therefore are not subject to NAFTA 302(4) or 302(5).

[51] While the expression "identical or similar good" is used in a general sense here, these words are used in NAFTA 303 as defined in NAFTA 415, which in turn defines this expression by reference to the GATT Customs Valuation Code. Section 82(1)(e) of the *Customs Act*, which sets forth Canada's version of this duty drawback rule, uses the expression "materials of the same class".

[52] See John S. Lambrinidis, *The Structure and Law of a Free Trade Area* (London, Steves & Sons, 1965), at p. 104.

[53] *Ibid.*

[54] See Gary C. Hufbrauer and Jeffrey J. Schott, *North American Free Trade — Issues and Recommendations* (Washington, D.C., Institute for International Economics, 1992), at p. 91. Chapter 5 of this book, entitled "The Maquiladora Phenomenon" contains a good general description of Mexico's maquiladora program.

[55] *Ibid.*, at pp. 91-2.

[56] Secretaria de Commercio y Fomento Industrial.

[57] Decree for the *Development and Operation of the In-Bond Assembly Industry*, Decree of August 9, 1983 (Decreto para el Fomento y Operacion de la Industria Maquiladora de Exportacion) (the "Maquiladora Decree"), Article 7.

[58] Maquiladora Decree Article 28.

[59] Maquiladora Decree Article 10.

[60] See Maquiladora Decree Article 12. A higher percentage can be allowed by special authori-

zation. In 1983, the percentage was 20%. This was increased to 50% in December, 1989. In Mexico's reservation respecting its performance requirement obligations under NAFTA 1106, the applicable percentage is 55%. See NAFTA Annex I, p. I-M-34. As discussed in §7.9(3)(d)(i), this requirement will be phased out and eliminated entirely seven years after NAFTA comes into effect.

[61] *Decreto que Establece Programas de Importacion Temporal para Producir Articulos de Exportacion.*

[62] *Decreto para el Fomento y Operacion de las Empresas Altamente Expotados.*

[63] *Customs Tariff*, s. 80.

[64] These are more fully described in *Comprehensive Guide*, §2.5(5), pp. 26-7.

[65] NAFTA 303(1). A Party is to require evidence of the amount of customs duty paid to another Party on the subsequent exportation of the good. See NAFTA 303(4).

[66] See NAFTA 303(2)(d).

[67] See NAFTA Annex 703.2, Section A, para. 12.

[68] NAFTA 303(3).

[69] In Canada, these provisions will be carried forward in a new s. 83.02 of the *Customs Tariff*. See s. 135 of the *North American Free Trade Agreement Implementation Act*, S.C. 1993, c. 44. The new s. 83.02 provides for the reduction of duties if evidence of payment of the duties to the other NAFTA country is presented within the sixty-day period. See s. 83.02(3). However, there is no provision for a refund of duties if the evidence of payment is subsequently presented. This is consistent with NAFTA 303(5)(b), which is permissive.

[70] These include tubes for high definition television.

[71] That would have been non-originating had NAFTA been in effect.

[72] See §3.1(9).

[73] As the only exception to the commingling rule for same-condition duty drawback is for the prohibition of same-condition substitution duty drawback for agricultural goods, the general prohibition on same-condition duty drawback discussed in §2.3(3)(b) does not apply in a commingling situation.

[74] NAFTA 303(6)(c).

[75] See NAFTA 303(6)(e).

[76] In Canada's implementing legislation, this is interpreted as "imported orange or grapefruit concentrates used in the manufacture or production of exported orange or grapefruit products ... that are exported to the United States". See new s. 83.02(5)(b) of the *Customs Tariff*.

[77] NAFTA Annex 303.6, subparagraph 2(c).

[78] NAFTA Annex 303.6, subparagraph 2(b). The HTSUS tariff items are 5811.00.20 (quilted cotton piece goods), 5811.00.30 (quilted man-made piece goods) and 6307.90.99 (furniture moving pads). The corresponding Canadian tariff items are 5811.00.10, 5811.00.20 and 6307.90.30 respectively.

[79] HTSUS tariff item 1701.11.02.

[80] Canadian tariff item 1701.99.00 or Mexican tariff items 1701.99.01 or 1701.99.99.

[81] See FTA 404(7).

[82] Such as producers of motor vehicles in Canada, whose imports of parts are subject to duties in the 9.2% range, but whose vehicles (unless they are trucks) are subject to duties of 2.5% entering the United States. If the 2.5% duty saved if the vehicle is originating is offset by the duty drawback or deferral lost on imported parts following January 1, 1996, the producer would be in no worse position if its vehicle were non-originating.

[83] Outerwear is comprised of various coats, jackets and snow and ski wear.

[84] "Greige" is fabric directly from the loom before undergoing any process to convert it into a finished fabric.

[85] See *Blouses and Shirts Remission Order*, SOR/88-332; *Denim Apparel Fabrics Remission Order*, SOR/88-333; *Outerwear Fabrics and Outerwear Remission Order*, SOR/88-334; *Outerwear Greige Fabrics for Converting Remission Order*, SOR/88-335; *Shirting Fabrics Remission Order*, SOR/88-331; and *Tailored Collar Shirts Remission Order, 1988*, SOR/88-330, all dated June 23, 1988. These orders were all retroactively amended by the *General Textile and Apparel Amendment Order (Customs Tariff), 1989*, SOR/89-83, dated January 19, 1989.

[86] The denim order applies to the end of the 1993 calendar year. The other orders extend to the end of 1997.

⁸⁷ NAFTA Annex 304.2(d).

⁸⁸ The expression "existing" is not defined in NAFTA 318. Therefore, the definition in NAFTA 201 applies, which means in effect on the date NAFTA enters into force. The cut-off date used elsewhere in the NAFTA provisions respecting Mexico's conditional duty waivers is July 1, 1991.

⁸⁹ See, for example, the Schedule to the *Temporary Importation Regulations* in Revenue Canada Customs and Excise Memorandum D8-1-1, January 1, 1991. Item 9 is "Rolls for embossing or printing short runs of fabrics or similar materials". Item 21 is "Equipment, not available from Canadian production, for use in the testing of microwave systems or of radiopath routing or for similar use". There are fifty-seven items altogether.

⁹⁰ Discussed in §9.3.

⁹¹ Other releasable security may be requested. No bond may be required for an originating good. In Canada's case, charges could include GST.

⁹² See NAFTA 306. The expressions "commercial samples of negligible value" and "printed advertising materials" are defined in NAFTA 318.

⁹³ The NAFTA text does not state whether Column I or II applies. For most goods in Section D, the rates are the same. Presumably Column I would apply because the repairs or alterations would not be considered to be of mixed Mexico-U.S. origin.

⁹⁴ The specific HS subheadings and tariff items for each country are set forth in Table 308.1.1 of NAFTA Annex 308.1.

⁹⁵ One Canadian exception is tariff item 8504.40.40, power supplies for the automatic data processing machines of heading No. 84.71. The MFN rate is 10.2% and the target rate is Free. Part A of Schedule I to the *Customs Tariff*, as amended by S.C. 1993, c. 44, provides for the reduction of the MFN rate to 8.2% on January 1, 1999, 6.2% on January 1, 2000, 4.2% on January 1, 2001, 2.2% on January 1, 2002 and Free on January 1, 2003. The U.S. rate for goods under HS subheading 8504.40 is 3% and Mexican rates are 10%, 15% or 20%, depending on the tariff item.

⁹⁶ The specific HS subheadings and tariff items for each country are set forth in Table 308.1.2 of NAFTA Annex 308.1.

⁹⁷ See §4.1.

⁹⁸ NAFTA 308(3). Annex 308.3 requires the NAFTA countries to consult regarding the tariff classification of these devices and come to an agreement no later than January 1, 1994.

⁹⁹ For examples, see *Comprehensive Guide*, pp. 21-2. A requirement that a good be used for a specified purpose is not a "performance requirement" as defined in NAFTA 318. Duty reductions of general application that are based on end use do not contravene NAFTA 304.

CHAPTER 3

TRADE IN GOODS: RULES OF ORIGIN, MARKING RULES, COUNTRY OF ORIGIN AND CUSTOMS PROCEDURES

As discussed in §1.4(2), an agreement creating a free trade area must establish rules of origin to determine which goods are entitled to preferential tariff treatment. NAFTA sets out new rules of origin that have replaced the rules of origin that applied under the FTA. The NAFTA rules of origin are described in §3.1 and the rules of origin for textile and apparel goods are described in §5.2(2). While eligibility for preferential tariff treatment applies only to "originating" goods,[1] it should be kept in mind that most other NAFTA obligations cover a wider range of goods. For example, the NAFTA disciplines respecting national treatment, export taxes and import and export restrictions and the NAFTA procedures respecting antidumping and countervailing actions apply to "goods of a Party". As discussed in §4.1, these are domestic products as understood under the GATT and include not only originating goods but other goods as well.[2]

The NAFTA rules of origin determine whether a good is "originating" and eligible for preferential NAFTA tariff treatment. However, applying the NAFTA rules of origin does not identify a country of origin. Because of the differing timing for elimination of tariffs among the NAFTA countries, the type of NAFTA preferential tariff treatment to which a good is entitled depends on whether it is "Canadian", "American" or "Mexican". The effect is to create a two-step process. Customs officials must first be satisfied that a good is originating and eligible for NAFTA treatment and then must know the country of origin of the good to ascertain which NAFTA treatment applies.[3] Once tariffs on a good have been fully eliminated in all three NAFTA countries, NAFTA treatment in most cases will cease to depend on the country of origin. However, the bilateral structure of NAFTA provisions respecting textile and apparel goods and agricultural goods will necessitate country of origin determinations even after tariffs have been eliminated. Country of origin determinations for goods other than textile and apparel goods and agricultural goods are discussed in §3.3. Country of origin determinations for textiles and apparel goods and for agricultural goods are discussed in §5.2(4) and §5.3(4) respectively.

Canada, the United States and Mexico all require that at least some imported goods be marked with the country of their origin. NAFTA sets out provisions respecting marking and each NAFTA country has established new Marking Rules under these provisions. The Marking Rules will also be used for country of origin determinations to determine which NAFTA preferential treatment applies. The NAFTA provisions respecting marking are described in §3.2.

NAFTA also sets out rules respecting the customs procedures to be followed by the NAFTA countries. These are described in §3.4.

3.1 RULES OF ORIGIN

(1) Approaches to Determining Origin

It is easy to establish a rule of origin for goods such as crops grown and harvested, trees cut, animals raised, and so on. These goods "wholly originate" in the preferential trading area. For example, lumber cut from white pine grown in Canada is wholly originating. Similarly, a table produced in Canada from Canadian white pine is also wholly originating. The determination of the origin of these goods is straightforward.

The more difficult origin determination arises with the good containing materials ("third country materials") from outside the preferential trading area. A rule of origin that treated all goods containing third country materials as non-originating would be far too restrictive and would defeat the purposes of creating a preferential trading area. On the other hand, to treat goods made entirely from third country materials and subject only to final assembly or finishing processes within the preferential trading area as eligible for preferential treatment would confer unintended benefits on producers in third countries. Rules of origin define the point at which third country materials have been sufficiently processed within the preferential trading area so that the good into which they are incorporated can be considered as "originating" and eligible for preferential tariff treatment.

This point can be defined in terms of "substantial transformation", which occurs when the third country materials have been transformed within the preferential trading area into a new and different good. This approach compares the imported materials with the finished good and ascertains whether the materials have been sufficiently changed within the preferential trading area so that the resulting good is something new and different. This point can also be defined in terms of value added within the preferential trading area. When the value of the third country materials has been counterbalanced by sufficient value imparted to the good through processing within the preferential trading area, the good is considered to be "originating".

American rules of origin have generally been based on substantial transformation while Canadian rules have relied on value-added requirements. The FTA rules of origin were based on both. The U.S. negotiators of the FTA recognized the defects in the case-by-case approach to substantial transformation. Accordingly, the FTA adopted a rules-based approach and set out good-specific rules specifying the transformation or change to materials that had to result from production activities in Canada or the United States for the finished good to be considered as originating. The required transformation was usually expressed as a change in tariff classification (or "tariff shift") that the material had to undergo as it was transformed through processing in Canada or the United States into the finished good. Some rules also imposed a value-added or "value-content" requirement. In a few situations in which a tariff classification change could not occur because of the way in which the Harmonized System is structured, originating status could be met solely on the basis of the content requirement.

NAFTA follows the same basic approach. The NAFTA change in tariff classification rules are frequently more detailed and sometimes more stringent than their FTA counterparts. NAFTA has completely overhauled the FTA content requirement. NAFTA has also introduced new *de minimis* and accumulation concepts designed to take some of the rigidity out of the application of both the change in tariff classification rules and the content requirement.

(2) Structure of the NAFTA Rules

The NAFTA rules of origin are set out in NAFTA Chapter Four and NAFTA Annex 401. NAFTA 511 obliged the NAFTA countries to implement, by January 1, 1994, Uniform Regulations respecting the "interpretation, application and administration" of the rules of origin in Chapter Four and the customs procedures in NAFTA Chapter Five. This NAFTA obligation has been satisfied by all three countries. The NAFTA countries adopted a "verbatim" approach to the Uniform Regulations affecting Chapter Four so that the regulations implementing the NAFTA rules of origin are virtually identical in all three countries.[4] In the course of negotiating the Uniform Regulations, the negotiators of the NAFTA countries effectively rewrote Chapter Four. The primary source for anyone working with the NAFTA rules of origin is the Uniform Regulations as enacted in the importing NAFTA country and not the NAFTA text.

(3) Establishing Origin

In rules of origin terminology, an "originating" good is one that satisfies the rules of origin and a "non-originating" good is one that does not. A "material" is any good used in the production of another good.[5] A "material" that qualifies as an originating good under the rules of origin that apply to it is an "originating" material and a material that does not so qualify is a "non-originating" material. A material must be produced within the

preferential trading area to be originating. Any material imported from outside the preferential trading area is a non-originating material. A material
produced within the preferential trading area can also be non-originating if
it contains imported materials that have not been sufficiently processed to
satisfy the rules of origin that apply to the material.

NAFTA Chapter Four and the Uniform Regulations set out five ways in
which it can be established that a good is originating.

A.   A good is originating if it wholly originates within the territories of the
      NAFTA countries. These goods are described in §3.1(4).

B.   A good that contains non-originating materials is originating if it satis-
      fies the requirements of any specific rule of origin that applies to the
      good. The specific rules of origin are discussed in §3.1(5).

C.   A good is originating if it is produced entirely from originating materials.

D.   In some cases, a change in tariff classification required by a specific
      rule of origin cannot occur because of the manner in which the Har-
      monized System is structured. In these situations, which are described
      in §3.1(8)(i), a good will be considered as originating if the regional value-
      content requirement is satisfied.

E.   As discussed in §2.7(1), once MFN rates on certain automatic data
      processing equipment and their parts are harmonized, any of these goods
      crossing a border between NAFTA countries will be considered as
      originating.

(4) Wholly Originating Goods

The NAFTA text defines "goods wholly obtained or produced entirely
in the territory of one or more of the Parties".[6] The definition is comprehensive but exhaustive. For a good to be "wholly originating", it must fall
under one or more of the nine categories listed in this definition or be
produced entirely from goods falling within those categories. The categories
are carried forward into Section 4(1) of the Uniform Regulations. Most of
the categories are straightforward. For example, the categories include a
mineral good extracted, a vegetable or other good harvested,[7] a live animal
born and raised and a good obtained from hunting, trapping or fishing in
one or more NAFTA countries. The categories covering marine life taken
from the sea require that the vessel be registered and recorded with a NAFTA
country and fly its flag. One category covers waste and scrap from production or used goods collected in one or more NAFTA countries. This category would include aluminum tailings resulting from machining imported
aluminum or steel scrap obtained from used cars originally manufactured
in non-NAFTA countries.

(5) The Specific Rules of Origin

The specific rules of origin are set out in NAFTA Annex 401 and have been carried forward in Schedule I of the Uniform Regulations. The organization of the specific rules follows that of the Harmonized System, with the same sections and chapters. The specific rules are grouped on an HS heading or subheading basis. In some cases there are specific rules for individual tariff items.[8] While the text of the NAFTA rules is longer than the FTA rules, this detailed format is much easier to work with because it is no longer necessary to read all the rules under a section to determine which rule applies to the goods being considered. Anyone making an origin determination must start with the specific rules and look up the rule that applies to the HS heading, subheading or tariff item under which the good under consideration is classified. Except for differences in tariff item numbers resulting from differences in the tariff schedules of the NAFTA countries below the subheading level, the specific rules of origin are the same in each NAFTA country.

Most of the specific rules prescribe the transformation of non-originating materials that must take place for the goods covered by the rule to be originating. The transformation requirements are expressed in terms of changes in tariff classification and sometimes include additional requirements. Many rules provide that meeting the transformation requirement will be sufficient to confer origin only if a "regional value-content" requirement is also satisfied. A few rules permit originating status to be established solely by meeting the content requirement without a transformation requirement.[9]

For most goods for which there is a rule prescribing a content requirement, there is an alternative rule that prescribes a more stringent change in tariff classification requirement without a content requirement. In some instances, the manner in which the value-content requirement is applied to a good depends on whether a material incorporated into the good is "subject to a regional value-content requirement". The Uniform Regulations make it clear in these alternative rule situations that the rule prescribing the content requirement must actually be relied upon to establish origin for the material to be "subject to a regional value-content requirement".[10]

(6) Categories of Materials

The NAFTA rules of origin define a number of categories of materials that are treated in different ways in applying both change in tariff classification requirements and value-content requirements.

"Indirect materials" are goods used in the production, testing or inspection of a good but not incorporated into the good. These include a variety of items such as fuel, energy, tools, dies, moulds, spare parts for maintenance, lubricants, gloves, glasses and safety equipment, catalysts and solvents and machinery and equipment.[11] Indirect materials are always considered as originating.

The NAFTA rules of origin distinguish between "packaging materials and containers" and "packing materials and containers".[12] "Packaging materials and containers" are materials used for packaging a good for retail sale. Plastic packaging in which a wrist watch is displayed for retail sale falls within this definition. "Packing materials and containers" are the materials used to protect a good during transportation. A crate containing wrist watches falls within this definition but the plastic packaging for retail sales purposes does not.

"Accessories, spare parts and tools" are goods that are delivered with a good as part of the good's standard accessories. These include items such as a bicycle tool kit or a car jack.[13]

The NAFTA rules of origin permit self-produced materials to be designated as "intermediate materials" in applying value-content requirements. These are discussed in §3.1(8)(h).

(7) Change in Tariff Classification and Other Transformation Requirements

(a) Change in tariff classification

The NAFTA specific rules rely upon the change in tariff classification approach as the principal means prescribing the transformation of non-originating materials that must take place for a good to be originating. The changes in tariff classification are expressed in terms of the chapters, headings and subheadings of the Harmonized System. Some required changes are expressed in terms of individual tariff items. Subject only to the *de minimis* rule described in §3.1(10), the prescribed change in tariff classification in each rule must be satisfied by every non-originating material incorporated into the good. However, the change need not be satisfied by originating materials. As all indirect materials are considered as originating, the change need not be satisfied by any indirect material. Packaging materials and containers that are classified with the good under the Harmonized System are disregarded in applying the change in tariff classification requirement.[14] Packing materials and containers are also disregarded, regardless of the manner in which they are classified. Accessories, spare parts and tools are also disregarded if the quantities and values are customary for the good within the industry and they are not invoiced separately from the good.

As a simple example of a change in tariff classification requirement, consider the rule for locks for use in motor vehicles classified under HS subheading 8301.20. There are two specific rules for this good. The first rule sets out a change in tariff classification without a regional value-content requirement. This rule is: "A change to subheading 8301.10 through 8301.50 from any other chapter." The "change" referred to is the change in tariff classification that results from processing non-originating materials into a finished good. The tariff classification to which the change must occur (in this case the group 8301.10 through 8301.50, which includes the locks under subheading 8301.20) is the tariff classification of the finished good. The tariff classification from which the change must occur (in this case, any HS chapter other than HS chapter 83). Suppose that the lock is made from imported stainless steel ingots classified under HS heading 72.18. Processing the steel ingot into a lock results in a change of tariff classification from HS heading 72.18 to HS subheading 8301.20. As heading 72.18 falls within HS chapter 72 and HS subheading 8301.20 falls within HS chapter 83, the change required by the rule has been satisfied.

Suppose that the lock producer uses one part that has been imported and is therefore non-originating. Parts for locks are classified under HS subheading 8301.60 which falls within the same HS chapter as the lock. Therefore the rule has not been satisfied. Unless the producer is in a position to use the *de minimis* rule described in §3.1(10), the producer will have to rely on the alternative rule of origin that applies to the lock, which is as follows:

> A change to subheading 8301.10 through 8301.50 from subheading 8301.60, whether or not there is also a change from any other chapter, provided that there is a regional value-content of not less than:
>
> (a) 60 percent where the transaction value method is used, or
>
> (b) 50 percent where the net cost method is used.

Under this rule the tariff classification from which the change must occur is the HS subheading under which the part is classified. Producing the lock from the part results in this change. However, a regional value-content requirement must also be satisfied.[15]

As will be discussed in §5.2(2)(a), the changes in tariff classification prescribed by NAFTA for a number of important categories of textile and apparel goods are more demanding than their FTA counterparts. However, the textile and apparel rules are a special case, and it would be incorrect to say that the NAFTA changes in tariff classification rules are more stringent overall than those in the FTA. Many are the same as under the FTA and others are simply expressed differently. In a number of instances, an FTA rule coupling a change in tariff classification with content requirement has been replaced with a more detailed change in tariff classification rule with no content requirement. For example, under the FTA, any combination of materials required to make an umbrella (frame and shaft, fabric, handle) could be non-originating, but a content requirement also had to be satisfied. Under the corresponding NAFTA rule, the content requirement has been dispensed with but the change in tariff classification requirement provides that a non-originating frame and shaft cannot be combined with non-originating fabric if the umbrella is to be originating. The NAFTA negotiators eliminated the value-content requirement with a number of other goods besides umbrellas.[16]

One obvious but very important factor to be kept in mind when working with any rule based on changes in tariff classification is that the rule cannot be applied unless tariff classifications of both goods and materials are correct.

(b) Other transformation requirements

Some specific rules of origin contain additional transformation requirements. These may be set out in the rule itself or in a special note accompanying the rule or in a note to the HS section or chapter in the Special Rules of Origin under which the rule falls.

Consider the rule for teleprinters under HS subheading 8517.20. In addition to prescribing a change in tariff classification, the rule requires that if the good contains less than three printed circuit assemblies all three must be originating and if the good contains more than three printed circuit assemblies, only one in nine may be non-originating. This printed circuit assembly requirement appears throughout the rules for items of equipment that contain printed circuit assemblies.

As another example, consider the rule for assemblies classified under Canadian tariff item 9009.90.10, U.S. tariff item 9009.90A or 9009.90B and Mexican tariff item 9009.90.02 used in photocopy machines. In addition to satisfying the prescribed change in tariff classification, at least one of a number of components used in the assembly must be originating. These components are listed in Note 3 to HS chapter 90 in the Special Rules of Origin.

A note at the beginning of HS chapter 20 provides that the fruit, nut and vegetable preparations prepared merely by freezing, packing in water, brine of natural juices or by roasting will be considered as originating only if the fresh good is wholly produced or obtained in a NAFTA country. A note to the rule covering HS headings 71.13 to 71.18 provides that pearls temporarily strung but without clasps or other ornamentation will be treated as originating only if the pearls were obtained in a NAFTA country. The rule for the goods of steel under HS heading 73.08 provides that changes resulting from certain processes will not satisfy the required change in tariff classification. Note 6 to HS chapter 85 provides that the origin of television combination units will be determined in accordance with the rule that would apply if the unit were comprised solely of the television receiver.

Some notes are relieving. A note at the beginning of HS Section II provides that agricultural and horticultural products grown in a NAFTA country will be originating even if the seed, bulbs, cuttings or slips come from non-NAFTA countries. A note in HS heading 38.08 provides that certain imported materials used to make pesticides will be treated as originating.[17] Note 2 to HS chapter 90 provides that the origin of the instruments and apparatus covered by that chapter will be determined without regard to the origin of any automatic data processing machines or parts that the good under consideration may include.

While the change in tariff classification is the primary means for prescribing transformation requirements, notes accompanying rules or set out as HS section or chapter notes may modify the manner in which the origin of the good is determined.

(8) The NAFTA Regional Value-Content Requirement

(a) Value-content requirements

Because of their complexity and the administrative burdens they impose on both producers and government officials, value-content requirements are a less attractive means than transformation requirements of prescribing origin requirements. Content requirements were used in the FTA because the HS-based tariff schedules of each of Canada and the United States are harmonized only down to the six digit subheading level. For a number of goods, this level of breakdown did not provide sufficient specificity to adequately prescribe required transformation in terms of changes in tariff classification so there was no alternative but to impose a content requirement. NAFTA solved the specificity problem by going below the subheading level to specific tariff items. However, mandatory content requirements have been retained for a few goods[18] and optional content requirements apply to many goods, such as the locks referred to previously.

There are a number of approaches which can be followed in measuring content. Values used in the content formula can be costs or customs values or selling prices or imputed values or some combination of these. The measurement of "domestic" or "regional"[19] value added can be determined by building up certain values which count towards regional value added, or by starting with a value and backing out items which do not count. The content formula can count the value of non-originating materials when they are acquired by the producer or require tracing back through chains of suppliers to the point that a non-originating material is imported into the preferential trading area. A cost-based formula can be restrictive or expansive in defining what non-material costs count towards regional value added. The content requirement can be applied on a shipment by shipment basis or averaged over a number of identical or generic or non-generic goods, produced at a certain place (such as a single plant) or places (such as all plants in a territory) over a certain period of time (such as the producer's fiscal year).

(b) The FTA regional value-content requirement

The FTA content requirement was based on costs and followed a build-up approach to regional value added. Materials were counted when acquired by the producer with no requirement for tracing back through chains of suppliers. Only production costs counted as regional, and not other non-material costs. Averaging was permitted for motor vehicles but not for other goods. Expressed as a formula, the FTA content requirement was:

$$\frac{\text{DCP plus VOM}}{\text{DCP plus VAM}} \text{ must be at least 50\%.}$$

Where:

DCP   = the direct cost of processing or direct cost of assembling
VOM   = the price paid by the producer for originating materials used or consumed in the production of the good
VAM   = the price paid by the producer for all materials (whether or not originating) used in the production of the good.

There was only one variation of the FTA content requirement and it applied to all goods subject to a regional value-content requirement under the FTA rules of origin.

(c) The NAFTA regional value-content requirement

There are two variations of the NAFTA content requirement. The first is the "transaction value method" and the second is the "net cost approach". Expressed as formulae, these are as follows:

Transaction Value Method:

$$\frac{\text{TV minus VNM}}{\text{TV}} \text{ must be at least 60\%.[20]}$$

Net Cost Method:

$$\frac{\text{NC minus VNM}}{\text{NC}} \text{ must be at least 50\%.[21]}$$

Where:

TV   = transaction value
NC   = the net cost of the good
VNM   = value of non-originating materials used by the producer in the production of the good.

(d) Transfer pricing and the GATT Customs Valuation Code

The NAFTA content requirement relies heavily on the principles of the GATT Customs Valuation Code ("CVC").[22] The CVC establishes a common set of principles applied by its signatories in valuing goods for the purpose of assessing *ad valorem* duties. Normally, the value of goods for the purposes of assessing duty is the amount actually paid or payable by the importer to the exporter. This "transaction value" is subject to a number of adjustments. For example, if the importer has given an "assist" to the exporter in the form of materials or tooling or design work, the value of these must be added to the transaction value.[23] If the exporter and importer are related to each other and the relationship has influenced the price, or if they have entered into arrangements which would result in the price charged by the exporter to the importer being understated, the transaction value will not be accepted as the value for duty purposes. If the price is unacceptable under these CVC principles, the CVC sets forth alternative means of determining the value of the good for duty purposes.[24]

The NAFTA rules of origin have adopted the principles of the CVC as transfer pricing disciplines. The acceptability of the price paid or payable for a good or a material for use as a value applying a regional value-content requirement is determined in accordance with the same principles set out in the CVC for determining whether the price paid or payable for an imported good is an acceptable basis for assessing duty. If the price paid for a material is unacceptable under these principles, NAFTA uses the alternative valuation methods set out in the CVC to assign a value to the material. NAFTA also applies adjustments to prices that are based on those set out in the CVC.

The CVC was adopted because it is the only code of transfer pricing disciplines common to all three NAFTA countries and customs authorities are familiar with it. However, the CVC was designed to cover transactions involving imports and was never intended to apply to a wholly domestic setting. The Uniform Regulations address this problem by restating the provisions of the CVC in a manner suitable for making origin determinations.

(e) Transaction value, net cost and value of materials

(i) Transaction value

The "transaction value" upon which the transaction value method is based is determined in accordance with Schedule II of the Uniform Regulations. Schedule II carries forward the relevant principles of the CVC and adapts them for rules of origin purposes. Schedule II defines "transaction value" as the amount actually paid or payable by the buyer of a good to the producer. The transaction used to determine the transaction value is the transaction in which the producer sells the good. This transaction may be the transaction in which the good is exported to another NAFTA country or it may be a domestic transaction involving a sale to a local distributor, who subsequently exports the good to another NAFTA country.

The transaction value is adjusted by adding buying commissions, royalties paid by the buyer and assists. For example, if the buyer provides an assist in the form of the dies and moulds needed to produce the good, Section 4(1)(b) of Schedule II requires that the "transaction value" used in applying the transaction value method be increased by the value of these items. The definition of "royalties" used in making these additions is the NAFTA definition discussed in §3.1(8)(e)(ii) and not the CVC concept of "royalties and licence fees". Costs of packaging (as opposed to packing) materials and containers are added if not already included in the price paid or payable for the good.

The transaction value is then "adjusted to an F.O.B. basis".[25] This means that transportation and associated costs to the "point of direct shipment" are included but costs after that point are excluded. The point of direct shipment is the location from which the producer usually ships its goods to the buyer. Consistent with the requirement in NAFTA 410 that packing (as opposed to packaging) materials and containers be disregarded in applying a value-content requirement, the cost of these items as recorded in the producer's books is deducted in making this adjustment.[26]

(ii) Net cost

The calculation of "net cost" begins with "total cost", which is the total of all "product costs", "period costs" and "other costs" incurred within one or more NAFTA countries. These expressions are defined in Section 2(1) of the Uniform Regulations. "Product costs" are costs associated with the production of a good, including the value of materials, direct labour costs and direct overhead. The "value of materials" is determined in the manner discussed in §3.1(8)(e)(iii). "Period costs" are costs other than product costs that are expensed in the period incurred, and "other costs" are costs that are not product or period costs.

"Net cost" is "total cost" minus "excluded costs", which are "sales promotion, marketing and after-service costs", "royalties", "shipping and packing costs", and "non-allowable interest costs". These expressions are all defined in NAFTA 415 and in Section 2(1) of the Uniform Regulations, and each definition must be reviewed before making any calculations. For example, "sales promotion, marketing and after-service costs" includes product liability insurance. "Royalties" do not include fees paid for distribution rights. "Shipping and packing costs" do not include costs incurred to prepare the product for retail sale. "Non-allowable interest costs" are interest costs on debt obligations that are more than 700 basis points above the yield on debt obligations of comparable maturities issued by the federal government of the NAFTA country where the producer is located. Schedule XI of the Uniform Regulations sets out rules for calculating non-allowable interest. Normal interest charges should not be captured by this definition.

Section 7(13) of the Uniform Regulations sets out several important points of clarification respecting excluded costs. Excluded costs included in the value of materials are not subtracted from total cost. For example, a producer of a good may purchase a part from a parts producer that is manufactured under licence agreement under which royalties are paid by the parts producer to a licensor. The royalty cost included in the value of the part is not subtracted from total cost in determining the net cost of the good. Also, excluded costs do not include amounts paid for research and development costs in any NAFTA country.

NAFTA 402(8) and Section 6(11) of the Uniform Regulations provide that net cost can be calculated by one of three basic methods: the producer may calculate its total cost, deduct excluded costs and "reasonably allocate" the difference to the good; or "reasonably allocate" total cost to the good and subtract excluded costs included in the amounts so allocated; or "reasonably allocate" each cost included in total cost so that the aggregate of costs allocated does not include any excluded costs. The acceptable methods for "reasonably allocating" costs are set out in Schedule VII of the Uniform Regulations. Schedule VII requires a producer to use a cost allocation method that it is using for internal management purposes provided that the method is based on the "criterion of benefit, cause or ability to bear". If this provision does not apply, the Appendices to the Schedule set out several methods that can be used to allocate overhead. The effect of Section 6 of Schedule VII is to exclude some further costs from the net cost calculation.[27]

Except for the cost of certain materials referred to in §3.1(8)(e)(iii), costs are those reflected in the producer's books, which must be maintained in accordance with the generally accepted accounting principles ("GAAP") of the NAFTA country in which it is situated. The authorities comprising GAAP in each country are listed in Schedule XII of the Uniform Regulations. Section 6(12) of the Uniform Regulations make it clear that the location of the payee of a cost is not a relevant factor in determining whether or not a cost is included.

(iii) Value of materials

The value of non-originating materials ("VNM") must be determined in applying either the transaction value method or the net cost method. The value of both originating and non-originating materials must be determined when applying the net cost method.

The value of indirect materials is their cost as recorded on the books of the producer.[28] The value of indirect materials, such as imported tooling or imported fuel, is included in net cost but, because indirect materials are considered originating, is never included in the VNM.

The value of packing (as opposed to packaging) materials and containers is their cost as recorded on the books of the producer. As packing materials and containers are disregarded when applying a value-content requirement, their value is not included in net cost when applying the net cost method or in the VNM when applying either method.

The value of packaging (as opposed to packing) materials and containers that the producer produces itself is the producer's total cost that can be reasonably allocated to these self-produced materials in accordance with the cost allocation rules set out in Schedule VII of the Uniform Regulations. This approach is the same as that followed for intermediate materials discussed in §3.1(8)(h).

The value of all materials other than indirect materials, intermediate materials, packing materials and containers and self-produced packaging materials and containers is determined in accordance with NAFTA 402(9) which applies the principles of the CVC and adds some further adjustments. It is very important to keep in mind that this method of valuation applies not only to the calculation of the VNM under either method but also to the calculation of the value of all these materials in the producer's total cost if the net cost method is being used.

NAFTA 402(9) and the principles of the CVC will be administered in each NAFTA country in accordance with Section 7(1) and Schedule VIII of the Uniform Regulations. If the producer imports a material from a non-NAFTA country, its value is the customs value used in the importation.[29] If the material is acquired within the NAFTA countries, the value is its "transaction value" determined in accordance with Schedule VIII. The transaction value is the price actually paid or payable for the material unless there is no sale or unless the price paid or payable is "unacceptable". The price paid or payable is unacceptable if the producer and the seller are related and the relationship affected the price[30] or if there are circumstances surrounding the sale which cause the price to be distorted or make calculation of the real consideration paid for the material impossible.[31] If the price paid or payable is acceptable, it is adjusted by adding commissions and brokerage fees (other than buying commissions), costs of containers classified with the material under the Harmonized System, assists such as tools, dies or materials supplied to the seller by the producer and any royalties that the producer must pay as a condition of the sale of the material.[32]

If the price paid for a material is unacceptable for the reasons described above, its value will be determined by using the alternative means in the CVC for establishing value for duty purposes. These have been carried forward, with some modification to make them applicable to domestic as well as international transactions, into Sections 6 to 11 of Schedule VIII. Section 6 provides that the transaction value used will be that for identical materials sold to a buyer in the NAFTA country where the producer is located at about the same time as the sale of the materials takes place. If Section 6 does not produce a value, the producer moves to Section 7, which is the same rule but with similar materials rather than identical materials. "Identical materials'' and ''similar materials'' are defined in Section 2(1) of the Uniform Regulations and the definitions are based on those set out in the CVC. Identical materials are materials that are the same in all respects, excluding minor differences in appearance, and similar materials are commercially interchangeable. If neither of these Sections produces a value, the producer has a choice between Section 9, which is the CVC deductive method, or Section 10, which is the CVC computed method. If all these fail, customs can rely on the ''reasonable means'' rule in Section 11, which carries forward Article 7 of the CVC.

Once the value of a material has been determined in the manner just described, there are additions of further amounts to the extent not included in such value. Transportation costs to the location of the producer are included. These include packing costs. Note that costs of packing materials and containers for the finished good are excluded in applying the value-content requirement but are included in respect of materials. Duties and taxes, other than those that are refundable,[33] customs brokerage fees and the cost of waste and spoilage are also added. It must be kept in mind that the ''origin'' of these costs is that of the material with which they are associated. Suppose that a U.S. producer buys an originating material in Seattle and ships it to its location in Chicago. The freight cost will be included in its net cost if the producer is using the net cost method but not in its VNM. Suppose, however, that the material is imported from Japan, entered in Seattle and shipped to Chicago. The freight cost from Japan to Seattle and from Seattle to Chicago would be included in the net cost if that method is being used and in the VNM with either method. The effect is that the domestic freight cost from Seattle to Chicago is treated as non-originating.

Accessories, spare parts and tools are taken into account as originating or non-originating materials, whichever is the case, in applying the value-content requirement and are valued in the manner just described. Purchased packaging (as opposed to packing) materials and containers are also valued in this manner.

There are special rules for determining the VNM for automotive goods described in §3.1(12).

(f) Which method applies?

Except in a few instances, a producer may choose between the transaction value method and the net cost method. The transaction value method is not available for footwear, word processing machines, motor vehicles and automotive goods that are listed on the tracing lists described in §3.1(12)(a). The transaction value method cannot be used if there is no transaction value, as will occur in a consignment situation, or if the transaction value is unacceptable under the CVC principles carried forward in Section 2(2) of Schedule III of the Uniform Regulations. These circumstances are the same as those for determining the acceptability of the price paid or payable for a material described in §3.1(8)(e)(iii). Even if the transaction value is acceptable, the "transaction value" method cannot be used if the good is sold to a related person and sales of at least 85% of identical or similar goods in the previous six months were also to related persons. The transaction value method is also not available for determining the origin of intermediate materials described in §3.1(8)(h) or by producers who are accumulating as described in §3.1(11).

A producer who chooses the transaction value method may recalculate the value-content under the net cost method under certain circumstances described in NAFTA 402(6) and in Section 6(7) of the Uniform Regulations. However, the choice of the net cost method is a one-way street. If customs determines that the required percentage has not been achieved by a producer who has chosen the net cost method, the producer cannot elect to use the transaction value method.

(g) Roll-up and roll-down

With roll-up and roll-down, a producer receives regional credit for the entire price paid for an originating material, even if it contains imported or non-originating sub-materials. The price of the imported sub-materials is "rolled up" into the price of the material. Similarly, the entire price of a non-originating material counts against the producer, even though it may contain some regional value-added. This regional value-added is "rolled down" to zero. NAFTA follows this approach for all goods except some automotive goods. The origin of each material acquired by the purchaser is determined under its own NAFTA rule of origin. If the material is originating, the value of non-originating or imported materials that it contains is not included in the VNM in applying either the transaction value or net cost method. If the material is non-originating, its entire value determined in the manner described in §3.1(8)(e)(iii) is included in the VNM.

Suppose that a producer of motor boats under HS heading 89.03 buys an engine. Suppose that the engine producer imported the pistons. The origin of the engine will be determined by its producer under the special rule of origin for engines under HS heading 84.07. If the engine is originating, the imported pistons will not be included in the motor boat producer's VNM. If the engine is non-originating, its entire value will be included in VNM, including the value added in NAFTA countries.

(h) Intermediate materials and internal roll-up

NAFTA explicitly recognizes the concept that a vertically integrated producer that manufactures its own parts should be in no worse a position than its non-integrated counterpart that receives the full benefit of roll-up on the parts that it buys. This concept might be termed as "internal roll-up". The NAFTA rules allow a producer to designate any self-produced material as an "intermediate material".[34] If a producer designates a self-produced originating material as an intermediate material, the VNM that it contains will not be included in the VNM of the good into which it is incorporated. The origin of the intermediate material is determined by using rules of origin that apply to it, including the specific rules in NAFTA Annex 401. If the applicable rule includes a content requirement, the net cost method must be used. However, the designation of an intermediate material does not preclude the use of the transaction value method for the finished good.

Suppose that the producer of motor boats referred to above is vertically integrated and produces its own engines and buys the pistons from a producer located in a non-NAFTA country. The producer may designate the engines as intermediate materials. The origin of the engines is determined under the specific rule of origin for heading 84.07, which includes a value-content requirement. The net cost method must be used. If the engines are found to be originating, the value of the imported pistons is not included in the VNM when calculating the value-content of the motor boat. The producer may use either the transaction value method or the net cost method in determining the regional value-content of the boat.

(i) Multiple designations

A producer can make multiple designations of intermediate materials. The only constraint on multiple designations is that if the intermediate material is subject to a content requirement, no other self-produced material that is subject to a content requirement used in its production can be designated as an intermediate material by the same producer. Suppose that the motor boat producer makes its own engine blocks from imported aluminum. Engine blocks fall under HS subheading 8409.91. The special rule for this subheading gives the producer a choice between a change in tariff classification requirement only and a regional value-content requirement only. As the imported aluminum falls under HS chapter 76, the block can be established as originating under the special rule requiring only a change in tariff classification. Therefore, the motor boat producer can designate the block as an intermediate material in applying the content requirement to the engine, and as a result of the designation the value of the imported aluminum can be excluded from the VNM in this calculation. Suppose, however, that the motor boat manufacturer incorporates the imported pistons into a piston assembly with originating connecting rods purchased from a local supplier. Both the piston and the piston assembly are classified under HS subheading 8409.91, and the producer would have to apply the specific rule providing for a content requirement to establish that the piston assembly is originating. The producer cannot designate the piston assembly as an intermediate material if it has designated the engine as an intermediate material. This constraint does not include designations of intermediate materials made by other producers.

However, if the producer is accumulating with another producer, as described in §3.1(11), the two producers are considered as one and the constraint on making multiple designations of intermediate materials applies.

(ii) Value of intermediate materials

The value of an intermediate material is the producer's total cost that can be reasonably allocated to it.[35] The allocation methodology is set out in Schedule VII of the Uniform Regulations. The expression "total cost" as opposed to "net cost" is used so that costs reasonably allocatable to the intermediate material that would otherwise be considered excluded can be included in the value of the intermediate material. If the producer elects to use the transaction value method for the good containing the intermediate material, the value of an originating intermediate material itself is irrelevant. The sole effect of the designation is to exclude the value of the non-originating materials contained in the intermediate material from the producer's VNM. If an intermediate material turns out to be non-originating the producer may rescind its designation,[36] so the value of a non-originating intermediate material should never appear in the VNM. However, the value of an intermediate material is relevant in applying the net cost method because any excluded costs included in the allocation of total cost to the intermediate material will not be included in the excluded costs that are subtracted from total cost to arrive at net cost. For example, a designated intermediate material may be a part manufactured under licence under which royalties are payable. Royalties are normally excluded costs. However, to the extent that they can be reasonably allocated to the cost of producing the designated intermediate material, they are included in value of the materials used to produce the good and, because of the rule in Section 7(13) of the Uniform Regulations referred to in §3.1(8)(e)(ii), will not be subtracted from total cost in calculating net cost. The result is that the royalties that would have been excluded if the designation had not been made are included in "net cost" and count as regional content.

If the integrated motor boat producer referred to above is producing the engines under a licence under which it pays royalties, the royalties, which are normally an excluded cost, would be included in the value of the engines and therefore in the net cost of the motor boats. However, in applying the value-content requirement to the engine itself, the royalties would be excluded from the engine's net cost because they are not included in the value of any materials used to produce the engine.

(i) The assembling rule

NAFTA carries forward the FTA concept that in certain situations in which the structure of the Harmonized System makes it impossible for a change in tariff classification to occur, origin can be established solely by satisfying the value-content requirement.[37] A change in tariff classification may not be possible because of the application of Rule 2(a) of the General Rules of Interpretation of the Harmonized System, which provides that unassembled or disassembled goods be classified under the same tariff provision as the finished good. Also, the Harmonized System frequently sets out separate parts headings and subheadings, goods and their parts are sometimes classified under the same heading or subheading. For example, while engines are classified under HS headings 84.07 (spark ignition) and 84.08 (diesel) and parts for engines are classified under the separate HS heading 84.09, HS heading 87.15 provides for baby carriages and their parts with no further breakdown into subheadings. The specific rule of origin for baby carriages requires a change in tariff classification from another heading. As another example, HS subheading 9402.10 covers dentists', barbers' or other similar chairs and parts thereof, and the applicable specific rule of origin requires a change from another chapter. Neither of these rules can be satisfied by a non-originating part and there are no alternative specific rules providing that originating status can be established on the basis of the value-content requirement. The assembling rule provides relief in this situation by permitting a producer of baby carriages or dentist chairs to use non-originating parts and establish that the good is originating solely on the basis of satisfying the value-content requirement.

The NAFTA language is more precise and the situations in which this approach may be followed are more clearly delineated than under the FTA. The rules as set out in the NAFTA text have been elaborated upon in the Uniform Regulations. For example, the rule in Section 4(4)(b)(iii) of the Uniform Regulations makes it clear that the rule cannot be used in connection with parts of parts under headings or subheadings that classify goods and their parts together. For example, a producer of parts for baby carriages who assembled its parts from other baby carriage parts that are non-originating cannot use the assembling rule to establish that its parts are originating.[38]

Subject only to the constraints described in §3.1(8)(f), a producer applying the assembling rule can choose between the transaction value method and the net cost method. Unlike the FTA, there is no difference in the wording of the content requirement applicable to this situation from that applicable in other situations. This precludes the possibility of customs authorities taking the approach of U.S. Customs in one of its Honda rulings that only ''assembling'' costs count when the assembling rule is used and ''processing'' costs are excluded.[39]

The assembling rule cannot be used with the apparel and textile made-up goods classified under HS chapters 61, 62 or 63.

(j) Averaging under the net cost method

The FTA provided that producers of motor vehicles could average their calculations over their fiscal years. The rules of origin as set out in the NAFTA text carry this provision forward and set out averaging options for parts manufacturers. These provisions are discussed in §3.1(12)(g).

The Uniform Regulations have extended the right to average calculations to any producer using the net cost method. Section 6(15) provides that calculations for a good can be averaged with identical or similar goods produced in the same plant. The calculations can be averaged over the producer's fiscal year or monthly, quarterly or half-yearly. Identical goods are those that are the same in all respects except for minor differences in appearance and similar goods are those that are commercially interchangeable for each other.[40] The producer applies the net cost method on the basis of the net costs incurred and the values of non-originating materials used in producing the goods under consideration and identical or similar goods over the averaging period elected. The averaging election applies to all goods produced during the averaging period and cannot be rescinded for the goods produced during that period.

(k) Inventory management and the transaction value method

Averaging is not permitted when applying the transaction value method. Calculations are made on a shipment by shipment basis. Section 6(1) of the Uniform Regulations provide that tracking the VNM of identical non-originating materials to the transaction value of each shipment may be done by using any of the inventory management methods set out in Schedule IX. The problem arises because materials in inventory will have been purchased at different times at different prices. Schedule IX sets out the first-in, first-out ("FIFO") method, the last-in, first-out method ("LIFO") and a rolling average method, and gives examples of how each is applied. Identical materials are those that are the same in all respects other than minor differences in appearance. Values of non-originating materials that are not "identical" must be separately tracked.

(9) Fungible Materials and Fungible Goods

Fungible goods and materials are goods or materials that are interchangeable for commercial purposes and whose properties are essentially identical.

The language of the FTA strongly implied that fungible originating and non-originating materials had to be kept physically separated.[41] In its Guidelines, Revenue Canada took the reasonable position that tracking fungible originating and non-originating materials through inventory accounting systems would be an acceptable alternative to physical separation.[42] However, U.S. Customs insisted that the words of the FTA meant that strict physical separation was required.[43]

The NAFTA rules clearly provide that when fungible originating and non-originating materials are used to produce a good, the determination of which materials are used in which good need not be by specific identification. This determination can be made through inventory management methods for the purpose of determining whether a required change in tariff classification has occurred or in applying a value-content requirement.[44] The inventory management methods are set out in Schedule X of the Uniform Regulations and are comprised of FIFO, LIFO and an "average method". Schedule X describes how each method is to be applied and Appendix A to Schedule X sets out examples. The producer is free to use specific identification if it wishes. If the producer chooses this method, the originating and non-originating materials can be physically segregated or segregated by means of marks identifying each material as originating or non-originating.

The inventory management methods set out in Schedule X are used for a different purpose than those set out in Schedule IX. The methods in Schedule X are used in applying a change in tariff classification or value-content requirement to determine the origin of materials drawn from an inventory of originating and non-originating materials that are fungible. The methods in Schedule IX are used by a producer applying the transaction value method to determine which values of identical non-originating materials to match with the transaction value of a shipment of goods.

NAFTA also provides for inventory treatment for commingled originating and non-originating goods. This can occur if a producer produces goods and supplements its inventory with goods imported from a non-NAFTA country. Under the FTA, the domestically produced goods had to be kept physically separate from the imported goods. Under NAFTA, the domestic and imported goods can be commingled and the origin of goods sold from the inventory of commingled goods can be determined using inventory management methods set out in Schedule X.[45]

(10) De Minimis

NAFTA sets out a *de minimis* provision that applies to both the change in tariff classification and the content requirement.[46] To remove some of the rigidity from the change in tariff classification rules, NAFTA provides that if the value of non-originating materials that do not undergo an applicable change in tariff classification is less than 7% of the transaction value of the good adjusted to an F.O.B. basis as described in §3.1(8)(e)(i) or the total cost of the good, the good will none the less originate so long as other requirements are satisfied.[47] The transaction value of the good is used in this calculation unless it is unacceptable under the rules set out in Schedule II of the Uniform Regulations described in §3.1(8)(e)(i). Consider the example involving barber chairs referred to in §3.1(8)(i). Assuming that other non-originating materials satisfy the required change in tariff classification, if the value of the non-originating parts used to make the chair amount to less than 7% of its transaction value or total cost, the non-originating parts can be disregarded and the producer does not have to rely on the assembling rule to establish that the good is originating.[48]

Yarns, textile and apparel goods classified under HS chapters 50 to 63 are not covered by the foregoing but by a special *de minimis* rule based on weight. If the weight of non-originating fibres and yarns that do not undergo a required change in tariff classification is less than 7% of the weight of the component of the good that determines its tariff classification, the good will be considered originating. This rule by weight does not apply to non-originating fabric.[49]

Under the FTA, the failure of a single insignificant non-originating material to satisfy a change in tariff classification requirement that did not include the content requirement could force the producer to apply the content requirement. NAFTA relieves the producer from having to satisfy the content requirement if the value of all non-originating materials used to produce the good is less than 7% of the transaction value or total cost of the good.[50]

There are a number of situations in which the NAFTA *de minimis* provision does not apply.[51] These include various agricultural products, dairy products, juices, certain sugar and cocoa products, lard, and various appliances such as stoves and trash compactors. The rule does not apply to any non-originating printed circuit assembly used to produce a good subject to the requirement respecting printed circuit assemblies described in §3.1(7)(b). The rule also does not apply to any non-originating material used in the production of a good classified under HS chapters 1 through 27, unless it is classified under a different subheading than the good.

(11) Accumulation

The NAFTA rules permit a producer to "accumulate" its production with that of another producer located in any NAFTA country for the purposes of determining whether a change in tariff classification has occurred or in applying a value-content requirement.[52] A producer who chooses to accumulate can pick and choose the materials to which accumulation is to apply, and does not have to accumulate with respect to all materials.

A producer of a good that purchases a non-originating material produced in a NAFTA country can avoid the harsh consequences of roll-down in applying the value-content requirement by "accumulating" its costs with those of the supplier as if they were a single producer. Regardless of the good produced, producers electing to "accumulate" must use the net cost method.

Consider the producer of motor boats referred to in §3.1(8)(g) who purchases a non-originating engine produced in a NAFTA country. There are two methods set out in the Uniform Regulations under which the motor boat producer and the engine producer can accumulate their costs. Under Section 14(2)(a) of the Uniform Regulations, the engine producer can give a statement to the motor boat producer stating the net cost and VNM of the engine. Instead of including the full value of the non-originating engine (determined in the manner described in §3.1(8)(e)(iii) above) in its net cost and VNM, the motor boat producer includes only the net cost and VNM figures received from the engine producer. Suppose that the motor boat producer pays $1,000 for the engine and that this amount is the value of the engine determined under Schedule VIII of the Uniform Regulations. Suppose that the engine producer's net cost is $800 and its VNM is $500. The motor boat manufacturer would not include the $1,000 in either its net cost or its VNM. Instead, it would include $800 in its net cost and $500 in its VNM.[53]

Under the alternative method in Section 14(2)(b) of the Uniform Regulations, the engine producer can state any amount that is part of its net cost and is not comprised of VNM. Suppose that the value of originating materials used by the engine producer is $100 and the engine producer does not want to disclose its profit margin to the motor boat producer. The engine producer issues a statement to the motor boat producer indicating an amount of $100. Using the figures set out above, the rule in Section 14(2)(b) requires that the motor boat producer include the value of the engine of $1,000 in its net cost. However, the amount required to be included in the motor boat producer's VNM is $1,000 less the amount of $100 stated by the engine producer. The motor boat producer includes $900 in VNM respecting the engine rather than the full amount of $1,000 that would have been included without accumulation.

Accumulation also applies to determining whether a prescribed change in tariff classification has occurred. As will be discussed in §5.2(2)(b), accumulation will be particularly useful for producers in the textile and apparel goods sector.

(12) Special Rules for Automotive Goods

The NAFTA rules of origin set forth special requirements respecting the application of the content requirement to motor vehicles and many other automotive goods. There are a number of variations of the value-content requirement that can apply to automotive goods. The variation that applies to vehicles depends on whether the vehicle is a light-duty vehicle or a heavy-duty vehicle. Light-duty vehicles are small trucks,[54] buses[55] and passenger vehicles[56] and heavy-duty vehicles are tractors,[57] larger trucks,[58] buses[59] and specialty vehicles.[60] The variation of value-content requirement that applies to other automotive goods depends on whether the good is intended for use as original equipment in a light-duty vehicle or a heavy-duty vehicle or whether it is produced for the aftermarket and whether it is included on the light-duty tracing list or the heavy-duty vehicle tracing list.

(a) The tracing lists

(i) The light-duty vehicle tracing list

The light-duty vehicle tracing list, which is set out in NAFTA Annex 403.1 and carried forward in Schedule IV of the Uniform Regulations, contains a list of tariff provisions. The tariff provisions listed cover many parts of a motor vehicle, such as rubber tubes and belts, tires, rear view mirrors, locks, engines and their parts, bearings, bearing housings, transmission shafts, transmissions, flywheels, electric motors, distributors, cassette decks and radios, windshield wipers and defrosters, switches and other electrical components, sealed beam head lamps, bodies and body stampings, chassis, safety seat belts, air bags, brakes and their parts, bumpers, axles, wheels, mufflers, air-conditioners, catalytic converters, radiators, clutches, steering wheels and columns and their parts, power train parts, suspension systems, various other parts, and seats. However, tariff provisions do not cover all parts. For example, the tariff provisions for spark plugs, batteries (other than for electric cars), brake linings and plastic tubes are not on the light-duty vehicle tracing list. Also, the tariff provisions for parts for a number of items on the light-duty vehicle tracing list, such as headlamps, clutches, road wheels, bumpers, radios and cassette decks, electric motors, air-conditioners, catalytic converters, locks and rear view mirrors are not on the list.

(ii) The heavy-duty vehicle tracing list

The heavy-duty vehicle tracing list is set out in NAFTA Annex 403.2 and is carried forward into Schedule V of the Uniform Regulations. This list uses noun descriptions rather than tariff provisions and lists only engines, vibration control goods, McPherson struts and transmissions, together with their parts, but does not include other parts of heavy-duty vehicles. In the terminology of the list, engines and transmissions are "components" in the NAFTA text and "automotive components" in the Uniform Regulations. The parts listed are called "materials" in the NAFTA text and "listed materials" in the Uniform Regulations. Henceforth, the terminology of the Uniform Regulations will be used.

For the automotive component comprised of gasoline or diesel engines, the list identifies such "listed materials" as the cast block, cast head, fuel injector pumps, glow plugs, turbochargers and superchargers, electronic engine controls, and so on. For the automotive component comprised of transmissions (or gear boxes), the list identifies as "listed materials" various parts for manual or torque converter type (automatic) transmissions. The listed materials include most but not all parts that comprise an automotive component. For example, the listed materials for engines do not include spark plugs, rocker arms or rocker arm assemblies.

76

(b) Application of the content requirement to automotive goods

The specific rules of origin for motor vehicles, engines, vibration control goods, McPherson struts and plastic tubes impose mandatory content requirements. The specific rules for many parts listed on the light-duty vehicle tracing list provide for a change in tariff requirement only. All other automotive goods are subject to a change in tariff classification alone or the alternative of either a less stringent tariff shift coupled with a content requirement or, in some instances, a content requirement alone.

The net cost method must be used in applying the value-content requirement to motor vehicles and to all automotive goods on the tracing lists. The transaction value method may be used for automotive goods such as plastic tubes (to which a mandatory content requirement applies) or spark plugs (to which a content requirement applies if the spark plug is made from parts) that are not on the tracing lists.

(c) Light-duty automotive goods

(i) Calculation of VNM

If the automotive good is light-duty vehicle, or a part falling under a tariff provision on the light-duty vehicle tracing list and intended for use as original equipment in a light-duty vehicle, the net cost method is applied in the manner described in NAFTA 403(1) and Section 9 of the Uniform Regulations. While net cost is determined in the same manner as for other goods, the calculation of the VNM is completely different. The VNM is the sum of the values, as determined under Section 9 of the Uniform Regulations, of non-originating materials imported from any non-NAFTA country under a tariff provision included on the light-duty vehicle tracing list. The rule applies regardless of who imported the materials. The producer must gather information from its suppliers that will enable it to determine the value of all materials incorporated into the vehicle imported under the specified tariff provisions. Materials imported under the specified tariff provisions are included in VNM even if they are incorporated into originating materials purchased or produced by the producer.

Consider a motor vehicle assembler who buys the engines for the light-duty vehicles that it produces. The engine may be originating under its own rule of origin. However, the tariff provision for parts of engines is included on the light-duty vehicle tracing list.[61] Therefore, if parts such as the pistons have been imported, their value is included in VNM for the content calculation for the vehicle. If the engine is non-originating, its value will not be included in VNM unless the engine itself has been imported. As with the originating engine, the value of all parts in the engine that have been imported under the listed tariff provisions will be included in VNM.

However, the value of materials imported under tariff provisions not included on the light-duty tracing list and of materials produced in a NAFTA country that are non-originating because they do not satisfy the requirements of their special rule will not be included in the VNM. For example, the value of imported spark plugs or an imported battery (except for an electric vehicle) will not be included in the VNM for the vehicle. Consider also a rear view mirror produced in a NAFTA country from imported glass. The mirror does not meet the change in tariff classification requirement in its specific rule because a change from the HS headings for glass to the HS heading for mirrors does not confer origin. Therefore the mirror would not be entitled to preferential tariff treatment crossing a NAFTA border. However, a mirror's value is included in the assembler's VNM only if it has been imported because the tariff provision for rear view mirrors is included on the light-duty vehicle tracing list. In this case, despite the fact that the mirror is non-originating, it has not been imported and its value is not included in the assembler's VNM for the vehicle. As the light-duty vehicle tracing list does not include the tariff provisions for glass, the value of the imported glass is not included in the VNM.

For a number of parts covered by tariff provisions on the light-duty vehicle tracing list, the value content will always be 100%. Consider the original equipment lock referred to in §3.1(7)(a) made from parts imported under HS subheading 8301.60. The lock producer must use the alternative specific rule that includes the value-content requirement to establish that the lock is originating. The tariff provision for the parts of locks is not on the light-duty vehicle tracing list. In fact, the tariff provisions included on the tracing list do not cover any materials from which a lock would be made. In applying the value-content requirement to the lock, the VNM will be zero and the regional value-content will be 100%.

(ii) Origin and tracing information distinguished

Tracing for light-duty vehicles leads to an important distinction between origin and tracing information. The origin of the engine referred to in the preceding paragraph is relevant to the vehicle assembler if the engine is being imported from another NAFTA country and the assembler wants NAFTA preferential duty to apply. However, except in one circumstance described below in the application of Section 9 of the Uniform Regulations, the fact that the engine is originating is not relevant for the purposes of the assembler's content calculation. What the assembler needs from the engine manufacturer is information respecting the values of materials contained in the engine that have been imported under tariff provisions included on the tracing list. Compare the situation of a vehicle assembler with that of the motor boat producer referred to in §3.1(8)(g), where the amount included in the VNM as well as the ability to receive preferential treatment when importing the engine from another NAFTA country depends on the origin of the engine.

(iii) Section 9 of the Uniform Regulations

Section 9 of the Uniform Regulations sets out the rules for determining the value of non-originating materials when applying the value-content requirement to light-duty automotive goods. Section 9 starts with the basic principle set out in NAFTA 403(1) that the VNM is the sum of the values of materials imported under the tariff provisions on the light-duty vehicle tracing list when received by the first person in the territory of a NAFTA country who takes title to them. Section 9 sets out rules for applying the principle and covers situations in which a producer cannot trace back to the point that a tracing list part first enters a NAFTA country or that title first passed.

The manner in which Section 9 functions may be illustrated with a simple example. Consider an importer in a NAFTA country who imports a piston with a customs value of $90 when reported or entered into a NAFTA country and transportation costs to that point of $10. The importer sells the piston to a wholesaler for $120. The wholesaler sells the piston to a subassembler for $150 who incorporates it into a piston sub-assembly with domestic materials. The piston sub-assembly is sold to an engine producer for $300 and is incorporated into an engine that is sold to a light-duty vehicle assembler for $1,000. The amount included by the vehicle assembler in the VNM in respect of the imported piston depends on information contained in a statement obtained from the engine producer. If title to the piston had passed to the importer at the time of importation, the amount included by the assembler in the VNM is the customs value of $90[62] and the transportation costs of $10. If title had not passed to the importer or if statement does not disclose these values, the amount included by the assembler in the VNM is the transaction value of $120 between the importer and the wholesaler. If the statement does not disclose this value, the amount included by the assembler in the VNM is the transaction value of $150 between the wholesaler and the sub-assembler. If the statement does not disclose this value, the amount included by the assembler in the VNM is the transaction value of $300 of the piston sub-assembly between the sub-assembler and the engine producer. If the engine producer will not divulge this information but is willing to state that the engine is originating, the vehicle assembler may calculate an amount for the VNM based on the content requirement applied to establish that the engine is originating. If the regional value-content requirement ("RVCR") necessary to establish that the engine is originating is 62.5%,[63] the amount included in VNM is equal to (1-RVCR) times the transaction value of $1,000 between the engine producer and the vehicle assembler.[64] On this basis, the vehicle assembler would include 37.5% of $1,000 (*i.e.*, $375) in its VNM. If the vehicle assembler fails to obtain any of these statements, the amount included in its VNM is $1,000.

All the transaction values referred to in the above example are established under Schedule VIII of the Uniform Regulations in the manner described in §3.1(8)(e)(iii). Non-refundable duties and taxes are included. Transportation costs are included only to the point that title to the material first passed to a person in a NAFTA country. In the example above, if the first person in a NAFTA country to receive title was the wholesaler, transportation costs to the point that the wholesaler took title would be included in the VNM. If transportation costs after that point can be separated from the transaction values, they may be excluded from the VNM.

To calculate the VNM, the assembler in the above example must obtain similar statements from producers of any other materials used in the vehicle that have been imported or that incorporate materials that have been imported from non-NAFTA countries under the tariff provisions on the light-duty vehicle tracing list. The assembler also includes in the VNM the customs value of each material that the assembler itself has imported from a non-NAFTA country under a listed tariff provision, together with transportation costs to the point in a NAFTA country at which it took title.

(iv) Designating intermediate materials

A producer whose good is subject to light-duty vehicle tracing cannot avoid tracing by designating self-produced materials as intermediate materials. However, the Uniform Regulations permit a producer to designate a self-produced material as an intermediate material for the purpose of calculating its net cost.[65] As discussed previously in §3.1(8)(h)(ii), this permits the producer to include costs in its net cost that would otherwise be excluded.

(v) Aftermarket

Except in certain circumstances described in §3.1(12)(g)(ii), when original equipment and aftermarket parts are being produced together, light-duty vehicle tracing does not apply to aftermarket parts. The net cost method or (for automotive goods not on the tracing lists) the transaction value method is applied in the same manner as for non-automotive goods.

(d) Heavy-duty automotive goods

(i) Tracing for heavy-duty automotive goods

NAFTA 403(2) and Section 10 of the Uniform Regulations provide that heavy-duty vehicles are subject to a limited form of tracing that applies only to the "automotive components" (e.g., the engines and transmissions) incorporated in them. In applying the content requirement to a heavy-duty vehicle, the assembler must obtain information respecting the origin of each of the listed materials included in the heavy-duty vehicle tracing list contained in the engine and the transmission. The origin of each listed material is determined by applying its own specific rule of origin. The amount included in the vehicle assembler's VNM for each of the engine and the transmission is the sum of the values of the listed materials that are non-originating, regardless of whether the engine or the transmission is originating. However, the origin of the engine or transmission will make a difference to the vehicle assembler's calculations. First, if the engine or transmission is originating, the vehicle assembler has the option of calculating its VNM by using the (1-RVCR) rule described in §3.1(12)(c)(iii). If the engine or transmission is non-originating, the (1-RVCR) rule cannot be used. Second, if the engine or transmission is originating, the values of any non-originating materials that it contains that are not on the heavy-duty vehicle tracing list are not included in the VNM. However, these values are included if the engine or transmission is non-originating. If the engine or transmission or an "automotive component assembly"[66] combining the engine or transmission with other automotive goods is imported, the entire value of the imported item is included in the VNM, regardless of whatever parts originating in NAFTA countries it might contain.

Consider the example of the engine, the piston and the piston assembly set out previously in §3.1(12)(c)(iii). Assume the same facts, except that the vehicle is a heavy-duty vehicle such as a tractor. The piston is a "listed material" and the piston assembly is a "sub-component".[67] Suppose that the engine contains an imported rocker arm assembly. A rocker arm assembly is not a listed material or a sub-component or an automotive component or an automotive component assembly. Assume that the engine is originating under its specific rule of origin. The piston is non-originating because it has been imported and the vehicle assembler will include its value in its VNM. If the piston assembly has been imported, its full value will be included in the vehicle assembler's VNM, even if the connecting rods have been produced in a NAFTA country. The value of the rocker arm assembly is not included in the VNM. The vehicle producer also has the option, if it cannot obtain better information, of determining the VNM of the engine by using the (1-RVCR) rule described in §3.1(12)(c)(iii). Thus, if the RVCR for the engine is 60% and its value when purchased by the producer is $1,000, the amount included in the VNM is $400. If the engine is non-originating, the (1-RCVR) rule cannot be used and the value of the rocker arm assembly must be included in the VNM.

The vehicle assembler can reduce the amount included in its VNM in respect of a non-originating listed material if it can isolate the values of the non-originating materials that it contains. Suppose that a truck assembler purchases a manual transmission that contains a clutch that is non-originating because it contains imported parts and the value-content requirement in the specific rule for clutches has not been satisfied. If the truck assembler can isolate the value of the non-originating parts contained in the clutch, it need only include their value in its VNM and not the entire value of the non-originating clutch.

The mode of tracing described above also applies to heavy-duty vehicle engines, transmissions and automotive component assemblies that are intended for use as original equipment in a heavy-duty vehicle. If an engine producer acquires a sub-component (such as a block assembly), it must trace each listed material in the sub-component and include in the VNM of the engine the value of those that are non-originating. As discussed in §3.1(12)(g)(iii), if engines, transmissions or automotive component assemblies are being produced for both heavy-duty and light-duty vehicles in the same plant and the producer does not know which item will be used for what purpose, the producer may apply the light-duty vehicle tracing method to its entire production and the heavy-duty vehicle producer to whom these items are sold may use the VNM calculated on this basis.

(ii) Normal roll-up and roll-down

For non-engine and non-transmission materials, the normal roll-up/roll-down approach applies in the same manner as with non-automotive goods regardless of whether the material is intended for use as original equipment or in the aftermarket. Applying the example respecting mirrors in §3.1(12)(c)(i) to heavy-duty vehicles, the value of the non-originating rear view mirror produced with imported glass would be included in the heavy-duty vehicle assembler's VNM. Tracing is also not required for a sub-component or a listed material before it is incorporated into an engine or transmission. This will occur when one of these items is imported into a NAFTA country from another NAFTA country and the applicable specific rule of origin contains a value-content requirement.

(iii) Origin and tracing information distinguished

Producers must be mindful of the distinction between origin and tracing information respecting heavy-duty engines, transmissions and automotive component assemblies. However, the distinction does not apply to other goods intended for use in heavy-duty vehicles.

(iv) Designating intermediate materials

A producer of a heavy-duty vehicle or of a good intended for use in a heavy duty vehicle may designate any self-produced material as an intermediate material other than an engine, a transmission, an automotive component assembly or a sub-component. The prohibition on designating these items as intermediate materials includes designating them for the purpose of calculating net cost. Unlike its light-duty counterpart, the producer of a heavy-duty vehicle or good cannot increase its net cost by otherwise excludable costs by designating self-produced materials as intermediate materials.[68]

(v) *Aftermarket*

Except in the circumstances described in §3.1(12)(g)(ii), heavy-duty vehicle tracing does not apply to goods intended for use in heavy-duty vehicles, including heavy-duty vehicle engines, transmissions or automotive component assemblies, produced for the aftermarket.

(e) Increased threshold percentages

The applicable percentage for light-duty vehicles, together with their engines and transmissions, will be 50% until the producer's fiscal year beginning on the day closest to January 1, 1998, 56% from then until the producer's fiscal year beginning on the day closest to January 1, 2002, and thereafter 62.5%. The applicable percentage for heavy-duty vehicles, together with their engines and transmissions, as well as parts (other than ball bearings, roller bearings and housed bearings) for all types of vehicles, will be 50% until the producer's fiscal year beginning on the day closest to January 1, 1998, 55% from then until the producer's fiscal year beginning on the day closest to January 1, 2002, and thereafter 60%. The threshold percentage for ball bearings, roller bearings and housed bearings remains at 50%. These increased percentages apply to aftermarket as well as original equipment parts.[69]

The applicable percentage remains at 50% for any five-year period for a vehicle not previously produced by the producer in any NAFTA country which is produced in a new plant. What constitutes a new vehicle is defined in the Uniform Regulations in terms of "class", "marque" or "size category" and type of "underbody". A new plant must include a "new building" and contain substantially new machinery.[70] The five-year period begins at the time that the "first prototype" of the new vehicle is produced at the new plant.[71] A similar rule applies in the case of a "refit", which is the closure of a plant for at least three consecutive months for plant conversion or retooling. The period is two years rather than five and the vehicle must be new, in terms of the criteria described above, in that it has not previously been produced at the refitted plant.[72]

(f) Permutations and combinations for parts producers

There are seven different combinations of the content requirement as applied to automotive goods that are on the tracing lists. Original equipment parts for light-duty vehicles are subject to light-duty vehicle tracing and a threshold percentage in the mature system of 62.5%, 50% or 60% depending on whether the good is an engine or transmission, a bearing or something else. Aftermarket parts and original equipment heavy-duty vehicle parts that are not engines or transmissions are subject to these same three percentages but are not subject to tracing. Original equipment heavy-duty vehicle engines and transmissions are subject to heavy-duty vehicle tracing and a threshold percentage of 60%.

The drafters of the Uniform Regulations recognized that these different combinations, particularly those driven by intended end use, could present difficulties in some cases and addressed this problem in the averaging provisions by permitting parts producers producing multi-purpose parts to select a single method for making their calculations.

(g) Averaging

The NAFTA rules retain averaging for motor vehicles and extends averaging to other automotive goods that are included on the tracing lists.

(i) Vehicle producers

Averaging calculations for vehicles are made over a producer's fiscal year.[73] Under the FTA, vehicle assemblers could average over classes of vehicles defined in terms of passenger and luggage volume. NAFTA expands these classes of vehicles into much broader categories. For example, all passenger vehicles are now in a single class, regardless of size. Under NAFTA, an assembler has several averaging options. The assembler can average over the same model line within the same class produced within the same plant, or over the same class within the same plant, or over the same model line within one of the NAFTA countries. The averaging calculations can be made over all vehicles of the chosen category produced during the fiscal year or just those exported to another NAFTA country. The Uniform Regulations describe how averaging elections are to be made. An averaging election cannot be rescinded or modified for the period during which it is in effect. A special averaging rule permits CAMI to average with General Motors Canada.[74]

(ii) Parts producers

Parts producers can average their calculations over goods of the same tariff provision included on the light-duty vehicle tracing list or goods that are automotive component assemblies, automotive components, sub-components or listed materials that are produced in the same plant.[75] Consider HS heading 84.09 (parts of engines) on the light-duty vehicle tracing list. This tariff provision covers all parts for both spark-ignition and diesel engines. The calculations for a whole variety of parts produced at the same plant can be averaged together in one calculation.

The averaging calculations are made for all those goods just described falling into a number of categories, which are: original equipment for light-duty vehicles; original equipment for heavy duty vehicles; aftermarket parts; and various combinations of these three basic categories.[76] A producer of engine parts for light-duty vehicle engines who also makes parts for the aftermarket may treat all these parts as being in a single category. Similarly, producer of engine parts for heavy-duty vehicles can choose that these be in the same category as engine parts for light-duty vehicles or for the aftermarket.

If a category contains any parts intended as original equipment in light-duty vehicles, value content will be calculated in the manner that applies to light-duty automotive goods. If a category contains any parts intended as original equipment in heavy-duty vehicles but none intended for light-duty vehicles, value content will be calculated in the manner that applies to heavy-duty automotive goods.[77] When these mixed-use categories are chosen, the value content of parts intended for use in heavy-duty vehicles may end up being calculated as if intended for light-duty vehicles, and aftermarket parts in these categories can be subject to either method. These provisions permit a parts producer to avoid a multiple calculations of value content if it chooses or if it is not sure of the intended end use. Parts producers can average across their total production within each category or only with those goods which they export.[78]

Averaging for original equipment is tied to the fiscal year of the motor vehicle producer to whom the parts are sold, while averaging for aftermarket equipment is tied to the producer's fiscal year or to the fiscal year of the vehicle producer to whom the equipment is sold. Parts producers may average over the full fiscal year or on a quarterly or monthly basis.

(iii) Averaging of tracing information

Parts producers issuing statements with tracing information being used either for light-duty or heavy-duty vehicle purposes may provide the information on an averaged basis, using the categories described above. The producer issuing the statement calculates the VNM of the parts in the category chosen and divides it by the number of units of the parts in the category that have been produced during the averaging period. The statement issued to the person to whom the information is being provided gives the VNM per unit.[79] Information respecting the VNM calculated in the manner for light-duty automotive goods may in some circumstances be used by a producer of heavy-duty automotive goods. For example, if an engine producer is producing engines for light-duty and heavy-duty vehicles in the same plant and the producer does not know which engines will be used for which vehicles, the producer may select a category comprised of all the engines and make its value-content calculations in the manner that applies to light-duty automotive goods. An assembler of heavy-duty vehicles who purchases engines from this producer may use the information respecting the VNM of the engines received from the engine producer even though this information has been calculated on the basis that applies to light-duty automotive goods.[80]

(13) Trans-shipment and Non-qualifying Operations

NAFTA 411 and Section 16(1) of the Uniform Regulations provide that if an originating good undergoes subsequent processing or other operations

in a non-NAFTA country, other than unloading, reloading or any other operation necessary to preserve the good or transport it to a NAFTA country.
If this occurs, the good is treated as entirely non-originating. Thus, if a good
produced in Mexico that qualifies as originating is transhipped to Guatemala
for further processing and is then imported into the United States, it will
be treated as entirely non-originating, including the value added in NAFTA
countries. The Uniform Regulations provide that the transhipment rule does
not apply to diodes, transistors, various semi-conductor devices, electronic
integrated circuits and microassemblies.[81]

NAFTA 412 and Section 17 of the Uniform Regulations provide that mere
dilution with water or another substance or any production or pricing practice the object of which, on the preponderance of evidence was to circumvent the rules, will not confer originating status on the good.

(14) Comments

The NAFTA rules of origin represent a substantial improvement over the
FTA rules. The NAFTA text is much clearer than that of the FTA. In drafting the Uniform Regulations, the negotiators of the three NAFTA countries
resolved a number of issues that, left unaddressed, had the potential to evolve
into disputes.

As discussed in §1.4(2), rules of origin are necessary in a free trade area.
However, they impede the free flow of goods by imposing additional administrative burdens on producers and customs administrations. Rules of origin
defeat the purpose of establishing a free trade area if compliance costs outweigh the benefits of preferential duty treatment.

For many producers, complying with the NAFTA rules of origin should
be relatively simple. Originating status for many goods may be established
without having to make a regional value-content calculation. While the
NAFTA rules of origin and the Uniform Regulations contain many pages
of text, producers who are able to establish origin through a change in tariff
classification alone should be able to comply by ascertaining the correct tariff classifications of their goods and the materials from which they are
produced and learning how to apply the specific rule of origin that applies
to their goods.

The application of the value content requirement is more problematic. The
negotiators have tried to make the value content requirement consistent with
accounting practices that producers will be applying in the ordinary conduct
of their businesses. However, the introduction of CVC principles as a means
for disciplining transfer pricing complicates this process as producers will
be required to make adjustments to values that they normally would not
make. Many producers will have to make more detailed cost allocations than
they would in the ordinary course of business. The tracing requirements that

apply to automotive goods require adjustments to accounting systems so that information can flow through chains of producers in the manner required by the Uniform Regulations. Customs administrations will have to learn how to audit the differing methods under NAFTA for calculating value content. All this imposes costs on both producers and governments.

The NAFTA negotiators and the computer industry established a very useful precedent with the establishment of the mini-customs union for automatic data processing equipment described in §2.7(1). The lowering of external tariffs under the Uruguay Round Agreements coupled with the pressure to harmonize tariffs that will occur when the NAFTA drawback and duty deferral provisions discussed in §2.3 become effective should make this innovative approach feasible for other sectors.

3.2 MARKING RULES

Many countries, including the NAFTA countries, require that at least some goods be marked as goods of a particular country so that domestic buyers know where goods come from.[82] The rules which determine the country of origin for this purpose are known as marking rules. Marking rules establish a specific country of origin for a good. In this they differ from the NAFTA rules of origin which treat all countries within a preferential trading area as interchangeable. Also, a good may be eligible to be marked as a good of a country within a preferential trading area but, because of differing criteria, not be eligible for preferential tariff treatment under the applicable rules of origin.

Marking requirements can be significant barriers to trade. Goods that are not properly marked can be detained by customs authorities and entry can be denied. Country of origin rules for determining eligibility for marking can lack transparency or be excessively onerous. Some goods by their very nature do not lend themselves to being marked.

(1) GATT Requirements

GATT Article IX sets out rules respecting Marks of Origin. GATT Article IX:1 establishes a most-favoured-nation principle in that products of other GATT contracting parties are to be no less favourably treated respecting marks of origin than goods from non-GATT countries.[83] Inconvenience is to be kept to a minimum.[84] Marking should be permitted at the time of importation[85] and not seriously damage products or reduce their value.[86] No special penalties should be imposed except in the case of unreasonable delay or deception.[87] The FTA is silent on the subject of marking. However, NAFTA contains provisions respecting the marking of goods which go well beyond the GATT requirements.

(2) Pre-NAFTA Canadian and U.S. Practice

Canadian marking rules in effect prior to January 1, 1994, required that certain listed goods be marked with their country of origin.[88] The country of origin was the country in which the goods were "substantially manufactured", meaning the country where the article essentially took the form in which it is imported.[89] This determination was made on a case-by-case basis.

U.S. marking rules required that all imported goods be marked with their country of origin except those to which an exception applied.[90] The regulations set out exceptions for certain goods, such as articles incapable of being marked, articles that cannot be marked without being subject to injury, and so on.[91] The country of origin was defined as the country of manufacture, production or growth of an article, and further work or materials added to an article in another country had to result in a "substantial transformation" if that other country was to be the country of origin.[92] As in Canada, the determination of whether a substantial transformation had occurred was made on a case-by-case basis.

(3) Marking Rules under NAFTA

NAFTA Annex 311(1) required the NAFTA countries to establish rules ("Marking Rules")[93] for determining whether a good is a "good of a Party" for the purposes of NAFTA Annexes 311, 300-B and 302.2 and for such other purposes as the NAFTA countries may agree. NAFTA Annex 311 covers country of origin marking. NAFTA Annex 300-B sets out special rules respecting textile and apparel goods discussed in §5.3. As discussed in §3.3, NAFTA Annex 302.2 provides that the Marking Rules will be used by the United States and Mexico and, in some instances, by Canada for determining the country of origin of goods for the purpose of applying the FTA Schedules and the NAFTA Schedules. However, the determination of whether a good is a "good of a Party" and covered by NAFTA provisions such as those relating to export taxes and import and export restrictions or antidumping and countervailing duties will not be determined in accordance with the Marking Rules.[94]

The negotiation of Marking Rules by the NAFTA countries did not result in verbatim regulations as occurred with the Uniform Regulations that were negotiated in respect of NAFTA Chapter Four. Each of Canada and the United States has implemented new NAFTA marking regulations based on the negotiations that took place pursuant to the requirement in NAFTA Annex 311.[95] The NAFTA marking regulations in these NAFTA countries are similar in approach and content, although there are differences in drafting style and in some differences in substance. A number of definitions and concepts in the NAFTA marking regulations are based on the NAFTA rules of origin and the Uniform Regulations.

(a) Hierarchy of rules

Each country's regulations establish a hierarchy of rules for establishing the country of origin.

(i) First rule

The first rule provides that the country of origin is: the country from which the good was wholly obtained or produced; or the country in which the good was produced from domestic materials; or the country in which all foreign materials satisfy the requirements set out in the tariff shift rules annexed to the regulations.[96] The concept of "wholly obtained or produced" is the same as in the NAFTA rules or origin described in §3.1(4). A "domestic material" is a material whose country of origin determined under the marking regulations is the same country where the good is produced, and a "foreign material" is a material with a different country of origin.

(ii) Tariff shifts under the first rule

The tariff shift rules are laid out in a similar manner to the specific rules of origin described in §3.1(5). Each rule prescribes a change in tariff classification and some rules (or chapter or section notes) prescribe additional requirements. There are no value-content requirements. Many changes in tariff classification are the same as in the specific rules of origin. Some are less onerous. For example, the tariff shift rule for the locks referred to in §3.1(7)(a) in both the Canadian and U.S. regulations is:

> A change to subheading 8301.10 through 8301.40 from any other subheading, including another subheading within that group, except a change from subheading 8301.60 when that change is pursuant to Rule 2(a) of the General Rules of Interpretation of the Harmonized System.

This rule permits the lock to be marked as a good of the country where it was produced even if foreign parts were to be used, as long as they are not part of the lock imported in an incomplete or unfinished or an unassembled or disassembled form.[97] As discussed in §3.1(7)(a), under the specific rules of origin a lock made from non-originating parts must satisfy a value-content requirement to be originating. Unlike the specific rules of origin, the requirements in the tariff shift rules set out in each country's regulations are not identical. For example, the U.S. requirements for apparel goods under HS chapters 61 and 62 are much more detailed than their Canadian counterparts.

(iii) Where no tariff shift occurs

Each country's regulations set out an assembling rule that provides an alternative means for establishing the country of origin of a good if the production of the goods does not result in a change in tariff classification for reasons similar to those set out in the assembling rule described in §3.1(8)(i). If the production results in a "substantial transformation" (*i.e.*, in goods that have a new and different name, character and use), the country in which the production took place is the country of origin.[98] While neither country's regulations is clear about where this rule stands in the hierarchy of application, this rule appears to be a special relieving provision that relates to the tariff shift requirement just described. This rule does not apply to the fibres, yarns, fabrics, apparel goods and textile goods classified under HS chapters 50 through to 63.

(iv) Second rule — essential character

If a country of origin cannot be established under the first rule, a second rule provides that the country or countries of origin of the good shall be the country or countries of origin of the single material that impart the essential character to the good unless the good is classified under Rule 3 of the General Rules of Interpretation of the Harmonized System as a set or mixture or composite good.[99] "Essential character" is not defined, but each country's regulations set out factors to be taken into consideration in making this determination. The factors include the nature, bulk, quantity, weight and value of the material and its role with regard to the good's use.[100] The concept of "essential character" appears in Rule 3(b) of the General Rules and these factors are cited in Explanatory Note (VIII) for Rule 3 of the Harmonized System Explanatory Notes.[101]

(v) Third rule — sets, mixtures and composite goods

If a country of origin cannot be established under either the first or the second rule and the good is classified under the Harmonized System as a set or mixture or composite good, a third rule provides that the country or countries of origin of the goods shall be the country or countries of origin of all the materials that "merit equal consideration" for determining or imparting "the essential character" of the goods.[102]

(vi) Fourth rule — country of last production

If a country of origin cannot be established under any of these rules, a fourth rule provides that the country or countries of origin of the good is the last country in which the goods underwent production, other than by "simple assembling" or "minor processing".[103] These expressions have the same definition in each country's regulations, with minor wording changes. The definition of "minor processing" lists a number of activities such as diluting with water, cleaning, testing, trimming, washing and so on. "Simple assembly" is fitting five or fewer foreign parts (other than screws and the like) without more than minor processing. If the good is produced by simple assembly, the fourth rule sets out additional rules for determining the country of origin of the good.

(b) The NAFTA override

Each country's regulations set out an important override provision that applies to any good that is determined to be originating under the NAFTA rules of origin. If a single NAFTA country is not established as the originating good's country of origin by applying the first or second rules described above, the country of origin will be the last NAFTA country in which the good underwent production that was more than minor processing.[104] A good can satisfy a change in tariff classification for rules of origin purposes and yet not meet the tariff shift requirements under an importing country's marking regulations because, unlike with rules of origin, the changes in tariff classification for marking purposes must all occur within a single country. This rule ensures that the country of origin of an originating good will always be a NAFTA country. This override concept is essential, given the use of the marking rules described in §3.3.

(c) NAFTA rules of origin concepts

Each country's regulations adopt a number of concepts from the NAFTA rules of origin and the Uniform Regulations. Packaging materials and containers, accessories and spare parts, packing materials and containers and indirect materials are all disregarded in determining whether a change in tariff classification has occurred.[105] The inventory management approach to fungible goods and fungible materials has been adopted.[106] There is a *de minimis* rule that applies when small amounts of foreign materials do not undergo a prescribed change in tariff classification.[107] There is a rule to cover transhipment when a good that would qualify to be marked as a good of Canada or a good of the United States undergoes further production in another country.[108]

(d) Comments

The Marking Rules just described represent a mix of objective and subjective approaches to determining a good's country of origin. The tariff shift rules are clearly objective. The "last country of production" rule is somewhat objective because of the definitions of "minor processing" and "simple assembly". However, the "essential character" rule and the "substantial transformation" concept in the assembling rule are clearly subjective. While one might be critical of this result, it must be kept in mind that drafting rules to pinpoint a country of origin is more difficult than drafting rules of origin for tariff preference purposes. Under rules of origin for tariff preference purposes, a good may either qualify or not qualify under wholly objective rules.

Country rules of origin must cover the contingency of the objective rules not providing an answer.

It is unfortunate that the negotiators of the NAFTA countries were unable to replicate for marking the verbatim approach that they successfully managed with the Uniform Regulations for NAFTA Chapter Four. The divergence in approach to marking is particularly apparent in the textile and apparel sector. Unlike the NAFTA rules of origin, producers will have to cope with somewhat differing marking obligations in each NAFTA country. Also, with differing rules from the outset, it is not clear how much coordination there will be among the NAFTA countries in the evolution of the Marking Rules over time. If a verbatim approach could not have been negotiated, the NAFTA countries could have at least established trilateral country of origin standards against which future amendments to an individual NAFTA country's marking regulations could be assessed.[109]

(4) Use of the Marking Rules

NAFTA Annex 311 sets out rules respecting the application by the NAFTA countries of requirements that goods be marked with their country of origin. Each NAFTA country may require that goods of another NAFTA country, determined in accordance with the Marking Rules described in §3.2(3), be marked with the name of the country of origin.[110] Country of origin marking in English, French or Spanish must be permitted, but a NAFTA country may require that a good be marked with its country of origin for general consumer information purposes in the same manner as its domestic goods.[111] As under the GATT, difficulties, costs and inconveniences are to be minimized.[112]

NAFTA countries are to exempt certain goods from the marking requirement. For example, a marking requirement cannot be imposed on a good that is incapable of being marked or cannot be marked without causing injury.[113] Building bricks, semiconductors and electronic integrated circuits and microassemblies are specifically exempted from marking requirements.[114] There are rules respecting the marking of containers.[115] Importers are to be permitted to mark goods subsequent to their being imported unless the importer has repeatedly violated marking requirements and has been notified that goods must be marked prior to importation.[116] No special duty or penalty is to be applied for failure to comply with marking requirements except in the case of importers who have been notified that goods must be marked prior to importation or where goods are removed from customs custody and control without being marked or where there has been deceptive marking.[117]

The Canadian Marking Regulations described above apply only to goods imported from NAFTA countries and only to goods listed on Schedule I of the regulations. Schedule I sets out the same goods listed in the Canadian Marking Regulations in effect prior to January 1, 1994. Canada has retained its pre-NAFTA marking rules for goods imported from non-NAFTA countries[118] and is not applying the NAFTA country of origin rules described above for non-NAFTA purposes. The United States, on the other hand, is in the process of adopting the country of origin rules described above as its general country of origin rules.

3.3 DETERMINATIONS OF COUNTRY OF ORIGIN

(1) Goods Entering the United States and Mexico

The United States will distinguish "Canadian" and "Mexican" goods on the basis of whether a good is eligible to be marked as a good of Canada or Mexico under the Marking Rules. To be eligible for FTA treatment, a good entering the United States from Canada will have to be originating under the NAFTA rules of origin and also be eligible to be marked as a good of Canada under the Marking Rules.[119] In this respect, the Marking Rules serve as supplemental rules of origin. While the expression "goods of a Party" generally means domestic products as understood under the GATT, for tariff elimination purposes for these NAFTA countries a "good of a Party" is a good that is eligible to be marked as a good of that Party under the Marking Rules. Mexico will also use the Marking Rules to distinguish between "American" and "Canadian" goods.[120]

American and Mexican determinations of the country of origin of textile and apparel goods are discussed in §5.2(4), and of agricultural goods in §5.3(4).

(2) Goods Entering Canada

Except for agricultural goods and textile and apparel goods, the country of origin of originating goods entering Canada will be determined by selectively applying the NAFTA rules of origin. To be "American" (and eligible for the United States Tariff), an originating good must also be originating under the NAFTA rules of origin applied as if Mexico were not a NAFTA country. The good may be further processed in Mexico after so qualifying so long as its transaction value is not increased by more than 7%. To be "Mexican", and eligible for the Mexico Tariff, an originating good must also be originating under the NAFTA rules of origin applied as if the United States were not a NAFTA country. The good may be further processed in the United States after so qualifying, so long as its transaction value is not increased by more than 7%, with permissible U.S. value added not exceeding 7%.[121]

Canadian determinations of national origin of agricultural goods and of textile and apparel goods entering Canada are discussed in §5.2(4) and §5.3(4) respectively.

(3) Uniform Regulations and Country of Origin Determinations

Article IX of the Uniform Regulations described in §3.4(1) sets out several clarifications respecting country of origin determinations for tariff preference purposes. If a NAFTA country gives duty-free treatment to originating goods from all NAFTA countries, the NAFTA country of origin need not be determined. Also, where the country of origin determination is made on the basis of the Marking Rules, these rules are applied only to goods processed in or incorporating materials from more than one NAFTA country. Otherwise the good is subject to the preferential rate that applies to the NAFTA country from which it is exported.

3.4 CUSTOMS PROCEDURES

One deficiency of the FTA was the absence of a uniform approach to applying of the rules of origin and other customs procedures. The customs administration of each of Canada and the United States followed its own independent course. After four years of experience under the FTA, the Canadian and U.S. NAFTA negotiators wished to establish common standards respecting a number of areas of customs procedures. The need for establishing standards was reinforced by the state of Mexico's customs laws, which needed reform in a number of significant respects. NAFTA Chapter Five is devoted entirely to establishing standards to be carried forward by each of the NAFTA countries into their customs laws and regulations. Chapter Five establishes standards respecting: certification of origin; administration and enforcement; advance rulings; and review and appeal. Chapter Five provides for the creation of working groups to monitor the implementation and administration of various customs-related NAFTA provisions.

(1) Uniform Regulations for Chapter Five

As required by NAFTA 511, the NAFTA countries successfully negotiated Uniform Regulations[122] covering various aspects of Chapter Five as well as certain aspects of NAFTA Chapter Three.[123] Because of the different structure of the customs laws in each of the NAFTA countries, the NAFTA negotiators adopted a "standards" rather than a verbatim approach to the Uniform Regulations. The Uniform Regulations set out standards to be observed that supplement those established by NAFTA Chapter Five. As discussed in

§1.3(2), each NAFTA country is free to determine the manner in which the standards are carried forward into its domestic law.

(2) Certification of Origin

NAFTA 501(1) obligated the NAFTA countries to establish, by January 1, 1994, a common form of Certificate of Origin for establishing that a good exported from one NAFTA country to another qualifies as originating. The NAFTA countries fulfilled this obligation and the common form of certificate of origin is discussed in §3.4(3). The NAFTA text allows an importing NAFTA country to provide that certificates be completed in a language required under its law.[124] However, the Uniform Regulations permit the exporter to choose between the language of the exporting and the importing country.[125] An exporter must complete and sign a Certificate of Origin for goods for which preferential tariff treatment is being claimed. NAFTA 501(3)(b) sets out the grounds upon which an exporter who is not the producer of a good can complete a Certificate of Origin.[126] Certificates of Origin can apply to single importations or to multiple importations of identical goods during a specified period of up to twelve months.

To claim preferential tariff treatment, the importer of a good must make a written declaration that the good qualifies as originating and have the exporter's Certificate of Origin in its possession when the declaration is made. The Certificate of Origin, including a written translation, must be provided to the customs authorities of the importing NAFTA country on request.[127] Provision is made for an importer to make a corrected declaration if it has reason to believe that a certificate contains incorrect information.[128] A claim for preferential tariff treatment for an imported originating good can be made up to twelve months after the good was imported.[129] Certificates of Origin are not required for commercial or non-commercial importations not exceeding $1,000 (US) or its Canadian dollar or Mexican peso equivalent.[130]

Exporters or producers who have provided Certificates of Origin to exporters must provide a copy of the certificate to its customs administration upon request.[131] Exporters or producers who become aware of an error in a certificate that they have provided must promptly inform in writing all persons to whom the certificate was given. Each NAFTA country must provide for penalties for false certification by an exporter or producer that are the same as those that would apply to an importer for a contravention of its customs laws and regulations.[132] However, a NAFTA country may not impose penalties on a producer or exporter who has made a notification of an error before an investigation has commenced.[133]

(3) Common Form of Certificate of Origin

The common form of Certificate of Origin is set out in Annex I.1a of the Uniform Regulations. The form provides for eleven fields, all of which must be completed in accordance with the instructions on the reverse side of the form. Field 1 and Fields 3 through to 6 require information respecting the exporter, the producer, the importer and the goods. If the certificate covers multiple shipments, the blanket period must be specified in Field 2. The "preference criterion", or basis for certifying that the goods covered by the certificate are originating, must be completed in Field 7. The preference criteria are identified by the letters "A" though to "F". Preference criteria "A" through to "E" correspond to those discussed in §3.1(3). Preference criterion "F" is used to identify agricultural goods traded between Mexico and either the United States or Canada as "qualifying goods" as discussed in §5.3(4)(b). In Field 8, the person signing the certificate indicates whether it is the producer of the goods and, if not, the basis for its completing the certificate. In Field 9, the exporter states whether the net cost method has been used in making any applicable regional value-content calculation and, if averaging applies, the period of time over which the calculation has been made. The country of origin, determined as described in §3.3, is identified in Field 10 and the exporter signs and dates the certificate in Field 11.

(4) Administration and Enforcement

(a) Records

Exporters and producers who complete Certificates of Origin and importers will be required to keep records of relevant documents and financial information for five years following the signing of the certificate or the importation of the good.[134] Article V of the Uniform Regulations requires that records be maintained in a manner that will permit a detailed verification by customs officers. The records may be maintained in machine-readable form. Preferential tariff treatment may be denied if a person obliged to keep records fails to do so or denies access to them. A producer who has not maintained its records in accordance with the GAAP of the NAFTA country where a good has been produced shall have sixty days to bring them into conformity with GAAP.

(b) Origin verification

NAFTA 506 establishes common rules for origin verifications. The customs administration of a NAFTA country can conduct a verification solely by written questionnaires[135] or visits or such other mutually agreed-upon means. Article VI of the Uniform Regulations provides that these other means include sending a "verification letter" to the exporter or producer. The verification letter must make specific reference to the goods and a determination may be made on the basis of the response received. If an exporter or producer does not respond to a questionnaire or verification letter within thirty days, the customs administration that sent it may send a subsequent verification letter or questionnaire with a notice of intent to deny preferential treatment. If the exporter or producer fails to respond in thirty days, preferential treatment may be denied.[136]

Visits must be preceded by written notification (containing certain prescribed information) to the exporter or producer and the customs administration of the NAFTA country in which the visit is to take place.[137] The exporter or producer must consent to the visit,[138] but if the consent is not given within thirty days, preferential tariff treatment can be denied.[139] An exporter or producer may designate two observers to be present during the visit.[140]

Customs authorities conducting a verification must provide the producer or exporter with a written determination of whether the good is originating.[141] A written determination shall include a notice of intent to deny preferential tariff treatment that specifies the date after which preferential treatment will be denied and a period for the exporter or producer to make additional comments regarding the determination.[142] Where a determination that a good is not originating is based on a tariff classification of or a value applied to materials, the determination is not effective until notification is given to both the importer and the person who signed the Certificate of Origin.[143] Such a determination shall not apply to an importation made before the effective date of the determination where an advance ruling or other ruling has been previously issued or consistent previous treatment has been given by the customs administration of the exporting NAFTA country with respect to the tariff classification or value at issue.[144] Where the importer or person signing the certificate has relied to its detriment on the tariff classification or value applied to identical materials by the customs administration of the exporting NAFTA country, the effective date of the determination will be postponed for up to ninety days.[145]

NAFTA 506(11) permits a NAFTA country to withhold preferential treatment when origin verifications disclose a pattern of conduct by an exporter or producer of false or unsupported representations until that person demonstrates compliance.[146]

Article VI of the Uniform Regulations sets out additional rules respecting origin verifications. Paragraph 3 provides that if regional value content of a good is calculated in accordance with the net cost method averaged over a time period, such as a producer's fiscal year, a verification of the value content may not be conducted during the time period. Paragraphs 10 to 12 provide that customs authorities may request cost submissions of actual costs from motor vehicle manufacturers who are averaging their calculations. Paragraphs 29 to 31 cover verifications of origin of materials. In applying both change in tariff classification and regional value-content requirements, producers will be relying on statements from other producers to the effect that materials are originating. Verifications of the origin of materials are to be conducted according to the same procedures that apply to verifying the origin of goods. If a producer of a material denies access to its records or fails to respond to a verification questionnaire or letter or refuses to consent to a visit, the customs administration conducting the verification may consider the material as non-originating.

NAFTA 507 sets out provisions respecting confidentiality and NAFTA 508 requires each NAFTA country to maintain criminal, civil or administrative penalties for violations of its laws and regulations respecting NAFTA Chapter Five.

(5) Advance Rulings, Review and Appeal

(a) Advance rulings

NAFTA 509 requires each NAFTA country to establish procedures for the issuance of written advance rulings respecting a variety of issues respecting importation of goods under NAFTA, including: whether materials undergo an applicable change in tariff classification; whether a good satisfies a regional value-content requirement; the basis for calculating the transaction value of a good or the value of materials in accordance with CVC principles; the appropriate basis or method for allocating costs; whether a good is originating; whether a good exported for alteration and repair qualifies for duty-free treatment upon re-entry; whether proposed or actual marking satisfies the requirements of NAFTA Annex 311; whether an originating good is "Canadian", "American" or "Mexican"; and whether a good is a qualifying good[147] under the NAFTA agricultural provisions.[148]

Advance rulings must be applied for prior to importation and shall be applied to importations made after the date of issuance or such later date as the ruling may specify. Unfavourable rulings must be accompanied by a full explanation.[149] Advance rulings issued by a customs authority must be consistent.[150]

An advance ruling may be revoked: if it is based on an error; if the ruling is not in accordance with an interpretation agreed to by all NAFTA countries; if there is a change in material facts or circumstances; to conform with a modification of certain provisions of NAFTA,[151] the Uniform Regulations[152] or the Marking Rules. A modification or revocation shall only be effective from the date it is issued and shall not apply to importations prior to that date, with provision for postponement in some cases. If a person to whom a ruling has been issued used reasonable care in presenting the facts and circumstances on which the ruling was based and acted in good faith, that person shall not be subject to penalties if it is subsequently determined that the ruling was based on incorrect information.

Article VII of the Uniform Regulations sets out additional provisions respecting advance rulings. Paragraph 1 makes it clear that a producer of materials in another NAFTA country for use in a good produced in another NAFTA country may apply to the customs administration of the NAFTA country to which the good is to be exported for an advance ruling. Applications for advance rulings must be in the language of the country issuing the ruling. Rulings must be issued within 120 days of receipt of all information reasonably required to process the application. The NAFTA countries are to establish by no later than January 1, 1995, common standards for required information. If information received is incomplete, a customs administration can decline to process further an application provided that it gives the applicant at least thirty days to produce supplemental information. A customs administration may decline to issue a ruling if it involves an issue that is the subject of an origin verification or a review.

The NAFTA advance ruling procedure substantially changes U.S. practice and has created an entirely new process for Revenue Canada.[153] The availability of advance rulings should be helpful to producers or exporters who have doubts as to how the rules of origin are to be applied. They will be particularly useful in dealing with the complexities of the regional value-content requirement.

(b) Review and appeal

NAFTA 510(1) requires that each NAFTA country must provide to persons completing Certificates of Origin or whose goods have been subject of a country of origin marking determination or who have received an advance ruling substantially the same rights of review and appeal as apply to importers generally. Paragraph 1 of Article VIII of the Uniform Regulations provides that an exporter or producer who completed a Certificate of Origin may appeal a denial of preferential tariff treatment. This requirement represents an important change to customs law in that exporters and producers, as well as importers, now have the right to challenge rulings made by customs administrations of importing NAFTA countries. Paragraph 2 of Article VIII of the Uniform Regulations extends the right of appeal to modifications or revocations of advance rulings.

NAFTA 510(2) requires access to at least one level of administrative review independent of the official or office making the initial determination and judicial or quasi-judicial review of the final level of administrative review.[154]

(6) Co-operation

The NAFTA countries have agreed to co-operate on a number of customs-related matters. The NAFTA countries will notify each other of determinations, measures and rulings with prospective application respecting: origin determinations arising from verifications; origin determinations that are contrary to rulings or practices of the customs administration of another NAFTA country respecting tariff classifications or valuation of goods and materials or allocation of costs; measures establishing or modifying administrative policies affecting future determinations of origin or country of origin marking requirements; and advance rulings and modifications and revocations of same.[155] These requirements are designed to identify areas of inconsistent application of the rules of origin and the Marking Rules.

The NAFTA countries will also co-operate in their enforcement of customs-related laws and regulations[156] and in the exchange of statistics, the standardization of forms and the acceptance of international syntax.[157] There is a special provision respecting detection and prevention of trans-shipments of non-Party textile and apparel goods.[158]

(7) Working Group and Customs Subgroup

The NAFTA will also establish a Working Group with a mandate to ensure the effective implementation and administration of the restrictions on duty drawback and deferral programs described in §2.3, the mini-customs union provisions respecting automatic data processing equipment and semiconductors described in §2.7, the marking of goods provisions in NAFTA Annex 311, the NAFTA rules of origin, the customs procedures in NAFTA Chapter Five, the Marking Rules and the Uniform Regulations.[159] The Working Group will meet at least four times a year. The Working Group will monitor the implementation of these NAFTA provisions and try to reach agreement on modifications or additions proposed by any NAFTA Party. The Working Group will propose modifications or additions to these NAFTA provisions required to conform with changes in the Harmonized System to the Free Trade Commission and will notify the Free Trade Commission of agreed modifications of or additions to the Uniform Regulations. The NAFTA text is silent as to what the Working Group is supposed to do with other agreed modifications or additions.

The Working Group will establish a Customs Subgroup that will try to agree on: the uniform interpretation, application and administration of the NAFTA provisions referred to above; tariff classification and valuation issues that arise in origin determinations; equivalency of procedures and other matters respecting advance rulings; revisions to the Certificate of Origin; matters referred to it by a NAFTA country of the Working Group or the

Committee on Trade in Goods; and other customs-related matters arising under NAFTA.[160] The Customs Subgroup will report to the Working Group periodically on agreements reached, and will refer to the Working Group any matter upon which it has not reached agreement within sixty days of the matter being referred to the Customs Subgroup. Like the Working Group, the Customs Subgroup will meet four times a year.

The Working Group and the Customs Subgroup will serve two important functions. First, modifications of and additions to the NAFTA provisions for which they have responsibility will flow through these bodies. The need for a modification or addition will probably be identified at the Subgroup level, and will flow up to the Working Group. The Working Group will notify the Free Trade Commission of agreed modifications of or additions to the Uniform Regulations. However, NAFTA does not make provision for how the Free Trade Commission is to proceed from there. The NAFTA text does not say what happens to agreed modifications of or additions to the other NAFTA provisions for which the Working Group has responsibility. With the exception of the Marking Rules, substantive changes to any of these provisions would be an amendment of NAFTA and subject to the provisions respecting the approval of international agreements in each NAFTA country.

The second important function of the Working Group and the Customs Subgroup will be to operate as a means for the expeditious resolution of disputes. The NAFTA text does not describe how the Working Group and the Customs Subgroup are to deal with disputes, and their respective mandates do not specifically cover dispute resolution. However, disputes concerning the application of NAFTA provisions for which they have responsibility will first be identified at the Working Group or Customs Subgroup level. A dispute concerning, say, the application of the rules of origin is a matter that could properly be referred by a NAFTA country to the Customs Subgroup. If the Customs Subgroup resolves the dispute, the resolution will be referred to the Working Group. If the resolution requires a modification of the Uniform Regulations, the Working Group will so agree and advise the Free Trade Commission. If the Customs Subgroup cannot resolve the dispute, the dispute would be referred to the Working Group which will try to resolve it. If the Working Group cannot resolve the dispute within thirty days, the dispute will be referred to the Free Trade Commission and be resolved in accordance with the NAFTA Chapter Twenty (described in §11.3(2)). The resolution of a dispute by the Customs Subgroup or the Working Group is not binding on a NAFTA country.

Expeditious resolution of disputes involving the application of the customs-related NAFTA provisions is highly desirable because importers and exporters must work with them on a daily basis. The experience under the FTA suggests that while NAFTA Chapter Twenty procedures will lead in the end to a resolution of a dispute, the result will not be expeditious. The Customs

Subgroup could evolve into an expeditious vehicle for resolution of customs-related disputes. On the other hand, it could exist merely as a conduit with little practical effect. Given that its role is not clearly defined in the NAFTA text, either of these results is possible.

ENDNOTES

[1] As discussed in §5.2(2)(d), NAFTA preferential treatment applies to certain non-originating textile and apparel goods.

[2] See NAFTA 201, which defines "goods of a Party" to include originating goods and also provides that the expression can include "such goods as the Parties may agree". "Goods of a Party" is defined separately in NAFTA 1911 for the purposes of the dispute settlement procedures for antidumping and countervailing duty actions. In NAFTA 1911, the meaning of "goods of a Party" is confined to domestic products as understood under the GATT.

[3] Subject to the exception discussed in §5.2(2)(d).

[4] The trilaterally agreed text of the *NAFTA Rules of Origin Regulations* appears in Part I of the *Canada Gazette*, Saturday, January 15, 1994 at p. 305. The references to "Uniform Regulations" in §3.1 and §3.2 are to this text and comments are based on this text. The text of the letters dated December 30, 1993, from The Honourable Roy MacLaren to each of The Honourable Jaime Serra Puche and Ambassador Michael A. Kantor to which these Uniform Regulations are appended appear on pages 301 to 305. The letters characterize the Uniform Regulations as "interim" and confirm that the NAFTA countries will incorporate them verbatim into their domestic regulations, subject only to the few exceptions outlined in the letters. The letters contemplate that there will be final Uniform Regulations after amendments (resulting from comments) have been agreed upon. At the time of writing, the form of the final Uniform Regulations had not been settled.

[5] NAFTA 415, Uniform Regulations Section 2(1).

[6] NAFTA 415.

[7] As discussed in §3.1(7)(b), the seeds, bulb cuttings or slips from which these goods are grown can come from a non-NAFTA country.

[8] A rule applicable to a tariff item takes precedence over a rule applicable to the HS heading or subheading under which the tariff item falls. See NAFTA Annex 401, Rule (b).

[9] See, for example, parts under HS subheadings 8409.91 and 8409.99 of spark ignition and diesel engines, certain centrifugal pumps under HS subheading 8413.92, parts under HS subheading 8414.90 of various air or vacuum pumps, parts under HS subheading 8419.90 of various types of heating equipment, parts under HS heading 8431 for machinery classified under HS headings 84.25 to 84.30, certain parts classified under HS heading 8473 and automotive parts classified under 8708.99.

[10] See definition of "subject to a regional value-content requirement" in Section 2(1) of the Uniform Regulations. This distinction is relevant to intermediate materials, discussed in §3.1(8)(h)(i) and in the application of the (1-RVCR) rule with light-duty and heavy-duty vehicles discussed in §3.1(12)(c) and (d).

[11] See definition in NAFTA 415 and Uniform Regulations Section 2(1). Machinery and equipment clearly falls within clause (h) of the definition.

[12] Both these expressions are defined in Section 2(1) of the Uniform Regulations.

[13] See Example 6 under Section 7 of the Uniform Regulations.

[14] See Rule 5(a) under General Rules for the Interpretation of the Harmonized System. For example, camera cases, gun cases, drawing instrument cases, necklace cases and similar containers are classified with the articles for which they are intended. However, this rule does not apply to "containers which give the whole its essential character".

[15] This rule applies to various types of padlocks, locks for furniture and other types of locks,

as well as to locks for use in motor vehicles. For the reasons discussed in §3.1(8)(f), only the net cost method may be used for locks for use in motor vehicles because HS subheading 8301.20 is a tariff provision included in the light-duty vehicle tracing list described in §3.1(12)(a).

[16] These include: refrigerators; gas and electric stoves and ovens; dishwashing machines; clothes washing machines; all forms of telecommunications equipment under HS heading 8517; most televisions and television tubes; most types of numerical control machine tools; photocopiers; anchors and grapnels; aluminum cable; inwrought lead and zinc; a wide range of small electrical appliances and consumer goods; burglar and fire alarms; parts of various aircraft, radar, radar navigation and radio remote control equipment; electrocardiographs; medical and industrial x-ray apparatus; and oscilloscopes and oscillographs.

[17] For example, if the MFN rate on an imported material used to produce the good is free in both the NAFTA country in which the good is produced and in the NAFTA country to which the good is exported, the material will be treated as originating.

[18] These are: pesticides under HS heading 38.08; plastics under HS chapter 39; engines under HS headings 84.07 and 84.08; certain colour televisions under HS subheading 8528.10; vehicles under HS headings 87.01 to 87.06; shock absorbers under Canadian tariff item 8708.80.10, U.S. tariff item 8708.80.10A or 8708.80.50A, and Mexican tariff item 8708.80.04; certain automotive parts under HS subheading 8708.99; yachts and pleasure boats under HS 89.03; and various parts for watches and clocks under HS headings 91.08 through to 91.13.

[19] The expression "regional", which NAFTA uses, denotes the same idea as "domestic" but applies to the entire region comprised of the NAFTA preferential trading area, and not just to a single NAFTA country. This chapter will use the expression "regional" in this sense.

[20] In some instances the applicable percentage is 65%. See, for example, goods described in HS chapters 34 (soaps, washing preparations, waxes, dental preparations), 35 (albuminoidal substances; modified starches; glues; enzymes) and 36 (explosives; pyrotechnic products; matches; pyrophoric alloys; certain combustible preparations). For pesticides under HS heading 38.08, the percentage can be 80% in the particular circumstances described in the rule.

[21] As discussed in §3.1(12)(e), the percentages for automotive goods will be increased over a phase-in period. The percentage applicable to footwear under HS headings 64.01 to 64.05 and to uppers under HS subheading 6406.10 is 55%. The percentage applicable to pesticides under HS heading 38.08 can be 70% in some instances.

[22] *The Agreement on Implementation of Article VII of the General Agreement on Tariffs and Trade.*

[23] There are a number of other adjustments, such as for commissions, cost of containers, packing costs and royalties. See CVC Article 8.

[24] The CVC requires that the transaction value accepted as the customs value of imported identical goods be used (CVC Article 2) and if none is found the CVC directs customs authorities to use the transaction value accepted as the customs value for imported similar goods (CVC Article 3). If neither is found, customs value is determined, at the choice of the importer, using a deductive method (CVC Article 5) or a computed method (CVC Article 6).

[25] Defined in Section 2(1) of the Uniform Regulations.

[26] See clause (a)(iii) of the definition of "adjusted to an F.O.B. basis" in Section 2(1) of the Uniform Regulations, and see also Section 7(13)(b) of the Uniform Regulations.

[27] Costs of a service provided by a producer where the service is unrelated to the good, gains or losses resulting from the disposition of discontinued operations, costs relating to cumulative effect of accounting changes, gains or losses resulting from sale of capital assets.

[28] Section 7(10) of the Uniform Regulations.

[29] Section 7(1)(a) of the Uniform Regulations. This value can be challenged under Section 7(2) of the Uniform Regulations if it is determined that it has not been correctly determined. For example, U.S. Customs could use this provision to challenge the customs value used by Revenue Canada respecting a material imported into Canada from a non-NAFTA country by a Canadian producer for incorporation into a good exported to the United States. In these circumstances, the value of the material would be determined in accordance with Schedule VIII of the Uniform Regulations. Hopefully, this provision will be used sparingly.

[30] The lengthy rules for applying this provision set out in the CVC are carried forward in Section 3 of Schedule VIII of the Uniform Regulations.

[31] These circumstances are set out in Section 2(3) of Schedule VIII of the Uniform Regulations.

[32] See Section 5 of Schedule VIII of the Uniform Regulations, which carries forward, with some adaptation and modification, the principles in Article 8 of the CVC. As with the adjustments made to transaction value described above, "royalties" are as defined in Section 2(1) of the Uniform Regulations.

[33] Such as the Canadian goods and services tax, for which an input credit can be claimed, or duty for which a drawback claim may be made.

[34] NAFTA 402(10) and Uniform Regulations, Section 7(4).

[35] NAFTA Article 402(11). See also Uniform Regulations, Section 7(6).

[36] NAFTA Note 22(e). See also Section 7(7) through to 7(9) of the Uniform Regulations which set out rules for rescinding designations.

[37] NAFTA 401(d). See also NAFTA Note 21. These provisions are carried forward and elaborated upon in Uniform Regulations, Section 4(4) and (5).

[38] Some special rules of origin have the effect of permitting the origin of parts assembled from other parts in the same tariff subheading to be established solely on the basis of satisfying the content requirement. See, for example, the alternative special rules for parts of engines under HS subheadings 8409.91 and 8409.99.

[39] U.S. Customs Service rulings CLA-2 CO:R:C:M 000155 VEA, February 10, 1992, and CLA-2 CO:R:I 000160 JLV, February 27, 1992.

[40] See Uniform Regulations, Section 2(1), definitions.

[41] See FTA Annex 301.2, Interpretation Rule 6.

[42] See Revenue Canada Customs and Excise Memorandum D11-4-12, December, 1988, Guidelines paragraph 30.

[43] See U.S. Customs Service Ruling CLA-2 CO:R:C:S: 556346 CW dated June 24, 1992.

[44] NAFTA 406(a). See also Uniform Regulations, Section 6(14)(a).

[45] NAFTA 406(b).

[46] NAFTA 405 and Uniform Regulations, Section 5.

[47] NAFTA 405(1) and Uniform Regulations, Section 5(1). The applicable percentage is 9% in the case of the cigarettes, cigars and other tobacco products classified under HS heading 24.02. See Uniform Regulations, Section 5(3).

[48] See Example 5 under Section 5 of the Uniform Regulations, upon which this is based.

[49] NAFTA 405(5). See also Uniform Regulations, Section 5(4)(m), (6).

[50] NAFTA 405(2) and Uniform Regulations, Section 5(2).

[51] NAFTA 405(3) and Uniform Regulations, Section 5(3).

[52] NAFTA 404 and Uniform Regulations, Section 14.

[53] The motor boat producer also adds to its net cost the transportation and other costs set out in Section 7(1)(c) through to (e) of the Uniform Regulations to the extent that these are not included in the net cost of the engine producer. Suppose that the motor boat producer had paid $50 to have the engine transported to its plant. This amount, which would not be included in the engine producer's net cost, is added to motor boat producer's net cost. However, even though the engine is non-originating, the transportation cost is not included in the motor boat producer's VNM, as would be the case if the motor boat producer and the engine producer were not accumulating.

[54] HS tariff subheadings 8704.21 or 8704.31 (motor vehicles for the transport of goods with g.v.w not exceeding 5 tonnes).

[55] Public-transport-type passenger motor vehicle under HS heading 8702 for the transport of fifteen or fewer persons.

[56] HS tariff subheadings 8703.21 to 8703.90.

[57] Vehicles under HS heading 8701.

[58] Vehicles under HS subheading 8704.10 (dumpers), 8704.22, 8704.23 and 8704.32 (motor vehicles for the transport of goods exceeding 5 tonnes g.v.w.), 8704.90 (other trucks).

[59] Public-transport-type vehicles, passenger motor vehicles under HS heading 8702 for transporting sixteen or more persons.

[60] Special purpose motor vehicles under HS heading 8705 and chassis fitted with engines under HS heading 8706.

[61] See HS heading 84.09 (parts of engines), which is a tariff provision included on the light-duty vehicle tracing list.

[62] The customs value can be challenged under Section 9(3) of the Uniform Regulations for the same reasons as discussed in note 29.

[63] As discussed in §3.1(12)(e), an engine intended for use in a light-duty vehicle will be subject to a value-content requirement of 62.5% once the phasing in of higher thresholds is complete.

[64] The formula is (1-RVCR) where RVCR is the regional value-content requirement expressed as a decimal. This approach is allowed only if the originating status of the material in question is established by applying a value-content requirement. While this will always be the case with an engine, the originating status of many automotive goods may be established by a change in tariff classification, and for some automotive goods, a change in tariff classification is the only means provided in the special rules of origin. If the originating status has been established solely by a change in tariff classification, the (1-RVCR) rule may not be used.

[65] Uniform Regulations, Section 9(9)(a)(i).

[66] This expression is defined in Section 2(1) of the Uniform Regulations as a good incorporating an automotive component.

[67] This expression is defined in Section 2(1) of the Uniform Regulations as a good comprised of listed materials and other materials or listed materials.

[68] Compare Section 10(9)(a) of the Uniform Regulations with Section 9(9)(a) of the same. The distinction flows from NAFTA 402(10), which clearly prohibits designating components in Annex 403.2 as intermediate materials but does not have the same effect respecting light-duty vehicle parts. The reference to NAFTA 403(1) in NAFTA 402(10) has the effect of causing the tracing requirement to override the effect of the designation on the calculation of VNM, but it does not prohibit the designation from being made.

[69] NAFTA 403(5) and Uniform Regulations, Section 13(1).

[70] Section 13(2)(a)(iii) of the Uniform Regulations fixes that value at 90%.

[71] See Uniform Regulations, Section 13(2)(a). The expressions in quotations are all defined in Section 8 of the Uniform Regulations.

[72] NAFTA 403(6)(b) and Uniform Regulations, Section 13(2)(b).

[73] For vehicle averaging, see NAFTA 403(3) and Uniform Regulations, Section 11.

[74] NAFTA Annex 403.3 and Uniform Regulations, Schedule VI.

[75] For parts averaging, see NAFTA 403(4) and Uniform Regulations, Section 12.

[76] For various combinations, see Uniform Regulations, Section 12(4).

[77] See Uniform Regulations, Section 12(6).

[78] Uniform Regulations, Section 12(4)(f).

[79] See Uniform Regulations, Sections 9(8), 10(8) and 12(3).

[80] Uniform Regulations, Section 10(4) and (5).

[81] Uniform Regulations, Section 16(3). As discussed in §2.7(1), the MFN rate of each NAFTA country became free upon NAFTA becoming effective.

[82] For Canada, see *Customs Tariff*, s. 64. The *North American Free Trade Agreement Implementation Act*, S.C. 1993, c. 44, s. 133, amends the *Customs Tariff* by adding a new s. 63.1 which covers marking. So long as s. 63.1 is in effect (which will be as long as NAFTA is in effect), s. 64 will be suspended.

[83] GATT Article IX:1.

[84] GATT Article IX:2.

[85] GATT Article IX:3.

[86] GATT Article IX:4.

[87] GATT Article IX:5.

[88] See the Schedule I to the *Marking of Imported Goods Order* in Revenue Canada Customs and Excise Memorandum D11-3-1, February 16, 1988. Section 3 of the order sets out a list of goods (for example, gifts, bequests, antiques) to which the regulations do not apply.

[89] See Revenue Canada Customs and Excise Memorandum D11-3-1, February 16, 1988, Guidelines and General Information, paragraph 21.

[90] 19 CFR Ch.I (4-1-93 Edition), §134.11.

[91] 19 CFR Ch.I (4-1-93 Edition), §134.32. See also the "J-List exceptions" in §134.33.

[92] 19 CFR Ch.I (4-1-93). See definition of "country of origin" in §134.1(b).

[93] NAFTA Annex 311 uses the expression "Marking Rules" to refer to the rules to be established by the NAFTA countries by January 1, 1994. In this book, the expression "Marking Rules" refers to the country of origin marking regulations described in this §3.2(3) that have been implemented by the NAFTA countries.

[94] Other than a reference to the Marking Rules in NAFTA 1004, the NAFTA text does not set out uses for the Marking Rules beyond those just described. NAFTA 1004 requires that for government procurement purposes, a NAFTA country will not apply rules of origin that are different from those it applies in its normal course of trade. NAFTA 1004 then suggests that these rules may be the Marking Rules "if they become the rules of origin applied by that Party in the normal course of its trade".

[95] At the time of writing, each of Canada and the United States had implemented its NAFTA marking regulations. For Canada, see the *Determination of Country of Origin for the Purposes of Marking Goods (NAFTA Countries) Regulations*, SOR/94-23, December 29, 1993 ("Canadian Marking Regulations"). Comments had been invited and the comment period had not expired. For the United States, see Federal Register, Vol. 59, No. 1, January 3, 1994, page 110, *Rules for Determining the Country of Origin of a Good for Purposes of Annex 311 of the North American Free Trade Agreement* ("U.S. Marking Regulations"). These had been enacted on an interim basis. Mexico has also implemented NAFTA marking regulations but these were not available to the author. Accordingly, the following discussion is confined to the Canadian Marking Regulations and the U.S. Marking Regulations.

[96] Section 4 of the Canadian Marking Regulations; §102.11(a) of the U.S. Marking Regulations.

[97] See Rule 2(a) of the General Rules of Interpretation of the Harmonized System.

[98] Section 12 of the Canadian Marking Regulations; §102.16 of the U.S. Marking Regulations.

[99] Section 4 of the Canadian Marking Regulations; §102.11(b) of the U.S. Marking Regulations.

[100] Section 2(2) of the Canadian Marking Regulations; §102.18(b) of the U.S. Marking Regulations.

[101] *Harmonized Commodity Description and Coding System — Explanatory Notes*, 1st ed. (Brussels, Customs Co-operative Council, 1986), Vol. I, p. 4.

[102] Section 6 of the Canadian Marking Regulations; §102.11(c) of the U.S. Marking Regulations. The Canadian regulations say "as imparting the essential character" while the U.S. regulations say "for determining the essential character".

[103] Section 7 of the Canadian Marking Regulations; §102.11(d) of the U.S. Marking Regulations.

[104] Section 8 of the Canadian Marking Rules; §102.19 of the U.S. Marking Regulations.

[105] Section 14(2) of the Canadian Marking Regulations; §102.15 of the U.S. Marking Regulations.

[106] Section 10 of the Canadian Marking Regulations; §102.12 of the U.S. Marking Regulations.

[107] Section 11 of the Canadian Marking Regulations; §102.13 of the U.S. Marking Regulations.

[108] Section 9 of the Canadian Marking Regulations; §102.14 of the U.S. Marking Regulations.

[109] As discussed below, NAFTA Annex 311 sets out rules respecting marking requirements but does not establish any standards for establishing the country of a good's country of origin for marking purposes.

[110] NAFTA Annex 311(2).

[111] NAFTA Annex 311(3).

[112] NAFTA Annex 311(4).

[113] NAFTA Annex 311(5)(b). There are fourteen exemptions altogether. These exemptions are similar to the exceptions set out in U.S. marking rules in §134.32 of 19 CFR Ch.I (4-1-93 Edition).

[114] NAFTA Annex 311(5)(b)(xiv).

[115] NAFTA Annex 311(6) and (7).

[116] NAFTA Annex 311(8).

[117] NAFTA Annex 311(9).

[118] Re-enacted as the *Determination of Country of Origin for the Purpose of Marking Goods (Non-NAFTA Countries) Regulations*, SOR/94-16, December 29, 1993.

[119] NAFTA Annex 302.2, para. 12.

[120] NAFTA Annex 302.2, paras. 10 and 11.

[121] See the *NAFTA Tariff Preference Regulations*, SOR/94-17, December 29, 1993. The concept of increasing the transaction value by not more than 7% has been translated into the

regulations by providing that the value of the subsequent Mexican or American production, as the case may be, not exceed 6.5421% (0.07 divided by 1.07 times 100%) of the value for duty of the goods when imported. See Sections 3(a)(ii) and 4(a)(ii) of this regulation.

[122] The trilaterally agreed text of the *Uniform Regulations for the Interpretation, Application, and Administration of Chapters Three (National Treatment and Market Access for Goods) and Five (Customs Procedures) of the North American Free Trade Agreement* appears in Part I of the *Canada Gazette*, Saturday, January 15, 1994, at p. 447. Unless otherwise indicated, the references to "Uniform Regulations" in §3.4 are to this text and comments are based on this text. The text of the letters dated December 30, 1993, from The Honourable Roy MacLaren to each of The Honourable Jaime Serra Puche and Ambassador Michael A. Kantor to which the Uniform Regulations are appended appear on pp. 446 and 447.

[123] Article IX of the Uniform Regulations sets out the provisions respecting country of origin determinations described in §3.3(3) and provisions respecting drawback and duty deferral programs referred to in §2.3(6).

[124] NAFTA 501(2).

[125] Uniform Regulations, Article I, Section 1(d).

[126] This rectifies a clear deficiency in the FTA, which did not recognize that the producer and the exporter may not be the same person.

[127] NAFTA 502(c); Uniform Regulations, Article II, para. 2(a).

[128] NAFTA 502(1)(d). Paragraph 2(b) of Article II of the Uniform Regulations also provides that an importer shall be granted five days to provide a corrected Certificate if a Certificate is illegible, defective on its face or incorrectly completed.

[129] NAFTA 502(3).

[130] NAFTA 503. A NAFTA country may require that commercial importations be accompanied by a statement certifying that the good qualifies. A NAFTA country may provide for a higher threshold. The exception does not apply if the importation is one of a series.

[131] NAFTA 504(1)(a).

[132] NAFTA 504(2).

[133] NAFTA 504(3); Uniform Regulations, Article IV, para. 2.

[134] NAFTA 505.

[135] Paragraph 9 of Article VI of the Uniform Regulations requires that the NAFTA countries establish common standards for written questionnaires by January 1, 1995.

[136] See paragraphs 1 and 2 and paragraphs 15 to 18 of the Uniform Regulations.

[137] If the NAFTA country in which the visit is to take place so requests, notice must also be given to the embassy of that NAFTA country in the NAFTA country whose customs administration proposes making the visit.

[138] NAFTA 506(2)(b).

[139] NAFTA 506(4). See also Uniform Regulations, Article VI, para. 5.

[140] NAFTA 506(7); Uniform Regulations, Article VI, para. 6.

[141] NAFTA 506(9). Paragraph 19 of Article VI of the Uniform Regulations sets out further requirements respecting the written determination.

[142] See Uniform Regulations, Article VI, paras. 19, 20. The period must be at least thirty days from the date of the determination or, if the exporting NAFTA country has so requested, confirmation of its receipt by the exporter or producer and any comments made must be taken into consideration.

[143] NAFTA 506(11).

[144] NAFTA 506(12). Paragraph 22 of Article VI of the Uniform Regulations explains what constitutes "consistent treatment".

[145] NAFTA 506(13).

[146] See also paragraph 21 of Article VI of the Uniform Regulations, which elaborates upon "pattern of conduct". There must be at least two determinations concluding as a finding of fact that Certificates of Origin contain false or unsupported representations.

[147] See §5.3(4)(b).

[148] NAFTA 509(1).

[149] NAFTA 509(3)(c).

[150] NAFTA 509(5).

[151] Chapters Three (National Treatment and Market Access), Four (Rules of Origin), Five (Customs Procedures) or Seven (Agriculture and Sanitary and Phytosanitary Measures).

[152] Which in this context include those respecting Chapter Four described in §3.1.

[153] Prior to NAFTA becoming effective, Revenue Canada issued rulings in income tax matters but not customs matters.

[154] In Canada, the *Customs Act* provides for redetermination of tariff classifications or origin determinations for U.S. goods (but not other goods) and re-appraisal of value for duty by a "designated" officer (ss. 59 and 60), and then to the Deputy Minister of National Revenue for Customs and Excise (ss. 63 and 64). The decision of the Deputy Minister can be appealed to the Canadian International Trade Tribunal (s. 67), which provides "quasi-judicial review". The decision of the Canadian International Trade Tribunal may be appealed, with leave, to the Federal Court. The *Customs Act* has been amended to replace origin determinations for U.S. goods with NAFTA origin determinations and extends the benefit of these procedures to advance rulings and marking determinations. See S.C. 1993, c. 44, ss. 90 to 96.

[155] NAFTA 512(1).

[156] NAFTA 512(2)(a).

[157] NAFTA 512(2)(c).

[158] NAFTA 512(2)(b).

[159] NAFTA 513(1).

[160] NAFTA 513(6).

CHAPTER 4

TRADE IN GOODS: NATIONAL TREATMENT, IMPORT AND EXPORT MEASURES, EXPORT TAXES, EMERGENCY ACTION

NAFTA Chapter Three incorporates the GATT national treatment principle and carries forward the FTA rules respecting import and export restrictions and export taxes. NAFTA Chapter Eight carries forward, with some modifications, the FTA provisions respecting emergency action.

4.1 GOODS OF A PARTY

The definition of "goods of a Party" in NAFTA 201 delineates the scope of the NAFTA provisions respecting national treatment, import and export restrictions[1] and export taxes. When the provision relates to imports, the "Party" is another NAFTA country. When the provision relates to exports, the "Party" is the NAFTA country enacting the measure.

"Goods of a Party" are domestic products as understood in the GATT. While the definition includes originating goods, a good does not have to be "originating" under the NAFTA rules of origin to fall within the definition. As discussed previously in §3.3(1), for tariff elimination and some other purposes the nationality attributed to a good is determined under the Marking Rules. This technical approach is not followed in determining whether a good is a "good of a Party" for purposes of applying the NAFTA provisions respecting national treatment, export taxes and import and export restrictions. These provisions apply to any good that is a "domestic product" of a NAFTA country as understood in the GATT.

The key to determining the scope of these provisions is the use of the word "product". As the GATT does not define "product", the meaning of this word is its ordinary meaning,[2] which is "something that is produced". For a thing to be produced, something must be done to it. It must be extracted, harvested, collected, stored, graded, transported, refined, processed, assembled, packaged or somehow transformed into an article of commerce. Unexploited resources such as oil or gas in the ground or water in lakes, rivers or aquifers are not "products" and therefore are not subject to these or any other NAFTA provisions. There is nothing in NAFTA by which a NAFTA country can be compelled to exploit and sell a resource. The governments of the NAFTA countries expressly confirmed this point with respect to water in a joint declaration issued in December, 1993. Once a resource is exploited by being extracted or collected, it becomes a product and is subject to these and other NAFTA provisions.

4.2   NATIONAL TREATMENT

(1) The GATT Obligation

The GATT national treatment requirements are set out in GATT Article III. GATT Article III covers a number of aspects of the general principle that, once duties have been paid, imported goods should be treated no less favourably than domestic goods. Discriminatory internal taxes and charges are prohibited,[3] as are quantitative restrictions that require the mixing, processing or use of imported products with domestic products.[4] Imported products are to be treated no less favourably than domestic products in measures affecting their internal purchase and sale, transportation, distribution or use.[5]

(2) Incorporation into NAFTA

NAFTA follows the same approach to national treatment as the FTA. NAFTA 301(1) incorporates GATT Article III without modification. NAFTA 301(2) requires that a state or province must provide treatment to goods of other NAFTA countries at least as favourable as the most favourable treatment that it provides to goods of the NAFTA country of which it is a part. If a Canadian province or U.S. or Mexican state provides more favourable treatment to products produced within the province or state than to products produced in other provinces or states, the more favourable treatment sets the standard for the treatment of products from other NAFTA countries.

4.3   IMPORT AND EXPORT RESTRICTIONS

(1) The GATT Regime

Except for duties and other charges on imports and exports, GATT Article XI:1 prohibits both import and export restrictions. However, there are many exceptions. GATT Article XI:2(a) permits restricting exports to relieve critical shortages. GATT Article XI:2(b) permits import or export restrictions necessary for the application of classification, grading or marketing standards or regulations. GATT Article XI:2(c), which forms the basis for Canada's dairy and poultry supply management system discussed in §5.3(2)(a)(i), permits import restrictions of agricultural and fisheries products that are part of government schemes to restrict domestic supply.

GATT Article XX contains ten more exceptions under which import and export restrictions or other GATT-inconsistent measures may be imposed. The exceptions apply to measures:

(a) necessary to protect public morals;

(b) necessary to protect human, animal or plant life or health;

(c) relating to the importation of gold and silver;

(d) necessary to ensure compliance with laws or regulations not inconsistent with the GATT, including those relating to customs enforcement, the enforcement of monopolies operated under GATT Articles II:4 and XVII; the protection of patents, trade marks and copyrights and the prevention of deceptive practices;

(e) relating to the products of prison labour;

(f) imposed for the protection of national treasures of artistic, historical or archaeological value;

(g) relating to the conservation of exhaustible natural resources if such measures are made effective in conjunction with restrictions on domestic production or consumption;

(h) undertaken in pursuance of obligations under any international commodity agreement;

(i) involving restrictions on exports of domestic materials necessary to assure essential quantities of such materials to a domestic processing industry during periods when the price of such materials is held below the world price as part of a government stabilization plan, provided that such restrictions not operate to increase the exports of or protection of such domestic industry and not depart from GATT non-discrimination principles; and

(j) essential to the acquisition of products in general or local short supply, subject to the principle of international sharing among contracting parties and provided that such measures which are otherwise inconsistent with the GATT are discontinued when the conditions giving rise to them have ceased.

Measures justified under any of the exceptions listed in GATT Article XX are subject to the "disguised restriction" and "arbitrary or unjustifiable discrimination" restrictions described in §1.3(4).

As discussed in §10.4, GATT Article XII permits restrictions to protect a contracting party's balance of payments.

(2) NAFTA and GATT Article XI

NAFTA 309(1) incorporates GATT Article XI and its interpretative notes by reference.[6] The incorporating language includes the equivalent provision to GATT Article XI contained in any successor agreement to which all NAFTA countries are party. This inclusion was designed to cover amendments to GATT Article XI resulting from the Uruguay Round. While the Uruguay Round agreements do not amend GATT Article XI, the tariffication requirements of the Uruguay Round *Agreement on Agriculture* significantly alter its application to agricultural goods. The implications are discussed in §5.3(7)(a).

(3) Minimum Import and Export Prices under NAFTA

NAFTA 309(2) confirms the NAFTA countries' understanding that GATT Article XI prohibits minimum export price requirements and, except for antidumping and countervailing duties, minimum import price requirements.[7] The text of the GATT itself makes no reference to minimum export or import prices. However, a GATT panel considered the question of minimum import price requirements in *EEC — Programme of Minimum Import Prices, Licences and Surety Deposits for Certain Processed Fruits and Vegetables* and found a minimum price requirement imposed by the Europen Union to be GATT-inconsistent.[8] The objection to minimum import prices is that they neutralize the effect of negotiated tariff reductions.

No GATT panel has dealt with the question of minimum export prices. In the context of GATT, the rationale that minimum prices frustrate bindings does not apply to exports, where export charges are unbound. However, in the context of both the FTA and NAFTA, where member countries have agreed not to levy discriminatory export charges, the prohibition of minimum export prices is based upon the same logic as the prohibition of minimum import prices. The NAFTA agricultural provisions create a limited exception to this rule for exports of agricultural goods between Canada and the United States.[9]

(4) Trans-shipments to and from Non-NAFTA Countries

NAFTA 309(3) carries forward the FTA provisions covering prohibitions and restrictions of imports from and exports to third countries.[10] If a NAFTA country such as the United States maintains a prohibition or restriction on imports from a country such as Cuba, it may limit the importation of goods of that non-NAFTA country[11] from a NAFTA country, such as Mexico.

Similarly, if a NAFTA country prohibits or restricts exports of a good to a non-NAFTA country, it may require that if that good is exported to another NAFTA country, it must be "consumed" there before being further exported to the non-NAFTA country. The expression "consumed" means actually consumed or "further processed or manufactured so as to result in a substantial change in value, form or use of the good or in the production of another good".[12] Under the FTA, "consumed" meant actually consumed or transformed so as to qualify under the FTA rules of origin.[13] The NAFTA rule differs from its FTA counterpart in that it switches from an objective to a subjective test.

(5) Incorporation of the GATT Article XX Exceptions

NAFTA 2101 incorporates GATT Article XX into NAFTA. Unlike FTA 1201, the NAFTA incorporating language includes the interpretative notes to GATT Article XX. Like the NAFTA incorporating language respecting GATT Article XI, the NAFTA text makes it clear that an equivalent successor provision to Article XX will also be incorporated. The text of Article XX was not altered by the conclusion of the Uruguay Round.

(a) Scope of incorporated GATT Article XX

The NAFTA language incorporating GATT Article XX is more explicit than that in the FTA[14] respecting the scope of the incorporation. NAFTA 2101 incorporates GATT Article XX for the purposes of Part Two of NAFTA (Trade in Goods), except to the extent that part applies to services or investment, and to Part Three of NAFTA (Technical Barriers to Trade), except to the extent that part applies to services. For example, paragraph 1 of NAFTA Annex 300-A (Trade and Investment in the Automotive Sector) requires that existing producers of vehicles be treated at least as favourably as new producers. While set out in NAFTA Part Two, this provision clearly applies to investment as well as trade in goods and, to the extent it does, is unaffected by the incorporation into NAFTA of GATT Article XX. NAFTA Part Three on Technical Barriers to Trade expressly applies to services as well as goods.[15] GATT Article XX as incorporated into NAFTA applies to provisions in NAFTA Part Three only in so far as they relate to goods, and not as they relate to services.

(b) Clarifications respecting certain exceptions

NAFTA 2101 clarifies the scope of two important GATT Article XX exceptions.

(i) Human, animal or plant life or health exception

There have been varying opinions as to the scope under the GATT of the "human, animal or plant life or health" exception in GATT Article XX(b). Some maintain that it was intended to apply to environmental measures while others contend that it applies only to sanitary measures related to imports.[16] NAFTA makes it clear that the "human, animal or plant life or health" exception includes "environmental measures necessary to protect human, animal or plant life or health".[17]

A GATT panel has held that a GATT member country cannot use the "human, animal or plant life or health" exception to justify restrictions to protect the life and health outside its boundaries.[18] NAFTA does not alter this limitation.

(ii) Exhaustible natural resources exception

There also has been some question as to the scope under the GATT of the "exhaustible natural resources" exception in GATT Article XX(g). One commentator has suggested that to consider renewable resources such as "animals, plants, soil, and water" as " 'exhaustible' robs that term of any meaning".[19] However, in two GATT disputes involving Canada and the United States, both countries agreed that fish stocks, which are renewable, are an "exhaustible" natural resource.[20] NAFTA makes it clear that the natural resources exception applies to both living and non-living exhaustible natural resources. A logical extension of this provision is that if living resources which are renewable are covered, the exception covers non-living renewable resources such as potable water that can be exhausted through misuse.

(6) The NAFTA Disciplines on Export Restrictions

NAFTA 315 carries forward, without modification, the disciplines imposed by FTA 409 on the use of certain GATT exceptions to justify export restrictions that would otherwise be GATT-inconsistent. The exceptions affected by the disciplines are the "critical shortages" exception in GATT Article XI:2(a), the "exhaustible natural resources" exception in GATT Article XX(g), the "governmental stabilization" exception in GATT Article XX(i) and the "products in short supply" exception in GATT Article XX(j).

The disciplines apply to restrictions on exports of a "good of a Party" to the "territory of another Party". While criticisms of these provisions in the FTA have focussed on their impact on resources and energy goods, they apply to any good that is a "domestic product" of a NAFTA country as understood under the GATT.

For the disciplines to apply, an export restriction must be inconsistent with the GATT but for one of the named exceptions. If the measure is consistent with the GATT or can be justified under a GATT exception not named in NAFTA 315, such as the "human, animal or plant life or health" exception, the disciplines do not apply.

(a) The three disciplines

(i) Proportionality

The first discipline, set out in NAFTA 315(1)(a), is a proportionality requirement. If a restriction justified under one of the identified GATT exceptions cuts back shipments of a good for export, shipments to domestic users must also be reduced so that the proportion of export shipments to total shipments that has prevailed over the preceding thirty-six months is maintained. This NAFTA discipline is clearly more rigorous than the loose requirements which the GATT attaches to some of the exceptions. The "exhaustible natural resources" exception, as expressed in the GATT, may be used only if the restriction is made effective in conjunction with restrictions on domestic production or consumption, but no proportion is set. The use of the "products in short supply exception" under the GATT is subject to principles of international sharing but the GATT does not say what these are. The GATT "government stabilization plan" exception is subject only to a vague non-discrimination requirement. Use of the "critical shortages" exception in GATT Article XI is not subject to any constraint, including the "arbitrary or unjustifiable discrimination" and "disguised restriction" constraints which apply to all GATT Article XX exceptions but not to those in GATT Article XI.

(ii) Pricing

The second discipline, set out in NAFTA 315(1)(b), requires that a restriction justified under one of the specified GATT exceptions not impose a higher price on exports of a good than the price charged when the good is consumed domestically. The operative word is "impose". The discipline does not apply to differences in prices for goods between NAFTA countries that may result from the operation of market forces. The discipline expressly does not apply to a higher price that results from a measure taken under the proportionality discipline that only restricts the volume of exports. This situation could arise if a NAFTA country, in compliance with the proportionality discipline, restricted exports to other NAFTA countries and market forces resulted in higher prices in those NAFTA countries than in the NAFTA country imposing the restriction.

(iii) Normal channels of supply

The third discipline, set out in NAFTA 315(1)(c) requires that a restriction justified under one of the enumerated exceptions not disrupt normal channels of supply or normal proportions among specific goods or categories of goods supplied to other NAFTA countries. In the late 1970s and early 1980s Canada continued to export heavy crude oil to the United States but severely curtailed the export of light crude. As discussed in *Comprehensive Guide*, the "normal proportions" requirement would likely have precluded these selectively applied restrictions.[21]

(b) The Mexican exemption

NAFTA Annex 315 provides that NAFTA 315 does not apply as between Mexico and the other NAFTA countries. The exemption works both ways.

Mexico is not obliged to observe the NAFTA 315 disciplines in imposing restrictions on exports to the United States and Canada. Similarly, neither Canada nor the United States is obliged to observe the disciplines in imposing restrictions on exports to Mexico. While the Mexican concern that gave rise to the exemption was with petroleum products, the exemption applies to all goods which are domestic products of Mexico, the United States and Canada.

The exemption only applies to the disciplines. Subject to the specific exceptions discussed below, all three countries must observe the other NAFTA requirements respecting export restrictions. For example, suppose that Mexico imposed a minimum export price on a good. While NAFTA Annex 315 exempts Mexico from the pricing discipline in NAFTA 315(1)(b), Mexico is still subject to the prohibition of minimum export prices in NAFTA 309(2).

(c) Comments

The disciplines on export restrictions imposed by the FTA and carried forward in NAFTA 315 have been subject to more critical comment in Canada than practically any other FTA provisions. The Canadian government was seen as having given up important policy instruments and to have acceded to U.S. demands for open access to Canadian resources. The most enthusiastic support for the disciplines in Canada has come from those who favour them because of the constraints they place on the ability of Canadian governments to implement resource policies. NAFTA 315 is arguably all the more objectionable because of the exemption granted to Mexico.[22]

While the NAFTA disciplines on export restrictions impose a constraint on the ability of those governments affected by them to regulate exports, their effect should not be over-estimated. Much critical Canadian commentary on the FTA disciplines ignores the fact that the principal constraint on the ability of Canadian governments to control export flows from GATT Article XI, to which Canada is subject with or without NAFTA. In order to impose an export restriction, a government must first justify it under one of the GATT exceptions. Suppose that a Canadian government decided to restrict exports of a resource in order to create jobs by encouraging more domestic processing. Job creation through restricting exports of raw materials cannot be justified under any GATT exception.[23] Canada surrendered its right to impose this sort of export restriction when it joined the GATT in 1947, and not when it entered the FTA in 1989.

Critical commentary on the disciplines has also suggested that the only circumstances under which export restrictions can be imposed are the four set out in NAFTA 315 (critical shortages, exhaustible natural resources, government stabilization plans, products in short supply). This is not so. The exceptions set out in NAFTA 315 are the only ones to which the disciplines apply and not the only ones that can be used. All the other GATT exceptions are clearly carried forward in NAFTA and can be used in appropriate circumstances to justify an export restriction.

To honestly assess the constraint on government action imposed by the NAFTA export restriction disciplines, one must first segregate those government actions already prohibited under the GATT from those additional government actions that are caught by the disciplines.

(7) Specific Exceptions to NAFTA 301 and NAFTA 309

NAFTA Annex 301.3 sets out specific exceptions to the national treatment obligations in NAFTA 301 and the obligations respecting imports and exports set out in §4.3(2), §4.3(3) and §4.3(4).

(a) Logs

Each NAFTA country retains the right to control the export of logs of all species.[24] The purpose of restrictions on the export of logs is to encourage further domestic processing. As this purpose does not fall within any of the GATT exceptions, restrictions on the export of logs would be inconsistent with GATT Article XI and NAFTA 301.3 if there were not an exception.

(b) Protocol of Provisional Application

The Protocol of Provisional Application (the "Protocol") was the instrument by which the original contracting parties to the GATT, which included Canada and the United States but not Mexico, became bound to its obligations. The Protocol contained a grandfathering provision which applied to legislation that existed on October 30, 1947. FTA 1202 exempted from FTA obligations any measure of Canada and the United States that was exempted from GATT obligations by virtue of the Protocol.

Consistent with its approach of identifying exemptions through specific reservations rather than general exempting provisions, there is no provision in NAFTA comparable to FTA 1202. Instead, NAFTA Annex 301.3 exempts specific Canadian and American measures to the extent that they were "mandatory legislation" when Canada and the United States acceded to the GATT and have not been amended to decrease their conformity with the GATT. The measures of Canada relate to prohibited goods, liquor exportation, certain preferential freight rates, excise taxes on absolute alcohol and foreign or non-duty paid ships used in Canada's coasting trade.[25] The measures of the United States relate to taxes on imported perfume containing distilled spirits and certain maritime measures.[26]

As Mexico was not a party to the original Protocol, there are no corresponding provisions in NAFTA 301.3 respecting Mexico. When Mexico acceded to the GATT in 1986, the applicable protocol of accession (the "Mexican Protocol")[27] included exemptions for a number of non-conforming

Mexican measures, including the Automotive Decree. There is no exemption in NAFTA for Mexican measures grandfathered under the Mexican Protocol of accession to the GATT. Instead, matters such as the Automotive Decree and Mexico's reservations respecting petroleum products are dealt with in specific provisions of NAFTA.

(c) Other exceptions in Annex 301.3

The four Atlantic provinces of Canada and Quebec may maintain controls on the export of unprocessed fish set out in the legislation listed in NAFTA Annex 301.3.[28] Mexico may maintain maritime measures reserving certain services exclusively to Mexican vessels.[29] Mexico may also maintain export permit measures respecting goods for exportation to other NAFTA countries that are subject to quantitative restrictions or tariff rate quotas of that NAFTA country.[30] These exceptions, and those of the United States and Canada discussed in §4.3(7)(b), apply to a continuation or prompt renewal of the specified measure or an amendment that does not make it more non-conforming with NAFTA 301 or 309.[31]

NAFTA Annex 301.3 contains an exception for Canada respecting import restrictions maintained by Canada respecting certain ships and vessels originating in the United States. The vessels are identified in FTA Annex 401.2.[32] The restrictions may be maintained so long as the United States maintains quantitative restrictions under its maritime legislation respecting the importation of comparable Canadian goods.

NAFTA Annex 301.3 permits Mexico to adopt or maintain, for a period of ten years after NAFTA became effective, prohibitions or restrictions on imports of certain used goods as provided in Mexico's tariff schedule as of August 12, 1992.[33] The items to which the exception applies are identified by Mexican tariff item codes listed in NAFTA Annex 301.3. The goods listed include a variety of manufactured goods such as cranes, graders, bicycles (except for racing bicycles), sewing machines, various types of trailers, and so on. Notwithstanding the exception, Mexico will not be permitted to prohibit or restrict the importation of certain of these goods when imported on a temporary basis to provide a cross-border service so long as certain conditions are satisfied.[34] This carve-out is necessary so that Mexico's obligations under the NAFTA services and government procurement provisions cannot be frustrated by the application of this exception.

4.4 EXPORT TAXES

NAFTA 314 carries forward the rule in FTA 408 respecting export taxes. A NAFTA country may not impose a tax on the export of a good to another NAFTA country unless the same tax is imposed on the good when destined for domestic consumption and when exported to all NAFTA countries. While export taxes are not prohibited, the requirement that a corresponding charge be imposed on goods destined for domestic consumption defeats their purpose. An export tax has the effect of favouring domestic buyers of a domestic good over foreign buyers. NAFTA 314 prohibits this discriminatory treatment.

Export taxes are generally used in government programs designed to keep domestic prices below international prices. A domestic price is set by the government and the price difference that domestic producers would earn by selling abroad at the higher international price is taxed away through the export tax. Canada imposed a tax on exports of crude oil during the 1970s and early 1980s as part of the federal government's policy of maintaining domestic prices below the world price.[35] However, apart from this example, Canada has made little use of export taxes. The only other recent instance was a federal tax on exports of softwood lumber imposed as part of settling a U.S. countervailing duty action.[36]

(1) Export Taxes and Embargos

Unlike other import and export restrictions, export taxes are not prohibited by the GATT Article XI, and unlike taxes on imports, there are no bindings limiting the amount of an export tax that can be charged.[37] Proponents of the view that the FTA seriously impaired Canada's ability to control exports of water argued that in agreeing not to impose taxes on exports of products to the United States, Canada gave up an important policy instrument for "embargoing" water exports.

Canadian governments have always used export licensing devices or outright prohibitions rather than export taxes to prohibit the export of goods or restrict quantities exported. The Export Control List in the *Export and Import Permits Act*[38] ("EIPA") lists many items subject to export controls, including logs, pulpwood and some other forestry products, various chemicals, unprocessed roe herring, some strategic industrial goods, various weapons, fissionable materials and equipment respecting atomic energy and nuclear reactors. Some Canadian export controls have been successfully attacked by other GATT member countries. In 1988, a GATT panel found that Canadian restrictions on the export of salmon and herring could not be justified under any of the GATT exceptions.[39] These restrictions were put in place long before the rule in FTA 408 respecting export taxes became effective. Why has Canada not restricted exports of these goods through prohibitive export taxes on goods and avoided GATT problems altogether?

The likely answer is that a tax set at such a high rate that no-one could ever possibly pay it is no longer a tax. An export tax of 100% might significantly restrict the amount of a good purchased by foreign consumers, but they could still pay the tax. A tax of 10,000% would completely "embargo" the export of a good because no-one would ever pay it.

There are no GATT panel decisions on prohibitive export taxes. Faced with complaints about a 10,000% export tax, a GATT panel might take one of three approaches. The first would be to find that the 10,000% export tax falls within the excepting language of GATT Article XI:1 and that GATT Article XI:1 did not apply. Such a finding would completely undermine the result that GATT Article XI:1 was intended to achieve. GATT members would be free of the "embargo" exports of goods through 10,000% export taxes, with "export tax quotas" applying to the volumes of goods whose exportation was to be permitted. The second would be to invoke GATT Article XXIII:1(b), which permits a GATT member country to complain about a measure applied by another GATT member country that nullifies or impairs GATT benefits even though the measure does not conflict with any provision of the GATT. However, GATT panels have tended to take a conservative approach to applying GATT Article XXIII:1(b).[40] While GATT Article XXIII:1(b) in its wording could apply to benefits arising from any GATT provision, the cases in which the article has been successfully invoked have involved tariff bindings on imported goods.[41] Also, a panel could find that freedom from export prohibitions or restrictions in the form of taxes is not a benefit contracted for in GATT Article XI or any other GATT article. The third approach that a panel might adopt to avoid the dire consequences of the first approach and the uncertainties of the second would be to find that a "tax" no-one could or ever would pay and from which no revenue would be derived is not a tax at all, and therefore does not fall within the excepting language of GATT Article XI:1. The author is of the view that this third approach is the most likely.

At worst, by agreeing to the export tax prohibition, Canada has given up the right to use a policy instrument that it has never used to "embargo" exports. As indicated above, a strong argument could be made before a GATT panel that a prohibitive export tax violates the GATT.

(2) Exception for Mexican Foodstuffs

NAFTA Annex 314 permits Mexico to adopt or maintain export charges on certain specified basic foodstuffs to limit the benefit of domestic food assistance programs to domestic consumers or in conjunction with government stabilization plans designed to keep domestic prices below world prices.[42] Mexico may adopt or maintain charges for periods of up to one year on the export of any foodstuffs for the purpose of relieving critical shortages.[43]

4.5 NATIONAL TREATMENT AND EXPORTS

Concern has been expressed in Canada that both the FTA and NAFTA extend the principle of national treatment to exports. National treatment when applied to imports requires that imported goods be treated as favourably as domestic goods. Extending national treatment to exports would require that consumers in other countries be treated as favourably as domestic consumers respecting access to domestic goods. The FTA and NAFTA prohibition of taxes charged on exports that are not also charged to domestic consumers has this effect. The proportionality and pricing disciplines described above ensure, in the specific circumstances in which they apply, even-handed treatment as between domestic consumers and those in other FTA or NAFTA countries.

However, some maintain that both the FTA and NAFTA impose broad national treatment obligations respecting exports that go well beyond these requirements. This interpretation forms the basis for the argument that the FTA and NAFTA have seriously impaired Canada's ability to regulate exports of water.[44]

Under the FTA, the argument was based on FTA 105, which required that each of Canada and the United States "to the extent provided in this Agreement, accord national treatment with respect to investment and to trade in goods and services". As "trade in goods" includes both imports and exports, the argument was advanced that the obligation to accord "national treatment" applied to both. However, the words "to the extent provided in this Agreement" made it clear that the operative national treatment requirements were to be found elsewhere than FTA 105. In any event, FTA 105 could not be read as establishing a general principle that national treatment applied to exports because the FTA expressly[45] preserved the entire GATT export restriction regime, subject only to the three disciplines described above and to the understanding respecting minimum export prices in FTA 407(2). While the GATT limits the circumstances in which export restrictions can be imposed, member countries clearly can treat domestic consumers more favourably than consumers in other member countries within those limits.

There is no equivalent to FTA 105 in NAFTA. The argument that NAFTA extends national treatment to exports is based on the lead-in language to each of the exceptions in NAFTA Annex 301 which refers to both NAFTA 301 and NAFTA 309. Some exceptions, such as the one respecting logs described in §4.3(7), apply only to exports. It is argued that NAFTA 301, which incorporates the national treatment provisions of GATT Article III, must therefore apply to exports as well as imports.

GATT Article III unequivocally applies only to imports and would have to be completely rewritten to apply to exports. NAFTA 301 does not alter the wording of GATT Article III. While the lead-in language of NAFTA

301.3 refers to NAFTA 301, the ordinary meaning of the GATT provision incorporated by NAFTA 301 is such that it can only apply to imports. As the *Vienna Convention on the Law of Treaties* requires that treaties be interpreted in accordance with their ordinary meaning,[46] this incorporated GATT provision that clearly applies only to imports cannot be read as applying to exports.

For these reasons, neither the FTA nor NAFTA extends the national treatment principle to exports beyond the export charge prohibition and the disciplines imposed on export restrictions.

4.6 MOST-FAVOURED-NATION PRINCIPLE

Unlike the NAFTA provisions respecting services, investment and financial services, NAFTA does not expressly establish a general most-favoured-nation principle among the three NAFTA countries respecting the trade in goods among them. However, all three countries are bound by the most-favoured-nation obligation in GATT Article I. As mentioned in §4.3(5)(a) and discussed more fully in §5.1(7), NAFTA Annex 300-A expressly sets out a most-favoured-nation obligation respecting automotive goods.

4.7 EMERGENCY ACTION

GATT Articles VI and XIX form the basis for the major trade remedies that can be taken against imports by domestic producers. GATT Article VI and the related GATT codes permit GATT-member countries to levy antidumping duties if imports are being dumped and countervailing duties if imports are being subsidized.[47] In both instances, a trade remedy is permitted to counteract a wrongful trade practice being followed by another country or its exporters if serious injury results or is threatened to a domestic industry. GATT Article XIX permits GATT members to take emergency action. Emergency action is a trade remedy that responds to a situation in which imports increase to an extent that causes or threatens serious injury to domestic producers of like or directly competitive products. Unlike the antidumping and countervailing duty trade remedies, the source of the injury is not the wrongful practice being followed by a trading partner but the importing country fulfilling its GATT obligations respecting the products of its trading partners. For this reason, the emergency action remedy is sometimes referred to as an "escape clause" or a "safeguard".

As under the FTA, the approach of NAFTA to the antidumping and countervailing duty remedies is quite different to that taken to the emergency action remedy. As discussed in §11.4, NAFTA sets out alternative judicial review procedures that, like their FTA predecessors, significantly affect the conduct of antidumping and countervailing duty actions, but do not otherwise affect the international obligations of the affected countries to each other respecting these remedies. On the other hand, the NAFTA emergency action provisions, which are based on those of the FTA, alter the provisions of GATT Article XIX as they apply among the three NAFTA countries. Like the FTA, NAFTA also sets out special bilateral emergency action provisions that apply when the increase in imports and resulting injury or threat of injury is caused by the reduction or elimination of tariffs.

(1) GATT Article XIX

GATT Article XIX requires that there be a causal link between the increase in imports and the GATT concessions given by the country taking the emergency action, although "unforeseen developments" can also be a factor. The importing country may withdraw or modify GATT concessions respecting the product being imported to the extent and for the time necessary to remedy the injury. The importing country must first consult with all GATT-member countries with a substantial interest as exporters. If the consultations do not result in an agreement, the importing country may none the less proceed with its emergency action.

As the emergency action remedy is not based on wrongdoing, GATT Article XIX permits the exporting country to retaliate by suspending substantially equivalent concessions. The other GATT contracting parties may veto this retaliatory action but it has not been their practice to do so.[48]

(2) Agreement on Safeguards

As discussed in §1.4(1), the agreements negotiated in the course of the Uruguay Round include a new *Agreement on Safeguards* ("GATT Safeguard Agreement").[49] This agreement defines "serious injury" and "threat of serious injury" and sets out a number of procedural requirements to be observed by a contracting party initiating an emergency or safeguard action.[50] Standards are established in applying certain safeguard measures, such as quantitative restrictions. Unlike GATT Article XIX, the GATT Safeguard Agreement sets time limits on safeguard actions. Measures may normally not exceed four years and must in no circumstances exceed eight years, or ten years for developing countries.[51] Rules are established respecting the suspension of concessions or obligations by countries whose goods are affected by safeguard actions. The GATT Safeguard Agreement prohibits contracting parties from seeking "voluntary export restraints", "orderly marketing arrangements" or similar measures and requires that such existing arrangements be phased out.[52]

As with other Uruguay Round Agreements, the NAFTA drafters have carried forward a number of ideas in the GATT Safeguard Agreement into the NAFTA text.

(3) Bilateral Actions

FTA 1101 set out a bilateral emergency action provision that applied to originating goods imported from either Canada or the United States to the other. As between Canada and the United States, FTA 1101 continues to apply to all goods except textile and apparel goods covered by NAFTA Annex 300-B. As discussed in §5.2(5), these goods are covered by special emergency action procedures. In applying FTA 1101, the origin of goods will be determined using the NAFTA rules of origin together with the country of origin rules in NAFTA Annex 302.2.[53] NAFTA 801 sets out emergency action procedures that will apply as between Mexico and each of Canada and the United States. As with FTA 1101, as incorporated by NAFTA Annex 801.1, NAFTA 801 does not apply to textile and apparel goods.[54]

The rules in NAFTA 801 are similar to those in FTA 1101. Emergency action is permitted when increases in imports from another NAFTA country "alone constitute a substantial cause of serious injury, or threat thereof".[55] The goods must be originating goods, and there must be a causal link between the increase in imports and the reduction or elimination of duties under the FTA Schedules in the case of FTA 1101 or under the NAFTA Schedules in the case of NAFTA 801.[56] Unlike GATT Article XIX, no mention is made of "unforeseen developments" as a cause. The FTA does not define "serious injury". NAFTA defines "serious injury" as "significant overall impairment of a domestic industry" and a "threat of serious injury" must be on the basis of facts and not allegation, conjecture or remote possibility.[57] The NAFTA definitions are based on those in the GATT Safeguard Agreement.[58] These definitions do not apply to the incorporated FTA 1101.

The FTA and NAFTA bilateral emergency action provisions apply only during the "transition period". Under FTA 1101, the transition period expires on December 31, 1998.[59] Under NAFTA, the transition period expires December 31, 2003, except for goods in staging category C + in the NAFTA Schedules of the United States and Mexico. Staging category C + , which removes tariffs in fifteen stages, is discussed in §2.2(5)(b)(iv). For these goods, the transition period expires on January 1, 2008.[60]

Under both FTA 1101 and NAFTA 801, the only emergency action permitted is the suspension of further duty reduction and increasing the duty to the lower of the MFN rate then applicable to the good or the MFN rate that applied just before the agreement in question came into effect.[61] In the case of a duty applied on a seasonal basis, the rate is increased to the MFN rate that applied to the good for the corresponding previous season.[62] Notification and consultation must proceed the action. Under NAFTA 801, notice of a proceeding that could result in emergency action being taken must be given to the affected NAFTA country, and the emergency action must be taken within one year of the notice being given. No action may be maintained against a good for more than three years unless, in an action taken under NAFTA 801, the good falls within staging category C +. In this case, the action may be extended for a further year, provided that the initial duty applied in the emergency action is substantially reduced at the beginning of the extension period. An emergency action may be extended beyond the end of the transition only if the affected country consents. Only one action may be taken against any particular good during the applicable transition period.

Under FTA 1101, once the emergency action is over, the rate reverts to what it would have been if tariff elimination had proceeded in the ordinary course. Under NAFTA 801 the rate reverts to what it would have been one year after the action was initiated, even though the action may have continued for the full three years. Tariff elimination starts again at the beginning of the next year, either according to the applicable NAFTA Schedule or, at the option of the NAFTA country initiating the action, in equal annual stages to the year that the tariff would have been completely eliminated under the applicable NAFTA Tariff Schedule. For example, assume that a good has a base rate of 10% and is in staging category C. The tariff will be eliminated in ten equal stages of 1% each. Suppose that an emergency action starts in 1996, when tariff elimination has progressed to the third stage and the rate is 7%. As a result of the emergency action, the tariff is raised back to 10%. If the action continues for three years and ends in 1999, the rate will be 6% (the level that would have applied in 1997, the year after the action was initiated) for the balance of 1999. Under one option, the tariff will then be reduced to 3%, which is what it would have been in 2000 if tariff elimination had run its ordinary course, and will continue to be reduced in annual 1% stages to complete elimination on January 1, 2003. Under the other option, the tariff of 6% will be reduced in four equal stages of 1.5% each beginning in 2000, with complete elimination in 2003.

This latter option does not take into account the fact that the date for complete elimination of the tariff under the NAFTA Tariff Schedule may have already passed at the time that the emergency action ends. This is a possibility as the goods most vulnerable to import competition are those with high base rates and short staging periods. A case in point is Canada's furniture industry. FTA base rates for furniture goods were generally over 12%. Tariff elimination proceeded in five stages with complete elimination on January 1, 1993. After the FTA entered into force, there were significant increases in imports from the United States into Canada of certain categories of furniture, and the Canadian industry was adversely affected.[63]

Under both FTA 1101 and NAFTA 801, the country taking the action must provide "mutually agreed trade liberalizing compensation" in the form of concessions that have "substantially equivalent trade effects" or that are "equivalent to the value of the additional duties expected to result from the action".[64] If agreement is not reached, the country against which the action is taken may take tariff action having substantially equivalent effect to the action taken against its goods.

(4) Global Actions

The NAFTA provision respecting emergency action taken under the GATT is set out in NAFTA 802. As between Canada and the United States, NAFTA 802 supersedes the corresponding FTA provision in FTA 1102. While NAFTA 802 is similar in concept to FTA 1102, there are some differences in detail.

The NAFTA countries retain their rights and obligations under GATT Article XIX and any safeguard agreement entered into pursuant to GATT Article XIX, except to the extent inconsistent with NAFTA 802. If the Uruguay Round agreements become effective, the safeguard agreement referred to in NAFTA 802 will be the GATT Safeguard Agreement. A NAFTA country taking emergency action under GATT Article XIX itself or a GATT Article XIX safeguard agreement must exclude imports from each other NAFTA country unless the imports from a NAFTA country account for a "substantial share" of total imports and "contribute importantly" to the serious injury or threat of serious injury. Imports from a NAFTA country will not normally constitute a "substantial share" if the NAFTA country has not been among the top five suppliers of the good.[65] Like the FTA, NAFTA defines "contribute importantly" as being an important cause but not necessarily being the most important cause of the injury.[66] NAFTA elaborates upon this concept by providing that imports from a NAFTA country will not normally be considered to "contribute importantly" to serious injury or threat of serious injury if the growth rate in those imports while the injurious surge[67] occurred was appreciably lower than the growth rate in imports from all sources over the same period.[68] Unlike in NAFTA 801, which applies only to originating goods, the imports referred to in NAFTA 802 do not have to be originating.[69]

Imports from a NAFTA country initially excluded from an action may be subsequently included if a surge of imports from that NAFTA country undermines the effectiveness of the action.[70] As under the FTA, action must be preceded with proper written notice and consultations.

NAFTA 802(6) carries forward the FTA obligation of the country initiating the action to provide "mutually agreed trade liberalizing compensation" on the same basis as described in §4.7(3) for bilateral emergency actions. Neither GATT Article XIX nor the GATT Safeguard Agreement contains a positive obligation to compensate. As in bilateral emergency actions, if agreement is not reached the NAFTA country against which the action is taken may take action having substantially equivalent effect to the action taken against its goods. However, unlike in bilateral emergency action proceedings, the action is not confined to tariff action. The concept of taking "action" confers a broader right than the GATT Article XIX and GATT Safeguard Agreement concept of suspending concessions or other obligations. Unlike GATT Article XIX and the GATT Safeguard Agreement, this NAFTA retaliatory provision does not contain time restrictions.[71]

Unlike NAFTA 801, NAFTA 802 can be applied to textile and apparel goods.

(5) Administration of Emergency Action Proceedings

NAFTA 803 and NAFTA Annex 803.3 establish criteria which must be followed by each NAFTA country in adopting procedures for both bilateral and global emergency action proceedings. The criteria are based on provisions of the GATT Safeguard Agreement as well as existing practice in the United States and Canada.

An emergency action may be instituted by a petition or complaint.[72] An entity filing a petition or complaint must demonstrate that it is representative of the domestic industry producing goods like or directly competitive with the goods being imported. An action may also be self-initiated by a NAFTA country or its "competent investigating authority". The competent investigating authorities are the Canadian International Trade Tribunal in Canada, the U.S. International Trade Commission in the United States and the designated authority within the Ministry of Trade and Industrial Development in Mexico.[73]

A petition or complaint must include a description of the imported good and the like or directly competitive domestic good concerned, and information establishing that the entity or entities filing the petition or complaint are representative of the domestic industry. The petition or complaint must contain import and domestic production data for the past five years and data showing injury, as well as a description of the causes of injury or threat of injury. In global actions, the petition or complaint must set out the criteria for including imports from other NAFTA countries. The competent investigating authority must be satisfied that the petition or complaint contains all the required information before continuing further.[74]

In the course of a proceeding, the competent investigating authority must hold a public hearing to allow interested parties, including consumer associations, to appear, present evidence, cross-examine and make presentations. This requirement goes beyond that in the GATT Safeguard Agreement, which requires that the investigation include "public hearings or other appropriate means in which importers, exporters and other interested parties could present evidence and their views".[75]

Notice of a proceeding must be published in the official journal of the NAFTA country instituting it. The notice must identify the petitioner and include information such as the times for various deadlines and the time and place of the public hearing.[76]

The competent investigating authority must gather all relevant information appropriate to the determination it must make. Like the GATT Safeguard Agreement, NAFTA requires the competent investigating authority to evaluate all relevant factors of an objective and quantifiable nature and lists such factors as the rate and amount of the increase in imports, the share of the domestic market taken by the increased imports, and changes in the level of sales, production, productivity, capacity utilization, profits and losses, and employment.[77] Both the GATT Safeguard Agreement and NAFTA require that an affirmative injury determination not be made unless there is a clear causal link between the imports and the injury or threat of injury. Both agreements require that findings be published in a report.[78]

Like the GATT Safeguard Agreement, NAFTA Annex 803.3 sets out obligations respecting the treatment of information provided on a confidential basis. Both agreements permit authorities to require that persons providing information on a confidential basis also provide non-confidential summaries or reasons why a summary cannot be provided. The obligations of competent investigating authorities to make petitions or complaints public and to publish findings in a report are subject to a confidentiality obligation.

Except in "critical circumstances" and "global actions involving perishable agricultural goods", the competent investigating authority must allow sufficient time for information gathering and for a public hearing to take place before making an affirmative determination.[79] Following the GATT Safeguard Agreement definition, critical circumstances occur where delay would cause damage that would be "difficult to repair".[80] However, when critical circumstances occur, the GATT Safeguard Agreement only permits provisional safeguard measures lasting not more than 200 days, during which time normal procedural requirements must be satisfied.[81] NAFTA does not contain a corresponding requirement. The exceptions in the NAFTA text for "critical circumstances" and "global actions involving perishable agricultural goods" apply only to the obligation to provide sufficient time to gather information and hold a public hearing, and not to the obligations themselves. Therefore, it is not clear what happens to these obligations if an exception applies and the competent investigating authority does not allow sufficient time to fulfil them before making its affirmative determination. It is unfortunate that the NAFTA drafters did not adopt the provisional measures approach of the GATT Safeguard Agreement, because this defect in the NAFTA text could result in disputes.

The NAFTA provisions respecting the administration of emergency action proceedings do not apply to the special emergency action provisions for textile and apparel goods described in §5.2(5).

(6) Concluding Remarks

The *quid pro quo* aspect of emergency action makes it a less attractive trade remedy than an antidumping or countervailing duty action. An industry seeking to invoke it must persuade its government that the negative implications of the domestic injury outweigh the cost of compensation or the risk of retaliation. Emergency action proceedings are much less common than antidumping or countervailing duty actions. Despite the occurrence of some situations in which they might have been invoked, such as that of Canada's furniture industry, the bilateral procedures in the FTA have not been used.

ENDNOTES

[1] As discussed in §5.3(6)(d), there is an exception to this general rule for import and export restrictions respecting agricultural goods as between Mexico and the United States and as between Canada and Mexico.

[2] See Article 31 of the *Vienna Convention on the Law of Treaties* (May 23, 1969, 8 I.L.M. 679) which provides that a treaty shall be interpreted in good faith in accordance with the ordinary meaning of the terms of the treaty in their context and in light of the treaty's object and purpose. While the United States is not a signatory to the Vienna Convention, the United States recognizes its principles. See, for example, the report of the FTA Chapter Eighteen binational panel in *Interpretation of and Canada's compliance with Article 701.3 with respect to durum wheat sales*, Case No. CDA-92-1807-01, February 8, 1993, paragraph 14. [1993] F.T.A.D. No. 2 (QL).

[3] GATT Articles III:1 and III:2. There is a grandfathering provision in GATT Article III:3 for internal taxes specifically authorized in a trade agreement in force on April 10, 1947.

[4] GATT Articles III:1, III:5 and III:8. There is a grandfathering provision in GATT Article III:6 respecting internal quantitative regulations in effect at certain dates.

[5] GATT Article III:4. A Canadian example of a violation of GATT Article III:4 has been Ontario's practice of permitting beer brewed in Ontario to be sold through outlets of Brewers Retail Inc., a monopoly owned by major Canadian brewers, but requiring that imported beer be sold only through government-owned liquor board outlets. These and other practices were the cause of a major trade dispute with the United States discussed in §5.5(4).

[6] In FTA 407(1), Canada and the United States merely affirmed their respective rights and obligations under the GATT, without specific reference to GATT Article XI. Only the exceptions in GATT Article XX were specifically incorporated by reference. See FTA 1201. The approach in NAFTA 309(1) corrects this drafting anomaly.

[7] The corresponding FTA provision is Article 407(2).

[8] The minimum prices were tied to a scheme for taking security from importers to ensure that minimum prices would be adhered to.

[9] See NAFTA Annex 702.1, para. 1 which incorporates by reference FTA 701. As discussed in §5.3(5)(a)(iii), FTA 701(3) prohibits public entities from selling agricultural goods at a price below acquisition cost. This has the effect of imposing a minimum export price.

[10] FTA 407(3).

[11] The expression used in NAFTA 309(3)(a) is "such good of that non-Party". This expression is not defined, but probably would be read in the same manner as "good of a Party", which, as discussed above, is a domestic product as understood under the GATT.

[12] NAFTA 318.

[13] FTA 410.

[14] FTA 1201.

[15] See NAFTA 901(1).

[16] Steve Charnovitz, "Exploring the Environmental Exceptions in GATT Article XX" (October 1991), 25 *Journal of World Trade* 37 at p. 44. Charnovitz states that looking narrowly at the drafting process for Article XX(b) may lead to the conclusion that it was intended to cover only sanitary measures, but that this approach neglects the historical background that shaped Article XX(b), which leads to the conclusion that environmental measures were also intended to be covered.

[17] NAFTA Article 2101(1).

[18] See Ted L. McDorman, "The 1991 U.S. — Mexico GATT Panel Report On Tuna And Dolphin: Implications For Trade And Environment Conflicts", 17 N.C. J. Int'l L. & Comm. Reg. 461 at p. 470. The panel was considering a U.S. measure restricting imports of tuna from Mexico caught using methods that endangered the lives of dolphins. The dolphins were in the high seas and Mexican territorial waters and not in U.S. territorial waters.

[19] Charnovitz, *op. cit.*, note 16, at p. 45.

[20] *Ibid.*, at p. 51.

[21] Jon R. Johnson and Joel S. Schachter, *The Free Trade Agreement: A Comprehensive Guide* (Aurora, Canada Law Book Inc., 1988), at pp. 70-71.

[22] If NAFTA Annex 315 creates a lopsided arrangement in Mexico's favour in respect of resources, the exemption in NAFTA 2106 respecting cultural industries creates an equally lopsided arrangement in Canada's favour. See §10.1.

[23] With the possible exception of the "government stabilization plan" exception in GATT Article XX(i). However, a number of conditions must first apply. See §1.3(4).

[24] In Canada, see item 5101, "Logs of all species of wood", on the Export Control List established under the *Export and Import Permits Act*, R.S.C. 1985, c. E-19.

[25] NAFTA Annex 301.3, Section A, paragraph 3. Schedule VII of the Customs Tariff covers prohibited goods.

[26] NAFTA Annex 301.3, Section C, paragraph 2.

[27] BISD 33S/3 (1986).

[28] See NAFTA Annex 301.3, Section A, paragraph 2. This exception carries forward the exception in FTA 1203(c).

[29] NAFTA Annex 301.3, Section B, paragraph 2(a).

[30] NAFTA Annex 301.3, Section B, paragraph 2(b).

[31] NAFTA Annex 301.3, Section A, paragraph 5; Section B, paragraph 3; Section C, paragraph 3.

[32] See NAFTA Annex 301.3, Section A, paragraph 4. The ships and vessels are identified by asterisks in Chapter 89 of the FTA Schedule of Canada. For these goods U.S. origin is determined by treating operations performed in Mexico as having been performed in a non-NAFTA country.

[33] NAFTA Annex 301.3, Section B, paragraph 4(a).

[34] NAFTA Annex 301.3, Section B, paragraph 4(b). The goods to which the exception to the exception applies are listed in paragraph 4(c).

[35] See *Comprehensive Guide*, p. 67.

[36] See FTA 2009. The Memorandum of Understanding referred to in FTA 2009, which has since been cancelled, required that taxes be imposed on exports of softwood lumber products. These had the same effect as countervailing duties, except that the taxes collected went to the Canadian government, rather than the U.S. government.

[37] This statement may not be quite correct. See *Canadian Water Exports and Free Trade, Rawson Academy Paper No. 2*, Rawson Academy of Aquatic Science, December 1989, Appendix A, p. 3, paragraph 9. According to the author of this paper, the Malayan Union bound its export tax on tin in negotiations with the United States. There may be a few other instances.

[38] R.S.C. 1985, c. E-19.

[39] *Canada-Measures Affecting Exports of Unprocessed Herring and Salmon*, 35th Supp. BISD (1987-1988) 114. The "exhaustible natural resources" exception was found not to apply because the measures challenged were not "primarily aimed" at conservation.

[40] See Mark N. Sills, "The Concept of Non-Violation Nullification and Impairment in the Investment and Services of the Canada-U.S. Free Trade Agreement" (1989), 3 *Review of International Business Law* 127 at pp. 134-5.

[41] See, for example, *European Economic Community — Payments and Subsidies Paid to Processors and Producers of Oilseeds and Related Animal Feed Proteins*. GATT Report L/6627 (December 14, 1989). Subsidies were being paid respecting European products that offset price advantages of imported products. Although not contrary to any express GATT provision, the subsidies were held to have nullified and impaired benefits to the United States from tariff concessions made by the European Union. See, however, in the matter of Puerto Rico regulation on the import, distribution and sale of U.H.T. milk from Quebec, Case No. USA-93-1807-01, QL Citation [1993] F.T.A.D. No. 7, a binational panel decision based on non-violation and impairment and unrelated to tariff bindings. The case involved standards.

[42] NAFTA Annex 314, paragraph 1. Paragraph 1(b) sets out several conditions respecting the government stabilization plan exception. The basic foodstuffs to which paragraph 1 applies are listed in paragraph 4.

[43] NAFTA Annex 314, paragraph 3.

[44] See, for example *Water Exports and Free Trade* by Mel Clark and Don Gamble, in *Canadian Water Exports and Free Trade, Rawson Water Academy Paper No. 2* (Rawson Academy of Aquatic Science, December 1989), at p. 7.

[45] FTA 407(1) which affirms the Parties' respective GATT rights and obligations respecting prohibitions and restrictions on bilateral trade in goods and FTA 1201 which expressly incorporates the GATT Article XX exceptions.

[46] See note 2, *supra*.

[47] What constitutes dumping and countervailable subsidization is discussed §11.4.

[48] John H. Jackson, *World Trade and the Law of GATT* (Indianapolis, Bobbs-Merrill Co., 1969), at p. 566.

[49] These comments are based on the Marrakesh text, April 15, 1994.

[50] See GATT Safeguard Agreement, Articles 3 and 4.

[51] *Ibid.*, paragraphs 1 and 3 of Article 7, paragraph 2 of Article 9.

[52] *Ibid.*, Article 11.

[53] See NAFTA Annex 801.1, which incorporates FTA 1101 by reference as between Canada and the United States, with the modification respecting determining the country or origin.

[54] NAFTA 801(5). These are the goods set out in Appendix 1.1 to Annex 300-B.

[55] NAFTA 801(1).

[56] The only non-originating goods to which tariff elimination applies are certain textile and apparel goods imported under tariff preference levels discussed in §5.2(2)(d). While emergency action may not be taken against these non-originating goods, these goods could be subject to the special bilateral emergency action procedures that apply to textile and apparel goods. These are discussed in §5.2(5).

[57] See NAFTA 804, definitions "serious injury" and "threat of serious injury". Neither of these expressions is defined in the FTA. It is not clear that these undefined expressions in FTA 1101 are to be read in accordance with the NAFTA definitions. Presumably if they were, the NAFTA text would have so provided.

[58] For "serious injury" see Article 4, paragraph 1(a) of the GATT Safeguard Agreement. For "threat of serious injury", see Article 4, paragraph 1(b) of the GATT Safeguard Agreement.

[59] FTA 201(1). The Parties may agree on an earlier date.

[60] See the definition of "transition period" in NAFTA 805. There are some goods for which tariff elimination is not complete until the year 2008 that are not described as being in staging category C+. See, for example, the sugar and sugar-containing goods described in Notes 2 and 8 to Chapter 17 of the NAFTA Schedule of the United States.

[61] FTA 1101(1)(b) and NAFTA 801(1)(b).

[62] FTA 1101(1)(c) and NAFTA 801(1)(c).

[63] Base rates on wooden office furniture under Canadian tariff items 9403.10.10 and 9403.10.90 were 15% and 16.1% respectively. See FTA Schedule of Canada. Imports of these goods from the United States almost doubled between 1989 and 1990, and increased by another 50% between 1990 and 1991. The furniture industry considered both antidumping proceedings and emergency action, but took neither.

64 FTA 1101(4) and NAFTA 801(4).
65 The FTA took a different approach. FTA 1102(1) provided that "imports in the range of five percent or ten percent or less of total imports would normally not be considered substantial".
66 NAFTA 804, FTA 1104.
67 A "surge" is a "significant increase in imports over the trend for a recent representative base period". See NAFTA 804. The corresponding FTA definition in FTA 1104 contained the additional words "for which data are available". It is a little difficult to see how one could use a base period for which data were not available. Perhaps the NAFTA drafters thought this obvious, and deleted the words for this reason.
68 NAFTA 802(2)(b).
69 GATT Safeguard Agreement, Article 2, paragraph 2 provides that safeguard measures shall be applied to a product being imported irrespective of its source.
70 NAFTA 802(3). The corresponding FTA provision is FTA 1102(2).
71 Contrast this with paragraph 3 of Article 8 of the GATT Safeguard Agreement, which provides that under certain circumstances the right of suspension shall not be exercised for the first three years that a safeguard measure is in effect.
72 The expression used in Canada is "complaint". The expression used in the United States is "petition".
73 NAFTA Annex 805. The definition for each country extends to the successor of the named authority.
74 This is the effect of NAFTA Annex 803.3(6).
75 GATT Safeguard Agreement, Article 3, paragraph 1(a). In Canada, the applicable legislation requires that the date upon which any hearing in an inquiry shall commence be published in the *Canada Gazette* (Canada's "official journal"), but does not expressly say that a hearing must be held. See the *Canadian International Trade Tribunal Act*, R.S.C. 1985, c. 47 (4th Supp.), s. 26(2) (en. 1993, c. 44, s. 42(2)). However, Canadian practice has been to hold hearings.
76 NAFTA Annex 803.3(5).
77 See GATT Safeguard Agreement, Article 4, paragraph 2(a); NAFTA Annex 803.3(9). The NAFTA text mentions other economic factors, such as changes in prices and inventories and the ability of firms to generate capital.
78 GATT Safeguard Agreement, Article 4, paragraph 2(c); NAFTA 803.3(12). The NAFTA requirement is a little more detailed.
79 NAFTA Annex 803.3(11).
80 NAFTA 804.
81 See GATT Safeguard Agreement, Article 6.

CHAPTER 5

TRADE IN GOODS: SPECIAL SECTORAL PROVISIONS

NAFTA sets out special sectoral provisions respecting automotive goods,[1] textiles and apparel, agriculture, energy and basic petrochemicals and wine, beer and distilled spirits.

5.1 AUTOMOTIVE GOODS

Given that the automotive industry is the biggest single generator of employment in each of Canada, the United States and Mexico, it was to be expected that NAFTA would contain special provisions respecting automotive goods. The disputes between Canada and the United States over the application of the FTA rules of origin to automotive goods led to the negotiation of the special rules respecting the application of the regional value content described in §3.1(12). NAFTA Annex 300-A sets out provisions relating to Canada's Auto Pact and other duty remission programs, the Mexican Automotive Decree, the U.S. Corporate Average Fuel Economy ("CAFE") rules and the trade in used cars. NAFTA Annex I phases out Mexican investment restrictions respecting the auto parts industry.

(1) Canadian Automotive Policy and the Auto Pact

Since the 1960s, Canadian automotive policy has balanced allowing integration of the Canadian and U.S. automotive industries with measures to ensure that an acceptable portion of the integrated industry remains in Canada. A productive Canadian automotive industry has been made possible through serving the larger U.S. market and continuing access to that market is a major Canadian policy objective. However, the by-product of allowing integration is permitting access by U.S. assemblers and parts producers to the Canadian market. Successive Canadian governments pursued a policy of making that access conditional on performance in Canada.

Canada achieved both these policy objectives when it entered into the Auto Pact[2] with the United States. The Auto Pact, which came into effect in 1966, combined duty-free access to the U.S. market based on origin with conditional duty-free access to the Canadian market based upon assemblers in Canada meeting performance requirements.

For automotive goods entering the United States, the Auto Pact is a sectoral free trade agreement with the criterion for duty-free entry into the United States being the origin of the goods. The focus on the Canadian side of the Auto Pact is not origin but the fulfilment of performance requirements by the importing assembler. The Auto Pact itself applied only to assemblers producing vehicles in Canada during the Auto Pact base year (August 1, 1963 to July 31, 1964). Those assemblers were the Big Three (*i.e.*, General Motors, Ford and Chrysler), and Volvo which had established an assembly operation in Nova Scotia. Following the Auto Pact coming into effect, the Canadian government began conferring "Auto Pact status" by company-specific duty remission orders on assemblers that met performance criteria similar to those contained in the Auto Pact.

To be eligible to import automotive goods into Canada duty-free under the Auto Pact, the importer must be a vehicle assembler maintaining a prescribed ratio between the value of the vehicles it produces in Canada and its sales of vehicles in Canada, together with a prescribed level of Canadian value added in its Canadian production. The production-to-sales ratio has the effect of requiring that an assembler wishing to import vehicles on a duty-free basis for sale in Canada produce vehicles in Canada. However, the vehicles produced need not be the same as those sold. So long as the ratio is maintained, an assembler entitled to Auto Pact benefits is free to supply the Canadian market with vehicles imported from anywhere. This flexibility permits specialization by allowing a U.S. assembler in Canada, such as General Motors, to limit the number of model lines produced in Canada and to supply the entire Canadian and U.S. markets for those model lines from Canadian plants. The Canadian value-added ("CVA") requirement ensures that Canadian production amounts to more than mere assembly. The production-to-sales ratio and the CVA requirement are the so-called Auto Pact safeguards. If the safeguards are met, the assembler can import new vehicles and original equipment ("OE") parts duty-free from anywhere, without regard to origin.[3]

While the Auto Pact served Canadian interests well, the arrangement was inherently unstable. At the time that the Auto Pact was entered into, the Big Three completely dominated the Canadian assembling industry. By the mid 1980s, the Asian transplants were becoming a significant factor in the North American automotive market. Toyota, Honda, Hyundai and CAMI were all in the process of establishing plants in Canada. In the mid 1960s, the disparity in the relative efficiencies of the Canadian and U.S. industries was so great that the need for safeguards for the Canadian industry in a sectoral-free trade arrangement was obvious. By the mid 1980s this disparity had disappeared, and so, from the U.S. perspective, had the rationale for the safeguards. U.S. interests were skeptical about the utility of a regime which provided for unqualified access to the U.S. market but conditional access to Canada, particularly when that conditional access was about to be extended to transplant assemblers.

(2) Effect of the Canada-U.S. Free Trade Agreement

Under the FTA, Canada surrendered its future ability to use duty remission as a means of ensuring performance in Canada in return for assurance that duty-free access to the U.S. market would continue. Like the Auto Pact, the FTA provided for duty-free access for Canadian automotive goods to the U.S. market based on origin, but replaced the Auto Pact origin rule with the FTA rules of origin.

While the FTA permitted duty remission under the Auto Pact and Canada's Auto Pact-based duty remission orders to continue in perpetuity, Canada surrendered its ability to extend the program. While an exception was made for CAMI, the other transplants in Canada, Toyota, Honda and Hyundai will never be permitted to receive Auto Pact status.

The FTA required the elimination of export-based and production-based duty remission orders which have been issued to various assemblers in Canada. Most notably, the production-based duty remission orders granted to Honda, Toyota and Hyundai, which tie duty remission to CVA in domestic production of vehicles, must be eliminated by January 1, 1996.

(3) The Mexican Automotive Decree

Mexican automotive policy[4] has been implemented through a series of decrees commencing in 1962 and culminating in the current Automotive Decree, which entered into force on November 1, 1990.[5] The Automotive Decree covers all vehicles except for tractors, buses and large trucks.[6] These vehicles are covered by the Autotransportation Decree.[7] The Automotive Decree substantially liberated previous Mexican rules governing the automotive industry. However, the regulatory framework imposed by the Automotive Decree is considerably more restrictive than that created by Canada's Auto Pact-based duty remission orders.

(a) Content requirement

Like the Auto Pact, the Automotive Decree requires automotive assemblers to maintain a level of national value added in their domestic production of motor vehicles.[8] However, only parts supplied by members of the Mexican "auto parts industry" or "national suppliers" count in the calculation of an assemblers national value added. Before NAFTA, under the content requirement the assembler's national value added from suppliers ("VANp") divided by the assembler's total national value added ("VANt") had to equal at least 36%. VANp is the total invoicing to the assembler for parts and components supplied by national suppliers and the auto parts industry minus imports incorporated in parts and components acquired from national suppliers and the auto parts industry *plus* exports "promoted" by the assembler *minus* imports incorporated in exports promoted. VANt is the assembler's total sales in the domestic Mexican market plus its trade balance. The calculation is made annually.

To qualify as a member of the auto parts industry, 60% of a producer's total sales had to be parts sold to the Mexican assembling industry. To qualify as national supplier, the producer had to be supplying the Mexican automotive industry with certain defined parts. Furthermore, for the parts supplied to be eligible for inclusion in an assembler's calculation of national value added, the supplier (whether a member of the Mexican auto parts industry or a national supplier) had to maintain a 30% level of national value added in its own production. An auto parts industry supplier had to be majority Mexican-owned.[9] A national supplier could be foreign-owned but not by the assembler it was supplying.[10] Maquiladoras were neither members of the auto parts industry nor national suppliers, and parts produced by them could not be included in the calculation of an assembler's national value added.

(b) Trade balance

Before NAFTA, the Automotive Decree required that assemblers maintain positive trade balances. An assembler's trade balance is the sum of the foreign exchange value of exports of automotive products *plus* exports of parts and components which it promotes *minus* the value of direct and indirect imports of parts and components that a manufacturer incorporates into vehicles produced in Mexico for sale in Mexico.[11]

(c) New vehicle imports

An assembler's ability to import new vehicles is determined by the amount of its extended trade balance.[12] An assembler's extended trade balance is its trade balance *plus* transfers of trade balances from other assemblers *plus* net trade balances of maquiladoras controlled by the assembler (up to an amount equal to 20% of the assembler's direct and indirect imports) plus 30% of its investment in fixed assets plus its unused entitlement to import vehicles carried forward from previous years. Before NAFTA, an assembler's extended trade balance was subject to a negative adjustment if the assembler did not meet the 36% content requirement. In this event, VANp was divided by 0.36 and an amount equal to the excess of VANt over this number was subtracted from the other values comprising the extended trade balance. An assembler in Mexico needed 1.75 units of positive value in its extended trade balance to import one unit of value of new vehicles.[13]

Regardless of the amount of the extended trade balance, imports of new vehicles could comprise only 20% of the total number of vehicles an assembler sold in Mexico. Restricting imports to a certain percentage of vehicles sold in Mexico made it impossible for an assembler in Mexico to specialize in the same manner as is possible under the Auto Pact for an assembler in Canada.

(d) Autotransportation Decree

The Autotransportation Decree which took effect on January 1, 1990, and covered buses and heavy trucks, was less restrictive. Assemblers were subject to trade balancing requirements and, during transition periods which have now expired, national value added requirements.[14]

(e) Canadian automotive trade balance with Mexico

The restrictive effect of policies such as the Automotive Decree on imports is apparent from Canada's balance of trade with Mexico in automotive goods. Consider the following figures for 1992:

AUTOMOTIVE GOODS — IMPORTS FROM AND EXPORTS TO MEXICO — JANUARY TO DECEMBER 1992

(CDN $'000s)[15]

	Imports	Export	Surplus (Deficit)
Parts[16]	1,490,578	246,360	(1,244,218)
Vehicles	602,074	176[17]	(601,898)
Total	2,092,652	246,536	(1,846,116)

(4) NAFTA Automotive Provisions

NAFTA permits the Auto Pact and Canada's duty remission program based on Auto Pact principles to continue indefinitely. However, NAFTA will phase out the Automotive Decree and will eliminate Mexican restrictions on investment in the auto parts sector. NAFTA will require that Mexican-produced vehicles be regarded as "domestic" under the CAFE rules. After a long phase-in period, NAFTA will eliminate restrictions on the trade in used cars.

(5) Effect of NAFTA on the Auto Pact

As discussed in §2.4, NAFTA contains provisions similar to those in the FTA prohibiting duty waivers which are conditional upon satisfying performance requirements.[18] However, Canada and the United States may continue the Auto Pact, as modified by the FTA, and Canada is permitted to maintain the Auto Pact duty remission orders which have been issued to the recipients listed in FTA Annex 1002.1. NAFTA has, in effect, preserved the *status quo* in so far as the Auto Pact and Canada's Auto Pact duty remission orders are concerned. The two-tier system is perpetuated, with only the Big Three and CAMI being entitled to Auto Pact benefits.

The HTSUS retains a "special" category for automotive goods imported under the Automotive Products Trade Act ("APTA"), the legislation that originally carried the U.S. Auto Pact obligations into effect. To qualify for duty-free APTA treatment, a good must now be originating under the NAFTA rules of origin and be eligible to be marked as a good of Canada under the Marking Rules. The good must also be imported as "original motor vehicle equipment" by a "bona fide motor-vehicle manufacturer" identified on a list maintained by the Secretary of Commerce. While the rate under the U.S. FTA Schedule for many goods eligible for APTA treatment is also free, some goods are still subject to duty. Once duty elimination between Canada and the United States is complete, the APTA category will cease to be relevant.

(a) Effect of duty elimination with Mexico

An Auto Pact assembler's sole incentive to meet the Auto Pact safeguards is duty remission. If there were minimal or no duty to remit, there would be no incentive to meet the safeguards and the Auto Pact would, for practical purposes, cease to exist. Duty remission on automotive goods will continue to be relevant for automotive goods imported from the United States until 1998 and from Mexico until 2003 for most vehicles and until 1999 or 2003 for many other automotive goods.[19] However, once duty elimination under the NAFTA is complete, Mexico will be added to the United States as a country from which automotive goods can be imported into Canada duty-free without meeting the safeguards. The question is whether free trade with both the United States and Mexico will reduce the benefits of duty remission so significantly that the Auto Pact safeguards will be ignored.

The continuing incentive to comply with the safeguards will be to save duty on vehicles and parts imported from third countries. Assemblers entitled to Auto Pact benefits will continue to have duty-free sources of duty-free new vehicles and parts other than the United States and Mexico. This advantage cannot be made available to their counterparts in the United States or Mexico so long as these countries choose to maintain external tariffs. How meaningful this advantage is depends on the volume of vehicles and parts imported from third countries, as opposed to the United States and Mexico, and Canada's level of external tariffs. Consider the following figures for the period January to December 1992:

IMPORTS OF AUTOMOTIVE GOODS INTO CANADA
JANUARY — DECEMBER 1992

(CDN $'000s)[20]

	Duty-free	Duty Paid	Total Imports
United States	35,361,913	7,710,495	43,068,208
Mexico	1,831,112	261,684	2,092,652
Third Countries			
Japan	2,839,435	3,748,452	6,587,485
Other	4,253,062	2,744,747	7,005,316
Subtotal	7,092,497	6,493,199	13,592,801
TOTAL	44,285,522	14,465,378	58,753,661

As Canada's published import statistics do not identify the basis for the duty-free treatment, the following analysis is based on several arbitrary assumptions. It is assumed that all imports from Mexico have been made by the Big Three under the Auto Pact. Toyota and Honda would have made duty-free imports from Japan under their production-based duty remission orders and some of the duty-free imports from the United States and from third countries besides Japan would have been made under non-Auto Pact remission programs. In the absence of better information, it is assumed that 75% of the duty-free imports from the United States, 50% of the duty-free imports from Japan and 75% of the duty-free imports from other third countries were made under the Auto Pact. Based on these assumptions, the breakdown is as follows:

ASSUMED DUTY-FREE IMPORTS UNDER THE AUTO PACT

(CDN $'000s)

United States	26,521,435	(75% of 35,361,913)
Mexico	1,831,112	
Third Countries		
Japan	1,419,718	(50% of 2,839,435)
Other	3,189,797	(75% of 4,253,062)
Subtotal	4,609,514	
TOTAL	32,962,061	

From these figures, it is obvious that without free trade with the United States and Mexico, the incentive to comply with the safeguards would be overwhelming. Assuming an average duty rate of 6%, duty saved on $32,962,061,000 would be $1,977,724,000. Removing United States and Mexico leaves $4,609,514,000 of Auto Pact imports, about 14% of the total. Assuming an average rate of duty of 6%, duty saved by meeting the safeguards would be $276,571,000. If Canada were to lower its external rate to 3.1% (the current U.S. MFN duty on most parts), duty saved would be $142,895,000. If it is assumed that only 50% of imports from all third countries are made under the Auto Pact, the duty saved with a 3.1% external rate of duty would still be $109,934,000. On the basis of these figures, it appears that there will continue to be a substantial incentive to earn the duty remission by meeting the safeguards even after the process of duty elimination under NAFTA is complete.

(b) Effect of the elimination of duty drawback

The elimination of duty drawback under NAFTA will have opposing effects on the incentive to comply with Auto Pact safeguards. On the one hand, elimination of duty relief through drawback will provide an added incentive for Auto Pact assemblers to earn duty remission through complying with the safeguards. On the other hand, the elimination of duty drawback will increase pressure to lower the external tariff on automotive goods to U.S. rates.

The elimination of duty drawback for exports to the United States will adversely affect the transplant assemblers in Canada. The production-based duty remission orders issued to each of the transplant assemblers must be terminated by January 1, 1996, which coincides with the NAFTA deadline for the elimination of duty drawback for exports to the United States. The only way that the Canadian government can assist the transplants when drawback is eliminated is to lower external tariffs to U.S. levels. However, this will weaken the incentive for Auto Pact assemblers to comply with the safeguards.

(6) Effect of NAFTA on Mexican Automotive Policies

(a) The Automotive Decree

NAFTA will eliminate the Automotive Decree by 2004. Up to that time, the Automotive Decree will remain in effect but a number of its restrictions are eased or eliminated.

(i) Content requirement

The 36% national value added requirement will be reduced to 34% from 1994 to 1998, to 33% in 1999, to 32% in 2000, to 31% in 2001, to 30% in 2002 and to 29% in 2003. Existing producers that did not satisfy the 36% content requirement for the 1992 model year may use the percentage that they did achieve for that year until that percentage is higher than the prescribed percentages. Thus, if the percentage achieved for the 1992 model year was 32%, the assembler may use that percentage until 2001.[21]

For existing assemblers, the basis for calculating the percentage of value added is the higher of VANt (described in §5.1(3)(a)) and the assembler's reference value for the year that the calculation is being made.[22] The reference value is the average of the assembler's sales for the 1991 and 1992 model years adjusted for inflation (*i.e.*, its base value) plus a prescribed percentage of the excess of its sales in the current year over that average amount.[23] The trade balance is not included in the reference value. However, the sales include imported vehicles and not just those produced domestically, so that the reference value could be higher than VANt. If this occurs, the assembler will require a higher level of domestic Mexican value added to satisfy the content requirement than would be the case if VANt is used. This provision affords protection to the Mexican autoparts industry, given the more lenient trade balancing requirements and the significantly enhanced capability to import new vehicles. This rule will not apply to new assemblers.[24]

The national value added required of the auto parts industry and national suppliers will be reduced from 30% to 20%. A maquiladora can now qualify as a national supplier, provided that it is not owned by the assembler that it is supplying.

(ii) Trade balance

In calculating its trade balance, the assembler will be required to include only a percentage of the imported parts and components in vehicles sold in Mexico rather than the entire amount. The initial percentage will be 80% for 1994 and will be phased down in more or less equal annual amounts to 55% in 2003.[25] This provision will enable assemblers to import more parts and components. For example, in 1999, when the applicable percentage is 66.1%, the importation of 1,513 units of parts and components would have the same impact on the assembler's trade balance as the importation of 1,000 units under the pre-NAFTA rules.[26] Thus, by 1999, an assembler's entitlement to import parts will have increased by 51.3%.

(iii) New vehicle imports

In determining the total value of new vehicles that an assembler may import, the assembler will be permitted to divide its extended trade balance by the percentages referred to in §5.1(6)(a)(ii) rather than by 1.75.[27] In 1994, the applicable percentage will be 80%. Dividing the extended trade balance by 0.8 rather than 1.75 will increase the ability of an assembler to import vehicles by 219%.[28] The value of the extended trade balance (upon which the ability to import new vehicles is based) is also enhanced by the more generous trade balance calculation described in §5.1(6)(a)(ii).

The negative adjustment to an assembler's extended trade balance for failure to meet the content requirement will be based on the percentages and, where applicable, the assembler's reference value described in §5.1(6)(a)(i).[29]

(b) Other requirements

The ownership restriction on enterprises of the auto parts industry will be eliminated for investors of Canada and the United States and their Mexican subsidiaries by 1999.[30] Parts produced in Mexico by suppliers owned by such investors will be eligible to be counted in the determination of national value added.

Mexico was required to eliminate the Autotransportation Decree when NAFTA became effective. However, until 1999 there will still be restrictions on the importation of these types of vehicles. Mexico may restrict the number of vehicles imported by an assembler to 50% of the number of vehicles produced in Mexico.[31] To qualify for the right to import vehicles during this period, the assembler must satisfy a 40% value added requirement.[32] Mexico is also required to permit persons who do not produce autotransportation vehicles in Mexico to import volumes of originating vehicles based on percentages of each type of these vehicles produced in Mexico. The percentages are 15% for 1994 and 1995, 20% for 1996 and 30% for each of 1997 and 1998.[33] Following 1998, the right to require import permits for these vehicles expires.

Mexico may continue to maintain import licensing measures to the extent necessary to administer the Automotive Decree, as modified by NAFTA, and the NAFTA provisions respecting autotransportation vehicles and used cars.

(7) Most-Favoured-Nation Obligation

Paragraph 1 of NAFTA Annex 300-A requires each NAFTA country to treat existing producers of vehicles as favourably as new producers. Existing producers are those that were producing vehicles in a NAFTA country before the 1992 model year. While this obligation applies to all three NAFTA countries, it has particular relevance to Mexico. Without a network of Mexican auto parts industry and national suppliers, it is unlikely that a new producer of vehicles could satisfy the content requirements of the Automotive Decree in its first several years of production. Unless the Mexican government were to allow a phase-in period, the new producer would face substantial financial penalties.[34] If the Mexican government allowed lower content levels over a phase-in period, the same lower content levels would have to apply to the existing vehicle producers in Mexico.

The definition of "vehicle" in paragraph 4 of NAFTA Annex 300-A expressly excludes motorcycles. Therefore, Honda, which produces motorcycles in Guadalajara, is not an "existing producer of vehicles" for the purposes of the most-favoured-nation rule in paragraph 1 of NAFTA Annex 300-A.

(8) CAFE Rules

The CAFE Rules impose fuel economy requirements on vehicles sold in the United States. The rules split the fleet of each assembler into a domestic fleet and imported fleet. The two fleets are treated the same but the calculations for each fleet must be made separately. As to whether a car line is domestic or imported depends on its meeting a 75% content test.[35]

In applying the test prior to NAFTA, Canadian production was considered domestic but Mexican production was considered imported. NAFTA requires that Mexican value added count as domestic, just as Canadian value added presently does. For manufacturers of automobiles not producing in any NAFTA country, the rule applies beginning with the model year next following January 1, 1994.[36] A manufacturer that started manufacturing automobiles in Mexico before model year 1992 and a manufacturer that produces automobiles in any NAFTA country may make a one time election at any time between January 1, 1997 and January 1, 2004 to have the rule apply beginning with the next model year after the election. However, if a manufacturer, such as Honda that manufactures automobiles in Canada and the United States but not Mexico, begins producing automobiles in Mexico after model year 1991, the rule will apply to the model year following the later of the commencement of production or January 1, 1994.[37] The rule applies to all manufacturers after January 1, 2004, including those entitled to make an election that have not done so.

The reason for delaying the application of the rule to existing manufacturers and permitting an election was to permit them to adjust. Ford's current sourcing practices are such that its fuel-efficient Escort produced in Hermasillo are "domestic" for CAFE purposes, while its less fuel-efficient Crown Victoria produced in Ontario are "imported". If Volkswagen wishes, it may continue to have its fuel efficient Mexican-produced Golf and Jetta treated as "imported" until January 1, 2004, to offset the less fuel-efficient Audi that it imports from Germany into the United States.

(9) Used Cars

A "used vehicle" is one that has been sold, leased or loaned, or driven a prescribed distance,[38] or manufactured prior to the current year where at least ninety days have elapsed since its manufacture. Canadian restrictions on imports of used vehicles from the United States were completely phased out by January 1, 1993, under FTA 1003. This obligation is carried forward in NAFTA in paragraph 2 of NAFTA Appendix 300-A.1. Canadian restrictions on imports of used vehicles from Mexico will be phased out over ten years starting in 2009. Mexican restrictions on imports of used vehicles from Canada and the United States will be phased out over the same time period. The restrictions which each of Canada and Mexico may maintain on used vehicle imports until the end of the phase-in period shall not derogate from their respective obligations respecting land transportation services.[39]

The removal of restrictions on imports of used vehicles will apply only to "originating" used vehicles. The NAFTA rules of origin will apply to determine the origin of a used vehicle. This may create difficulties because the vehicle may have originally been produced for domestic consumption without any origin calculations being made. While it may be obvious that a vehicle manufactured in the 1970s by one of the Big Three is "North American", it is much less obvious with a vehicle manufactured in the 1990s by a transplant assembler for, say, the domestic U.S. market.

(10) Aftermarket Parts

Under the FTA, tariffs on aftermarket parts were phased out over five stages rather than ten. The parts to which the five stage phasing applied were identified in the FTA Schedules for each of Canada and the United States. The phasing out of tariffs as between Canada and the United States on these goods is now complete. As the FTA Schedules have been incorporated into NAFTA, the differing treatment of OE and aftermarket parts traded between the United States and Canada will continue until 1998, when the phasing out of tariffs will be complete. Otherwise, NAFTA does not distinguish between OE and aftermarket parts for tariff elimination purposes.[40]

(11) Concluding Remarks

Except for the changes in the rules of origin, NAFTA maintains the FTA status quo as between Canada and the United States. The significance of NAFTA for the trade in automotive goods is that it sets the stage for the full integration of the Mexican automotive industry into the North American automotive industry. Assemblers in Mexico will no longer have to satisfy Mexican demand with locally produced vehicles and will be able to specialize. Because of Mexico's liberalization commitments respecting the maquiladoras described in §7.9(3)(d)(i), the distinction in the Mexican parts industry between the maquiladoras and the auto parts industry will disappear. Subject only to the constraints imposed by the NAFTA rules of origin, assemblers in Mexico will be able to source parts from wherever they choose.

By phasing out and ultimately eliminating tariffs on automotive goods imported from Mexico, NAFTA weakens the incentive for Auto Pact assemblers in Canada to comply with the Auto Pact safeguards by opening another country besides the United States from which automotive goods can be imported duty-free without having to comply with the safeguards. Duties saved on vehicles and parts imported from non-NAFTA countries will be a continuing incentive to comply with the safeguards. However, this incentive will not be sufficient to ensure that production of automotive goods remains in Canada if costs in Canada exceed those in the United States and Mexico by any substantial amount.

The significance of the Auto Pact to preserving jobs in Canada's automotive industry should not be over-estimated. In the years immediately following the introduction of the Auto Pact in 1966, the Auto Pact safeguards served as an effective defence mechanism to maintain automotive production and employment in Canada while the Canadian industry was significantly less efficient than that in the United States. However, the success of Canada's automotive industry in the 1980s and 1990s has depended on its ability to compete in the U.S. market. With the integration of the Mexican automotive industry into the North American, Mexico's assemblers and parts producers could become formidable competitors with their Canadian counterparts for the U.S. market. While the Auto Pact and similar policies may protect Canadian jobs that depend on serving the Canadian market, they will not protect Canadian jobs that depend on serving the U.S. market. The only way those jobs will be protected is for Canadian costs to remain competitive with those in the United States and Mexico.

The degree to which the Canadian automotive industry depends on serving the U.S. market is evident from the following figures:

AUTOMOTIVE GOODS — IMPORTS FROM AND EXPORTS TO
THE UNITED STATES — JANUARY TO DECEMBER 1992

(CDN $'000s)[41]

	Imports	Exports	Surplus (Deficit)
Parts[42]	33,359,442	19,736,254	(13,623,188)
Vehicles	9,708,766	27,560,283	17,851,517
Total	43,068,208	47,296,537	4,228,329

These figures emphasize the role of the Canadian automotive industry as being primarily assembling. The production-to-sales ratio which the Big Three must meet is 75 to 100, which could be satisfied with a negative balance of trade in vehicles. The ratio of vehicles exported to those imported in 1992 was almost three to one.[43] The Canadian jobs that depend on this trade surplus in vehicles are clearly not being secured by the production-to-sales safeguard. Also, the CVA requirement does not prevent a significant trade deficit in parts.

The most significant barrier to the trade in automotive goods among the three NAFTA countries is the Mexican Automotive Decree. Its phasing-out and ultimate elimination should provide significant export opportunities for automotive producers in both Canada and the United States. The biggest adjustment resulting from NAFTA will occur in Mexico. While the greatest potential beneficiary of the full integration of the Mexican automotive industry into the North American is the Mexican industry, the Mexicans are also most at risk. The Mexican auto parts industry has, for over thirty years, operated under the protection of import-substitution regulatory environments. Within five years of NAFTA becoming effective, that environment will be largely dismantled. In ten years it will be gone.

There was concern during the NAFTA negotiations that NAFTA would create a managed trade regime for automotive goods. This did not occur. In fact, in dismantling the Automotive Decree, NAFTA eliminates managed trade as between Mexico and Canada and the United States. There was also concern that the NAFTA would prejudice the transplant assemblers. This certainly has not occurred overtly. However, complying with the new rules of origin will be more difficult for the transplant assemblers than the Big Three. Also, unless Mexico chooses to relax the provisions of the Automotive Decree for all assemblers, it will probably not be practical for a transplant assembler to commence assembling vehicles in Mexico until the phase-out period for the Automotive Decree has been largely completed.

5.2 TEXTILES AND APPAREL GOODS

Many developed countries, including both Canada and the United States, regard their textile and apparel sectors as particularly vulnerable to imports, especially those from developing countries. With the introduction of Mexico into the Canada-U.S. free trade area, it was inevitable that the trade in textile and apparel goods would receive considerably more attention than under the FTA. Special provisions respecting textile and apparel goods are set out in NAFTA Annex 300-B.

With one exception, the NAFTA provisions respecting originating textile and apparel goods operate in much the same manner as with other goods. Originating goods are entitled to preferential tariff treatment and tariffs will be phased out according to the respective tariff schedules of each NAFTA country. NAFTA Annex 300-B sets out the special bilateral tariff elimination arrangements between Mexico and each of Canada and the United States that have been described in §2.2(4)(b)(i) and §2.2(5)(b)(i) respectively. As with other goods, originating textile apparel goods are entitled to the benefit of the NAFTA obligations described previously in Chapter 4. The one exception is that originating textile and apparel goods are subject to the tariff action safeguard procedure set out in NAFTA Annex 300-B and described in §5.3(5).

The NAFTA provisions respecting textile and apparel goods depart from the rules applicable to other goods in so far as the trade in non-originating goods is concerned. Normally, non-originating goods are not entitled to the benefits of tariff elimination. However, NAFTA Annex 300-B follows and elaborates upon the FTA approach of applying a relatively strict rule of origin but allowing preferential treatment to prescribed annual quantities of certain categories of non-originating textile and apparel goods. Also, NAFTA takes into account the fact that the trade in many categories of textile and apparel goods is governed by rules that are outside the GATT and contrary to basic GATT principles. These rules are to be found in bilateral restraint agreements between many developing countries and developed countries. The terms of these restraint agreements and the conditions under which they can be negotiated are prescribed by a multilateral set of rules known as the Multifibre Arrangement ("MFA"), to which all three NAFTA countries are party. MFA issues were not addressed in the FTA because there was no restraint agreement between Canada and the United States nor any prospect of one coming into existence. However, there is a restraint agreement between the United States and Mexico. While there is no restraint agreement between Canada and Mexico, circumstances could arise under which one could be negotiated. NAFTA Annex 300-B sets out provisions covering restraint arrangements generally, and phases out the existing restraint arrangements between the United States and Mexico. These provisions apply only to non-originating goods and take into account the effect of the Uruguay Round, which will phase out bilateral restraint arrangements so that all textile and apparel goods will eventually be "integrated into the GATT"[44] and subject to normal GATT disciplines.

(1) Textile and Apparel Goods Defined

The expression "textiles and apparel goods" used throughout NAFTA Annex 300-B means the goods listed in Appendix 1.1 to NAFTA Annex 300-B.[45] Appendix 1.1 includes the yarns, threads and fabrics referred to in HS chapters 50 to 55, fibres under HS chapter 55, the textile goods in HS chapters 56 to 60, the apparel goods in HS chapters 61 and 62 and the made-up textile items in HS chapter 63. Appendix 1.1 also covers: wadding, gauze and bandages; certain plastic goods; various leather goods such as luggage and handbags; footwear; headgear and parts thereof; umbrellas; yarn and woven fabric of fiberglass; seat belts for motor vehicles; parachutes; watch straps, bands and bracelets of textile materials; various articles of bedding; garments for dolls; and woven ribbons.

Not every provision in NAFTA Annex 300-B applies to this extensive list of goods. Most of the provisions in NAFTA Annex 300-B apply only to fibres, yarns, threads, fabrics, apparel goods and made-up textile articles.

(2) Rules of Origin and Tariff Preference Levels

NAFTA follows the FTA approach of establishing relatively onerous rules of origin for most fabrics, apparel goods and other made-up textile articles but allowing preferential tariff treatment to annual volumes of imports of specified categories of textile and apparel goods that do not meet the strict rules of origin so long as certain requirements are met. With some exceptions, the NAFTA rules of origin for yarns, fabrics, apparel goods and made-up textile articles are generally more stringent than their FTA counterparts. As between Canada and the United States, the more onerous rules are offset by the considerable increase in the volumes of certain categories of non-originating goods that can be imported from Canada into the United States and receive preferential tariff treatment.

(a) NAFTA rules of origin for textile and apparel goods

While the NAFTA rules of origin for a few goods listed in Appendix 1.1 impose a regional value content requirement,[46] the rules for most textile and apparel goods, including those for fibres, yarns, threads, fabrics, apparel goods and made-up textile goods are, like their FTA counterparts, based solely on prescribed tariff shifts. Unlike the rules of origin for automotive goods, there is no unique approach to determining the origin of textile and apparel goods.[47] However, NAFTA Annex 300-B sets out special bilateral rules for a few categories of goods and provides for review and possible revision of the rules affecting a number of goods.

Most textile and apparel goods begin as fibre (such as wool, animal hair, cotton, flax, jute, vegetable fibre or man-made staple fibres) which is spun into yarn. The yarn is then woven into fabric. The fabric may be further processed into a textile good or cut, sewn and assembled to make an apparel good. A "fabric-forward" rule of origin means that, for the finished good to be originating, the fabric must be made in the free trade area but the yarn and fibre can be from outside the free trade area. A "yarn-forward" rule of origin means that both the fabric and the yarn must be made in the free trade area but the fibre can be from outside the free trade area. With a "fibre-forward" rule of origin, the yarn and fabric must be produced in the free trade area and the fibre from which the yarn is made must come from one of the countries in the free trade area.

(i) Apparel goods (HS chapters 61 and 62)

The FTA rules for apparel goods (HS chapters 61 and 62) imposed a fabric-forward requirement. Most of the NAFTA rules respecting apparel goods impose a yarn-forward rule, meaning that for the apparel good to be originating, both the fabric and the yarn must be originating. Consider, as a typical example, men's and boys' jackets and blazers falling under tariff headings 6103.31-6103.33.

The FTA rule was: "A change to any heading of Chapter 61 from any heading outside that chapter other than headings 5111-5113, 5208-5212, 5309-5311, 5407-5408, or 5512-5516."

The specified headings from which the change cannot occur are fabrics of wool, cotton, vegetable fibres (including flax), man-made filaments and man-made staple fibres. The corresponding NAFTA rule is:

> A change to subheading 6103.31 through 6103.33 from any other chapter, except from heading 51.06 through 51.13, 52.04 through 52.12, 53.07 through 53.08 or 53.10 through 53.11, Chapter 54, or heading 55.08 through 55.16 or 60.01 through 60.02, provided that:
> (a) the good is both cut (or knit to shape) and sewn in the territory of one or more Parties, and
> (b) the visible lining fabric listed in Note 1 to Chapter 61 satisfies the tariff change requirements provided therein.[48]

The wool, cotton and man-made staple fibre categories have all been expanded so that a yarn-forward rule applies. The man-made filament category has been expanded so that the filaments from which a fabric is made must be extruded in a NAFTA country. Except for linen, a yarn-forward rule applies to apparel made from fabric produced from vegetable fibre. However, the NAFTA rule is more lenient for apparel made from linen. Under the FTA, a fabric-forward rule applied, while under NAFTA the linen can be imported. NAFTA applies a fabric-forward rule if the article is made from knitted or crocheted fabric (HS chapter 60). Under the FTA, these fabrics could be imported. Under both the FTA and NAFTA, an article can be made from imported silk fabric and still be originating. NAFTA prescribes separate rules for visible linings in apparel goods covered by both Chapters 61 and 62.

There are some exceptions in NAFTA to the yarn-forward rule for apparel goods. Apparel goods of Chapter 62 (Articles of Apparel and Clothing Accessories, Not Knitted or Crocheted) made from fabric from a non-NAFTA country will originate if they are both cut and sewn or otherwise assembled in one or more NAFTA countries and if the fabric of the outer shell, exclusive of collars or cuffs, is wholly of five prescribed fabrics, including certain cotton velveteens and corduroys, Harris Tweeds and batiste fabrics. Men's and boys' shirts of cotton or man-made fibres under HS subheadings 6205.20 and 6205.30 made from fabric from a non-NAFTA country will originate if they are both cut and assembled in one or more NAFTA countries and if the fabric of the outer shell, exclusive of collars or cuffs is wholly one of nine prescribed fabrics.[49] Brassieres, which fall under HS subheading 6212.10, may be made from imported fabric provided that they are both cut and sewn or otherwise assembled in one or more NAFTA countries. Men's or boys' pajamas or nightshirts made entirely from knitted or crocheted cotton fabric (excluding collar, cuffs, waistband or elastic) that are cut and sewn or otherwise assembled in a NAFTA country will be considered as originating even if the fabric is non-originating. The same rule applies to women's or girls' briefs made entirely from the same fabric (excluding waistband, elastic or lace). As discussed in §5.2(2)(c), each of these exceptions is subject to review. For the goods identified in each of these exceptions, the NAFTA rule is less stringent than the FTA rule.

As between the United States and Mexico, a special bilateral rule of origin applies respecting certain categories (described by individual tariff items) of sweaters, pullovers, sweatshirts and similar articles of HS subheading 6110.30, including those that are parts of ensembles that are knitted or crocheted from man-made fibres. This special rule replaces the usual yarn-forward requirement with a fibre-forward requirement.[50]

(ii) Yarns and fabrics (HS chapters 50 to 55)

With some yarns and fabrics, the NAFTA rules are clearly more stringent than their FTA counterparts. For others, the FTA rules have remained essentially unchanged.

Silk: With silk yarn and fabric, the rule is unchanged from the FTA. Under both agreements, yarn made from non-originating fibre will be originating and silk fabric made from non-originating yarn will be originating.

Wool and Animal Hair: Under both the FTA and NAFTA, woollen yarn and yarn from fine or coarse animal hair can be spun from non-originating fibre and still be originating. Woollen fabric and fabric of coarse or fine animal hair are subject to a yarn-forward rule under both the FTA and NAFTA, meaning that the yarn must be originating for the fibre to be originating. However, unlike the FTA, NAFTA requires that if the yarn in the fabric includes synthetic yarns, those yarns must also be originating.

Cotton: Under the FTA, cotton thread and yarn could be spun from non-originating fibre and still be originating. NAFTA applies a fibre-forward rule to these goods, which means that the fibre must be originating for the thread or yarn to be originating. If the thread or yarn includes fibres that are man-made filaments or man-made staple fibres, those fibres must also be originating. Like the FTA, NAFTA applies a yarn-forward rule to cotton fabric, meaning that for the cotton fabric to be originating, the cotton yarn must also be originating. Unlike the FTA, NAFTA requires that any woollen yarn or synthetic yarn included in the cotton fabric also be originating.

Vegetable Fibres: Under the FTA, yarn of vegetable fibres such as flax, jute and true hemp could be spun from non-originating fibre. A yarn-forward rule applied to fabric made from vegetable fibres. Under NAFTA, the rule is the same, except for flax fabrics (linen). Like silk but unlike other fabrics, linen woven in a NAFTA country will be considered originating regardless of the origin of the yarn.

Man-made Filaments: With threads, yarns and fabrics of man-made filaments, the NAFTA rule is essentially the same as under the FTA. Man-made filament yarns and threads must be extruded in a NAFTA country to be originating. NAFTA also provides that if a yarn or thread from man-made filaments also includes cotton fibre or man-made staple fibre, that fibre must also be originating. Fabrics of various synthetic or artificial filaments must be woven from originating yarn. NAFTA also provides that if such fabrics include woollen or cotton yarn or yarn made from man-made staple fibres, that yarn must also be originating for the fibre to be originating. NAFTA contains a more lenient rule for woven fabric identified under specific Canadian, U.S. and Mexican tariff items[51] that are at least 85% non-textured polyester filament. These fabrics can be woven in a NAFTA country from non-originating polyester filament yarn and still be originating. However, as described in §5.2(2)(c)(ii), this rule is subject to possible review.

Man-made Staple Fibres: With yarn made from man-made staple fibres, the FTA treated yarn spun from non-originating fibre as originating. Under NAFTA, the yarn must be spun from originating fibre. Under both the FTA and NAFTA, a yarn-forward rule applies to fabrics.

(iii) Carpets and textile floor coverings (HS chapter 57)

The FTA and NAFTA rules are virtually the same. Any thread, yarn or fabric of wool, cotton, man-made filaments or man-made staple fibres used in the production of the carpet or floor covering must be originating, while jute woven fabrics can be non-originating. Jute yarn had to be originating under the FTA rule, which made little sense given that jute fabric could be non-originating. NAFTA corrects this anomaly by providing that the jute yarn can also be non-originating.

As between the United States and Mexico, a special modification of the rule applies for tufted carpets of nylon and other man-made textile materials (HS subheadings 5703.20 and 5703.30) and for felt carpets and tiles (HS heading 5704). In addition to the restrictions described above, any man-made staple fibre material (HS chapter 55) must be originating.[52]

(iv) Coated fabrics (HS chapter 59)

The FTA applied a fabric-forward rule to coated fabrics under HS chapter 59 if the fabrics were of wool, cotton, vegetable fibres, man-made filaments and man-made staple fibres. For tire cord fabric of HS heading 59.02 and transmission or conveyor belts of HS heading 59.10, NAFTA imposes a yarn-forward rule respecting materials of wool or other animal hair or vegetable fibres[53] and a fibre-forward rule respecting materials of man-made staple fibres. The NAFTA rules for other coated fabrics are essentially the same as their FTA counterparts.

(v) Knitted or crocheted fabrics (HS chapter 60)

Both the FTA and NAFTA apply a yarn-forward rule to knitted or crocheted fabrics of HS chapter 60 to materials that are of wool or other animal hair or of cotton. Under both rules, materials of man-made filaments or man-made staple fibres must be originating. The FTA imposed a fabric-forward rule for materials of vegetable fibres. NAFTA imposes a yarn-forward rule for these materials unless they are of flax, in which case both yarn and fabric can be non-originating.

(vi) Other textile made-up articles (HS chapter 63)

These goods include blankets, bed and table linens, toweling, curtains and related items, bed spreads and so on. The FTA and NAFTA rules are essentially the same. Both rules impose a yarn-forward requirement for materials of wool or cotton. Also, any materials of man-made filaments or man-made staple fibres must be originating. The FTA imposed a yarn-forward rule respecting materials of vegetable fibres. NAFTA exempts flax yarns and fabrics from this requirement. NAFTA also makes an exception for curtains, interior blinds and curtain or bed valances of synthetic fibre under HS sub-heading 6303.92 from the requirement that man-made filaments must be originating. Provided that these goods are cut and sewn or otherwise assembled in a NAFTA country, yarn of certain polyester filaments can be non-originating. However, as discussed in §5.2(2)(c)(ii), this exception is subject to review.

(b) Accumulation

Under the FTA, a yarn-forward rule applied to cotton fabric and a fabric-forward rule applied to cotton apparel goods. If a single producer wove the fabric and made the apparel good, the cotton yarn from which the fabric was made could be imported. However, if the producer of the apparel good purchased cotton fabric from a supplier who had imported the yarn, the fabric would be non-originating and the producer would not be able to satisfy the fabric-forward rule that applied to the apparel good. The apparel good would be non-originating, even though the processing activities of the producer and the supplier, taken together, satisfied the fabric-forward requirement. The effect was to apply a yarn-forward rule in these circumstances.

Consider the same situation under NAFTA. Most apparel goods are subject to a yarn-forward requirement, while cotton fabric is subject to a fibre-forward requirement. As discussed in §3.1(11), in determining whether a required tariff shift has occurred, NAFTA permits several producers to accumulate their processing activities. Suppose that the fabric supplier had spun the yarn from imported cotton fibre. The fabric, considered by itself, would be non-originating. However, NAFTA permits the activities of the fabric supplier and the apparel good producer to be accumulated. Between them, they satisfy the yarn-forward requirement applicable to the apparel good, and this good is originating. As Section 2(2)(a) of NAFTA Annex 300-B states, this result would follow even if the supplier and the producer were located in different NAFTA countries.[54]

(c) Review and possible future revision of rules of origin

Section 7 of NAFTA Annex 300-B provides for the review and possible revision of the rules of origin affecting textile and apparel goods.

(i) Brassieres

Section 7(1) of NAFTA Annex 300-B provides that the rule of origin for brassieres, which permits the use of non-originating fabric, is subject to review. Any NAFTA country may request consultations to find a solution to any "difficulties" resulting from the application of the rule. Presumably the "difficulties" would be the inability of producers in the NAFTA country requesting the consultations to compete with brassieres imported from other NAFTA countries made with imported fabric. If the consultations do not result in a "satisfactory solution" within ninety days, any NAFTA country may request that the rule of origin for brassieres be changed to the yarn-forward rule that applies to most apparel goods.[55] The new rule will take effect 180 days after the request.

(ii) Availability of fibres, yarns or fabrics

Section 7(2) of NAFTA Annex 300-B provides that any NAFTA country may request consultations to consider whether particular goods should be subject to different rules of origin. The purpose of different rules would be to address issues of availability of the supply of fibres, yarns or fabrics within the three NAFTA countries. The thrust of this provision is that if a NAFTA country demonstrates substantial production of a particular fibre, yarn or fabric by showing that its producers are capable of supplying commercial quantities in a timely manner, the rule of origin for the end product should be made more stringent.

While the request can be made respecting any textile and apparel good, five specific rules of origin are identified for possible review and amendment. These are: the rule for certain fabrics of non-textured polyester filament described in §5.2(2)(a)(ii) under Man-made Filaments; the exceptions (other

153

than the brassiere exception discussed in §5.2(2)(c)(i)) to the yarn-forward requirement for apparel goods described in §5.2(2)(a)(i); and the exception for curtains, interior blinds and curtain or bed valances of synthetic fibre described in §5.2(2)(a)(vi). Consider, for example, the rule respecting curtains. A NAFTA country may request review of this rule of origin if it can demonstrate that its producers are capable of supplying commercial quantities of the polyester filaments in a timely manner referred to in the rule. The NAFTA country making the request would be seeking to have the rule amended to conform with the more general requirement for made-up textile articles that man-made filaments be originating.

Consultations are to be concluded within sixty days, and two NAFTA countries can bilaterally agree on an amended rule that will only apply as between them. However, unlike the review procedure for the brassiere rule of origin, there is no automatic substitution upon request of a more stringent rule. If no agreement is reached, the NAFTA country requesting the consultations may request consultations to adjust the annual tariff preference levels that apply between it and the other NAFTA countries. Tariff preference levels are discussed in §5.2(2)(d). Tariff preference levels cannot be altered without the mutual consent of the NAFTA countries concerned.

(iii) Review of textile and apparel rules of origin

Section 7(3) of NAFTA Annex 300-B requires the NAFTA countries to review the NAFTA rules of origin for textile and apparel goods within five years of NAFTA becoming effective. The review will take into account increasing global competition for these goods and the implication of the integration of these into the GATT as the result of any successor agreement to the MFA (which is the *Agreement on Textiles and Clothing* discussed in §5.3(3)(c)). This provision does not set out any consequence if the NAFTA countries cannot agree on what to do with the textile and apparel rules of origin as a result of such review.

(d) Tariff rate quotas and tariff preference levels

The FTA rules of origin provided that prescribed annual quantities of imports of apparel goods and non-wool fabric and made-up textile articles could receive preferential FTA tariff treatment on importation into each of Canada and the United States without having to meet the FTA rule of origin. These annual quantities were known as tariff rate quotas ("TRQs"). The TRQs were negotiated to take into account the fact that Canadian textile and apparel manufacturers rely more heavily than their U.S. counterparts on imported inputs. However, rather than treating apparel and made-up goods produced from imported fabric as originating, the FTA negotiators opted for the TRQ approach, which limits imports of these goods under preferential FTA tariffs to prescribed annual volumes.

NAFTA applies this same approach to all three NAFTA countries and applies and expands it to include cotton and man-made fibre spun yarn. The prescribed annual quantities in NAFTA are referred to as tariff preference levels ("TPLs") rather than tariff rate quotas because the tariff rate quota concept used elsewhere in NAFTA applies to originating goods. Provided that certain conditions are satisfied, imports during a calendar year of non-originating goods from another NAFTA country up to the applicable TPL receive preferential NAFTA tariff treatment, and imports above the TPL are subject to the importing NAFTA country's MFN rate.

TQRs in the FTA are expressed in terms of square yard equivalents (SYEs). TPLs in NAFTA are expressed in terms of square metre equivalents (SMEs). Schedule 3.1.3 of NAFTA Annex 300-B sets out conversion factors by which the square metre equivalent textile and apparel goods not primarily measured in terms of square metres can be determined.

(i) Apparel goods (HS chapters 61 and 62)

As mentioned previously, the FTA applied a fabric-forward rule to apparel goods. Notwithstanding this, provided that the goods were both cut and sewn in the United States or Canada or both countries, the following annual quantities of apparel goods made from fabric from third countries would receive preferential tariff treatment.[56]

	TRQ for Imports from Canada into United States	TRQ for Imports from United States into Canada
Non-wool apparel	50 million SYE (i.e., 41,806,500 SME)	10.5 million SYE (i.e., 8,779,365 SME)
Wool apparel	6 million SYE (i.e., 5,016,780 SME)	1.1. million SYE (i.e., 919,743 SME)

Consider imports of non-wool apparel from Canada into the United States. Imports up to a total of 50 million SYE in any year would be subject to the applicable FTA preferential rate in the U.S. tariff schedule. All imports over this volume for the balance of the year would be subject to the applicable U.S. MFN rate. The same would apply in the following year, with the first 50 million SYE being subject to preferential FTA treatment and imports over that volume being subject to the MFN rate. There was no provision for annual increase of these volumes. However, at least as far as imports into the United States from Canada were concerned, the TRQs represented about six times the volume of actual imports.[57] As a percentage of the TRQ, actual imports of non-wool apparel into the United States from Canada for 1989, 1990 and 1991 were 9%, 17% and 27% respectively.[58] The corresponding percentages for actual imports of wool apparel for 1989, 1990 and 1991 were 20%, 20%

and 51% respectively. While TRQ utilization by Canadian producers and exporters of both categories of apparel goods was well below the limit, utilization was growing.

As discussed above, NAFTA applies a yarn-forward requirement to most apparel goods. The NAFTA TPLs function like the FTA TRQs.[59] To qualify, the apparel good must be cut and sewn or otherwise assembled in a NAFTA country. TPLs apply to apparel goods made from fabric or yarn produced or obtained from outside the NAFTA countries. Imports in any year up to the TPL are subject to the applicable NAFTA rate, and imports over the TPL for the balance of the year are subject to the applicable MFN rate. NAFTA introduces some elaborations. For example, only 75% of the TPL of imports of non-originating cotton or man-made fibre apparel goods into the United States from Canada may be used for goods made from non-NAFTA country fabric. The remainder of the TPL may only be used for apparel goods which are made from fabric woven in Canada from non-NAFTA country yarn.

The TPLs of imports into the United States from Canada and Mexico are as follows:[60]

Imports into United States	From Canada	From Mexico
Cotton or Man-made Fibre Apparel		
(a) Total NAFTA TPL	80,000,000 SME	45,000,000 SME
(b) Maximum from non-NAFTA country fabric	60,000,000 SME	45,000,000 SME
(c) FTA TRQ	41,806,948 SME	N/A
Wool Apparel		
(a) NAFTA TPL	5,066,948 SME	1,500,000 SME
(b) FTA TRQ	5,016,780 SME	N/A

Respecting imports into the United States from Canada, the NAFTA TPL for cotton or man-made fibre apparel has been increased from the corresponding FTA TRQ by almost 44%.[61] However, the NAFTA TPL for wool apparel is almost the same as the corresponding FTA TRQ. Of the NAFTA TPL of 5,066,948 SME, only 5,016,780 SME can be used for men's or boys' wool suits. Unlike the FTA, under which TRQs did not increase, NAFTA provides that the TPLs of imports from Canada into the United States be increased annually for five consecutive years starting January 1, 1995, as follows: the total TPL for cotton or man-made fibre apparel, by 2% each year; the portion of the TPL for cotton or man-made fibre apparel made from non-NAFTA country fabric, by 1% each year; and the TPL for wool apparel, by 1% each year.

NAFTA does not provide for the growth of the TPLs of imports into the United States from Mexico.

The TPLs of imports into Canada and Mexico are as follows:[62]

Imports into Canada	From United States	From Mexico
Cotton or Man-made Fibre Apparel		
(a) NAFTA TPL	9,000,000 SME	6,000,000 SME
FTA TRQ	8,779,365 SME	N/A
(b) Wool Apparel	919,740 SME	250,000 SME
FTA TRQ	919,740 SME	N/A

Imports into Mexico	From United States	From Canada
(a) Cotton or Man-made Fibre Apparel	12,000,000 SME	6,000,000 SME
(b) Wool Apparel	1,000,000 SME	250,000 SME

For imports into Canada from the United States, the TPL of cotton or man-made fibre apparel has been increased by about 2.5% from the FTA TRQ, and the TPL of wool apparel is the same as the FTA TRQ. NAFTA does not provide for growth of any of the TPLs of imports into either Canada or Mexico.

As between the United States and Mexico, the sweaters, pullovers, sweatshirts and similar articles to which the special rule of origin described in §5.2(2)(a)(i) applies are not eligible for preferential treatment under the respective TPLs for each country. Also not eligible are apparel goods made from denim or oxford cloth and T-shirts, singlets, tank tops and similar garments and men's and boys' underpants or briefs made from certain circular knit fabrics.

(ii) Fabric and made-up goods

Notwithstanding its yarn-forward requirements, the FTA provided that an annual quantity of 30,000,000 SYE (*i.e.*, 25,083,900 SME) of non-wool fabric and non-wool made-up textile articles[63] woven or knit in Canada from third country yarn would receive FTA preferential tariff treatment upon entry into the United States. This TRQ was to apply from January 1, 1989 to December 31, 1992, after which time it was to be renegotiated. Canadian textile producers and exporters utilized this TRQ extensively. As a percentage of the TRQ, actual imports of these items into the United States from Canada for 1989, 1990 and 1991 were 79%, 98% and 81% respectively.[64]

157

There was no corresponding TRQ for imports into Canada from the United States.

NAFTA establishes TPLs for these goods on a trilateral basis without time limitations. To qualify, the good must be woven or knit in a NAFTA country from non-NAFTA country yarn. A good is also eligible if it is knit from yarn spun in a NAFTA country from non-NAFTA country fibre. This latter feature is included because of the fibre-forward requirements that NAFTA applies to cotton fabric and fabric of man-made staple fibres. NAFTA also extends the TPL concept to pillows, cushions, quilts, eiderdowns, comforters and similar articles[65] that are finished, cut, sewn or otherwise assembled in a NAFTA country from specified categories of non-NAFTA country cotton or man-made fabric.[66]

In applying the TPL of imports into the United States from each of Canada and Mexico, goods eligible for the TPL are split into two categories. The first is knitted or crocheted fabrics of HS chapter 60 and for knitted and crocheted bed linen, table linen, curtains and related items, bedspreads and furnishing articles. The second is eligible textile and made-up goods other than these knitted or crocheted articles. TPL usage for each of these categories is subject to limits, or "sublevels". Once imports of a category reach the sublevel, the TPL cannot be used for that category for the balance of the year.

The TPL of imports into Canada of fabrics and made-up goods from the United States applies only to the knitted and crocheted fabrics of HS chapter 60. The TPL of imports into Canada from Mexico is not subject to such a restriction.

The TPLs of these goods for the three NAFTA countries are as follows:[67]

Imports into Canada	*From Mexico*	*From United States*
	7,000,000 SME	2,000,000 SME (only goods of HS chapter 60)

Imports into Mexico	*From Canada*	*From United States*
	7,000,000 SME	2,000,000 SME

Imports into United States	*From Canada*	*From Mexico*
Total TPL	65,000,000 SME	24,000,000 SME
Sublevel Knitted or Crocheted Articles	35,000,000 SME	18,000,000 SME
Sublevel Other Articles	35,000,000 SME	6,000,000 SME
FTA TRQ	25,083,900 SME	N/A

The TPLs of imports from Canada into the United States, together with the sublevels will be increased by 2% each year for five consecutive years starting January 1, 1995.[68] No increase is provided for any of the other TPLs. There is also a special rule that applies to the TPLs as between Canada and the United States that takes into account dual sourcing of textile materials. If the non-originating textile materials in the good are 50% or less by weight of the materials contained in that good, only 50% of the SME of the good counts against the TPL. Otherwise, 100% of the SME of the good counts against the TPL.[69] There is no corresponding rule as between the United States and Mexico.

The TPL of imports from Canada into the United States has been increased by 159% over the FTA TRQ.[70] Even with the constraints imposed by the sublevels, this increase is substantial. If the NAFTA TPL had been in effect during 1989, 1990 and 1991, utilization would have been 30%, 39% and 31% respectively, rather than 79%, 98% and 81% as indicated above.[71]

(iii) Spun yarn

Because of the shift from a yarn-forward to a fibre-forward rule of origin for cotton yarn and yarn of man-made staple fibres, NAFTA includes TPLs for each NAFTA country for yarn spun from non-NAFTA country fibre.[72] The TPLs for the three NAFTA countries are as follows:[73]

Imports into Canada	From Mexico 1,000,000 kg	From United States 1,000,000 kg
Imports into Mexico	From Canada 1,000,000 kg	From United States 1,000,000 kg
Imports into United States	From Canada 10,700,000 kg	From Mexico 1,000,000 kg

The TPLs of imports into the United States from Canada will increase by 2% each year for the five-year period starting January 1, 1995.[74] No increase is provided for the other TPLs.

(iv) Goods imported from Mexico under U.S. tariff item 9802.00.80.60

As discussed in §2.3(1)(b)(ii), HTSUS tariff item 9802.00.80 is a U.S. tariff provision that complements Mexico's maquiladora program by levying duties only on the value added abroad of imported goods manufactured outside the United States from U.S. materials. To qualify for importation into the United States under this tariff item, the non-U.S. operations performed with respect to the good are confined to assembling and very limited processing. Tariff item 9802.00.80.10 applies to goods imported under U.S. textile and apparel restraint arrangements and is discussed in §5.2(3)(e). Tariff item 9802.00.80.60 applies to imports that are not subject to these arrangements.

Schedule 6.B.1 to Appendix 6 of NAFTA Annex 300-B provides for an annual TPL of 25,000,000 SME for apparel (HS chapters 61 and 62) and made-up goods (HS chapter 63), sewn or otherwise assembled in Mexico from imported fabric and imported from Mexico into the United States under tariff item 9802.00.80.60. This provision will apply to U.S. producers who import fabric from non-NAFTA countries, cut the fabric and export the cut material to Mexico for assembly and reimportation into the United States. This TPL expires at such time as the quantitative restrictions under the MFA (discussed in §5.2(3)(a)) are eliminated.[75]

(v) Review of TPLs and consultation

A NAFTA country that wishes to adjust a TPL based on availability of fibres, yarns or fabrics, may request consultations. Upon such request, the NAFTA countries will consult with a view to adjusting the TPL. However, adjustment of any TPL requires the mutual consent of the NAFTA countries concerned.

In the review of rules of origin referred to in §5.2(2)(c)(iii), Canada and the United States shall decide whether the annual increases in the U.S. TPLs of goods imported from Canada will continue. If the increases are not continued, Canada may request consultations with a view to adjusting the applicable TPLs. However, as stated above, TPLs may be adjusted only with the mutual consent of the NAFTA countries concerned.

(3) Import and Export Restrictions

Appendix 3.1 of NAFTA 300-B sets out rules regarding the administration of prohibitions, restrictions and consultation levels respecting non-originating textile and apparel goods. These NAFTA rules are necessitated by the unique international trading rules that apply to the textiles and apparel.

Textiles and apparel have been described as receiving "more comprehensive and persistent protection than any other industrial sector".[76] While successive rounds of GATT negotiations progressively reduced trade barriers for other goods, increasingly restrictive international arrangements have been entered into in the textile and apparel sector. The first such post-GATT arrangement was the Short Term Arrangement ("STA") which arose out of GATT negotiations in 1959 and 1960 at the instigation of the U.S. negotiators and was entered into in 1961. The STA was based on a concept of "market disruption" that went beyond the safeguard mechanism provided for in GATT Article XIX. Restrictions did not have to be applied on a MFN basis as under the GATT. Also, unlike GATT Article XIX, this concept did not permit the party subjected to restrictions to suspend concessions of equivalent value. By July, 1961, one-year restrictions had been authorized on sixty-four categories of cotton textiles.[77]

The STA was replaced in 1962 by the Long Term Arrangement Regarding

Cotton Textiles ("LTA"). The LTA was renewed in 1967 and again in 1970 through to 1973. During the late 1960s and early 1970s, there was increasing pressure in the United States for the inclusion of woollen goods and man-made fibres in these restrictive arrangements. The result was the negotiation and entry into force on January 1, 1974, of the Arrangement Regarding International Trade in Textiles, otherwise known as the Multifibre Arrangement.

(a) The Multifibre Arrangement

Like the STA and LTA, the Multifibre Arrangement ("MFA") permits action to be taken by a party on the occurrence of "market disruption". Market disruption occurs with the "existence of serious damage to domestic producers or actual threat thereof".[78] The market disruption must be caused by a "sharp and substantial or imminent increase of imports"[79] or products being "offered at prices substantially below those prevailing for similar goods of comparable quality in the market of the importing country",[80] or a combination of these factors. Market disruption caused by "technological changes" or "changes in consumer preferences" will not constitute a situation of "market disruption" for MFA purposes.

The MFA covers "textiles", which are "tops, yarns, piece-goods, made-up articles, garments and other textile manufactured products" of cotton, wool, man-made fibres or combinations thereof.[81] Artificial and synthetic staple fibre, tow, waste, and simple mono-filaments and multi-filaments, while not "textiles", are subject to certain key provisions of the MFA.[82]

If the market of a participating importing country is being "disrupted" by imports of a textile product, it can seek consultations with the exporting country.[83] If the consultations lead to a mutual understanding that the situation calls for restrictions, the annual level of restriction is, according to the MFA, generally not to be less than the level of actual imports and exports during the twelve-month period ending two months before the request for consultations was made.[84] If agreement is not reached within sixty days, the country requesting the consultations can, subject to some constraints, impose restrictions unilaterally.[85] Alternatively, either country can refer the matter to a GATT organization known as the Textiles Surveillance Body, which will examine the matter and make recommendations.[86] Measures taken may be introduced for limited periods not exceeding a year, but upon agreement these may be renewed for one-year periods.[87]

MFA Article 4 permits participating countries to enter into bilateral agreements to eliminate the risk of market disruption, provided that the agreements are consistent with MFA principles. One example of an MFA principle is that if a restraint is in effect for sequential twelve-month periods, in the absence of exceptional circumstances, the level for each subsequent period is to be at least 6% greater than that for the previous period.[88] The terms of bilateral agreements are to be communicated to the Textiles Surveillance Body.[89]

The original MFA was for a term of four years and has been renewed several times. In 1986, the MFA was renewed for a period until 1991. Since 1991, the MFA has been extended on a year to year basis, pending the conclusion of the Uruguay Round.

(b) Bilateral restraint agreements

Since the MFA came into effect, many bilateral restraint agreements have been negotiated between developed countries, as importers, with developing countries, whose exports are subjected to restraint. Both Canada and the United States are party to a number of such agreements.[90] The United States has entered into a bilateral agreement with Mexico which restrains exports of Mexican textiles into the United States. Canada does not have a bilateral restraint agreement with Mexico.

A restraint agreement typically sets out maximum levels of exports from the exporting country for a base year of various categories of "textiles", as defined in the MFA. The expression "growth" means the percentage of annual increase in the restraint level for each product.[91] The expression "swing" means that a level may be exceeded for a product category by a prescribed percentage provided that an equivalent amount is deducted from some other product category.[92] The expression "carryover" means that the portion of a restraint level for a product not used in one calendar year can be carried forward and added to the restraint level for the next year, up to a prescribed percentage.[93] "Carryforward" is the opposite of "carryover". With "carryforward", a restraint level for a year can be increased by up to a prescribed amount, expressed as a percentage, provided that the restraint level for the same product for the following year is reduced by the same amount.[94]

A restraint agreement is administered by both the exporting and the importing country. An exporter in the exporting country must obtain an "export permit" or "export visa" from a government official. Each time during a year that a permit or visa is issued, the exporter's share of the restraint level, or quota, is reduced by the number of items in the shipment. Once the exporter's quota has been used up, no further permits or visas will be issued until the next calendar year. The importing country's customs officials will not admit goods from the exporting country that are subject to the restraint agreement unless the shipment is accompanied by an export permit.

Restraint agreements sometimes contain "consultation levels". If a "consultation level" is in effect, the importing country agrees not to seek consultations unless imports of a product exceed a pre-agreed "consultation level" during a restraint period.[95] If the level is exceeded, consultations are initiated with the objective of negotiating a restraint level. Restraint agreements may also contain "consultation mechanism standards". If the importing country believes that market disruption in respect of a previously unrestrained item might occur, it may request consultations with a view to reaching an arrangement within a ninety-day period. During the ninety-day period, the other government will hold exports of the product in question to pre-agreed levels, and if agreement is not reached, a pre-agreed minimum restraint level shall take effect.[96]

While the basis for requesting restraint under the MFA is supposed to be the extraordinary circumstance of "market disruption", the effect of the MFA and the bilateral restraint agreements which have been negotiated both under its provisions and independently from them has been to make routine the existence of quotas in developed countries for many categories of textile and apparel goods imported from developing countries.

(c) The Uruguay Round and "Integration into GATT"

One of the objectives of the Uruguay Round was to eliminate this restrictive regime and to return the textile and apparel sector to normal GATT disciplines. This objective will have been accomplished once the ten-year transition period set out in the *Agreement on Textiles and Clothing* (the "GATT Textile Agreement")[97] is over. For the purposes of NAFTA Annex 300-B, the GATT Textile Agreement is the successor agreement to the MFA.

(i) Integration into GATT

Once the GATT Textile Agreement becomes effective, the parties must notify a GATT body known as the Textiles Monitoring Body ("TMB") of all quantitative restrictions maintained under bilateral agreements.[98] No new restrictions may be introduced except as provided in the GATT Textile Agreement transitional safeguard rules or justified under some other GATT provision.[99] Products are to be "integrated into GATT" in stages. The expression "integrated into GATT" means that a product is subject to normal GATT disciplines and free from MFA-style export restraint levels. The first stage occurs upon the GATT Textile Agreement becoming effective, which is anticipated to be sometime in 1995. The second and third stages take place in 1998 and 2002 respectively, with complete "integration into GATT" occurring in 2005.[100] Each stage is expressed in terms of a percentage of the total volume of imports in 1990 of the products listed in the Annex (the "GATT Textile Annex") to the GATT Textile Agreement. The products listed in the GATT Textile Annex are the same as those listed in Appendix 1.1 to NAFTA Annex 300-B, referred to in §5.2(1), but include a wider range of products than the "textiles" and other products described in §5.2(3)(a) that are covered by the MFA. The percentage that applies when the GATT Textile Agreement becomes effective is 16%,[101] and the percentages for 1998 and 2002 are 17% and 18% respectively.[102] The products to be "integrated into GATT" are "tops and yarns, fabrics, made-up textile products and clothing",[103] which are the "textiles" covered by the MFA.

163

(ii) Safeguard provisions

The GATT Textile Agreement sets out transitional safeguard procedures that will apply to textile and apparel goods not integrated into the GATT during the ten-year transition period. These procedures apply to all the goods listed in the GATT Textile Annex. As discussed in §5.2(3)(c), these goods are the same as the textile and apparel goods listed in Appendix 1.1 of NAFTA Annex 300-B.

The basis for invoking the procedures closely follows the concept of "market disruption" in the MFA discussed in §5.2(3)(a). A product must be imported in such increased quantities as to cause or threaten serious damage to a domestic industry producing like or directly competitive goods. The serious damage or threat of serious damage must be caused by the increased imports and, as under the MFA, not by factors such as technological changes or changes in consumer preferences.[104] In making a determination, the effect of those imports on the state of the particular industry will be examined as reflected in changes in variables such as output, productivity, utilization of capacity, inventories, market share, exports, wages, employment, domestic prices, profits and investment. None of these factors is to be considered decisive.[105] Unlike the GATT Safeguard Agreement, the GATT Textile Agreement does not set out any procedural requirements in making determinations as to whether a domestic industry has sustained or is threatened with serious injury.

The safeguards in the GATT Textile Agreement are to be applied on a country by country basis. A country proposing taking action must first seek consultations and try to reach an agreement. If agreement is reached, the level of restraint shall be fixed at a level not lower than the actual level of exports or imports from the member country concerned during the twelve-month period ending two months before the request for consultation was made.[106] Details of restraint agreements must be communicated to the Textile Monitoring Body. If agreement is not reached, the matter is referred to the Textile Monitoring Body, which can make recommendations.[107] In some cases, provisional action can be taken.[108] Measures may remain in effect for up to three years or until the affected product is integrated into the GATT, whichever occurs first. The safeguard provisions provide for a growth rate of 6% and set out criteria for "swing", "carryover" and "carryforward".[109]

(d) The NAFTA rules respecting import and export restrictions

Appendix 3.1 of NAFTA Annex 300-B sets out rules respecting maintaining a "prohibition, restriction or consultation level" in respect of the importation of textile and apparel goods. These rules, which may be applied only in respect of non-originating goods, prevail over the MFA and will prevail over the GATT Textile Agreement.[110] However, consistent with the requirements of the GATT Textile Agreement, NAFTA Annex 300-B requires that such measures be eliminated for any product which has been "integrated into GATT".[111] Therefore, the NAFTA Annex 300-B rules in Appendix 3.1 apply only to non-originating goods that have not been "integrated into GATT" under the GATT Textile Agreement. NAFTA Annex 300-B expressly states that goods imported under a TPL that receive preferential tariff treatment are to be otherwise considered as non-originating goods.[112] The effect of this is that notwithstanding that a good may qualify for importation under a TPL, until it has been "integrated into GATT" it may be subjected to a prohibition, restriction or consultation level.

Appendix 3.1 is split into two parts. The first part is comprised of rules of general application to trade between Canada and Mexico and between Mexico and the United States. The second part deals with existing restrictions and consultation levels between the United States and Mexico. Appendix 3.1 does not set out any rules respecting trade between Canada and the United States.

(i) General rules

The rules in Part A apply as between Mexico and the United States and will apply to any restraint arrangement entered into by Canada with Mexico under the MFA or the GATT Textile Agreement. Part A requires that exporting NAFTA countries whose products are subject to a "prohibition, restriction or consultation level" are obliged to limit their annual exports of the affected product categories to the specified limits or levels[113] and to endeavour to "space" exports evenly throughout a calendar year, having regard to seasonal factors.[114] While expressed in general terms, the only NAFTA country to which this provision applies is Mexico. The Part A rules provide for consultation on various matters.[115]

Part A sets out "flexibility" rules respecting adjustment through "swing", "carryover" and "carryforward" to the "annual specific limit" (*i.e.*, the restraint level) that applies to a product category subject to a restriction. As discussed in §5.2(3)(b), "swing" is the ability to increase the limit of one category by deducting an equivalent amount from another. The Part A rules fix the permitted amount of "swing" at 6%.[116] The maximum "carryover" of unused portion (or "shortfall") for a calendar year to the following calendar year is 11%.[117] The maximum "carryforward" to a calendar year from the following calendar year is 6%.[118] The combination of adjustments to a calendar year through "carryover" from the previous year and "carryforward" from the following year cannot exceed 11%.[119] The Part A rules make no provision for "growth".

(ii) Trade as between the United States and Mexico

Part B of Appendix 3.1 sets out rules that apply only to the United States and Mexico. These rules are in addition to those set out in Part A.

The existing bilateral restraint agreement (the "Bilateral Agreement") between the United States and Mexico terminated upon NAFTA becoming effective[120] and is replaced by the rules set out in Appendix 3.1. Restrictions and consultation levels on many categories of goods exported by Mexico into the United States were eliminated immediately upon NAFTA becoming effective.[121] Schedule 3.1.2 to Appendix 3.1 sets out the annual restrictions and designated consultation levels that continue to apply.

Restrictions or designated consultation levels continue on the following goods until January 1, 2001:[122] cotton and man-made fibre duck fabric; cotton sheeting fabric; cotton poplin and broadcloth fabric; cotton printcloth fabric; cotton twill fabric; cotton and man-made fibre knit shirts and blouses; cotton and man-made fibre woven shirts; cotton and man-made fibre trousers and pants; men's and boys' man-made fibre suit-type coats; and man-made fibre suits for men and boys. Restrictions or consultation levels continue on the following goods until January 1, 2004:[123] woven wool fabric; wool men's and boys' suit-type coats; wool men's and boys' suits; and artificial staple fibre woven fabric. Only cotton and man-made fibre woven shirts and wool men's and boys' suits are subject to restrictions by way of annual specific limits of exports. The remaining categories of goods are subject to designated consultation levels.

Subject to the "flexibility rules" in Part A described above, Mexico may carry forward any unused portions of its 1993 limit for a product category under the Bilateral Agreement against exports made in 1994, and may carry forward the 1994 limit for a product category still subject to restraint to exports made in 1993.

(e) U.S. tariff item 9802.00.80.10

HSTUS tariff item 9802.00.80.10 is the subset of U.S. tariff item 9802.00.80 (discussed in §2.3(1)(b)(ii)) that applies to goods eligible for entry into the United States under a bilateral textile agreement. The United States will eliminate restrictions, consultation levels[124] and customs duties[125] on textile and apparel goods assembled in Mexico from fabrics wholly formed and cut in the United States and exported from and reimported into the United States under U.S. tariff item 9802.00.80.10. These requirements also apply to goods exported from and reimported into the United States under HS chapters 61 and 62 (apparel goods) or HS chapter 63 (made-up textile articles such as blankets, bed linen, curtains and similar products) if the assembled goods that would have qualified for treatment under 9802.00.80.10 have been subject to further processing in Mexico in the form of bleaching, garment dyeing, stone-washing, acid washing or perma-pressing.[126]

(f) Hand-loomed fabrics, hand-made and handicraft goods

The MFA exempts developing country exports of hand-loomed fabrics of a cottage industry, hand-made cottage industry goods made from such fabrics or traditional folklore handicraft goods, provided that these products are certified under arrangements established between the importing and exporting countries.[127] The rules respecting prohibitions, restrictions and consultation levels as between the United States and Mexico described in §5.2(3)(d)(ii) carry forward this exception and express it so that it could apply to exports from either country to the other.[128]

NAFTA Annex 300-B also sets out a special trilateral tariff elimination rule respecting these products.[129] An importing NAFTA country will grant duty-free treatment to goods identified and certified by an exporting NAFTA country as hand-loomed fabrics of a cottage industry, hand-made cottage industry goods made from such fabrics or traditional folklore handicraft goods. The rule does not require that the goods be originating under the NAFTA rules of origin.

(4) Country of Origin of Textile and Apparel Goods

The country of origin has particular significance for textile and apparel goods that goes beyond determining which tariff schedule applies for tariff elimination purposes. The country of origin of non-originating textile and apparel goods is relevant to the administration by each NAFTA country of its TPLs. The country of origin is also relevant for many textile or apparel goods entering Canada or the United States because of the bilateral restraint agreements that each of these NAFTA countries will continue to maintain until the process of "integration into GATT" is complete.

(a) The country of origin of originating goods

NAFTA Annex 300-B provides that, for tariff elimination purposes, the country of origin of an originating good will be determined by each NAFTA country's regulations, practices or procedures or, if the NAFTA countries can agree, the Marking Rules.[130] Since the NAFTA text was finalized, all three NAFTA countries have agreed to use the Marking Rules to determine the country of origin of textile and apparel goods.

(b) Administration of TPLs

Each NAFTA country's TPLs are country-specific respecting non-originating goods imported from the other two NAFTA countries. Consider non-originating apparel goods imported into Canada from another NAFTA country. Canadian officials will have to determine whether the apparel good is "American" or "Mexican" in order to count the good against the U.S. TPL or the Mexican TPL for that category of good.

To qualify for preferential treatment under a TPL, a non-originating apparel good must be both cut or knit to shape and sewn or otherwise assembled within a NAFTA country and, apart from being made from non-NAFTA country fabric or yarn, meet "other applicable conditions for preferred tariff treatment". These conditions are those set out in the applicable rule of origin. A good that meets these requirements should be eligible for preferential tariff treatment regardless of the rules that the importing NAFTA country applies to determine the country of origin of apparel goods.

(c) Country of origin and bilateral restraint agreements

With most non-originating goods, the country of origin is relevant only to determine the tariff rate which applies and, as most countries are GATT members, the usual worst result is that the importing country's MFN rate applies. However, until integration into the GATT is complete under the GATT Textile Agreement, the determination that a textile or apparel good is from a country and of a category that is subject to a bilateral restraint agreement will result in entry being denied unless the good is accompanied by the required export permit or export visa. Suppose that a textile good has been produced in Canada from materials imported from a country with which the United States has a restraint agreement. If U.S. authorities determine that the good is a good of that country rather than a good of Canada, the good will be denied entry to the United States unless it is accompanied by an export visa issued by the authorities of that country. The transhipment of the materials through Canada and their transformation into a different category of good would make the required export documentation virtually impossible to obtain.

Until NAFTA, each of Canada and the United States had its own rules for determining the country of origin of goods for these purposes. Once NAFTA became effective, the United States proposed using the Marking Rules for this purpose. Differences between the Marking Rules and former U.S. practice could result in goods that were formerly regarded as "Canadian" as being goods of some other country. Canadian textile and apparel manufacturers and government officials should monitor the application by the United States of the Marking Rules to ensure that this does not happen.

(5) Safeguard Provisions for Textile and Apparel Goods

As mentioned in §4.7(2), the bilateral emergency action provisions in NAFTA 801 and FTA 1101 do not apply to textile and apparel goods. NAFTA Annex 300-B sets out two special bilateral emergency action procedures for textile and apparel goods that will apply until January 1, 2004. The tariff action procedure set out in Section 4 of NAFTA 300-B is closely analogous to the emergency action provision in NAFTA 801. However, the basis for invoking it and the procedures to be followed are different. The quantitative restriction procedure set out in Section 5 of NAFTA Annex 300-B has no other parallel in NAFTA but is analogous to the safeguard procedure set out in the GATT Textile Agreement described in §5.2(3)(c)(ii).

(a) Scope of the procedures

The goods covered by the tariff action and quantitative restriction procedures are all the goods listed in Appendix 1.1 to NAFTA 300-B discussed in §5.2(1). The tariff action procedure applies only to goods that are eligible for tariff elimination. These are originating goods, goods eligible for entry under TPLs, and goods eligible for entry into the United States from Mexico described in §5.2(3)(e).[131] The quantitative action procedure may only be invoked against non-originating goods that have not been integrated into GATT. These goods include goods eligible for entry under TPLs but are not confined to them.

The tariff action procedure may be invoked by any NAFTA country against goods imported from any other NAFTA country. The quantitative restriction procedure does not apply as between Canada and the United States.[132]

(b) Basis for invoking the procedures

The basis for invoking either procedure is the same as set out in the safeguard provisions of the GATT Textile Agreement described in §5.2(3)(c)(ii). Goods must be imported in such increased quantities as to cause or threaten serious damage to a domestic industry producing like or directly competitive goods. The factors to be considered and to be ignored are the same as set out in the GATT Textile Agreement.[133] Serious damage is intended as a less stringent standard than serious injury which is discussed in §4.7. To invoke the tariff action procedure, the increase in imports that causes or threatens the damage must result from the reduction or elimination of tariffs. It is not necessary in invoking the quantitative restriction procedure to link the increase in imports to any cause. This is consistent with the approach in the MFA and the GATT Textile Agreement safeguard provisions but is not consistent with the general GATT approach to emergency action.

(c) Tariff action procedure

A NAFTA country taking a tariff action must notify the NAFTA country against which the action is being taken of the intent to take the action and, upon request, will enter into consultations. The reductions of duty permitted in a tariff action are similar to those in NAFTA 801, described in §4.7(3).[134] As under NAFTA 801, the action cannot be maintained for more than three years and cannot, without the affected Party's consent, extend beyond the transition period, which for all three NAFTA countries is the ten-year period commencing January 1, 1994.[135] At the end of the action, tariffs are reduced in the same manner as under NAFTA 801.[136] As under NAFTA 801, a tariff action can be taken only once against any particular good originating within the territory of another Party.[137] Goods entered under TPLs are non-originating and would not be subject to this limitation. The trade liberalizing compensation requirements are the same as set out in NAFTA 801, except that the concessions must be restricted to textile and apparel goods described in Appendix 1.1, unless the NAFTA countries agree otherwise.

(d) Quantitative restriction procedures

Consistent with the MFA and the safeguard procedure in the GATT Textile Agreement, the quantitative restriction procedure commences with a request for consultations. The consultations must begin within sixty days of the request being made and the NAFTA countries involved have ninety days to reach an agreement. If agreement is not reached, the NAFTA country that requested the consultations may act unilaterally and impose quantitative restrictions. The quantity can be no less than imports during the first twelve months of the fourteen-month period preceding the month in which consultations were requested, plus 20% of such quantity for cotton, man-made fibre and other non-vegetable categories and 6% for wool good categories.[138] The first period of any quantitative restriction imposed begins on the day after the date on which the request for consultations was made and that period runs to the end of the current calendar year.[139] A quantitative restriction imposed before July 1st of a year may remain in effect for the balance of that year and for two more calendar years, and after July 1st of a year for three more calendar years. Quantitative restrictions for subsequent calendar years must increase by 6% each year for cotton, man-made fibre and other non-vegetable goods and by 2% each year for wool goods.[140] The flexibility provisions set out in Appendix 3.1 and described in §5.2(3)(d)(i) apply. Quantitative restrictions must terminate when the transition period expires. No quantitative restriction action may be taken after the transition period without the consent of the NAFTA country against which the action is taken.

(e) Absence of procedural standards

As stated in §4.7(5), the procedural standards established by NAFTA for emergency action procedures do not apply to either of the special textile and apparel emergency action procedures. The NAFTA text does not set out any procedural requirements for making determinations of such matters as the existence or threat of serious damage or, in a tariff action, the establishment of a nexus between tariff reduction or elimination and the increase in imports. It is left to each NAFTA country to establish its own.

(6) Concluding Remarks

The NAFTA provisions described in §5.2(3) and §5.2(5) respecting import restrictions and special safeguards are transitional and will fall away with the integration of textile and apparel goods into the GATT. However, the NAFTA TPL provisions described in §5.2(2) are permanent and, unlike the tariff rate quotas that appear elsewhere in NAFTA, they are not a transitional device that falls away over time. With their prescribed volumes, the TPLs establish a form of managed trade. However, as imports above the prescribed annual volumes are subject to tariffs that may be high but are by no means prohibitive, the managed trade regime constituted by the TPLs is significantly less severe than one administered through quotas or through prohibitive over-quota tariff rates as will apply to agricultural goods with the Uruguay Round tariffication process described in §5.3(1)(b)(iii).

The review of some of the more lenient rules of origin described in §5.2(2)(c) may lead to a future tightening of the regime for some goods. Country of origin determinations will be critical and, with the country-specific TPLs, will be another permanent feature of the NAFTA textile and apparel regime.

5.3 AGRICULTURE

Like textile and apparel goods, world trade in agricultural products, particularly primary agricultural products, is subject to significant trade barriers. However, with textile and apparel goods the barriers are generally erected by developed countries against developing countries. With agricultural goods, both developed and developing countries nurture their agricultural sectors with subsidies and protect them with quantitative restrictions and other non-tariff barriers against goods from other countries. The three NAFTA countries are no exception. The need for special agricultural provisions in NAFTA stems from the substantial non-tariff barriers on agricultural goods existing among the three NAFTA countries. The end result of the NAFTA negotiations is three bilateral agreements rather than a single trilateral set of trading rules. As between Canada and the United States, NAFTA maintains the FTA status quo with a few technical changes. As between Canada and Mexico, NAFTA will reduce non-tariff barriers for a few goods but maintains both tariff and non-tariff barriers respecting many other goods. The only significant elimination of non-tariff barriers on agricultural goods provided for in NAFTA is between Mexico and the United States.

(1) The GATT and the Uruguay Round Agreements

Like textiles and apparel, the trade in agricultural goods is conducted largely outside of GATT disciplines. The problems with the world trade in agricultural products stem from support programs maintained by countries for their agricultural sectors. These programs are based on subsidies and quantitative restrictions. Subsidies take the form of domestic support programs or export subsidies. Quantitative restrictions are usually imposed in conjunction with domestic price support programs which take a variety of forms such as controlling the amount of product supplied to keep prices high.

(a) Provisions of the GATT

(i) Subsidies and GATT Article XVI

GATT rules distinguish between domestic support programs that apply to all domestic production and export subsidies that are paid only if products are exported.[141] GATT Article XVI prohibits export subsidies on all products except primary products. The only restriction imposed on export subsidies on primary products is that the subsidy not result in the subsidizing member country having "more than an equitable share of the world export trade" in the subsidized product, having regard to the shares of other member countries over "a previous representative period". The GATT Subsidies Code provides some clarification as to the meaning of these expressions[142] but does not alter the general exemption of export subsidies on primary products from GATT disciplines.

Neither GATT Article XVI nor the Subsidies Code imposes any meaningful discipline on domestic support programs. GATT member states may impose countervailing duties on exports of subsidized products if the conditions set out in the GATT Subsidies Code are fulfilled. However, other than in situations in which domestic support programs have been directed at negating the effect of tariff concessions,[143] domestic support programs are untouched by the GATT and the Subsidies Code.

(ii) Quantitative restrictions and GATT Article XVI:2(c)

Quantitative restrictions on agricultural goods are imposed under the authority of GATT Article XI:2(c). This GATT provision sets out a special exception for agricultural and fisheries products from the general prohibition of quantitative restrictions set out in GATT Article XI:1. GATT Article XI:2(c)(i) exempts import restrictions on agricultural products that are necessary for enforcing governmental measures which restrict the quantities of like domestic products that are permitted to be marketed or produced. GATT Article XIII sets out disciplines respecting the allocation of import quotas among GATT member countries. These requirements are supplemented by the *Agreement on Import Licensing Procedures* that sets out procedures to be followed in implementing import licensing systems.[144]

(b) Uruguay Round Agreement and agriculture

The Uruguay Round *Agreement on Agriculture* (the "GATT Agricultural Agreement") is the first serious attempt under the GATT to provide a framework for the resolution of the problems encountering the world trade in agricultural goods. As has occurred elsewhere in NAFTA, the concepts developed in this Uruguay Round agreement have significantly influenced NAFTA provisions.[145]

(i) Agricultural goods

The NAFTA definition of "agricultural goods" in NAFTA 708 covers the same products as those covered by the GATT Agricultural Agreement. The products listed in Annex 1 of the GATT Agricultural Agreement include all products in HS chapters 1 to 24 (other than fish and fish products), as well as certain other products such as manitol, sorbitol, essential oils, albumoidal substances, starches and glues, hides and skins, furskins, raw cotton, silk, flax, hemp, and wool and animal hair.

(ii) Domestic support programs and export subsidies

Part IV of the GATT Agricultural Agreement requires that each participant submit a schedule of domestic support reduction commitments, other than with respect to certain exempt programs.[146] Part V of the GATT Agricultural Agreement lists the types of export subsidies subject to reduction commitments, and each participant will identify its reduction commitments in a schedule.[147]

As discussed below, the FTA went further than the GATT Agricultural Agreement respecting export subsidies by prohibiting them. However, other than incorporating the FTA export subsidies provision as between Canada and the United States, NAFTA does not go as far as the GATT Agricultural Agreement respecting either domestic support programs or export subsidies. The negotiators obviously decided to let these issues be addressed through the multilateral GATT process rather than attempting to deal with them in NAFTA.

(iii) Tariffication

Under Part III of the GATT Agricultural Agreement, each member country will convert border measures other than customs duties into customs duties. These measures include quantitative import restrictions, variable import levies, minimum import prices, discretionary import licensing, non-tariff measures maintained through state trading enterprises and voluntary export restraints. The process of conversion is called "tariffication".

The NAFTA agricultural provisions adopt the Uruguay Round tariffication approach to quantitative restrictions, particularly as between Mexico and the United States and, to a lesser extent, to Canadian goods entering Mexico. Tariffication under NAFTA goes much further than under the GATT Agricultural Agreement in that the duties resulting from the conversion of quantitative restrictions to tariffs will eventually be eliminated. NAFTA does not provide for tariffication in respect of any goods traded between Canada and the United States.

(iv) Special safeguards

The GATT Agricultural Agreement provides for special safeguards respecting agricultural products for which participants have made concessions. The safeguards may be invoked upon imports exceeding a trigger level or import prices falling below a trigger price. The safeguard measure takes the form of additional duties calculated in accordance with a formula.[148]

NAFTA adopts the concept of special safeguards as between Mexico and each of Canada and the United States, although not as between Canada and the United States. However, these safeguard provisions apply to specifically identified products and function quite differently from the special safeguard provisions set out in the GATT Agricultural Agreement.

(2) Canadian, American and Mexican Restrictions

Each of Canada, the United States and Mexico applies non-tariff barriers to protect agricultural goods. The non-tariff barriers in all three countries are elements of broader regulatory schemes covering the entire process of producing and marketing particular products.

(a) Canadian restrictions

Canada's supply management programs respecting dairy, poultry and egg products, and Canada's grain marketing practices through the Canadian Wheat Board have significant trade implications.

(i) Supply management — dairy, poultry and egg products

Canada's dairy supply management system is administered by the Canadian Dairy Commission ("CDC"), a federal agency established under the *Canadian Dairy Commission Act*.[149] The CDC chairs the Canadian Milk Supply Management Committee, which is comprised of producers and provincial government representatives. Each year this committee sets a national production target for industrial milk, which is called the "market sharing quota", or MSQ. The MSQ is based on anticipated domestic demand for dairy products plus a small amount for anticipated exports less anticipated imports. The objective of the MSQ is to achieve national self-sufficiency and avoid over-production. The CDC also sets target prices to be paid to producers for industrial milk.

The MSQ is allocated among the provinces, with Quebec holding the largest share at 47% and Ontario the second largest share at 31%. Marketing boards or government agencies within each province set quotas for individual producers within that province for both industrial and fluid milk. Processors within a province must purchase their industrial milk from the provincial marketing boards and agencies.[150]

Supply management of poultry and egg products functions in a manner similar to that for dairy products. Yearly production quotas are established by federal agencies for chicken (Canadian Chicken Marketing Agency), turkey (Canadian Turkey Marketing Agency), shell eggs (Canadian Egg Marketing Agency) and broiler hatching eggs (Canadian Broiler Hatching Egg Marketing Agency). Provincial agencies allocate production quotas to individual producers and regulate prices.[151]

The regulatory schemes for controlling the supply of dairy, poultry and egg products are complemented by import controls imposed under the *Export and Import Permits Act* ("EIPA").[152] Imports of cheese, ice cream and related products, yoghurt, buttermilk, evaporated and condensed milk, broiler hatching eggs and chicks, chicken and chicken products and turkey and turkey products are all subject to quantitative restrictions.[153] Imports of certain other milk products are not permitted at all.

Import controls under Canada's supply management programs have been imposed under the cover of GATT Article XI:2(c). The applicability of GATT Article XI:2(c) to ice cream and yoghurt has been successfully challenged by the United States. A GATT panel held that as these products are processed, they are not "like products" within the meaning of this GATT exception.

Canada's supply management programs are under pressure from several directions. Tariffication under the GATT Agricultural Agreement will replace import controls with duties which, while very high, will be reduced over time, lowering the level of protection. Supply management is also under increasing pressure because of tariff elimination between Canada and the United States on processed food products. Canadian food processors who use supply-managed products as inputs maintain that they are increasingly at a competitive disadvantage with their U.S. counterparts.

Canada does not maintain quantitative restrictions against imports of agricultural goods other than those mentioned above.

(ii) Wheat, oats, barley and their products

The interprovincial and international trade in wheat, oats and barley and prescribed products made from these grains is governed by the Canadian Wheat Board ("CWB"). No one may import or export wheat, oats, barley or prescribed wheat, oat or barley products without a licence issued by the CWB, or as otherwise permitted under the applicable regulations.[154] Prescribed wheat products include flour, breakfast foods, cereals, macaroni, spaghetti, vermicelli, noodles, animal and poultry feeds, wheat starch and wheat malt. Prescribed oat products include ground oats, crimped oats and crushed oats. Prescribed barley products include ground barley, crimped barley, barley meal and barley flour.[155] The CWB purchases grain from Canadian producers at initial prices representing about 75% of expected market return. The grain is sold to customers in other provinces and countries. Distributions less deductions for CWB expenses are made to producers.

These goods are not subject to supply management. The GATT permits state trading monopolies such as the CWB so long as they act in a non-discriminatory and commercial manner.[156]

(b) U.S. restrictions

The United States applies quantitative restrictions against a number of agricultural goods.

(i) Section 22 of the Agricultural Adjustment Act

The principal statutory provision under which quantitative restrictions are imposed is s. 22 of the Agricultural Adjustment Act ("AAA"). This provision authorizes fees of up to 50% *ad valorem* or import quotas if imports "render or tend to render ineffective or materially interfere with" U.S. Department of Agriculture programs respecting agricultural commodities or their products.[157] On March 5, 1955, the United States was granted a waiver by the GATT in respect of these statutory powers.[158]

Products covered by s. 22 fees and quotas are set out in Chapter 99, Subchapter IV of the HTSUS (under HS heading 9904). These include: milk and cream; butter and butter substitutes; milk-based drinks; various products derived from dried milk or buttermilk or whey, cheeses and cheese substitutes, edible articles containing butterfat; peanuts and peanut products (except peanut butter); sugar and sugar-containing products, various chocolate and other food preparations containing cocoa, various malt extract products and mixes and doughs for bakers' wares; and cotton.

For some goods, s. 22 quotas amount to an embargo. For example, the quota quantity for certain mixtures containing dried milk, whey and buttermilk is none.[159] For others, the quota quantity for each calendar year period is specified. Sometimes the quota is a global quota. For example, for butter and fresh sour cream containing over 45% by weight of butterfat there was a global quota in 1993 of 320,689.[160] Sometimes the quota is specified by country. For example, for ice cream under tariff heading 21.05, the quota allotments in litres for 1993 were: Belgium (922,315), New Zealand (589,312), Denmark (13,059), Netherlands (104,477), Jamaica (3,596) and Other, which includes both Canada and Mexico (None).[161]

The GATT waiver respecting s. 22 of the AAA has been a point of contention between the United States and its GATT trading partners, and its existence has undermined U.S. attempts to break down barriers against its agricultural exports. Under the GATT Agricultural Agreement, quotas maintained under the authority of s. 22 of the AAA and the cover of the GATT waiver will be subject to tariffication.[162] Special rules respecting sugar and sugar-containing products are described in §5.3(10)(g).

(ii) The Meat Import Act of 1979

The United States also imposes quantitative limitations on the importation of fresh, chilled and frozen cattle meat, meat of sheep and goats and prepared and preserved beef and veal under the authority of the Meat Import Act of 1979.[163] The statutory amount is set at 1,147,000 pounds, subject to some adjustments.[164] The United States has also entered into voluntary restraint agreements to protect its domestic meat producers. At the time of writing, meat from Australia and New Zealand is subject to voluntary restraint agreements. Imports of Mexican meat have been limited through voluntary restraint agreements.[165]

(c) Mexican restrictions

The Mexican agricultural sector is structured differently from that in Canada and the United States. Small scale agriculture is more prevalent, with the bulk of arable land being held in parcels of five acres.[166] Much of this land is held through *ejidos*, a form of collective farm organization created during the Mexican revolution. The Salinas administration has endeavoured to reform the agricultural sector by taking steps to encourage agriculture on a larger scale.[167]

Mexican tariffs on agricultural imports are significantly higher than those in Canada and the United States. Base rates set out in the NAFTA Schedule of Mexico for most agricultural goods as defined in NAFTA 708 are at least 10% and many are 20%. The Mexican government also controls the volume of imports of agricultural products through import licensing requirements. The quantities of imports of many agricultural products are restricted because of price support programs for basic foods, oilseeds and feed grains that maintain domestic prices above world prices.[168] Products subject to import licensing include dairy and poultry products, potatoes, beans, barley and corn.

(3) Overview of NAFTA Provisions

The NAFTA provisions respecting agriculture are set out in Section A of Chapter Seven. The special bilateral arrangements are set out in the Annexes to Section A. NAFTA Annex 702.1 applies only between Canada and the United States and incorporates most of the FTA agricultural provisions. Section A of NAFTA Annex 703.2 sets out rules that apply only between Mexico and the United States. Section B of NAFTA Annex 703.2 sets out rules that apply only between Canada and Mexico. Section A prevails over all other NAFTA provisions in the event of an inconsistency.

(4) Country of Origin of Agricultural Goods

Because different bilateral rules apply among the NAFTA countries, the country of origin of agricultural goods acquires particular significance. As a practical matter, the country of origin of primary products such as live animals or crops such as grains, fruit and vegetables should not be an issue, as it is unlikely that these products will be raised or grown and harvested in more than one country. The country of origin of processed products will be more difficult to determine. Pork or beef can be processed in the United States from animals raised in Canada. Frozen orange juice can be processed in Mexico from oranges grown in California. Bakery products can be produced in Mexico from Canadian wheat.

(a) Country of origin for tariff elimination

As with other goods, to be eligible for preferential tariff treatment under NAFTA an agricultural good must be an originating good under the NAFTA rules of origin. The country of origin will then determine which Schedule applies. All three NAFTA countries will determine the country of origin of originating agricultural goods by use of the Marking Rules. With the United States and Mexico, the use of the Marking Rules for determining the country of origin of agricultural goods conforms to the approach for other goods. With Canada, use of the Marking Rules for determining the country of origin of originating agricultural goods is an exception to the general Canadian approach under NAFTA to determining country of origin described in §3.3(1).[169]

Under Canada's tariff schedule, there are only two possible Canadian tariff treatments for originating agricultural goods rather than three. An originating agricultural good entering Canada is either eligible to be marked as a good of the United States and be eligible for the United States Tariff, or to be marked as a good of Mexico and be eligible for the Mexico Tariff.[170] Canada's Mexico-United States Tariff does not apply to agricultural goods.

(b) Qualifying goods

The applicability of the Mexico-U.S. bilateral rules and the Canada-Mexico bilateral rules is based on an agricultural good being a "qualifying good". For the purposes of the Mexico-U.S. bilateral rules, a "qualifying good" is an originating agricultural good where, in determining whether the good is originating, Canadian operations are considered as having been performed in a non-NAFTA country.[171] With a "qualifying good" under the Canada-Mexico bilateral rules, U.S. operations are treated as non-NAFTA country operations.[172] The approach in each case is similar to the general Canadian approach to determining country of origin for tariff elimination purposes described above in §3.3(1), without the latitude of 7% value-added for the NAFTA country whose operations are considered as non-NAFTA country operations.

(c) Country of origin between Canada and the United States

The concept of the "qualifying good" is not used to determine the applicability of the bilateral rules respecting agricultural goods that apply between Canada and the United States. As discussed below, these bilateral rules are comprised of most of FTA Chapter Seven, which has been incorporated into NAFTA by reference in NAFTA 702.1. The expression "originating goods" is used throughout FTA Chapter Seven and "originating" is defined in FTA 201 as qualifying under the FTA rules of origin. Unlike NAFTA Annex 805, which makes it clear that the NAFTA country of origin rules in NAFTA Annex 302.2 apply to determine whether a good is "originating" under the incorporated FTA safeguard provisions,[173] NAFTA Annex 702.1 is silent as to the meaning of "originating" in the incorporated FTA provisions. Arguably, "originating", when used in these articles has its original FTA meaning, and the FTA rules of origin continue to apply. However, the intent of the negotiators was that the NAFTA rules of origin apply and that the country of origin for the purposes of the incorporated FTA provisions be determined in the same way as the country of origin for tariff elimination purposes.

(5) Incorporation of FTA Provisions as Between Canada and the United States

NAFTA Annex 702.1 incorporates FTA 701 (Agricultural Subsidies), 702 (Special Provisions for Fresh Fruit and Vegetables), 703 (Market Access for Agriculture), 704 (Market Access for Meat), 705 (Market Access for Grain and Grain Products), 706 (Market Access for Poultry and Eggs), 707 (Market Access for Sugar-Containing Products) and 710 (International Obligations).

The only articles of FTA Chapter Seven that have not been incorporated are FTA 708 and FTA 709. FTA 708 requires Canada and the United States to work toward the harmonization of standards respecting "agricultural, food, beverage and certain related goods".[174] Canada and the United States have agreed through a separate agreement to maintain this provision in effect.[175] FTA 709, which provides for semi-annual consultations on agricultural issues, has been superseded by the establishment under NAFTA 706 of a Committee on Agricultural Trade, discussed in §5.3(6)(c).

The defined expressions in FTA 711 continue to have the same meanings in the incorporated articles. For example, the meaning of the expression "agricultural good" in the incorporated articles FTA 701 and FTA 703 will continue to be as defined in FTA 711 and not as in NAFTA 708. There are differences in the definitions. The NAFTA 708 definition includes meat preparations, beer, wine and spirits, while the FTA 711 definition does not.

References to the dispute settlement procedures in FTA Chapter Eighteen will be read in the incorporated FTA articles as references to NAFTA Chapter Twenty. These references appear in paragraphs 16 and 18 of FTA Annex 705.4, and relate to the arbitration of disputes over levels of government support for wheat, oats and barley, discussed in §5.3(10)(e).

(a) Agricultural export subsidies

(i) Export subsidies

As discussed in §5.3(1)(b)(ii), FTA 701(2) goes much further than the GATT Agricultural Agreement in that it completely eliminates export subsidies on trade in agricultural goods between Canada and the United States. Consistent with the GATT concept, an export subsidy is defined in FTA 711 as a subsidy which is conditional upon exportation of agricultural goods, and specific reference is made to the list of examples in the Annex to the Subsidies Code.

Canada provides export subsidies in respect of supply-managed products. In response to subsidy practices of the European Union, the United States has adopted an Export Enhancement Program ("EEP") which makes use of export subsidies to improve the competitive position of U.S. exports. However, the major agricultural subsidies in both Canada and the United States are through domestic support programs.

(ii) Transportation and other domestic subsidies

FTA 701(5) requires that Canada exclude from the transport rates under the *Western Grain Transportation Act* ("WGTA") agricultural goods originating in Canada and shipped via west coast ports for consumption in the United States. However, this requirement does not apply to grain that is shipped east from Canada's western provinces to Thunder Bay. Much of this grain is sold into the domestic Canadian market but some is exported to the United States. Canada views these subsidies as being justifiable domestic subsidies, while U.S. grain producers consider them as unfair. At the time of writing, WGTA subsidies continue to be a trade irritant between Canada and the United States.

FTA 701(4) requires each of Canada and the United States to take into account the export interests of the other in applying subsidies to exports to third countries. On June 24, 1993, the United States Secretary of Agriculture announced that the EEP would be extended to the Mexican market to win back market share that had been lost through allegedly unfair Canadian practices. Canada has taken the position that this action violates FTA 701(4) and had, at the time of writing, invoked a Chapter Eighteen panel to resolve the issue.[176]

(iii) Selling below acquisition cost

FTA 701(3) requires that the governments of Canada and the United States not sell agricultural goods for export to the other country at prices below the cost of acquisition plus storage, handling or other costs. This obligation extends to federally established public entities, such as the "CWB", but not to provincial or state public entities or to private sector entities.

FTA 701(3) has been the subject of an on-going dispute between Canada and the United States respecting the marketing of durum wheat in the United States by the CWB. Following 1986, sales of Canadian durum wheat into the United States increased significantly. The U.S. government alleged that the pricing practices of the CWB contravened FTA 701(3). The issue was considered by a Chapter Eighteen panel that issued its final report on February 8, 1993. The panel considered what constituted "acquisition costs" and "other costs". The panel found that only costs incurred by the marketing agency counted and not other government outlays, such as domestic subsidies.[177] WGTA subsidies paid for shipment to Thunder Bay were held to be valid domestic subsidies and were not to be included.[178] The acquisition cost included only the initial payment to producers and not subsequent distributions of profit.[179] Other costs were held to be variable costs, like storage and handling, and not fixed costs, such as administrative expenses.[180]

The panel's report was not favourably received by either the U.S. growers or the U.S. administration, and CWB marketing practices continue to be a trade issue between Canada and the United States.

(b) Retention of GATT rights

Except as otherwise provided in FTA Chapter Seven, Canada and the United States retain their GATT rights and obligations under FTA 710 respecting all "agricultural, food, beverage and certain related goods". This expression covers "agricultural goods" as defined in FTA Article 711 together with some other goods including beer. The incorporating language in NAFTA Annex 702.1(4) provides that the rights and obligations retained include exemptions under the *Protocol of Provisional Application* and waivers granted under GATT Article XXV.

The incorporation of FTA 710 and NAFTA Annex 702.1(4) have two significant results. First, in retaining its rights under GATT Article XI, particularly GATT Article XI:2(c), Canada has retained its supply management system under NAFTA as against the United States, subject only to FTA 706 which requires that Canada permit prescribed percentages of its chicken, turkey and egg markets to be served with imported U.S. product. Second, as pointed out in the U.S. Statement of Administrative Action, the waivers referred to in NAFTA Annex 702.1(4) include the waiver granted to the United States respecting s. 22 of the AAA.[181] Therefore, the fees and quantitative restrictions implemented under s. 22 of the AAA may continue in effect as regards Canada, subject only to exceptions in the incorporated FTA articles. There are exceptions in FTA 704 (Meat), FTA 705 (Grain and Grain Products) and FTA 707 (Sugar-Containing Products) discussed in §5.3(10)(c), §5.3(10)(e) and §5.3(10)(g) respectively.

Neither FTA 710 nor NAFTA Annex 702.1(4) refer to future agreements. However, there is no NAFTA or incorporated FTA provision expressly permitting Canada to maintain its supply management system or the United States to maintain its s. 22 fees and quotas. Therefore, Canada and the United States will each have to convert their quotas to tariffs when the Uruguay Round agreements come into effect. As will be discussed in §5.3(7)(a), the Canadian and U.S. governments disagree on whether the tariffs resulting from the conversion are subject to the NAFTA tariff elimination requirements.

(c) The other incorporated FTA articles

The incorporated FTA Articles 702 through to 707 relate to specific product groups and are discussed further under the relevant product headings in §5.3(10).

(6) The NAFTA Provisions

The NAFTA agricultural provisions are divided into separate bilateral arrangements between Mexico and the United States and Canada and Mexico. Much of the detail of the Mexico-United States arrangement is found in the notes to the NAFTA Schedules of each of these countries, and not in the main NAFTA text. To a lesser extent this observation also applies to the Canada-Mexico arrangement.

The NAFTA text sets out a few trilateral provisions. There are also some common provisions in the Mexico-United States bilateral arrangement and the Canada-Mexico bilateral arrangement.

(a) Domestic support

NAFTA 704 is a trilateral measure covering domestic support measures. Each NAFTA country is to "work toward domestic support measures" that have minimal trade distorting or production effects and that are exempt from the domestic support reduction commitments negotiated under GATT that are described in §5.3(1)(b)(ii). This provision is essentially an affirmation of GATT rights and obligations and nothing more.

(b) Export subsidies

NAFTA 705 is a trilateral measure covering export subsidies. NAFTA 705 is expressed so as not to derogate from the elimination of export subsidies provided for in FTA 701 and is therefore irrelevant as between the United States and Canada. NAFTA 705 requires that an exporting NAFTA country give notice to an importing NAFTA country prior to adopting export subsidy measures, and enter into consultations with a view to eliminating the subsidy or minimizing its adverse impact. The NAFTA countries recognize that export subsidies are inappropriate when there are no other subsidized imports of the subsidized good into the importing NAFTA country. The NAFTA countries agree to take each others interests into account when using export subsidies. A Working Group on Agricultural Subsidies is established to work toward the elimination of export subsidies. The NAFTA countries expressly retain their rights to levy countervailing duties against subsidized imports of agricultural goods.

(c) Committee on Agricultural Trade

NAFTA 706 establishes a Committee on Agricultural Trade which is to monitor the implementation of the NAFTA provisions respecting agricultural goods and to provide a forum for consultation.

(d) NAFTA 309(1) and (2) and qualifying goods

The Mexico-U.S. and Canada-Mexico bilateral arrangements each provide that NAFTA 309(1) and (2) applies only to qualifying goods.[182] As discussed in §4.3(2) and §4.3(3), NAFTA 309(1) incorporates GATT Article XI and NAFTA 309(2) confirms understandings respecting minimum export and import requirements.

Consider high quality beef cuts prepared in the United States from unprocessed Canadian beef from Canadian-grown animals and exported to Mexico. The beef cuts would be originating goods under NAFTA rules of origin. As such they would clearly be a "good of a Party" and the prohibition of quantitative restrictions under GATT Article XI incorporated by NAFTA 309(1) would normally apply. However, as between Mexico and the United States, NAFTA 309(1) applies only to qualifying goods and because the unprocessed beef came from Canada, the beef cuts are not qualifying goods. Therefore, the prohibition of quantitative restrictions incorporated by NAFTA 309(1) would not apply to the beef cuts.

(e) Changes to rules of origin

The Mexico-United States bilateral arrangement provides that certain categories of cocoa powder containing sugar and syrups from cane or beet sugar exported from Mexico to the United States, or vice versa, containing any sugar under subheading 1701.99 that is not a qualifying good of the exporting country will be treated as non-originating.[183] A similar provision is set out in the Canada-Mexico bilateral arrangement.[184]

The Mexico-United States bilateral arrangement also provides that peanuts and peanut products such as peanut butter exported from Mexico to the United States, or vice versa, must be made from material wholly obtained in the exporting country to be originating.[185] The normal rule of origin for peanut butter permits non-NAFTA country peanuts to be used. There is no corresponding rule in the Canada-Mexico bilateral arrangement.

(f) Agricultural grading and marketing standards

Each of the Mexico-United States and the Mexico-Canada bilateral arrangements provides for the establishment of a bilateral Working Group to review agricultural grade and quality standards and to resolve disputes.[186] The Mexico-United States arrangement sets out a national treatment obligation respecting measures respecting the classification, grading and marketing of agricultural goods.[187] There is no corresponding provision in the Canada-Mexico bilateral arrangement.

(g) Voluntary restraint agreements

Canada and Mexico have agreed not to seek voluntary restraint agreements from each other respecting any agricultural good that is a qualifying good.[188] The corresponding provision in the Mexico-United States bilateral arrangement applies only to meat.[189] As noted in §4.7(2), the GATT Safeguards Agreement contains a similar provision that applies to all goods.

(7) Tariff Rate Quotas

The Mexico-United States bilateral arrangement makes extensive use of tariff rate quotas. Tariff rate quotas are less frequently used in the Canada-Mexico bilateral arrangement, but they do apply to some goods.

As discussed in §2.2(8), under a tariff rate quota imports up to a certain annual quantity (the "in-quota quantity") are admitted free of duty or at a low rate of duty (the "in-quota tariff rate"). Imports above the in-quota quantity are subject to a higher rate of duty (the "over-quota tariff rate"). Tariff rate quotas result from the tariffication of quantitative restrictions. A tariff rate quota has the same practical effect as a quantitative restriction if the over-quota tariff rate is prohibitively high. However, the prohibitive rate of duty can be reduced over time and eventually eliminated.

Consider tariff item 0701.90.90 (fresh or chilled potatoes other than seed potatoes) in the NAFTA Schedule of Mexico. The in-quota quantity in 1994 for potatoes originating from the United States and Canada are 15,000 and 4,000 tonnes respectively. These quantities increase by 3% annually. Imports within the in-quota quantity are admitted free of duty. The over-quota tariff rates are as follows:

Base rate	greater of 272% and $US 0.354 per kilogram
January 1, 1994	greater of 261.1% and $US 0.339 per kilogram
January 1, 1995	greater of 250.2% and $US 0.325 per kilogram
January 1, 1996	greater of 239.3% and $US 0.311 per kilogram
January 1, 1997	greater of 228.4% and $US 0.297 per kilogram
January 1, 1998	greater of 217.6% and $US 0.283 per kilogram
January 1, 1999	greater of 206.7% and $US 0.269 per kilogram
January 1, 2000	greater of 155.0% and $US 0.201 per kilogram
January 1, 2001	greater of 103.3% and $US 0.134 per kilogram
January 1, 2002	greater of 56.6% and $US 0.067 per kilogram
January 1, 2003	free[190]

In this example of tariffication, the over-quota tariff rate is very high and this tariff rate quota will operate much like a quantitative restriction. However, towards the end of the period, some over-quota imports will be feasible. At the end of the period, the tariff rate quota comes to an end and originating American and Canadian potatoes will enter Mexico free of duty or quantitative restrictions.

Eligibility under the NAFTA Schedule of the United States for the in-quota tariff rates in the tariff rate quotas resulting from tariffication depends upon goods being qualifying goods. If a good is originating and eligible to be marked as a good of Mexico but not a qualifying good, it will be subject to the over-quota tariff rate. The tariff rate quotas in the NAFTA Schedule of Mexico resulting from tariffication do not contain this requirement.[191]

(a) Relationship with GATT and GATT Uruguay Round agreements

As the above example shows, over-quota tariff rates resulting from tariffication can be very high. These rates will exceed bound rates under the GATT. Accordingly, each of Mexico-United States and the Canada-Mexico bilateral arrangements provide for waivers of GATT rights respecting over-quota tariff rates that exceed rates set out in the GATT Schedule of Concessions as of July 1, 1991. However, if as the result of tariffication under an agreement negotiated under the GATT a lower rate applies to a good than the over-quota rate set out in the NAFTA Schedule of the United States or Mexico, the lower GATT rate will apply to goods that are qualifying goods.[192] These provisions do not apply to any of the goods that are subject to special safeguards described in §5.3(7)(b) or, in the Mexico-United States bilateral arrangement, to orange juice.[193]

The bilateral Mexico-United States and Canada-Mexico arrangements each provide that any in-quota quantity that applies to qualifying goods under a NAFTA tariff rate quota may be counted towards the in-quota quantity provided for in a tariff rate quota adopted as a result of an agreement under the GATT.[194] Therefore, if under a GATT agreement Mexico establishes a tariff rate quota on fresh or chilled potatoes, U.S. potatoes counted in the in-quota quantity under NAFTA tariff rate quota described above would also be counted in the in-quota quantity in the GATT tariff rate quota. The GATT in-quota quantity would not have to be treated as additional to the NAFTA in-quota quantity.

The bilateral Canada-United States arrangement does not refer to the Uruguay Round agreements or take into account the process of tariffication that will occur when those agreements become effective. Tariffication will affect dairy products entering both countries, poultry and eggs entering Canada, and peanuts, sugar-containing products and cotton entering the United States. The United States has taken the position that tariff elimination under NAFTA applies to tariffs resulting from tariffication and that these must be eliminated by January 1, 1998.[195] One U.S. trade expert has stated that the United States could take the stronger position that the prohibition of new tariffs in NAFTA 302(1) applies to tariffs arising from tariffication so that quotas will have to be eliminated when the Uruguay Round agreements come into effect but they cannot be replaced by the high protective tariffs that Canada contemplates imposing in meeting its GATT tariffication obligations.[196] Canada has taken the position that tariffs that replace quotas on supply managed goods are import restrictions imposed pursuant to a "successor agreement" to GATT Article XI and, as such, are justified under NAFTA 309(1). At the time of writing, this dispute had not been resolved.

(b) Special safeguard provisions

NAFTA 703 permits special safeguards in the form of tariff rate quotas to be maintained by each country in respect of agricultural goods listed in NAFTA Annex 703.3. The safeguards apply as between Mexico and the United States and between Canada and Mexico but not between Canada and the United States. The tariff rate quota adopted or maintained for any of these goods must be in accordance with the applicable NAFTA schedule of the importing NAFTA country, and the over-quota tariff rate cannot exceed the lower of the MFN rate in effect on January 1, 1991, or the current rate. A NAFTA country may not maintain a safeguard against a good under NAFTA 703 and also invoke NAFTA emergency action proceedings respecting that good. With a few exceptions in the NAFTA Schedule of Canada, where some measure of discretion is provided, the special safeguards appear as fixed elements in the NAFTA Schedule of each country.

(i) Canadian safeguards

The list for Canada applies only to goods from Mexico and includes certain categories of cut flowers, fresh and chilled tomatoes, onions and shallots, cucumbers and gherkins, strawberries and prepared or preserved tomatoes.[197] With all of these goods, when the tariff rate quota applies the in-quota quantity is zero and the over-quota tariff rate is Canada's MFN rate. With fresh and chilled tomatoes, onions and shallots, and cucumbers and gherkins, the tariff rate quota may be applied for any period not exceeding prescribed numbers of weeks in any twelve-month period and ending on March 31st. With the other goods, the tariff rate quota is in effect continuously. The tariff rate quotas with MFN over-quota tariff rates all expire on January 1, 2003, and from then these goods will be duty-free.

(ii) U.S. safeguards

The list for the United States applies only to goods from Mexico and includes certain categories of tomatoes, onions and shallots, eggplants, squash and watermelons.[198] The tariff rate quotas are all fixed in the NAFTA Schedule of the United States, and operate on a seasonal basis. In-quota quantities are fixed in the chapter notes for imports during a specific period in each year. For example, the in-quota quantity for 1994 for fresh or chilled tomatoes entered from March 1st to July 14th is 165,500,000 kilograms. This quantity increases to 209,650,000 kilograms for that same period in 2002, the last year that the tariff rate quota is in effect. Imports up to the in-quota quantity are subject to duties phased out in staging category C. The over-quota tariff rate equals the base rate, with no phasing. These tariff rate quotas all end on January 1, 2003, and from then on these goods will be duty-free.

(iii) Mexican safeguards

The list for Mexico applies to goods from each of Canada and the United States and includes certain categories of live swine, swine meat, dried and prepared potatoes, apples and coffee extracts, essences and concentrates.[199] Tariff rate quotas for these goods are set out in the NAFTA Schedule of Mexico. None is seasonally based. For each good, separate in-quota quantities are established for originating goods from the United States and of originating goods from Canada. For example, in-quota quantity for U.S. live swine weighing less than 50 kilograms is 49,500 head for 1994, subject to annual increase for 1995 and following years of 3%. The corresponding figures for Canada are 1,000 head with an annual increase of 5%. In-quota tariff rates in all the special safeguard tariff rate quotas is the applicable base rate reduced in accordance with staging category C. Over-quota tariff rates are equal to the lesser of the base rate (without reduction) or the MFN rate. All special safeguards end on January 1, 2003, and from then these goods will be duty-free.

(8) Mexico-United States Bilateral Arrangement — GATT Article XI:2(c), Section 22 and Tariffication

Each of Mexico and the United States waives its rights under GATT Article XI:2(c) as against each other.[200] The United States has agreed not to impose fees under s. 22 of the AAA.[201] While the NAFTA text does not mention quantitative restrictions under s. 22 of the AAA, the combined effect of NAFTA 309(1), the waiver of rights under GATT Article XI:2(c) and the rule of prevalence in NAFTA 103, is to prohibit quantitative restrictions as between Mexico and the United States.[202] These obligations apply only to qualifying goods.

Tariffication is the singular most important aspect of the bilateral arrangement between Mexico and the United States. Section 22 import quotas have been converted to tariff rate quotas. Mexican import licensing requirements have been converted to tariff rate quotas and, in some cases, to simple tariffs. These will be discussed under the product headings in §5.3(10). The Mexico-United States bilateral arrangement also sets out special rules respecting sugar and syrup goods that are discussed in §5.3(10)(g).

Goods processed in Mexican maquiladoras and re-exported to the United States and goods processed in U.S. foreign trade zones and re-exported to Mexico will not be counted in respect of the in-quota quantity of a tariff rate quota.[203]

(9) Canada-Mexico Bilateral Arrangement — GATT Article XI:2(c) and Dairy, Poultry and Egg Goods

Each of Canada and Mexico reserve their rights under GATT Article XI:2(c)(i) with respect to dairy, poultry and egg goods specified for each country in NAFTA Appendix 703.2.B.7. The lists are extensive and cover all of Canada's supply managed goods. The effect of the reservation is that quantitative restrictions may be applied against these goods by both Canada and Mexico.[204]

Canada and Mexico will not maintain quantitative restrictions against each other with respect to other agricultural goods. As with goods from the United States, Mexican import licensing requirements respecting goods from Canada will be converted to tariff rate quotas. Canada does not maintain quantitative restrictions against agricultural goods other than its supply managed goods. Therefore, there are no quantitative restrictions on the Canadian side to which tariffication applies.

Canada and Mexico each retain the right to apply customs duties and other restrictions in respect of these goods to the extent permitted under the GATT.[205] The effect of this provision is that, as between Canada and Mexico, tariff elimination does not apply to these goods. Tariff elimination will also not apply to sugar and syrup goods.[206]

(10) Treatment of Major Product Groups

The following sections compare the treatment of major product groups under the three bilateral arrangements.

(a) Poultry and egg goods

(i) Canada and the United States

FTA 706 requires Canada to permit limited quantities of poultry and egg products to be imported. The limit for chicken and chicken products for a year is not less than 7.5% of the previous year's domestic production. The limit for turkey and turkey products for a year is not less than 3.5% of the domestic turkey quota for that year. The limits for shell eggs, frozen, liquid and further processed eggs and powdered eggs for a year are 1.647%, 0.714% and 0.627% respectively of the previous year's domestic production. Subject only to these requirements and those imposed by the Uruguay Round agreements, Canada's quantitative restrictions on these goods are unaffected.

The United States does not maintain quantitative restrictions respecting these products, but, subject to the Uruguay Round agreements, its rights under s. 22 of the AAA continue to apply.

(ii) Mexico and the United States

Mexican import licensing requirements respecting various poultry products have been converted to tariff rate quotas. The tariff rate quotas are structured in the same manner as that described in §5.3(7). In-quota tariff rates are free and the NAFTA Schedule of Mexico sets out in-quota quantities for the affected tariff items. Over-quota tariff rates vary, but all start from high base rates. For example, base rates for turkey products are the higher of 133% or $1.85 (US) per kilogram and base rates for products of chickens, ducks, geese and guineas are the higher of 26% and $1.68 (US) per kilogram.[207] All the over-quota tariff rates are reduced in ten stages and will be completely eliminated on January 1, 2003. A tariff rate quota has also been established for fresh eggs.[208]

Because there are no U.S. quantitative restrictions respecting these products, there are no U.S. tariff rate quotas.

(iii) Canada and Mexico

Because these products included in the "dairy, poultry and egg" goods listed in Appendix 703.2.B.7, Canada and Mexico may continue to apply quantitative restrictions, even after the Uruguay Round agreements become effective. Tariffs on these goods will not be eliminated.

(b) Dairy products

(i) Canada and the United States

FTA Chapter Seven does not contain any provision respecting dairy products. Accordingly, subject to the Uruguay Round agreements, each country may continue to maintain the quantitative restrictions against the other's dairy products described in §5.3(2)(a)(i) and §5.3(2)(b).

(ii) Mexico and the United States

U.S. quantitative restrictions on dairy products (milk, cream, buttermilk, yoghurt, other milk products, butter and cheese, preparations of fats and oils containing butterfat, ice cream, infants' preparations containing milk solids, mixes and doughs containing butterfat and animal feeds containing milk or milk derivatives) have been converted to tariff rate quotas. Consider, for example, milk and cream classified under HSTUS tariff item 0401.30.10. The quota quantity is 5,678,117 litres for New Zealand and none for other countries, including Mexico.[209] In 1994, the in-quota quantity for qualifying goods from Mexico is 366,000 litres. This amount increases annually to 464,000 litres in the year 2002. The in-quota tariff rate is free. The over-quota tariff rate for 1994 is 55.5 cents per litre for goods valued at less than 61.7 cents per litre and 84.5% for goods with a higher value. These rates diminish to 6.2 cents per litre and 9.4% in 2002, and become free on January 1, 2003. The U.S. tariff rate quotas for dairy products, which expire on January 1, 2003, apply only to qualifying goods.

The NAFTA Schedule of Mexico establishes tariff rate quotas for two categories of powdered milk.[210] The base rate for the over-quota tariff rate is 139%, and it is phased out over fifteen stages, with complete elimination on January 1, 2008. Other dairy products are subject only to simple tariffs phased out under staging category C.

(iii) Canada and Mexico

As with poultry and eggs, because these products included in the "dairy, poultry and egg" goods listed in Appendix 703.2.B.7, Canada and Mexico may continue to apply quantitative restrictions even after the Uruguay Round agreements become effective. Tariffs on these goods will not be eliminated.

(c) Meat and livestock

(i) Canada and the United States

FTA 704 eliminates quantitative import restrictions on originating meat goods other than restrictions necessary to preserve the integrity of quantitative import restrictions or voluntary agreements limiting meat imports from third countries. Meat articles in The Meat Import Act of 1979 do not include meat originating in Canada.[211] There are no quantitative restrictions in effect in either country respecting livestock, but rights under GATT Article XI:2(c) and s. 22 of the AAA continue to apply.

Imports of Canadian swine and pork have been subjected to U.S. countervailing duty actions alleging unfair subsidization. Canada has achieved substantial success in these actions before FTA Chapter Nineteen binational panels, but the question of support programs remains an issue between Canada and the United States.

(ii) Mexico and the United States

Mexican meat products that are qualifying goods are exempt from any quantitative limitations that may be imposed by the United States.[212] The Meat Import Act of 1979 has been amended so that meat articles do not include meat originating in Mexico.[213] No U.S. restrictions apply to imports of livestock. Live swine and swine meat entering Mexico are subject to the special safeguard tariff rate quotas described in §5.3(7)(b)(iii).

(iii) Canada and Mexico

Other than the Mexican special safeguards for live swine and swine meat described in §5.3(7)(b)(iii), there are no quantitative restrictions respecting these goods between Canada and Mexico.

(d) Fresh fruits and vegetables

(i) Canada and the United States

FTA 702(1) permits the application of temporary or "snapback" duties on fresh fruits and vegetables under limited circumstances.[214] The fruits and vegetables to which the temporary duty may be applied are listed in FTA 702(7). The temporary duty may be applied on a national or regional basis.[215] The duty may be applied only once in a twelve-month period and must not exceed the lesser of the MFN rate that applied on January 1, 1989, or the current MFN rate. A consultation period of two working days must precede the application of a temporary duty. The right to apply these temporary duties expires on January 1, 2009.

(ii) Mexico and the United States, Canada and Mexico

Potatoes (except for seed) and kidney beans (except for seed) are subject to tariff rate quotas under the NAFTA Schedule of Mexico. The tariff rate quota for potatoes is described in §5.3(7). The in-quota tariff rate is free. The base rate for the over-quota tariff rate for kidney beans is 139% and is phased out in fifteen stages, with complete elimination on January 1, 2008. The in-quota quantities for 1994 are 50,000 tonnes and 1,500 tonnes respectively for the United States and Canada. These quantities increase by 3%

each year.[216] Certain other categories of fruits and vegetables are subject to the special safeguard tariff rate quotas described in §5.3(7)(b).

(e) Grain products and corn

(i) Canada and the United States

FTA 705(1) requires Canada to eliminate import permit requirements for wheat, oats, barley or products made from them originating in the United States if the level of U.S. government support for any of these grains becomes equal to or less than the level of Canadian government support. The level of government support is compared in accordance with producer subsidy equivalent formulae set out in FTA Annex 705.4.

In 1991, Canadian government support exceeded that of the United States for wheat and permission was granted for the importation of wheat and wheat products.[217] Consistent with FTA 705(1), the regulation granting the permission requires that the product be accompanied by an end use certificate, be denatured if for feed use and be accompanied by a certificate issued under the *Seeds Act* if imported for seed. The U.S. legislation implementing NAFTA contains a *quid pro quo* provision that will require end use certificates for wheat or barley imported from any country that imposes a similar requirement on U.S. wheat.[218] These requirements will be suspended on a reciprocal basis.[219]

In 1993, the Canadian government eliminated CWB licensing requirements for barley and barley products imported from and exported to the United States. This unilateral step was taken to improve efficiency in the barley market through greater integration with the U.S. market. The certification and denaturing requirements that apply to wheat and wheat products do not apply to these products.[220]

FTA 705(5) permits Canada or the United States to introduce or, if previously eliminated, reintroduce restrictions or import fees on imports of grain or grain products originating in the territory of the other Party if such imports significantly increase as a result of a substantial change in that Party's support programs.[221] This provision has the effect of prohibiting quantitative restrictions on grain products unless a substantial change occurs in support programs and a substantial increase in imports ensues. Canadian exports of durum wheat to the United States increased substantially since the FTA became effective, although not because of changes in support programs. This none the less provoked a trade dispute which was settled in August, 1994, with a one year truce limiting Canadian exports of durum wheat to 1.5 million tonnes.

There are no special provisions respecting corn as between Canada and the United States. The Canadian government has challenged U.S. subsidies to corn growers and has levied countervailing duties against imports of corn from the United States.[222]

(ii) Mexico and the United States

There are no tariff rate quotas for these goods in the NAFTA Schedule of the United States, and there are no quantitative restrictions as against Mexico. There are tariff rate quotas in the NAFTA Schedule of Mexico for barley and corn (except for seed) under HS headings 10.03 and 10.05 respectively. The in-quota tariff rate is free. The base rate for the over-quota tariff rate is 128% for barley and 215% for corn. The over-quota tariff rate for barley will be phased out by January 1, 2003, and the rate for corn by January 1, 2008.[223] There is also a tariff rate quota in the NAFTA Schedule of Mexico for malt under heading 1107. The in-quota tariff rate is free. The base rate for the over-quota tariff rate is 139%, and it will be phased out by January 1, 2003.[224]

(iii) Canada and Mexico

CWB licensing requirements will apply to imports of Mexican grain products. The tariff rate quotas for barley, corn and malt in the NAFTA Schedule of Mexico all apply to goods originating in Canada, with different in-quota quantities from those for U.S. goods.[225]

(f) Peanuts and peanut products

(i) Canada and the United States

The United States maintains quantitative restrictions against peanuts and peanut products except peanut butter.[226] Products from Canada are subject to these restrictions which, in turn, are subject to the tariffication requirements of the GATT Agricultural Agreement. Canada does not maintain quantitative restrictions respecting these products.

(ii) Mexico and the United States, Canada and Mexico

U.S. quantitative restrictions have been converted to tariff rate quotas for qualifying goods of Mexico. The aggregate in-quota quantity for these products is 3,377,000 kilograms for 1994 and increases to 4,959,000 kilograms for 2007. In-quota tariff rates are free. Over-quota tariff rates vary but are all high at the beginning. For example, the over-quota tariff rate for 1994 for shelled peanuts valued over 65.2 cents per kilogram is 181.4%. This rate is phased out over fifteen stages, with complete elimination on January 1, 2008. Peanut butter is subject to a simple tariff in staging category C. There are no Mexican tariff rate quotas for these goods from either the United States or Canada.

(g) Sugar and sugar-containing products

The NAFTA provisions respecting sugar and syrup goods between the United States and Mexico and the issues respecting the trade in these goods between the United States and Canada are both tied to the U.S. import restrictions respecting these goods. Briefly, U.S. import restrictions break down into two broad categories: products subject to tariff rate quotas and products subject to quantitative restrictions.

The products subject to tariff rate quotas are described in Additional Notes 2 and 3 to HTSUS Chapter 17. These products consist of cane and beet sugar and chemically pure sucrose in various forms, certain other sugars such as maltose, fructose and glucose, chocolate and other foods containing cocoa over 90% by weight of sugar, and syrups derived from cane or beet sugar.[227] Prior to 1990 these products were subject to quantitative restrictions. However, a GATT panel decided in 1989 that these restrictions were inconsistent with GATT Article XI:1,[228] and shortly thereafter the United States adopted a tariff rate quota system. The in-quota quantity[229] for all these goods is established by the Secretary of Agriculture and is allocated among various specifically identified countries. Mexico falls in the category of "other specified countries and areas", each of which receives the greater of the share allocable under Additional Note 3(b)(i) and 7,258 tonnes.[230] Some of these goods are also subject to fees under s. 22 of the AAA.[231]

The in-quota and over-quota tariff rates are identified by the tariff item. Consider cane sugar under HTSUS subheading 1701.11. Tariff item 1701.11.01 is sugar entered within the in-quota quantity (i.e., entered under HTSUS Additional Notes 3(a) and 3(b) of Chapter 17), and the MFN in-quota tariff rate is 1.4606 cents per kilogram.[232] Tariff item 1701.11.02 is the same good imported for distilling certain alcohols, and the rates of duty are the same as for tariff item 1701.11.01. Tariff item 1701.11.03 applies to the same goods imported outside the in-quota quantity described in tariff item 1701.11.01 and not covered by the special purpose described in tariff item 1701.11.02. The MFN over-quota tariff rate is 37.386 cents per kilogram, which is over twenty-five times as great as the MFN in-quota tariff rate. The in-quota and over-quota tariff rates for the other goods for which there are tariff rate quotas are identified in the same way.[233]

Other sugar-containing goods are subject to quantitative restrictions imposed under s. 22 of the AAA. These are set out in HTSUS tariff items 9904.50.20 (which applies to certain blended syrups, capable of being further processed and not for retail sale) and 9904.50.40 (certain articles containing 65% by dry weight of sugar, capable of being further processed and not for retail sale) and subheading 9904.60 (certain articles containing over 10% by dry weight of sugar except articles for retail sale in the identical form and packaging as imported).[234] There is no overlap in the goods described in these provisions and the goods subject to tariff rate quotas described above.

(i) Canada and the United States

FTA 707 requires that the United States not maintain any quantitative import restriction or import fee on any good originating in Canada which contains 10% or less sugar by dry weight for the purposes of restricting its sugar content. The United States does not maintain fees or quantitative restrictions against goods falling within this description. Other U.S restrictions are unaffected by FTA 707, and, subject to the GATT Agricultural Agreement, the quantitative restrictions described above apply to Canadian goods.

The current sugar difficulties between Canada and the United States arise from the fact that the United States adopted the tariff rate quotas described above after the FTA came into effect. FTA 401(1) prohibited the United States from applying the high over-quota tariff rates to Canadian goods. Therefore, both the in-quota and over-quota tariff rate that applies to Canadian goods imported into the United States under the relevant tariff items is the tariff rate set out in the FTA Schedule of the United States.[235] Canada is therefore exempted from the U.S. tariff rate quota system. Since the FTA became effective, Canadian exports of these products to the United States have increased, although the Canadian share of the U.S. market continues to be very small. On June 3, 1993, the U.S. Secretary of Agriculture requested that emergency restraints in the form of additional s. 22 fees and quantitative restrictions be imposed on imports of these products from Canada.[236] At the time of writing, the U.S. government had not taken action on this request. NAFTA does not address the issue.

(ii) Mexico and the United States

The provisions of the Mexico-United States bilateral arrangement respecting sugar and sugar-containing goods fall into the same two broad categories as the U.S. import restrictions described above.

The provisions affecting the goods subject to U.S. tariff rate quotas described above are set out in paragraphs 13 to 22 of Section A of NAFTA Annex 703.2 under the heading "Trade in Sugar and Syrup Goods". These provisions also apply to the goods described in the corresponding tariff provisions in the NAFTA Schedule of Mexico. The tariff items in the NAFTA Schedule of each of the United States and Mexico set out tariff rate quotas. The sugar and syrup goods provisions set out the manner in which the aggregate in-quota quantity is to be established for all of these sugar and syrup goods for each of the fourteen "marketing years" following NAFTA becoming effective. A "marketing year" is a twelve-month period beginning October 1st. A determination will be made each year as to whether each of the United States and Mexico is projected to be a "net surplus producer" for the next marketing year. A "net surplus producer" has a "net production surplus", which is the quantity by which domestic consumption exceeds total sugar consumption in a marketing year.[237] For each of the first four-teen marketing years, the aggregate in-quota quantity for each of the United States and Mexico respecting the tariff quotas applied to goods of the other will be the greater of the allocation of U.S. quota to any country within the category of "other specified countries and areas" described above and the Mexican projected net production surplus in the case of the U.S. tariff rate quota on Mexican goods and the U.S. projected net production surplus in the case of the Mexican tariff rate quota on U.S. goods.[238] For the first six marketing years there is a cap of 25,000 tonnes on this in-quota quantity. In the seventh marketing year, the cap increases to 150,000 tonnes and esca-lates by 10% per marketing year through to the fourteenth marketing year.[239] In certain circumstances after the sixth marketing year, such as if Mexico or the United States is a net surplus producer for two consecutive marketing years, the caps do not apply. The in-quota tariff rate is free. The tariff rate quotas in both tariff schedules apply only to qualifying goods.

Except for the complex manner of determining the in-quota quantity just described, the tariff rate quotas for these goods operate as those elsewhere. Consider the example respecting cane and beet sugar in the HTSUS described above. Tariff item 1701.11.01 in the NAFTA Schedule of the United States continues to be sugar entered under Additional Note 3 and tariff item 1701.11.02 continues to apply to the special purpose situation described above. Tariff item 1701.11.03 is split into separate tariff items. Tariff items 1701.11.03A and 1701.11.03C provide for tariff-free treatment for sugar that is over the Additional Note 3 in-quota quantity and up to the NAFTA in-quota quantity just described.[240] Tariff items 1701.11.30B and 1701.11.30D[241] cover over-quota entries and provide for over-quota tariff rates that start from a base rate of 37.386 cents per kilogram (as described above) and dimin-ish year by year to complete elimination by 2008.[242] A variety of over-quota tariff rates apply, depending on the product.

The corresponding Mexican tariff rate quotas function in a similar man-ner, except that the NAFTA Schedule of Mexico does not set out what over-quota tariff rates apply. The combined effect of paragraphs 17 and 18 of the sugar and syrup provisions is that Mexican over-quota tariff rates on U.S. qualifying goods may not exceed their U.S. counterparts.

The sugar and syrup goods provisions set out some other requirements concerning these goods, including a reciprocal requirement that duty-free treatment apply, outside the tariff rate quotas, to raw sugar imported from one country to be refined in the other for re-export, and to refined sugar imported from one of the countries that has been refined from raw sugar from the other country.[243]

Sugar-containing goods subject to U.S. quantitative restrictions are not covered by the sugar and syrup provisions. However, the same principle of tariffication in the NAFTA Schedule of the United States applies to these goods as to other goods. Consider maple sugar blended with other sugars under HTSUS tariff item 1702.20.20. This good is not covered by Additional Note 3 but is covered by the quantitative restriction in HTSUS tariff 9904.50.40. In the NAFTA Schedule of the United States, tariff item 1702.20.20.A applies the in-quota tariff rate of free and tariff items 1702.20.20.B and 1702.20.20.C apply the over-quota tariff rates. The in-quota quantities increase from 1,500,000 kilograms to 1,900,000 kilograms from 1994 to 2002,[244] and the over-quota rates diminish to free by 2003.[245] Tariff item 1702.20.20.D applies to goods of this description that are not subject to the quantitative restriction. The NAFTA Schedule of Mexico provides for simple tariff elimination for all of these goods.

(iii) Canada and Mexico

Mexico will continue to apply its MFN rate to Canadian sugar and syrup goods. Canada may continue to apply a rate to these goods that is equal to the rate applied by Mexico. The goods to which this provision applies in the NAFTA Schedule of each of Mexico and Canada are the same categories of goods that are covered by the sugar and syrup provisions in the Mexico-United States bilateral arrangement. The effect is that the elimination of tariffs under NAFTA does not apply to these goods. For other sugar-containing goods, simple tariff elimination applies under the NAFTA Schedules of both countries, under various staging categories.

(h) Orange juice, coffee, lard, cotton

(i) Canada and the United States

There are no special FTA or NAFTA provisions as between Canada and the United States respecting these goods. None of these goods is on Canada's Import Control List. Except for cotton, which is subject to U.S. s. 22 quantitative restrictions under HTSUS subheading 9904.30, none of these goods is subject to U.S. quantitative restrictions.

(ii) Mexico and the United States

The NAFTA Schedule of the United States sets out tariff rate quotas for various forms of orange juice. These tariff rate quotas are not based on tariffication. Notes to the schedule establish in-quota quantities, in-quota tariff rates and higher over-quota tariff rates.[246] The in-quota and over-quota tariff rates are phased out by January 1, 2008. The s. 22 quantitative restrictions on cotton have been converted to tariff rate quotas, with an in-quota tariff rate of free and over-quota tariff rates being phased out by January 1, 2003.[247]

In the NAFTA Schedule of Mexico, orange juice products from the United States are also subject to tariff rate quotas, although like their U.S. counterparts, these are not the result of tariffication. The over-quota tariff rate will be phased out by January 1, 2008.[248] The NAFTA Schedule of Mexico sets out a tariff rate quota for lard and other pig and poultry fat. The in-quota tariff rate is free. The base rate for the over-quota tariff rate is 282%, and it will be phased out by January 1, 2003.[249]

(iii) Canada and Mexico

Orange juice products from Canada enter Mexico free of duty. The tariff rate quota for lard and other pig and poultry fat applies to goods of Canada, with different in-quota quantities.[250] Canada and Mexico have agreed not to adopt or maintain measures pursuant to an international coffee agreement that restricts trade in coffee between them.[251]

(i) Water — Canada and the United States

While water is an "agricultural good", unlike other agricultural goods the issues affecting water revolve about the export controls rather than import controls. The fact that water is an "agricultural good" has been raised by Canadian proponents of the water export issue as further evidence that the FTA and NAFTA constrain the ability of Canadian governments to restrict water exports. The only FTA provisions dealing with exports of agricultural goods are those in FTA 701 relating to export subsidies and selling below acquisition cost. The effect of these provisions is that a Canadian government is prohibited from subsidizing the export of water or, either directly or through a public entity, selling water into the United States at a price below acquisition cost. If anything, these provisions should make it easier and not more difficult to restrict the export of water.

(11) Concluding Remarks

The provisions respecting agricultural goods are among the most complicated in NAFTA. Most of the complication arises from the fact that the NAFTA countries went in separate directions and made no pretense at adopting a trilateral approach. The bilateral approach followed with agricultural goods underscores the merits of the trilateral approach that had been followed in most other sectors.

The NAFTA provisions respecting agricultural goods will result in free trade between Mexico and the United States for most goods by 2003 and for all goods by 2008. Trade will be free not just from tariffs but from quantitative restrictions as well. Canada chose not to join in this exercise. As between Canada and the United States, NAFTA maintains the *status quo*. Unfortunately that *status quo* includes a host of trade disputes that NAFTA does nothing to resolve and, as discussed in §5.3(7)(a), tariffication under the GATT Agricultural Agreement raises additional issues. As between

Canada and Mexico, NAFTA does not even remove tariffs on dairy, poultry, egg and sugar goods, let alone quantitative restrictions.

5.4 ENERGY AND BASIC PETROCHEMICALS

Energy goods have particular strategic importance and the energy sectors in all three NAFTA countries are highly regulated. Energy policy is directed primarily at assuring a secure supply of energy goods. However, security of supply means different things to different countries. For net importers of energy goods, like the United States, security of supply means securing access to foreign sources of energy goods. For producers of energy goods such as Canada and Mexico, security of supply means ensuring that domestic supplies of energy goods are not exploited for the benefit of foreign consumers at the expense of domestic needs. While Canada and Mexico share a common concern that their energy resources not be unduly exploited to serve U.S. interests, their relations vis à vis the United States respecting their energy sectors have been very different. Canadian nationalism respecting the energy sector, which reached its height in the 1970s and early 1980s, was relatively mild and counterbalanced by powerful export-oriented domestic interests. In Mexico, national control of the exploitation of energy goods, particularly hydrocarbons, occupies a place in the political psyche that transcends mere economic concerns.

Energy issues are addressed in the NAFTA provisions respecting trade in goods and in the NAFTA investment provisions. The NAFTA provisions affecting the trade in energy goods are described in this section. The NAFTA provisions affecting investment in the energy sector are described in §7.10(1).

(1) Energy Goods and International Agreements

Energy goods do not receive special treatment under the GATT or any of the Uruguay Round agreements. Some GATT exceptions, such as the natural resources exception in GATT Article XX(g) and the national security exemption in GATT Article XXI have more relevance for energy goods than for many other goods. However, there are no major exceptions or separate trading regimes for energy goods comparable to those for agricultural goods and textile and apparel goods. It is debatable as to whether the GATT applies to electricity as the original drafters of the GATT appear to have considered it to be a service rather than a good.[252]

Canada and the United States, together with a number of other OECD countries, are parties to the *Agreement for an International Energy Program* ("IEP"). This agreement, which is discussed in §5.4(6)(b)(ii), applies only to oil and is activated only in emergency circumstances. One commentator stated that the creation of the IEP reflects the ineffectiveness of the GATT in dealing with energy-related trade issues.[253] This statement was prompted by the fact that the GATT imposes more comprehensive disciplines on import restrictions than export restrictions.[254] Unlike most goods, where major trade issues arise over import restrictions, energy-related trade issues between producing and consuming countries arise mainly from concerns over access to sources of supply and export restrictions that impede that access.

(2) Export Restrictions and the Canada-U.S. Experience

U.S. concern over the ineffectiveness of GATT rules respecting export controls was the driving force behind the energy provisions of the FTA and arose from Canadian government policy towards the petroleum sector from 1974 to 1985.

The major oil and gas producing areas of Canada, located primarily in Alberta and to a lesser extent in British Columbia and Saskatchewan, came into production after World War II. Following the development of these resources, Canadian petroleum demand from Ontario westward was satisfied from domestic supply, while demand in Quebec and the Atlantic provinces was met by imported oil, principally from Venezuela. Oil was exported from Western Canada to U.S. markets. The National Energy Board ("NEB") was established in 1959 under the *National Energy Board Act* and was empowered to regulate the export and import of oil and gas and, later, electricity. These goods may be imported and exported only under the authority of a licence issued by the NEB, and the NEB must approve the import or export price.

Until 1973, imported oil was substantially cheaper than the domestically produced Canadian oil. However, with the embargo of the Organization of Arab Oil Exporting Countries ("OAPEC") of 1973-74, world oil prices increased dramatically. The federal government reacted by establishing a Canadian price for oil substantially below the world price. The domestic industry was required to sell oil to Canadian consumers at the Canadian regulated price. However, the NEB determined that exports to the United States should not be priced at the Canadian regulated price but at prices prevailing in the United States which were world prices. The price paid by Canadian refiners in Quebec and the Atlantic provinces for imported oil was brought down to the Canadian regulated price by a subsidy financed by an export charge on oil exported to the United States[255] and an excise tax on gasoline. From 1974 to 1979, the Canadian regulated price was increased semi-annually and, by 1978, was approaching world prices. However, with the doubling of world oil prices between 1979 and 1980, the difference between the Canadian price and the world price widened substantially.[256] During this period, the NEB altered its estimates of Canadian reserves and exports of light crude to the United States, which had dropped steadily from 1974, were all but eliminated.

In 1980, the Canadian federal government introduced its National Energy Policy ("NEP"), which consisted of a variety of conservation measures, taxes, price controls and Canadian ownership rules, as well as a reserved Crown interest in petroleum-producing properties and developed lands controlled by the federal government.[257] The NEP was the watershed of the Canadian nationalist approach to the energy sector. However, the NEP was based on projections of oil prices that never materialized. World oil prices fell and exports of crude oil to the United States resumed. With the election of the Mulroney government in 1984, the NEP was largely dismantled. Oil prices were deregulated by agreement with the producing provinces on March 28, 1985,[258] and the export charge was discontinued. Gas markets were effectively deregulated later that year[259] and a federal tax on exports of natural gas and gas liquids was discontinued.[260]

A prime U.S. objective in the FTA negotiations was to prevent a repetition of the two-price policy, the export charges and the disruption of supply that had occurred in the 1970s and early 1980s respecting oil. In this objective, they had powerful Canadian allies in the Canadian oil-producing provinces and the Canadian oil industry, who had bitterly opposed the Canadian regulated price and the NEP. The major provisions of the FTA affecting the trade in energy goods are directly responsive to these issues. These provisions are the prohibition of minimum export prices in FTA 902(2), the prohibition of discriminatory export charges in FTA 903 and the disciplines attached to the use of certain GATT exceptions in FTA 904. While these provisions repeat provisions of general application,[261] they were first negotiated in respect of energy goods, and the provisions of general application were modelled after them rather than the other way around.[262]

(3) Energy Goods and Mexican Attitudes

The most politically sensitive area of the Mexican economy is its energy sector, particularly hydrocarbons. As one Mexican commentator expressed it: "Energy derived from hydrocarbons is, without doubt, a subject that evokes singular interest within my country. Its fascination does not stop with legal aspects. Rather, it scans every aspect of society: politics, domestic and international economics, labor relations and sociology."[263]

Mexico has adopted a much more nationalistic approach to its energy sector than has Canada. The Canadian Constitution deals with energy only in the context of providing that natural resources within a province fall under provincial rather than federal ownership and control. In Mexico, exclusive public ownership and control of energy production and distribution is unequivocally mandated by Article 27 of the Mexican Constitution, which reads in part as follows:

> In the case of petroleum, and solid, liquid, or gaseous hydrocarbons or radioactive minerals, no concessions or contracts shall be granted nor may those that have been granted continue, and the nation shall carry out the exploitation of those products, in accordance with the provisions indicated in the respective regulatory law. It is exclusively the function of the nation to generate, conduct, transform, distribute, and supply electric power which is to be used for public service. No concessions for this purpose shall be granted to private persons and the nation shall make use of the property and the natural resources which are required for these ends.

> The use of nuclear fuels for the generation of nuclear energy and the regulation of its application to other purposes is also a function of the nation.

In the late nineteenth and early twentieth centuries, the Mexican government granted oil concessions to foreign companies. However, a nationalist approach to resource exploitation evolved during the Mexican Revolution and was reflected in the original version of Article 27 of the Mexican Constitution which came into effect on May 1, 1917. A series of disputes between the U.S. and Mexican governments followed the Revolution, as the Mexican government tried to assert what it viewed as being its constitutional rights over resources and the U.S. government tried to protect what it viewed as property rights of U.S. citizens.[264] This process culminated in the expropriation of the petroleum industry on March 18, 1938. The Mexican state acquired exclusive control over oil and gas exploration and production, other hydrocarbon development and basic petrochemical production, and created a government monopoly, Petroleos Mexicanos ("PEMEX"), to administer these activities. The commentator referred to above described the expropriation decree as "a transcendental act within the public life of my country".[265]

(4) NAFTA Provisions Respecting Energy Goods

NAFTA Chapter Six sets out NAFTA provisions respecting the trade in energy goods. As between Canada and the United States, NAFTA carries forward the FTA provisions respecting energy goods virtually in their entirety, with a single modification respecting energy regulatory measures. However, the FTA *status quo* has not been extended to Mexico. The Mexican negotiators were largely successful in exempting Mexico's energy sector from NAFTA obligations. The exemptions are reciprocal in that Canada and the United States need not meet NAFTA requirements vis à vis Mexican goods from which Mexico is exempt.

(5) Scope and Coverage of NAFTA Chapter Six

(a) Energy and basic petrochemicals

The FTA energy chapter covered "energy goods" which were comprised of: uranium ores and concentrates, natural uranium and uranium compounds (HS subheadings 2612.10 and 2844.10 to 2844.50); heavy water (HS heading 2845.10); coal, lignite, peat, coke, coal gas and tar (HS headings 27.01 to 27.06); pitch and pitch coke (HS heading 27.08); crude petroleum oils and other petroleum oils (HS subheadings 27.09 and 27.10); petroleum gases and other gaseous hydrocarbons (HS subheading 27.11); petroleum coke, petroleum bitumen and other residues (HS heading 27.13), bitumen and asphalt, oil shale, tar sands and bituminous mixtures (HS headings 27.14 and 27.15); and electricity (HS heading 27.16).

The NAFTA chapter covers "energy and basic petrochemical goods" which include almost all goods covered by the FTA energy chapter. They also include: aromatic hydrocarbon mixtures under HS subheading 2707.50; solvent naphtha, rubber extender oils and carbon black feedstocks under subheading 2707.99; petroleum jelly and various waxes under HS heading 2712; and acyclic hydrocarbons (respecting ethane, butanes, pentanes, hexanes and heptanes) under HS subheading 2901.10. A few goods covered by the FTA are not included in "energy and basic petrochemical goods".[266]

The inclusion of the additional petrochemical goods relates to the treatment of basic petrochemicals under Mexican law and has little practical effect as between Canada and the United States.[267] The expression "basic petrochemicals", which is used in a number of places in the NAFTA text without definition, is discussed in §7.10(1)(a).

(b) NAFTA Annex 602.3

NAFTA Annex 602.3 sets out reservations and special provisions affecting the energy and petrochemical sector that for the most part relate to Mexico's NAFTA obligations respecting services and investment. Paragraph 1 of NAFTA Annex 602.3, which prevails over all other NAFTA provisions, reserves most energy-related activities to the Mexican State and paragraph 2 relates to investment and the provision of services in respect of those activities. Paragraph 4, which applies to all three NAFTA countries, relates to performance requirements in service contracts negotiated by state enterprises. Paragraph 5, which relates only to Mexico, sets out rules respecting investment in electricity generation facilities. All these provisions are discussed in §7.10(1).

Only paragraph 3 of NAFTA Annex 602.3 applies to trade in goods. This provision requires each NAFTA country to permit end-users, suppliers, and state enterprises as required under domestic law, to negotiate supply contracts respecting natural gas and petrochemicals. These contracts are permitted to be subject to regulatory approval. This paragraph does not indicate whether or not regulatory approval must be administered in a manner consistent with NAFTA requirements. If a derogation from NAFTA obligations is intended by this paragraph, it is not clear what it is.

(6) Import and Export Restrictions, Export Taxes and Other Export Measures

With slight changes in wording, NAFTA 603, NAFTA 604 and NAFTA 605 repeat for energy goods and basic petrochemicals the provisions respecting import and export restrictions, export charges and other export measures set out in NAFTA 309, NAFTA 314 and NAFTA 315 respectively. NAFTA 603, NAFTA 604 and NAFTA 605 are based on FTA 902, FTA 903 and FTA 904 with slight wording changes.

(a) Import and export restrictions and export taxes

(i) Incorporation of GATT provisions

As discussed in §4.3(2), NAFTA 309(1) incorporates GATT Article XI and its interpretative notes. NAFTA 603(1) incorporates all the provisions of GATT respecting prohibitions or restrictions on the trade in energy goods and basic petrochemical goods. While this language incorporates a broader range of GATT provisions than NAFTA 309(1), it is unlikely that this makes any practical difference.

NAFTA 603(1) expressly excludes the protocols of provisional application to the GATT from this incorporating language.[268] This provision is relevant to Mexico. The *Protocol for the Accession of Mexico to the General Agreement on Tariffs and Trade* (the "Mexican Protocol") provides that Mexico will exercise its sovereignty over natural resources in accordance with its constitution. While NAFTA 603(1) excludes this Mexican Protocol provision from NAFTA, NAFTA 601(1) confirms full respect for the constitutions of the NAFTA countries and the reservations in NAFTA Annex 602.3 and the NAFTA Annexes discussed in §7.9 carry forward Mexico's constitutional rights. However, the Mexican Protocol also has the effect of expanding the natural resources exception in GATT Article XX(g) by permitting export restrictions to which this exception relates to be based on "social and development needs".[269] The effect of NAFTA 603(1) is to ensure that this provision of the Mexican Protocol does not apply among the NAFTA countries.

(ii) Minimum import and export prices and export charges

NAFTA 603(2) repeats the understanding in NAFTA 309(2), discussed in §4.3(3), that the GATT prohibits minimum import and export prices. Canadian academics disagree as to whether the provisions of the GATT actually have this effect.[270] However, the expression of the understanding in NAFTA puts the matter beyond dispute as among the NAFTA countries. This understanding has particular relevance to the energy sector because, as discussed above respecting past Canadian practices, energy administrators sometimes impose minimum export prices as a regulatory device to maximize the value earned from exploiting a scarce resource. This is particularly the case if the government mandates domestic prices that are below international prices and wishes to ensure that only domestic consumers benefit from the mandated domestic price. NAFTA 603(2) has the same effect as FTA 902(2) in precluding these practices.

NAFTA 604 repeats for energy and basic petrochemical goods the prohibition of discriminatory export charges set out for in NAFTA 314 and discussed in §4.4. As with the understanding respecting minimum export charges, the prohibition of discriminatory export charges has particular relevance to the energy sector. Export taxes may be ineffective policy instruments for export embargoes but they are very useful in maintaining two-price systems such as the Canadian system for oil between 1973 and 1985. If a government mandates domestic prices that are lower than international prices, producers must be prevented from selling into the international market. The government can prohibit or restrict exports, but the export restriction must be justified under a GATT exception. Alternatively, the government may remove the incentive to export by taxing away the price difference through an export charge that does not require justification under the GATT.

(iii) Trans-shipment, consultation, import and export licensing

NAFTA 603(3) repeats the trans-shipment rule in NAFTA 309(3) discussed in §4.3(4). Following the general requirement in NAFTA 309(4), NAFTA 603(4) requires that a NAFTA country maintaining import restrictions against energy and basic petrochemical goods from non-NAFTA countries must, upon request, consult with a view to avoiding disrupting arrangements in other NAFTA countries.

NAFTA 603(5) permits the NAFTA countries to administer import and export licensing systems for energy and basic petrochemical goods so long as they are operated consistently with NAFTA requirements. Mexico may restrict the granting of import and export licences respecting the energy and basic petrochemical goods identified in NAFTA Annex 603.6 for the sole purpose of reserving the foreign trade in these goods to itself.[271]

(iv) Application to Mexico

Other than the reservation respecting import and export licences just referred to, NAFTA 603 and NAFTA 604 apply to all three NAFTA countries, including Mexico.

(b) Other export measures

NAFTA 605 repeats for energy and basic petrochemical goods the three disciplines set out in NAFTA 315 applicable to the use of the GATT "critical shortages", "exhaustible natural resources", "government stabilization plans" and "products in short supply" exceptions. The disciplines are discussed in §4.3(6). As with NAFTA 315, the three disciplines do not apply to Mexico and Canada and the United States, while bound to each other, do not have to observe these disciplines in respect of Mexico. All three NAFTA countries continue to be bound by conditions attached by the GATT to the use of these exceptions. These conditions are discussed in §4.3(6)(a)(i).

(i) The three disciplines and the energy sector

While applicable to all goods, the NAFTA disciplines on export restrictions have particular relevance to energy and basic petrochemical goods and were directly responsive to U.S. concerns over security of supply. The Canadian oil policies described above are a case in point. From 1973 to 1980, exports of crude oil were significantly reduced without domestic cutbacks. Under the FTA and NAFTA, proportional domestic cutbacks would be required so that the proportion could be maintained. From 1973 to 1985, Canadian regulatory authorities imposed export prices that were higher than the Canadian regulated price. This practice would be prohibited under the FTA and NAFTA pricing discipline if it were tied to an export restriction that was justified under one of the GATT exceptions. If this were not the case, the practice would still be caught by the understanding respecting minimum export prices described above. In 1979 and 1980, the Canadian government virtually shut down exports of light crude to the United States but continued shipments of heavy crude. Under the FTA and NAFTA, this policy would be subject to the NAFTA discipline respecting disrupting normal channels of supply.

Of the three disciplines, the proportionality discipline has been of greatest concern to Canadians.[272] The proportion is based on shipments. The denominator of the proportion is "total supply", which is comprised of shipments to domestic and foreign users from domestic production, domestic inventory and from "other imports, as appropriate". The numerator of the proportion is "total export shipments", which is comprised of shipments to the other NAFTA country. The NAFTA proportionality requirement is breached only if the reduction in the proportion of total export shipments to total supply results from the imposition of an export restriction as opposed to the operation of market forces. Accordingly, the proportionality requirement merely assures a level of access but does not guarantee a level of supply. Export restrictions are clearly permitted so long as they remain within the parameters set by the proportionality requirement.

A supply crisis is more likely to occur with oil than with other energy goods because oil, unlike the others, is imported in significant quantities from off-shore into both the United States and Canada. The inclusion of imports in the calculation of the proportion could be important. If imported oil was still available in a shortages situation, Canada could reduce its exports from domestic reserves and maintain the proportion through increased imports so long as "normal channels of supply" were not disrupted. Canada's degree of flexibility in this situation would depend on the meaning of "other imports, as appropriate", about which there is much speculation but no hard experience. However, these considerations may be irrelevant in a shortages situation because of the pooling requirements of the IEP.

(ii) Proportionality and the IEP

As mentioned above, Canada and the United States are both parties to the IEP, but Mexico is not. NAFTA Annex 608.2 provides that, as between Canada and the United States, the IEP prevails over NAFTA to the extent of any inconsistency between them.[273]

The IEP was established by a number of OECD countries as a direct result of the world oil crisis in 1973-74. The IEP applies only to oil and not to other forms of energy. The IEP requires countries that are net oil importers to establish strategic reserves of crude oil sufficient to cover ninety days' worth of imports.[274] Canada has been exempted from this obligation in recent years because it has been a net exporter of oil.[275] In the event of a disruption of supply, each country is required to reduce domestic consumption. A disruption of supply occurs when imports available to any country or all countries as a whole fall by 7% or more. The occurrence of a disruption triggers an oil pooling and sharing mechanism, under which each country is assigned a "supply right" for each month of the disruption. Each country then is assigned an "import right", comprised of the difference between a country's supply right and its available supply of oil from domestic production and net imports. A negative import right becomes an export obligation to the other IEP countries. The administration of these arrangements is entrusted to the International Energy Agency ("IEA").

The IEP pooling arrangements have never been invoked, so the extent of the obligations under the IEP is a matter of conjecture. One commentator who has made an extensive review of the available literature concludes that there is a divergence of views as to whether Canada would have export obligations or import rights in the event of a disruption, with "conventional wisdom" supporting the former and several studies suggesting that the latter could occur in some instances.[276] Canadian supporters of the FTA and NAFTA countered critics of the proportionality requirement with the argument that Canada was already bound to sharing arrangements under the IEP. Obviously this argument applies only to oil and not to other energy goods.

The IEP obligations are difficult to compare with those under NAFTA because they are structured differently. On the one hand, IEP obligations do not apply to production sources shut in before the pooling mechanism is triggered.[277] On the other hand, the occurrence of a disruption under the IEP triggers an express obligation to reduce consumption together with a possible export obligation, while the NAFTA operates by restraining government action and relying on market forces to distribute scarce oil supplies between Canada and the United States. While it is not possible to say with any certainty that the IEP obligations are more or less onerous than those of NAFTA, the fact that Canada and the United States were already bound by a sharing arrangement for oil significantly reduces the relative impact of the NAFTA proportionality obligation.

Several commentators have observed that unlike the FTA the IEP does not contain any sanctions for its enforcement.[278] This seems a meaningless distinction because reneging on international obligations is generally an unacceptable course of action because it is open to aggrieved parties to retaliate regardless of what the agreement says.

(iii) Electricity and GATT

While the NAFTA provisions respecting energy and basic petrochemical goods clearly apply to electricity, the disciplines in NAFTA 604 relate to restrictions justified under exceptions to GATT obligations. It would not be necessary to justify a restriction of electricity exports under a GATT exception if GATT obligations do not apply to electricity. Following this logic, since the disciplines apply only to restrictions justified under the exceptions, the disciplines do not apply to electricity. This is clearly contrary to the intent of the NAFTA countries and that fact coupled with the treatment of electricity elsewhere in NAFTA as a good rather than a service should prevent a panel from arriving at this result. The "exhaustible natural resources" exception would not be available as cover for restrictions on electricity exports because if electricity is a good, it is clearly not a "natural resource".

Trade issues respecting electricity between Canada and the United States are as likely to arise on the import side as the export side. Some U.S. electric utilities view Canadian electricity produced by provincially owned competitors as dumped or subsidized. Also, U.S. environmental opposition to the second phase of the Hydro Quebec-James Bay project will likely continue and could adversely affect imports of Canadian electricity.

(7) Market Access, National Security and Regulatory Measures

The United States is an important market for Canadian energy goods. While Canadian nationalists have been concerned with the effect of the FTA and NAFTA on Canada's ability to control its energy resources, Canada's oil and gas sector has been more interested in maintaining secure access to the U.S. market for Canadian energy goods. Tariff elimination is not an important factor respecting market access for energy goods as U.S. tariffs are low or non-existent. Market access concerns for Canadian energy goods have arisen from the expansive interpretation by some U.S. administrations of the national security exception in GATT Article XXI and from the actions taken from time to time by U.S. regulatory authorities.

(a) National security

As discussed in §10.2, GATT Article XXI sets out exceptions to GATT obligations for reasons related to national security. This exception is carried forward in NAFTA 2102. Some of the language in GATT Article XXI is capable of being broadly construed and has been used by the United States to justify oil import quotas[279] and other restrictive policies.[280] The oil import quotas, from which Canada was exempt, were maintained from the 1950s to the early 1970s. Like its predecessor in FTA 907, NAFTA 607 limits the scope of the national energy exception in its application to energy goods to purely military situations and to matters relating to the non-proliferation of nuclear weapons. Mexico is neither bound by NAFTA 607 nor entitled to its benefits.

(b) Regulatory measures

The other Canadian concern respecting access to the U.S. markets arises from the powers and actions of U.S energy authorities. Federal U.S. authority for energy matters in the United States is divided between the Federal Energy Regulatory Commission ("FERC") and the Economic Regulatory Administration ("ERA"). These authorities exercise considerable control over imports of energy goods such as natural gas. There are also authorities at the state level with the power to interfere in contracts relating to the sale and distribution of energy goods.

Shortly before the FTA was negotiated, the FERC issued Opinion 256 which allowed the reasonableness of charges billed by exporters of Canadian natural gas to be questioned and disallowed if found to be inconsistent with FERC rate-making principles. As these charges are approved by the NEB, the Canadian government regarded Opinion 256 as objectionable as departing from usual U.S. practice of deferring to Canadian regulatory practice.[281]

FTA 905 addressed issues arising from the actions of regulatory authorities. FTA 905(1) required consultations if one of Canada or the United States considered that the regulatory actions of the FERC, the ERA or the NEB would discriminate against its energy goods. This provision was criticized in Canada as ineffective because it provides only for consultations and was not responsive to the Opinion 256 situation, where the issue did not involve discrimination but, rather, the application by the FERC of its standards in a way that could affect Canadian energy policy.[282] FTA 905(1) has not been carried forward into NAFTA.

NAFTA 606 covers energy regulatory measures. Energy regulatory measures are broadly defined to include any measure by a federal or sub-federal entity that directly affects the transportation, transmission, distribution, purchase and sale of an energy or basic petrochemical good. NAFTA 606(1) confirms that energy regulatory measures are subject to the NAFTA requirements respecting national treatment requirements, import and export restrictions and export taxes. NAFTA 606(2) requires the federal government of each NAFTA country to seek to ensure that in applying energy regulatory measures, regulatory bodies avoid disrupting contractual relationships as much as possible. The expression "seek" means "to try to bring about or effect", and is used a number times in NAFTA to soften the obligation imposed by NAFTA 105 on each federal government to ensure that provincial and state governments observe NAFTA provisions. As noted in §6.6(2), "seek" has been interpreted as imposing a "best efforts" obligation.

NAFTA 606(2) is responsive to a dispute between Alberta natural gas exporters and the California Public Utilities Commission ("CPUC") that arose when NAFTA was being negotiated and underscored weaknesses in the FTA. The CPUC was attempting to alter contracts between these producers and California gas utilities. NAFTA 606(2) obliges the U.S. government to try to ensure that the CPUC not disrupt these contractual relationships. However, the CPUC is controlled by the state of California and not by the U.S. federal government, and the "seek to ensure" language means that unless the actions of the CPUC amounted to a failure to accord national treatment so that NAFTA 606(1) applies, there is no recourse under NAFTA if the U.S. government fails in its efforts to prevent the CPUC from disrupting these contractual relationships.[283] The obligation of the U.S. government imposed by NAFTA 606(2) is much stronger in respect of actions taken by the FERC or the ERA that disrupt contractual relationships because these are federal entities.

NAFTA 606 binds all three NAFTA countries, including Mexico.

(8) Existing and Future Incentives

NAFTA 608, like its predecessor in FTA 906, expressly allows existing or future incentives for oil and gas exploration, development and related activities in order to maintain reserve bases. Neither the FTA nor NAFTA prohibit subsidies other than export subsidies on agricultural goods, and paragraph 8(b) of GATT Article III, which is incorporated into NAFTA by NAFTA 301, clearly permits subsidies paid exclusively to domestic producers. Expressly allowing what is not disallowed seems unnecessary and can be misinterpreted.[284] While it is arguable that NAFTA 608 creates an exception to countervailing duty laws, it is unlikely that this result was intended. The right to impose countervailing duties does not depend on whether or not a subsidy is "allowed".[285]

(9) Incorporation of FTA Provisions

Paragraph 1 of NAFTA Annex 608.2 incorporates FTA Annexes 902.5 and 905.2 into NAFTA as between Canada and the United States. Mexico is not affected by these provisions.

(a) FTA Annex 902.5

Paragraphs 1 and 2 of FTA Annex 902.5 apply to uranium. Canada agreed to permit uranium to be exported to the United States rather than being upgraded domestically.[286] The United States exempted Canada from its restrictions on the enrichment of foreign uranium. Paragraph 3 of FTA Annex 902.5 exempts Canada from a U.S. embargo on the exportation of Alaskan oil, up to a maximum of 50,000 barrels a day. The oil must be shipped to Canada from the lower forty-eight states rather than directly from Alaska.

(b) FTA Annex 905.2

Paragraph 1 of FTA Annex 905.2 required Canada to eliminate the NEB's "least cost alternative test" in issuing permits for the export of energy goods to the United States. Under this requirement, an export price could not result in a cost in the U.S. market which was materially less than the cost of alternative energy from indigenous sources. The other two NEB requirements, namely, that an export price should recover its appropriate share of costs incurred and, under normal conditions, not be less than the price to Canadians for similar deliveries in the same area, were not mentioned in the FTA. One commentator has observed that these requirements can be interpreted as minimum export price requirements that are inconsistent with minimum export price prohibitions.[287]

Paragraphs 2, 3 and 5 of FTA Annex 905.2 relate specifically to issues between the Bonneville Power Authority and British Columbia Hydro. The Bonneville Power Authority is British Columbia Hydro's principal competitor in California and controls the transmission lines that grant access to that market. FTA Annex 905.2 requires the Bonneville Power Authority to grant British Columbia Hydro as favourable treatment as other utilities located outside the Pacific Northwest.

Paragraph 4 of FTA Annex 905.2 requires that "surplus tests" on the export of energy goods be administered in a manner consistent with FTA 902, FTA 903 and FTA 904. Under a "surplus test", only exports that are surplus to domestic needs are permitted. As to whether a "surplus test" requirement is consistent with the GATT depends upon its falling within GATT exceptions such as those for "exhaustible natural resources" or "products in short supply". Under NAFTA, these requirements may be applied, but only in a manner that is consistent with the rules governing export restrictions described above.

(10) Concluding Remarks

As between Canada and the United States, NAFTA continues the FTA *status quo* in the trade of energy goods between them. The effect of the market-oriented FTA and NAFTA provisions has yet to be tested because there has been little disruption of energy supplies since the FTA became effective. The real test of these provisions will take place at such time as an energy crisis does occur.

Mexico has opted out of most of the provisions of the NAFTA chapter on energy goods, and has surrendered the benefits of these provisions in exchange for not being bound by their requirements. Mexico has preserved the right to continue its nationalistic policies with respect to its energy sector. Having regard to Mexico's need for capital and desire for economic expansion, the degree to which Mexico exercises this right remains to be seen.

5.5 WINE, BEER AND DISTILLED SPIRITS

Most countries control the distribution and consumption of alcoholic beverages because excessive consumption of alcohol is a major cause of death and disease. As an Advisory Committee on Liquor Regulation reported to the government of Ontario in 1987:

> In an ideal society, there would be no need for regulation of the manufacture, sale and service of alcoholic beverages. If alcohol were a consumer commodity like soup, special regulations would be unnecessary. However, we live in an imperfect world and we must recognize that alcohol is not an ordinary substance. The fact that it is an enjoyable commodity does not obviate its potentially destructive consequences for individuals and society in general.[288]

However, controls often serve a secondary purpose of protecting domestic producers from foreign competition and, as such, provide fertile ground for trade disputes. This has been particularly the case between Canada and the United States, and discriminatory practices have been followed on both sides of the border. The FTA and NAFTA provisions covering alcoholic beverages reflect a resolution of disputes over the practices of Canada's provincial liquor monopolies respecting wine and distilled spirits. Canadian complaints over U.S. practices and U.S. complaints over the practices of

Canadian liquor monopolies respecting beer have been dealt with through the GATT rather than the FTA or NAFTA.

(1) Discriminatory Practices

(a) Canada

In the early years of Confederation, the Canadian federal government made various legislative attempts to control the distribution of alcoholic beverages. These were frustrated by adverse constitutional decisions, and in 1928 the federal government passed responsibility for alcoholic beverages to the provinces by enacting the *Importation of Intoxicating Liquors Act*.[289] Under this legislation, a province may establish an agency with the exclusive authority to import alcoholic beverages into the province from anywhere, including another province.

During the 1920s and early 1930s, both the U.S. federal government and the Canadian provincial governments prohibited the trade in alcoholic beverages. As prohibition ended, trade in alcoholic beverages resumed under strict regulation.[290] Every province established a monopoly to import and distribute these products, and the distribution of alcoholic beverages in Canada continues to be dominated by these provincial monopolies.

Provincial governments pursue a variety of objectives through their liquor monopolies. Their original purpose was to control access to alcoholic beverages and curb excessive consumption. However, they have become significant revenue sources, and entities such as the Liquor Control Board of Ontario ("LCBO") are major customers for beverage alcohol producers all over the world. Provincial governments have also used their monopolies as vehicles for protecting Canadian producers of wine, spirits and beer through discriminatory mark-ups and listing practices and discriminatory practices respecting points of sale.

(i) Mark-ups

Each provincial monopoly purchases alcoholic beverages and sells them at a profit. The retail price established by monopoly is equal to the base price plus a mark-up. The mark-up is the percentage increase over a base price, which is the invoice price plus freight to a pre-set destination plus federal charges such as customs duties and excise taxes.[291] Historically, the provincial monopolies have applied higher mark-ups to imported products than to domestic products.

(ii) Listings

If a supplier of alcoholic beverages wishes to sell its products through a provincial monopoly, it must obtain a listing. A listing is a decision by a provincial monopoly that a product may be sold in its outlets.[292] A listing request is assessed on a number of criteria (quality, price, marketability, etc.) and may be granted subject to conditions (such as minimum sales quotas and packaging requirements). Provincial monopolies historically have made listings for imported products more difficult to obtain than for domestic products.[293] Without a listing, an alcoholic beverage cannot be sold in a province.

(iii) Points of sale

In some provinces, domestic products receive more favourable treatment than imported products in points of sale. For example, until recently in Ontario, beer brewed in the province could be purchased in LCBO outlets or outlets of Brewers' Retail Inc., a retail monopoly owned by the major breweries in the province, but imported beer was available only in the LCBO outlets. Domestic wineries may sell their wine either through the LCBO outlets or their own stores, but imported wine is available only in LCBO outlets.

(iv) Other practices

Other practices complained of have included restrictions on private delivery of imported products to points of sale, minimum price requirements, discriminatory packaging requirements and discriminatory application of deposit/return systems.[294]

(b) The United States

The regulation of the distribution of alcoholic beverages in the United States occurs primarily at the state level. While the private sector has a much greater role in the distribution of alcoholic beverages in the United States than in Canada, some states maintain government liquor monopolies. Like the Canadian provinces, U.S. states view beverage alcohol as a revenue source and levy a variety of excise and other taxes. Some states have local option requirements, under which political subdivisions within the state can apply prohibition laws.

Canadian producers have complained of a number of requirements in effect in some states that discriminate against imported products. These include: discriminatory rates of excise taxes and tax credits; requirements that imported beer and wine be sold through wholesalers while exempting local producers from such requirements; price affirmation requirements setting maximum prices at which imported beer and wine can be sold to wholesalers that do not apply to local producers; requirements that imported beer and wine be transported by common carriers while exempting local producers from such requirements; discriminatory licensing fees; listing and delisting practices followed by some state liquor monopolies; and discriminatory application of local option laws.[295]

(2) The Provincial Liquor Monopolies and the GATT

Practices followed by the Canadian provincial liquor monopolies have conflicted with Canada's GATT obligations. Although U.S. producers have long complained of these practices, they first came to a head as a result of actions taken by the EC. The EC negotiators met with their Canadian counterparts during the Tokyo Round of GATT negotiations. However, the only result was a non-binding Provincial Statement of Intentions with Respect to Sales of Alcoholic Beverages by Provincial Marketing Agencies ("Provincial Statement") with the EC.[296] The Provincial Statement provided that mark-up differentials would reflect "normal commercial considerations" and would not increase beyond current levels and made some general statements respecting listing policy and application of standards.

In 1984, the EC requested consultations with Canada over the practices of the provincial liquor monopolies respecting beer, wine and distilled spirits. When no resolution was reached, a GATT panel was requested, and the report of the panel was adopted on March 22, 1988. The United States made submissions before the panel in support of the EC position. The panel's report focussed on mark-ups, listing and points of sale. The panel held that the discriminatory mark-ups were contrary to GATT Article II because Canada was bound to maximum tariffs for these products and the mark-up differentials, when added to Canadian tariffs, exceeded the bound levels in Canada's GATT schedule. The listing and delisting practices were found to be restrictions under GATT Article XI:1.[297]

Following the adoption of the panel report, Canada and the EC negotiated the *Agreement between Canada and the European Economic Community concerning Trade and Commerce in Alcoholic Beverages* (the "EC Alcoholic Beverages Agreement"). Under this agreement, mark-up differentials in Ontario, British Columbia and Nova Scotia between EC wine and 100% Canadian wine were to be phased out by 1998. Other discriminatory mark-ups were to be phased out by 1995. Discriminatory mark-ups on beer were not to be increased above the levels that existed on December 1, 1988. Canada agreed to accord national treatment in the listing and delisting of beer and wine. Canada undertook to accord national treatment in the distribution of wine, with the permitted exception of the private wine store outlets of Canadian wineries in Ontario and of Quebec regulations requiring that wine sold in grocery stores be bottled in Quebec.

(3) Provisions of the FTA

The FTA was negotiated at the time that the EC GATT case was being heard by the panel but before the decision was adopted and before the EC

Alcoholic Beverages Agreement was concluded.[298] The FTA addressed the same issues that were brought by the EC before the GATT panel.

(a) Wine and distilled spirits

FTA Chapter Eight covered wine and distilled spirits. FTA 801 permitted non-conforming measures existing on October 4, 1987,[299] to be maintained provided that they were not made more non-conforming and that the additional requirements of Chapter Eight were satisfied. FTA 802 required that listing practices conform with the national treatment obligations of FTA Chapter Five (which incorporates GATT Article III) and sets out a number of specific requirements relating to such matters as transparency and appeal procedures. There is an exception for automatic listing procedures in British Columbia for estate wineries producing less than 30,000 gallons annually. FTA 803 required that discriminatory mark-ups on distilled spirits be eliminated immediately and that mark-up differentials on wine be phased out by January 1, 1995, in all provinces. Like the EC Alcoholic Beverages Agreement, FTA 804 required that national treatment apply to distribution, with slight differences in the exceptions. The exception for on-premises sales includes distilled spirits. The exception for private wine stores includes British Columbia and applies to measures existing on October 4, 1987. FTA 805 required Canada to eliminate blending requirements for bulk imports of distilled spirits from the United States. Under FTA 806, Canada agreed to prohibit the sale of any product described as "Bourbon Whiskey" unless the product had been produced in the United States in accordance with its prescribed standards. The United States entered into a similar agreement respecting "Canadian Whiskey". FTA 807 reserves GATT rights, but these are subject to FTA Chapter Eight.

(b) Beer

FTA 1204 provided that the national treatment obligations in FTA Chapter Five not apply to measures related to the internal sale and distribution of beer and malt-containing beverages existing on October 4, 1987, provided that they were not made more non-conforming. FTA 1205 set out an unqualified reservation of GATT rights. Given that the GATT panel in the EC case based its findings on GATT Articles II and XI rather than on the national treatment obligations set out in GATT Article III, the FTA beer provision represented nothing more than a temporary truce in the Canada-U.S. beer wars.

(4) GATT Actions Following the FTA

In 1989, the Province of Ontario introduced minimum cost-of-service and profit charges which resulted in price increases of a number of lower priced imported beers.[300] In 1990, at the instigation of several U.S. breweries, the United States commenced consultations with Canada under the GATT over the practices of the provincial liquor monopolies respecting the sale and distribution of beer. The consultations failed to produce a resolution and a panel was requested. The panel report, which was adopted on February 18, 1992, reiterated the findings of the 1988 panel and found against Canada on a number of additional grounds. For example, Ontario's requirement that imported beer could only be sold in six packs was found to be contrary to GATT Article III:4. Restrictions on private delivery of imported beer in most Canadian provinces and minimum price requirements based on the prices of competing domestic products were also found to be inconsistent with GATT Article III:4 as denying "competitive opportunities" to the imported products.[301]

Canada initiated its own GATT complaint against the practices of U.S. states referred to above. The panel report was adopted on June 19, 1992, and decided in Canada's favour. All the practices referred to in §5.5(1)(b) were held to violate GATT Article III.[302]

(5) Provisions of NAFTA

(a) Wine and distilled spirits

NAFTA sets out two separate bilateral arrangements respecting wine and distilled spirits. The bilateral arrangement between Canada and the United States is comprised of FTA Chapter Eight, which has been incorporate into NAFTA. A bilateral arrangement between Canada and Mexico is set out in NAFTA Annex 312.2. There is no special bilateral arrangement between the United States and Mexico, and the trade in wine and distilled spirits between them is governed by NAFTA rules of general application.

The bilateral arrangement between Canada and Mexico is structured in a manner similar to FTA Chapter Eight. There are similar grandfathering and listing provisions, including the exception for the B.C. estate wineries, as those in the FTA. Section 4(b) of NAFTA Annex 312.2 incorporates the timetables for phasing out discriminatory mark-ups on wine set out in the EC Alcoholic Beverages Agreement, which for wine sold in Ontario, British Columbia and Nova Scotia are less favourable than under the FTA. Discriminatory mark-ups on distilled spirits are eliminated upon NAFTA becoming effective. National treatment is to be accorded in respect of distribution, subject to the exceptions for on-premises sales, private wine stores in Ontario and British Columbia, and the Quebec bottling requirement described above.

(b) Distinctive products

NAFTA Annex 313 requires that Canada and Mexico not permit the sale of any product as "Bourbon Whiskey" or "Tennessee Whiskey" unless manufactured in the United States in accordance with U.S. regulations. The

United States and Mexico will not permit the sale of any product as "Canadian Whisky" unless manufactured in Canada in accordance with Canadian regulations. Canada and the United States shall not permit the sale of any product as "Tequila" or "Mezcal" unless manufactured in Mexico in accordance with Mexican regulations.

(c) Beer

Negotiations took place between Canada and the United States following the GATT beer decision and continued after NAFTA was signed. The negotiations were complicated by an environmental levy on beer cans introduced by Ontario, which the United States viewed as discriminatory because most U.S. beer is sold in cans while most Canadian beer is sold in bottles. When negotiations failed to produce a resolution, the United States imposed a 50% duty on Ontario-brewed beer,[303] and the Canadian government reciprocated. The dispute was ultimately resolved by an agreement signed in August, 1993. Ontario retained its environmental levy, but dropped its minimum prices, lowered its fees and agreed to permit U.S. brewed beer to be sold in the Brewers' Retail outlets. The provinces have also agreed not to introduce new discriminatory measures.[304]

NAFTA does not contain any special provisions respecting beer or malt-containing beverages. There is no equivalent in NAFTA to FTA 1204. As evident from the incorporation into NAFTA of FTA 710 discussed in §5.3(5)(b), these products are subject to GATT rules of general application.

(6) Concluding Remarks

The trade in alcoholic beverages presents particularly difficult issues in trade law because of the unique nature of the product and the legitimate public policy objective in minimizing its abuse. The sale and distribution of these products will always be subject to a greater degree of regulation than other products, and regulators will continue from time to time to cross the line from protecting the public interest to discriminating against imported products. The three GATT decisions which have been described above and which have all been adopted after the FTA was originally negotiated provide a much clearer picture than existed previously of where that line is.

ENDNOTES

[1] For a more detailed discussion by the author, see Jon R. Johnson, "NAFTA and the Trade in Automotive Goods" in *Assessing NAFTA: A Trinational Analysis*, Steven Globerman and Michael Walker, eds. (Vancouver, The Fraser Institute, 1993), p. 87.

[2] The full name of the Auto Pact is the *Agreement Concerning Automotive Products between the Government of Canada and the Government of the United States*.

[3] Not quite anywhere. Under the *Motor Vehicles Tariff Order, 1988*, SOR/88-71, which covers the assemblers producing in Canada during the Auto Pact base year, the countries from which duty-free importations may be made are those entitled to the benefit of Canada's MFN Tariff. This includes most countries in the world. Tires and tubes are excluded.

[4] For a good summary of the Mexican Automotive Decrees of 1962, 1972, 1977, 1983 and 1989 (the current Automotive Decree), see Gary C. Hufbrauer and Jeffrey J. Schott, *North American Free Trade — Issues and Recommendations* (Washington, D.C., Institute for International Economics, 1992), pp. 215-19.

[5] The full name is the *Decree for Development and Modernization of the Automotive Industry* ("Decreto para el Fomento y Modernización de la Industria Automotriz") (December 11, 1989). See NAFTA Annex 300-A.2, para. 1.

[6] Gross vehicular weight exceeding 8,864 kilograms. See Article 2:IV of the Automotive Decree for the classes of vehicles covered.

[7] The full name of which is the *Decree for Development and Modernization of the Autotransportation Vehicle Manufacturing Industry* ("Decreto para el Fomento y Modernización de la Industria Manufacturera de Vehiculos de Autotransporte"). See NAFTA Annex 300-A.2, para. 20.

[8] The calculation of CVA under Canada's Auto Pact duty remission orders is not comparable to the calculation of national value added under the Automotive Decree. In calculating CVA, only the cost of imported components count as foreign and virtually all other costs count as domestic. Under the Automotive Decree, only the domestic content of parts supplied by auto parts industry and national suppliers and of parts exported by these suppliers where the exportation has been promoted by the assembler count as domestic.

[9] See Hufbrauer and Schott, *op. cit.*, note 4, at p. 218. Prior to NAFTA becoming effective, a Mexican auto parts firm had to be at least 60% Mexican-owned. NAFTA Annex I — Mexico, p. I-M-33, reduced this restriction to 51% Mexican ownership immediately upon NAFTA becoming effective.

[10] See Hufbrauer and Schott, *ibid.*

[11] The formula is set forth in rule 9 of the Acuerdo que Determina Reglas para la Aplicación para el Fomento y Modernización de la Industria Automotriz (the "Auto Decree Implementing Regulations").

[12] The formula is set forth in rule 8 of the Auto Decree Implementing Regulations.

[13] But for NAFTA, the ratio of 1.75:1 would have come into effect at the beginning of 1994 and replaced a 2:1 ratio which applied in 1993.

[14] See Hufbrauer and Schott, *op. cit.*, note 4, at p. 219. See the definition of "auto transportation vehicle" in NAFTA Appendix 300-A.2, para. 27 for a precise description of the vehicles covered.

[15] These figures are taken from *Imports by Commodity for 1992* and *Exports by Commodity for 1992* published by Statistics Canada.

[16] The parts are those listed in Code 9450 in Schedule I to the *Motor Vehicles Tariff Order, 1988*, SOR/88-71.

[17] Comprised of one concrete mixer under HS subheading 8705.40 for $145,000 and one truck with a g.v.w. of less than 5 tonnes under HS subheading 8704.31 for $31,000.

[18] See NAFTA 304. See also FTA 405, which is incorporated by reference by NAFTA Annex 304.2(c) to apply as between Canada and the United States as regards measures predating the NAFTA entering into force.

[19] As discussed above, engines are a significant exception.

[20] These figures are taken from *Imports by Commodity for 1992* published by Statistics Canada, and are comprised of vehicles classified under HS headings 87.01 to 8706, together with all articles listed in Code 9450 in Schedule I to the *Motor Vehicles Tariff Order, 1988*, SOR/88-71.

[21] Only Ford achieved the required percentage in the 1992 model year. The percentage which this relieving provision permits an assembler to use is calculated on a basis which includes purchases from independent maquiladoras. Under the current Automotive Decree, these are excluded but, as indicated below, under the NAFTA rules these will be included.

[22] NAFTA Appendix 300-A.2, para. 5.

[23] See NAFTA Appendix 300-A.2, para. 8. "Base value" is defined in NAFTA Appendix

219

300-A.2, para. 27. The prescribed percentage is 65% for 1994-97, 60% for 1998-2000, and 50% for 2001-03.

[24] New assemblers being assemblers beginning production of vehicles after the model year 1991. See NAFTA Appendix 300-A.2, para. 5.

[25] The percentages are: 80% for 1994, 77.2% for 1995, 74.4% for 1996, 71.6% for 1997, 68.9% for 1998, 66.1% for 1999, 63.3% for 2000, 60.5% for 2001, 57.7% for 2002 and 55.0% for 2003.

[26] 1,000 is 66.1% of 1,513.

[27] NAFTA Appendix 300-A.2, para. 14.

[28] In 2003, the last year of the transition period, the applicable percentage is 55% (or 0.55) and the ability to import new vehicles will have increased by 318% over what would have been the case if 1.75 had been used.

[29] NAFTA Appendix 300-A.2, para. 15. For example, in 2002 the applicable percentage is 30%. If the assembler was using its reference value as the basis for its calculation, the negative adjustment would be equal to the reference value minus (VANp/0.30).

[30] NAFTA Annex I—Mexico, p. I-M-31.

[31] See NAFTA Appendix 300-A.2, para. 22. Note that the imported vehicles must be originating.

[32] See clause (c) of the definition of "manufacturer of autotransportation vehicles" in NAFTA Appendix 300-A.2, para. 27 for this requirement.

[33] NAFTA Appendix 300-A.2, para. 23.

[34] In the Automotive Decree Implementing regulations, the negative adjustment to the extended trade balance for failing to meet the content requirement is referred to as "Y". If "Y" exceeds the assembler's trade balance "S", or if "Y" results in the extended trade balance becoming negative, rule 28 requires that the assembler pay a penalty equal to 50% of the excess or the deficit.

[35] See 40 CFR Ch.I (7-1-89 Edition), Section 600.511-80.

[36] See NAFTA Appendix 300-A.3, para. 2(d). The expressions "manufacturer", "automobile" and "model year" all have the meanings attributed to them in the *Energy Policy and Conservation Act of 1975*, 42 U.S.C. §6201 *et seq.* See NAFTA Appendix 300-A.3, para. 6.

[37] This is the combined effect of NAFTA Appendix 300-A.3, paras. 2(c), 2(b).

[38] One thousand kilometres if the vehicle has a gross vehicle weight of less than five metric tons; otherwise 5,000 kilometres. See the definition of "used vehicle" in NAFTA Annex 300-A, para. 4.

[39] See para. 5 of NAFTA Appendix 300-A.1 in Canada's case and para. 25(b) of NAFTA Appendix 300-A.2 in Mexico's case. Specific reference is made to NAFTA Annex I which, in Mexico's case, includes liberalization commitments. These are discussed in §7.10(2)(b).

[40] However, a distinction is made for rules of origin purposes in that tracing does not apply to aftermarket parts. See §3.1(12)(c)(v) and §3.1(12)(d)(v).

[41] These figures are taken from *Imports by Commodity for 1992* and *Exports by Commodity for 1992* published by Statistics Canada.

[42] The parts are those listed in Code 9450 in Schedule I to the *Motor Vehicles Tariff Order, 1988*, SOR/88-71.

[43] Total imports of vehicles from all sources in 1992 was $14,636,781,000, as compared to total exports in the same period of $27,785,615,000. Exports to countries other than the United States amounted to only $225,332,000, slightly less than 1% of the total.

[44] This expression is defined in NAFTA Annex 300-B, Section 10, and is discussed in §5.2(3)(c).

[45] The list in Appendix 1.1 corresponds to the products listed in the Annex to the Agreement on Textiles and Clothing that has been negotiated under the Uruguay Round. This agreement is discussed in §5.2(3)(c).

[46] Plastics, footwear and watchstraps, bands and bracelets are subject to mandatory required value content requirements. With footwear, the net cost method must be used. Wadding, gauze and bandages and seat belts for motor vehicles are subject to a value content requirement in one of the two rules for establishing origin. The other is based on a tariff shift alone.

[47] One exception is the *de minimis* rule in NAFTA 405(6), which applies to goods under HS chapters 50 to 63 and provides that the 7% *de minimis* rule be determined on the basis of weight rather than value. See §3.1(2)(j)(i).

[48] The required tariff shift for visible lining fabrics for apparel goods falling under each of HS chapters 61 and 62 is set forth in a note at the beginning of the chapter.

[49] See the Note in NAFTA Annex 401, Section B, Section XI, Chapter 62, 6205.20—6205.30.

[50] NAFTA Annex 300-B, Appendix 6, Part A, para. (b).

[51] Canadian tariff item 5407.60.10; U.S. tariff items 5407.60.05A, 5407.60.10A and 5407.60.20A; Mexican tariff item 5407.60.02.

[52] NAFTA Annex 300-B, Appendix 6, P.A, para. (a).

[53] For transmission or conveyor belts, flax yarns or fabrics can be non-originating.

[54] This result follows from NAFTA 404, in any event. It was hardly necessary to state it in Section 2(2)(a).

[55] The rule that would apply is that for goods under headings 62.06 through 62.11.

[56] FTA Annex 301.2, Rules, Section XI, Rule 17.

[57] Eric Barry and Elizabeth Siwicki, "NAFTA: The Textile and Apparel Sector" in *Assessing NAFTA: A Trinational Analysis*, Steven Globerman and Michael Walker, eds. (Vancouver, The Fraser Institute, 1993), p. 135, Table 3.

[58] *Ibid.*

[59] The TPL categories are "cotton or man-made fibre apparel" and "wool apparel". The NAFTA "cotton or man-made fabric" corresponds for practical purposes to the FTA "non-wool apparel" because linen apparel made from imported fabric is originating and yarns and fabrics of other vegetable fibres are not generally used to make apparel goods.

[60] NAFTA Annex 300-B, Schedule 6.B.1.

[61] The FTA TRQ of 41,806,500 SME has been increased by 18,193,500 SME to 60,000,000 SME, an increase of 43.52%.

[62] NAFTA Annex 300-B, Schedule 6.B.1.

[63] HS chapters 52-55, 58, 60 and 63. See FTA Annex 301.2 Rules, Section XI, Rule 18.

[64] Barry and Siwicki, *op. cit.*, note 57, p. 135, Table 3.

[65] Set out in HS subheading 9404.90.

[66] These categories are identified by HS subheadings in NAFTA, Annex 300-B, Appendix 6, Part B, para. 4(a).

[67] NAFTA Annex 300-B, Appendix 6, Schedule 6.B.2.

[68] NAFTA Annex 300-B, Appendix 6, Part B, para. 4(b).

[69] NAFTA Annex 300-B, Appendix 6, Part B, para. 5.

[70] This disregards the limitations on the use of the TPL resulting from the sublevels.

[71] This calculation has been done as follows: If utilization in 1989 was 79% with a TRQ of 25,083,900 SME, 19,816,281 SME must have been exported. If the TRQ had been the NAFTA TPL of 65,000,000 SME, the utilization percentage based on exports of 19,816,281 SME would have been 30.49%. The percentages for 1990 and 1991 are calculated the same way. The split of the NAFTA TPL into sublevels is ignored.

[72] NAFTA Annex 300-B, Appendix 6, Part B, para. 6(a).

[73] NAFTA Annex 300-B, Appendix 6, Schedule 6.B.3.

[74] NAFTA Annex 300-B, Appendix 6, Part B, para. 6(b).

[75] NAFTA Annex 300-B, Appendix 6, Part B, para. 2.

[76] William R. Cline, *The Future of World Trade in Textiles and Apparel*, rev. ed. (Washington, D.C., Institute for International Economics, 1990), at p. 1.

[77] *Ibid.*, at p. 147.

[78] Multifibre Arrangement "MFA" Annex A, para. I.

[79] MFA Annex A, para. II(i).

[80] MFA Annex A, para. II(ii).

[81] MFA Article 12(1).

[82] MFA Article 12(2). MFA Article 3 (which provides for restrictions and is discussed further on) and provisions related thereto apply, as does the obligation to notify set out in MFA Article 2(1).

[83] MFA Article 3(3).

[84] MFA Article 3(4) and Annex B, para. 1.

[85] MFA Article 3(5)(i).

[86] MFA Article 5(ii) and (iii).

[87] MFA Article 3(8).

88 MFA Annex B, paras. 2 and 3.

89 MFA Article 4(4).

90 In 1993, Canada had bilateral restraint agreements with Bangladesh, Brazil, Bulgaria, Columbia, the Czech and Slovak republics, the Dominican Republic, Hong Kong, Hungary, India, Indonesia, Macau, Malaysia, Mauritius, North Korea, Pakistan, the People's Republic of China, the Philippines, Poland, Romania, Singapore, South Africa, South Korea, Sri Lanka, Taiwan, Thailand, Turkey, the United Arab Emirates, Uruguay and Vietnam.

91 See *Summary of Canada's Restraint Arrangements—Textiles and Clothing 1992* (Import Controls Division, Export and Import Permits Bureau, External Affairs and International Trade Canada, March 1992), p. 2. The growth factors for Canadian restraint agreements frequently deviate from the MFA 6% requirement. A few, such as those for some categories of products from Bangladesh, are higher. Others are lower. For example, the growth factor for a number of categories of textile products from Hong Kong is only 0.75%.

92 *Ibid.*

93 *Ibid.*

94 *Ibid.*

95 *Ibid.*, at pp. 5-6.

96 For a description of Canada's version of this, see *ibid.*, pp. 4-5.

97 For the draft version of this agreement that was available to the NAFTA negotiators, see *"The Dunkel Draft" from the GATT Secretariat, op. cit.*, note 45, pp. 0.1 to 0.36. The discussion of this agreement that follows is based on the Marrakesh text.

98 GATT Textile Agreement, Article 2, para. 1.

99 GATT Textile Agreement, Article 2, para. 4.

100 See GATT Textile Agreement, Article 2, para. 6. For the second and third stages, see paras. 8(a) and 8(b) respectively. For complete "integration into GATT", see para. 8(c). The second and third stages enter into effect on the first day of the thirty-seventh and eighty-fifth months respectively following the WTO Agreement becoming effective. Full integration takes place on the first day of the 121st month.

101 GATT Textile Agreement, Article 2, para. 6.

102 GATT Textile Agreement, Article 2, paras. 8(a) and 8(b).

103 GATT Textile Agreement, Article 2, paras. 6, 8(a) and 8(b).

104 GATT Textile Agreement, Article 6, para. 2.

105 GATT Textile Agreement, Article 6, para. 3

106 GATT Textile Agreement, Article 6, para. 8.

107 GATT Textile Agreement, Article 6, para. 10.

108 GATT Textile Agreement, Article 6, para. 11.

109 See GATT Textile Agreement, Article 6. For "carryover" and "carryforward", see para. 13 and for "swing", see para. 14. As among the NAFTA countries, these criteria would be superseded by the criteria set out in Appendix 3.1(A)(8), described in §5.2(3)(d)(i).

110 NAFTA Annex 300-B, Section 1(2).

111 NAFTA Annex 300-B, Section 3(2).

112 NAFTA Annex 300-B, Appendix 6(B)(7).

113 NAFTA Annex 300-B, Appendix 3.1, Part A, Section 2.

114 NAFTA Annex 300-B, Appendix 3.1, Part A, Section 4.

115 Annex 300-B, Appendix 3.1, Part A, Sections 5 (on any matter), 6 (inequity) and 7 (increase in annual Designated Consultation Levels).

116 NAFTA Annex 300-B, Appendix 3.1, Part A, Section 8(b). The NAFTA text simply says that an exporting Party may increase the annual specific limit ("SL") for a calendar year by no more than 6%. The NAFTA text calls this "swing" but does not explain that "swing" means transferring from one category and is not the same as "growth".

117 NAFTA Annex 300-B, Appendix 3.1, Part A, Section 8(c)(i).

118 NAFTA Annex 300-B, Appendix 3.1, Part A, Section 8(c)(ii).

119 NAFTA Annex 300-B, Appendix 3.1, Part A, Section 8(c)(iii).

120 *Bilateral Textile Agreement Between the United States of America and the United Mexican States.* See NAFTA Annex 300-B, Appendix 3.1, Part B, Section 12.

121 See NAFTA Annex 300-B, Appendix 3.1, Schedule 3.1.1. Restrictions are removed for all categories of goods identified in the Schedule as being in staging category 1. See Appendix

3.1, Part B, Section 9(a). To determine the HS provisions contained in a category, see *Correlation: Textile and Apparel Categories with the Harmonized Tariff Schedule of the United States* (1992 or successor document), referred to in NAFTA Annex 300-B, Appendix 3.1 Part C.

[122] Those categories in staging category 2 in Schedule 3.1.1. See Appendix 3.1, Part B, Section 9(b).

[123] Those categories in staging category 3 in Schedule 3.1.1. See Appendix 3.1, Part B, Section 9(c).

[124] See NAFTA Annex 300-B, Appendix 3.1, Part B, Section 10.

[125] See NAFTA Annex 300-B, Appendix 2.4.

[126] To be eligible for entry under U.S. tariff item 9802.00.80, an article must be assembled abroad from U.S. components that are exported in condition ready for assembly without further fabrication, and not advanced in value or improved in condition abroad except by being assembled and by incidental operations such as cleaning, lubricating and painting. Processes described in the NAFTA text such as dyeing and perma-pressing probably go beyond this limitation.

[127] MFA Article 12, para. 3.

[128] NAFTA Annex 300-B, Appendix 3.1, Part B, Section 11.

[129] NAFTA Annex 300-B, Section 2, para. 3.

[130] NAFTA Annex 300-B, Section 2, para. 2(b).

[131] See NAFTA 300-B, Section 4, paras. 1 and 7.

[132] The NAFTA text is not this direct. See Appendix 5.1 to NAFTA Annex 300-B, which states that actions otherwise permitted under Section 5 shall be governed by FTA 407, which is incorporated into NAFTA. Under FTA 407, Canada and the United States affirm their respective rights under the GATT with respect to "prohibitions or restrictions on bilateral trade in goods". As between Canada and the United States, this has the effect of integrating textile and apparel goods into the GATT and rendering Section 5 inapplicable.

[133] See NAFTA Annex 300-B, Section 4, para. 2 for tariff actions and NAFTA Annex 300-B, Section 5, para. 4 for quantitative restrictions; compare with Article 6, para. 2 of the GATT Textile Agreement. See also Note 16 to the NAFTA text.

[134] See NAFTA 300-B, Section 4, para. 1. One minor difference is that instead of referring to the MFN rate in effect on the day NAFTA becomes effective, the text says December 31, 1993. The "seasonal basis" provision is obviously not included.

[135] Note that for bilateral emergency procedures affecting other goods, as between Canada and the United States the transition period expires on December 31, 1998. See §4.7(3).

[136] See NAFTA Annex 300-B, Section 4, para. 4(c).

[137] NAFTA Annex 300-B, Section 4, para. 4(b).

[138] NAFTA Annex 300-B, Section 5, paras. 7(a) and 7(b). The time period in (a) is based on the time period in Article 6, para. 8 of the GATT Textile Agreement.

[139] NAFTA Annex 300-B, Section 5, para. 8. Note that this start date falls at a time before consultations have commenced.

[140] NAFTA Annex 300-B, Section 5, para. 9(a). The NAFTA country imposing the restriction must also accelerate the growth rate for cotton, man-made fibre and other non-vegetable goods, but not wool goods, if required under any successor agreement to the MFA. Article 6, para. 13 of the GATT Textile Agreement provides for a growth rate of 6%.

[141] John Jackson, *World Trade and Law of GATT* (Indianapolis, Bobbs-Merrill Co., 1969), pp. 365-6.

[142] GATT Subsidies Code Article 10:2(a).

[143] See, for example, the *Panel Report on "European Economic Community—Payments and Subsidies paid to Processors and Producers of Oilseeds and Related Animal-feed Proteins"*, L/6627, adopted on January 25, 1990, C/M/228.

[144] Report of the Canadian International Trade Tribunal, *An Inquiry into the Allocation of Import Quotas* (Minister of Supply and Services, 1992), at p. 9.

[145] The version of the GATT Agricultural Agreement available to the NAFTA negotiators was that set out in The Dunkel Draft. The Marrakesh text of the GATT Agricultural Agreement differs in a number of material respects from the version set out in The Dunkel Draft, but the basic principles are essentially the same.

223

[146] Exempt programs are listed in Annex 2 of the GATT Agricultural Agreement. For example, programs providing general services to the agricultural sector, such as research or pest and disease control, are exempt.

[147] See *The Dunkel Draft, op. cit.*, note 45, at pp. L.6 to L.8. The forms of the schedules for commitments respecting domestic support programs are set out on pages L.67 to L.73, and commitments respecting export subsidies are set out on page L.74. The Marrakesh text of the GATT Agricultural Agreement sets out substantially the same provisions, with some modifications. See Articles 6 to 9.

[148] GATT Agricultural Agreement, Article 5. The trigger level and trigger price is described in paragraph 1 and the schedule for calculating the additional duty is set out in paragraph 5.

[149] R.S.C. 1985, c. C-15.

[150] *Op. cit.*, note 144, at p. 22.

[151] *Ibid.*, pp. 48 to 50 for chickens, p. 50 for turkey, p. 55 for shell eggs and p. 42 for broiler hatching eggs.

[152] R.S.C. 1985, c. E-19.

[153] For a concise summary of the quantitative restrictions in effect for 1991, see *op. cit.*, note 144, p. 7, Table 1.1.

[154] *Canadian Wheat Board Act*, R.S.C. 1985, c. C-24, s. 45(a) for wheat. Section 45(b) sets out a similar provision for interprovincial trade. These provisions were extended to oats and barley by s. 9 of the *Canadian Wheat Board Regulations*, C.R.C. 1978, c. 397. The authority for the CWB to issue licences is set out in s. 14 of the *Canadian Wheat Board Regulations*.

[155] *Canadian Wheat Board Regulations, ibid.*, ss. 17 and 18.

[156] GATT Article XVII. As discussed in §9.2(2), NAFTA sets out rules respecting monopolies and state enterprises. Neither set of rules should have any material impact on the operations of the CWB.

[157] 7 U.S.C. § 624(a) and (b). The process is initiated by the Secretary of Agriculture and an investigation is conducted by the United States International Trade Commission. If the investigation supports the facts required by the legislation, the President must impose the fees or the quantitative restrictions. Immediate action may be taken in emergency situations before the investigation is complete. See 7 U.S.C. §624(b).

[158] See 3rd Supp BISD 32 (1955).

[159] HTSUS tariff item 9904.10.72.

[160] HTSUS tariff item 9904.10.21.

[161] HTSUS tariff item 9904.10.72.

[162] See Note 1 to Article 4, paragraph 2 of the GATT Agricultural Agreement.

[163] 19 U.S.C. § 2253. The tariff items covered are 106.10, 106.22, 106.25, 107.55 and 107.62. Sausage and lamb meat are not included. See the definition of "meat articles" 19 U.S.C. §2253, s. 808(b)(2).

[164] See 19 U.S.C. §2253, s. 808(c).

[165] *Op. cit.*, note 4, at p. 291. The voluntary restraint agreements are negotiated under the authority of the U.S. Agricultural Act of 1956.

[166] *Ibid.*, at p. 284.

[167] For a description of these measures, see, *ibid.*, at pp. 284-5.

[168] *Ibid.*, at p. 289. According to Hufbrauer and Schott, in 1990 over 50% of U.S. agricultural goods exported to Mexico were subject to import controls.

[169] NAFTA Annex 302.2, para. 8.

[170] Where there is one. As will be discussed, tariff elimination does not apply to the "dairy, poultry and egg goods" identified by tariff item in NAFTA Appendix 703.2.B.7.

[171] NAFTA Annex 703.2, Section A, para. 26.

[172] NAFTA Annex 703.2, Section B, para. 14.

[173] Discussed in §4.7(3).

[174] This expression is defined in FTA 711.

[175] U.S. Statement of Administrative Action, H.R. 3450, 103rd Congress, 1st Session (1993), p. 68.

[176] W. M. Miner, "Agricultural Trade Under the Klieg Lights: Domestic Pressures and Bilateral Frictions" (paper presented at a seminar on Canada-U.S. Economic Relations, November

10, 1993), sponsored by the Center for Trade Policy and Law (Ottawa) and the Centre for Strategic & International Studies (Washington). See Annex I, *Canada-U.S. Wheat Dispute* by Karen Hurlburt, p. 4.

[177] See report of the binational panel entitled *Interpretation of and Canada's compliance with Article 701.3 with respect to durum wheat sales*, [1993] F.T.A.D. No. 2, para. 47 (QL).

[178] *Ibid.*, para. 107.

[179] *Ibid.*, para. 70.

[180] *Ibid.*, paras. 110 and 111.

[181] *Op. cit.*, note 175, at pp. 67-8.

[182] See NAFTA Annex 703.2, Section A, para. 2 (Mexico-U.S.) and Section B, para. 2 (Canada-Mexico).

[183] NAFTA Annex 703.2, Section A, para. 10(c) for goods under HSTUS tariff items 1806.10.42 and 2106.90.12 exported from Mexico and para. 11(c) for goods of Mexican tariff items 1806.10.01 and 2106.90.05 exported from the United States.

[184] NAFTA Annex 703.2, Section B, paras. 9 and 10. The Canadian tariff items are 1806.10.10 and 2106.90.21.

[185] NAFTA Annex 703.2, Section A, paras. 10(a) and 10(b), which apply to peanuts (heading 12.02) and peanut products (subheading 2008.11) respectively exported from Mexico to the United States. The corresponding provisions for goods exported from the United States to Mexico are paragraphs 11(a) and 11(b).

[186] NAFTA Annex 703.2, Section A, para. 25, and Section B, para. 13.

[187] NAFTA Annex 703.2, Section A, para. 23.

[188] NAFTA Annex 703.2, Section B, para. 8.

[189] NAFTA Annex 703.2, Section A, para. 9.

[190] See NAFTA Schedule of Mexico, Chapter 7, Notes 3 and 4 for the in-quota quantities. See Note 1 for the base rate and Note 2 for the staging. This example is typical of the Mexican tariff rate quotas.

[191] See, for example, Note 3 under Chapter 7 of the NAFTA Schedule of Mexico. The expression used is "los bienes originarios provenientes de EE.UU". If a qualifying good had been intended, the expression "los bienes calificados de EE.UU." would have been used.

[192] NAFTA Annex 703.2, Section A, paras. 4 and 5 (Mexico and the United States); Section B, paras. 3 and 4 (Canada and Mexico). The Mexico-U.S. waiver also applies to certain customs duties that may result from the special provisions respecting sugar set out in Section A.

[193] See NAFTA Appendix 703.2.A.4 for exact tariff items.

[194] NAFTA Annex 703.2, Section A, para. 6 and Section B, para. 5.

[195] See "Tariffs must go by 1998, U.S. says", *The Globe and Mail*, December 18, 1993, p. A-1.

[196] See, *ibid.*, at p. A-2. The expert in question was Bill Merkin.

[197] See NAFTA Annex 703.3, Section A. The Canadian tariff items are: 0603.10.90, 0702.00.91, 0703.10.31, 0710.80.20, 0710.80.20, 0811.10.10, 0811.10.90 and 2002.90.00.

[198] NAFTA Annex 703.3, Section C. The U.S. tariff items are: 0702.00.60, 0702.00.20, 0703.10.40, 0709.30.20, 0709.60.00, 0709.90.20 and 0807.10.40.

[199] NAFTA Annex 703.3, Section B. The Mexican tariff items listed are: 0103.91.99, 0103.92.99, 0203.11.01, 0203.12.01, 0203.19.99, 0203.21.01, 0203.22.01, 0203.29.99, 0210.11.01, 0210.12.01, 0210.19.99, 0710.10.01, 0712.10.01, 0808.10.01, 2004.10.01, 2005.20.01, 2101.10.01

[200] NAFTA Annex 703.2, Section A, para. 3.

[201] NAFTA Annex 703.2, Section A, para. 8.

[202] See United States Statement of Administrative Action, pp. 70-71.

[203] NAFTA Annex 302.2, Section A, para. 7.

[204] NAFTA Annex 703.2, Section B, para. 7(a). According to the notes in the NAFTA Schedule of Mexico, this provision extends to goods from the United States that are not qualifying goods of the United States. See, for example, the note under column (1), U.S. Goods, for tariff item 0401.10.01 of the NAFTA Schedule of Mexico. As discussed in §5.3(1)(b)(iii), the GATT Agricultural Agreement requires tariffication of quantitive restrictions.

[205] NAFTA Annex 703.2, Section B, para. 7(b).

[206] NAFTA Annex 703.2, Section B, paras. 11 and 12.

[207] NAFTA Schedule of Mexico. See the notes to Chapter 2. Respecting over-quota tariff rates, note 3 establishes the base rate for turkey products and note 5 establishes the base rate for most other poultry products. Note 4 establishes the phase-out schedule for the over-quota tariff rate for turkey products under Mexican tariff item 0207.10.01, as well as an in-quota quantity of 2,000 tonnes for 1994 that increases annually by 3%. Other tariff items are covered by other notes.

[208] See NAFTA Schedule of Mexico, tariff item 0407.00.01.

[209] See HSTUS tariff item 9904.10.03 and Statistical Note 1 at the beginning of HSTUS Chapter 4.

[210] Mexican tariff items 0402.10.01 and 0402.21.01.

[211] 19 U.S.C. §2253, under LIMITATION OF MEAT IMPORTS, (b)(2).

[212] See Note to Chapter 2 of the NAFTA Schedule of the United States.

[213] North American Free Trade Agreement Implementation Act, H.R. 3450, 103rd Congress, 1st Session (1993), Section 321(a).

[214] See FTA 702(1)(a).

[215] The right to apply duties on a regional basis only applies to Canada because the only regions described in FTA 702(9) are Canadian.

[216] See NAFTA Schedule of Mexico, Chapter 7, Notes 27 (base rate), 28 (staging), 29 (in-quota quantity for the United States) and 30 (in-quota quantity for Canada).

[217] *Canadian Wheat Board Regulations*, C.R.C. 1978, c. 397, s. 15.1 (am. SOR/91-302, s. 1).

[218] *Supra*, note 213, Section 321(f)(1).

[219] *Ibid.*, Section 321(f)(4).

[220] SOR/93-360. The reasons for the deregulation are discussed in the Regulatory Impact Analysis Statement accompanying the Regulation.

[221] The United States at one time did maintain quantitative restrictions on imports of wheat. See HTSUS tariff item 9904.20.10, which at the time of writing has been suspended.

[222] See *National Corn Growers Assn. v. Canada (Canadian Import Tribunal)* (1988), 58 D.L.R. (4th) 642, [1989] 2 F.C. 517, 18 C.E.R. 268, 92 N.R. 264 (C.A.), affd 74 D.L.R. (4th) 449, [1990] 2 S.C.R. 1324, 45 Admin. L.R. 161, 114 N.R. 81.

[223] NAFTA Schedule of Mexico, Chapter 10, Notes 1 (barley base rate), 2 (barley staging), 3 (barley in-quota quantity), 5 (corn base rate), 6 (corn staging) and 7 (corn in-quota quantity).

[224] NAFTA Schedule of Mexico, Chapter 11, Notes 1 (base rate), 2 (staging) and 3 (in-quota quantity).

[225] NAFTA Schedule of Mexico, Chapter 10, Note 4 (barley) and Note 8 (corn); Chapter 11, Note 4 (malt).

[226] See HSTUS tariff item 9904.20.20. The global quota is 775,189 kilograms. The tariff subheadings affected are 1202.10, 1202.20 and 2008.11.

[227] HTSUS tariff provisions 1701.11, 1701.12, 1791.91.21, 1791.91.22, 1701.99, 1702.90.31, 1702.90.32, 1806.10.41, 1806.10.42, 2106.90.11 and 2106.90.12.

[228] United States Restrictions on Imports of Sugar, Report of the Panel, adopted on June 22, 1989 (L/6514).

[229] The in-quota quantity is comprised of a "base quota amount", a "quota adjustment amount" and an amount reserved for the importation of specialty sugars. See HTSUS Additional Note 3(a)(i) to Chapter 17.

[230] 15 CFR Ch XX (1-1-93 Edition), §2011.303(b)(1) and (2).

[231] See HTSUS tariff items 9904.40.20 and 9904.40.60. The fees are "2.2 cents per kilogram, but not in excess of 50%", which reflects the s. 22 limitation.

[232] The sugar rates are actually on a sliding scale, based on international sugar degrees, with the maximum number being 100. The per kilogram rates quoted here are those that apply to 100 degrees.

[233] The in-quota tariff rates are identified in tariff items 1701.11.01, 1701.12.01, 1701.91.21, 1701.99.01, 1702.90.31, 1806.10.41 and 2106.90.11. The over-quota tariff rates are identified in tariff items 1701.11.03, 1701.12.02, 1701.91.22, 1701.99.02, 1702.90.32, 1806.10.42 and 2106.90.12.

[234] The quota quantity for tariff items 9904.50.20 and 9904.50.40 is None. Subheading 9904.60 is broken down into three tariff items that prescribe quota quantities in tonnes for specific products.

[235] In 1993, this rate for tariff items 1701.11.01, 1701.11.02 and 1701.11.03 was 0.7303 cents per kilogram as opposed to the MFN in-quota tariff rate of 1.4606 cents per kilogram and the MFN over-quota tariff rate of 37.386 cents per kilogram. To this is added the s. 22 fee of 2.2 cents per kilogram provided for in HTSUS tariff item 9904.40.20.

[236] *Agricultural Trade Under the Klieg Lights: Domestic Pressures and Bilateral Frictions*, a paper presented by W.M. Miner at a Seminar on Canada-U.S. Economic Relations on November 10, 1993, sponsored by the Center for trade Policy and Law (Ottawa) and the Centre for Strategic & International Studies (Washington). See Annex I, *Canada-U.S. Sugar Dispute* by Karen Hurlburt, pp. 8-9.

[237] The calculation is set out in a complex formula in NAFTA Appendix 703.2.A.13.

[238] NAFTA Annex 703.2, Section A, para. 14. Subsections (a) and (b) reflect 15 CFR §2001(b)(2) and (1) respectively.

[239] NAFTA Annex 703.2, Section A, para. 15.

[240] See NAFTA Schedule of the United States, Chapter 17, Note 1(a).

[241] The reason for the split into four categories rather than two is that some goods covered by tariff item 1701.11.03 are also subject to s. 22 fees under HTSUS 9904.40.20, whereas others are not.

[242] See NAFTA Schedule of the United States, Chapter 17, Note 2.

[243] NAFTA Annex 703.2, Section A, para. 22.

[244] See NAFTA Schedule of the United States, Chapter 17, Note 6.

[245] See *ibid.*, Chapter 17, Notes 5 and 7.

[246] See *ibid.*, Chapter 20, Notes 3 to 7 inclusive.

[247] *Ibid.*, Chapter 52, Notes 1 to 4.

[248] NAFTA Schedule of Mexico, Chapter 20, Notes 17 to 20.

[249] *Ibid.*, Chapter 15, Notes 1 (base rate), 2 (staging) and 3 (in-quota quantity).

[250] *Ibid.*, Chapter 15, Note 4.

[251] NAFTA Annex 702.3.

[252] Jackson, *op. cit.*, note 141 at p. 745. See also Andre Plourde, "Canada's International Obligations in Energy and the Free-Trade Agreement with the United States" (1990), 24 *Journal of World Trade* 36, at pp. 36-7.

[253] J. Owen Saunders, "The Mexico Factor in North American Free Trade Agreement" (1991), 9 *Journal of Energy and Natural Resources Law* 239 at p. 248.

[254] See Plourde, *op. cit.*, note 252, who comments on the asymmetry between the GATT rules respecting import restrictions and those involving export restrictions.

[255] See the *Petroleum Administration Act*, S.C. 1974-75-76, c. 47, now the *Energy Administration Act*, R.S.C. 1985, c. E-6.

[256] In April, 1979, the official price for Arabian light marker crude (34 degrees API) was $14.55 (US). The Canadian regulated price for conventional oil in effect at that time was $12.75 (Cdn). By January 1980, these prices were $26.00 (US) and $14.75 (Cdn) respectively.

[257] In Canada, as between the federal and provincial governments, resources within a province are owned by the province, while resources in the Northwest Territories and the Yukon are owned by the federal government.

[258] The Western Accord, An Agreement between the Governments of Canada, Alberta, Saskatchewan and British Columbia on Oil and Gas Pricing and Taxation, March, 1985.

[259] Agreement Among the Governments of Canada, Alberta, British Columbia and Saskatchewan on Natural Gas Markets and Prices, October 31, 1985.

[260] See Saunders, *op. cit.*, note 253, at p. 249.

[261] See FTA 407(2), 408 and 409 respectively.

[262] Saunders, *op. cit.*, note 253, at p. 248.

[263] Fernando Flores-Garcia, "Aspects of Mexican Energy Regulation" (1990), *Texas International Law Journal* 359 at p. 361.

[264] F. Reuben Clark, Jr., "The Oil Settlement with Mexico" (1927), *Foreign Affairs* 600.

[265] Flores-Garcia, *op. cit.*, note 263, at p. 362.

[266] These include certain paraffin mixtures under HS heading 27.10 and ethylene, propylene, butylene and butadiene under HS 27.11 in purities over 50%.

[267] See Andre Plourde, *Energy and the NAFTA*, C.D. Howe Institute Commentary, No. 46, May 1993, at p. 5.

[268] Compare this with FTA 1202, which expressly exempted measures that were exempt under the original GATT Protocol of Provisional Application. See also §4.3(7)(b).

[269] See Basic Instruments and Selected Documents, 33rd Supplement, pp. 3 to 6. These provisions of the Mexican Protocol are set out in paragraph 5 on p. 4 of this report. The author assumes that "their respective protocols of provisional application" in NAFTA 603(1) means, in Mexico's case, the Mexican Protocol.

[270] Compare Plourde, *op. cit.*, note 252, at p. 46, who believes that this understanding is consistent with GATT Article XI, with Saunders, *op. cit.*, note 253, at p. 249, who considers it "at best questionable".

[271] For a discussion of possible ambiguities between the exception in NAFTA Annex 603.6 and the requirement respecting supply contracts in paragraph 3 of NAFTA Annex 602.3 (discussed in §5.4(5)(b)), see Plourde, *op. cit.*, note 267, at p. 7.

[272] For a useful analysis of Canadian exports as a percentage of Canadian production for oil, natural gas and electricity, see G.C. Watkins, "NAFTA and Energy: A Bridge not Far on Enough" in *Assessing NAFTA: A Trinational Analysis*, Steven Globerman and Michael Walker, eds. (Vancouver, The Fraser Institute, 1993) p. 193 at pp. 195-201.

[273] This carries forward FTA 908.

[274] In its unilateral declaration on energy and NAFTA on December 2, 1993, the measures that the Canadian government stated that it may deem necessary to take would include the establishment of strategic reserves. In the case of oil, Canada already has this obligation under the IEP, at least in circumstances in which it is a net importer.

[275] Plourde, *op. cit.*, note 252, at p. 44.

[276] See, *ibid.*, at pp. 44-5. This article sets out an excellent summary of the issues arising under the IEP. As the footnotes in this article indicate, there are a number of articles and studies describing the IEP pooling mechanism.

[277] *Ibid.*, at p. 52.

[278] See, for example, J. Owen Saunders, "Energy, Natural Resources and the Canada-United States Free Trade Agreement" (1990), 8 *Journal of Energy and Natural Resources Law* 3 at p. 10.

[279] Plourde, *op. cit.*, note 252.

[280] Saunders, *op. cit.*, note 278, at p. 9.

[281] *Ibid.*, at p. 11. Pages 10 and 11 of this article discuss a number of issues surrounding Opinion 256.

[282] *Ibid.*

[283] Plourde, *op. cit.*, note 267, at p. 9. Plourde believes that the requirement in NAFTA 601(1) that the NAFTA countries respect their constitutions reinforces this conclusion, particularly in the case of Canada where ownership of natural resources is so clearly an area of provincial responsibility.

[284] See, for example, Maude Barlow, *Parcel of Rogues: How Free Trade is Failing Canada* (Toronto, Key Porter Books Limited, 1990), at p. 140. Barlow concluded that the only subsidies permitted under the FTA are those for defence-industry production and searching for new energy sources. Having regard to GATT Article III:8(b) and the binational panel report discussed in §5.3(5)(a)(iii), this conclusion is clearly incorrect.

[285] See *Comprehensive Guide*, at p. 71, which raises the possibility of this argument.

[286] The upgrading requirement had been a point of contention between Canada and the United States. In November 1986 the United States challenged the requirement under the GATT. See Bill Charnetski, *The Energy Sector and the Free Trade Agreement: Entrenching Free Market Principles*, a draft paper prepared for The International Business and Trade Law Programme of the Ontario Centre for International Business, at p. 35.

[287] Plourde, *op. cit.*, note 252, at p. 48. On p. 49, Plourde observes that recent Canadian policy changes have moved away from export price regulation.

[288] *Report of the Advisory Committee on Liquor Regulation*, February, 1987, p. 24.

[289] R.S.C. 1985, c. I-3.

[290] Canadian provinces ended prohibition at various times. For example, prohibition in Ontario ended in 1927.

[291] *Canada — Import, Distribution and Sale of Alcoholic Drinks by Canadian Provincial Marketing Agencies*, BISD 35S/37, pp. 39-40.

[292] See the definition of "listing" in *Agreement between Canada and the European Community concerning Trade and Commerce in Alcoholic Beverages* dated February 28, 1989, which is referred to in NAFTA Annex 312.2, Section B, para. 4(b).

[293] *Op. cit.*, note 291, p. 40.

[294] All these practices are described in *Report of the Panel on "Canada—Import, Distribution and Sale of Certain Alcoholic Drinks by Provincial Marketing Agencies"* GATT Doc. DS17/R.

[295] These practices are all described in *Report of the Panel on "United States—Measures Affecting Alcoholic and Malt Beverages"*, GATT Doc. DS23/R.

[296] *Op. cit.*, note 291, at pp. 94-5. See the text of the letter accompanying the Provincial Statement from the Canadian Ambassador and Head of Delegation to the EC Head of Delegation, on pp. 93-4, which characterizes the Provincial Statement as "non-contractual in nature".

[297] *Ibid.* For discussion on mark-ups, see pp. 85-9. For discussion on points of sale and listing, see pp. 89-91.

[298] The U.S. delegation was heard by the panel on March 26, 1987. See, *ibid.*, at p. 38. The FTA negotiations were underway at that time. The FTA was signed in early January, 1988. As indicated above, the report of the GATT panel was not adopted until March 22, 1988.

[299] This is the date that the Elements of Agreement that formed the basis for the FTA were signed.

[300] See, *op. cit.*, note 294, at para. 4.29.

[301] See, *ibid.*, para. 6.1.

[302] See, *op. cit.*, note 295.

[303] See HTSUS tariff item 9903.22.03.

[304] See John Saunders and Casey Mahood, "Deal means cheaper beer: U.S. brewers will get access to Ontario stores", *The Globe & Mail*, August 6, 1993, p. A1. See, however, Peter Morton, "U.S. urged to bar Canadian beer", *The Financial Post*, January 6, 1994, which suggests that the agreement may be coming unravelled. For the text of the U.S.-Canada Memorandum of Understanding on Provincial Beer Marketing Practices of August 5, 1993, see News Release No. 152 dated August 5, 1993, Media Relations Office, Foreign Affairs and International Trade Canada, Ottawa. See also News Release No. 89 dated May 5, 1994.

CHAPTER 6

TECHNICAL BARRIERS TO TRADE, ENVIRONMENTAL AND LABOUR ISSUES

Technical standards have increasingly become a fact of life as governments have tried to address issues of product safety, occupational health and safety, public health and degradation of the environment. From a trade perspective, standards can be used as effective non-tariff barriers. The GATT itself does not deal with standards. The first major attempt to deal with non-tariff barriers to trade was made during the Tokyo Round of negotiations in the 1970s. These negotiations led to the signing by a number of GATT members of the *Agreement on Technical Barriers to Trade* (the "1980 Technical Barriers Agreement") which came into effect on January 1, 1980. The FTA affirmed the respective obligations of Canada and the United States to each other under the 1980 Technical Barriers Code and established some additional standards. The Uruguay Round negotiations resulted in a new *Agreement on Technical Barriers to Trade* (the "1994 GATT Technical Barriers Agreement")[1] and an *Agreement on the Application of Sanitary and Phytosanitary Measures* (the "GATT Sanitary and Phytosanitary Measures Agreement") covering measures respecting pests or diseases in animals or plants and contaminants in food. The NAFTA provisions respecting standards are based largely on these Uruguay Round agreements.

Like the GATT, the FTA dealt minimally with environmental issues because of the generally held view that trade agreements were not appropriate vehicles for solving environmental problems. The prospective impact of the FTA on the environment became a major issue in Canada after the FTA was signed but U.S. environmentalists did not express similar concerns. However, the U.S. environmental movement became very concerned with NAFTA because environmentalists were increasingly making links between trade policy and environmental policy and because of Mexico's relatively poor record of environmental enforcement. The original NAFTA text addresses the environment in a number of provisions. However, these were considered as inadequate both by the U.S. environmental movement and by the incoming Clinton administration which had campaigned on the basis of negotiating stronger environmental controls in NAFTA. As a result, the NAFTA countries negotiated and signed the *North American Agreement on Environmental Cooperation* (the "Environmental Cooperation Agreement") discussed in §6.9.

Organized labour in both Canada and the United States bitterly opposed NAFTA. Canadian labour had opposed the FTA for many reasons, one of the more significant of which was perceived wage differentials and labour standards between Canada and certain parts of the United States. This issue was greatly magnified vis à vis Mexico because of the dramatic real wage gap between Mexico and each of the United States and Canada. The concern was that U.S. and Canadian workers would lose their jobs because businesses would move to Mexico to take advantage of low Mexican wages and lax enforcement of labour standards. Many Democrats supported the labour's position and Mr. Clinton had promised in his election campaign to protect U.S. workers. These pressures resulted in the negotiation and signing of the *North American Agreement on Labour Cooperation* (the "Labour Cooperation Agreement") discussed in §6.10.

6.1 1980 GATT TECHNICAL BARRIERS AGREEMENT

The 1980 GATT Technical Barriers Agreement established the basic principle that technical standards not create obstacles to trade. Goods from other contracting parties must receive no less favourable treatment than domestic goods as regards technical standards.[2] Where international standards exist they should be used by the contracting parties.[3] Wherever appropriate, technical standards should be specified in terms of performance rather than design or descriptive characteristics.[4] When international standards do not exist, the contracting parties must follow a notification and discussion process in introducing technical standards.[5] In cases involving urgent problems of health, safety, environmental protection or national security, the discussion process may be deferred until after the standard has come into effect.[6] All technical standards adopted must be published[7] and, except in urgent situations, with a reasonable interval between publication and entry into force.[8]

This agreement sets out provisions to ensure that testing procedures are not applied in a discriminatory manner[9] and that, where possible, reciprocity governs the recognition of certifications of other contracting parties.[10] Certification systems may not create obstacles to international trade[11] and must be formulated so that suppliers of products originating in other contracting parties have access to the system under conditions no less favourable than those accorded suppliers of domestic products.[12] A Committee on Technical Barriers to Trade was established to provide a vehicle for consultation and dispute settlement.[13]

6.2 PROVISIONS OF FTA

The FTA established two separate sets of provisions relating to standards. FTA 708 applied to "agricultural, food, beverage and certain related goods" and FTA Chapter Six applied to other goods.

FTA Chapter Six unequivocally applied only to federal government measures. Following the 1980 GATT Technical Barriers Agreement, FTA 603 established the basic principle that "standards-related measures" and "product approval procedures" not create unnecessary obstacles to trade. Measures to achieve a "legitimate domestic objective" were deemed not to create an unnecessary obstacle to trade. A "legitimate domestic objective" was defined as protecting health, safety, essential security, the environment or consumer interests.[14] FTA 604 required that Canada and the United States "make compatible" their standards-related measures. The expression "make compatible" was defined to mean mutual recognition of differing standards, technical regulation systems and certification systems. FTA Chapter Six included provisions respecting mutual recognition of accreditation systems. The provisions of FTA Chapter Six are superseded by NAFTA.

FTA 708 established procedures for Canada and the United States to work towards the harmonization of technical regulations and standards for "agricultural, food, beverage and certain related goods". These are defined in FTA 710 as including agricultural goods, fish and other types of seafood, various types of alcoholic beverages, provitamins and vitamins, hormones, glands, human blood, antibiotics and other organic goods, medicaments, fertilizers, vegetable colouring matter, synthetic food, dyes, pesticides, sausage casings and various wood products. FTA Annex 708.1 set out schedules covering specific product groups and generally provided for the two countries to work towards the harmonization of standards. As noted in §5.3(5), FTA 708 was not incorporated by reference into NAFTA but Canada and the United States have collaterally agreed to maintain the provision in effect. A binational panel held *In the Matter of Puerto Rico regulations on the import, distribution and sale of U.H.T. milk from Quebec*[15] that FTA 708 imposed only a best efforts obligation but none the less decided that a Puerto Rico ban on imports of milk from Quebec for failure to meet newly imposed standards nullified and impaired FTA benefits because the ban was imposed before an equivalency study of procedures in Quebec had been completed.

6.3 THE URUGUAY ROUND AGREEMENTS

As indicated previously, the Uruguay Round negotiations resulted in two agreements respecting standards. The GATT Sanitary and Phytosanitary Measures Agreement covers measures respecting pests or diseases in animals or plants and contaminants in food. The 1994 GATT Technical Barriers Agreement, which will supersede the 1980 Technical Barriers Agreement, covers technical regulations and standards not covered by the GATT Sanitary and Phytosanitary Measures Agreement. The 1994 GATT Technical Barriers Agreement is largely based on the 1980 Technical Barriers Agreement while the GATT Sanitary and Phytosanitary Measures Agreement is entirely new. Each of these agreements will come into effect in 1995. The provisions of these agreements are discussed below with the corresponding provisions in the NAFTA text.

6.4 PROVISIONS OF NAFTA

The NAFTA provisions respecting technical regulations and standards are based largely on these two Uruguay Round agreements. As under the Uruguay Round, the NAFTA provisions respecting technical regulations and standards are divided into two discrete categories. The NAFTA provisions respecting sanitary and phytosanitary measures are set out in Section B of NAFTA Chapter Seven. The NAFTA provisions respecting technical regulations, standards and conformity assessment procedures are set out in NAFTA Chapter Nine. Chapter Nine and Section B of Chapter Seven do not overlap.

When applying the NAFTA provisions to a measure, one first determines whether the measure is a "sanitary or phytosanitary measure" as defined in NAFTA 724. If it is, Section B of Chapter Seven (Sanitary and Phytosanitary Measures) applies and NAFTA Chapter Nine does not. If the measure is not a sanitary or phytosanitary measure, one determines whether it is a "standards-related measure" as defined in NAFTA 915. If it is, NAFTA Chapter Nine applies.

(1) Definition of Sanitary and Phytosanitary Measures

The NAFTA definition of "sanitary and phytosanitary measures" is set out in NAFTA 724 and is based on the corresponding definition in the GATT Sanitary and Phytosanitary Measures Agreement with some wording changes. NAFTA 724 defines a "sanitary or phytosanitary measure" as a measure to: (a) protect animal or plant life or health in its territory from risks arising from the introduction, establishment or spread of a pest or disease; (b) protect human or animal life or health in its territory from risks arising from the presence of an additive, contaminant, toxin or disease-causing organism in a food, beverage or feedstuff; (c) protect human life or health in its territory from risks arising from a disease-causing organism or pest carried by an animal or plant, or a product thereof; or (d) prevent or limit other damage in its territory arising from the introduction, establishment or spread of a pest. A "contaminant" includes pesticide and veterinary drug residues and extraneous matter and a "pest" includes a weed. Each branch of the definition is qualified by the words "in its territory", meaning that a measure purporting to have extraterritorial application is not a "sanitary or phyto-sanitary measure". The definition sets out examples of measures included.[16]

There are some subtle distinctions in this definition and each of its branches has to be carefully considered. Consider a measure enacted to prevent the spread of AIDS through the human blood supply. Branch (a) of the definition would not cover the measure because only animal and plant life are covered. Branch (b) of the definition would not cover the measure because, while human life and health are included, the "disease-causing organism" must be "in a food, beverage or feedstuff". Branch (c) of the definition also covers human life and health but the "disease causing organism" must be carried by "an animal or plant, or a product thereof". Branch (d) of the definition, which refers only to "pests", would not cover the measure because other branches of the definition refer to both "disease-causing organisms" and "pests", suggesting that the expression "pest" does not include a "disease carrying organism" such as the AIDS virus. Therefore, the measure would not be covered by the definition and the NAFTA obligations affecting the measure would depend on whether it was a "standards-related measure" as defined in NAFTA 915.

(2) Definition of Standards-related Measures

A "standards-related measure" is a "technical regulation", a "standard" or a "conformity assessment procedure". All these expressions are defined in NAFTA 915 and the definitions are similar to their counterparts in the 1994 GATT Technical Barriers Agreement.[17]

(a) Application to land transportation and telecommunication services

The definitions of "technical regulation" and "standards" in the 1994 GATT Technical Barriers Agreement apply only to goods and not to services. The "services" referred to in the corresponding NAFTA definitions and throughout NAFTA Chapter Nine are land transportation services and telecommunication services. Chapter Nine applies only to these services and to service-providers providing these services, and not to other services or service providers.

(b) Technical regulation

A "technical regulation" is a document which lays down "goods' characteristics or their related processes and production methods or services' characteristics or their related operating methods", with which compliance is mandatory. For example, an occupational health and safety requirement set out in a statute or regulation prescribing maximum exposure limits for substances such as lead or isocyanates would be a "technical regulation". Failure to comply results in the imposition of a penalty.

(c) Standard

A "standard" is a document "approved by a recognized body, that provides, for common and repeated use, rules, guidelines or characteristics for goods or related processes and production methods, or for services or related operating methods, with which compliance is not mandatory". A standard established by a standards association requiring that an appliance be wired in a certain manner would be a "standard". Failure to observe the standard does not result in the imposition of a penalty but may seriously affect the marketability of the product and may be used as evidence by claimants in civil liability claims.

(d) Conformity assessment procedure

A "conformity assessment procedure" is a procedure used to determine whether a technical regulation is fulfilled.[18] Unlike its counterpart in the 1994 GATT Technical Barriers Agreement, the NAFTA definition of "conformity assessment procedure" expressly excludes "approval procedures". These are defined as registration, notification or other mandatory administrative procedures for granting permission for a good or service to be marketed or used for a stated purpose or under stated conditions. Approval procedures are not subject to any of the provisions of Chapter Nine respecting conformity assessment procedures. Approval procedures are covered by the provisions of Chapter Nine respecting "standards-related measures" to the extent that they can be characterized as "technical regulations". The definition of "technical regulation" in NAFTA 915 does not refer to "approval procedures" but does include "applicable administrative provisions, with which compliance is mandatory".

6.5 SANITARY AND PHYTOSANITARY MEASURES

The NAFTA provisions respecting sanitary and phytosanitary measures are based on the GATT Sanitary and Phytosanitary Measures Agreement.

(1) Scope and Coverage

The scope and coverage of the NAFTA sanitary and phytosanitary provisions are delineated by the definition of "sanitary and phytosanitary measures" described in §6.4(1).

NAFTA 710 provides that NAFTA 301 (National Treatment, discussed in §4.2), NAFTA 309 (Import and Export Restrictions, discussed in §4.3) and the "human, animal or plant life and health" exception in Article XX(b) of the GATT incorporated into NAFTA by NAFTA 2101 (discussed in

§4.3(5)) do not apply to sanitary or phytosanitary measures. As a result, the NAFTA sanitary and phytosanitary measures provisions are a self-contained code. For example, a measure falling within the definition that complies with the requirements of the NAFTA sanitary and phytosanitary provisions cannot be attacked as failing to accord national treatment under NAFTA 301. Similarly, a measure covered by the definition that fails to conform with these provisions cannot be defended under the general "human, animal or plant life and health" exception in GATT Article XX(b).

The GATT Sanitary and Phytosanitary Measures Agreement approaches the issue of the relationship with other GATT obligations a little differently. Sanitary and phytosanitary measures conforming with the GATT Sanitary and Phytosanitary Measures Agreement are presumed to conform with GATT obligations, including GATT Article XX(b).[19]

(2) States and Provinces and Non-governmental Bodies

With one exception discussed in §6.5(7)(a), the NAFTA provisions respecting sanitary and phytosanitary measures are subject to NAFTA 105 that obliges NAFTA countries to take all necessary measures to ensure compliance by state and provincial governments. The GATT Sanitary and Phytosanitary Measures Agreement does not clearly establish the obligations of member countries respecting ensuring compliance by sub-national governments.[20] NAFTA 711 requires that each NAFTA country ensure that non-governmental entities on which it is relying in applying a sanitary or phytosanitary measure act consistently with these provisions. The GATT Sanitary and Phytosanitary Measures Agreement contains a similar provision.[21]

(3) Basic Rights and Obligations

(a) Basic right to adopt

NAFTA 712(1) sets out the basic right of NAFTA countries to adopt sanitary and phytosanitary measures and provides that a measure adopted can be more stringent than an international standard, guideline or recommendation.[22] Paragraph 1 of Article 2 and paragraph 3 of Article 3 of the GATT Sanitary and Phytosanitary Measures Agreement have a similar effect.[23]

(b) Level of risk and risk assessment

(i) Level of risk

NAFTA 712(2) states that each NAFTA country may establish its appropriate levels of protection in accordance with the risk assessment procedures set out in NAFTA 715. This provision, which applies notwithstanding any of the other NAFTA sanitary or phytosanitary provisions, is significant because it makes it clear that the NAFTA countries do not have to harmonize their standards. The effect of paragraph 3 of Article 3 of the GATT Sanitary and Phytosanitary Measures Agreement is that member countries can determine their own levels of protection but this is not stated in the unequivocal manner as in NAFTA 712(2).

(ii) Risk assessment

NAFTA 712(3)(c) requires that sanitary and phytosanitary measures be based on a risk assessment.[24]

NAFTA 715 sets out factors that NAFTA countries must take into account in assessing risk and determining levels of protection. NAFTA 715(1) lists as factors relevant risk assessment techniques and methodologies developed by international or North American standardizing organizations, relevant scientific evidence, processes and production methods, prevalence of relevant diseases or pests, relevant ecological and other environmental conditions and relevant treatments. NAFTA 715(2) requires that, where relevant, loss of production or sales from and costs of control or eradication of a pest or disease, as well as the relative cost-effectiveness of alternative approaches must be taken into account. NAFTA 715(3)(a) provides that NAFTA countries "should" take into account the objective of minimizing negative trade effects and NAFTA 715(3)(b) requires that NAFTA countries "shall" avoid distinctions in levels of protection that result in "arbitrary or unjustifiable discrimination" against goods of other NAFTA countries or disguised restrictions in trade. These provisions all have somewhat differently worded counterparts in the GATT Sanitary and Phytosanitary Measures Agreement.[25] NAFTA 715(5) provides for the phased application of sanitary and phytosanitary measures.

(c) Scientific principles and other limitations

Like paragraph 2 of Article 2 of the GATT Sanitary and Phytosanitary Agreement, NAFTA 712(3) requires that sanitary and phytosanitary measures be based on scientific principles and not be maintained when there is no longer a scientific basis for them. Paragraph 2 of Article 2 also requires that these measures be applied only to the extent necessary to protect human, animal or plant life or health. NAFTA 715(4) permits provisional measures when relevant scientific evidence or other information is incomplete. Paragraph 7 of Article 5 of the GATT Sanitary and Phytosanitary Measures Agreement sets out a similar provision.

NAFTA 712(5) requires that a sanitary or phytosanitary measure be applied only to the extent necessary to achieve the level of protection that the NAFTA country has determined is appropriate. This requirement, which relates to the application of a measure, does not derogate from a NAFTA country's right in NAFTA 712(2) to determine the appropriate level of protection. Paragraph 6 of Article 5 of the GATT Sanitary and Phytosanitary Measures Agreement takes a different approach by requiring that a measure not be more trade restrictive than necessary to achieve the appropriate level of protection. There is no express "least trade-restrictive" requirement in the NAFTA sanitary and phytosanitary provisions.

(d) Non-discriminatory treatment

As discussed in §1.3(4), NAFTA 712(4) and 712(6) provide respectively that sanitary and phytosanitary measures not arbitrarily or unjustifiably discriminate against goods of other NAFTA countries or constitute disguised restrictions on trade. This is consistent with the approach taken in Paragraph 3 of Article 2 of the GATT Sanitary and Phytosanitary Agreement but constitutes a weaker non-discrimination obligation than the national treatment obligation in NAFTA 301 which, as discussed in §6.5(1), does not apply to sanitary and phytosanitary measures. Some individual provisions do contain national treatment requirements. There is no general MFN obligation but some individual provisions contain MFN provisions.

(4) International Standards and Equivalence

NAFTA 713(1) requires NAFTA countries to use international standards, guidelines or recommendations, defined in NAFTA 724,[26] in establishing sanitary and phytosanitary measures so long as levels of protection are not reduced. One stated objective of this requirement is to make these measures equivalent or, where appropriate, identical, in the NAFTA countries. NAFTA 713(2) provides that if a measure conforms to these defined international norms it will be presumed to comply with the NAFTA sanitary and phytosanitary provisions, but that a measure that is different will not, for that reason alone, be presumed to fail to comply. NAFTA 713(3) reiterates the right of NAFTA countries in NAFTA 712(1) to adopt more stringent standards. NAFTA 713(4) provides that if a NAFTA country believes that a measure maintained by another NAFTA country that is not based on a defined international norm may adversely affect its exports, it may request written reasons explaining why the measure is being maintained. NAFTA 713(5) requires the NAFTA countries to participate in international and North American standardizing organizations. These NAFTA provisions all have somewhat differently worded counterparts in the GATT Sanitary and Phytosanitary Measures Agreement.[27]

NAFTA 714 requires the NAFTA countries to "pursue equivalence" in their sanitary and phytosanitary measures so long as levels of protection are not reduced. An importing NAFTA country is required to treat a measure of exporting NAFTA countries as equivalent to its own if it is objectively demonstrated that the measure achieves the importing NAFTA country's level of protection. A similar but differently worded provision is set out in Paragraph 1 of Article 4 of the GATT Sanitary and Phytosanitary Measures Agreement. Exporting NAFTA countries must facilitate access for inspection, testing and other relevant procedures. A NAFTA country may reject another NAFTA country's measure as equivalent if it has a scientific basis for so doing and provides written reasons.

It is apparent from the decision *In the Matter of Puerto Rico regulations on the import, distribution and sale of U.H.T. milk from Quebec* discussed in §6.2, that a NAFTA country imposing a new and more stringent measure would have to give another NAFTA country the opportunity to demonstrate the equivalency of its measures unless it was clear that the measures were not equivalent.

(5) Adaptation to Regional Conditions

NAFTA 716 requires NAFTA countries to adapt sanitary and phytosanitary measures relating to the introduction, establishment or spread of animal or plant pests or diseases to the characteristics of the area where a good is produced and the area to which it is destined. NAFTA countries must take into account the prevalence of relevant pests or diseases in an area, the existence of eradication or control programs and relevant defined international norms. A NAFTA country concerned about the introduction of a pest or disease must take into account the fact that a good produced in another NAFTA country comes from a pest-free or disease-free area in that country. A NAFTA country will recognize an area of another NAFTA country as pest-free or disease-free if the other NAFTA country can so demonstrate to that NAFTA country's satisfaction, with reasonable access being required to be given to the importing country for inspection and testing. Implicit in this obligation is the requirement that the NAFTA country be given the opportunity to so demonstrate. Similar but differently worded obligations are set out in Article 6 of the GATT Sanitary and Phytosanitary Measures Agreement.

NAFTA also provides that NAFTA countries may maintain different risk assessment procedures for pest or disease-free areas than for low pest or disease areas and may make different final determinations for the disposition of goods produced in these different areas. In the one instance in the NAFTA sanitary and phytosanitary provisions of an MFN obligation, a measure must accord a good produced in a pest or disease-free area of another NAFTA country no less favourable treatment than a good posing the same level of risk produced in a pest or disease-free area of another country. These provisions do not have equivalents in the GATT Sanitary and Phytosanitary Measures Agreement.

(6) Control, Inspection and Approval Procedures

NAFTA 724 distinguishes between "approval procedures" and "control or inspection procedures". An "approval procedure" is a registration, notification or other mandatory administrative procedure for approving the use of an additive or a tolerance for a contaminant in a food, beverage or feedstuff. A "control or inspection procedure" is any procedure other than an "approval procedure" used to determine that a sanitary or phytosanitary measure is fulfilled.[28]

NAFTA 717[29] requires that both types of procedures be applied as expeditiously as possible and in a manner consistent with both national treatment and MFN treatment. The normal processing period must be published or the anticipated processing period must be communicated to an applicant upon request. NAFTA 717 imposes obligations respecting the processing of applications, the information that may be requested and the extent to which specimens or samples may be required. Confidential and proprietary information respecting goods of other NAFTA countries is subject to a national treatment requirement and legitimate commercial interests must be protected. Fees imposed for conducting procedures are subject to both national treatment and MFN treatment requirements. The criteria for locating facilities and selecting samples of goods should not result in unnecessary inconvenience. A mechanism must be provided for reviewing complaints and taking corrective action when they are justified. If a good is modified subsequent to fulfilling a requirement, the procedure is limited to the extent necessary to determine that the good continues to comply.

If a control or inspection procedure must be implemented at the level of production, an exporting NAFTA country will at the request of an importing NAFTA country facilitate access and provide assistance necessary to facilitate the conducting of the procedure. A NAFTA country maintaining an approval procedure may require that approval be obtained before access to its market for a food, beverage or feedstuff is granted, but must consider using a relevant defined international norm as a basis for granting access pending completion of the procedure.

Annex C of the GATT Sanitary and Phytosanitary Measures Agreement sets out similar but differently worded requirements.

(7) Notification, Publication and Provision of Information and Inquiry Points

(a) Notification, publication and provision of information

NAFTA 718(1) imposes notification, publication and provision of information requirements on federal governments which go beyond the general requirements set out in NAFTA 1802 (Publication) and NAFTA 1803 (Notification and Provision of Information). Federal governments must, at least sixty days prior to the adoption or modification of a sanitary or phytosanitary measure other than a law, publish a notice of the proposed measure and notify other NAFTA countries. The good to which the proposed measure is to apply must be identified, as must deviations from the defined international norms. Copies of the measure must be provided to other NAFTA countries and interested persons. Federal governments must allow comments from other NAFTA countries and interested persons, discuss the comments with those making them and take them into account.

NAFTA 718(2) requires NAFTA countries to seek, through appropriate means, to ensure that state and provincial governments, "at an early appropriate stage", give notice and notification of sanitary measures and otherwise comply with the requirements just described. As discussed in §6.6(2), this amounts to a "best efforts" obligation.

NAFTA 718(3) permits the notice and notification requirements just described to be abridged in the case of an urgent problem, provided that other NAFTA countries are notified and apprised of the problem. A copy of the measure must be provided to other NAFTA countries and interested persons and comments must be allowed, discussed and taken into account.

Except where there is an urgent problem, there must be a reasonable time between the publication of a measure and its coming into effect so that interested persons can adapt. NAFTA countries must designate a government authority at the federal level responsible for the implementation of the notification requirements in NAFTA 718 and so notify other NAFTA countries. An importing NAFTA country that denies entry to a good of another NAFTA country because it does not comply with a sanitary or phytosanitary measure, must on request provide a written explanation identifying the measure and the reason for non-compliance.

Paragraph 5 of Annex B of the GATT Sanitary and Phytosanitary Measures Agreement requires notification only when measures are not substantially the same as international standards, guidelines or recommendations or when such international norms do not exist and where the regulation may have a significant effect on the trade of other members. Notification can be abridged in the case of urgent problems, subject to requirements similar to the NAFTA requirements described above.

(b) Inquiry points

NAFTA 719 requires each NAFTA country to ensure that there is at least one inquiry point to answer all reasonable inquiries from other NAFTA countries and interested persons and provide relevant documents regarding a number of matters respecting sanitary and phytosanitary measures maintained at the federal, state or provincial level, including control or inspection procedures, approval procedures, risk assessment procedures and the location of notices and other relevant information, as well as the membership and participation of relevant federal, state or provincial government authorities in international and regional sanitary and phytosanitary organizations and in relevant bilateral and multilateral arrangements. There is a provision similar to NAFTA 719 in paragraph 3 of Annex B of the GATT Sanitary and Phytosanitary Measures Agreement.

(8) Limitations on Provision of Information, Technical Co-operation

NAFTA 721 provides that the NAFTA sanitary and phytosanitary provisions will not require a NAFTA country to provide information in a language other than its (or one of its) official language(s) or to furnish information that would impede law enforcement or be otherwise contrary to the public interest or prejudice legitimate commercial interests of particular enterprises. This latter limitation has the potential of being broadly construed. The corresponding provision in the GATT Sanitary and Phytosanitary Measures Agreement mentions law enforcement solely in the context of sanitary and phytosanitary legislation and does not refer to the public interest.[30]

NAFTA 720 sets out provisions respecting technical co-operation between the NAFTA countries.

(9) Establishment of Committee, Technical Consultations, Committee and Burden of Proof

NAFTA 722 establishes a Committee on Sanitary and Phytosanitary Measures which is to serve a number of purposes, including the facilitation of consultations when disputes arise. In the event of a dispute, a NAFTA country may notify the Committee and the Committee may serve as a vehicle for facilitating consultations through considering the matter itself or referring the matter to a working group for non-binding technical advice. The Committee is to consider matters referred to it expeditiously and provide the NAFTA countries with any technical advice or recommendations that it develops.

NAFTA 723(6) provides that a NAFTA country asserting that a sanitary or phytosanitary measure is inconsistent with the NAFTA sanitary and phytosanitary measures has the burden of proof of establishing the inconsistency. There is no corresponding provision in the GATT Sanitary and Phytosanitary Measures Agreement.

6.6 STANDARDS-RELATED MEASURES

The NAFTA provisions respecting standards-related measures are based primarily on the 1994 GATT Technical Barriers Code. Some concepts have been carried forward from the FTA.

(1) Scope and Coverage

The scope of the provisions of NAFTA Chapter Nine is delineated both by the definitions of "standards-related" measure and "sanitary and phytosanitary" measures discussed in §6.4. Chapter Nine applies to all standards-related measures other than sanitary and phytosanitary measures. An exception is also made for technical specifications prepared by governmental bodies for their own production or consumption requirements. These are governed by the government procurement provisions of NAFTA Chapter Ten discussed in §9.1(10).[31]

There is no exclusion of the human, animal and plant life and health exception in GATT Article XX(b) as with the NAFTA sanitary and phytosanitary provisions. A standards-related measure may be justified under this GATT exception which, as discussed in §4.3(5)(b)(i), has been clarified by NAFTA as including environmental measures.

(2) States and Provinces and Non-governmental Bodies

Unlike the NAFTA provisions respecting sanitary and phytosanitary measures, the obligation to ensure observance of NAFTA provisions by state and provincial governments set out in NAFTA 105 does not apply to NAFTA Chapter Nine. The weaker obligation to "seek, through appropriate measures, to ensure observance" by states and provinces and by non-governmental standardizing bodies applies to NAFTA 904 (Basic Rights and Obligations), NAFTA 905 (Use of International Standards), NAFTA 906 (Compatibility and Equivalence), NAFTA 907 (Assessment of Risk), NAFTA 908 (Conformity Assessment) and to some provisions of NAFTA 909 (Notification, Publication and Provision of Information). These provisions are discussed in §6.6(3) through to §6.6(7). The dictionary definition of "seek" is "to try to bring about or effect"[32] and the panel in *In the Matter of Puerto Rico regulations on the import, distribution and sale of U.H.T. milk from Quebec* interpreted "shall seek" in FTA 708(1) as imposing a "best efforts" obligation.[33]

With some exceptions, the 1994 GATT Technical Barriers Agreement requires central governments to "take such reasonable measures as may be available to them to ensure compliance" by state and provincial governments with provisions respecting technical regulations, standards and conformity assessment procedures.[34] While this obligation may not be as strong as the general requirement in NAFTA 105 to "take all necessary measures", it is clearly stronger than the "seek, through appropriate measures" obligation that applies in NAFTA Chapter Nine.

(3) Basic Rights and Obligations

(a) Basic rights and legitimate objectives

NAFTA 904(1) states that NAFTA countries may adopt standards-related measures so long as they are in accordance with NAFTA. These measures may include the prohibition of the importation of goods of other NAFTA countries or the provision of land transportation or telecommunications services from other NAFTA countries if approval procedures are not completed or measures are not in compliance. Specific reference is made to the right to adopt measures relating to "safety" and the "protection of human, animal or plant life or health, the environment or consumers". NAFTA 915 defines these objectives, together with "sustainable development", as "legitimate objectives". The NAFTA concept of "legitimate objective" is similar to the FTA concept of a "legitimate domestic objective"[35] and the concept of the "legitimate objective" set out in the 1994 GATT Technical Barriers Agreement.[36] Unlike its FTA and 1994 GATT Technical Barriers Agreement counterparts, the NAFTA concept of a "legitimate objective" does not include "essential security" or "national security".[37]

(b) Level of protection and assessment of risk

NAFTA 904(2) provides that a NAFTA country may, in pursuing its legitimate objectives,[38] establish the level of protection that it considers appropriate. As with the corresponding provision for sanitary and phytosanitary measures discussed in §6.5(3)(b)(i), this provision is significant because it makes it clear that NAFTA does not oblige NAFTA countries to harmonize their standards. One NAFTA country can adopt a zero-tolerance approach to a problem while another NAFTA country may choose to tolerate a certain level of risk. There is no counterpart to this provision in the 1994 GATT Technical Barriers Code.

Unlike with sanitary and phytosanitary measures, an assessment of risk is not mandatory with standards-related measures. NAFTA 907(1), which covers risk assessments, is permissive and sets out factors such as available scientific or technical information that a NAFTA country may take into account in making an assessment of risk but does not confine a NAFTA country to the listed factors or require that technical regulations or standards have a scientific basis as is the case with sanitary and phytosanitary measures. NAFTA 907(3) permits NAFTA countries to adopt provisional regulations where scientific or other information is insufficient to complete the assessment.

NAFTA 907(2) provides that NAFTA countries "should", in establishing levels of protection and conducting risk assessments, avoid distinctions between similar goods and services where the distinctions result in arbitrary or unjustifiable discrimination against goods or service providers of other NAFTA countries, or constitute a disguised restriction on trade or discriminate between similar goods or services for the same use under the same conditions posing the same levels of risk. Unlike its counterpart in NAFTA 715(3)(b) discussed in §6.5(3)(b)(ii), this non-discrimination obligation uses the ambiguous expression "should" rather than the unambiguous expression "shall", suggesting that there are circumstances in which this obligation does not apply.

(c) Non-discriminatory treatment

NAFTA 904(3)(a) requires the NAFTA countries to accord national treatment in respect of their standards-related measures in accordance with NAFTA 301 and NAFTA 1202. The inclusion of NAFTA 301 contrasts with the express exclusion in NAFTA 710 of NAFTA 301, discussed in §6.5(1), respecting sanitary and phytosanitary measures. NAFTA 1202 is referred to because standards-related measures include measures affecting land transportation and telecommunications services. NAFTA 904(3)(b) sets out an MFN obligation requiring NAFTA countries to accord to goods and service providers of other NAFTA countries treatment no less favourable than that accorded to like goods and service providers in similar circumstance of other countries. The 1994 GATT Technical Barriers Agreement also contains both national treatment and MFN obligations.[39]

(d) Unnecessary obstacles

NAFTA 904(4) carries forward the basic principle established in the 1980 GATT Technical Barriers Code and the FTA that standards-related measures not create unnecessary obstacles to trade. Paragraph 2.2 of the 1994 GATT Technical Barriers Agreement sets out a similar provision respecting technical regulations but also requires that they not be more trade-restrictive than necessary to fulfil a legitimate objective. There is no express "least trade-restrictive" requirement in NAFTA Chapter Nine.

Following the approach in the FTA, NAFTA 904(4) provides that an unnecessary obstacle to trade "shall not be deemed to be created" where the demonstrable purpose of the measure is to achieve a legitimate objective and the measure does not exclude goods of other NAFTA countries that meet that objective. Paragraph 2.5 of the 1994 GATT Technical Barriers Code provides that a technical regulation that meets a legitimate objective and is in accordance with an international standard shall be "rebuttably presumed" not to create an obstacle to international trade.

(4) International Standards

NAFTA 905(1) requires the NAFTA countries to use international standards as the basis for their standards-related measures. An international standard is defined in NAFTA 915 as standards-related measures or other guides or recommendations adopted by an international standardizing body[40] and made public. This obligation does not apply if the international standard would be ineffective or inappropriate because of factors related to climate, geography, infrastructure, scientific justification or the level of protection that a NAFTA country considers appropriate. The 1994 GATT Technical Barriers Agreement sets out similar but differently worded provisions that do not include level of protection considered appropriate as a factor.[41] NAFTA 905(3), which does not have a counterpart in the 1994 GATT Technical Barriers Code, permits NAFTA countries to apply standards-related measures providing for higher levels of protection than international standards.

NAFTA 905(2) provides that a standards-related measure that conforms to an international standard is presumed to be consistent with the provisions respecting non-discrimination and obstacles to trade. The corresponding provision in the 1994 GATT Technical Barriers Code is paragraph 2.5, which differs in that a technical regulation complying with the international standard must also meet a legitimate objective for the presumption to apply.

(5) Compatibility and Equivalence

NAFTA 906 elaborates upon the FTA concept of making standards-related measures compatible. The expression "make compatible" is defined in NAFTA 915 as bringing different standards-related measures of the same scope approved by differing standardizing bodies to a level that they are identical, equivalent or have the effect of permitting goods or services to be used in place of one another to fulfil the same purpose. The corresponding FTA definition differed in that it was based on reciprocal recognition of differing standards as being technically identical or equivalent. NAFTA 906(2) requires that the NAFTA countries, to the greatest extent practicable and taking international standardizing activities into account, make compatible their standards-related measures to facilitate trade in goods or land transportation or telecommunications, but not so as to reduce levels of safety or protection and without prejudice to other rights under Chapter Nine. The corresponding requirement in FTA 604(1) was based on the greatest extent "possible" rather than "practicable" and was not subject to these other qualifications. There is no counterpart to these "make compatible" provisions in the 1994 GATT Technical Barriers Agreement.

An importing NAFTA country must treat a technical regulation of an exporting NAFTA country as equivalent to its own if the exporting NAFTA country can satisfy the importing NAFTA country that the technical regulation fulfils the importing country's legitimate objectives. An exporting NAFTA country may request written reasons if the importing NAFTA country does not treat its technical regulation as equivalent. As with the corresponding provision for sanitary and phytosanitary provisions discussed in §6.5(4), the decision *In the Matter of Puerto Rico regulations on the import, distribution and sale of U.H.T. milk from Quebec* leads to the conclusion that a NAFTA country imposing a new and more stringent measure would have to give another NAFTA country the opportunity to demonstrate equivalency unless it was clear that the measures were not equivalent.

Paragraph 2.7 of the 1994 GATT Technical Barriers Code contains a somewhat weaker requirement in that members are only required to give "positive consideration" to accepting the technical regulations of other members as equivalent.

(6) Conformity Assessment

(a) Conformity assessment procedures and approval procedures applied by a NAFTA country

NAFTA 908(3) sets out requirements to be observed by the NAFTA countries in applying their own conformity assessment procedures. Procedures must not be stricter than necessary to be satisfied that the good or service conforms. Procedures must be expeditious and undertaken in a non-discriminatory order. NAFTA 908(3) imposes obligations respecting publishing or communicating processing periods, processing applications, information that may be requested, treatment of confidential and proprietary information, imposition of fees, location of facilities, requiring samples dealing with modifications subsequent to approval similar to those set out in NAFTA 717 for sanitary and phytosanitary standards described in §6.5(6). The 1994 GATT Technical Barriers Agreement sets out similar but differently worded procedures.[42] Unlike NAFTA 717 and the GATT Technical Barriers Agreement, NAFTA 908(3) does not require that the procedure include a process for reviewing complaints.[43] NAFTA 908(4) provides that these requirements also apply to approval procedures with such modifications as may be necessary.

(b) Conformity procedures of other NAFTA countries

NAFTA Chapter Nine sets out several provisions respecting recognition of conformity assessment procedures of other NAFTA countries. NAFTA 906(6) requires that, where possible, a NAFTA country accept the results of the conformity assessment procedure conducted in another NAFTA country where it is satisfied that the procedure offers assurance that the good or service complies with its own applicable technical regulation or standard. NAFTA 908(1) imposes a "make compatible" obligation respecting conformity assessment procedures maintained by the NAFTA countries and NAFTA 908(2) requires that each NAFTA country accredit conformity assessment bodies in other NAFTA countries on terms no less favourable than its own. This accreditation obligation does not apply to Mexico until January 1, 1998.[44]

(7) Notification, Publication and Provision of Information and Inquiry Points

(a) Notification, publication and provision of information

NAFTA 909(1) sets out requirements respecting notification and provision of information respecting the adoption and modification of technical regulations that are virtually identical to those applicable to sanitary and phytosanitary measures in NAFTA 718(1) described in §6.5(7)(a). The one difference is that NAFTA 909(1) provides that in the case of perishable goods the period can be shortened to thirty days. NAFTA 909(3) sets out a requirement similar to that in NAFTA 718(2) that NAFTA countries seek, through appropriate means, to ensure that state and provincial governments, "at an early appropriate stage", give notice and notification of technical regulations and otherwise comply with these requirements. Like NAFTA 718(3), NAFTA 909(4) permits the notice and notification requirements just described to be abridged in the case of an urgent problem so long as other NAFTA countries are notified and apprised of the problem, a copy of the measure is provided to other NAFTA countries and interested persons and comments are allowed, discussed and taken into account.

NAFTA 909(2) requires notification at an "early appropriate stage" of standards and conformity assessment procedures where a relevant international standard does not exist or the proposed measure is not the same as an international standard, and where the measure may have a significant effect on the trade of other NAFTA countries. This requirement is similar to that imposed by the 1994 GATT Technical Barriers Agreement for technical regulations and conformity assessment procedures.[45] However, the notification requirement for standards in Annex 3 of the GATT Technical Barriers Agreement more closely corresponds to the requirements in NAFTA 909(1) for technical regulations.[46]

If a NAFTA country permits its own non-government persons to be present during the development of a standards-related measure, non-government persons from other NAFTA countries must also be permitted to be present. NAFTA countries must notify other NAFTA countries of the development of, amendment to or change in the application of a standards-related measure no later than when it notifies its own non-government persons or the relevant sector. NAFTA countries must seek, through appropriate measures, to ensure compliance with these requirements by state and provincial governments.

Except where there is an urgent problem, there must be a reasonable time between the publication of a measure and its coming into effect so that interested persons can adapt. NAFTA countries must designate a government authority at the federal level responsible for the implementation of the notification requirements in NAFTA 909 and so notify other NAFTA countries.

(b) Inquiry points

NAFTA 910(1) sets out requirements respecting inquiry points for standards-related measures that are similar to those in NAFTA 719, described in §6.5(7)(b), for sanitary and phytosanitary measures. If more than one inquiry point is designated, NAFTA 910(2) requires a NAFTA country to provide complete and unambiguous information respecting the responsibility of each point and to redirect incorrectly addressed inquiries. NAFTA 910(3) requires NAFTA countries to provide inquiry points to answer inquiries respecting standards and conformity assessment procedures maintained by non-governmental standardizing bodies.

(8) Limitation on Provision of Information, Technical Co-operation

NAFTA 912 applies the same requirement respecting limitation on provision of information set out in NAFTA 721, described in §6.5(8), to the obligations set out in NAFTA Chapter Nine. The counterpart in paragraph 10.8 of the 1994 GATT Technical Barriers Code refers only to essential security interests and does not mention law enforcement, the public interest or legitimate commercial interests. NAFTA 911 sets out provisions similar to those in NAFTA 720 respecting technical co-operation between the NAFTA countries and NAFTA 914 sets out provisions for technical consultations.

(9) Committee on Standards-related Measures and Subcommittees

Under NAFTA 913, the NAFTA countries have established a Committee on Standards-Related Measures to monitor the implementation of Chapter Nine, facilitate the process of making standards-related measures compatible and provide a vehicle for consultation. The Committee is required to establish a Land Transportation Subcommittee, a Telecommunications Standards Subcommittee, an Automotive Standards Council, a Subcommittee on Labelling of Textile and Apparel Goods and such other subcommittees as it considers appropriate. The functions of the four specifically identified committees are described in NAFTA Annexes 913.5.a-1 through to 913.5.a-4 respectively.

The Land Transportation Subcommittee and the Telecommunications

Standards Subcommittee are required to establish work programs to make various standards-related measures compatible. The requirements respecting the Land Transportation Subcommittee, which covers bus, truck and rail transportation, are the most specific and NAFTA Annex 913.5.a-1, which describes the functions of this subcommittee, sets out specific time limits for making certain standards-related measures compatible.[47] The work of the Telecommunications Subcommittee described in NAFTA Annex 913.5.a-2 relates to measures respecting "authorized equipment", which is defined in NAFTA 1310 as terminal or other equipment approved for attachment to the public telecommunications transport network discussed in §7.11(3). The functions of the Automotive Standards Council described in NAFTA Annex 913.5.a-3 are somewhat more general. NAFTA Annex 913.5.a-4 provides for the establishment by the Subcommittee of Labelling and Apparel Goods of a work program to harmonize labelling requirements of textile and apparel goods through the adoption of uniform labelling provisions. It must be emphasized that none of these provisions harmonizes or "makes compatible" any standards-related measures.

(10) Technical Consultations and Burden of Proof

As under the NAFTA sanitary and phytosanitary measures, in the event of a dispute, a NAFTA country may notify the Committee on Standards-Related Measures and the Committee may serve as a vehicle for facilitating consultations by considering the matter itself or referring the matter to a working group for non-binding technical advice. The Committee must expeditiously consider matters referred to it and provide the NAFTA countries with any technical advice or recommendations that it develops.

NAFTA 914(4) provides that a NAFTA country asserting that a standards-related measure is inconsistent with NAFTA Chapter Nine, has the burden of proof of establishing the inconsistency. There is no corresponding provision in the 1994 GATT Technical Barriers Agreement.

6.7 RELATION BETWEEN NAFTA PROVISIONS AND URUGUAY ROUND AGREEMENTS

The NAFTA sanitary and phytosanitary measures do not refer to the GATT Sanitary and Phytosanitary Measures Agreement. However, paragraph 3 of Article 11 of the GATT Sanitary and Phytosanitary Measures Agreement provides that nothing in it shall impair the rights of member countries under other international agreements. While this provision is included with a group of provisions relating to consultations and dispute settlement, it is general in its wording. Article 30(2) of the Vienna Convention on the

Law of Treaties provides that when a treaty specifies that it is not to be considered as incompatible with an earlier or later treaty, the other treaty prevails. Based on this rule of interpretation, the NAFTA sanitary and phytosanitary measures would prevail as among the NAFTA countries over the GATT Sanitary and Phytosanitary Measures Agreement in the event of incompatibility.

In NAFTA 903, the NAFTA countries affirm, but do not incorporate, their rights and obligations under the 1980 Technical Barriers Agreement.[48] The rights and obligations affirmed are those that existed on January 1, 1994, so, as discussed in §1.6(5), the rule of prevalence in NAFTA 103 applies. NAFTA Chapter Nine makes no reference to the 1994 GATT Technical Barriers Agreement, either specifically or by reference to a successor agreement to the 1980 Technical Barriers Agreement and the 1994 GATT Technical Barriers Agreement does not contain any provision similar to that in paragraph 3 of Article 11 of the GATT Sanitary and Phytosanitary Measures Agreement. Therefore, the considerations discussed in §1.6(6)(b) apply as between NAFTA Chapter Nine and the 1994 GATT Technical Barriers Agreement.

6.8 THE NAFTA TEXT AND ENVIRONMENTAL ISSUES

While trade disciplines have always had an obvious relationship to environmental measures that prohibit or limit imports or exports or establish conditions under which products may be sold, environmental issues per se were not considered by the negotiators in the GATT rounds preceding the Uruguay Round and environmentalists did not focus on the strictures imposed by trade disciplines on environmental measures. This has changed in recent years as environmental problems have become more compelling. Some environmentalists have come to view the GATT and agreements based on GATT principles as heavily biased in favour of the market and against environmental goals such as sustainable development.

The interaction of the disciplines imposed by trade agreements with environmental policy can be broken down into three broad categories. The first relates to the potentially negative effect of trade disciplines on the ability of a country to take measures to protect its own environment through prohibiting the importation of dangerous goods, setting product standards and encouraging its own industries to use environmentally friendly production processes. The second relates to whether trade disciplines should permit retaliation against countries that attract investment through weak environmental laws and lax environment enforcement and thereby undermine more rigorous environmental measures in other countries. The third relates to whether trade agreements should address global and cross-border environmental problems or whether these issues are better dealt with through other means. The purpose of this discussion is to review briefly the provisions of the main NAFTA text in relation to environmental concerns and to identify the major issues that arise under each of these categories.

(1) Measures to Protect the Domestic Environment

Measures to protect the domestic environment can affect both products themselves and the processes by which they are produced. Some measures directed at products take the form of quantitative restrictions or outright prohibitions. In trade terms, these translate into import restrictions. In some instances, a country may wish to protect its environment by imposing export restrictions on resources to prevent their excessive exploitation. Product standards to protect human, animal or plant life or health affect the conditions under which imported as well as domestic products can be offered for sale. Encouraging the use of environmentally friendly production processes through subsidies can expose exporting domestic industries to GATT-sanctioned countervailing duties.

(a) Import and export controls

As discussed in §4.3, NAFTA carries forward the GATT regime respecting import and export controls virtually intact. The most significant modifications made by NAFTA from an environmental perspective are those discussed in §4.3(5)(b) respecting the human, animal or plant life or health exception in GATT Article XX(b) and the exhaustible natural resources exception in GATT Article XX(g). The clarification that GATT Article XX(b) includes environmental measures necessary to protect human, animal and plant life and health should remove doubts that the scope of this exception is confined to sanitary measures only. The NAFTA disciplines on export controls discussed in §4.3(6) have a potentially negative impact on environmental policy to the extent that they inhibit the ability to maintain conservation policies. However, these disciplines may have an indirect positive environmental effect to the extent that they encourage Americans to use Canadian natural gas rather than domestic coal or imported oil.

(b) Standards

The ability to set standards is critical to protecting the domestic environment and trade disciplines potentially undermine environmental policy by creating grounds under which standards can be challenged. Standards are always trade inhibiting to some extent because they impose additional requirements that must be satisfied by both domestic and foreign producers in order to sell their goods. The trade-off is increased environmental protection. However, standards can be potent protectionist weapons and the objective of trade policy is to distinguish between measures that protect the environment and those that protect domestic producers from foreign competition. As always, the difficult case is the measure that has both effects.[49] Free traders will lean towards combatting protectionism while many environmentalists would prefer to give any benefit of doubt to the environment.

The NAFTA provisions respecting standards are the sanitary and phytosanitary measures and the standards-related measures discussed in §6.5 and §6.6 respectively. Concerns have been expressed by environmentalists that these NAFTA provisions provide a basis for challenging environmental standards in the United States and Canada.

(i) Level of protection, risk assessment and scientific basis

It seems clear in both the NAFTA sanitary and phytosanitary provisions and in NAFTA Chapter Nine that it is up to each NAFTA country to choose the level of protection that will be provided by its measures. However, according to at least some environmentalists, the fact that sanitary and phytosanitary measures must be based on a risk assessment and have a scientific basis leaves some standards, such as the zero-risk standard under the U.S. Food, Drug and Cosmetic Act for carcinogenic pesticides, open to challenge because the zero-risk standard is based on policy rather than scientific judgments.[50] The response in this particular case is that scientific evidence that the pesticides in question present a risk of cancer should satisfy both the risk assessment and scientific basis requirements and that choosing a zero-risk level of protection falls within a NAFTA country's right to choose its own level of protection. The risk assessment requirement requires that it be determined that there actually is a risk. Once that is determined, a NAFTA country may, as a matter of policy, choose the level of protection that it wishes to apply against that risk. This right applies notwithstanding other NAFTA sanitary or phytosanitary provisions. Measures to which Chapter Nine applies do not have to be based on a risk assessment and need not have a scientific basis.

(ii) Necessary and least-trade-restrictive

The concept of necessity applies to both sanitary and phytosanitary measures and to standards-related measures. Sanitary and phytosanitary measures must be applied only to the extent necessary to achieve a level of protection; standards-related measures cannot constitute unnecessary, as opposed to necessary, obstacles to trade. While NAFTA does not expressly impose a least-trade-restrictive requirement, concern has been expressed that the GATT jurisprudence respecting the term "necessary" leads to the same result.[51]

The concept of necessity does not apply to the choice of the level of protection afforded by a sanitary and phytosanitary measure because the right to establish a level of protection in NAFTA 712(2) applies notwithstanding any other NAFTA sanitary or phytosanitary provision. So long as a product like a pesticide presents a risk, a NAFTA country is free to adopt a zero-tolerance policy. The "extent necessary" requirement applies to achieving the level of protection once it is chosen. A NAFTA country choosing a zero-tolerance policy in respect of residues of a pesticide could breach the "extent necessary" requirement by banning all imports of a food product from another NAFTA country on the grounds that the product might contain residues of the pesticide. The zero-tolerance result could be achieved by permitting imports and inspecting them.

The deeming provision in NAFTA 904(4) should go a long way to shielding standards-related measures from challenge under NAFTA on the basis that they are "unnecessary". As indicated in §6.6(3)(d), the corresponding provision in the 1994 GATT Technical Barriers Agreement offers less protection from challenge as the presumption is rebuttable.

(iii) Arbitrary and unjustifiable discrimination and disguised restriction

Environmentalists are troubled by the arbitrary and unjustifiable discrimination and disguised restriction requirements that apply to both sanitary and phytosanitary measures and standards-related measures. One concern expressed respecting the arbitrary and unjustifiable discrimination requirement is that inconsistent levels of protection in U.S. pesticide and food safety regulations could constitute arbitrary or unjustifiable distinctions that would be open to challenge.[52] As discussed in §1.3(4), the scope of the arbitrary and unjustifiable discrimination requirement that qualifies a number of GATT exceptions and requirements is unclear. However, for the requirement to apply at all a measure must discriminate on the basis of nationality. Tolerance amounts that vary from good to good would not normally constitute discrimination so long as the tolerance amount for each category applied equally to all goods, regardless of nationality. However, if a high tolerance amount applied to a category of good that happened to be a domestic product and a low tolerance amount applied to a category of good that happened to be imported there would be a basis for a claim of discrimination. The next step would be to determine whether the discrimination was arbitrary or unjustifiable.

As discussed in §1.3(4), the disguised restriction requirement has been narrowly construed in GATT jurisprudence.

(iv) International standards

Some U.S. environmentalists have been critical of the provisions in the NAFTA sanitary and phytosanitary measures requiring harmonization with international standards, as well as international standards-setting organizations referred to in the NAFTA definitions such as the Codex Alimentarius Commission. This international body is jointly funded by the World Health Organization and the Food and Agriculture Organization and establishes recommended food, safety and nutritional standards and suggested maximum residue limits for contaminants such as pesticides.[53] The standards published by Codex have been characterized as much weaker than U.S. public health standards.[54] Other studies suggest that while some Codex standards are weaker than U.S. standards, many are the same and some are stronger.[55] In any event, NAFTA 713(3) and NAFTA 905(3) clearly permits NAFTA countries to adopt more stringent standards.

(c) Environmental subsidies

Rather than following the "polluter pays principle", a concept adopted by the Organization for Economic Cooperation and Development,[56] governments sometimes defray the cost of pollution prevention and control through outright subsidies or other financial concessions. One prime motive for doing this is to avoid job loss that results from producers who cannot or will not pay for pollution control equipment out of their own funds. While subsidies that are generally available are not open to attack, subsidies paid to specific producers are vulnerable to challenge through countervailing duty actions if they can be linked to lower priced exports that cause material injury to industries in the importing country. As discussed in §11.4(7), NAFTA does not alter the countervailing duty laws among the three NAFTA countries and makes no special exception for subsidies or other governmental assistance given to firms for environmental reasons. However, the Uruguay Round *Agreement on Subsidies and Countervailing Duties*, discussed in §11.4(3)(c)(ii), identifies as non-actionable government assistance for adapting existing facilities to new environmental requirements so long as certain conditions are met.[57] NAFTA 1902(2)(d) has the effect of requiring that amendments to a NAFTA country's countervailing duty laws must be consistent with this requirement once it comes into effect in 1995.

(2) The Pollution Haven Question

From an environmental point of view, countries that create pollution havens through weak or non-existent environmental laws and enforcement undermine strict environmental laws and stringent enforcement by encouraging industries to relocate to avoid compliance costs. U.S. and Canadian environmentalists have had particular concerns with Mexico because of its relatively poor record in environmental matters and because of the perception that its environmental laws were not accompanied with effective regulations and were inadequately enforced.[58] The concern expressed by many was that with the removal of tariffs and other trade restrictions at least some U.S. and Canadian businesses would relocate to Mexico to lower production costs by avoiding having to meet U.S. and Canadian environmental standards. The goods produced would have an unfair competitive advantage[59] over U.S. and Canadian goods produced in accordance with strict environmental standards. Governments would have to choose between lowering standards or facing higher unemployment levels.

The only provision in the NAFTA text that directly addresses the pollution haven issue is NAFTA 1114, under which the NAFTA countries recognize that it is "inappropriate to encourage investment by relaxing health, safety or environmental measures". Accordingly, NAFTA countries "should not" waive or otherwise derogate from such measures in order to attract investment. A NAFTA country that considers that another NAFTA country has encouraged investments by these means may request consultations. NAFTA 1114 has been criticized for using the ambiguous "should" rather than the mandatory "shall" and, in referring only to waiving or derogating from measures, does nothing to prevent a NAFTA country from adopting measures that provide low levels of protection.

There are several approaches to pollution havens advocated by environmentalists. One is to permit restrictions on the importation of products produced using environmentally unsound processes. GATT rules do not permit import restrictions based on process. As discussed in §4.3(5)(b)(i), the "human, animal and plant life or health" exception in GATT Article XX(b) does not have extra-territorial application. Therefore, while the importation of dangerous products can be prohibited or restricted, the importation of benign products produced through environmentally unsound processes that threaten human, animal and plant life or health in other countries cannot be restricted. NAFTA does not alter this GATT approach.

Another approach advocated by environmentalists follows from the notion that products produced in pollution havens have an unfair competitive advantage over those produced in countries with appropriate environmental standards and levels of enforcement. Such products should be charged with a countervailing duty on the basis that the failure to maintain or to enforce adequate standards amounts to a subsidy.[60] The countervailing duty would be equal to the cost of complying with adequate standards. Under present international trading rules, as reflected in both the GATT and NAFTA, a countervailing duty could not be justified on this basis. Such a duty would be a breach of GATT tariff concessions and the NAFTA commitment to eliminate duties.

There are several responses to these concerns. First, it is questionable as to how likely businesses are to move to take advantage of substandard environmental norms and weak environmental enforcement. Several studies suggest that pollution abatement costs represent a relatively small percentage of production costs in most industries and that the cost saving would not be worth the trouble of moving.[61] Also, businesses contemplating a move to Mexico to save on pollution abatement costs must consider future and not past Mexican environmental policies. Second, international trading rules based on notions of process-based import restrictions and environmental countervailing duties presuppose a consensus of what constitutes appropriate environmental standards. While this may be feasible within international structures with a supranational institutional structure such as the European Union, it becomes much more difficult within loose arrangements such as NAFTA and even looser arrangements such as the GATT.

One economist has characterized looking for "policy and institutional differences as sources of unfair trade" as "opening up a Pandora's box" that will "diminish greatly the possibility of agreeing to a rules-oriented trading system".[62] Environmentalists question the value of rules-oriented trading systems if the rules inhibit the application of measures that protect the global environment while developing countries with few comparative advantages resist the concept of "green" trade barriers. The GATT Trade and Environment Committee formed at Marrakesh in April 1994 will have to consider these conflicting positions.

(3) Global and Cross-border Environmental Issues

Two broad issues arise when considering trade agreements in the context of global and cross-border environmental problems. First, do the disciplines imposed by the trade agreement frustrate the implementation of measures designed to address the environmental problem? Second, should the trade agreement sanction the use of trade remedies to force countries to address environmental problems?

The trade disciplines most likely to work at cross purposes with environmental measures are those that inhibit the imposition of import and export controls. The basic premise under GATT Article XI and NAFTA 309 is that import and export restrictions are prohibited. If an import or export restriction is to be GATT or NAFTA consistent, it must be justified under an exception. The GATT exceptions give ample scope for enacting measures to protect the domestic environment but do not have extra-territorial application. Global environmental problems cannot be solved at a national level. Solutions may require countries to enact measures primarily directed at circumstances beyond their borders. For example, the prevention of the extinction of an endangered species may require that the trade in products derived from that species be banned. To bring this into effect, countries must ban imports on products derived from animals indigenous to other countries but not their own, which is contrary to the general approach taken by GATT panels that the GATT exemptions do not have extra-territorial application. NAFTA addresses this limitation in the scope of the NAFTA exceptions by providing that certain international environmental agreements described in §6.8(4) take precedence over NAFTA. However, there is no general principle that NAFTA countries can take measures, either unilaterally or in concert with other countries, otherwise inconsistent with NAFTA, if the measures are necessary to address a global environmental problem.

As discussed previously respecting pollution havens, some environmentalists advocate the use of trade remedies as a response to environmental problems. One reason is because of the general absence of effective dispute settlement and enforcement procedures in international law as it pertains to the environment and in international environmental agreements. While the dispute settlement and enforcement procedures in trade agreements such as NAFTA and the GATT may not be well suited for addressing environmental problems, they are perceived as at least providing a possible means for dealing with these issues. The drafters of the NAFTA text resisted demands for specific environmentally based trade remedies or "green" taxes on cross-border trade among the NAFTA countries to provide funding to remedy cross-border pollution problems. However, the Environmental Cooperation Agreement discussed in §6.9 addresses some of these issues and provides for remedies.

(4) Prevalence of Specified International Agreements over NAFTA

NAFTA 104 identifies a number of major international environmental agreements and provides that each prevails in the event of an inconsistency with NAFTA. Where alternative means exist for complying with the international agreement, NAFTA countries must choose the means that is least inconsistent with NAFTA. The agreements identified are:

(a) Convention on International Trade in Endangered Species of Wild Fauna and Flora

This Convention, to which each NAFTA country is a party, was completed March 3, 1973 and amended June 22, 1979. The Convention prohibits the trade in endangered species and products derived from them. Restrictions enacted pursuant this Convention on imports of products derived from endangered species, such as a Canadian prohibition on the importation of products made from ivory from African elephants, do not protect domestic animal life in foreign countries and are not covered by the "human, animal or plant life or health" exception in GATT Article XX(b). NAFTA 104 ensures that restrictions such as these are not open to challenge under NAFTA.

(b) Montreal Protocol on Substances that Deplete the Ozone Layer

The Montreal Protocol, to which each NAFTA country is a party, was completed September 16, 1987[63] and amended June 29, 1990.[64] The Protocol sets out timetables for the signatory countries to reduce consumption of substances that deplete the earth's ozone layer such as chlorofluorocarbons and halons. Consumption is defined in the Protocol as production plus imports minus exports of controlled substances,[65] and provisions enacted in signatory countries include import and export controls.[66] In the absence of the Protocol and NAFTA 104, it is at least open to question as to whether a GATT member country could justify import and export controls of these substances under GATT Article XX(b) when there is no direct connection between the use of the substances and domestic human life or health.

(c) Basel Convention on the Control of Transboundary Movements of Hazardous Wastes and their Disposal

The Basel Convention, which was completed March 22, 1989,[67] sets out rules respecting the generation, transboundary movement and disposition of hazardous wastes. These rules include both import and export controls. For example, signatories must prohibit the export of hazardous wastes to non-signatories and to other signatories that prohibit their importation. Imports of hazardous wastes from non-signatories are prohibited. Transboundary movement of hazardous wastes should be allowed only if a signatory does not have appropriate facilities for disposing of them.

(d) Bilateral agreements

NAFTA 104 also provides that *Agreement Between the Government of Canada and the Government of the United States Concerning the Transboundary Movement of Hazardous Waste*, signed at Ottawa, October 28, 1986, and the *Agreement Between the United States of America and the United Mexican States on Cooperation for the Protection and Improvement of the Environment in the Border Area*, signed at La Paz, Baja California Sur, August 14, 1983, prevail over NAFTA.

6.9   THE ENVIRONMENTAL COOPERATION AGREEMENT

The Environmental Cooperation Agreement, which was entered into force on January 1, 1994, is a comprehensive arrangement among the three NAFTA countries that sets out general commitments of each NAFTA country respecting its environment. It creates an institutional structure, provides for cooperation and the provision of information among the NAFTA countries and, perhaps most significantly, establishes a dispute resolution process that can result in the withdrawal of NAFTA benefits or the imposition of monetary penalties.

(1)   General Commitments

The general commitments of the NAFTA countries are set out in Part Two of the Environmental Cooperation Agreement. Article 3 recognizes the right of each NAFTA country to establish its own levels of environmental protection but requires each NAFTA country to ensure that its laws and regulations provide for "high" levels of environmental protection. While "high" is not defined, this commitment, when read together with the obligations in NAFTA 713 and NAFTA 905 respecting the use of international standards, could make it difficult for a NAFTA country to ignore in its domestic laws a situation that was generally recognized as an environmental problem requiring remedial action, particularly when there were internationally recognized means for dealing with it. However, failure to observe this requirement is not subject to the enforcement procedures discussed in §6.9(4).

Article 4 requires that environmental laws, regulations and administrative rulings of general application be published or otherwise made available so that interested persons can become familiar with them. Proposed measures must be published in advance and interested persons and other NAFTA countries must be given a reasonable opportunity to comment. Article 5 commits the NAFTA countries to enforcing their environmental laws and regulations through appropriate government action. Various means are listed. NAFTA countries must ensure that judicial, quasi-judicial or administrative proceedings are available to enforce environmental laws and criteria are set out for sanctions and remedies. Article 6 sets out commitments respecting private access to remedies and Article 7 establishes procedural guarantees.

Article 2(3) takes a tentative step towards extra-territorial application of the GATT "human, animal or plant life or health" exception by requiring NAFTA countries to "consider prohibiting" the export to other NAFTA countries of pesticides or toxic substances, the use of which it prohibits. Presumably this provision could be invoked to justify such a export restriction despite the absence of an available exception under current GATT jurisprudence.

(2) Commission for Environmental Cooperation

Part Three of the Environmental Cooperation Agreement establishes a Commission for Environmental Cooperation comprised of a Council, a Secretariat and a Joint Public Advisory Committee.

(a) The Council

The Council is comprised of the cabinet level or equivalent representatives of the NAFTA countries. The Council is the governing body of the Commission and performs a variety of functions, the principal of which are making recommendations and serving as a vehicle for dispute resolution. The Council establishes its rules and procedures. The Council may consider and develop recommendations regarding a wide range of environmental issues listed in Article 10(2). The Council will also develop recommendations regarding public access to information and appropriate limits for specific pollutants. The Council will serve as a point of inquiry and receipt for comments from non-governmental organizations and will provide assistance in any consultations requested under NAFTA 1114 discussed in §6.8(2). The Council will promote the exchange of information on criteria and methodologies used in establishing environmental standards and develop procedures for developing greater compatibility of environmental technical regulations, standards and conformity assessment procedures.

(b) The Secretariat

(i) General functions

The Secretariat is comprised of an Executive Director, an office which rotates consecutively between nationals of each NAFTA country, and a staff. The Secretariat provides technical, administrative and operational support to the Council and prepares an annual report and other reports.

(ii) Submissions of failure to enforce effectively

The Secretariat performs the important function of considering submissions from non-governmental organizations or persons assenting that a NAFTA country is failing to enforce effectively its environmental laws. Article 14(1) sets out a number of criteria that must be satisfied by the Secretariat before it will be considered. For example, the identity of the person or organization, who must reside in a NAFTA country, must be clearly identified and the submission must contain sufficient information. The submission must appear to be aimed at promoting enforcement rather than at harassing industry. The submission must indicate that the matter has been communicated to the NAFTA country in question and set out the response, if any, to such communication. If the submission meets these criteria, Article 14(2) requires the Secretariat to determine whether to request a response from the NAFTA country in question. In making this determination, the Secretariat will take into account whether the submission alleges harm to the person or organization making it, whether the submission raises matters whose further study would advance the goals of the Environmental Cooperation Agreement, whether available private remedies have been pursued and whether the submission is drawn exclusively from mass media reports. If the Secretariat makes a request for a response, the NAFTA country has thirty days, or sixty days in exceptional circumstances, to advise the Secretariat whether the matter is the subject of a pending judicial or administrative proceeding, in which case the Secretariat proceeds no further. The NAFTA country can provide the Secretariat whatever other information it wishes.

The one further step that the Secretariat can take following receipt of the response is to inform the Council that the submission, in light of the response received from the NAFTA country, warrants the development of a factual record. The Secretariat shall proceed to develop a factual record if the Council, by a vote of two-thirds, instructs it to do so. In developing the factual record, the Secretariat may consider relevant technical, scientific or other information from a variety of sources, including non-governmental organizations and persons. Once a draft report is prepared, any NAFTA country may provide comments. The Council may, on a two-thirds vote, make the report available to the public.

This process is significant for two reasons. First, the publicity resulting from a factual record documenting a failure to enforce environmental laws will put pressure on a NAFTA country to rectify the situation. Second, a factual record could form the basis for an action against a NAFTA country for persistent failure to enforce its environmental laws discussed in §6.9(4).

(c) Joint public advisory committee

The Joint Public Advisory Committee is comprised of fifteen members, unless the Council decides otherwise, and is to act in an advisory capacity to the Council.

(3) Co-operation and Provision of Information

Part Four of the Environmental Cooperation Agreement sets out obligations respecting co-operation and the provision of information. For example, NAFTA countries must inform other NAFTA countries of actual or proposed environmental measures that may materially affect the operation of the agreement. NAFTA countries are obliged to provide information to the Council or the Secretariat that may be required for the preparation of a report or factual record.

(4) Consultation and Resolution of Disputes

(a) Consultations

Article 22(1) provides that any NAFTA country may request consultations with another NAFTA country regarding whether there has been a persistent pattern of failure by that other NAFTA country to enforce effectively its environmental law. The expression "persistent pattern" is defined in Article 45 as "a sustained or recurring course of action or inaction beginning after the date of the entry into force of this Agreement". A single instance of failure to enforce, which may be documented in a factual record, will not be sufficient to give rights under this provision.

The resolution of the dispute commences with consultations. A third NAFTA country that considers that it has a substantial interest may participate unless rules established by the Council otherwise provide. If the matter is not resolved within sixty days, a NAFTA country may request a special session of the Council. The Council shall convene within twenty days of the delivery of the request and shall endeavour to resolve the dispute.

(b) Arbitral panel

If the matter has not been resolved within sixty days of the Council being convened, Article 24 provides that the Council shall, on the written request of the NAFTA country that requested the consultations and on a two-thirds vote, convene an arbitral panel. A panel may be convened only where the persistent pattern of failure to enforce effectively relates to a situation involving workplaces, firms, companies or sectors that produce goods or provide services that are traded between NAFTA countries or that compete in the NAFTA country against which the complaint is made with goods or services from other NAFTA countries. This limitation reflects the general notion that failure to enforce effectively environmental laws results in an unfair competitive advantage. However, there is no requirement that such an unfair advantage be established as a condition for bringing the matter before a panel. A third NAFTA country with a substantial interest can join as a complaining NAFTA country.

Article 25(1) requires the Council to maintain a roster of panelists and Article 25(2) and Article 26 set out the qualifications of panelists. Article 27 sets out the procedure for panel selection. Article 28 provides that the Council will establish model rules of procedure which must include the right to at least one hearing. Article 29 provides that non-disputing NAFTA countries that notify the disputing NAFTA countries may attend panel hearings and make and receive submissions. Article 30 permits panels to seek technical advice. Article 31 provides that a panel will present an interim report within 180 days of the last panelist being selected. The disputing NAFTA countries may make comments. Article 32 provides that a final report will be submitted within sixty days and will be published five days after it is submitted to the Council.

(c) Implementation of panel decision

If a panel determines that there has been a persistent pattern of failure by a NAFTA country to enforce effectively its environmental laws, the disputing parties may agree on a mutually satisfactory action plan which should normally conform with the recommendations of the panel. Article 34 provides for the panel to be reconvened if the disputing parties do not agree on an action plan or whether a NAFTA country is implementing an action plan. If the NAFTA countries have not been able to agree on an action plan, paragraph 4 of Article 34 provides that the panel shall determine whether an action plan proposed by the NAFTA country against which the complaint was made is sufficient to remedy the situation and may approve such plan or establish a plan consistent with that NAFTA country's laws. In these circumstances the panel may, where warranted, impose a monetary enforcement assessment. Paragraph 5 of Article 34 covers the situation in which the NAFTA country complained against is alleged not to be implementing an action plan. If the panel finds that the plan is not being fully implemented, the panel must impose a monetary enforcement assessment.

(d) Monetary enforcement assessment and suspension of benefits

Annex 34 sets out factors, such as pervasiveness and duration of the non-enforcement and the level of enforcement that could be expected given resource constraints, that a panel must consider when determining the amount of a monetary enforcement assessment. Annex 34 also provides that the maximum amount of an assessment in the first year will be twenty million dollars (U.S.) or its equivalent in the currency of the NAFTA country complained against. In following years, the maximum amount will be .007% of the total trade in goods among the NAFTA countries during the most recent year for which data are available. Monetary enforcement assessments must be paid in the currency of the NAFTA country complained of to a fund established by the Council in the Commission's name. The funds will be expended at the Council's direction to improve or enhance environmental law or law enforcement in the NAFTA country complained against.

If a NAFTA country fails to pay an assessment, a complaining NAFTA country can suspend NAFTA benefits, but only to the extent necessary to collect the amount of the assessment. Annex 36B sets out rules respecting the suspension of benefits and provides that tariffs cannot be increased to rates higher than the lesser of the MFN rate on January 1, 1994, or on the date of suspension of benefits. A special procedure is set out for Canada in Annex 36A which provides for the collection of an assessment by the Commission through the Canadian courts. So long as such procedures apply, the suspension of benefits provisions do not apply to Canada.

(5) General Provisions

The Environmental Cooperation Agreement does not empower authorities in a NAFTA country to undertake environmental enforcement activities in other NAFTA countries. No private rights of action are created. There are provisions in Articles 39 and 42 respectively respecting the protection of information and national security. There are provisions respecting amendments and accession by other countries. A NAFTA country may withdraw after giving six months' notice. If this happens, the agreement remains in effect between the remaining NAFTA countries.

Article 41 and Annex 41 take into account the constitutional limitations in Canada upon the federal government's authority to act in environmental matters. The Canadian government is required to submit a declaration setting out those provinces for which the federal government is to be bound for matters arising within their jurisdiction. To the extent that provinces are not included on the declarations, certain limitations apply to Canada's rights under the Environmental Cooperation Agreement.

(6) Concluding Remarks

The effective scope of the Environmental Cooperation Agreement is confined to issues of enforcement rather than substance of environmental laws. Also, environmentalists have been critical of the fact that the dispute settlement procedures do not provide for direct participation by non-governmental organizations or persons. The reason for these deficiencies is that the Environmental Cooperation Agreement comes close to the fine line defining national sovereignty. A Commission with the power to impose minimum standards and a panel system with the authority to hear and adjudicate the complaints of non-governmental organizations and persons would be supranational institutions along the lines of those in the European Union. While from an environmental viewpoint this may be desirable, sovereignty concerns in all three NAFTA countries make the implementation of this sort of model very difficult. Notwithstanding its shortcomings, the fact remains that the Environmental Cooperation Agreement is unique amongst international environmental agreements in that it sets out a process which results in a resolution and, in the event of non-compliance, a penalty.

6.10 THE LABOUR COOPERATION AGREEMENT

The Labour Cooperation Agreement, which was entered into force on January 1, 1994, was negotiated and concluded because of concerns in the United States and Canada that businesses would move to Mexico to take advantage of low wages and weak enforcement of labour standards. Like the Environmental Cooperation Agreement, the Labour Cooperation Agreement sets out general commitments, creates an institutional structure, provides for co-operation and the exchange of information and establishes a dispute settlement process.

Part One of the Labour Cooperation Agreement sets out its basic objectives, which include the promotion of the labour principles set out in Annex 1 of the agreement. These include freedom of association and protection of the right to organize, the right to bargain collectively, the right to strike, the prohibition of forced labour, labour protection for children, minimum employment standards, the elimination of employment discrimination, equal pay for men and women, the prevention of and compensation in cases of occupational injuries and illnesses and the protection of migrant workers. However, only issues of enforcement of laws and regulations respecting occupational safety and health, child labour and minimum wages are subject to the dispute resolution and enforcement provisions of the agreement.

(1) Obligations

Part Two of the Labour Cooperation Agreement sets out the respective obligations of the NAFTA countries. Article 2 requires each NAFTA country to ensure that its labour laws and regulations provide for "high" standards but, as under the Environmental Cooperation Agreement, these are not defined. Moreover, this obligation is qualified by affirmation of full respect for each NAFTA country's constitution and a recognition of the right of each NAFTA country to establish its own domestic labour laws. The meaning of the constitutional reference is not clear, but the Canadian federal government has very limited scope to regulate labour matters.[68] Articles 3 to 6 set out provisions respecting government enforcement, private rights of action, procedure guarantees and publication of laws and regulations similar to those in the Environmental Cooperation Agreement.

(2) Commission for Labour Cooperation

Part Three of the Labour Cooperation Agreement establishes the Commission on Labour Cooperation comprised of a Council and a Secretariat. The Commission will be assisted by the National Administrative Office in each NAFTA country.

(a) The council

The Council is comprised of the labour ministers of each of the NAFTA countries, or their designates. The Council establishes its own rules and procedures and convenes at least yearly or whenever a NAFTA country requests a special session. The Council performs a variety of functions including facilitating consultations between NAFTA countries and promoting the collection of data on enforcement, labour standards and labour market indicators. The Council also promotes co-operative activities between the NAFTA countries regarding matters such as occupational safety and health, child labour and migrant workers.[69]

(b) The Secretariat, the National Administrative Offices and national committees

The structure of the Secretariat is similar to that under the Environmental Cooperation Agreement. The Secretariat performs an advisory role to the Council. There is nothing in the Labour Cooperation Agreement corresponding to the right of the Secretariat under the Environmental Agreement to consider submissions of non-governmental organizations and persons described in §6.9(2)(b)(ii).

Each NAFTA country is to establish a National Administrative Office ("NAO") to serve as a point of contact and to provide publicly available information. The Labour Cooperation Agreement permits each NAFTA country to convene a national advisory committee comprised of members of the public to act in an advisory capacity.

(3) Consultations and Dispute Resolution

Part Four of the Labour Cooperation Agreement sets out procedures for consultations. Article 21 sets out procedures for consultations at the NAO level. Article 22 sets out procedures for consultations at the ministerial level. These consultations can relate to any matter covered by the agreement, which would include any of the labour principles listed in Annex 1 described in §6.10.

(a) Evaluation Committee of Experts

If the ministerial consultations under Article 22 do not lead to a resolution, the matter is referred under Article 23 to an Evaluation Committee of Experts ("ECE"). However, an ECE cannot be convened if the matter is not "trade-related", which is not defined, or covered by "mutually recognized labour laws". These are laws of both a NAFTA country requesting consultations and laws of the NAFTA country whose laws were the subject of consultations that address the same general subject-matter in a manner that provides enforceable rights, protections or standards. The determination as to whether these circumstances apply is made by an independent expert chosen by the Council at the request of the NAFTA country whose laws are in question. If the expert determines that the matter is not trade-related or not covered by mutually recognized labour laws, the ECE is not convened and the matter proceeds no further.

Article 24 sets out rules respecting the composition and procedures of ECEs. Article 25 requires the ECE to report within 120 days or such other period determined by the Council. Each NAFTA country may submit comments. Article 26 requires that the final report be made within sixty days after the presentation of the draft report.

(b) Consultations

If the ECE final report addresses the enforcement of a NAFTA country's labour laws and regulations respecting occupational safety and health, child labour or minimum wages, a NAFTA country may, under Article 27, request consultations with another NAFTA country as to whether there has been a persistent pattern of failure by that NAFTA country to enforce such laws and regulations. If the report does not address these issues, the matter proceeds no further. A "pattern of practice" is a course of action or inaction beginning after the Labour Cooperation Agreement became effective and does not include a single instance; a "persistent pattern" is a sustained or recurring pattern of practice.

(c) Arbitral panels

If the matter is not resolved through these consultations within sixty days, the matter proceeds from there in much the same manner under the Environmental Cooperation Agreement. A NAFTA country may request a special session of the Council and if the matter is not resolved within sixty days after the Council has convened, the matter proceeds to an arbitral panel. Articles 30 through to 35 cover panel rosters, the qualifications of panelists, panel selection, rules of procedure, participation by third NAFTA countries and the role of experts. Article 36 requires that the panel present an initial report to the disputing parties within 180 days of the last panelist being selected and a disputing NAFTA country has thirty days to submit written comments. The panel then has sixty days to present a final report to the disputing NAFTA countries. The report is delivered to the Council and published.

(d) Enforcement

If the panel has determined that there has been a persistent pattern of failure by the NAFTA country complained against to enforce effectively its occupational safety and health, child labour or minimum wage laws or regulations, the matter continues in much the same manner as under the Environmental Cooperation Agreement. The NAFTA countries agree on an action plan. Failure to agree or failure to comply can lead ultimately to monetary enforcement assessments in the same amounts as under the Environmental Assessment Agreement and, if these are not paid, to the suspension of NAFTA benefits. Annex 41A sets out procedures for Canada similar to those set out in Annex 36A of the Environmental Cooperation Agreement.

(4) General Provisions

There are provisions in the Labour Cooperation Agreement similar to those described in §6.9(5) to the effect that the agreement does not empower authorities in NAFTA countries to undertake enforcement activities in other NAFTA countries. No private rights are created. There are provisions respecting the provision of information but there is no national security provision. Section 46 and Annex 46 address Canada's constitutional limitations in the same manner as Section 41 and Annex 41 of the Environmental Cooperation Agreement. As under the Environmental Cooperation Agreement, there are provisions respecting amendments and accession by other countries. A

NAFTA country may withdraw after giving six months' notice. If this happens, the agreement remains in effect between the remaining NAFTA countries.

(5) Concluding Remarks

The Labour Cooperation Agreement is more limited in scope than the Environmental Cooperation Agreement. Like the Environmental Cooperation Agreement, the enforcement provisions apply only in cases of failure to enforce laws and regulations. However, unlike the enforcement provisions of the Environmental Cooperation Agreement which cover the full range of environmental laws and regulations, the enforcement provisions of the Labour Cooperation Agreement cover only laws and regulations pertaining to occupational safety and health, child labour and minimum wages. None of the other matters listed in Annex 1, such as the right to organize and bargain collectively, the right to strike, equal pay for men and women, and so on are covered. Also, the process in the Labour Cooperation Agreement is significantly more convoluted than that under the Environmental Cooperation Agreement, in that a report of an ECE must first be prepared before the consultations leading ultimately to enforcement can commence. Like the Environmental Cooperation Agreement, the dispute settlement process is government to government. However, unlike the Environmental Cooperation Agreement, there is no procedure for non-governmental organizations and persons to make submissions to the Secretariat. The principles enunciated in the Labour Cooperation Agreement have within them the makings of a social charter, but the absence of effective enforcement procedures for all but a few of these principles make this agreement much less effective than its environmental counterpart.

ENDNOTES

[1] The comments in this Chapter are based on the Marrakesh text of the 1994 GATT Technical Barriers Agreement.

[2] Article 2:1 of the 1980 GATT Technical Barriers Agreement, 26th Supp. BISD (1980) 56, reprinted in Kenneth R. Simmonds and Brian H.W. Hill, *Law and Practice under the GATT* (New York, Oceana Publications, 1988) at pp. 99-153.

[3] *Ibid.*, Article 2:2.

[4] *Ibid.*, Article 2:4.

[5] *Ibid.*, Article 2:5.

[6] *Ibid.*, Article 2:6.

[7] *Ibid.*, Article 2:7.

[8] *Ibid.*, Article 2:8.

[9] *Ibid.*, Article 5:1.

[10] *Ibid.*, Article 5:2.

[11] *Ibid.*, Article 7:1.

[12] *Ibid.*, Article 7:2.

[13] *Ibid.*, Article 13.

[14] The FTA concept of deeming standards-related measures whose demonstrable purpose is to achieve a legitimate domestic objective as not creating an unnecessary obstacle to trade, as well as the FTA definition of "legitimate domestic purpose", appears to be based on language in the legislation enacted by the United States to implement the 1980 GATT Technical Barriers Agreement. See Seymour J. Rubin, "A Predominantly Commercial Policy Perspective" in *Environment and Trade: The Relation of International Trade and Environmental Policy*, Seymour J. Rubin and Thomas R. Graham, eds. (Totowa, N.J., Allanheld, Osmun & Co. Publishers Inc., 1982) at p. 10.

[15] *In the Matter of Puerto Rico regulations on the import, distribution and sale of U.H.T. milk from Quebec*, [1993] F.T.A.D. No.7 (Q.L.).

[16] These are: end product criteria; a product-related processing or production method; a testing, inspection, certification or approval procedure; a relevant statistical method; a sampling procedure; a method of risk assessment; a packaging and labelling requirement directly related to food safety; and a quarantine treatment, such as a relevant requirement associated with the transportation of animals or plants or with material necessary for their survival during transportation.

[17] *Op. cit.*, note 1, Annex 1.

[18] The definition sets out a number of examples.

[19] GATT Sanitary and Phytosanitary Measures Agreement, Article 2, para. 4.

[20] See Article 13 of the GATT Sanitary and Phytosanitary Agreement, which covers implementation. Article 13 states that members are "fully responsible" for the "observance of all obligations", which could be construed as an obligation to ensure compliance by sub-national governments.

[21] *Op. cit.*, note 19, Article 13.

[22] *Ibid.*, Article 2, para. 1, for comparable GATT Sanitary and Phytosanitary Agreement provision.

[23] Article 3, para. 3, permits higher levels of protection if there is a scientific justification or as a consequence of the level of protection determined to be appropriate in following the risk assessment procedures in Article 5. The statement in NAFTA 712(1) is unqualified.

[24] Risk assessment is defined in NAFTA 724 as an evaluation of the potential for the introduction, establishment or spread of a pest or disease and associated biological and economic consequences or the potential for adverse effects on human or animal life and health from the presence of an additive, contaminant, toxin or disease-causing organism in a food, beverage or feedstuff. The counterpart to NAFTA 712(3)(c) in the GATT Sanitary and Phytosanitary Measures Agreement is Article 5, para. 1.

[25] The counterparts in the GATT Sanitary and Phytosanitary Measures Agreement to NAFTA 715(1), (2), (3)(a) and (3)(b) are paras. 2, 3, 4 and 5 of Article 5, respectively.

[26] The organizations referred to are the Codex Alimentarius Commission (including the Codex Committee on Fish and Fishery Products), the International Office of Epizootics and the Secretariat of the International Plant Protection Convention in co-operation with the North American Plant Protection Organization, as well as any other international organization agreed upon by the NAFTA countries.

[27] The counterparts in the GATT Sanitary and Phytosanitary Measures Agreement to NAFTA 713(1), (2), (3), (4) and (5) are paras. 1, 2 and 3 of Article 3, para. 8 of Article 5 and para. 4 of Article 3, respectively. The NAFTA definition of "international standard, guideline or recommendation" in NAFTA 724 closely follows that in paragraph 3 of Annex A of the GATT Sanitary and Phytosanitary Agreement.

[28] The definition includes a lengthy list of examples.

[29] NAFTA 717(1) applies to control or inspection procedures and NAFTA 717(2) applies the same provisions to approval procedures.

[30] *Op. cit.*, note 19, Annex B, para. 11(b).

[31] This is consistent with para. 1.4 of the 1994 GATT Technical Barriers Agreement.

[32] See *The Shorter Oxford English Dictionary on Historical Principles*, 3rd ed., which contains a number of definitions of "seek", the most likely of which is intended to apply in NAFTA is "to try to bring about or effect".

271

[33] *Supra*, note 15, at para. 5.28. Note that while the panel refused in para. 5.29 of the decision to find that the United States had breached this "best efforts" obligation in FTA 708(1), the panel ultimately found in Canada's favour on the basis of nullification and impairment. See para. 5.60.

[34] See 1994 GATT Technical Barriers Agreement, Article 3 respecting technical regulations, Article 4 respecting standards and Article 7 respecting conformity assessment. The corresponding provisions of the 1980 GATT Technical Barriers Code are similar.

[35] FTA 609.

[36] *Op. cit.*, note 1, Article 2, para. 2.2.

[37] The FTA definition includes "essential security" and the GATT definition includes "national security".

[38] Sustainable development is omitted from this provision.

[39] See para. 2.1 respecting technical regulations, para. 5.1.1 respecting conformity assessment and paragraph D. of Annex 3 respecting standards.

[40] This expression is also defined in NAFTA 915. Specific organizations mentioned are: the International Organization for Standardization (ISO), the International Electrotechnical Commission (IEC), Code Alimentarius Commission, the World Health Organization (WHO), the Food and Agriculture Organization (FAO) and the International Telecommunication Union (ITU). The NAFTA countries may designate other bodies.

[41] See para. 2.4 for technical regulations, para. 5.4 for conformity assessment and Annex 3, paragraph F for standards. However, para. 5.4 includes national security requirements, the prevention of deceptive practices and the protection of human health or safety, animal or plant life and health or the environment as reasons for not adopting an international standard.

[42] See paras. 5.2.2 through to 5.2.7. There is no provision dealing with samples.

[43] Paragraph 5.2.8 of the 1994 GATT Technical Barriers Agreement covers complaints.

[44] NAFTA Annex 908.2.

[45] See paras. 2.9 and 2.9.1 for technical regulations and paras. 5.6 and 5.6.1 for conformity assessment procedures.

[46] See para. L.

[47] For bus and truck operations: one and one-half years for non-medical measures respecting drivers; two years for medical measures respecting drivers; and three years for various measures affecting vehicles, motor carriers' safety compliance and road signs. For rail operations: one year for measures respecting operating personnel, locomotives and rail equipment. For transportation of dangerous goods, six years, using the United Nations *Recommendations on the Transportation of Dangerous Goods* as a basis or such other standards as may be agreed upon. The time limits run from January 1, 1994. NAFTA is silent as to what happens if these time limits are not met.

[48] NAFTA 903 also affirms rights and obligations existing on January 1, 1994, under other international agreements, including environmental and conservation agreements. As discussed in §6.8(4), NAFTA 104 provides that some of these agreements prevail over NAFTA.

[49] One example is the tax levied by the Province of Ontario on aluminum beer cans, which are recyclable but, unlike bottles, not reusable. From an environmental standpoint, reusable containers are preferable to recyclable ones. However, from a trade perspective, the measure arguably discriminates against U.S. beer which, unlike Canadian beer, is mostly in cans. The environmental justification for the measure would have been more convincing if the tax had applied to all beverages in cans and not just beer.

[50] See paragraphs 35 and 37 of the Affidavit of Lori Wallach, referred to in the Opinion of Charles R. Richey, United States District Judge, in *Public Citizen, Sierra Club, and Friends of the Earth v. Office of the United States Trade Representative* (unreported, June 30, 1993, Civil Action No. 92-2102 (CRR), D.D.C.).

[51] *Ibid.*, para. 39. The GATT decisions cited are *United States — Section 337 of the Tariff Act of 1930*, BISD 36th Supp. 345 and *Thailand — Restrictions on Importation of and Internal Taxes on Cigarettes*, BISD 37th Supp. 200.

[52] *Op. cit.*, note 50, para. 36.

[53] *Canada, North American Free Trade Agreement: Canadian Environmental Review: Executive Summary* (Ottawa, Queen's Printer, October 1992), p. 25.

[54] *Op. cit.*, note 50, para. 25.

[55] *Op. cit.*, note 53, pp. 25-6. Of 941 U.S. and Codex data points respecting residue limits, limits were equal in 398 instances, Codex was more stringent in 382 cases and U.S. limits were more stringent in 161 cases. There is no qualitative analysis of these numbers.

[56] See Rubin, *op. cit.*, note 14, at pp. 15-16 for a discussion of the "polluter pays principle", which means that: "The polluter should be charged with the cost of whatever pollution prevention and control measures are determined by public authorities."

[57] The assistance is a one time non-recurring measure, is limited to 20% of the cost of the adaptation, does not cover the cost of replacing and operating the assisted investment, is directly linked and proportionate to the firm's planned reduction of nuisances and pollution, does not cover manufacturing cost savings and is available to all firms that can adopt the new equipment or production processes. See Article 8.2(c) of the *Agreement on Subsidies and Countervailing Duty Measures.*

[58] See paragraph 14 of the affidavit of John Audley referred to, *op. cit.*, note 53. Audley states in reference to Mexico's *Federal Law of Ecological Equilibrium and Environmental Protection* passed in 1988: "While that law sets out the general authority for Mexico to regulate various environmental problems, it does not establish the regulatory standards or apply them to particular environmental problems." See also paragraph 18 in which Audley states that Mexico's enforcement capabilities are inadequate.

[59] See affidavit of John Audley, *ibid.*, para. 20.

[60] For a brief discussion of the concept of environmental countervailing duties, see *Canada, North American Free Trade Agreement: Canadian Environmental Review: Executive Summary, op. cit.*, note 53, pp. 33-4.

[61] See, *ibid.*, at pp. 55-9. See also p. 226 of *Review of U.S.- Mexico Environmental Issues* February, 1992, plaintiffs' Exhibit D referred to in the Opinion of Charles R. Richey, United States District Judge, *op. cit.*, note 53.

[62] Jagdish Bhagwati, *The World Trading System at Risk* (Princeton, Princeton University Press, 1991), at pp. 21-2.

[63] See 26 I.L.M. 1541 (1987) for text of the original Protocol.

[64] See 30 I.L.M. 537 (1991), 30 I.L.M. 539 (1991) and 30 I.L.M. 541 (1990).

[65] Article 2, para. 6.

[66] The amendments that became effective on January 1, 1992, contemplate bans on imports and exports of controlled products. See 30 I.L.M. 541 under Article 4: Control of Trade with Non-Parties. The Canadian government banned the importation of a number of these substances at the beginning of 1994.

[67] See 28 I.L.M. 649 (1989) for the text of this Convention. As of March 28, 1989, Canada and Mexico were signatories but the United States was not. The Canadian government ratified the Convention on August 28, 1992, and enacted the *Export and Import of Hazardous Wastes Regulations*, SOR/92-637, which became effective on November 12, 1992.

[68] Federal labour standards apply only to direct federal government employees and to federal works and undertakings, which include railway companies, airlines, banks and a number of other specific businesses. Otherwise, labour standards fall within the exclusive jurisdiction of the provinces.

[69] See Article 11 for the full list.

CHAPTER 7

INVESTMENT, SERVICES AND RELATED MATTERS

The NAFTA provisions respecting investment, services and financial services go well beyond the rather tentative provisions of the FTA. The NAFTA investment provisions carry forward on a trilateral basis all of the key provisions of U.S. bilateral investment treaties. The NAFTA services chapter, unlike that of the FTA, is general in application. While the FTA financial services chapter is concession-based, its NAFTA counterpart is principle-based.

This chapter describes the NAFTA investment provisions set forth in Section A of NAFTA Chapter Eleven. The NAFTA investor state dispute settlement procedures set forth in Section B of NAFTA Chapter Eleven will be described in §11.3. This chapter will discuss NAFTA Chapter Twelve (Cross-Border Trade in Services) and Chapter Thirteen (Telecommunications). NAFTA Chapter Fourteen (Financial Services) will be described in Chapter 8.

7.1 BASIC ISSUES

Some basic issues are common to the investment, services and financial services provisions of the FTA and NAFTA.

The scope of the investment, services and financial services provisions of NAFTA depends on the delineation of who is entitled to their benefit and in respect of what. For example, the investment provisions of NAFTA protect "investors" in respect of their "investments". The scope of the protection accorded by these provisions depends on how these expressions are defined.

The national treatment and MFN principles can apply to investments, services and financial services as readily as to the trade in goods. National treatment requires that investors or service providers of other member countries be treated no less favourably than one's own. MFN treatment requires that investors or service providers of each member country be treated no less favourably than investors or service providers of other member countries or non-member countries.

Under the FTA, provincial and state measures were covered by the investment and services chapters but not the financial services chapter. Under

NAFTA, provincial and state measures are covered by all three chapters. In applying national treatment, a provincial or state government must accord to investors or service providers of other NAFTA countries treatment no less favourable than the most favourable treatment it accords to investors or service providers of the NAFTA country of which it forms a part. This means that if a provincial or state government treats its own residents more favourably than residents of other provinces or states, this more favourable treatment sets the standard for investors or service providers of other NAFTA countries.

An international agreement must address the problem of existing measures that do not conform with the new norms being established. One approach is to require that existing measures be made to conform with the new norms. A second approach is to grandfather existing non-conforming measures. This means that existing non-conforming measures may continue in effect so long as they are not made more non-conforming. A third approach is to require each country to take a reservation specifically identifying each non-conforming measure that it intends to maintain. Non-conforming measures not listed must be brought into conformity with the new norms. The grandfathering approach, which the FTA follows, is simple to draft but not necessarily simple to apply because of uncertainty as to what non-conforming measures are maintained by each member country. The reservation approach, which NAFTA adopts, is more transparent and forces each member country to identify the non-conforming measures that it intends to continue.

7.2 RELATIONSHIP OF NAFTA CHAPTERS ELEVEN TO FOURTEEN

NAFTA Chapters Eleven (Investment), Twelve (Cross-Border Trade in Services) and Thirteen (Telecommunications) are not self-contained codes. An enterprise may provide services covered by the telecommunications provisions of Chapter Thirteen. However, the general NAFTA services provisions in Chapter Twelve and the investment provisions in Chapter Eleven also apply to the enterprise. Conflict between Chapter Eleven and other NAFTA chapters is resolved by NAFTA 1112(1) which provides that the other chapters prevail. Thus, if there is an inconsistency, Chapters Twelve and Thirteen, as well as other NAFTA chapters, prevail over Chapter Eleven. NAFTA 1307 provides that Chapter Thirteen prevails over other chapters to the extent of any inconsistency, so if Chapters Twelve and Thirteen conflict, Chapter Thirteen prevails.

NAFTA Chapter Fourteen (Financial Services) on the other hand operates independently from Chapters Eleven and Twelve. Neither Chapter Eleven nor Twelve apply to any measure covered by the financial services provisions of Chapter Fourteen. However, Chapter Fourteen incorporates several important provisions of Chapter Eleven by reference, together with the Chapter Eleven investor state dispute procedures in so far as they apply to the incorporated provisions.

Under the FTA, the financial services chapter was self-contained for financial services other than insurance services. For insurance services, there was overlap with the FTA investment and services provisions. Under NAFTA, insurance services are clearly covered only by the NAFTA financial services provisions.

7.3 BILATERAL INVESTMENT TREATIES

There are principles of customary international law that are relevant to the protection of direct foreign investment. However, effective multilateral procedures for enforcing these principles have not evolved, and there is a lack of international consensus on several key issues. Because of the deficiencies of customary international law, developed capital-exporting countries have endeavoured to protect direct foreign investments of their nationals in developing capital-importing countries through the negotiation of bilateral investment treaties, or "BITs". BITs have been entered into by the United States, Canada,[1] various European countries and Japan with many developing countries. By 1989, over 300 BITs had been concluded, involving all the world's capital-exporting countries and over eighty developing countries.[2] However, BITs are a developed country vis à vis developing country phenomenon. Until the FTA, capital exporting countries had not entered into BITs with one another.[3]

For many years, the United States used Friendship, Commerce and Navigation treaties ("FCNs") to protect U.S. interests in foreign countries. The earlier versions of these treaties had dealt with trade and navigation, but following World War II and the dramatic increase in U.S. direct foreign investment, the emphasis shifted to the protection of investment.[4] FCNs typically provided for MFN treatment and some other protections for investors. However, they came to be regarded as inadequate to protect U.S. investors and the need for a treaty dealing solely with investment became evident.[5]

By 1982, the office of the United States Trade Representative ("USTR") had developed a prototype BIT ("Model BIT").[6] The provisions of the Model BIT include:

(a) right of establishment and the better of MFN or national treatment;[7]
(b) investments to be accorded fair and equitable treatment and to enjoy full protection and security;[8]
(c) prohibition of performance requirements as a condition of establishing, expanding or maintaining an investment;[9]

(d) no expropriation unless for a public purpose accomplished under due process of law on a non-discriminatory basis and accompanied by prompt, adequate and effective compensation at fair market value;[10]

(e) all transfers related to an investment, such as the transfer of earnings, to be made freely and without delay;[11]

(f) resolution of disputes between a national or company of one party and the government of another through arbitration, using the facilities of the International Centre for the Settlement of Investment Disputes ("ICSID").

The United States has entered into BITs with a number of developing countries.[12] While the BITs are bilateral in form, they are asymmetrical as investment in the United States by nationals of the developing countries with which BITs have been concluded is virtually non-existent. One commentator has suggested that if the United States had followed the less-exacting European approach, which is more flexible on matters such as performance requirements and transfer of foreign exchange earnings, it might have signed BITs with more countries.[13]

The provisions of the Model BIT reflect U.S. objectives of encouraging a freer international flow of capital investment.[14] Some provisions, such as the investor-state dispute settlement procedures, also reflect the typical concerns that developed capital exporting countries have in dealing with legal systems in developing capital importing countries that they do not trust. The U.S. negotiators used the Model BIT as the basis for negotiating the FTA and achieved partial success in having its provisions incorporated. In negotiating NAFTA, with the addition of a developing country to the Canada-U.S. free trade area, the process of incorporating the provisions of the Model BIT was completed.

The significance of the relationship between NAFTA and the Model BIT is that U.S. interpretation of Model BIT provisions gives a fair indication of the approach that the United States will adopt in respect of NAFTA. Similarly, academic literature on Model BIT provisions and their origins should be consulted by anyone who wishes to draw informed conclusions respecting the meaning of the NAFTA investment provisions.

7.4   THE FTA INVESTMENT PROVISIONS

The FTA investment chapter is a BIT entered into between the governments of Canada and the United States.

The scope of the FTA investment chapter is delineated by the FTA definitions of "investment" and "investor". Only investments that are business enterprises or controlling interests in business enterprises are covered by the FTA. Other types of investments, such as portfolio investments and real estate, are not covered. An "investor" cannot be controlled by persons who are nationals of countries other than the United States or Canada. Thus, an enterprise incorporated in Canada with extensive Canadian business activities that is controlled by European or Asian shareholders would not be entitled to the protections accorded by the FTA in respect of its investments in the United States.

The FTA followed the Model BIT in imposing a national treatment obligation but did not require MFN treatment. The national treatment obligation respecting the conduct and operation (as opposed to the establishment, acquisition or disposition) of services businesses was confined to businesses providing "covered services" identified in the FTA services chapter. The FTA prohibited minimum equity requirements, requirements that a local presence be maintained, the imposition of certain performance requirements as a condition precedent for being permitted to invest and (subject to prudential exceptions) restrictions on the repatriation of funds. The FTA also incorporated the standard Model BIT provision respecting expropriation and nationalization.

The FTA did not impose "fair and equitable treatment" or "full protection and security" obligations, and made no special provision for resolution of investment disputes beyond the general state-to-state procedures in FTA Chapter Eighteen. Canada retained the right to restrict the ability of U.S. investors to acquire interests in privatized corporations. Transportation and financial services (except insurance services) were excluded from the FTA investment obligations. Financial services were covered by the limited provisions of the FTA financial services chapter. Cultural industries were also exempt from the provisions of the FTA investment chapter under the general cultural exemption in FTA 2005, discussed in §10.1.

The FTA investment chapter grandfathered non-conforming measures existing at the time that the FTA came into effect, provided that they not be made more non-conforming. The FTA permitted Canada's investment screening legislation, the *Investment Canada Act* ("ICA") to continue in effect, but required the threshold levels for review of direct acquisitions by U.S. investors to be raised from five million dollars to 150 million constant dollars by 1993 and the review of indirect acquisitions by U.S. investors to be eliminated by 1992. These requirements did not apply to transportation, financial services (except insurance) or cultural industries, or, because of a special exemption in the FTA provision requiring amendment of the ICA, to the oil, gas[15] and uranium sectors.

7.5 MEXICAN BACKGROUND

The Mexican government that negotiated NAFTA placed a high priority on developing the Mexican economy through attracting direct foreign investment. The extent of this priority is evident when one compares traditional Mexican approaches with the position ultimately reached in the NAFTA negotiations.

(1) The Calvo Doctrine

The governments of Canada and the United States are in broad agreement as to the principles of customary international law that apply to direct foreign investment. For example, Canada shares the view of the United States and other developed countries that prompt, adequate and effective compensation at fair market value should be paid to a foreign investor in the event of an expropriation, even if nationals of the expropriating state receive less favourable treatment.[16]

Mexico's historical position on these issues is consistent with that of other Latin American countries but quite different from that of the United States and Canada. As part of a long tradition of resisting outside interference, Latin American countries have employed "Calvo clauses" in their laws as applied to foreigners. The general rule in customary international law is that a foreigner is obliged to exhaust local remedies as a prerequisite to international redress.[17] Carlos Calvo, an Argentine jurist, took this rule a step further in a treatise published in 1868:

> (1) that sovereign states, being free and independent, enjoy the right on a basis of equality to freedom from 'interference of any sort' by other states; (2) that aliens are not entitled to rights and privileges not accorded to nationals, and that therefore they may seek redress for grievances only before the local authorities.[18]

A Calvo clause requires that a foreigner waive the diplomatic protection of its home state and rights under international law, and rely solely on local remedies. Foreigners may be treated as favourably as nationals but are not entitled to better treatment. Mexico has followed the Calvo approach, both in its constitution and in some of its domestic laws. Article 3 of the Law to Promote Mexican Investment and to Regulate Foreign Investment (the "Mexican Investment Law")[19] provides:

> Foreigners who acquire properties of any kind in the Mexican Republic agree, because of such action, to consider themselves as Mexican nationals with regard to these properties and not to invoke the protection of their governments with respect to such properties, under penalty, in case of violation, of forfeiting to the Nation the properties thus acquired.[20]

A U.S. academic, writing in 1975, explained the penalty provisions as a matter of honour:

> Honor underpins the forfeiture provision: One who enjoys the benefits of the country must commit his honor and loyalty to Mexico; diplomatic interposition undermines that commitment and must accordingly be penalized.[21]

Adherence by Mexico to the Calvo doctrine in matters respecting the property of U.S. nationals in Mexico has been a source of friction between Mexico and the United States. Also, because of the Calvo principles historically followed in most of Latin America, the United States has, until NAFTA, been unsuccessful in negotiating BITs with Latin American countries.

(2) Mexican Regulation of Direct Foreign Investment

The Mexican Investment Law was originally enacted in 1973.[22] It has been characterized as the centrepiece of the "Escheverrian Wall" of protectionist legislation, and represented a change to a foreign investment policy of strict control.[23] Some relaxation began under President de la Madrid, with the announcement of new investment guidelines in 1984.[24] The Regulation of the Law to Promote Mexican Investment and to Regulate Foreign Investment (the "Mexican Investment Regulation")[25] was enacted in 1989 by President Salinas and substantially liberalized the Mexican investment regime.[26]

The Mexican Investment Law and the Mexican Investment Regulation prescribe foreign ownership limits for a wide range of economic activities and provide for screening by the National Commission on Foreign Investment (the "National Commission")[27] in circumstances in which prescribed limits will be exceeded. Ownership restrictions affecting specific activities are also set forth in various other Mexican measures.

Article 4 of the Mexican Investment Law reserves certain activities to the state and certain others exclusively for Mexicans. Article 5 permits participation by foreigners of up to 34% respecting the exploitation and/or processing of mineral carbon, phosphoric rock and sulphur, and of up to 40% the manufacture of secondary petrochemical products and autoparts. Article 5 also establishes a general rule that where laws or regulations do not specify a percentage, foreign investment of an enterprise may not exceed 49% without the authorization of the National Commission.

The Mexican Investment Regulation includes a schedule entitled Specific and General Regulation for the Direct Foreign Investment based on the Mexican Classification of Economic Activities and Products (the "Classification"). The Classification lists various activities and identifies for each the applicable foreign investment restrictions.

The combined effect of the Mexican Investment Law and the Classification is that the following activities are reserved for the Mexican state: petroleum and other hydro carbons (including oil and natural gas extraction); oil refining and manufacture of basic petrochemical products; exploitation of radioactive minerals (including treatment of uranium and processed nuclear combustibles); the generation of nuclear energy; certain mining activities; generation, transmission and supply of electricity; railroad transportation services; telegraphic and wireless communications; banking; and minting of currency.[28] The following activities are reserved exclusively for Mexicans or Mexican companies with an exclusion-of-foreigners clause: radio and television; urban and interurban automotive transportation and federal highways transport; domestic air and maritime transportation; exploitation of forestry resources (including tree nurseries); gas distribution (including the retail trade of liquid combustible gas); credit unions; general bonded warehouses; exchange houses; various financial services; stock exchange services; services by bonding companies, insurance companies and independent pension funds; notary public services.[29]

The Classification includes the activities referred to above in which foreign participation is restricted to 34% and 40% and provides that participation by foreigners of up to 49% is permitted regarding the following activities: fishing; extraction, exploitation and/or processing of various minerals; manufacture of explosives, firearms and cartridges; retail trade of firearms, cartridges and munitions; transportation services inside ports; telephone and other telecommunication services; and financial leasing companies. The Classification also provides that majority foreign participation is permitted with the consent of the National Commission in the following activities: certain forestry activities; periodical and review publishing; manufacture of coke; various construction and installation activities; special works, including drilling oil and gas wells; high seas maritime transportation; tourist boat rentals; private schools; legal and accounting services; management services for roads and vehicle towing services; air navigation and airport administration services; and certain financial services.

Article 5 of the Mexican Investment Regulation permits foreign investors to incorporate and operate an enterprise without the authorization of the National Commission to carry on activities not on the Classification provided certain conditions are met. For example, investment in fixed assets cannot exceed $100 million (US) and must be funded from non-Mexican sources. The industrial site cannot be located in areas of high industrial concentration, and foreign exchange balancing requirements must be satisfied during the first three years.[30] As many activities are not listed in the Classification, this liberalizing measure has been considered by some to contradict the general 49% limitation in the Mexican Investment Law and therefore to be unconstitutional.[31] Article 6 of the Mexican Investment Regulation provides that no authorization is required for foreign investors to acquire any proportion of companies constituted as maquiladoras. Subject to these exceptions, acquisition by foreign investors of more than 49% (or other prescribed percentage) of an enterprise requires the authorization of the National Commission, regardless of whether or not the activity is listed on the Classification.[32]

The National Commission may increase or decrease the applicable percentages in specific cases, decide the participation of foreign investment in new economic activities and set conditions for foreign investment.[33] The

Mexican Investment Law sets out criteria to be taken into account in determining whether or not to authorize a foreign investment and establishing percentages and conditions respecting investments that are authorized.[34]

Trust mechanisms using financial institutions as trustees have been developed to permit foreigners to hold beneficial interests in investments that would otherwise be prohibited under Mexico's foreign investment laws.

7.6 URUGUAY ROUND AGREEMENTS

(1) The GATT TRIMS Agreement

The Uruguay Round did not result in a comprehensive investment agreement along the lines of the Model BIT. The *Agreement on Trade-Related Investment Measures* ("GATT TRIMS Agreement") resulting from the Uruguay Round deals with the much narrower issue of trade-related investment measures ("TRIMS").[35] The GATT TRIMS Agreement prohibits TRIMS that are inconsistent with GATT Articles III and XI and sets out examples of non-conforming TRIMS in an Annex. The TRIMS prohibited by the GATT TRIMS Agreement are performance requirements that require enterprises to favour domestic over imported products or restrict imports on a basis related to exports of local production or impose trade balancing requirements or export requirements.[36] Member countries are required to identify all their TRIMS within ninety days of the GATT TRIMS Agreement becoming effective and eliminate them within two years (or five or seven years for developing or least developed members). Unlike the NAFTA performance requirements, there is no provision for reservations.

(2) The General Agreement on Trade in Services

The Uruguay Round resulted in the negotiation of a General Agreement on Trade in Services ("GATS"),[37] which is a comprehensive agreement on services. The approaches adopted in the GATS had a substantial impact on the NAFTA investment and services provisions. The NAFTA concept of the "cross-border provision of a service" is based on Section 2 of GATS Article I. The reservation approach that is so important throughout the NAFTA investment, services and financial services provisions is taken from the GATS. The GATS market access obligations are based on a schedule of commitments prepared by each GATS signatory. A similar approach is followed in the NAFTA concept of liberalization commitments discussed in §7.9.

7.7   THE NAFTA INVESTMENT OBLIGATIONS

(1) Scope and Coverage

NAFTA has extended the scope and coverage of the FTA investment provisions by expanding the concepts of "investment" and "investor".

(a) Investment

Besides enterprises and controlling interests in enterprises, an "investment" under NAFTA includes: equity securities; debt securities with terms of at least three years; debt securities regardless of term where the issuing enterprise is an affiliate of the investor; interests entitling sharing in an enterprise's assets on dissolution or income or profits; real estate and other tangible and intangible property acquired for economic benefit or other business purposes; and various other contractual interests. The NAFTA "investment" does not include debt securities of or loans to state enterprises, or accounts receivable.

The expanded concept of "investment" means that more types of measures are subject to NAFTA disciplines than was the case under the FTA. For example, securities legislation, except in so far as it affected the acquisition of control of business enterprises, was unaffected by the FTA. Under NAFTA, virtually all aspects of securities legislation are subject to NAFTA disciplines. Legislation affecting interests in real estate, such as land transfer tax or rent control legislation, was unaffected by the FTA but is covered by NAFTA.

(b) Investor

The NAFTA investment provisions apply to "investors" of Canada, the United States and Mexico and, in a few instances, to investors of non-NAFTA countries.

To be an investor of Canada, the United States or Mexico, an individual must be a citizen or permanent resident of the NAFTA country in question. An investor can also be the government of a NAFTA country or a state enterprise of a NAFTA country. With these investors, status depends on nationality. However, unlike the FTA, the status of an enterprise as an investor of Canada, the United States or Mexico does not depend on nationality. An "enterprise" is a corporation or any other type of juridical entity.[38] To be an "investor of a Party", an enterprise must be organized under the laws of a NAFTA country, but need not be controlled by nationals of that country. Under NAFTA 1113, if the enterprise is controlled by investors of a non-NAFTA country, benefits can be denied if the enterprise does not have substantial business activities in the NAFTA country under which it is constituted. A NAFTA country may also deny benefits if it does not maintain diplomatic relations with the non-NAFTA country or if it maintains measures respecting the non-NAFTA country that prohibit transactions with the enterprise, or if its laws would be violated if the benefits were not denied.[39]

This means that a Canadian subsidiary of a Japanese-controlled transnational with a substantial business in Canada is as much an investor of Canada for NAFTA purposes as a Canadian company controlled by Canadians. The United States or Mexico could deny benefits to the Canadian subsidiary only if diplomatic relations were not maintained with Japan or the other circumstances just described applied respecting Japan. The practical effect is that the beneficiaries of the NAFTA investment chapter will include the subsidiary of any European, Asian or Australasian enterprise with substantial business activities in Canada, the United States or Mexico. This approach is more expansive than under the Model BIT which, like the FTA, provides for the denial of benefits to enterprises based on the nationality of their controllers.[40]

The NAFTA provisions respecting performance requirements apply to investors of non-NAFTA countries as well. The benefits of other NAFTA provisions do not apply directly to investors of non-NAFTA countries, but may apply indirectly to them through their Canadian, American or Mexican subsidiaries.

(2) National Treatment and MFN Treatment

As under the FTA, NAFTA 1102 requires each NAFTA country to accord national treatment to investors of other NAFTA countries respecting the establishment, acquisition, expansion, management, conduct, operation, and sale or other disposition of investments.[41] NAFTA makes it clear that this obligation extends to the "investments" and not just the "investors". This means, for example, that U.S. obligations under NAFTA extend not only to an investor of Canada establishing a subsidiary in the United States, but to the subsidiary itself.

NAFTA 1102(3) provides that the standard of treatment for a province or state is the most favourable treatment that it accords to investors of the NAFTA country of which it forms a part. If the province or state treats its own investors better than investors from other provinces or states, the treatment of its own investors sets the standard.

As under the FTA, NAFTA 1102(4) prohibits minimum equity requirements and forced disposition by investors of other NAFTA countries on the basis of nationality.[42]

Unlike the FTA but like the Model BIT, NAFTA 1103 imposes an MFN obligation by requiring each NAFTA country to treat investors of another NAFTA country and their investments, no less favourably than investors of any other NAFTA country or any non-NAFTA country, and their investments, respecting the establishment, acquisition, expansion, management, conduct, operation, and sale or other disposition of investments.[43] This means, for example, that if Mexico were to enter into a BIT with the European Union providing for a more favourable phasing out of restrictions on direct foreign investment than applies under NAFTA, Mexico would be required to apply the more favourable rules to investors of Canada and the United States.

NAFTA requires that investors of other NAFTA countries receive the better of national treatment or MFN treatment.[44]

(3) Minimum Standard of Treatment

Unlike the FTA but like the Model BIT, NAFTA requires each NAFTA country to accord to investments of another NAFTA country treatment in accordance with international law, including fair and equitable treatment and full protection and security.[45]

Fair and equitable treatment has been described as a "classical international law standard" that is not precisely defined but has been shaped by "State practice, doctrine and decisions of international tribunals".[46] The concept is derived from the doctrine of State responsibility for injury to aliens and their property. According to this doctrine, States must observe "an international minimum standard in the treatment of aliens and their property".[47] Under traditional international law, but contrary to the Calvo principles referred to previously, it is not sufficient for a State to assert compliance with its own laws in respect of an alien if those laws do not meet the international standard of fair and equitable treatment.

The textbooks on international law do not give much guidance to what constitutes the international minimum standard. The *Restatement of the Law Second, Foreign Relations Law of the United States* ("Second Restatement") states that one looks to the usual sources of what constitutes international law but when the authority from such sources is conflicting or absent, international law "adopts analogous law from reasonably developed legal systems".[48] The discussion of State responsibility in the *Restatement of the Law Third, Foreign Relations Law of the United States* ("Third Restatement")[49] gives as an example the failure of a state to:

> . . . provide reasonable police protection. A state does not guarantee the safety of an alien or alien property, but it is responsible for injury when police protection falls below a minimum standard of reasonableness. What constitutes reasonable police protection depends on all the circumstances, including the state's available resources; ordinarily, the standard of police protection for foreign nationals is unreasonable if it is less than provided generally for the state's nationals.[50]

The Third Restatement also gives as an example of state responsibility the failure to:

. . . provide to an alien remedies for injury to person or property, whether inflicted by the state or by persons in circumstances in which a remedy would be provided by the major legal systems of the world . . .[51]

It is difficult to define with precision what is meant by the NAFTA obligation to accord treatment "in accordance with international law". However, the standard is fairly basic and presumably one which a country with a "major legal system" like Canada should have no difficulty in satisfying.

(4) Performance Requirements

Like the FTA and the Model BIT, NAFTA 1106(1) prohibits imposing performance requirements in connection with the establishment, acquisition, expansion, management, conduct or operation of an investment of an investor of either a NAFTA country or a non-NAFTA country. NAFTA carries forward the FTA prohibitions against the following performance requirements: exporting given levels or percentages of goods or services; achieving given levels of domestic content; and purchasing or preferring local goods and services. The FTA prohibition of substituting local for imported goods and services is not carried forward. However, NAFTA also prohibits: trade or foreign exchange balancing requirements; restrictions on domestic sales; technology transfer requirements; and exclusive supplier or world product mandate requirements.[52] The NAFTA prohibitions of technology transfer requirements and trade or foreign exchange balancing requirements are directed at Mexican laws requiring transfer of technology as a condition of direct foreign investment[53] or that foreign companies maintain positive balances in their trading accounts.[54]

Unlike both the FTA and the Model BIT, NAFTA 1106(3) prohibits the following performance requirements as conditions for investments of investors of NAFTA countries or non-NAFTA countries receiving advantages such as subsidies: achieving given levels of domestic content; purchasing or preferring local goods and services; trade or foreign exchange balancing requirements; and restrictions on domestic sales. However, NAFTA 1106(4) expressly permits requirements to locate production, provide a service, train or employ workers, construct or expand particular facilities or carry on research and development activities. NAFTA 1108(8)(c) provides that the prohibition of domestic content levels and purchasing or preferring local goods and services do not apply to qualifications imposed by importing NAFTA countries for receiving advantages in the form of preferential tariff treatment or preferential quotas. This exception is necessary because preferential tariff treatment programs, including the elimination of tariffs under NAFTA, depend on domestic content levels being achieved in the exporting countries. NAFTA 1106(5) makes it clear that the prohibited performance requirements, whether as conditions of investment or receiving an advantage, are confined to those specifically identified.[55] For example, while a world product mandate requirement is prohibited as a condition of investment, it is neither prohibited or expressly permitted as a condition for receiving a subsidy. The effect of NAFTA 1106(5) is that because world product mandate requirements tied to subsidies are not prohibited, they are permitted.

The purpose of extending the prohibition of performance requirements to investors of non-NAFTA countries is to maintain the integrity of the MFN principle. The objective of prohibiting performance requirements is to prevent NAFTA countries from distorting investment decisions in their favour. From the investor's perspective, this NAFTA provision may be as much a detriment as a benefit. While the investor would prefer to receive permission to invest or an advantage such as a subsidy free from performance requirements, a NAFTA government, being unable to impose a performance requirement, may choose not to grant permission or extend the advantage. If the option of granting permission or extending an advantage subject to performance requirements is foreclosed respecting investors of NAFTA countries, it follows from the MFN principle that this option cannot remain open respecting investors of non-NAFTA countries.

NAFTA 1106(6) provides that the prohibition of performance requirements shall not prevent requirements that given levels of domestic content be achieved or that local goods and services be purchased or preferred if they are necessary: to secure compliance with laws and regulations consistent with NAFTA; to protect human, animal or plant life and health; or for the conservation of exhaustible natural resources. The exception is subject to the "arbitrary or unjustifiable discrimination" and "disguised restriction" qualifiers discussed in §1.3(4). The utility of this exception is debatable. It is difficult to see how imposing a requirement that a certain level of domestic content be maintained could be necessary to protect human, animal or plant life and health or to conserve natural resources. Perhaps such a requirement could be justified if the domestic content were demonstrably more environmentally benign than its imported substitute.

(5) Senior Management and Boards of Directors

Unlike the FTA, NAFTA 1107 prohibits requirements that the senior management of businesses owned by investors of other NAFTA countries be of any particular nationality. Resident or nationality requirements[56] are permitted for the majority of boards of directors or any committee thereof, so long as the requirement does not impair the ability of the investor to exercise control.

(6) Transfers

Like both the FTA[57] and the Model BIT,[58] NAFTA 1109 requires each NAFTA country to permit transfers relating to investments of investors of other NAFTA countries to be made freely and without delay. The NAFTA follows the Model BIT language quite closely and, because of the wider scope of the NAFTA concept of "investment", is broader than the corresponding FTA language.[59] As under the FTA, transfers may be prevented through the "equitable, non-discriminatory and good faith" application of laws respecting bankruptcy and insolvency, securities, criminal or penal offences, reports of currency and other transfers or ensuring satisfaction of judgments. The NAFTA provisions respecting transfers are also subject to measures taken by the NAFTA countries to protect their balance of payments (discussed in §10.4) and to taxation measures (discussed in §10.3).

Unlike the FTA, NAFTA 1109(3) prohibits a NAFTA country from requiring its own investors to repatriate earnings from investments in other NAFTA countries. For example, the Mexican government could not require a Mexican company to repatriate the earnings of its subsidiary in the United States.

(7) Expropriation and Compensation

Like both the FTA and the Model BIT, NAFTA 1110(1) prohibits a NAFTA country from directly or indirectly nationalizing or expropriating an investment of an investor of another NAFTA country except for a public purpose, on a non-discriminatory basis, in accordance with due process and on payment of compensation. This provision states the traditional view of customary international law respecting nationalization or expropriation. This is consistent with the historical positions of both Canada and the United States. However, because of the Calvo approach common in Latin America, the NAFTA formulation represents a significant departure from the traditional Mexican position.

(a) Nationalization and expropriation

There is no ready distinction between a "nationalization" and an "expropriation". The FTA does not define either expression. The drafters of the NAFTA text attempted to craft definitions but, because of the complexity of the issues involved, wisely opted for the FTA approach of leaving the expressions undefined.

Canadian, U.S. and customary international law all distinguish between state action that constitutes an expropriation, or taking, and requires compensation and state action that constitutes regulation and does not require compensation.[60] Some state actions clearly amount to the taking of property. However, many actions taken by government adversely affect the economic interests of property owners. Examples include land use laws, taxation measures, environmental measures, measures regulating rents and other prices, government licensing and quota allocation practices, and so on. These sorts of measures are generally, but not always, regarded as regulation and property owners are not entitled to compensation for resulting economic loss. This notion flows from the concept that there are actions that a government must be able to take, in the public interest, without having to pay compensation, even if the interests of individual property owners may be adversely affected. There is considerable U.S. jurisprudence on the taking versus regulation issue because of the constitutional protections given to property in the U.S. constitution. While the Canadian constitution does not protect property rights, there is a large body of Canadian jurisprudence on the taking versus regulation because of the common law presumption that the state will compensate if it takes property unless the expropriating measure clearly provides otherwise. American and Canadian courts have approached the issue in broadly the same manner, but results in specific fact situations differ.

The taking versus regulation distinction clearly exists in customary international law and there is a great deal of analysis of the question to be found in the academic literature. However, while there is ample international jurisprudence covering state actions clearly constituting expropriation, there is very little international jurisprudence dealing with the difficult question of where a state action implemented for clear public policy reasons crosses over the line from non-compensable regulation to compensable taking. An example would be the creation of a monopoly to provide an essential service such as health or automobile insurance.

Other than following the FTA and Model BIT precedent by ensuring, through the addition of the words "tantamount to nationalization or expropriation", that the concept of the "creeping expropriation" is included, NAFTA does not address the thorny issue of where non-compensable regulation crosses over into compensable taking. This issue will be addressed by adjudicators on a case by case basis.

The NAFTA describes several situations that are not to be subject to the expropriation and compensation provisions. The issuance of compulsory licences respecting intellectual property rights, and measures revoking, limiting or creating intellectual property rights are not compensable so long as they are consistent with NAFTA Chapter Seventeen (discussed in §9.4).[61] Non-discriminatory measures of general application that impose costs on a debtor that cause it to default will not be considered as expropriation of the defaulted debt instruments.[62]

(b) Public purpose, non-discriminatory basis, due process

The requirements that an expropriation be for a public purpose and be carried out on a non-discriminatory basis in accordance with due process are customary international law standards.

Customary international law clearly recognizes that a government has the right to take property for a public purpose. For example, a municipality may need a strip of land abutting a highway for road widening purposes. The taking is clearly for a public purpose, namely, widening the road. The fact that it is for a public purpose justifies the taking, so long as compensation is paid. An expropriation motivated by a desire to enrich private interests would be wrongful under international law, even if compensation were paid.

The non-discrimination requirement entails more than merely according national or MFN treatment. As one commentator expressed it:

> "Non-discrimination" is not merely redundant of national treatment/Most Favoured Nation (MFN) treatment provisions secured by other provisions of the treaty. It is meant broadly to preclude discrimination, whether based on foreign nationality, a particular foreign nationality, a particular corporate or personal identity that may be in disfavour, where expropriating measures fall unequally on persons in like circumstances.[63]

The same commentator also made the following observation respecting the due process requirement:

> "Due process of law" is intended to refer to observance of requirements of substance and procedure under national laws, and is formulated with sufficient breadth to encompass concepts of international due process.[64]

Observing the due process requirement entails more than merely adhering to domestic legal requirements. An express denial of compensation or of judicial review in Canadian expropriating legislation could be enacted in accordance with Canadian legal requirements and also be consistent with the *Canadian Charter of Rights and Freedoms* and none the less constitute a denial of due process in international law.

(c) Compensation

The FTA and the Model BIT[65] both use the traditional customary international law standard of prompt, adequate and effective compensation at fair market value. "Prompt" means payment as soon as is reasonable under the circumstances. "Adequate" requires that fair market value be used as the standard for setting compensation. "Effective" means that the compensation must be in effectively realizable form.[66]

The NAFTA provisions respecting compensation make explicit the requirements that are implicit in the traditional "prompt, adequate and effective" formulation. Compensation is to be at the fair market value of the expropriated investment immediately prior to the expropriation without regard to depressing effects on value resulting from prior knowledge that the expropriation was going to take place. Valuation criteria such as "going concern value" are cited. Compensation shall be paid without delay, and fully realizable and freely transferable. NAFTA also sets forth requirements respecting currency of payment and interest.[67]

(d) Some observations

The NAFTA provisions respecting expropriation and compensation are essentially the same as those of the FTA. The NAFTA provisions respecting compensation make explicit what is implicit in the FTA and Model BIT formulation. However, the effect of the NAFTA expropriation and compensation provisions will be more far reaching than those of the FTA for two reasons. First, the expanded concept of "investment" under NAFTA brings a much wider range of property interests under their protection.[68] Second, the investor state dispute settlement procedures described in §11.3 provide a direct means for investors to enforce their rights under NAFTA.

The extension of justiciable rights to compensation to investors of NAFTA countries has particular significance to Mexico and to Canada. For Mexico, these NAFTA provisions represent an abandonment of the Calvo doctrine. However, these NAFTA provisions are consistent with Mexico's constitution which, like that of the United States, protects property rights.[69] The extension of justiciable rights to compensation to investors of NAFTA countries is consistent with Canada's views of its obligations under customary international law. However, being alone among the three NAFTA countries in not protecting property rights in its constitution, Canada is in the anomalous position of having guaranteed protections to investors of other NAFTA countries that it does not provide to its own citizens.

(8) Special Formalities and Information Requirements

NAFTA 1111(1) permits governments of NAFTA countries to prescribe special formalities in connection with the establishment of investments that do not materially impair the protection that NAFTA affords to investors of other NAFTA countries and their investments. NAFTA 1111(2) permits governments of NAFTA countries to require investors of other NAFTA countries and their investments to provide routine information for information and statistical purposes, provided that confidential information is protected.

(9) Exceptions to the Investment Obligations

Exceptions to the NAFTA investment obligations are primarily by way of the reservations discussed in §7.9. However, there are several general exceptions to the NAFTA investment obligations.

(a) Government procurement

NAFTA 1108(7) provides that NAFTA 1102 (National Treatment), 1103 (Most-Favoured-Nation Treatment) and 1107 (Senior Management and Boards of Directors) do not apply to procurement by a NAFTA country or a state enterprise. As discussed in §9.1, NAFTA Chapter Ten imposes national treatment and other obligations respecting procurement at the federal level, but not at the provincial or state levels.

NAFTA 1108(8)(a) provides that the prohibition of the following performance requirements do not apply to procurement by a government or a state enterprise: achieving given levels of domestic content; purchasing or preferring local goods and services; technology transfer requirements; and exclusive supplier or world product mandate requirements. However, a procurement by a government from a domestic subsidiary of an investor of a NAFTA or non-NAFTA country that was tied to an export requirement or a trade or foreign exchange balancing requirement would be caught by the NAFTA prohibition.

(b) Subsidies and grants

NAFTA 1108(7) provides that NAFTA 1102 (National Treatment), 1103 (Most-Favoured-Nation Treatment) and 1107 (Senior Management and Boards of Directors) do not apply to subsidies or grants provided by governments of NAFTA countries or state enterprises; these include government-supported loans, guarantees and insurance. The FTA excepted subsidies from all FTA investment obligations. However, the FTA exception was subject to the "arbitrary or unjustifiable discrimination" and "disguised restriction" qualifiers discussed in §1.3(4). The exception in NAFTA 1108(7) is unqualified.

NAFTA 1108(8)(a) provides that the prohibition of the following performance requirements in NAFTA 1106 does not apply to export promotion and foreign aid programs: exporting given levels or percentages of goods or services; achieving given levels of domestic content; and purchasing or preferring local goods and services.

(c) Cultural industries

As between Canada and the United States and Canada and Mexico, cultural industries are exempt from the investment obligations of NAFTA under the exemption for cultural industries discussed in §10.1.

7.8 THE NAFTA SERVICES OBLIGATIONS

(1) Scope and Coverage

The delineation between what is covered under the services as opposed to the investment chapter is much more precise under NAFTA than under the FTA. Under the FTA, a measure that was covered by the services provisions could also be covered by the investment provisions in so far as they applied to the conduct and operation of a business. The emphasis in the NAFTA chapter on services is on the cross-border provision of services. Cross-border provision of services means providing services from one NAFTA country into another, or within a NAFTA country by one of its nationals or enterprises to a national or enterprise of another NAFTA country, or by a national (*i.e.*, individual) of one NAFTA country within another NAFTA country.[70] However, the NAFTA services chapter, unlike the FTA services chapter and unlike the GATS,[71] does not apply to the provision of services within a NAFTA country by an investment, such as a branch or subsidiary, of an investor of another NAFTA country.

For example, the NAFTA services obligations cover a Canadian service provider who provides services from Canada into the United States or within Canada to a U.S. national or a company owned by U.S. investors. The services obligations also cover a Canadian individual providing services in the United States. However, the NAFTA services provisions do not apply to a U.S. subsidiary of a Canadian investor providing services in the United States. The subsidiary would look to the investment chapter for NAFTA coverage.

NAFTA 1201 provides that the NAFTA services obligations cover government measures that affect: the production, distribution, marketing, sale and delivery of services; the purchase, use of and payment for services; the access by service providers to transportation and distribution systems for providing their services; the maintenance by service providers of a local presence; and the provision by service providers of financial security as a condition of being permitted to provide a service.

NAFTA substantially expands the range of services covered over that in the FTA. The FTA applied only to listed "covered services". Services that were not covered services were not subject to FTA disciplines. The NAFTA services provisions are general in application and apply to all services, with the sole exception of financial services covered by NAFTA Chapter Fourteen, certain air services (discussed in §7.10(2)(a)(i)) and services affected by the cultural exemption (discussed in §10.1). The NAFTA services chapter also widens the circle of persons entitled to its benefits. As with the concept of "investor", an enterprise that is a service provider does not have to be controlled by nationals of the NAFTA country under which it was organized. The provisions in NAFTA 1211 respecting denial of benefits respecting service providers are similar to those that apply to investors in NAFTA 1113 that are described in §7.7(1)(b). As with investors, the critical factor for determining entitlement to NAFTA benefits is not the nationality of those who control the service provider but whether the service provider has substantial business activities in any NAFTA country.[72]

(2) Non-discriminatory Treatment and Local Presence

NAFTA 1202 and 1203 impose national treatment and most-favoured-nation requirements similar to those that apply to investors described in §7.7(2). As under the investment provisions, the treatment accorded by a province or state to its own service providers sets the national treatment standard that must be applied to service providers of other NAFTA countries. NAFTA 1204 requires each NAFTA country to accord service providers of other NAFTA countries the better of national treatment and MFN treatment. NAFTA 1205 carries forward the FTA obligation to not require service providers of other NAFTA countries to establish a local presence. Just as a foreign investor wants the right to establish a business in another country, a service provider wants to be relieved from the burden of establishing a local presence when services can be provided effectively from across the border. The NAFTA services chapter does not contain the investment chapter requirement of "fair and equitable treatment and full protection and security".

(3) Licensing and Certification Requirements

(a) General provision

NAFTA 1210(1) sets out general standards respecting measures relating to licensing or certification of nationals of other NAFTA countries respecting the provision of services. The measures are to be based on objective and transparent criteria, not be more burdensome than necessary to ensure quality and not constitute a disguised restriction on the cross-border provision of a service.

(b) Where MFN does not apply

NAFTA 1210(2) is a derogation from the MFN principle in that it provides that if a NAFTA country recognizes the education, experience, licences or certifications obtained in another country (which need not be a NAFTA country), the NAFTA country is not also required to recognize these attributes when obtained in another NAFTA country. However, the NAFTA country must afford another NAFTA country an opportunity to demonstrate that these attributes obtained in its territory should also be recognized. Under this provision, a Canadian province would be entitled to recognize educational qualifications obtained in the United States or the United Kingdom, but not those obtained in Mexico. However, Mexican authorities would have to be given the opportunity to demonstrate that the Mexican educational qualifications should also be recognized.

(c) Citizenship and permanent residency requirements

NAFTA 1210(3) obliges each NAFTA country to eliminate, within two years of NAFTA becoming effective, citizenship or permanent residence requirements set out in its Annex I reservations (discussed in §7.10(4)) that it maintains respecting the licensing or certification of professional service providers. If a NAFTA country does not comply with this requirement, other NAFTA countries may maintain or reinstate an equivalent requirement in the same sector but may not otherwise retaliate. NAFTA 1210(4) provides for consultation respecting the feasibility of removing remaining citizenship or permanent residency requirements.

(d) NAFTA Annex 1210.5

NAFTA Annex 1210.5 sets out a number of provisions respecting professional services that for the most part provide for consultations with a view to future liberalization. Under the General Provisions in Section A, each NAFTA country is to ensure that determinations are made regarding applications for licence of certification from nationals of other NAFTA countries and applicants are informed as to the determination or as to what additional information may be required. The NAFTA countries are to encourage licensing bodies to develop mutually acceptable standards and criteria for licensing and certification. Sections B and C cover foreign legal consultants and temporary licensing of engineers and are discussed in §7.10(4).

(4) Liberalization of Quantitative Restrictions and Other Non-discriminatory Measures

For the purposes of the NAFTA services provisions, quantitative restrictions are non-discriminatory measures that limit the number of service providers or their operations. NAFTA Annex V sets forth quantitative restrictions maintained by each NAFTA country at the federal level. The structure of the Annex V reservation is discussed in §7.9(6). Quantitative restrictions maintained at the provincial and state (but not local) levels are to be listed within one year of NAFTA becoming effective. Quantitative restrictions subsequently adopted at any level except local are to be added to the list.

NAFTA 1207 requires that the federal governments of the NAFTA countries meet at least every two years to negotiate the liberalization or removal of quantitative restrictions. However, there is no firm obligation to liberalize or remove any of the restrictions. Canada has listed measures respecting postal services, radio communications, electricity transmission, oil and gas pipelines, provincial monopolies respecting importation of intoxicating liquors and extra-provincial bus services. Mexico has listed measures respecting telecommunications, private educational services and various land transportation services. The United States has listed measures respecting radio communications, cable television services, natural gas transportation services, postal services and national parks concessions.

(5) Exceptions for Procurement and Subsidies

Procurement by governments and state enterprises and subsidies provided by these entities are exempt from the NAFTA services provisions.[73]

7.9 RESERVATIONS AND LIBERALIZATION COMMITMENTS

As indicated previously, the NAFTA investment and services provisions adopt the reservations approach to non-conforming measures existing at the time NAFTA became effective. No reservations are permitted in respect of the minimum standard of treatment obligation (NAFTA 1105), the transfers obligation (NAFTA 1109) or the expropriation and compensation obligation (NAFTA 1110). Any measures that do not conform with these requirements must be amended so as to conform.

(1) The NAFTA Annexes

NAFTA contains seven annexes numbered I through to VII. The reservations applicable to the NAFTA investment and services Chapters are categorized into four different reservation types set forth in NAFTA Annexes I (Reservations for Existing Measures and Liberalization Commitments), II (Reservations for Future Measures), III (Activities Reserved to the State) and IV (Exceptions from Most-Favoured-Nation Treatment). NAFTA Annexes I, II and III set out reservations to the national treatment (NAFTA 1102), MFN treatment (NAFTA 1103), performance requirements (NAFTA 1106) and senior management obligations (NAFTA 1107) of the investment chapter and from the national treatment (NAFTA 1202), MFN treatment (NAFTA 1203) and local presence (NAFTA 1205) obligations of the services chapter. NAFTA Annex IV applies only to the MFN treatment obligation (NAFTA 1103).

Each reservation in NAFTA Annex I exempts specific non-conforming measures of a NAFTA country from one or more of these obligations. A "measure" is "any law, regulation, procedure, requirement or practice".[74] A measure which is "non-conforming" is a measure that does not conform to the requirements of NAFTA. For example, a law that requires that nationals hold at least 51% of the equity of enterprises in a specified sector, such as telecommunications, does not conform with the prohibition of minimum equity requirements in NAFTA 1102(4)(a). A law permitting a non-national to establish a factory only if a certain percentage of output is exported does not conform with the prohibition of performance requirements in 1106(1)(a). Many of the reservations in Annex I set out liberalization commitments. Some of these take effect immediately while others are phased in over time. With a number of non-conforming measures, the fully phased-in liberalization commitment will eliminate the measure.

The NAFTA Annex II reservations are much broader in scope than the NAFTA Annex I reservations in that each one exempts an entire sector, sub-sector or activity from the NAFTA provisions referred to above. NAFTA Annex III reserves to the state the exclusive right to perform certain activities. Only Mexico has taken reservations under Annex III. The reservations in NAFTA Annex IV apply to the most-favoured-nation obligation in NAFTA 1103 respecting international agreements to which the NAFTA country taking the reservation is a party. There are no liberalization commitments in NAFTA Annexes II, III or IV.

NAFTA Annex V (Quantitative Restrictions) has been discussed in §7.8(4). Annex VI (Miscellaneous Commitments), as its name suggests, sets out specific liberalization commitments relating to certain service sectors. Annex VII (Reservations, Specific Commitments for Other Items) sets out reservations and liberalization commitments respecting financial services discussed and is discussed in Chapter 8.

The sectoral discussions in §7.10 cover energy and petrochemical goods in §7.10(1), air and land transportation in §7.10(2), maritime activities in §7.10(3) and professional services in §7.10(4). Telecommunications is discussed in §7.11. These sectors are all covered by several annexes and some are also affected by special provisions set out elsewhere in the NAFTA text. The reservations and liberalization commitments affecting each of these sectors are described in those sectoral discussions.

Otherwise, the following discussion of reservations and liberalization commitments is organized by annex rather than by sector. The NAFTA Annex I and III reservations are discussed together because, while they differ, both are referenced in the same excepting provision in each of the investment and the services chapters. The discussion then covers Annexes II, IV, V and VI.

(2) General Structure of Reservations

Annexes I, II, V, VI and VII each begin with a brief description of the structure of each reservation and rules of interpretation. The rules of interpretation are particularly important respecting Annexes I and VII and must be read carefully to understand properly the meaning of each reservation. Except for Annex III, which is comprised solely of a Schedule of Mexico, each Annex is split into a Schedule of Canada, a Schedule of Mexico and a Schedule of the United States. The Schedules to Annexes I, II, V, VI and VII are broken down into reservations that are in turn broken into elements.

The first three elements in each reservation are the "Sector" (the general sector in which the reservation is taken), the "Sub-Sector" (the specific sector in which the sector is taken) and, where applicable, the "Industry Classification" (the activity covered by the reservation). The activities under Industry Classification are identified by domestic industry classification codes. The Canadian and the U.S. Schedules use the Standard Industrial Classification ("SIC") numbers[75] and the Mexican Schedules use Clasificion Mexicana de Actividades y Productos ("CMAP") numbers.[76] Central Product Classification ("CPC") numbers are also used.[77] The next element is the "Reservation Type", which sets out the NAFTA obligation from which the reservation is being taken, and, in the case of Annexes I, V, VI and VII, the Level of Government to which the reservation applies. The reservation then sets out a "Measures" element and a "Description" element, the meaning and significance of which vary from annex to annex. Annexes I and VII reservations also contain an element called "Phase-Out", which sets out liberalization commitments.

Consider, for example, the Mexican reservation respecting the Auto Parts Industry set out on page I-M-31 of Mexico's schedule to Annex I. The Sector is "Manufacturing and Assembly of Goods". The Sub-Sector is the "Auto Parts Industry". The Industry Classification sets out five CMAP numbers, the first of which is CMAP 383103, which is Manufacturing of Parts and Accessories for Electrical Automotive Systems. The Type of Reservation is National Treatment (Article 1102) and the Level of Government is Federal.

(3) NAFTA Annex I and NAFTA Annex III Reservations

NAFTA 1108 and NAFTA 1206 provide that NAFTA Articles 1102 and 1202 (National Treatment), NAFTA Articles 1103 and 1203 (Most-Favoured-Nation) and NAFTA Article 1106 (Performance Requirements), 1107 (Senior Management and Boards of Directors) and 1205 (Local Presence) do not apply to federal non-conforming measures as set out in NAFTA Annexes I or III, to provincial or state non-conforming measures as set out in Annex I or to local government non-conforming measures. These exceptions apply only to non-conforming measures that existed on January 1, 1994.

Non-conforming federal measures not set out in Annex I or Annex III and not relating to a sector or activity covered by an Annex II reservation or otherwise exempt must be amended to conform with NAFTA. Non-conforming measures maintained by states and provinces do not have to be set out on

Annex I until January 1, 1996. After that date, non-conforming state and provincial measures that are not set out in a NAFTA country's schedule to Annex I are subject to the same requirement to conform as federal measures. Reservations under Annex III cannot be taken for provincial or state measures. Non-conforming measures maintained by local governments do not have to be set out in an annex for the exception in NAFTA 1108 and NAFTA 1206 to apply.

If a non-conforming measure set out in Annex I is made less non-conforming or eliminated, whether by unilateral action or because of a liberalization commitment, it cannot subsequently be amended by or replaced with a new measure that is more non-conforming. If an activity reserved to the Mexican state by NAFTA Annex III is privatized or opened to private investment, foreign participation may, notwithstanding NAFTA 1102, still be restricted. However, the restriction must be described in Mexico's Schedule to NAFTA Annex I at the time it becomes effective. In effect, Mexico may at a future time replace a reservation of an activity reserved to the state with a non-conforming measure set out on its NAFTA Annex I schedule. From that point on, the rules respecting NAFTA Annex I reservations would apply.

(a) Structure of NAFTA Annex I reservations

The preamble to Annex I sets out rules for interpreting the reservations. The three key elements in each reservation are the Measures element, the Description element and the Phase-Out element. The Measures element sets out the measures in respect of which the reservation is taken. The Description element describes the measure and sets out any changes to the measure that will occur forthwith upon NAFTA becoming effective. The Phase-Out element describes any future liberalization following NAFTA becoming effective. As a result of this format, the reader must examine both the Description and the Phase-Out elements to determine the liberalization commitment. The Phase-Out element prevails over all other elements. The Description element prevails over the Measures element if it qualifies the measure by immediate liberalization. Otherwise, the Measures element prevails, and one looks to the measure itself rather than to the narrative description of it under the Description element to determine what has been reserved.

Consider the Mexican Auto Parts Industry reservation referred to in §7.9(2). The Measures element of this reservation lists four measures, namely, the Mexican Investment Law, the Mexican Investment Regulation, the Automotive Decree and the Auto Decree Implementing Regulations. The Mexican Investment Regulation in effect when NAFTA was signed on December 17, 1992, restricted foreign ownership in an "enterprise of the autoparts industry" to 40% which does not conform with the NAFTA national treatment obligation in NAFTA 1102. The Description element of the reservation provides that investors of other NAFTA countries may own, directly or indirectly, 49% of an "enterprise of the autoparts industry". Because the Description element prevails over the Measures element, the applicable percentage became 49% when NAFTA became effective on January 1, 1994, with the result that the level of permitted ownership by investors of NAFTA countries was liberalized by 9%. The Phase-Out element provides that the permitted percentage be increased to 100% within five years of NAFTA becoming effective. Thus, the liberalization commitment eliminates this non-conforming measure by January 1, 1999.

For the purposes of the Annex I reservations, a Mexican enterprise is an enterprise organized under the law of Mexico. A "foreigner's exclusion clause" is a provision in the by-laws of an enterprise excluding foreigners from becoming partners or shareholders.

At the time of writing, the provincial and state non-conforming measures had not been set out in the schedules to NAFTA Annex I. Therefore, the following discussion of the NAFTA Annex I reservations does not include the reservations that will be taken by provinces or states. Significant barriers to the cross-border trade in services and to cross-border investment can result from provincial and state non-conforming measures.

(b) NAFTA Annex I reservations and investment screening

(i) Canada and the Investment Canada Act

Canada has taken a reservation from NAFTA 1102 (National Treatment), NAFTA 1106 (Performance Requirements) and NAFTA 1107 (Senior Management and Boards of Directors) in respect of the *Investment Canada Act*.[78] The only liberalization commitment made by Canada in its *Investment Canada Act* reservation is that the benefits of the higher thresholds conferred on investors of the United States under the FTA are extended to investors of Mexico. However, for purposes of the *Investment Canada Act*, the narrower concept of investor of the United States or Mexico, based on the *Investment Canada Act* requirement of control by nationals or entities controlled by nationals, has been retained.

The reservation provides that the higher thresholds will not apply to uranium production and ownership of uranium producing properties, oil and gas,[79] financial services, transportation services and cultural businesses. Canada has retained the right to impose undertakings respecting technology transfer, notwithstanding NAFTA 1106(1)(f). However, reservations were not taken respecting the other new prohibitions of performance requirements introduced by NAFTA such as those relating to trade or foreign exchange balancing requirements (NAFTA 1106(1)(e)) or exclusive supplier or world product mandate requirements (NAFTA 1106(1)(g)).

(ii) Mexico and the Mexican Investment Law and Regulation

Mexico has taken a reservation from NAFTA 1102 (National Treatment) respecting most provisions of the Mexican Investment Law and the Mexican Investment Regulation from the national treatment obligation in NAFTA 1102.[80] However, the Description and Phase-out elements of the reservations provide for substantial liberalization.

Once NAFTA becomes effective, the National Commission will only review direct or indirect acquisitions by investors of Canada or the United States of more than a 49% ownership interest of Mexican enterprises in unrestricted sectors if the gross assets of the enterprise exceed prescribed threshold amounts.[81] An "unrestricted sector" is one not listed in the Classification described in §7.5(2). The threshold amounts will be $25 million (US) for the years 1994 to 1996, $50 million (US) for the years 1997 to 1999, $75 million (US) for the years 2000 to 2002 and $150 million (US) thereafter. Beginning in 1995, these amounts will be adjusted annually for inflation.[82]

This liberalization does not apply to acquisitions of interests in existing or newly created enterprises carrying on activities in restricted sectors. Except as modified by liberalization commitments discussed in §7.9(3)(d), §7.10 and Chapter 8, the restricted sectors described in §7.5(2) continue.

The criteria that may be taken into account by the National Commission in reviewing the acquisition or establishment of an investment have been narrowed to its effects on employment and training, its technologies contribution and its general contribution to increase Mexican industrial productivity and competitiveness. Criteria that have been dropped include: not displacing national businesses that are operating satisfactorily; positive effects on balance of payments; incorporation of domestic imports and components; extent of financing from resources abroad; contribution to development of less developed regions; respect of social and cultural values; and identification of the foreign investor with Mexico's interest and investor's involvement with foreign centres of economic decision.[83]

These reservations do not cover NAFTA 1106 (Performance Requirements) or 1107 (Senior Management and Boards of Directors). Therefore, any conditions imposed by the National Commission in authorizing an investment must be consistent with these NAFTA requirements.

Unlike the reservation taken by Canada in respect of the *Investment Canada Act*, the expansive NAFTA concept of investor applies, and an "investor" of Canada or the United States does not have to be controlled by nationals or entities controlled by nationals of those countries.

(iii) The United States and Exon Florio

Unlike Canada and Mexico, the United States does not have laws of general application providing for screening of foreign direct investment. However, the Exon Florio Amendment[84] ("Exon Florio") enacted in 1988 and made permanent in 1991 permits the President to prohibit or reverse an acquisition of a U.S. business by a foreign person or entity if he believes that it would harm national security in a manner not adequately addressed by other laws. The President has delegated this power to the Committee on Foreign Investment in the United States. The Committee may conduct reviews and investigations within prescribed time periods. Parties to transactions have no obligation to notify the Committee of a transaction but provision is made for parties to file notices and to have their proposed transactions reviewed. Exon Florio does not define national security, and the regulations[85] give only general guidance for determining whether a transaction constitutes a threat to national security.

The United States has not taken a reservation in respect of the Exon Florio and is presumably relying on the exception in NAFTA 2102 for measures affecting national security. However, the scope of NAFTA 2102 is limited. The exception covers access to information, actions respecting traffic in implements of war and transactions respecting goods, services and technology for supplying military or security establishments, and actions taken under the United Nations Charter for the maintenance of international peace and security. NAFTA 2102 would not support an expansive application of Exon Florio. Without a reservation, an application of Exon Florio to an investment of an investor of Canada or Mexico that did not fall within the limited scope of the NAFTA 2102 exception would be contrary to the national treatment obligation in NAFTA 1102.

The status of Exon Florio under the FTA was less clear. Exon Florio was enacted after the FTA was signed but before it came into effect. The grandfathering provision in the FTA investment chapter applied to laws that existed at the time that the FTA came into effect, which included Exon Florio. However, letters exchanged on January 2, 1988, between Canada's Minister of International Trade and the United States Trade Representative amounted to a standstill arrangement. FTA 2003 is almost identical to NAFTA 2102, and an application of Exon Florio beyond its limited scope would have been contrary to the FTA national treatment obligation were it not for the grandfathering. In such a case, Canada would have had to rely on the standstill arrangement. Because of the NAFTA reservation approach and the absence of a reservation for Exon Florio, the application of Exon Florio by the United States must be consistent with NAFTA. If its application is extended beyond the confines of NAFTA 2102, investors of Canada and Mexico will have their direct remedies against the U.S. government under the investor-state dispute settlement procedures described in §11.3.

(c) Other Canadian NAFTA Annex I reservations

(i) State enterprises

Canada has reserved the right to impose ownership restrictions and limitations on the ability of investors of the other NAFTA countries to control state enterprises ("Crown corporations") and governmental entities that are being sold.[86] The reservation applies to such entities existing at the time that NAFTA comes into effect. Canada may also adopt and maintain measures respecting the nationality of the boards of directors and senior management of such entities. The reservation applies to the provinces.

The FTA investment chapter contained special provisions respecting Crown corporations. The FTA permitted the enactment of new measures respecting Crown corporations that were inconsistent with the FTA national treatment and minimum equity obligations, provided that once enacted, the inconsistent measures were not made more inconsistent.[87] The NAFTA reservation does not contain such a restriction. On the other hand, the FTA permitted the enactment of measures inconsistent with the FTA national treatment and minimum equity obligations respecting the initial acquirors of a Crown corporation that was established after the FTA came into force.[88] The NAFTA reservation makes no provision for Crown corporations established after NAFTA becomes effective.

Canada has taken reservations[89] respecting measures that restrict nonresident ownership of a number of former Crown corporations to prescribed percentages. The corporations and corresponding prescribed percentages are: Air Canada (25%), Canada Development Corporation (25%), Petro-Canada (25%), Canadian Arsenals Limited (25%), Eldorado Nuclear Limited (5%), Nordion Limited (25%), Theatronics Limited (49%) and Co-operative Energy Corporation (49%).

(ii) Corporate statutes

Canada has taken several reservations respecting its legislation for the incorporation of companies at the federal level. Canada has taken a reservation respecting the constrained share provisions of the *Canada Business Corporations Act* ("CBCA").[90] Under these provisions, the articles of a federally incorporated company may restrict the transfer of shares so that prescribed levels of "Canadian" ownership may be maintained. A reservation has also been taken respecting the CBCA requirement that a majority of the board of directors be "resident Canadians".[91] This requirement is also present in provincial corporate statutes and presumably each province will take its own reservations.

(iii) Other reservations

Canada has taken a reservation respecting nationality limitations that apply to loans made by the Farm Credit Corporation.[92] A reservation has been taken respecting federal restrictions respecting nationality that apply to the ownership of certain land in the Province of Alberta.[93] Canada has reserved the requirement in the *Export and Import Permits Act*[94] that recipients of export, import or transit permits be individuals ordinarily resident in Canada, enterprises having their head offices in Canada or branch offices of foreign enterprises.[95] Canada has reserved its nationality requirements respecting duty free shops[96] and for expert examiners of cultural property under the *Cultural Property Export and Import Act*.[97]

(iv) No liberalization commitments

None of the foregoing reservations contain any liberalization commitments.

(d) Other Mexican NAFTA Annex I reservations and liberalization commitments

Mexico has taken more Annex I reservations than either Canada or the United States. However, some of the Mexican Annex I reservations contain liberalization commitments.

(i) Duty deferral programs

Mexico has taken a reservation respecting the requirement that maquiladoras not sell to the domestic market more than 55% of the value of their annual exports in the previous year.[98] However, the percentage will be increased in 5% annual increments to 85% six years after NAFTA comes into force, and the requirement will be eliminated entirely seven years after the NAFTA becomes effective. This commitment will set the stage for the maquiladora plants to become fully integrated into the Mexican economy.

Mexico has also taken reservations respecting the export requirements in the ALTEX Decree and the PITEX Decree.[99] However, these requirements will be eliminated seven years after NAFTA becomes effective.

(ii) Mining

Mexico has reserved the right with respect to a wide range of mining activities to restrict ownership by investors of other NAFTA countries, or their investments, to 49%.[100] As some of these activities were subject to a 34% foreign ownership restriction, this reservation liberalizes the previous rule. Five years after NAFTA becomes effective, and subject to review by the National Commission for investments exceeding the thresholds described in §7.9(3)(b)(ii), Mexico will allow 100% ownership in all these activities.

(iii) Construction

Mexico has reserved the right with respect to a wide range of construction activities to require approval by the National Commission of ownership by investors of other NAFTA countries, or their investments, of more than

49%.[101] However, five years after NAFTA becomes effective, and subject to review by the National Commission for investments exceeding the thresholds described in §7.9(3)(b)(ii), Mexico will allow 100% ownership in these activities.

(iv) Ownership of land

Mexico has reserved its restriction respecting the acquisition by foreigners of land in the 100 kilometre strip along the country's borders or in the fifty kilometre strip inland from its coasts.[102] Mexican law provides for certain trust arrangements through which foreigners can acquire interests in these lands.[103] Only Mexican nationals or enterprises may own land for agricultural, livestock or forestry purposes. An enterprise must issue special shares representing the value of the land at the time of its acquisition and investors of another NAFTA country or their investments may own only 49% of such shares.[104] There is no liberalization commitment respecting either of these reservations.

(v) Entertainment and media

Mexico has reserved the right to restrict ownership by investors of other NAFTA countries, and their investments, to 49% of enterprises that own or operate cable television services.[105] This reservation is a liberalization because these services were previously reserved solely to Mexican nationals. There is no liberalization commitment but the reservation is subject to discussion in five years. The thresholds for review discussed in §7.9(3)(b)(ii) do not apply. Only Mexican nationals and Mexican enterprises may receive concessions to operate cable television systems.[106] As noted in §7.9(4)(b), Mexico has taken an Annex II reservation respecting broadcasting.

Mexico has reserved restrictions respecting importation of radio or television programming for broadcast or cable distribution[107] and requirements respecting the use of the Spanish language in radio and television programming.[108] Advertising included in programs transmitted directly from outside Mexico may not be distributed in those programs when retransmitted in Mexico.[109] Thirty percent of screen time of theatres must be reserved for films produced by Mexicans.[110] There are no liberalization commitments respecting these reservations.

Investors of other NAFTA countries, and their investments, may own up to 49% of enterprises publishing daily newspapers distributed in Mexico for Mexican audiences, and 100% of enterprises that print and distribute in Mexico newspapers published outside of Mexico.[111]

These reservations are relevant only as between Mexico and the United States because the activities covered are "cultural industries" and, as between Canada and Mexico, fall within the cultural exemption discussed in §10.1.

(vi) Other reservations

Mexico has reserved the right to limit participation by foreign nationals in co-operatives to 10%.[112] Only Mexican nationals can apply for a licence to qualify as a "microindustry enterprise" and such enterprises may not have foreign partners.[113] Prior approval by the National Commission must be obtained for investors of other NAFTA countries, or their investors, to own more that 49% of enterprises that provide educational services. The thresholds for review do not apply. Investors of other NAFTA countries, and their investments, may own up to 49% of enterprises manufacturing artificial explosives and fireworks, firearms, cartridges and ammunition,[114] or that sell firearms, cartridges and ammunition,[115] and no foreign national may be a director or officer of such an enterprise. Representatives of religious associations in Mexico must be Mexican nationals.[116] Concessions to provide road and bridge administration and ancillary services, to construct and/or operate marine or river works or roads, and to construct and/or operate pipelines other than energy or basic petrochemicals may only be obtained by Mexican nationals and Mexican enterprises.[117] None of these reservations contains a liberalization commitment.

Only Mexican nationals and Mexican enterprises may obtain concessions to spray pesticides. However, six years after NAFTA becomes effective, the requirement of a concession will be replaced with a permit requirement without a citizenship requirement.[118]

(e) Other U.S. NAFTA Annex I reservations

Of the three NAFTA countries, the United States has taken the fewest Annex I reservations. The United States has taken a reservation respecting certain provisions of the Export Trading Company Act of 1982[119] that provide for issuance of certificates to the effect that export activities of a person do not have the anti-competitive effects proscribed by the Act. Only U.S. residents, partnerships and corporations can apply for and be protected by such a certificate. Certain export licences may be applied for only by persons subject to U.S. jurisdiction.[120] Information supplied by applicants under certain U.S. federal insecticide, fungicide and rodenticide legislation cannot be provided by the Environment Protection Agency, without consent, to foreign or multinational businesses or their employees.[121]

Insurance and loan guarantees provided by the Overseas Private Investment Corporation are not available to certain foreign entities.[122] Other than certain Canadian issuers, foreign firms cannot utilize certain procedures under the Securities Act of 1933.[123] Grants under the Clean Water Act[124] for the construction of treatment plants for municipal sewage of industrial waste will be made only if the materials used in the works are manufactured in the United States.

None of these reservations contains liberalization commitments.

(f) Annex III reservations

Mexico's schedule to NAFTA Annex III reserves to the Mexican state the exclusive right to perform certain activities and to refuse to permit investment in same.[125] These activities include the energy and petrochemical sectors discussed in §7.10(1)(a). The other reserved activities are: satellite communications; telegraph services; radiotelegraph services; postal services; railroads; issuance of currency and minting of coinage; control, inspection and surveillance of maritime and inland ports; and control, inspection and surveillance of airports and heliports.

NAFTA Annex III identifies the major measures relevant to each activity reserved. These measures are listed for "transparency purposes" and include subordinate measures adopted under and consistent with the listed measures. The subordinate measures are not listed.

If an activity was reserved to the Mexican state on January 1, 1992, but is not reserved to the Mexican state when NAFTA enters into force, Mexico may none the less restrict foreign participation in the initial sale of state-owned assets or state enterprises that performed that activity to enterprises with majority Mexican ownership. The restriction may continue in effect for three years following the sale. After three years, the national treatment obligations in NAFTA 1102 apply unless the restriction is covered by a reservation in Mexico's schedule to NAFTA Annex I or the activity is listed in Mexico's schedule to NAFTA Annex II.[126]

(4) NAFTA Annex II Reservations

The NAFTA Annex II schedule of each NAFTA country lists sectors, subsectors and activities that are exempt from the national treatment (NAFTA 1102), MFN treatment (NAFTA 1103), performance requirements (NAFTA 1106) and senior management obligations (NAFTA 1107) of the investment chapter and from the national treatment (NAFTA 1202), MFN treatment (NAFTA 1203) and local presence (NAFTA 1205) obligations of the services chapter.[127] A NAFTA country may maintain existing non-conforming measures respecting the listed sectors and activities and may adopt new measures that are more non-conforming. The effect of the NAFTA Annex II reservations is to remove completely the sectors and activities identified from the disciplines imposed by these NAFTA provisions. The ability to adopt more non-conforming measures is constrained only by the requirement that an investor of another NAFTA country cannot be forced to dispose of an investment because of its nationality.[128]

NAFTA does not provide for Annex II reservations to be taken by provinces or states, and is silent as to the effect of the listed Annex II reservations on provincial and state laws. However, it has been agreed that reservations respecting the sections and activities listed in NAFTA Annex II apply to provincial, state and local, as well as to federal, laws.

(a) Structure of NAFTA Annex II reservations

The focus of Annex II reservations is not on measures but on sectors, sub-sectors and activities. In some cases, the reservation covers an entire sector. For example, the reservation on page II-C-1 of the Schedule of Canada covers Aboriginal Affairs. With others, activities are identified by industrial classification code numbers. For example, the reservation on page II-U-9 of the Schedule of the United States identifies the Sector as "Transportation", the Sub-Sector as "Water Transportation". Under Industry Classification the reservation sets out twelve SIC numbers, the first one of which is SIC 091, Commercial Fishing (limited to fishing vessels within the Exclusive Economic Zone). The precise scope of this reservation is determined by these SIC numbers. The scope of Annex II reservations is further delineated by the Description, which is critical and prevails over all other elements. Unlike the measure-specific Annex I reservations, the Measures element is not the focal point of Annex II reservations, and is included only for "transparency purposes".

(b) Sectors affected by NAFTA Annex II reservations

All three NAFTA countries have taken Annex II reservations respecting public law enforcement and correctional services. Reservations have also been taken respecting income security insurance, social welfare, public education, public training, health and child care, to the extent that these are social services established or maintained for a public purpose. A Canadian province could, under this reservation, require that operators of health care clinics be Canadian residents. Each NAFTA country has also taken reservations respecting rights and privileges accorded to socially or economically disadvantaged minorities. The U.S. reservation includes corporations organized in accordance with the Alaska Native Claims Settlement Act. Canada has taken a separate reservation respecting rights and privileges provided to aboriginal peoples.

Mexico has taken reservations respecting broadcasting and certain related services, telecommunication services relating to air navigation, postal services, telegraph and radiotelegraphy services, satellite communications services, services associated with energy and basic petrochemical goods, and nationality requirements respecting occupations related to vessels and aircraft, harbour pilots and masters, airport administrators and customs brokers.

Canada and the United States have each taken reservations respecting the ownership of oceanfront property. The Canadian reservation is general, while the U.S. reservation only applies to investors of Canada and their investments. There is no corresponding Mexican NAFTA Annex II reservation respecting oceanfront property. As indicated in §7.9(3)(d)(iv), Mexico has taken an Annex I reservation respecting coastal and border lands.

The United States has reserved the right to adopt or maintain any measure that accords equivalent treatment to persons of a country that limits ownership by U.S. persons in cable television systems or daily newspapers.[129] This reservation permits the U.S. government to respond in kind to Mexico's reservations respecting cable television and newspapers discussed in §7.9(3)(d)(v). As between Canada and the United States, these activities are covered by the cultural exemption discussed in §10.1.

(5) Annex IV Reservations

NAFTA 1108(6) provides that NAFTA 1103 (MFN Treatment) does not apply to international agreements or to sectors set out in Annex IV. The need for NAFTA 1108(6) and the Annex IV reservations flows from the fact that preferential treatment to a third country contrary to NAFTA 1103 may result from complying with an international agreement rather than maintaining a domestic measure.

Annex IV is broken into three identical schedules, one for each NAFTA country.[130] Each NAFTA country reserves from NAFTA 1103 all bilateral and multilateral international agreements signed prior to NAFTA becoming effective. Each NAFTA country has also taken a reservation respecting future international agreements involving aviation, fisheries, maritime matters and telecommunications transport networks and services.[131] Concessions to foreigners for matters such as routes for air services, fishing rights and the provision of international maritime services are based largely on reciprocal arrangements under which the basis for granting the concession is the receipt of a comparable concession in the foreign country. Without the reservation, NAFTA 1103 would make negotiating future concessions difficult because third countries granting concessions to one NAFTA country in return for reciprocal concessions may not wish those reciprocal concessions to be granted to other NAFTA countries that are not party to the arrangement.

Each NAFTA country has also taken a reservation to NAFTA 1103 for international agreements signed during the two-year period allowed in NAFTA 1108(2) for listing provincial and state measures. The international agreement must relate to a provincial or state measure set out in a NAFTA country's schedule to NAFTA Annex I within the two-year time frame. While provinces and states obviously do not enter into international agreements, some obligations under international agreements are carried out through measures enacted by co-operating provinces or states. While an international agreement respecting which this Annex IV reservation is taken can be signed at any time between January 1, 1994 and December 31, 1995, the provincial or state measure to which the agreement relates must have been in effect prior to January 1, 1994. This reservation is therefore directed at international agreements negotiated prior to January 1, 1994, and which have been carried into effect by provincial or state legislation in anticipation of their being signed.

The schedules to NAFTA Annex IV also take a reservation for current or future foreign aid programs.[132]

(6) Annex V Reservations

The contents of the Annex V reservations have been discussed in §7.8(4). In each reservation, the Measures element identifies the measures under which the quantitative restriction is contained and the Description element sets out the scope of the sector, subsector or activity covered by the quantitative restriction. There are no rules of interpretation.

(7) Annex VI Reservations

Under NAFTA 1208, Annex VI, the schedule of each NAFTA country sets out specific commitments to liberalize specified non-discriminatory measures respecting various services. In each reservation, the Measures element identifies the measure to be liberalized and the Description element sets out the liberalization commitment. The United States has made a commitment respecting certain retransmission applications under s. 325 of the Communications Act of 1934 and Mexico has made commitments respecting film distribution and use of equipment in bus and truck transportation services.[133] The commitments of all three NAFTA countries in Annex VI respecting legal services are discussed in §7.10(4).

7.10 SECTORAL DISCUSSIONS

(1) Energy and Petrochemical Goods

All three NAFTA countries have taken reservations respecting their energy sectors. Those taken by Mexico are by far the most extensive because, as discussed in §5.4(3), the energy sector, and particularly the hydrocarbon sector, is the most politically sensitive sector of the Mexican economy.

(a) Mexico

(i) Hydrocarbons

As described in §5.4(3), extensive state participation in the hydrocarbon sector flows from Article 27 of the Mexican constitution and the creation of PEMEX as a state monopoly to administer activities in this sector following the expropriation of the petroleum industry in 1938. The nationalist approach to the hydrocarbon sector is reflected in the Mexican Investment Law. Article 4 reserves the activities of petroleum and other hydrocarbons, as well as basic petrochemicals, exclusively to the state. Gas distribution is reserved exclusively for Mexicans or Mexican companies with exclusion-of-foreigners clauses. Article 5 permits foreign participation in secondary petrochemicals of up to 40%.

When the Mexican Investment Regulation came into effect in 1989, these restrictions were reflected in the Classification. However, the Mexican Investment Regulation provides for indirect foreign participation, which can be up to 100%, in gas distribution and secondary petrochemical production through twenty-year trust arrangements.[134] Also, the extent to which foreign investment is permitted in the Mexican hydrocarbon sector depends on the classification of petrochemicals as "basic" as opposed to "secondary". The Petroleum Resolution of 1989[135] reclassified a number of basic petrochemical products as secondary, and thereby expanded the scope for foreign participation. As a result of this regulation, only twenty petrochemicals are classified as "basic", while sixty-six are classified as "secondary".[136] Petrochemicals not classified as "basic" or "secondary" are covered by the rules that apply to unrestricted sectors. There was also some liberalization prior to NAFTA respecting the manufacture of certain derivatives of oil refining.

NAFTA Annex 603.2 and NAFTA Annex III reflect the provisions of the Mexican Investment Law, and reserve the following activities to the Mexican state: exploration, exploitation, refining and processing of crude oil and natural gas; production of artificial gas, basic petrochemicals and their feedstocks and pipelines; and foreign trade and transportation, storage and distribution to the first-hand sale of crude oil, natural and artificial gas, basic petrochemicals and goods covered by Chapter Six obtained from refining or processing crude oil and natural gas. These reservations are more expansive than the Mexican Investment Law in so far as the distribution of natural gas is concerned. As indicated above, this activity is reserved for Mexicans but not to the state, and foreigners have been permitted to participate through temporary trusts.

Mexico has taken several NAFTA Annex I reservations from NAFTA 1102 (National Treatment). Mexico has taken a reservation to the effect that only Mexican nationals or Mexicans with a foreigners' exclusion clause may engage in various activities respecting the distribution of liquified petroleum gas[137] or in operating retail outlets selling gasoline, diesel fuel, lubricants, oils or additives.[138] Mexico has also taken an Annex I reservation requiring the prior approval of the National Commission for an investor of Canada or the United States to own more than 49% of an enterprise involved in "non-risk sharing" contracts for the "exploration and drilling works of petroleum and gas wells and the construction of means for the transportation of petroleum and its derivatives".[139] This reservation relates to a 1958 Mexican law implementing Article 27 of the Mexican constitution that permits PEMEX to engage private contractors for these purposes so long as they are paid in cash rather than by a participation, or "risk sharing" basis.[140]

The scope of Mexico's reservations under NAFTA Annex 602.3 and NAFTA Annex III in the hydrocarbon sector depends on what is meant by a "basic petrochemical". While NAFTA 602(2) describes what "energy and basic petrochemical goods" are, the expression "basic petrochemicals" is undefined. However, "basic petrochemicals" are defined in the Petroleum Resolution of 1989 and, presumably, the scope intended by the Mexicans of these reservations was based on their own domestic law definition of a "basic petrochemical". While various activities respecting "basic petrochemicals" are reserved to the Mexican state, foreign investment is permitted in activities respecting other petrochemicals. Investment by investors of Canada or the United States in enterprises producing petrochemicals that are not basic petrochemicals will be governed by the principles described in §7.9(3)(b)(ii).

The tendency in recent years has been for the number of "basic petrochemicals" defined by Mexican law to diminish. Reservations in NAFTA Annexes I and III are subject to the requirements in NAFTA 1108(1)(c) and 1206(1)(c) that amendments not make non-conforming measures more non-conforming. An amendment to the Petroleum Resolution of 1989 that expanded the list of basic petrochemicals would contravene these provisions.[141]

(ii) Electricity

Consistent with Article 27 of the Mexican constitution set out in §5.4(3), Article 4 of the Mexican constitution reserves electricity exclusively for the state. This reservation applies only to the provision of electricity as a public service and does not extend to the generation of electricity for private use.[142] The state monopoly entrusted with providing electricity as a public service is the Comision Federal de Electricidad ("CFE").

Both NAFTA Annex 602.3 and NAFTA Annex III reserve to the state the supply of electricity as a public service, including its generation, transmission, transformation, distribution and sale. Paragraph 5 of NAFTA Annex 602.3 sets out rules respecting activities and investment in electricity generation facilities. Enterprises of Canada or the United States may acquire or establish generation facilities to meet their own needs or cogeneration facilities, provided in either case that excess power is sold to the CFE. Such enterprises may also acquire or establish independent power production facilities. Power produced for sale in Mexico must be sold to the CFE. Provision is made for the negotiation, with CFE as a participant, for the cross-border sale of electricity.

(iii) Nuclear energy

As required by Section 27 of the Mexican constitution, Article 4 of the Mexican Investment Law reserves the exploitation of radioactive minerals and the generation of nuclear energy to the Mexican state. These activities are entrusted to the National Commission of Nuclear Energy, which was formed in 1955.[143] The reservation of nuclear energy to the Mexican state is carried forward in both NAFTA Annex 602.3 and in NAFTA Annex III.

(iv) Annex II reservation respecting cross-border services

Mexico has taken a reservation under Annex II reserving the right to adopt or maintain any measure not inconsistent with NAFTA Annex 602.3 related to services associated with energy and petrochemical goods.[144] Such measures can be inconsistent with the national treatment, most-favoured-nation and local presence requirements of the NAFTA services chapter, and can cover cross-border services related to hydrocarbons, basic petrochemicals, electricity, nuclear power and treatment of radioactive materials. As the reservation is under NAFTA Annex II, such measures can be new non-conforming measures or amendments to non-conforming measures making them more non-conforming.

(b) Canada

In addition to retaining the lower threshold limits for review of investments in oil, gas and uranium properties referred to in §7.9(3)(b) and the ownership restrictions on certain former energy-sector Crown corporations referred to in §7.9(3)(c), Canada has taken several other reservations under Annex I respecting its energy sectors. Production licences for oil and gas in "frontier lands" and "offshore areas" are subject to Canadian ownership requirements.[145] A reservation has been taken retaining requirements that authorization for oil and gas developments in the Northwest Territories, the Yukon, Nova Scotia and Newfoundland offshore areas be conditional upon approval of a "benefits plan" that ensures employment and other benefits to Canadians.[146] A reservation has been taken respecting the Hibernia project off Newfoundland respecting benefit plans and transfer of technology.[147] A reservation has been taken respecting ownership requirements relating to uranium producing properties.[148] There is no Phase-out provided in any of these reservations.

Subject only to these reservations, Canadian energy sectors are subject to the requirements of the NAFTA services and investment chapters.

(c) The United States

The United States has taken a reservation under Annex I respecting ownership restrictions that apply to licences to transfer, manufacture, produce, or to the use of import facilities that produce or use nuclear materials.[149] There is no Phase-out provided. The United States has also taken a reservation respecting requirements that an alien or foreign corporation may not acquire rights-of-way for oil or gas pipelines or pipelines carrying products refined from oil and gas across on-shore federal lands or acquire leases or interests in certain minerals, such as coal and oil, on such lands. However, non-U.S. citizens can acquire 100% of the ownership of domestic corporations with such interests.[150] Subject only to these reservations, U.S. energy sectors are subject to the requirements of the NAFTA services and investment chapters.

(2) Air and Land Transportation

Unlike the FTA, the NAFTA investment chapter covers all forms of transportation services. The NAFTA services chapter also covers all transportation services, except for certain air services. Each NAFTA country has taken reservations respecting air and land transportation services, so that these sectors continue to be restricted. However, except to the extent that reservations have been taken under NAFTA Annex II, the reservations fix the limits of permissible discrimination. Substantial liberalization respecting specialty air services has been achieved in all three NAFTA countries. NAFTA will also significantly liberalize the provision of truck and bus services across the U.S.-Mexico border.

(a) Air transportation services

(i) Exception from services provisions

NAFTA 1201(2)(b) provides that the services chapter does not apply to air services, including domestic and international transportation services. Air services are covered by their own international conventions. Related services in support of air services are also exempt, other than aircraft repair and maintenance services and specialty air services.

(ii) Commercial air services

Commercial air services are covered by the NAFTA investment chapter but all three NAFTA countries have taken Annex I reservations. Canada has reserved its requirements that only "Canadians" (citizens, permanent residents or entities, 75% of the voting interests of which are controlled by such persons) may provide air services between points in Canada or scheduled or unscheduled services from Canada to points in other countries that have been reserved to Canadian carriers in bilateral agreements.[151] Canadian air carriers must use Canadian registered aircraft. The United States and Mexico have both taken reservations that are similar in effect to that taken by Canada.[152]

(iii) Specialty air services

Specialty air services consist of aerial mapping, aerial surveying, aerial photography, forest fire management, fire fighting, aerial advertising, glider towing, parachute jumping, aerial construction, heli-logging, aerial sightseeing, flight training, aerial inspection and surveillance, and aerial spraying services.[153] These services are covered by both the investment and services chapters. All three NAFTA countries have taken Annex I reservations respecting these activities. Canada has also taken an Annex II reservation.

In all three NAFTA countries, permission from applicable federal authorities[154] must be obtained to provide specialty services. In their respective Annex I reservations[155] Canada and the United States have agreed that persons of other NAFTA countries may, upon NAFTA becoming effective, receive permission to provide aerial mapping, aerial surveying, aerial photography, forest fire management, fire fighting, aerial advertising, glider towing and parachute jumping services. The corresponding Mexican commitment applies to flight training, forest fire management, fire fighting, glider towing and parachute jumping services.

Canada and the United States have agreed that permission may be given to persons of the other NAFTA countries to provide: aerial construction and heli-logging services two years after NAFTA becomes effective; aerial sightseeing, flight training and aerial inspection and surveillance services three years after NAFTA becomes effective; and aerial spraying services six years after NAFTA becomes effective. Mexico has agreed that permission may be given to persons of other NAFTA countries to provide: aerial advertising, aerial sightseeing services, aerial construction and heli-logging three years after NAFTA becomes effective; and aerial inspection and surveillance, mapping, photography, surveying and spraying six years after NAFTA becomes effective.

Canada has also reserved the right under Annex II to restrict the acquisition or establishment in Canada of investments providing specialty air services to Canadian nationals and 75% Canadian-owned corporations.[156] This reservation would not affect the ability of U.S. or Mexican persons from providing such services in Canada on a cross-border basis.

(iv) Repair and maintenance services

The NAFTA investment and services chapters apply to repair and maintenance services. However, all three NAFTA countries have taken Annex I reservations in respect of these services. In Canada, aircraft repair, overhauls or maintenance activities to maintain the airworthiness of Canadian registered aircraft must be performed by Canadian-certified aircraft maintenance organizations and engineers. Certifications are not provided to persons outside Canada.[157] In Mexico, only Mexican nationals and enterprises may receive concessions to establish and/or operate an aircraft repair

316

facility.[158] In the United States, aircraft repair, overhaul or maintenance performed outside the United States on U.S. registered aircraft must be certified by the Federal Aviation Administration, with continuing oversight.[159] Under an airworthiness agreement between Canada and the United States, each country recognizes the certifications and oversight provided by the other country for individuals and facilities performing work in the other country.[160]

(v) Air navigation services, airport and heliport administration

In Mexico, concessions to construct and operate airports and heliports and to provide air navigation services may only be granted to Mexican nationals and enterprises.[161] Neither Canada nor the United States has taken a similar reservation.

(vi) Remarks

The only liberalization commitments in respect of air services are those respecting specialty services. Otherwise, the provision of air services remains a restricted sector in all three countries.

(b) Land transportation services — truck and bus

(i) Between Canada and the United States

Notwithstanding the exclusion of transportation services from the FTA, there has been significant deregulation in freight transportation services between the United States and Canada in recent years. Deregulation began in the United States in the early 1980s and Canadian deregulation began several years later.[162] In the trucking industry, the result has been the replacement of a "public convenience and necessity" standard with a new entry control system based on fitness. A public interest test applies but the onus is on the objector to establish that issuance of the licence to the applicant would not be in the public interest.[163] In both the United States and Canada, the nationality of the owners of firms is not a factor in the granting of licences. Except for cabotage (transporting passengers or cargo between two points in the same country), U.S. transportation firms are permitted to operate in Canada and Canadian firms are permitted to operate in the United States.

(ii) Between the United States and Mexico

The situation between the United States and Mexico is quite different. Truck transportation between the United States and Mexico is regulated by a variety of discriminatory restrictions on the Mexican side. Transportation of most cargo in Mexico is reserved exclusively for Mexicans, the only exception being the transportation of dangerous substances. Trucking permits and commercial drivers' licences are reserved exclusively for Mexicans. Mexican unions have successfully blocked reform of these measures. There are a few

317

examples of deregulation. Owners of a maquiladora in Mexico can use their own fleets to transport intermediate components and final products back and forth across the U.S.- Mexico border.[164] Bus and taxi services are reserved exclusively to Mexicans under the Classification.

The United States has retaliated with its own measures against Mexico. A moratorium has been placed on the Interstate Commerce Commission granting to Mexicans operating authority for interstate and cross-border bus and truck services. Mexicans without operating authority can operate only within prescribed border zones, and Mexicans providing trucking services must obtain a certificate of registration to enter the United States and to provide services to and from these zones.[165]

(iii) NAFTA and cabotage

Cabotage is providing transportation services between points in the same country. Each NAFTA country has taken a reservation respecting the provision of truck and bus services between points within its country. In each of Canada and the United States, only persons of Canada or the United States using domestically built or duty-paid vehicles may provide these services.[166] A person of Canada or the United States includes enterprises organized under the laws of these countries, but these need not be controlled by Canadian or U.S. nationals.

The Mexican rule that will apply to cabotage when NAFTA becomes effective is similar, except that a Mexican enterprise will not be eligible without a foreigner's exclusion clause. Three years after NAFTA becomes effective, investors of Canada or the United States, or their investments, will be able to own up to 49% of enterprises that provide inter-city bus services, tourist transportation services or truck services for transporting international cargo between points in Mexico. This percentage increases to 51% seven years after NAFTA becomes effective and to 100% ten years after NAFTA becomes effective.[167] This liberalization commitment does not apply to local bus services, school bus services or taxi or other collective transportation services.[168]

(iv) Services to and from points between NAFTA countries

NAFTA substantially liberalizes access to and from Mexico by Canadian and U.S. providers of truck and bus services. Within three years of NAFTA becoming effective, Canadian and U.S. nationals and enterprises will be permitted to provide cross-border truck services to and from the border states of Baja California, Chihuahua, Coahuila, Neuvo Leon, Sonora and Tamaulipas, and such persons will be permitted to enter and depart Mexico through different ports of entry. This commitment will extend to all of Mexico six years after NAFTA becomes effective. Within three years of NAFTA becoming effective, Canadian and U.S. nationals and enterprises will be permitted to provide cross-border bus services to and from Mexico.[169]

The United States has reciprocated by undertaking to remove similar restrictions that it applies to Mexico. Within three years of NAFTA becoming effective, Mexican nationals and enterprises will be permitted to provide cross-border truck services to and from the border states of California, Arizona, New Mexico and Texas, and such persons will be permitted to enter and depart Mexico through different ports of entry. This commitment will extend to all of the United States six years after NAFTA becomes effective. Within three years of NAFTA becoming effective, Mexican nationals and enterprises will be permitted to provide cross-border bus services to and from the United States.[170]

(v) Monitoring

NAFTA Annex 1212 requires the Free Trade Commission to complete, receive and consider a report from the NAFTA countries during the fifth year and every second year after that until the bus and truck liberalization commitments are complete assessing the effectiveness of the liberalization, specific problems and possible modifications to periods for liberalization. The primary impact of this monitoring and consultative process will be on the provision of truck and bus services across the U.S.-Mexico border.

(vi) No discriminatory re-regulation

While NAFTA does not require changes in current practices as between Canada and the United States, NAFTA will have the effect of preventing either country from re-regulating the truck and bus transportation industries in a manner inconsistent with the requirements of the NAFTA investment or services chapters.

(c) Land transportation services — rail

Mexico has taken Annex II and Annex III reservations respecting a broad range of activities respecting railroads, including their operation and administration, the control of traffic, the supervision and management of railway rights-of-way and the operation, construction and maintenance of basic railway infrastructure.[171] Mexico has also taken an Annex I reservation requiring that railway crews be Mexican nationals.[172] The rail service sector will continue to be highly restricted in Mexico under NAFTA.

Neither Canada nor the United States has taken any reservations respecting rail services. As a result, Canadian and U.S. measures respecting the provision of rail services will be subject to the disciplines of the NAFTA investment and services chapters.

(3) Maritime Activities

Maritime activities continue to be highly restricted in all three NAFTA countries.

(a) Fisheries

Unlike the European Union, NAFTA makes no pretense whatever at establishing a common fisheries policy. Fishing will remain a highly restricted activity in all three NAFTA countries.

Canada has taken Annex I reservations respecting measures relating to the management of Canadian fisheries. Foreign vessels are prohibited from entering Canada's exclusive economic zone unless they are licensed or permitted to do so under a treaty. Fish processing enterprises cannot hold Canadian commercial fishing licences if they are more than 49% foreign owned. Port privileges are granted only to vessels from countries with which Canada has favourable fishery relations.

Mexico has reserved the right under NAFTA Annex I to limit ownership by investors of other NAFTA countries, and their investments, in enterprises performing coastal fishing, fresh water fishing and fishing in the exclusive economic zone to 49%. With enterprises performing fishing on the high seas, prior approval of the National Commission must be obtained for investments by investors of other NAFTA countries, or their investments, exceeding 49%.[173] A concession or permit issued by the Secretaria de Pesca (Secretary of Fisheries) is required to fish in "Mexican jurisdictional waters". Only Mexican nationals and Mexican enterprises (subject to the foregoing ownership limitations) using Mexican-flagged vessels may receive such a concession or permit. Permits to fish in Mexico's exclusive economic zone may be issued to vessels flagged in countries that give reciprocal treatment to Mexican vessels. Authorization for a variety of other fishing-related activities will be issued only to Mexican nationals and Mexican enterprises.[174]

The United States has reserved the right under NAFTA Annex II to adopt or maintain measures prescribing requirements for investment in, ownership or control of and the operation of vessels engaged in fishing and related activities in U.S. territorial waters and the U.S. exclusive economic zone. Unlike the Canadian and Mexican Annex I reservations, the U.S. Annex II reservation permits the adoption of more restrictive measures than those existing when NAFTA becomes effective.

(b) Other maritime activities

(i) The United States

All the reservations taken by the United States respecting maritime activities fall under NAFTA Annex II. The United States has reserved the right to adopt or maintain measures respecting the provision of maritime transportation services and the operation of U.S.-flagged vessels.[175] The reservation lists twenty-seven different existing measures and covers a wide range of matters such as: requirements for investment in, ownership and control of, and operation of vessels and other maritime structures in maritime cabotage services and in foreign trades; documentation and manning requirements for U.S.-flagged vessels; certification, licensing and citizenship requirements for crews and for pilots performing pilotage services in U.S. territorial waters; and so on. Vessel construction and repair and landside aspects of port activities are not included.

(ii) Canada

Canada has taken a reciprocal Annex II reservation reserving the right to maintain measures denying benefits to service providers or investors of the United States (but not Mexico) equivalent to the measures reserved in the U.S. reservation.[176] Canada has reserved the right in Annex II to adopt or maintain measures relating to investment in or provision of maritime cabotage services which, besides transporting goods or passengers between points in Canada and its exclusive economic zone, include the engaging by vessels in any commercial maritime activity in Canada and its exclusive economic zone, as well as activities respecting minerals and non-living resources on the continental shelf.[177] Canada has also reserved the right to adopt or maintain measures implementing arrangements with other countries respecting maritime activities in areas such as pollution control, safe navigation, barge inspection standards, water quality, pilotage, salvage, drug abuse control and maritime communications.

Canada has reserved in NAFTA Annex I its requirement that to register a vessel in Canada, the owner must be a Canadian or Commonwealth citizen or a corporation incorporated under the laws of and having its principal place of business in Canada or a Commonwealth country.[178] Only Canadian citizens or permanent residents may be certified as ship's officers[179] or be licensed to provide pilotage services.[180]

(iii) Mexico

All Mexico's reservations respecting maritime activities are in Annex I.

Maritime cabotage services, including off-shore maritime services, are reserved to Mexican-flagged vessels. Only Mexican nationals or a Mexican enterprise with a foreigners' exclusion clause may own Mexican-flagged vessels, and the directors and managers of such vessels must be Mexican. Foreign-flagged vessels may provide international maritime services on the basis of reciprocity with the country concerned.[181]

Prior approval of the National Commission must be obtained for investors of Canada or the United States, or their investments, to own more than 49% of enterprises operating foreign-flagged vessels providing international maritime transport services[182] or enterprises providing a variety of landside services including operating and maintaining docks and piers, loading and unloading vessels, ship and boat cleaning, stevedoring, transfer of cargo to other transportation facilities and waterfront terminal operations.[183]

Only Mexican nationals and Mexican enterprises may obtain concessions to construct and/or operate maritime and inland port terminals[184] and to establish and/or operate shipyards. To obtain government cargo preferences, subsidies and tax benefits, Mexican-flagged vessels must carry out repairs and maintenance in shipyards and repair facilities in Mexico.[185] Port workers must be Mexican nationals.[186]

(4) Professional Services

All three NAFTA countries have taken reservations and given liberalization commitments respecting various professional services. However, in Canada and the United States, much of the regulation of professional services takes place at the provincial or state level. The extent of reservation and liberalization will not be fully known until all provinces and states have completed their reservation lists.

(a) Patent and trade mark agents

Canada has taken Annex I reservations maintaining residency requirements for patent and trade mark agents,[187] and the United States has taken an Annex I reservation maintaining similar requirements for patent attorneys and patent agents.[188] These will be phased out by January 1, 1996, in accordance with NAFTA 1210(3), discussed in §7.8(3)(c). The U.S. reservation also reserves certain requirements respecting practitioners in trade mark and non-patent cases.

(b) Lawyers and foreign legal consultants

NAFTA Annex VI provides that the Canadian Provinces of British Columbia, Ontario and Saskatchewan and the U.S. States of Alaska, California, Connecticut, Florida, Georgia, Hawaii, Illinois, Michigan, New York, Ohio, Oregon, Texas and Washington, as well as the District of Columbia, will permit lawyers authorized to practise in the other two NAFTA countries and law firms located there to provide foreign legal consultancy services.[189] NAFTA Annex VI sets out a similar Mexican commitment, which operates on a reciprocal basis.[190]

Subject to their respective liberalization commitments in NAFTA Annex VI, the United States and Mexico have taken reciprocal NAFTA Annex II reservations respecting the provision of legal services and foreign legal consultancy services. The Mexican reservation relates to the provision of these services by U.S. persons and the U.S. reservation relates to the provision of these services by Mexican persons. Neither applies to Canadian persons.

Mexico has taken an Annex I reservation maintaining a requirement that only lawyers licensed in Mexico may have an interest in a law firm established in Mexico.[191] There are some reciprocating provisions in this reservation respecting lawyers licensed in Canada, but not the United States. Mexico has also taken reservations under NAFTA Annex I respecting both the federal government and a number of states maintaining citizenship requirements and business affiliation requirements respecting public notaries. The citizenship requirements maintained at the federal level will be phased out by January 1, 1996, in accordance with NAFTA 1210(3) discussed in §7.8(3)(c). There is no provision for phasing out the citizenship requirements maintained by the states identified in the reservation.

Subject to reservations, which include the foregoing as well as those that will be taken by states and provinces, Section B of NAFTA Annex 1210.5 requires each NAFTA country to ensure that a national of another NAFTA country is permitted to practise or advise on the law of any country in which that national is entitled to practise as a lawyer. The balance of Section B provides for consultation with relevant professional bodies to obtain recommendations on various matters, including the development of standards and criteria for the authorization of foreign legal consultants, and to work towards future liberalization.

(c) Custom brokers

Each NAFTA country has taken an Annex I reservation that maintains citizenship or residency requirements for customs brokers.[192] Mexico has also taken a reservation to the effect that shipper's export declarations must be processed by a Mexican-licensed customs broker.[193] All these reservations are subject to discussion in 1999.

(d) Other professions

Mexico has taken a reservation under NAFTA Annex I maintaining a requirement that only Mexican nationals may be licensed in professions that require a professional licence.[194] Mexico has also taken reservations under Annex I that maintain citizenship requirements respecting medical doctors providing in-house medical services in enterprises,[195] accountants performing certain types of tax audits[196] and veterinarians involved with enterprises that manage chemical, pharmaceutical and biological goods for application to animals.[197] Consistent with NAFTA 1210(3), the citizenship and permanent residency requirements in these reservations will be removed by January 1, 1996.

Section C of NAFTA Annex 1210.5 provides for the NAFTA countries to establish work programs with a view to achieving the temporary licensing of nationals of other NAFTA countries who are licensed as engineers in those countries. In Mexico's case, this only applies to civil engineers and to other specialties that Mexico may designate.

7.11 TELECOMMUNICATIONS

The technically complex and highly regulated telecommunications sector presents a unique set of international trade and investment issues. Telecommunication is communicating by transmitting and receiving signals by electromagnetic means.[198] Providers of telecommunication services must own or have access to an expensive and technically sophisticated telecommunications network or infrastructure in order to carry on their businesses.

Telecommunication services are categorized as either "basic" on the one hand or "enhanced" or "value-added" on the other. Basic services include communication by telephone, telegraph or telegram, telex and facsimile. The customer accesses the telecommunications network and uses it to communicate information, such as by making a telephone call or sending a fax. The essence of a "basic" service is that the information is carried through the telecommunications network without being changed. More sophisticated telecommunications services involving customer interaction are referred to as "enhanced" or "value-added". Examples of "enhanced services" include electronic and voice mail, protocol conversion and packet switching. Examples of "value-added" services include commercial databases and other on-line computer services. Consider the customer interaction involved with an on-line computer service. The customer uses a computer to search through information stored in a database to which it is linked through the telecommunications network. The customer selects the information by issuing commands through the computer and retrieves it into the computer's memory.

Telecommunications networks in many countries are owned and operated by public monopolies. Regardless of ownership, telecommunications networks have attributes of a natural monopoly and public access to the network is a regulatory issue. Basic services can be provided by a state enterprise or a private monopoly with regulated rates, or by competing service providers in a deregulated environment. In many countries, basic services like telephone or telegraph services are provided by the public monopoly that owns the telecommunications network, while in the United States these services are provided by competing companies. One basic regulatory question is what basic services should be required to be made generally available to the public and at what rates. Rate regulation raises public interest issues, such as whether the rates charged on one type of service should be such so as to cross-subsidize the provision of another type of service. For example, charges for long distance telephone service, which is used mainly by business, can be used to keep rates charged on local service affordable for the general public.

Enhanced or value-added services are provided over telecommunications networks by both providers of basic services and independent companies. One question that arises when telecommunications services, whether basic or enhanced, are being provided in a competitive environment is the terms upon which the owner of a telecommunications network who provides basic or enhanced telecommunications services itself should be obliged to grant access to the network to a competing service provider.

Producers of infrastructure equipment are affected by the standards and procurement practices of governments, telecommunications monopolies and major providers of basic telecommunications services, and by the procurement practices of these entities. Producers of terminal equipment are also affected by standards and by decisions respecting compatibility and equipment approvals.

These issues become more complex in an international environment. Telecommunications infrastructure and the services provided through it are regarded as being of strategic importance and, as with other strategic sectors such as energy, foreign involvement becomes a sensitive issue. Telecommunications industries are highly regulated and protection of domestic interests often becomes a regulatory objective. These interests are frequently powerful forces in the local economy because the telecommunications industry in many countries produces national champions, either in the form of state enterprises or domestically owned private sector network owners and service providers with ancillary interests in manufacturing sophisticated telecommunications equipment.

(1) The Canadian Model

A brief description of the Canadian telecommunications industry will highlight some of the issues discussed previously. The Canadian telecommunications carriage industry is comprised of the networks and the providers of basic telecommunications services. The telecommunications carriage industry and the telecommunications equipment manufacturing industries are very important to the Canadian economy. In 1990, the Canadian telecommunications carriage industry and the telecommunications equipment manufacturing industry employed approximately 125,000 people. In that year, the telecommunications carriage industry generated over $15 billion in revenue and comprised a higher percentage of gross domestic product than any of the agricultural sector, the logging and forestry sector or the mining sector.

Historically, the Canadian telecommunications industry was characterized by a separation between telephone and telegraph companies, with the result that there are two distinct national telecommunications in Canada. One system, Stentor Canadian Network Management (formerly Telecom Canada), is an unincorporated association comprised primarily of the Canadian telephone companies. Through this arrangement, the networks of the member companies are fully interconnected within an integrated system for the provision of telecommunication services. However, Canada never has had a single national carrier of telephone services and the networks are owned by the

member companies and not by Stentor. The other system is Unitel Communications, formerly CNCP Telecommunications or CNCP, and had its roots
in the telegraph services originally established by the railway companies.
Unitel is controlled by two Canadian companies, Canadian Pacific Limited
and Rogers Communications, Inc. Unitel has entered into an alliance with
AT&T, under which AT&T has invested equipment and technology in Unitel
in exchange for 20% of its shares. Unitel competes with Stentor in business
telecommunications services and operates its own microwave and fibre-optic
relay system and switching centres.

The Canadian telephone companies are regionally based with a mix of public and private ownership. The largest telephone company is Bell Canada,
which provides service throughout most of Canada's two largest provinces,
Ontario and Quebec, and is owned by BCE, a widely held Canadian company. MT&T (Nova Scotia), NBTel (New Brunswick), Island Tel (Prince
Edward Island) and Newfoundland Tel provide telephone service in the Atlantic provinces. These companies are owned by private investors, with Bell
Canada having a substantial interest in each of these companies. The telephone companies in Saskatchewan and Manitoba (SaskTel in Saskatchewan
and MTS in Manitoba) are owned by the governments of those provinces.
The shares of Telus (formerly Alberta Government Telephones or AGT) in
Alberta are publicly traded. BCTel, which provides telephone service in British
Columbia, is owned by GTE Corporation, a U.S. company. There are also
some independent carriers.

The federal government established Teleglobe as the overseas carrier and
Telesat as the domestic satellite carrier. Teleglobe operates international gate-
way switches in Montreal, Toronto and Vancouver that route traffic between
Canadian domestic carriers and overseas countries. Telesat leases satellite
capacity to the telephone companies and to broadcasters and provides some
telecom services directly to customers.[199] Both these companies have now
been privatized.

Much of Canada's telecommunications equipment industry is controlled
by the carriers, with Northern Telecom the manufacturing arm of Bell Canada
and Microtel Ltd. the manufacturing arm of BCTel.

The question as to which level of government has jurisdiction to regulate
the telecommunications industry has only recently been settled. In May, 1979,
the competent federal regulatory body, the Canadian Radio-Television and
Telecommunications Commission ("CRTC") approved an application made
by CNCP, Unitel's predecessor, to interconnect its system with that of Bell
Canada.[200] CNCP then pursued a similar arrangement with AGT. The
Alberta government challenged the right of the CRTC to consider the application. The resulting litigation led to a decision of the Supreme Court of
Canada in 1989 granting the federal government exclusive jurisdiction.[201]

Until recently, the telephone companies have had monopolies on public telephone service in their respective operating territories, while Unitel has had a monopoly on telegram services. This is changing. The CRTC turned down an application for long distance competition in 1985 but reversed this position in a decision in 1992 that opened up competition in long distance telephone service to Unitel. As one commentator expressed it:

> This was a very important decision, since it means that *any* entrant that compensates the telephone companies for lost contribution and pays for interconnection and related services will be allowed to enter through equivalent access arrangements.[202]

The Canadian approach to foreign investment in the telecommunications industry has been ambivalent. Telephone service in Canada was originally developed by American Bell. Canadian involvement in the Bell Telephone Company of Canada (Bell Canada's predecessor) evolved because American Bell had a policy of raising capital locally. American Bell's successor, AT&T, progressively allowed its position to be diluted, so that by 1934 AT&T held only 24% of the stock. AT&T divested itself of this interest in 1962 as the result of an anti-trust action. As one commentator observed, Bell Canada became Canadian not because of Canadian government policy but because of American Bell's approach to raising capital and the outcome of a U.S. anti-trust action.[203] BCTel, Canada's second largest telephone company, continues to be U.S. owned. However, a regulatory policy has evolved over the years that foreign ownership in facilities-based carriers should be restricted to 20%. This policy is reflected in Canada's new *Telecommunications Act*,[204] which was proclaimed into force in 1993.

(2) Provisions of NAFTA

NAFTA Chapter Thirteen sets out provisions that address some unique concerns respecting telecommunications. The telecommunication sector is otherwise subject to the obligations of NAFTA Chapters Eleven and Twelve. The obligations are significantly affected by reservations that have been taken by the three NAFTA countries described in §7.11(4). As indicated in §7.2, NAFTA 1307 provides that Chapter Thirteen prevails over other NAFTA chapters. As a result of this rule of prevalence, reservations taken in respect of obligations under Chapters Eleven and Twelve cannot derogate from obligations under Chapter Thirteen. Reservations cannot be taken from the obligations in Chapter Thirteen.

(3) NAFTA Chapter Thirteen

NAFTA Chapter Thirteen, which builds upon the provisions set out in FTA Annex 1404.C, is essentially a code of regulatory behaviour. NAFTA

1310 sets out key definitions used throughout the chapter. A "public telecommunication transport network" (a "public network"), is a public telecommunications infrastructure permitting telecommunications between defined network termination points. A "network termination point" is the final demarcation of the public network at the customer's premises. A simple example would be a telephone jack. A "public telecommunications transport service" (a "basic service"), is a basic service that must be provided to the public.

NAFTA 1310 defines "enhanced or value-added services" (hereafter simply referred to as "enhanced services") as telecommunications services employing computer processing applications that: act on the format, content, code, protocol or similar aspects of a customer's transmitted information; or provide a customer with additional, different or restructured information; or involve customer interaction with stored information.[205] This definition is critical because the NAFTA disciplines affecting the provision of enhanced services are considerably stricter than those regarding basic services. The FTA distinguished between basic and enhanced services but left it to the regulators to define where the line was crossed from one to the other.

(a) Scope and coverage

As indicated in §7.8(1), the measures covered by the NAFTA services chapter include those respecting access to distribution systems. Much of Chapter Thirteen is concerned with access to public networks and basic services. NAFTA 1301(1) provides that Chapter Thirteen applies to measures relating to access to public networks and basic services within a NAFTA country by persons of other NAFTA countries, the terms upon which persons of other NAFTA countries may provide enhanced services within or into a NAFTA country and standards respecting the attachment of terminal and other equipment to the public networks in each NAFTA country. NAFTA 1301(2) provides that Chapter Thirteen does not affect the distribution of radio or television programming other than to ensure access by operators of broadcast stations and cable systems to telecommunications public networks and basic services.

NAFTA 1301(3) sets out several important limitations with regard to the scope of Chapter Thirteen respecting public networks and basic services. Chapter Thirteen does not confer any right upon persons of other NAFTA countries to establish networks or provide basic services. This is an important limitation on the scope of Chapter Thirteen as it leaves these rights to be governed by Chapters Eleven and Twelve, from which reservations have been taken. The effect of NAFTA 1301(3)(b) is that Chapter Thirteen does apply to networks or basic services that are not generally available to the public. Also, NAFTA 1301(3)(c) provides that Chapter Thirteen cannot prevent a NAFTA country from prohibiting owners of private networks from using them to provide basic services.

(b) Access to public networks and basic services

NAFTA 1302(1) requires each NAFTA country to ensure that persons of other NAFTA countries have access to the public network and the basic services offered within its territory and across its borders on reasonable and non-discriminatory terms. NAFTA 1302(2) to 1302(7) elaborate upon this general principle. NAFTA 1302(2) ensures such rights as attaching equipment and interconnecting private leased or owned circuits to public networks, performing switching functions and operating protocols. NAFTA 1302(3) sets out certain pricing requirements respecting basic services, such as requiring that pricing reflect economic costs. However, the provision is not to be construed to prevent cross-subsidization between basic services. NAFTA 1302(4) covers the use of public networks and basic services for the cross-border movement of information. NAFTA 1302(5) to 1302(7) elaborate upon the regulatory measures that may or may not be adopted respecting public networks and basic services.

(c) Conditions for the provisions of enhanced services

NAFTA 1303 covers enhanced services. NAFTA 1303(1) requires that any licensing, permit, registration and other procedure respecting the provision of enhanced services must be transparent and non-discriminatory, and that the provision of information under such procedures must be confined to demonstrating financial solvency and compliance with applicable standards or technical regulations. NAFTA 1303(2) prevents NAFTA countries from requiring providers of enhanced services to provide their services to the public generally, cost-justify rates, file tariffs,[206] interconnect with any particular customer or public network, or conform to any standard other than that relating to interconnecting with a public network.

(d) Standards-related measures

NAFTA 1304 sets out requirements respecting standards relating to the attachment of terminal and other equipment to public networks that supplement the general principle in NAFTA 904(4) that standards not create unnecessary obstacles to trade. Standards respecting attachment may be maintained only to the extent necessary to prevent technical damage, interference or billing equipment malfunction, or to ensure users' safety. Network termination points for public networks are to be defined on a reasonable basis. NAFTA 1304(5) requires that conformity assessment procedures be transparent and non-discriminatory and sets out requirements respecting testing.

(e) Other provisions

NAFTA 1305 sets out provisions respecting monopolies that are discussed in §9.2(2)(b)(ii). NAFTA 1306 sets out a transparency requirement respecting access to and use of public networks and basic services. NAFTA 1308 provides for promoting international standards through the work of international bodies, and NAFTA 1309 provides for consultation for determining the feasibility of future liberalization.

(4) Reservations

(a) Telecommunications networks and basic services

All three NAFTA countries have taken Annex II reservations respecting networks and basic services.[207] All three reservations apply to the national treatment (NAFTA 1102) and most-favoured-nation treatment (NAFTA 1103) obligations in the investment chapter. The U.S. and Canadian reservations also apply to the investment obligation respecting senior management and boards of directors and the U.S. and Mexican reservations apply to the national treatment and local presence requirements in the services chapter. Mexico has also taken an Annex III reservation respecting telegraph services and radio telegraph services. The effect of these reservations is that the major NAFTA investment and services disciplines do not apply to telecommunication networks or the provision of basic services. However, while foreign investment and other restrictions in these sectors may be maintained, NAFTA Chapter Thirteen ensures that the activities of investors and service providers of NAFTA countries will not be frustrated in the operation of their business in other NAFTA countries by being denied reasonable access to the public networks or basic services.

(b) Enhanced services

The reservations taken by Canada and the United States expressly exclude enhanced services. The Mexican reservation does not explicitly refer to enhanced services but the telecommunications services covered by the reservation are described in a manner that is consistent with the concept of basic services.

Mexico and the United States have taken Annex I reservations affecting the provision of enhanced services.[208] Under the Mexican reservation, videotext and enhanced packet switching services may not be provided on a cross-border basis and enterprises investment by investors of Canada and the United States may not exceed 49%. These limitations are phased out as of July 1, 1995. The Description in the reservation has the effect of removing ownership restrictions and local presence requirements respecting the provision of other enhanced services. The U.S. reservation relates to a U.S. requirement respecting foreign-owned providers of enhanced services operating in the United States that negotiate operating agreements with foreign governments.

The NAFTA countries have not taken any other reservations respecting the provision of enhanced services, and these activities are subject to the disciplines of the NAFTA investment and services chapters. NAFTA Chapter Thirteen ensures that these disciplines will be meaningful by ensuring access to the public networks over which these services are provided on reasonable terms.

ENDNOTES

[1] Canadian BITs are called Foreign Investment Protection Agreements (or "FIPAs")

[2] Jeswald W. Salacuse, "BIT by BIT: The Growth of Bilateral Investment Treaties and Their Impact on Foreign Investment in Developing Countries" (1990), 24 *The International Lawyer* 655.

[3] The treaties creating the European Union which establish principles such as the free movement of capital, as well as Union legislation and jurisprudence, constitute a body of principles that protect direct foreign investment among the Union member states on a multilateral basis. However, because the institutional structure of the Union is so different from that desired by the governments of the three NAFTA countries in structuring NAFTA, the Union model was not used as a precedent.

[4] Kathleen Kunzer, "Recent Development: Developing a Model Bilateral Investment Treaty" (1983), 15 *Law & Policy in International Business* 273 at p. 276.

[5] *Ibid.*, at p. 277.

[6] *Ibid.*, at Appendix 1. The U.S. Government issued a revised prototype on February 24, 1984.

[7] Model BIT, *ibid.*, Article II:1

[8] *Ibid.*, Article II:4.

[9] *Ibid.*, Article II:7.

[10] *Ibid.*, Article III:1.

[11] *Ibid.*, Article V:1.

[12] As of January 1, 1990, the United States had concluded treaties with Senegal, Zaire, Morocco, Turkey, Cameroon, Bangladesh, Egypt and Grenada. BITs had been signed with Panama and Haiti, but had not been ratified.

[13] Patricia McKinistry Robin, "The BIT Won't Bite: The American Bilateral Investment Treaty Program" (1984), 33 *The American University Law Review* 931 at p. 957.

[14] *Op. cit.*, note 4, at p. 273.

[15] The Canadian government unilaterally agreed to raise the threshold for the review of oil and gas acquisitions by U.S. investors to the general FTA threshold limits. See *An Act to Amend the Investment Canada Act*, S.C. 1993, c. 35, s. 3.

[16] See, for example, *Agreement Between the Government of Canada and the Government of the Union of Soviet Socialist Republics for the Promotion and Reciprocal Protection of Investments*, Article VI.

[17] See Roger C. Wesley, "The Procedural Malaise of Foreign Investment Disputes in Latin America: From Local Tribunals to Factfinding" (1975), 7 *Law & Policy in International Business* 813 at p. 816.

[18] *Restatement of the Law Second: Foreign Relations Law of the United States* ("Second Restatement") as adopted and promulgated (St. Paul, American Law Institute Publishers, 1965), §202, p. 603.

[19] Ley para Promover la Inversión Mexicana y Regular la Inversión Extranjera.

[20] Article 27(1) of the Mexican constitution contains a similar provision respecting foreigners acquiring "ownership of lands, waters, and their appurtenances, or obtaining concessions for the exploitation of mines or waters".

[21] *Op. cit.*, note 17, at p. 821.

[22] Ignacio Gomez-Palacio, "The New Regulation on Foreign Investment in Mexico: A Difficult Task" (1989), 12 *Houston Journal of International Law* 253 at p. 256, note 19.

[23] See Dale A. Kimball Jr., "Recent Development: Secondary and Tertiary Petroleum Operations in Mexico: New Foreign Investment Opportunities" (1990), 25 *Texas International Law Journal* 411 at p. 413. Luis Escheverria was the President of Mexico at the time that the Mexican Investment Law was enacted.

[24] The do not appear to have had the force of law. See Dale A. Kimball Jr., *ibid.*, at p. 419, note 54.

[25] Reglamento de la Ley para Promover la Inversión Mexicana y Regular la Inversión Extranjera.

[26] *Op. cit.*, note 23, at p. 419.

[27] Comisión Nacional de Inversiones Extranjeras. The National Commission was created by Article 11 of the Mexican Investment Law.

[28] Some of these activities, such as "banking" and "minting of currency", are not referred to in Article 4 of the Mexican Investment Law, but are identified in the Classification as activities reserved to the state.

[29] None of the activities listed from "credit unions" on to the end of this list are referred to in Article 4 of the Mexican Investment Law, but are identified in the Classification as activities reserved for Mexicans.

[30] There are several other requirements. See Kimball Jr., *op. cit.*, note 23, at p. 420, note 59 for a description of these requirements. The requirements themselves are listed in Sections I to VI of the Mexican Investment Regulation.

[31] Gomez-Palacio, *op. cit.*, note 22, at pp. 260-62.

[32] Article 7 of the Mexican Investment Regulation.

[33] See Article 12 of the Mexican Investment Law, which sets out the powers of the National Commission.

[34] See Article 13 of the Mexican Investment Law.

[35] These comments are based on the Marrakesh text of the GATT TRIMS Agreement.

[36] See the Illustrative List set out in the Annex to the GATT TRIMS Agreement. The Mexican Automotive Decree discussed in §5.1(3) falls within the measures described in this list.

[37] The comments are based on the Marrakesh text of the GATS.

[38] Unlike under the FTA, the NAFTA concept of "enterprise" includes non-profit entities.

[39] NAFTA 1113.

[40] Model BIT Article I:(a), under definition of "company".

[41] NAFTA 1102(1). The references to "expansion", "management" and "other disposition" are not in the FTA text.

[42] NAFTA 1102(4); FTA 1602(2) and 1602(3).

[43] NAFTA 1103; Model BIT Article II:2.

[44] NAFTA 1104.

[45] NAFTA 1105; Model BIT Article II:4.

[46] United Nations Centre on Transnational Corporations, *Bilateral Investment Treaties*, published in co-operation with the United Nations (London, Graham & Trotman Ltd., 1988), at p. 41.

[47] *Ibid.*, at p. 240.

[48] *Restatement of the Law Second, Foreign Relations Law of the United States* (St. Paul, Minn, American Law Institute Publishers, 1965), p. 503 ("Second Restatement").

[49] *Restatement of the Law Third, Foreign Relations Law of the United States* (St. Paul, Minn., American Law Institute Publishers, 1987) ("Third Restatement").

[50] Third Restatement, *ibid.*, Volume 2, pp. 187-8.

[51] Third Restatement, *ibid.*, Volume 2, p. 188.

[52] For example, a transnational with a number of product lines could be required to use its foreign subsidiary as the sole supplier of one of those product lines for its entire world market.

[53] See *Reglamento de la Ley sobre el Control y Registro de la Transferencia de Tecnologia y el Uso y Explotacion de Patentes y Marcas*, Diario Oficial, January 9, 1990.

[54] For example, Mexico's trade balancing requirements in respect of its automotive industry, discussed in §5.1(3)(b).

[55] The Model BIT language is more general, using language such as "or which impose any other similar requirements".

[56] These are common in corporate statutes in Canada, both at the federal and provincial levels.

[57] FTA 1606.

[58] Model BIT Article V:1.

[59] NAFTA also requires that transfers be permitted in freely usable currencies.

[60] In U.S. jurisprudence and customary international law, taking is sometimes referred to as exercising the "power of eminent domain", which is compensable, and regulation as exercise of "police power", which is not compensable. These expressions are not generally used

in Canadian jurisprudence but the reasoning in the Canadian cases is similar to that in the United States.

[61] NAFTA 1110(7).

[62] NAFTA 1110(8).

[63] K. Scott Gudgeon, "Valuation of Nationalized Property" in *The Valuation of Nationalized Property in International Law*, vol. IV, Richard B. Lillich, ed. (Charlottesville, University Press of Virginia, 1986), at p. 103.

[64] *Ibid.*

[65] Model BIT Article III:1.

[66] Samuel K.B. Asante, "International Law and Foreign Investment: A Reappraisal" (July 1988) *International and Comparative Law Quarterly* 588 at p. 596.

[67] See NAFTA 1110(2) through to 1110(6) for compensation criteria.

[68] Consider, for example, s. 6 of the *Customs Act*, R.S.C. 1985, c. 1 (2nd Supp.), which requires operators of certain cross-border facilities to provide free of charge to Revenue Canada Customs and Excise buildings and other amenities. This measure does not affect "investments" as defined in the FTA, but clearly affects "investments" as defined in NAFTA.

[69] Article 27 of the Mexican Constitution provides: "Private property shall not be expropriated for reasons of public use and subject to payment of indemnity."

[70] See definition of "cross-border provision of services" in NAFTA 1213. Paragraphs (a), (b) and (c) of this definition are taken from paragraphs (a), (b) and (d) of Section 2 of GATS Article I.

[71] GATS Article I, Section 2(c).

[72] There is a slight point of departure here from the criteria that apply to an "investor", whose substantial business activities must be with the NAFTA country under whose law it is constituted or organized. See NAFTA 1113(2) and compare it with NAFTA 1211(2).

[73] NAFTA 1201(2)(c) and 1201(2)(d) respectively.

[74] NAFTA 201(1).

[75] For Canada, see Statistics Canada, *Standard Industrial Classification*, 4th ed., 1980. For the United States, see United States Office of Management and Budget, *Standard Industrial Classification Manual*, 1987.

[76] See Institutio Nacional de Estadistica, Geografia e Informatica, *Clasificacion Mexicana de Actividades y Productos*, 1988.

[77] See Statistical Office of the United Nations, Statistical Papers, Series M, No. 77, *Provisional Central Product Classification*, 1991.

[78] R.S.C. 1985, c. 28 (1st Supp.). See NAFTA Annex I, p. I-C-2.

[79] Note, however, that the provision excluding oil and gas from the higher thresholds for U.S. investors was repealed in 1993. See *An Act to Amend the Investment Canada Act*, S.C. 1993, c. 35, s. 3. Therefore, this reservation will not apply to U.S. investors in respect of oil and gas. The amendments to the *Investment Canada Act* made when NAFTA became effective do not make an exception for oil and gas from the higher thresholds for investors of either the United States or Mexico. See the new s. 14.01(6) of the *Investment Canada Act* added by s. 181 of the *North American Free Trade Agreement Implementation Act*, S.C. 1993, c. 44.

[80] NAFTA Annex I, pp. I-M-2 and I-M-4.

[81] NAFTA Annex I, p. I-M-4.

[82] According to the implicit price deflator for U.S. Gross Domestic Product or any successor index published by the Council of Economic Advisors in "Economic Indicators". See NAFTA Annex I, p. I-M-5.

[83] See Article 13 of the Mexican Investment Law.

[84] Section 5021 of the Omnibus Trade and Competitiveness Act of 1988 (Pub. Law 100-418). The following discussion is based on a paper delivered by Wilson Chu of Vial, Hamilton, Koch & Knox at the Inter-Pacific Bar Association Third Annual Meeting and Conference, Taipei, May 2-5, 1993.

[85] 56 Federal Register 58774 (31 C.F.R. Part 800).

[86] NAFTA Annex I, p. I-C-7.

[87] FTA 1602(5) and (6).

[88] FTA 1602(7).

[89] NAFTA Annex I, p. I-C-14.

90 R.S.C. 1985, c. C-44. NAFTA Annex I, p. I-C-9. In Canada, corporations may be incorporated under federal law or provincial law.
91 NAFTA Annex I, p. I-C-10.
92 NAFTA Annex I, p. I-C-1.
93 NAFTA Annex I, p. I-C-12.
94 R.S.C. 1985, c. E-19.
95 NAFTA Annex I, p. I-C-16.
96 NAFTA Annex I, p. I-C-19.
97 R.S.C. 1985, c. C-51. The reservation is in NAFTA Annex I, p. I-C-20.
98 NAFTA Annex I, p. I-M-34.
99 Annex I, pp. I-M-36 and I-M-37 respectively.
100 NAFTA Annex I, p. I-M-40. In the Appendix to the Mexican Regulation, most of these activities fall under System 5, which limits foreign ownership to 49%. However, a number, such as exploitation of mineral carbon and extraction of phosphoric rock and sulphur fall under System 3, which limits the participation of foreigners to 34%.
101 NAFTA Annex I, p. I-M-21. All of these activities fall under System 6 in the Appendix to the Mexican Regulations, so the reservation preserves the status quo.
102 NAFTA Annex I, p. I-M-1.
103 See Chapter IV of the Mexican Investment Law and Chapter III of the Mexican Investment Regulation.
104 NAFTA Annex I, p. I-M-9.
105 NAFTA Annex I, p. I-M-15.
106 NAFTA Annex I, p. I-M-16.
107 NAFTA Annex I, p. I-M-10.
108 NAFTA Annex I, p. I-M-12.
109 NAFTA Annex I, p. I-M-14.
110 NAFTA Annex I, p. I-M-17.
111 NAFTA Annex I, p. I-M-42. Previously all periodical and review publishing was included in System 6 on the Classification, so that approval of the National Commission was required for majority ownership.
112 NAFTA Annex I, p. I-M-7.
113 NAFTA Annex I, p. I-M-8. A "microindustry enterprise" includes enterprises with up to fifteen workers and sales of amounts periodically determined by SECOFI.
114 NAFTA Annex I, p. I-M-39.
115 NAFTA Annex I, p. I-M-52.
116 NAFTA Annex I, p. I-M-53.
117 NAFTA Annex I, p. I-M-65 for road and bridge administration services and ancillary services, p. I-M-72 for marine or river works and roads, and p. I-M-73 for pipelines. Concessions are granted by the Secretaria de Communicaciones y Transportes (Secretary of Communication and Transport).
118 NAFTA Annex I, p. I-M-54.
119 15 U.S.C. §§4011-4021. For the reservation, see NAFTA Annex I, p. I-U-2.
120 NAFTA Annex I, p. I-U-4.
121 NAFTA Annex I, p. I-U-6.
122 NAFTA Annex I, p. I-U-11.
123 15 U.S.C. §§ 77C(b), 77f, 77g, 77h, 77j and 77s(a).
124 33 U.S.C. §§1251 et seq. The reservation is at NAFTA Annex I, p. I-U-23.
125 NAFTA 1101(2).
126 See NAFTA Annex III, Schedule of Mexico, Section C.
127 See NAFTA 1108(3) for investment chapter and NAFTA 1206(3) for services chapter.
128 NAFTA 1108(4).
129 NAFTA Annex II, p. II-U-8.
130 For Canada, see p. IV-C-1. For Mexico, see p. IV-M-1. For the United States, see p. IV-U-1. The schedules are identical to the extent that the Schedule of Canada refers to "state measures" when "provincial measures" was obviously intended.
131 Except to the extent covered by NAFTA Chapter Thirteen (Telecommunications).
132 By way of example, each NAFTA country's schedule refers to the programs governed by

the Energy Economic Cooperation Program with Central America and the Caribbean (Pacto de San José) and the OECD Agreement on Export Credits.

[133] Annex VI, p. VI-U-1 for U.S. commitment and pp. VI-M-1 and VI-M-3 for Mexican commitments.

[134] Kimball Jr., *op. cit.*, note 23, at p. 422. See Article 23 of the Mexican Investment Regulation. The need for new investment is one criterion applied in permitting these arrangements.

[135] See Kimball Jr., *ibid.*, at pp. 413-14, note 11. The full title is Resolution that Classified the Indicated Petrochemical Products as Basic or Secondary Petrochemicals (Resolucion que clasifica los productos petroquimicos que se indican, dentro de la petroquimica basica o secundaria).

[136] See Kimball Jr., *ibid.*, at pp. 427-31, which sets out the text of the Petroleum Resolution of 1989.

[137] NAFTA Annex I, p. I-M-27.

[138] NAFTA Annex I, p. I-M-28.

[139] NAFTA Annex I, p. I-M-23.

[140] Ewell E. Murphy Jr., "The Dilemma of Hydrocarbon Investment in Mexico's Accession to the North American Free Trade Agreement" (1991), 9 *Journal of Energy & Natural Resource Law* 239 at p. 263. The law is the *Ley Reglamentaria del Articulo 27 Constitucional en el Ramo del Petrolea.*

[141] As noted above, this would not be the case if the reservations had been taken under NAFTA Annex II.

[142] Andre Plourde, "Energy and the NAFTA", C.D. Howe Inst. Commentary, No. 46, May 1993, p. 5.

[143] Fernando Flores-Garcia, "Aspects of Mexican Energy Regulation" (1990), 25 *Texas International Law Journal* 359 at p. 361.

[144] NAFTA Annex II, p. II-M-8.

[145] NAFTA Annex I, p. I-C-23. These regulations apply in parts of Canada, such as the Northwest Territories and the Yukon, that are not under provincial jurisdiction.

[146] NAFTA Annex I, p. I-C-25.

[147] NAFTA Annex I, p. I-C-28.

[148] NAFTA Annex I, p. I-C-29.

[149] NAFTA Annex I, p. I-U-1.

[150] NAFTA Annex I, p. I-U-7.

[151] NAFTA Annex I, p. I-C-32.

[152] For the United States, see NAFTA Annex I, p. I-U-13. For Mexico, see NAFTA Annex I, p. I-M-55. The United States is less restrictive than the other two countries respecting the provision of air freight forwarding and charter activities (other than the actual operation of the aircraft). Non-U.S. citizens may provide these services under authority from the Department of Transportation. U.S. citizens do not require such authority.

[153] NAFTA 1213.

[154] In Canada, an operating certificate issued by the federal Department of Transport; in the United States, authorization from the federal Department of Transportation; in Mexico, a permit issued by the Secretaria de Communicionnes y Transportes (Secretary of Communication and Transport).

[155] NAFTA Annex I, p. I-C-34 for Canada, p. I-U-15 for the United States and p. I-M-57 for Mexico.

[156] NAFTA Annex II, p. II-C-10.

[157] NAFTA Annex I, p. I-C-36.

[158] NAFTA Annex I, p. I-M-59.

[159] NAFTA Annex I, p. I-U-12.

[160] NAFTA Annex I, pp. I-C-36 and I-U-12.

[161] NAFTA Annex I, p. I-M-60.

[162] In Canada, see the *National Transportation Act, 1987*, R.S.C. 1985, c. 28 (3rd Supp.) and the *Motor Vehicle Transport Act, 1987*, R.S.C. 1985, c. 29 (3rd Supp.).

[163] See Dean Saul, "The National Transportation Act 1987: A Brief Overview Federal Motor Vehicle Transport Regulation in Canada", in *Transportation Deregulation: The New Frontiers* (Toronto, Insight Press, 1988), at p. 8.

[164] These examples of Mexican restrictions on truck transportation are taken from Gary C. Huf-brauer and Jeffrey J. Schott, *North American Free Trade: Issues and Recommendations* (Washington, D.C., Institute for International Economics, 1992), pp. 84-5.

[165] These restrictions are described in NAFTA Annex I, p. I-U-19. See also Hufbrauer and Schott, *ibid.*, at p. 85.

[166] For Canada, see NAFTA Annex I, p. I-C-37. For the United States, see NAFTA Annex I, p. I-U-18 at p. I-U-19, para. 4.

[167] NAFTA Annex I, p. I-M-68. See pp. I-M-70 and 71.

[168] NAFTA Annex I, p. I-M-66. This reservation does not contain a liberalization commitment.

[169] NAFTA Annex I, p. I-M-68. See pp. I-M-69 and I-M-70.

[170] NAFTA Annex I, p. I-U-18.

[171] NAFTA Annex III, p. III-M-3.

[172] NAFTA Annex I, p. I-M-64.

[173] NAFTA Annex I, p. I-M-29.

[174] NAFTA Annex I, p. I-M-75.

[175] NAFTA Annex II, p. II-U-9.

[176] NAFTA Annex II, p. II-C-13.

[177] NAFTA Annex II, p. II-C-11.

[178] NAFTA Annex I, p. I-C-38.

[179] NAFTA Annex I, p. I-C-39.

[180] NAFTA Annex I, p. I-C-40. Canada has also taken reservations on pp. I-C-41 (Shipping Conferences) and I-C-42 (Exception in Coasting Trade Act for U.S. Government Vessels Supplying Distant Early Warning Sites).

[181] NAFTA Annex I, p. I-M-78.

[182] NAFTA Annex I, p. I-M-78. See p. I-M-79.

[183] NAFTA Annex I, p. I-M-81.

[184] NAFTA Annex I, p. I-M-83. These include docks, cranes and related facilities.

[185] NAFTA Annex I, p. I-M-77.

[186] NAFTA Annex I, p. I-M-80.

[187] NAFTA Annex I, pp. I-C-21 (Patent Agents) and I-C-22 (Trade Mark Agents).

[188] NAFTA Annex I, p. I-U-9.

[189] NAFTA Annex VI, pp. VI-C-1 (Canada) and VI-U-2 (United States).

[190] NAFTA Annex VI, p. VI-M-2.

[191] NAFTA Annex I, p. I-M-46.

[192] NAFTA Annex I, pp. I-C-18 (Canada), I-M-74 (Mexico) and I-U-21 (United States).

[193] NAFTA Annex I, p. I-M-44.

[194] NAFTA Annex I, p. I-M-45.

[195] NAFTA Annex I, p. I-M-43.

[196] NAFTA Annex I, p. I-M-48.

[197] NAFTA Annex I, p. I-M-51.

[198] See the definition of "telecommunications" in NAFTA 1310.

[199] Hudson N. Janisch, "Canadian Telecommunications: The World Turned Upside Down", *The Canadian Law Newsletter*, Vol. XVIII, Summer 1993, published by the Committee on Canadian Law/Section of International Law and Practice, American Bar Assn., at p. 6.

[200] *Ibid.*, at p. 10. The decision is *CNCP Telecommunications—Interconnection with Bell Canada* (1979), Telecom. Decision C.R.T.C. 79-11.

[201] *Alberta Government Telephones v. Canada (Canadian Radio-Television & Telecommunications Commission)* (1989), 61 D.L.R. (4th) 193, [1989] 2 S.C.R. 225, [1989] 5 W.W.R. 385, 68 Alta L.R. (2d) 1, 26 C.P.R. (3d) 289, 98 N.R. 161 (S.C.C.).

[202] Janisch, *op. cit.*, note 199, at p. 12. The decision is *Competition in the Provision of Public Long Distance Telephone Services and Related Resale and Sharing Issues* (1992), Telecom. Decision C.R.T.C. 92-12.

[203] Hudson N. Janisch, "Emerging Issues in Foreign Investment in Telecommunications", *International Business and Trade Law Programme*, Working Paper Series, 1988-89, p. 10.

[204] *Telecommunications Act*, S.C. 1993, c. 38. See s. 16, which contains grandfathering language.

[205] No distinction is made in NAFTA between "enhanced" services and "value-added" services.

NAFTA 1303(3) sets out some circumstances in which NAFTA country may require that a tariff be filed.
[207] NAFTA Annex II, pp. II-C-3 (Canada), II-M-4 (Mexico) and II-U-3 (United States).
[208] NAFTA Annex I, pp. I-M-18 (Mexico) and I-U-5 (United States).

CHAPTER 8

FINANCIAL SERVICES

A viable financial sector is an essential component in any economy. The ability of businesses to finance their activities depends on the existence of a stable and efficient banking sector. Government macro-economic policy is implemented largely through its ability to regulate the country's banking system and the banking system is critical to a government's ability to finance its own activities.

Financial intermediaries such as banks and other lending institutions are the vehicles through which savings are made available to finance economic activity. Banks accept deposits from people with excess cash and lend money to people or business with cash needs. Banks are the custodians of "other people's money".[1] Depositors must have confidence that deposits will be available to be withdrawn when the money is needed. Without this confidence, deposits will not be made and savings will not be channelled to finance economic activity. Permitting enterprises to accept deposits and make loans without proper regulation is an open invitation to fraud and mismanagement.

The ability of businesses to raise equity capital depends on the existence of creditable and efficient securities markets. Governments promote the credibility of securities markets by regulating the trade in securities to ensure adequate and truthful disclosure to investors and minimize fraud.

Insurance companies perform the important function of spreading the risk of unforeseen contingencies such as premature death, personal injury, sickness and property damage. Governments have public policy concerns that insurance companies be in a position to honour the policies that they have underwritten.

Financial sectors are highly regulated. The objective of financial regulation is to ensure that financial institutions such as banks and other deposit taking and lending entities, securities firms and insurance companies are financially sound and able to honour their obligations, and that members of the public dealing with financial obligations have confidence that these obligations will be met.

8.1 CROSS-BORDER FINANCIAL REGULATION

Financial regulation is more complex in a cross-border context because foreign providers of financial services are more difficult to regulate than their domestic counterparts. Also, aggressive foreign competition may undermine the stability of the domestic financial system. For these reasons, financial regulation in many countries restricts foreign ownership of domestic financial institutions and foreign participation in the domestic market for financial services.

Regulation of foreign providers of financial services can be based on reciprocity, national treatment, most-favoured-nation treatment or a combination of these principles.

(1) Reciprocity

In its simplest form, reciprocity entails a unilateral *quid pro quo* approach under which one country allows financial institutions of another country to participate in its market only to the extent that its financial institutions are permitted to participate in the other country's market.[2] However, reciprocity can result in the most open arrangement in the trade in financial services between countries. If regulatory authorities in one country (a "host" country) are satisfied that financial institutions are adequately supervised in the country where they are incorporated or which is their principal place of business (the "home" country), they can defer to the home country supervision in agreed areas of regulatory responsibility. If this occurs on a reciprocal basis, the financial institutions of one country should be relatively free to provide financial services in the other through branches, subsidiaries or on a cross-border basis.

Principles for allocating regulatory responsibility between home and host country regulators have been developed by the Governors of the central banks of the major OECD countries, including the United States and Canada, through the Committee on Banking Regulations and Supervisory Practices (the "Basle Committee"). The Basle Committee was established as the result of international banking disruptions in the early 1970s and concerns over regulation of international banking institutions. The Basle Committee established guidelines in a 1975 Concordat and promulgated a Revised Concordat in 1983.[3] The Revised Concordat establishes that home country supervision must be consolidated if it is to be adequate.[4] This means that home country supervisors must monitor such matters as capital adequacy and risk exposure of the banks and banking groups for which they are responsible on the basis of the totality of their business, wherever conducted. The Revised Concordat lays down principles for supervising such matters as solvency and liquidity. For example, the prime responsibility for supervising solvency when the home country's bank carries on business in the host country through a branch rests with the home country because the solvency of a branch is indistinguishable from that of the bank. The host country has a general responsibility to monitor the "financial soundness" of foreign branches. However, the supervision of solvency when subsidiaries are involved is a joint responsibility.[5] The host country is responsible for supervising foreign subsidiaries operating in its territory and the home country must take the condition of foreign subsidiaries into account in its consolidated supervision. The Basle Committee has done further work on capital adequacy measurement and the United States and the United Kingdom covered similar issues in a non-binding accord released in 1987.[6]

Some of the difficulties in deferring to home country supervision have been illustrated by the Bank of Credit and Commerce ("BCCI") affair. The BCCI was incorporated in Luxembourg but almost all of its activities were conducted outside this home country.[7] BCCI operated without any supervision on a consolidated basis, so that no financial regulators were aware of its complete financial situation.[8] Regulators of financial institutions may be sympathetic with principles of "consolidated bank supervision" and "home country" supervisory control but they are concerned that the BCCI affair not be repeated and see gaps in the principles laid down in the Basle Concordat and a need for continued host country regulation.[9]

(2) National Treatment

According national treatment does not require recognizing the adequacy of the financial supervision of other countries. It is consistent with national treatment to require that financial institutions from other countries satisfy all the regulatory requirements to which domestic financial institutions are subject. The application of the national treatment principle to financial regulation does not result in as free a flow of financial services among countries as the reciprocity model described above. A financial institution wishing to provide financial services in the other country must satisfy two sets of financial regulations — those that apply in its home jurisdiction and those that apply in the other country.

Application of the national treatment principle to financial regulation is complicated by the fact that financial regulation focuses on the corporate structure of the financial institution and the quality of its balance sheet. While it may not matter in other service sectors whether a foreign service provider operates through a branch or a domestic subsidiary, it can make a significant difference to financial regulators. Canadian requirements that foreign banks operate in Canada only through domestic subsidiaries reflect a regulatory concern that Canadian standards for banks cannot be adequately applied to a branch operation. In 1991, the U.S. Treasury Department, in proposing revisions to the U.S. bank regulatory system, advocated requiring that foreign banks in the United States conduct banking operations only through subsidiaries. While this approach was not adopted in the legislative changes that were subsequently enacted,[10] the Department advocated it because regulators can more easily protect persons dealing with a subsidiary with its own capital, assets and liabilities than with a branch that stands or falls with its foreign owners.[11]

(3) Most-Favoured-Nation Principle

The MFN principle can have significant implications if one of the member countries in an international arrangement wishes to enter into reciprocal recognition arrangements with non-member countries or selected member countries. The MFN principle requires that such reciprocal arrangements be entered into with all member countries or not be entered into at all.

8.2 REGULATION OF FINANCIAL SERVICES IN THE NAFTA COUNTRIES

There is extensive communication between financial regulators in the NAFTA countries, particularly between those of the United States and Canada. Arrangements based on reciprocal recognition of home jurisdiction regulation such as the Multijurisdictional Disclosure System implemented by Canadian and U.S. securities regulators in 1991 do exist and both Canadian and U.S. bank supervisors have participated in the work of the Basle Committee.[12] However, reciprocity arrangements are not the norm among the three NAFTA countries.

The Mexican financial sector is the most restricted in terms of the ability of non-Mexicans to participate. Canadian laws impose some foreign ownership restrictions and limit activities that can be carried on by some foreign-owned financial institutions. U.S. financial regulation, which is based largely on national treatment, is the most open in terms of the ability of foreigners to participate; but in some respects, it is the most restrictive in terms of the activities that can be carried on by financial institutions, whether domestic or foreign.

(1) Canada

The major Canadian financial institutions are the chartered banks, the trust and loan companies, the life insurance companies, the co-operative credit associations and the securities dealers. Other participants in the Canadian financial sector include property and casualty companies, pension funds, venture capital companies and sales finance companies.

The Canadian constitution provides that jurisdiction over banks and banking falls within the exclusive jurisdiction of the federal government. However, other financial institutions in Canada are regulated at both the federal and provincial levels. Trust, loan and insurance companies may be incorporated under federal or provincial law. Federally incorporated trust and loan corporations control the bulk of assets in this sector but some are provincially incorporated and all are subject to provincial licensing requirements.[13] Most life insurance companies are federally incorporated and supervised.[14] The securities industry, which includes securities dealers and underwriters, investment advisors and portfolio managers, is regulated at the provincial level and by provincial and national self-regulatory bodies.[15] Financial co-operatives such as credit unions and caisse populaires are regulated by the province where they are incorporated and the federal government if registered under federal legislation.

Financial institutions governed by federal law are supervised by the Office of the Superintendent of Financial Institutions ("OSFI").[16] Each province has its own department for supervising the activities of financial institutions falling within its jurisdiction.

The fact that banks are regulated exclusively at the federal level has made possible the development of a nationwide branch banking system. A Canadian chartered bank can establish branches in any part of Canada without any provincial restriction. Federally incorporated trust and loan companies and insurance companies may, as of right, establish branch operations in any province.

(a) Recent reforms

Regulation of the Canadian financial services industry used to be based on the "four pillars" (banks, trust and loan companies, insurance companies, securities dealers) remaining separate and distinct. Each "pillar" was prohibited from carrying on activities assigned to another.

This situation has changed dramatically as the result of a process of reform that began in the early 1980s. The reform process focussed on the question of what products and services various types of financial institutions should be able to provide and what ownership linkages should be permitted between financial institutions and other enterprises. The federal government's position in this process was outlined in a series of discussion papers which set out proposals for dismantling the "four pillars" approach to financial regulation.[17]

A first step towards reform took place in 1987 when the federal government enacted legislation permitting federally regulated financial institutions to own security dealer subsidiaries.[18] The comprehensive reform package came into effect on June 1, 1992, with the proclamation into force of the *Bank Act*, the *Trust and Loan Companies Act*, the *Insurance Companies Act* and the *Co-operative Credit Associations Act*.[19]

(i) Merging functions and downstream ownership

Subject to some limitations, trust, loan and life insurance companies have been given full consumer and commercial lending powers and banks and loan companies may provide portfolio management and investment advice.[20] Banks may carry on the business of insurance to a limited extent[21] and may acquire federally regulated insurance companies. The ability of federally regulated financial institutions to invest other commercial entities is generally subject to a 10/25 limitation, meaning that investment is limited to not more than 10% of voting shares and not more than 25% of shareholders equity. However, financial institutions may exceed the 10/25 limitation in acquiring other financial institutions and other entities engaged in financial activities such as factoring, financial leasing, providing information services, providing investment advice and portfolio management, mutual funds and mutual fund distribution, certain activities relating to real estate and certain other financial services.[22] As a result of the completion of the reforms, federal financial institutions, regardless of whether they are banks, loan companies or insurance companies may, either directly or through subsidiaries, offer a wide range of financial services.

(ii) Upstream ownership

The *Bank Act* provides for the incorporation of two types of chartered banks — Schedule I banks and Schedule II banks. The major Canadian chartered banks are all Schedule I banks. No more than 10% of any class of shares of a Schedule I bank may be held by a person or associated group of persons.[23] All but two of the Schedule II banks are owned by foreign banks. Schedule II banks owned by foreign banks can be closely held indefinitely.[24] Otherwise, a Schedule II bank must become widely held after the first ten years of its existence,[25] unless it is owned by a widely held federally regulated financial institution.[26]

Federal trust, loan and life insurance companies may be held on a closely held basis subject to the requirement that 35% of the shares be widely held and publicly traded within five years of its consolidated capital exceeding $750 million.[27] This requirement is satisfied if the shares are held by another financial institution that satisfies the requirement.

(b) Foreign financial institutions

(i) Financial institutions providing banking, lending and similar financial services

The definition of "foreign bank" in the *Bank Act* is sufficiently broad to include foreign financial institutions that are not called banks. For example, any entity in a foreign country that engages in the business of lending money and accepting deposit liabilities transferable by cheque or other instrument is a foreign bank, regardless of what it might be called.[28]

A foreign bank may maintain a representative office in Canada for promotion and liaison purposes.[29] Otherwise, a foreign bank may operate in Canada only through a Schedule II foreign bank subsidiary and cannot directly carry on a "banking business" in Canada.[30] The effect is to prohibit the cross-border provision of banking services. Foreign-owned Schedule II banks are not subject to the requirement that they become widely held after ten years but can in some circumstances be subject to the 35% rule described above.[31] Foreign banks with foreign bank subsidiaries may not without consent acquire Canadian entities engaged in providing various types of specified financial services.[32] However, a foreign bank subsidiary may make the investments in entities providing financial services described in §8.2(1)(a)(i).

Foreign bank subsidiaries can be owned by certain other types of foreign financial institutions, such as those engaged in the trust, loan or insurance business, or co-operative credit societies or securities firms. The institution must satisfy the criteria set out in the legislation.[33]

Foreign bank subsidiaries are subject to some limitations in their operations. The average outstanding total domestic assets of all foreign banks subsidiaries, excluding those controlled by U.S. and Mexican nationals, cannot exceed 12% of "total domestic assets" of all banks.[34] The average outstanding domestic assets of a foreign bank subsidiary, unless controlled by U.S. or Mexican nationals, may not in any three-month period exceed the amount fixed by the Minister for that subsidiary.[35]

No more than 25% of the voting shares of a Schedule I bank may be held by non-resident persons.[36] This restriction does not apply to U.S. and Mexican residents. However, U.S. and Mexican residents are subject to the general 10% limitation referred to in §8.2(1)(a)(ii).

(ii) Other financial institutions

Non-resident ownership of federally incorporated trust and loan corporations and financial institutions governed by the *Co-operative Credit Associations Act* are subject to the same 25% limitation as are Schedule I banks.[37] This restriction does not apply to U.S. and Mexican residents.

No more than 25% of the voting shares of a federally regulated life insurance company, loan and trust company or co-operative credit association may be held by non-resident persons.[38] This restriction does not apply to U.S. and Mexican residents.

Foreign insurance companies can carry on business in Canada without having to incorporate a domestic subsidiary. However, subject to some exceptions,[39] a foreign insurance company may not insure a risk in Canada without the approval of OSFI.[40] One condition of approval is that the foreign insurance company maintain assets vested in trust in Canada of a prescribed value.[41] The foreign insurance company also must establish the place where its chief agency will be located.[42]

Foreign ownership restrictions on the provincially regulated securities industry have been removed. Ontario took the lead in December 1986 by permitting non-residents to hold 50% of securities dealers operating in the province, and removed the limitation on June 30, 1988. However, some provincial statutes governing financial institutions contain foreign ownership restrictions. For example, the *Loan and Trust Corporations Act (Ontario)* limits the percentage of voting shares of provincially incorporated loan and trust corporations that can be held by non-residents.[43]

(c) Comments

As a result of the reforms in recent years, Canadian financial regulation permits the "universal banking model" of financial institution that may provide a wide range of financial services, either through a single entity or related entities. Branching throughout Canada is permitted. Subject to some restrictions, such as the requirement that banking be conducted through foreign bank subsidiaries, non-residents may provide financial services in Canada.

(2) The United States

Unlike Canada, regulation of financial institutions in the United States continues to be based largely on "separation of functions". Banks in the United States have also been restricted in their ability to carry on business through branches outside their "home" state. As discussed in §8.7, the restrictions on interstate branching will be largely dismantled by the Riegle-Neal Interstate Banking and Branching Efficiency Act of 1994 (the "Interstate Banking Act") which was signed into law on September 29, 1994. U.S. financial regulation at the federal level generally adopts a non-discriminatory approach to foreigners. However, non-U.S. financial institutions are subject to the same restrictions as U.S. financial institutions in their ability to deliver a wide range of financial services and, in the case of banks, to establish inter-state branch networks.

(a) The Dual banking system and the McFadden Act

In the United States, banks are regulated at both the federal and state levels. Until 1863, banks were chartered solely at the state level. Congress enacted the National Bank Act of 1963,[44] which provided for chartering banks at the federal level. The objective at the time was to drive state banks out of existence and establish a national banking system. The states successfully resisted this attempt and many banks continue to be chartered and regulated at the state level.[45] However, many state banks are also regulated at the federal level through membership in the Federal Reserve System[46] and through insuring their deposits with the Federal Deposit Insurance Corporation.[47]

(b) Inter-state branching and the McFadden Act

The situation respecting the ability of banks to branch or to otherwise establish a presence outside their home state has been summarized by one commentator as follows:

> Commercial banking enterprises are unique among major American businesses. Unlike their counterparts in industry, which may transact business throughout the United States, commercial banking enterprises may not engage in "the business of banking", either directly or through branch offices or by affiliation with a commonly owned bank, in more than one state.[48]

The National Bank Act was interpreted by early regulators as prohibiting the establishment of branches. In 1927, Congress passed the McFadden Act[49] which authorized limited branching by national banks[50] within their home states. In 1933 Congress "adopted a policy of 'competitive equality' between national and state banks with respect to branching"[51] by permitting national banks to branch throughout their home states to the same extent as state banks were permitted under state law. The "competitive equality" doctrine has been applied by the courts in the extensive litigation over the ability of national banks to branch. For example, the court in *Walker Bank & Trust Co.*[52] based its decision that national banks must comply with state law regulations regarding the establishment of branches on the legislative intent to establish competitive equality between national and state banks. In *First National Bank v. Dickinson*,[53] the court noted the legislative intent that neither state nor national banks obtain any competitive advantage over the other in the area of branch banking.[54] National banks do not have authority to open branches outside their home state. Most states do not permit their own state banks to open branches in other states or permit banks from other states to open branches. Banks have established loan production offices in other states and most banks belong to automated teller machine ("ATM") networks with inter-state ATM facilities.[55] As discussed in §8.7, the Interstate Banking Act will have the effect of removing the limitations imposed by the McFadden Act.

(c) Bank holding companies

U.S. banks have used bank holding companies ("BHCs") to circumvent the restrictions on branch banking. The BHC establishes separate bank subsidiaries to carry on banking activities at different locations. BHCs were subject to little federal regulation until Congress enacted the Bank Holding Company Act of 1956. Under this legislation, Federal Reserve approval is required before an organization controlling one bank can acquire more than 5% of the shares or substantially all of the assets of another.[56] Multibank BHCs were also required to dispose of businesses that were not closely related to the business of banking.[57] In 1970, the Bank Holding Company Act was amended to include one-bank holding companies. The amendments were prompted by concern over the ability of BHCs to diversify into non-bank areas. Non-bank activities were viewed as higher risk than banking and thus a threat to the stability of banking businesses. Also diversification of banks into non-bank businesses was viewed as a competitive threat to those businesses because BHCs could cause banking subsidiaries to deny credit to non-banking subsidiaries.[58]

BHCs and their subsidiaries are prohibited from engaging in or acquiring the assets of or a controlling interest in any company engaged in an activity other than banking or activities "closely related to banking".[59] Certain non-bank acquisitions, such as voting securities comprising no more than 5% of the voting shares of a company, are exempted.[60] A BHC must first obtain approval to engage in permissible non-banking activities listed in the regulations.[61] These activities are characterized as being so "closely related to banking" as to be a "proper incident thereto"[62] and include: making, acquiring and servicing loans and other extensions of credit; operating an industrial bank;[63] trust company functions;[64] providing investment or financial advice in certain defined capacities;[65] certain leasing functions;[66] making community development investments;[67] providing data processing and data transmission services;[68] providing management consulting services to depository institutions[69] and providing certain other financial services. BHCs and their subsidiaries are permitted to operate insurance agencies and to engage in underwriting to a limited extent. For example, banks may provide insurance directly related to the extension of credit to ensure that a balance of a loan is repaid in the event of the death, disability or involuntary unemployment of the borrower.[70] BHCs and their subsidiaries are also permitted to engage to a limited extent in securities brokerage. The services are restricted to buying and selling securities on behalf of customers and do not include securities underwriting or dealing.[71] National banks may carry on these same activities except for underwriting credit insurance and operating an industrial bank.[72]

A number of activities have been held not to be closely related to banking. These include: combined sale of mutual funds and insurance; underwriting life insurance not sold in connection with a credit transaction; real estate brokerage; land development; management consulting; and property management.[73] Activities that have been denied to BHCs and their subsidiaries have also been denied to national banks.[74]

The Bank Holding Company Act of 1956 effectively blocked the spread of interstate banking through the creation of separate bank subsidiaries. This situation will change, however, as the provisions of the Interstate Banking Act come into effect. The 1970 amendments and related regulations have permitted BHCs to diversify to some extent in the range of financial services that they can provide, and some BHCs have expanded their permissible non-banking businesses on a nation-wide basis. However, the regulations also preclude BHCs and their subsidiaries from providing a number of major financial services. The activities permitted to U.S. banks are further limited by the provisions of the Glass-Steagall Act.

(d) The Glass-Steagall Act

The Glass-Steagall Act is comprised of sections 16, 20, 21 and 32 of the Banking Act of 1933. The objective of this Depression era legislation was to create a barrier between commercial and investment banking. The perception at the time was that links between these financial institutions was a major contributing factor to the stock market crash in 1929.[75]

Section 16 applies to national banks and state banks in the Federal Reserve System and establishes three limitations on commercial bank involvement in securities activities.[76] First, purchase of equity securities are limited to transactions for bank customers. Second, the investment authority of national banks is limited to investments sanctioned by regulation. Third, the underwriting and dealing activities of commercial banks are limited to U.S. Treasury and agency obligations and general obligations of state and local governments.[77] Section 20 prohibits national banks and state banks under the Federal Reserve System from affiliating with organizations engaged principally in the investment banking business.[78] Section 21 prohibits organizations in the business of issuing, underwriting, selling or distributing securities from accepting deposits.[79] This prohibition does not apply to banks from dealing in or underwriting securities to the extent permitted by section 16. Section 32 prevents interlocking managements between national banks and other banks under the Federal Reserve System and firms engaged in the securities business.[80]

There has been considerable litigation over the Glass-Steagall provisions as the banking industry and bank regulators have tested its limits. In *Investment Co. Institute v. Camp*,[81] the U.S. Supreme Court, in ruling that banks could not operate open-ended mutual funds, discussed the rationale behind the Glass-Steagall provisions as follows:

> The legislative history of the Glass-Steagall Act shows that Congress also had in mind and repeatedly focussed on the more subtle hazards that arise when a commercial bank goes beyond the business of acting as fiduciary or managing agent and enters the investment banking business either directly or by establishing an affiliate to hold and sell particular investments. This creates new promotional and other pressures on the bank which in turn create new temptations. For example, pressures are created because the bank and the affiliate

are closely associated in the public mind, and should the affiliate fare badly, public confidence in the bank might be impaired. And since public confidence is essential to the solvency of a bank, there might exist a natural tendency to shore up the affiliate through unsound loans or other aid.[82]

There are a limited number of activities engaged in by banks that the courts have held not to be prohibited by the Glass-Steagall provisions. The U.S. Supreme Court has upheld the authority of national banks and BHC subsidiaries to provide investment advice to closed-end mutual funds,[83] and banks appear to have the authority to act as investment advisors in other limited capacities.[84] Banks manage agency accounts, with discretion to make investments.[85] Banks can offer brokerage services so long as they act solely as agents between their customer and the broker who executes the transaction.[86] As the result of several court decisions, banks are permitted to offer discount brokerage services.[87]

However, the Glass-Steagall provisions represent a real impediment to the development in the United States of the "universal banking model" as the U.S. banking industry is for the most part still precluded from participating in the investment banking business.

(e) Regulation of foreign banks

Until 1978, foreign banks operated under state law and were not covered by federal law. Laws affecting foreign banks varied from state to state. The majority of states had no special statutory rules respecting foreign-owned banks.[88] Iowa, Missouri, South Carolina, Texas, Vermont and Oklahoma prohibited foreign banks from entering their markets.[89] Alaska, California, the District of Columbia, Florida, Georgia, Hawaii, Illinois, Massachusetts, New York, Oregon and Washington had enacted statutory provisions permitting foreign banks to enter their jurisdictions and regulating their activities to varying degrees.[90] Foreign banks established branches in states where they were permitted and also established foreign bank subsidiaries. A number of foreign banks established operations in more than one state.

(i) The International Banking Act of 1978

Foreign bank operations in the United States increased substantially during the 1970s. In 1978, Congress enacted the International Banking Act of 1978[91] ("IBA") in response to Federal Reserve Board concerns over the lack of federal control and concerns of domestic banks over competitive equality. Prudential concerns were not a significant motivating factor behind this legislation.[92] Congress considered a reciprocity approach which would have permitted a foreign bank to operate in the United States to the same extent as U.S. banks were permitted in the foreign bank's home jurisdiction.[93] However, Congress opted for national treatment. With some exceptions,[94] the

IBA has the effect of subjecting foreign banks to similar regulatory requirements as apply to U.S. federally regulated banks.

Under the IBA, the Comptroller of the Currency has the power to charter branches and agencies of foreign banks. Federal charters cannot be awarded to a foreign bank already operating a branch or agency under state law or in a state prohibiting foreign bank operations. A foreign bank may not maintain both a federal branch and a federal agency in the same state. Interstate banking was limited by Congress by restricting each foreign bank to a single state for deposit-taking. As discussed in §8.7, this situation will change as the provisions of the Interstate Banking Act become effective. Although foreign bank branches and agencies (as opposed to subsidiaries) cannot be members of the Federal Reserve System, the Federal Reserve Board has authority to set reserve requirements for foreign bank branches and agencies as if they were member banks. Federal deposit insurance has been made available to foreign banks and coverage is mandatory for branches that accept deposits of under $100,000. Non-banking activities of foreign banks were brought under the restrictions of the Bank Holding Company Act with the effect that foreign banks are subject to Glass-Steagall restrictions. Securities operations of foreign banks existing in the United States as of July 26, 1978, were grandfathered.

(ii) Foreign Bank Supervision Enhancement Act of 1991

The BCCI scandal and problems encountered with other foreign banks[95] in the late 1980s resulted in the enactment of the Foreign Bank Supervision Enhancement Act of 1991 ("Enhancement Act"). Unlike the IBA, the Enhancement Act was prompted by prudential concerns. Deposit insurance requirements were tightened up.[96] Foreign banks must obtain Federal Reserve Board approval before opening any branch, agency or representative office, regardless of whether chartered under federal or state law. Approval shall not be given unless the Federal Reserve Board is satisfied that the foreign bank is subject to comprehensive regulation in its home country.[97] The regulations set out factors for assessing the adequacy of home country supervision, such as whether the home country supervisor receives financial reports that are consolidated on a world-wide basis.[98] The Federal Reserve Board may require a foreign bank operating a state branch or agency or commercial lending company to terminate operations if the foreign bank is not subject to comprehensive supervision or regulation on a consolidated basis by its home country or if there is reason to believe that it has violated the law or is engaging in unsound banking practice.[99] The Enhancement Act increased Federal Reserve Board examination powers respecting foreign banks, expanded various other supervisory powers and increased powers to assess penalties for violations.[100]

The Enhancement Act and the regulations enacted under its authority bring foreign bank operations in the United States under closer federal supervision than ever before. Except for some grandfathered operations, the domestic banking industry has achieved competitive equality with foreign banks in so far as regulatory supervision is concerned. The Enhancement Act and its regulations include home country supervision on a consolidated basis as a factor in determining whether to permit a foreign bank to open an office. However, comprehensive host country regulation is maintained even though the home country supervision meets the required criteria.

(f) Regulation of other financial institutions

Unlike in Canada, the United States constitution permits effective regulation of the securities industry under federal law.[101] Securities dealers and financial intermediaries engaged in the investment banking business are regulated primarily by the federal Securities Exchange Commission, although states also regulate dealing in securities. Lending institutions such as thrifts and savings associations, as well as insurance companies, are subject to regulation at both the federal and state levels.

(3) Mexico

Mexican laws respecting the regulation of financial institutions are the most restrictive of the three NAFTA countries in so far as foreign participation is concerned.

(a) Nationalization and privatization of the banks

In 1982, the Portillo administration nationalized all but two of Mexico's commercial banks and the Mexican constitution was amended to grant to the government a monopoly in the provision of banking and credit services.[102] Some private participation in the banking system was permitted during the de la Madrid administration. However, it was not until June 28, 1990, that the constitution was changed to permit Mexican individuals and financial holding companies to hold controlling interests in Mexican banks.[103]

During the period of government ownership the number of commercial banks was reduced from over sixty to eighteen. Following the constitutional change in 1990, all of the government-owned commercial banks were privatized.[104] The buyers were generally groups of Mexican investors organized around wealthy families or individuals.[105] At the time of writing, the Mexican commercial banking system is comprised of the eighteen privatized banks together with Citibank and Banco Obrero. The three largest commercial banks are Banamex, Bancomer and Banca Serfin.

The government continues to own seven "development" banks. These banks are dedicated to the development of certain sectors of the economy. The two major development banks are Nacional Financiera S.N.C. (Nafin) and Banco Nacional de Comercio Exterior S.N.C. (Bancomext). Foreign investment in development banks is not permitted.[106]

(b) Mexican financial regulation

There are some similarities between the regulation of banks in Mexico and of those in Canada. Banks in both countries are regulated exclusively at the federal level and may branch throughout the country.[107] With the exception of Citibank, which operates a limited number of branches in Mexico under a grandfathering provision, foreign banks cannot operate branches in Mexico. Like Canada, Mexico has adopted the universal banking model. Mexican law permits the creation of financial groups, with a single holding company owning financial services subsidiaries such as banks, securities firms, exchange houses, leasing companies, factoring companies, insurance companies, bonding companies, general warehouses and fund managers.[108]

A number of the privatized commercial banks, including the three largest Mexican banks, were acquired by financial groups. Banamex is part of the Banacci group which owns the Accival brokerage house. Bancomer is part of the Bancomer group which owns the Bancomer (formerly Acciones Bursatil) brokerage house and is affiliated with Seguros Monterrey, an insurance company. Banca Serfin is part of the Serfin group which includes a brokerage company (Operadora de Bolsa) and an insurance company (Seguros Serfin).[109]

In addition to the twenty commercial banks, in January 1993 the Mexican financial sector included twenty-six brokerage firms, forty insurance companies, forty-six leasing companies and various other financial concerns such as factoring companies and foreign exchange houses.[110]

(c) Mexican foreign ownership restrictions

Privatization of the banking sector was not accompanied by liberalization of foreign ownership restrictions. At the time that NAFTA became effective, Mexican laws restricted foreign participation in practically every type of financial institution. At least 51% of the capital stock of financial holding companies must be Class A shares, which may be held only by Mexican individuals and certain institutions. Class B shares may be held by Mexican corporations (without foreign investment) and Mexican institutional investors such as pension funds. Foreign investment of up to 30% of issued capital stock is permitted through Class C shares, with prior approval of the Ministry of Finance.[111] Permitted foreign ownership of commercial banks corresponds to the requirements for financial holding companies. Foreign investment in securities firms is limited to 30% of capital stock and Ministry of Finance approval is required. Participation by a foreign individual in a securities firm may not exceed 10%.[112] Foreign investment in insurance companies, general deposit warehouses, financial leasing companies, factoring companies and bonding companies must be less than 50% and is subject to Ministry of Finance approval.[113] Foreign investment in credit unions, financial agents and foreign exchange firms is prohibited.[114]

8.3 PROVISIONS OF THE FTA

The financial services provisions in FTA Chapter Seventeen were negotiated separately from the rest of the FTA. Other than insurance services, financial services were not subject to the national treatment and other requirements of FTA Chapters Fourteen and Sixteen. Chapter Seventeen did not cover provincial or state measures. Disputes under FTA Chapter Seventeen were not covered by the normal FTA Chapter Eighteen dispute settlement procedures. Instead, disputes were to be resolved through consultations between the Canadian Department of Finance and the U.S. Department of the Treasury.[115]

The FTA financial services provisions are concession-based rather than principle-based. Each side granted specific and limited concessions to the other and agreed to continue to allow financial institutions of the other the same access that applied at the time that the FTA was signed.[116]

(1) Canadian Concessions

Canada exempted U.S. residents and companies controlled by U.S. residents from the ownership restrictions that applied and continues to apply to banks and federally chartered insurance companies, loan companies, trust companies and investment companies.[117] However, the 10% limitation described in §8.2(1)(a)(ii) was unchanged by the FTA.

Canada exempted U.S.-controlled Schedule II banks from the limitation on total domestic assets that applied and continues to apply to foreign bank subsidiaries[118] and from limitations on average outstanding domestic assets that individual foreign bank subsidiaries may hold.[119] U.S.-controlled foreign bank subsidiaries were exempted from having to obtain the approval of the Minister of Finance to open branches in Canada[120] and were permitted to transfer loans to parent corporations.[121]

(2) U.S. Concessions

The United States made only one concession to Canada in FTA Chapter Seventeen. FTA 1702(1) required that the Glass-Steagall Act be amended to permit domestic and foreign banks and BHCs to deal in, underwrite and purchase debt obligations backed by the government of Canada and Canadian provincial governments. This provision benefitted Canadian bank-owned dealers operating in the United States[122] and also broadened the market for Canadian government-backed securities.[123]

The United States agreed in FTA 1702(2) not to adopt any federal measure that would accord to Canadian-controlled banks treatment less favourable than that existing on October 4, 1987, respecting their ability to establish and operate any state branch, state agency or bank or lending company subsidiary outside their home states.[124] As discussed in §8.2(2)(e)(ii), the Enhancement Act, which became effective in 1991, requires foreign banks to obtain Federal Reserve Board approval before establishing a branch, agency or acquiring control of a commercial lending company. By imposing a requirement that approval be obtained where none was previously required, this federal measure arguably accords less favourable treatment than existed on October 4, 1987.

The United States agreed in FTA 1702(3) to accord to Canadian financial institutions the same treatment as U.S. financial institutions respecting any amendments to the Glass-Steagall Act. As of the time of writing, the Glass-Steagall restrictions had not been liberalized.

(3) Mutual Dissatisfaction

Each of Canada and the United States was clearly dissatisfied with the results of the FTA negotiations. As discussed in §8.2(1)(a), at the time that the FTA was negotiated Canada was in the process of dismantling its "four pillar" approach to financial regulation. As a result of Canada's concessions previously described, U.S.-controlled foreign bank subsidiaries in Canada became the full beneficiaries of the liberal environment resulting from the collapse of the four pillars while the operations of Canadian banks operating in the United States continued to be limited by McFadden and Glass-Steagall restrictions. The U.S. negotiators were dissatisfied at failing to obtain from Canada concessions respecting Canada's requirement that foreign banks may carry on banking in Canada only through foreign bank subsidiaries.

In somewhat unusual provisions, each of Canada and the United States expressly acknowledged in the FTA text that Chapter Seventeen did not represent their mutual satisfaction concerning the treatment of their respective financial institutions.[125]

8.4 NAFTA — GENERAL PROVISIONS

The NAFTA provisions respecting financial services set out in Chapter Fourteen represent a significant departure from those of the FTA. While the FTA financial services provisions amounted to no more than an exchange of concessions, the NAFTA financial services provisions are principle-based.

The NAFTA obligations respecting financial services are based almost exclusively on principles of national treatment and MFN treatment similar to those in NAFTA Chapters Eleven and Twelve. This reflects the fact that the negotiators of the NAFTA financial services provisions were significantly influenced by the negotiation of the GATS which applies the GATT national treatment and MFN treatment concepts to the trade in services.[126] The NAFTA financial services provisions do not deal with the home versus host country supervisory issues that have been considered by the Basle Committee, and the obligations under Chapter Fourteen are not based on reciprocity.

Unlike the FTA financial services provisions, the provisions of NAFTA Chapter Fourteen apply to provincial and state as well as federal measures.

(1) Scope and Coverage

As mentioned in §7.2, NAFTA Chapter Fourteen operates independently from Chapters Eleven and Twelve. NAFTA 1101(3) provides that Chapter Eleven (Investment) does not apply to measures adopted or maintained by NAFTA countries to the extent that they are covered by Chapter Fourteen. NAFTA 1201(2)(a) provides that Chapter Twelve (Services) does not apply to financial services as defined in Chapter Fourteen. While the obligations of the NAFTA countries to each other in Chapter Fourteen are based on the same broad principles as those set out in Chapters Eleven and Twelve, there are differences in application. There are also differences in the remedies available if these obligations are breached.

(a) Chapter Fourteen and Chapter Eleven

Chapter Eleven covers measures of each NAFTA country affecting investors of the other NAFTA countries and investments made by those investors. Chapter Fourteen is analogous in that it covers measures of each NAFTA country affecting financial institutions of the other NAFTA countries and investments in financial institutions in that NAFTA country by investors of the other NAFTA countries. NAFTA 1101(3) has the effect of carving these measures out of Chapter Eleven. If an investor of a NAFTA country is a financial institution or if an investment being made by an investor of another NAFTA country is in a financial institution, Chapter Fourteen applies and Chapter Eleven does not. The scope of Chapter Fourteen depends on the meaning of "financial institution".

(i) Financial institution

NAFTA 1416 defines "financial institution" as any financial intermediary or other enterprise authorized to do business and regulated or supervised as a financial institution under the laws of the NAFTA country in which it is located. A financial institution is not defined in terms of the activities that an enterprise carries on. Rather, it is defined in terms of how it is regulated in the NAFTA country in which it is located. If an enterprise carrying on a particular activity is regulated as a financial institution in a NAFTA country, it is a financial institution. If an enterprise carrying on the identical activity in another NAFTA country is not regulated as a financial institution, it is not a financial institution.

A "financial institution of another Party" is a financial institution, including a branch, located in one NAFTA country that is controlled by persons of another NAFTA country. Persons are natural persons who are citizens or permanent residents of a NAFTA country or enterprises of a NAFTA country but do not include branches of enterprises of non-NAFTA countries. A "financial institution of another Party" would include a branch of a Canadian Schedule I bank located in the United States, or a Schedule II subsidiary in Canada of a U.S.-owned bank. The definition would also include a financial institution in Canada controlled by the incorporated U.S. subsidiary of an enterprise of a non-NAFTA country, such as a European bank. However, it would not include a financial institution controlled by a U.S. branch of a European bank.

(ii) Investor and investment

An "investor" for the purposes of Chapter Fourteen is defined in the same manner as in Chapter Eleven. As under Chapter Eleven, an investor need not be controlled by nationals of a NAFTA country to be an investor of that country. Chapter Fourteen incorporates the Chapter Eleven definition of "investment" with technical modifications to "loans" and "debt securities". Loans to or debt securities issued by financial institutions are "investments" only if they are not treated as regulatory capital by the authorities of the NAFTA country where it is located. Loans granted by or debt securities owned by financial institutions are not investments.

(iii) Scope and coverage

Chapter Fourteen covers measures of NAFTA countries that affect financial institutions of other NAFTA countries. For example, Canadian laws requiring foreign banks to establish by incorporating a subsidiary are covered by Chapter Fourteen. U.S. laws that govern what Canadian financial institutions such as banks can own in the United States are covered by Chapter Fourteen. Chapter Fourteen also covers measures affecting the ability of investors of NAFTA countries to invest in financial institutions of other NAFTA countries. Mexican laws restricting foreign ownership in Mexican banks are covered by Chapter Fourteen. As these measures are covered by Chapter Fourteen, they are not covered by Chapter Eleven.

Chapter Fourteen does not cover laws of general application in a NAFTA country that affect the ability of investors of other NAFTA countries to invest. A Mexican law that restricts investment by any non-Mexican in a business that is not a financial institution is covered by Chapter Eleven, even if an investor of another NAFTA country is a financial institution. However, if the Mexican law restricting the ability to invest is directed at non-Mexican financial institutions, it is governed by Chapter Fourteen and not by Chapter Eleven.

(b) Chapter Fourteen and Chapter Twelve

Just as Chapter Twelve covers measures of a NAFTA country affecting the cross-border trade in services, Chapter Fourteen covers the cross-border trade in financial services.

(i) Financial services

"Financial services" are defined in NAFTA 1416 as services of a financial nature or services ancillary to such services. The definition includes insurance but does not mention any other activity, and "financial nature" is not defined. Besides insurance, services of a financial nature would include: lending money; various other banking services such as taking deposits, access to cash by automated teller machines, payroll services, and so on; services relating to the securities industry such as brokerage and underwriting; leasing; providing financial advice; financial leasing; factoring, providing bonding services; and dealing in foreign exchange.

The definition of "financial services" is not linked to the definition of "financial institution". A service provided by a "financial institution" has to be "of a financial nature" in order to be a "financial service". A "financial service" need not be provided by a "financial institution" because a "financial institution" is defined in terms of how it is regulated and not in terms of what it does. Many companies whose primary business has nothing to do with financial services none the less provide financial services to their customers by way of loans or other credit facilities to enable them to buy their products.

A financial service provider of a NAFTA country is a national or an enterprise of a NAFTA country that provides financial services within that NAFTA country. A financial service provider may be, but does not have to be, a financial institution.

(ii) Cross-border

The concept of "cross-border" is identical to that in Chapter Twelve.[127] Cross-border provision of or trade in financial services means providing financial services from one NAFTA country into another, or within a NAFTA country by one of its nationals or enterprises to a national or enterprise of another NAFTA country, or by a national (*i.e.*, individual) of one NAFTA country within another NAFTA country. For example, the cross-border financial services provisions of Chapter Fourteen would cover U.S. measures affecting the ability of a financial service provider in Canada (whether or not regulated as a financial institution) to provide financial services to customers in the United States or to a Canadian national, such as a financial advisor, to provide financial services within the United States. These provisions would also cover Canadian measures affecting the ability of a financial service provider in Canada to provide financial services to customers in Canada who are U.S. or Mexican nationals or enterprises.

(c) Example of scope and coverage of Chapter Fourteen

Consider a company with its principal place of business in Ontario that is in the business of leasing automobiles. If the company is operating a car rental business, where a customer rents a car for a short period of time, it is unlikely that the service being provided is of a "financial nature". The service is a transportation service rather than a financial service and measures affecting the cross-border provision of these services would be covered by Chapter Twelve rather than by Chapter Fourteen. However, suppose that the company is leasing automobiles on a long-term basis and the customers leasing the automobiles are fully responsible for repairs and maintenance. The leasing company is providing its customers with an alternative means to borrowing of financing the acquisition of automobiles and, as such, is providing a service of a financial nature. Measures affecting the cross-border provision of these services would be covered by Chapter Fourteen and not by Chapter Twelve.

An automobile leasing company operating in Ontario is not "regulated or supervised" as a financial institution and, therefore is not a financial institution. Measures affecting investments in such a company by U.S. and Mexican investors and their investments would be covered by Chapter Eleven and not by Chapter Fourteen. However, if the company only leases vehicles with a gross vehicle weight of over twenty-one tonnes, it is a "financial leasing corporation" that can be acquired by a federally regulated financial institution, such as a bank. If it is owned by a federally regulated financial institution it will be regulated as a financial institution, and measures affecting investments in it by U.S. and Mexican investors and their investments will be governed by Chapter Fourteen and not Chapter Eleven.

(2) Provisions Incorporated from Chapter Eleven

NAFTA 1401(2) incorporates NAFTA 1109, NAFTA 1110, NAFTA 1111, NAFTA 1113, NAFTA 1114 and NAFTA 1211 into Chapter Fourteen. NAFTA 1109 relates to transfers and is discussed in §7.7(6). Without limiting the scope of NAFTA 1109(4) that allows a NAFTA country to prevent transfers through the "equitable, non-discriminatory and good faith" application of various laws, NAFTA 1410(4) permits a NAFTA country to prevent or limit transfers by financial institutions and financial service providers to affiliates in the application of measures relating to the maintenance of the "safety, soundness, integrity or financial responsibility of financial institutions or cross-border financial service providers". NAFTA 1110 relates to expropriation and compensation and is discussed in §7.7(7). NAFTA 1111 relates to special formalities and information requirements and is discussed in §7.7(8). NAFTA 1114 relates to environmental measures and is discussed in §6.8(2).

NAFTA 1113 and NAFTA 1211, discussed in §7.7(1)(b) and §7.8(1) respectively, set out the circumstances under which the benefit of the NAFTA investment and services provisions may be denied to enterprises controlled by investors of non-NAFTA countries and establish the "substantial business activities" test. NAFTA 1113 applies to those provisions of Chapter Fourteen that are analogous to Chapter Eleven and NAFTA 1211 applies to the provisions of Chapter Fourteen relating to the cross-border provision of financial services.

The investor-state dispute settlement procedures described in §11.3 are incorporated into NAFTA Chapter Fourteen solely for breaches of the incorporated provisions of Chapter Eleven referred to above. If a NAFTA country expropriates a bank owned by investors of another NAFTA country, NAFTA 1110 applies and those investors can invoke these procedures to secure a remedy. However, if a NAFTA country breaches its obligations (described in §8.4(5)) to accord national treatment to a bank owned by investors of another NAFTA country, the Chapter Eleven investor-state dispute settlement procedures are not available to those investors. The dispute can only be resolved on a government-to-government basis under Chapter Twenty, as modified by NAFTA 1414 and discussed in §11.2.

(3) Establishment of Financial Institutions

NAFTA 1403 sets out an operative set of principles and a prospective set of principles that may apply in the future under certain circumstances. An investor for the purposes of NAFTA 1403 must be in the business of providing financial services, although it need not be a financial institution.

(a) Operative principles

Each NAFTA country has agreed in NAFTA 1403(4) to permit an investor of another NAFTA country to establish a financial institution in its territory if the investor has not already done so. The investor may be required to incorporate the financial institution under the laws of the host NAFTA country and the host NAFTA country may impose terms and conditions consistent with the national treatment obligations in NAFTA 1405.

(b) Prospective principles

In NAFTA 1403(1), each NAFTA country recognizes the principle that it should permit investors of other NAFTA countries to choose the juridical form of financial institutions that they establish. This principle is directed at requirements that financial institutions be established as subsidiaries rather than as branches. In NAFTA 1403(2)(a) and (b), each NAFTA country recognizes the principle that investors of other NAFTA countries should be able to provide a range of financial services in its territory through separate financial institutions and expand geographically. The reference to a range of financial services is an endorsement of the universal banking model and is directed at the separation of functions approach required by the Glass-Steagall Act and other U.S. laws. The reference to separate financial institutions is consistent with Canadian and Mexican laws that permit a variety of financial institutions within a corporate group but requires each to be incorporated separately. The reference to geographic expansion is directed at U.S. restrictions on branching. NAFTA 1403(2)(c) sets out the principle that NAFTA countries should not maintain ownership requirements specific to foreign financial institutions. This reference is directed at measures such as Canada's requirement that foreign banks operate in Canada only through "foreign bank subsidiaries".

NAFTA 1403(3) sets the stage for a renegotiation of the NAFTA market access provisions for financial services based on these principles. If the United States eliminates its interstate branching restrictions and permits Canadian and Mexican commercial banks to expand through branches or subsidiaries into substantially the entire U.S. market, the NAFTA countries will review market access in relation to these principles with a view to permitting investors to choose the juridical form for establishing commercial banks. Until this occurs, these principles remain prospective. However, the condition for the review required by NAFTA 1403(3) may be fulfilled once the provisions of the Interstate Banking Act, discussed in §8.7, become fully effective in 1997.

(4) Cross-border Trade in Financial Services

NAFTA 1404 sets out a standstill respecting the cross-border trade in financial services. NAFTA 1404(1) provides that NAFTA countries may not introduce more restrictive measures than existed when NAFTA came into effect. It is consistent with this obligation for Canada to maintain its restriction on the cross-border provision of banking services. However, the United States could not prohibit the cross-border provision of banking services by Canadian and Mexican banks and insist that they carry on business in the United States only through subsidiaries.

NAFTA 1404(2) requires each NAFTA country to permit its persons in its territory and its nationals to purchase financial services provided by financial service providers of other NAFTA countries but does not have to permit these service providers to do or solicit business in its territory. This provision is consistent with Canadian practice respecting foreign banks. Canadians frequently borrow money directly from foreign banks. There is no legal impediment to this so long as the foreign bank does not solicit or arrange the loan in Canada.

NAFTA 1404(3) permits NAFTA countries to require registration of financial service providers of other NAFTA countries. NAFTA 1404(4) and NAFTA Annex 1404.4 provide for consultations respecting future liberalization of financial services.

(5) National Treatment

(a) Investors, investments and financial institutions

NAFTA 1405(1) and (2) set out national treatment obligations that closely follow those set out in NAFTA 1102 described in §7.7(2). These obligations to provide no less favourable treatment benefit investors of other NAFTA countries, investments of those investors in financial institutions within a NAFTA country, and financial institutions of other NAFTA countries. These obligations cover measures affecting the establishment, acquisition, expansion, management, conduct, operation, and sale or other disposition of financial institutions and investments in financial institutions within a NAFTA country. Consider, for example, the scope of these obligations in so far as they apply to U.S. measures affecting Canada. The obligations cover Canadian investors (whether or not they are financial institutions) who invest in U.S. financial institutions and investments of Canadian investors in U.S. financial institutions. The obligations would also cover a Canadian financial institution with branch operations in the United States or that wishes to establish a financial institution in the United States by way of a branch.

(b) Cross-border financial service providers

NAFTA 1405(3) requires each NAFTA country to accord no less favourable treatment to cross-border service providers than it accords to its own service providers. However, this obligation applies only when a NAFTA country permits the cross-border provision of a financial service and is subject to the standstill in NAFTA 1404.

(c) States and provinces

NAFTA 1405(4) sets out rules relating to the application of these principles to state and provincial measures in greater detail than in the corresponding provisions in the investment and services chapters.[128] These provisions

are best explained by way of an example. Consider a Canadian financ
tution with operations in the United States. If the Canadian financ
tution is located in a state, the state must accord to it treatment no less
favourable than U.S. financial institutions located in that state. If the Canadian financial institution is not located in that particular state but is located
in other states, the state must accord to it treatment no less favourable than
that accorded to U.S. financial institutions in like circumstances. If the laws
of that state prohibit U.S. financial institutions established in other states
from establishing in that state, the same measure could be applied to the
Canadian financial institution. If the Canadian financial institution is located
in that state and in other states as well, the state must accord to it treatment
no less favourable than that accorded to U.S. financial institutions in like
circumstances. If the operations of a U.S. financial institution within that
state are restricted because of its presence in other states, the same restrictions could be applied to the Canadian financial institution.

The effect of these provisions is that U.S. states may maintain restrictions
on interstate branching so long as they are maintained on a non-discriminatory
basis.

(d) Equal competitive opportunities

Treatment by a NAFTA country of financial institutions and cross-border
service providers of other NAFTA countries will comply with the obligations
described above if it affords "equal competitive opportunities". This requirement is met if the treatment does not "disadvantage" these entities in their
ability to provide financial services as compared with the ability of their
domestic counterparts. Differences in market share, profitability or size will
not themselves establish a denial of equal competitive opportunities but may
be used as evidence regarding whether a NAFTA country is fulfilling this
NAFTA obligation.

National treatment does not mean identical treatment. It only means no
less favourable treatment. The effect of the "competitive opportunities test"
of compliance allows somewhat greater latitude for differential treatment
than applies with national treatment provisions set out elsewhere in NAFTA.

(e) National treatment and FTA concessions

The national treatment obligation described above would not prevent the
U.S. federal government from prohibiting all banks governed by U.S. federal law from dealing in Canadian government securities. The U.S. federal
government could also enact measures that were consistent with national treatment but that further restricted the ability of Canadian-controlled banks to
branch outside their home states. Therefore, NAFTA Annex 1401.4 preserves
the U.S. concessions in FTA 1702(1) and FTA 1702(2) described in §8.3(2)
by incorporating them into NAFTA.

As discussed in §8.5(2)(b), the Canadian FTA concessions are covered in NAFTA by way of reservation rather than by incorporation by reference.

(6) Most-Favoured-Nation Treatment

NAFTA 1406(1) sets out an MFN obligation analogous to those in the investment and financial services chapters. However, NAFTA 1406(2) sets out an important qualification that is very similar to a provision that appears in the GATS Annex on Financial Services.[129] A NAFTA country may recognize prudential measures of another NAFTA country or a non-NAFTA country. Such recognition can be unilateral, achieved through harmonization or other means or based on an agreement or other arrangement. If this occurs, the NAFTA country according the recognition must give a NAFTA country to which recognition has not been accorded the opportunity to demonstrate that its prudential measures are comparable and should also be recognized[130] and provide the other NAFTA country with an opportunity to negotiate accession to the agreement or arrangement or negotiate something comparable. However, the obligations of a NAFTA country in these circumstances to other NAFTA countries do not extend beyond this.

The effect of these provisions is that NAFTA countries may enter into arrangements with non-NAFTA countries respecting prudential measures without being bound to accord comparable treatment to other NAFTA countries. For example, the Revised Concordat could evolve into a formal arrangement under which supervisory responsibilities were divided between home and host countries. The United States and Canada, as G-10 countries, could recognize home country supervision by other member countries in the areas agreed to be the responsibility of the home country supervisors. Mexico would have to be given the opportunity to demonstrate that its home country supervision in these areas was comparable and be afforded the opportunity to negotiate accession to the arrangement. However, Canada and the United States would not be obliged under the NAFTA MFN obligation to recognize Mexican home country supervision in these areas.

(7) New Financial Services and Data Processing

NAFTA 1407(1) requires each NAFTA country to permit financial institutions of other NAFTA countries to provide any new financial services[131] that it permits its own financial institutions to provide. The NAFTA country may determine the institutional and juridical form through which the service is provided and require that authorization first be obtained, provided that a decision is made within a reasonable time and authorization is not refused for other than prudential reasons. NAFTA 1407(2) requires each NAFTA country to permit financial institutions of other NAFTA countries to transfer information out of its territory for data processing required in the ordinary course of business.

(8) Senior Management and Boards of Directors

NAFTA 1408 sets out a provision similar to that in NAFTA 1107 described in §7.7(5) respecting senior management and boards of directors. The provision applies to financial institutions of other NAFTA countries. Like NAFTA 1107, NAFTA 1407 permits nationality or residency requirements respecting boards of directors but, unlike NAFTA 1107, without the *caveat* that the requirement does not impair the ability to exert control.

(9) Transparency

NAFTA 1411 sets out transparency rules respecting publication of measures and applications to provide financial services. NAFTA 1411(1) requires each NAFTA country, to the extent practicable, to provide advance notice to all interested persons of measures of general application that it proposes adopting and allow an opportunity for comment.

NAFTA 1411(2) through to NAFTA 1411(4) cover applications respecting the provision of financial services. Regulatory authorities are to make requirements for completing applications available to interested persons and, upon request, advise applicants of the status of applications. Decisions on completed applications are to be made within 120 days and promptly notify the applicant. Regulatory authorities must also inform the applicant if it is not practicable for the decision to be made within 120 days, and in such case shall try to make the decision within a reasonable time.

NAFTA 1411(5) provides that nothing in NAFTA Chapter Fourteen requires a NAFTA country to furnish confidential information or information respecting the financial affairs of individual customers. NAFTA 1411(6) requires each NAFTA country to establish inquiry points to respond to reasonable inquiries from interested persons respecting measures of general application covered by Chapter Fourteen.

(10) Self-Regulatory Organizations

NAFTA 1402 requires each NAFTA country to ensure that self-regulatory organizations to which financial institutions or cross-border financial service providers must belong or participate in observe the obligations in Chapter Fourteen.

(11) Exceptions

(a) Retirement plans

NAFTA 1401(3) provides that Chapter Fourteen shall not prevent a NAFTA country or its public entities from exclusively conducting or providing activities or services forming part of a public retirement plan or statutory system of social security or activities or services for the account of or with the guarantee of or using the financial resources of the NAFTA country.

(b) Prudential measures and monetary policy

NAFTA 1410(1) provides that nothing in Part Five of NAFTA, which includes not only Chapter Fourteen but also Chapters Eleven, Twelve, Thirteen, Fifteen and Sixteen, prevents a NAFTA country from adopting and maintaining reasonable measures for prudential reasons. These include measures to protect investors, depositors, financial market participants, policy holders, policy claimants and persons to whom fiduciary duties are owed. These also include measures relating to the maintenance of the "safety, soundness, integrity or financial responsibility of financial institutions or cross-border financial service providers" and ensuring the integrity and stability of a NAFTA country's financial system. The GATS Annex on Financial Services sets out a similar exception using similar wording.[132] NAFTA 1410(1) does not require that these "reasonable measures" be non-discriminatory.

NAFTA 1410(2) provides that Part Five does not apply to non-discriminatory measures of general application taken by public entities in pursuit of monetary and related credit policies or exchange rate policies. However, this exception does not affect the obligations respecting performance requirements in NAFTA 1106 (discussed in §7.7(4)) or transfers in NAFTA 1109 (discussed in §7.7(6)).

8.5   RESERVATIONS AND LIBERALIZATION COMMITMENTS

As with investment and services, the financial services provisions adopt the reservations approach to non-conforming measures existing at the time NAFTA became effective. The reservations of each NAFTA country are set out in Annex VII.

(1) Annex VII

The general structure of Annex VII is as described in §7.9(2) and the structure of the Measures, Description and Phase-Out elements corresponds to that of Annex I described in §7.9(3)(a). The Schedule of each NAFTA country attached to is divided into Sections A, B and C.

(a) Section A reservations

Section A sets out the measures reserved under NAFTA 1409(1) which corresponds to NAFTA 1108 and NAFTA 1206 described in §7.9(3). NAFTA 1409(1) provides that NAFTA 1403 (Establishment of Financial Institutions), 1404 (Cross-Border Trade), 1405 (National Treatment), 1406 (Most-Favoured-Nation Treatment), 1407 (New Financial Services and Data Processing) and 1408 (Senior Management and Boards of Directors) do not apply to federal non-conforming measures set out in Section A, provincial or state non-conforming measures as provided in NAFTA Annex 1409.1 or to local government non-conforming measures. NAFTA Annex 1409.1 required non-conforming measures of the Canadian provinces and the states of California, Florida, Illinois, New York, Ohio and Texas to be set out in Section A of the Canadian and U.S. Schedules respectively by January 1, 1994. The non-conforming measures of other U.S. states may be maintained until January 1, 1995, and after that date if they are set out in Section A of the U.S. Schedule. Non-conforming measures of Mexican states may be maintained without being set out in Section A.

As under NAFTA 1108 and NAFTA 1206, these exceptions apply only to measures that existed on January 1, 1994. As with Annex I reservations described in §7.9(3), non-conforming measures made less non-conforming or eliminated cannot subsequently be amended or replaced with a new measure that is more non-conforming.

(b) Section B reservations and Section C commitments

NAFTA 1409(2), which corresponds to NAFTA 1108(3) and 1206(3) described in §7.9(4), provides that NAFTA 1403 to 1408 do not apply to non-conforming measures adopted and maintained in accordance with Section B of its Schedule. Section C of each NAFTA country's schedule sets out specific commitments of that country.

(c) Application of reservations in other annexes

NAFTA 1409(4) provides that reservations in Annexes I, II, III or IV to the national treatment obligations in NAFTA 1102 and NAFTA 1202 and the MFN obligations in NAFTA 1103 and NAFTA 1203 are deemed to be reservations to the corresponding obligations in NAFTA 1405 and NAFTA 1406 to the extent that the measures referred to in the reservation are covered by Chapter Fourteen. Under this provision, reservations from NAFTA 1102 such as that taken by Canada under Annex I in respect of the *Investment Canada Act* and the *Investment Canada Regulations* apply as well to NAFTA 1405.[133] Canada's Annex II social services reservation from NAFTA 1102, NAFTA 1202 and NAFTA 1203 applies as well to NAFTA 1405 and NAFTA 1406.[134] Without this reservation, measures respecting the provision of health insurance by provincial governments would be covered by Chapter Fourteen.

(2) Schedule of Canada

(a) Section A reservations

The Canadian federal government has taken a Section A reservation respecting limitations on the purchase of reinsurance services from non-resident reinsurers.[135] Reservations have also been taken under Section A respecting various provincial measures. For example, a reservation has been taken respecting the ownership restrictions in the *Loan and Trust Corporations Act* (Ontario) described in §8.2(1)(b)(ii).[136] Reservations have been taken respecting other Ontario laws covering credit unions, mortgage brokers, insurance agencies and brokers, mutual insurance companies, insurance adjusters, securities brokers and dealers and commodity futures registrants. Similar reservations cover laws of other provinces.

(b) Section B reservations

Canada has reserved the right under Section B to adopt measures respecting the cross-border trade in securities services that derogates from the standstill provision in NAFTA 1404(1) or, respecting the United States only, from the MFN treatment obligation in NAFTA 1406. As discussed in §8.5(6)(b), the United States has taken a similar reservation respecting Canada.

Canada has also reserved the right under Section B to adopt or maintain measures requiring enterprises of other NAFTA countries controlled by residents of those countries to be entitled to the benefits of Chapter Fourteen. The reservation sets out rules for determining control. Under this reservation, Canada may deny the benefits of Chapter Fourteen to an enterprise of another NAFTA country controlled by residents of non-NAFTA countries even though the enterprise has substantial business activities in that NAFTA country. The limits imposed by this limitation are consistent with the obligations that Canada had under the FTA to remove ownership restrictions described in §8.3(1).

(c) Section C commitments

Canada agreed under Section C to extend to Mexico the same treatment that was extended under the FTA to U.S. residents and institutions controlled by U.S. residents.

(3) Schedule of Mexico

The Schedule of Mexico establishes a process of liberalization that will be phased in over a transition period that began on January 1, 1994, and will end on January 1, 2000. The expression "foreign financial affiliate" used in the Schedule of Mexico means a financial institution established in Mexico and controlled by an investor of either the United States or Canada.[137]

(4) Mexican Schedule A Reservations

Mexico has taken Section A reservations respecting all of the measures containing the ownership restrictions described in §8.2(3)(c).[138] The percentage ownership restrictions in these measures do not apply to foreign financial affiliates.

Mexico has taken a reservation respecting measures prohibiting foreign governments and foreign state enterprises from investing in a wide range of enterprises providing financial services.[139] There is no exception in this reservation for foreign financial affiliates.

Mexico has maintained its prohibition on foreign investments in development banks[140] and has reserved activities of acting as custodian for certain funds and seized goods and managing the saving funds, retirement plans and other property of certain public sector personnel.[141]

Mexico has reserved its existing prohibitions and restrictions on the cross-border trade in insurance services. However, restrictions respecting the ability of Mexicans to purchase some types of insurance from cross-border insurance providers is excluded from the reservation.[142] The types of insurance include tourist insurance and certain types of cargo insurance. In this, the reservation constitutes a liberalization commitment.

(5) Mexican Section B Reservations and Section C Commitments

Sections B and C of Mexico's Schedule to NAFTA Annex VII must be read together. Section B sets out the limits, expressed in terms of percentages of the aggregate capital or assets of all financial institutions of a type that may be comprised of authorized capital or assets of foreign financial affiliates, that apply to the establishment of foreign financial affiliates in Mexico during and after the transition period. Section B is structured as a reservation but in Mexico's case constitutes a commitment to liberalize. Section C sets out specific commitments.

(a) During the transition period

(i) General rules

During the transition period, the maximum capital authorized for an individual commercial bank or a casualty or life and health insurance company owned by Canadian or U.S. investors cannot exceed 1.5% of the authorized capital for all institutions of the same type. The percentage applicable to securities firms is 4%.[143] If an investor of Canada or the United States acquires a financial institution in Mexico, the sum of the authorized capital of the acquired institution and that of foreign financial affiliates already controlled by the acquirer may not exceed these limits.

There are also limits on the percentage that the aggregate authorized capital of financial institutions of various types owned by Canadian or U.S. investors can comprise of the total capital of all financial institutions of the corresponding type. For example, at the beginning of the transition period, the total capital of Mexican commercial banks owned by Canadian and U.S. investors cannot exceed an initial limit of 8% of the total capital of all Mexican commercial banks. This percentage will increase to a final limit of 15% by the end of the transition period. For securities firms, factoring companies and leasing companies, the initial limit is 10% and the final limit 20%. For insurance companies, the initial limit is 6% and the final limit 12%.[144] The limits for insurance companies controlled by Canadian and U.S. investors are 6% for 1994, 8% for 1995, 9% for 1996, 10% for 1997, 11% for 1998 and 12% for 1999.[145]

(ii) Alternative for insurance companies

The individual and aggregate limits for insurance companies just described do not include existing or new insurance companies for which a Canadian or U.S. investor has elected an alternative procedure for investing in Mexico. To qualify, the Canadian or U.S. investor must phase in its ownership, so that Mexicans own prescribed levels of common voting stock of the company during the transition period. These levels are 70% for 1994, 65% for 1995, 60% for 1996, 55% for 1997, 49% for 1998 and 25% for 1999. The requirement ceases January 1, 2000.[146] Mexico will permit these limits to be exceeded in certain cases where Canadian or U.S. investors owned more than 10% of an insurance company prior to July 1, 1992, and had an option at that time to acquire further ownership interests.[147]

(iii) Limited scope financial institutions

Section C requires Mexico to permit non-bank investors of Canada and the United States to establish "limited scope financial institutions to separately provide consumer, commercial and mortgage lending or credit card services". These institutions may raise money in the securities market but may not take deposits.[148]

During the transition period, Section B limits the aggregate assets of these foreign financial affiliates to 3% of the aggregate assets of all commercial banks and all types of limited scope financial institutions in Mexico.[149] Lending by affiliates of automobile manufacturing companies respecting their vehicles are not taken into account in this calculation. NAFTA Annex 1413.6 provides for consultations on these limits following January 1, 1997.

(iv) Other provisions

Paragraph 3 of Section B sets out rules for administering the capital limits in Section B and paragraph 4 prohibits foreign financial affiliates from issuing subordinate debentures, other than to controlling investors.

(b) Following the transition period

At the end of the transition period, Mexico must remove the limits described in §8.5(5)(a)(i) and §8.5(5)(a)(iii). However, if the authorized capital of commercial banks and securities firms controlled by Canadian or U.S. investors exceeds 25% and 30% respectively of total capital for all such financial institutions in Mexico, Mexico shall have the one-time right to freeze the permitted aggregate capital percentage firms for a further three years. This right expires at the end of 2004.[150]

NAFTA Annex 1413.6 provides that Mexico may request consultations once this threshold of 25% for commercial banks is reached. The consultations will address the potential adverse effects arising from the presence of Canadian and U.S. banks in the Mexican market and the possible need for remedial action, such as further temporary limitations on market participation. If no consensus is reached in the consultations, any NAFTA country may invoke an arbitration under NAFTA 1414 or NAFTA 2008.

(c) Other provisions in Section B

Paragraphs 12 to 17 of Section B apply from January 1, 1994, and at all times thereafter. However, amendments to measures made pursuant to paragraphs 12 to 15 cannot decrease the conformity of a measure as it existed on January 1, 1994, with NAFTA 1403 to 1408.

Paragraph 12 provides that Mexico may require that financial institutions owned by Canadian or U.S. investors be wholly owned and prohibited from establishing agencies, branches or subsidiaries outside Mexico.[151] Paragraph 13 provides that after the transition period, the capital of a Mexican commercial bank acquired by a Canadian or a U.S. investor (together with other commercial banks owned by that investor) will only be authorized if it does not exceed 4% of the aggregate capital of all commercial banks in Mexico.[152] Paragraph 14 permits Mexico to limit the ability of Canadian and U.S. investors to establish foreign financial affiliates if they are providing similar financial services in Canada or the United States. Such investors may be limited to no more than one institution of the same type in Mexico.[153] Paragraph 15 excludes the operations of certain Mexican government insurance programs. Paragraph 16 prohibits cross-border financial services in transactions dominated in pesos.

Paragraph 17 applies to the Citibank branches.[154] The benefits of NAFTA shall not be extended to such branches and the existing rules continue to apply so long as the branches continue in that form. A branch may be converted into a subsidiary and will then be covered. However, in the event of conversion the capital of the branch existing on January 1, 1994, will not be counted against the individual or aggregate capital limits described in §8.5(5)(a)(i).

(d) Other provisions in Section C

Paragraph 1 sets out criteria for approving affiliations between commercial banks and securities firms with commercial or industrial corporations but provides that the discretion to approve is retained by Mexico. Paragraph 3 requires Mexico to conduct a study into the desirability of permitting the establishment of limited scope securities firms. If Mexico permits a Canadian or U.S. investor to establish or acquire a commercial bank or securities firm, paragraph 5 requires Mexico to permit the investor to establish a financial holding company in Mexico, through which other financial institutions may be acquired.

(6) Schedule of the United States

(a) Section A reservations

The United States has taken a reservation respecting a measure requiring that all directors and the president of a national bank be U.S. citizens.[155] A reservation has been taken respecting certain provisions of the Bank Holding Act and the International Banking Act that result in foreign banks with direct deposit-taking branches or subsidiaries in the United States not being able to acquire interests in banks in some states on the same terms as their domestic counterparts.[156] A reservation has been taken respecting ownership restrictions applicable to non-bank foreign persons of specialized international banking companies known as "Edge" corporations.[157] The United States has reserved the requirement referred to in §8.2(2)(e)(i) that foreign banks must have insured banking subsidiaries in order to accept retail deposit accounts of less than $100,000.[158] The United States has taken a reservation respecting the rule referred to in §8.2(2)(e)(i) that foreign banks with branches or agencies may not be members of the foreign reserve system.[159]

Other reservations have been taken respecting primary dealers in U.S. government debt obligations,[160] trustees under indentures for debt securities,[161] reserve requirements for broker-dealers with principal places of business in foreign countries,[162] futures contracts on unions,[163] provision of surety bonds for U.S. government contracts[164] and registration of foreign banks as investment advisors.[165]

The United States has not taken any reservation respecting the Enhancement Act,[166] presumably because U.S. financial supervisors are of the view that this measure is covered by the prudential exception discussed in §8.4(11)(b).

As indicated in §8.5(1)(a), reservations respecting non-conforming state measures were taken as of January 1, 1994, or will be taken by January 1, 1995, depending on the state.

(b) Section B reservations

The United States has reserved the right with respect to Canada to adopt measures respecting the cross-border trade in securities services that derogates from the standstill provision in NAFTA 1404(1) or from the MFN treatment obligation in NAFTA 1406.

(c) Section C commitment

Section C sets out a very limited exception to the provisions of the Glass-Steagall Act. Subject to some limitations, the United States has agreed to permit a Mexican financial group formed before January 1, 1994, that in its formation acquired a Mexican bank and a Mexican securities company owning or controlling a U.S. securities company to continue to engage in the activities in which the U.S. securities company was engaged for a period of five years from the acquisition.

8.6 COMMITTEE ON FINANCIAL SERVICES, CONSULTATIONS AND DISPUTE RESOLUTION

NAFTA 1412 establishes a Financial Services Committee to supervise the implementation of Chapter Fourteen and its further elaboration, to consider issues referred to it by a NAFTA country and to participate in dispute settlement procedures. The Committee is to meet annually to assess the functioning of NAFTA as it applies to financial services.

NAFTA 1413 provides that any NAFTA country may request consultations regarding any matter arising under NAFTA affecting financial services. Rules are established respecting the participation of regulatory authorities in such consultations. NAFTA Annex 1413.6 provides for consultations on the matters discussed in §8.5(5)(a)(iii) and §8.5(5)(b).

NAFTA 1414 and NAFTA 1415 set out provisions respecting disputes arising out of Chapter Fourteen. These are discussed in §11.2(10)(b) and §11.3(10).

8.7 CONCLUDING REMARKS

In terms of practical changes, the NAFTA financial services provisions have little impact on the Canadian and U.S. financial services sectors. Canada has extended to Mexico the concessions that it made to the United States in the FTA, and the United States has made a minor concession to Mexico in respect of its Glass-Steagall restrictions. The NAFTA financial services provisions will have a significant practical impact on the Mexican market for financial services. Before NAFTA, the Mexican financial services market was virtually closed to Canadian and U.S.-controlled financial institutions. At the end of the ten-year transition period, Canadian and U.S.-financial institutions should have substantial scope to operate in the Mexican market, although there will still be restrictions.

In terms of conceptual changes, the approach taken in the NAFTA financial services provisions represents a substantial change from that taken under the FTA. Rather than exchanging concessions, the three NAFTA countries have applied to financial services, with some modification, the principles of national treatment and MFN treatment that govern investment and services. Future measures of the NAFTA countries affecting financial institutions and financial services must be consistent with these principles. The fact that the financial services provisions apply to states and provinces is significant for both the United States and Canada because states and provinces have substantial supervisory power in the financial sector. The NAFTA financial services provisions do not address any of the home versus host country supervisory issues that have been considered by other international bodies. However, the flexible MFN provisions leave each NAFTA country free to negotiate reciprocal arrangements with other countries respecting these matters.

The unresolved issues of the negotiations are reflected in the NAFTA provisions respecting the establishment of financial institutions described in §8.4(3). The U.S. negotiators failed to persuade either Canada or Mexico to surrender their requirements that foreign banks carry on business through subsidiaries. However, as discussed in §8.1(2), the U.S. Treasury Department has advocated this same approach in some of its proposals to revise U.S. banking laws. The Canadian and Mexican negotiators and the financial services industries in each country were dissatisfied with the failure to obtain any movement by the United States on the interstate bank branching and the Glass-Steagall restrictions.

The Glass-Steagall restrictions and the other U.S. restrictions on bank diversification continue. However, as the provisions of the Interstate Banking Act become fully effective by 1997, the U.S. restrictions on interstate branching will be largely dismantled.[167] Subject to some limitations, the Federal Reserve Board will be authorized to permit bank holding companies to acquire the assets of banks located outside their own states. Following June 1, 1997, mergers between banks in different states may be approved and the establishment of branches by banks outside their home states may be authorized. The IBA has been amended so that foreign banks will be able to establish branches or agencies outside their home states to the same extent as national banks. These changes may set the stage for the completion of the unfinished business of juridical forms discussed in §8.4(3)(b).

ENDNOTES

[1] Douglas H. Ginsburg, "Interstate Banking" (1981), 9 *Hofstra Law Review*, No. 4, p. 1133 at p. 1142.

[2] For example, *Bank Act*, S.C. 1991, c. 46, s. 24 and *Insurance Companies Act*, S.C. 1991, c. 47, s. 574(2).

[3] Daniel B. Gail, Joseph J. Norton, Michael K. O'Neal, "The Foreign Bank Supervision Act of 1991: Expanding the Umbrella of 'Supervisory Regulation'", *The International Lawyer*, Winter 1992, Vol. 26, No. 4, p. 993 at p. 997. The Revised Concordat is reprinted in (1983), 22 I.L.M. 900. See also Richard Dale, "Reflections on the BCCI Affair: A United Kingdom Perspective", *The International Lawyer*, Winter 1992, Vol. 26, No. 4, p. 949 at p. 949, note 1.

[4] Dale, *ibid.*, p. 950.

[5] Committee on Banking Regulations and Supervisory Practices: Revised Basle Concordat on Principles for the Supervision of Banks Foreign Establishments (1983), 22 I.L.M 900. See IV. *Aspects of the supervision of banks' foreign establishments* under 1. *Solvency*.

[6] Joseph J. Norton, "The Work of the Basle Supervisors Committee" (1989), 23 *International Law* 245 for a discussion of the 1983 Revised Concordat and the subsequent work of the Basle Committee, as well as the "Agreed proposal of the United States federal banking supervisory authorities and the Bank of England on primary capital and capital adequacy assessment" released January 8, 1987.

[7] Dale, *op. cit.*, note 3, at pp. 949-50.

[8] *Ibid.*, at p. 950.

[9] Gail, Norton and O'Neal, *op. cit.*, note 3 at p. 997.

[10] The Foreign Bank Supervision Act of 1991, discussed in §8.2(2)(e).

[11] Michael L. Whitener, "New Federal Reserve Board Regulations Regarding Foreign Banks in the United States", *The International Lawyer*, Winter 1992, Vol. 26, No. 4, p. 1007 at p. 1013. This approach was dropped because of resistance from foreign banks and because of concerns over foreign retaliation.

[12] The Multijurisdictional Disclosure System ("MJDS") permits single-jurisdiction regulation of certain securities offerings and continuous reporting obligations. The objective is to make cross-border securities offerings in Canada and the United States to be made more efficiently at less expense.

[13] Bank of Canada Review (Ottawa, Publications Distribution Bank of Canada, Winter 1992-1993) p. 22.

[14] *Ibid.*

[15] Each of the provinces and the territories has legislation regulating the trading in securities and the licensing of securities dealers. Self-regulatory bodies include the Investment Dealers Association of Canada and the Toronto, Montreal, Vancouver and Alberta stock exchanges.

[16] OSFI was created in 1987 by merging the Office of the Inspector General of Banks and the Department of Insurance (which was responsible for supervising trust and mortgage loan companies and insurance companies). Bank of Canada Review, Winter 1992-1993, p. 43.

[17] See *The Regulation of Canadian Financial Institutions* (the "Green Paper", April 1985), *New Directions for the Financial Sector* (the "Blue Paper" or "Hockin Paper", December 1987), the *Proposed Legislation to Revise and Amend the Law Governing Federal Trust and Loan Companies* (December 1987) and *Reform of Financial Institutions Legislation: Overview of Legislative Proposals*. See Bank of Canada Review, Winter 1992-1993, at p. 30. The Hockin Paper is discussed on pp. 114-15 of *Comprehensive Guide*.

[18] *An Act to amend certain Acts relating to financial institutions*, S.C. 1987, c. 26. There were some jurisdictional issues between the federal government and the Province of Ontario when this change was first implemented as to which level of government had the power to regulate

the activities of a securities firm controlled by a federally regulated financial institution. Through an understanding known as the Hockin-Kwinter Accord, it was agreed that the OSFI would regulate the federal financial institution but the Ontario Securities Commission would regulate the securities firm.

[19] S.C. 1991, c. 46; S.C. 1991, c. 45; S.C. 1991, c. 47; and S.C. 1991, c. 48, respectively. Each of these Acts replaced previous legislation.

[20] Bank of Canada Review, Winter 1992-1993, p. 32.

[21] *Bank Act*, S.C. 1991, c. 46, s. 416 and the *Insurance Business (Banks) Regulations*, SOR 92/330.

[22] *Bank Act*, S.C. 1991, c. 46, s. 468; *Trust and Loan Companies Act*, S.C. 1991, c. 45, s. 453; *Insurance Companies Act*, S.C. 1991, c. 47, s. 495; and *Co-Operative Credit Associations Act*, S.C. 1991, c. 48. There are limitations on some of these activities. For example, the activities of a "financial leasing corporation" do not include leasing motor vehicles with a gross vehicle weight of less than twenty-one tonnes.

[23] *Bank Act*, S.C. 1991, c. 46, ss. 8, 372.

[24] *Bank Act*, s. 375.

[25] *Bank Act*, s. 373(1).

[26] *Bank Act*, s. 374.

[27] *Insurance Companies Act*, S.C. 1991, c. 47, s. 411; *Trust and Loan Companies Act*, S.C. 1991, c. 45, s. 379.

[28] Paragraph (*d*) of the definition of foreign bank in s. 2 of the *Bank Act*.

[29] *Foreign Bank Representative Offices Regulations, 1992*, SOR/92-299.

[30] *Bank Act*, s. 508.

[31] *Bank Act*, s. 381.

[32] *Bank Act*, ss. 518(1) and 521. There is a grandfathering provision in s. 518(3).

[33] *Bank Act*, s. 399(2); "foreign institution"; and paragraph (*b*) of the definition of "eligible foreign institution" in s. 370(1).

[34] *Bank Act*, s. 424.

[35] *Bank Act*, s. 423(1).

[36] *Bank Act*, s. 399.

[37] *Trust and Loan Companies Act*, S.C. 1991, c. 45, s. 397; *Insurance Companies Act*, S.C. 1991, c. 47, s. 427; and *Co-Operative Credit Associations Act*, S.C. 1991, c. 48, s. 365.

[38] *Insurance Companies Act*, S.C. 1991, c. 47, s. 429; *Trust and Loan Companies Act*, S.C. 1991, c. 45, s. 397; and *Co-operative Credit Associations Act*, S.C. 1991, c. 48, s. 366.

[39] Such as marine insurance, insurance against injury or damage caused by nuclear energy, fire insurance on Canadian properties but not effected or solicited in Canada. See the *Insurance Companies Act*, s. 572(1).

[40] *Insurance Companies Act*, s. 573.

[41] *Insurance Companies Act*, s. 581(1)(*a*).

[42] *Insurance Companies Act*, s. 581(1)(*c*).

[43] R.S.O. 1990, c. L.25, ss. 60, 61.

[44] Chapter 58, 12 Stat. 665. See 12 U.S.C. §§21-215(b) (Supp. III 1979).

[45] Ginsburg, *op. cit.*, note 1, at pp. 1140-41.

[46] Membership in the Federal Reserve System is mandatory for national banks and is permitted for state chartered banks. Each member bank must subscribe 6% of capital as a condition for stock in its regional Federal Reserve Bank, and comply with reserve and other regulatory requirements. See 12 U.S.C. §222 for national banks and 12 U.S.C. §321 for state banks. Many state banks are members. See Ginsburg, *op. cit.*, note 1, at pp. 1151-2.

[47] Ginsburg, *op. cit.*, note 1, at pp. 1150-51. National banks must insure their deposits with the Federal Deposit Insurance Corporation ("FDIC") and most states require state chartered banks to insure their deposits with FDIC. Almost all state chartered banks carry FDIC insurance. All banks with FDIC insurance are subject to reserve requirements, whether or not they are members of the Federal Reserve System.

[48] Ginsburg, *op. cit.*, note 1, at p. 1137.

[49] Act of February 25, 1927, ch. 191, §7, 44 Stat. 1224, 1228-9.

[50] A national bank is one incorporated under U.S. federal law as opposed to state law.

[51] Ginsburg, *op. cit.*, note 1, at p. 1154.

[52] 385 U.S. 252 (1966).

[53] 369 U.S. 122 (1969).

[54] See the comments on this case in Frank J. Marinaro, "Banking Law: The Clash Between the McFadden Act and a National Banking Market", 1990 Ann. Surv. Am. L. 203 at p. 208. The court upheld an order of the Florida state comptroller that the plaintiff national bank discontinue an armoured car messenger service and an off-premises receptacle for receiving deposits on the grounds that these activities contravened a state branching prohibition.

[55] See Marinaro, *ibid.*, at pp. 220-22 for a discussion of whether or not loan production offices and ATMs are "branches" within the meaning of the McFadden Act. Marinaro observes that the courts have refused to classify LPOs and ATMs as branches but the decisions have not resulted in a clear exemption under the McFadden Act. If an ATM is a "branch", a national bank would not be permitted to maintain one outside its home state.

[56] Ginsburg, *op. cit.*, note 1, at p. 1157.

[57] *Ibid.*, p. 1158. The legislation did not result in a significant divestiture.

[58] *Ibid.*, p. 1160.

[59] 12 CFR Ch.II (1-1-93 Edition), §225.21. See generally Regulation Y of the Federal Reserve Board, Par 225, 12 CFR Ch. II(1-1-93 Edition) for the activities that can and cannot be undertaken by BHCs.

[60] Approval is given by the Board of Governors of the Federal Reserve System.

[61] 12 CFR Ch.II (1-1-93 Edition), §225.23.

[62] 12 CFR Ch.II (1-1-93 Edition), §225.25(a).

[63] 12 CFR Ch.II (1-1-93 Edition), §225.25(b)(2).

[64] See 12 CFR Ch.II (1-1-93 Edition), §225.25(b)(3). These include fiduciary activities and limited ability to accept deposits, but not making loans.

[65] 12 CFR Ch.II (1-1-93 Edition), §225.25(b)(4). §225.25(b)(4)(ii) permits BHCs and their subsidiaries to act as advisors to closed-end investment companies. This regulation was challenged under the Glass-Steagall Act (discussed in §8.2(2)(d)) in *Investment Co. Institute v. Board of Governors of the Federal Reserve System.* The D.C. Circuit Court upheld the challenge but was overturned by the Supreme Court. See 606 F.2d 1004 and 450 U.S. 46 (1981). For a discussion of this case, see Joseph J. Norton, "Up Against 'The Wall': Glass-Steagall and the Dilemma of a Deregulated ('Reregulated') Banking Environment" (1987), 42 *The Business Lawyer* 327 at pp. 338-9. See also 12 CFR Ch.II (1-1-93 Edition), §225.25(b)(17) which permits BHCs and their subsidiaries to provide advice respecting foreign exchange exposures and §225.25(b)(19) which permits BHCs and their subsidiaries to provide investment advice on financial futures and options on futures.

[66] 12 CFR Ch.II (1-1-93 Edition) §225.25(5) and (6). For example, leases must serve as the functional extension of credit to the lessee and must be on a non-operating basis. In other words, the lessee must be responsible for such matters as repair and maintenance.

[67] 12 CFR Ch.II (1-1-93 Edition), §225.25(b)(6).

[68] 12 CFR Ch.II (1-1-93 Edition), §225.25(b)(7).

[69] 12 CFR Ch.II (1-1-93 Edition), §225.25(b)(11).

[70] 12 CFR Ch.II (1-1-93 Edition), §225.25(b)(8)(i). The remaining permitted activities in §225.25(b)(8) are confined to insurance agency activities, with grandfathering provisions for certain agency activities in §225.25(b)(iv) and (vi).

[71] 12 CFR Ch.II (1-1-93 Edition), §225.25(b)(15)(i). §225.25(b)(15)(ii) sets out a number of limitations.

[72] Ginsburg, *op. cit.*, note 1, at p. 1162.

[73] 12 CFR Ch.II (1-1-93 Edition), §225.126.

[74] Ginsburg, *op. cit.*, note 1, at p. 1162.

[75] Norton, *op. cit.*, note 65, at p. 327. See Norton's description of the "Underlying Policy" on p. 334.

[76] 12 U.S.C. §24 (Seventh).

[77] As discussed in §8.3(2), FTA 1702(1) extended this authority to include obligations backed by Canada or its political subdivisions and agents thereof.

[78] 12 U.S.C. §377 (1982). Some Canadian banks and their U.S. counterparts have expanded their underwriting powers through exemptive orders. See Cally Jordan, "Financial Services

under NAFTA: The View from Canada'', Standard & Poor's Corp., Vol. 9, No. 6, March 24, 1993, p. 45 at p. 49.

79 12 U.S.C. §378.
80 2 U.S.C. §78 (1982).
81 401 U.S. 617 (1971).
82 401 U.S. 617 at 630-33. For a discussion of this case and the *subtle hazards* test it creates, see Norton, *op. cit.*, note 65, at pp. 335-7.
83 450 U.S. 46 (1981). For a discussion of this case, see Norton, *op. cit.*, note 65, at pp. 338-40.
84 *Ibid.*, p. 353.
85 *Ibid.*, pp. 346-7.
86 Section 16 of the Glass-Steagall Act grants this power. See Norton, *ibid.*, pp. 353-4.
87 See Norton, *ibid.*, pp. 358-9.
88 Philip Hablutzel and Carol Richards Lutz, ''Foreign Banks in the United States after the International Banking Act of 1978: The New Dual System'', *The Banking Law Journal*, Vol. 96, No. 1, January 1979, p. 133 at p. 141.
89 *Ibid.*, at p. 141.
90 *Ibid.*, at p. 141, note 16.
91 Pub. L. No. 95-369, 92 Stat. 607.
92 Gail, Norton and O'Neal, *op. cit.*, note 3, at p. 995.
93 Hablutzel and Lutz, *op. cit.*, note 88, at p. 147.
94 Note the U.S. reservation in NAFTA Annex VII(A)—United States, p. VII-U-2, discussed in §8.5(6)(a).
95 Such as the Italian Banca Nazionale Lavarro. See Gail, Norton and O'Neal, *op. cit.*, note 3, at p. 993.
96 See Whitener, *op. cit.*, note 11, at p. 1011. Foreign banks must establish a federally insured subsidiary to maintain deposit accounts of less than $100,000 unless the foreign bank was accepting or maintaining such deposit accounts at an insured branch when the Enhancement Act was enacted. See Whitener's discussion of some drafting problems with this legislation.
97 Gail, Norton and O'Neal, *op. cit.*, note 3, at p. 997. See also 12 U.S.C. §3105 (1988 Edition, Supp. IV).
98 See Whitener, *op. cit.*, note 11, at pp. 1008-9 for a discussion of these criteria.
99 *Ibid.*, at p. 1008.
100 Gail, Norton and O'Neal, *op. cit.*, note 3, at pp. 1002-3 for description of civil money penalties and p. 1005 for criminal sanctions for violating the IBA.
101 See the Securities Act of 1933 (48 Stat. 74) and the Securities and Exchange Act of 1934 (48 Stat. 881).
102 The banks not nationalized were Citibank and Banco Obrero, a small institution associated with the trade unions. See ''Booming Banks Must Stay Vigilant'', Euromoney Supplement — Mexico, January 1993, Euromoney Publications PLC, at p. 2.
103 Antje Zaldivar, ''Financial Services in Mexico'', *The North American Free Trade Agreement: Provisions and Implications — An Introduction*, Beatriz Boza, ed., at p. 197. Papers presented at the North American Regional Meeting of the Association Internationale des Jeunes Avocats, March 26-27, 1993, Mexico City.
104 As of January, 1993, the government still held 22.5% of Bancomer, 15.9% of Banca Serfin and 21% of Banco Internacional.
105 *Op. cit.*, note 102, at pp. 4-5.
106 See *Ley de Instituciones de Credito*, Article 33.
107 As of September, 1992, the twenty Mexican commercial banks operated 4,400 branches throughout Mexico. See, *op. cit.*, note 102, at p. 8.
108 Zaldivar, *op. cit.*, note 103, at pp. 198-9.
109 See, *op. cit.*, note 102, at p. 4 for a summary of the affiliations through financial groups of the eighteen privatized banks with brokerage houses and insurance companies.
110 *Ibid.*, at p. 8.
111 See *Ley para Regular las Agrupaciones Financieras*, Article 18, referred to in NAFTA Annex VII, p. VII-M-1. See also Zaldivar, *op. cit.*, note 103, at p. 199. Additional foreign invest-

ment may be made through Class L shares so that through a combination of Class C shares and Class L shares, foreign investors can own up to 46% of total capital stock.

[112] See *Ley del Mercado de Valores*, Article 17-II, referred to in NAFTA Annex VII, p. VII-M-2. Individual participation by Mexicans, other than financial holding companies, can be increased to 15% of capital stock with the approval of the *Secretaria de Hacienda y Credito Publico*.

[113] For insurance companies, see *Ley General de Instituciones y Sociedades Mutualistas de Seguros*, Article 29-I referred to in NAFTA Annex VII, p. VII-M-6. Individual participation of both foreigners and Mexicans in insurance companies, other than financial holding companies, is restricted to 15%. See Zaldivar, *op. cit.*, note 103, at p. 201. For the remaining types of financial institutions referred included in this list, see *Ley General de Organizaciones y Actividades Auxiliares del Credito*, Article 8-III-1, and *Ley Federal de Instituciones de Fianzas*, Article 15-XIII, referred to in NAFTA Annex VII, p. VII-M-3.

[114] *Ley General de Organizaciones y Actividades Auxiliares del Credito*, Articles 8-II-1, 82-III; *Ley de Instituciones de Credito*, Article 92; and *Reglas de la Secretaria de Hacienda y Credito Publico*; all referred to in NAFTA Annex VII, p. VII-M-4.

[115] FTA 1704(2).

[116] FTA 1703(4) for Canada and FTA 1702(4) for the United States.

[117] FTA 1703(1).

[118] FTA 1703(2)(a). The limitation on total domestic assets of foreign bank subsidiaries at the time that the FTA was signed was 16%. This was reduced to the present level of 12% at the time that the *Bank Act* was amended to implement the requirements of FTA 1703(2).

[119] FTA 1703(2)(b).

[120] FTA 1703(2)(c).

[121] FTA 1703(2)(d).

[122] Jordan, *op. cit.*, note 78, at p. 49.

[123] Leonard Bierman and Donald R. Fraser, "The Canada-United States Free Trade Agreement and U.S. Banking: Implications for Policy Reform" (1988), 29 *Virginia Journal of International Law* 1.

[124] FTA 1702(2).

[125] FTA 1702(4) and FTA 1703(4).

[126] See Pierre Sauve and Brenda Gonzalez-Hermosillo, "Implications of the NAFTA for Canadian Financial Institutions", C.D. Howe Institute Commentary, No. 44, April 1993, p. 5, for a discussion of the influence of the GATS on the NAFTA financial services provisions.

[127] See §7.8(1).

[128] NAFTA 1102(3), described in §7.7(2) and NAFTA 1202(2), described in §7.8(2), respectively.

[129] Paragraph 3 of the GATS Annex on Financial Services.

[130] This is a rough translation of NAFTA 1406(3), the actual wording of which is: "to demonstrate that circumstances exist in which there are or would be equivalent regulation, oversight, implementation of regulation, and if appropriate, procedures concerning the sharing of information between the Parties".

[131] The expression "new financial service" is defined in NAFTA 1416.

[132] See para. 2 of the GATS Annex on Financial Services.

[133] NAFTA Annex I, p. I-C-2. See para. 8 under Description, which makes specific reference to financial services as one of the sectors to which the higher review thresholds do not apply.

[134] NAFTA Annex II, p. II-C-9.

[135] NAFTA Annex VII—Canada, p. VII-C-1.

[136] NAFTA Annex VII—Canada, p. VII-C(Ont.)-3.

[137] See the definitions set out following Schedule C of the Schedule of Mexico.

[138] See NAFTA Annex VII, p. VII-M-1 for financial holding companies and commercial banks; p. VII-M-2 for securities firms; p. VII-M-3 for general deposit warehouses, financial leasing companies, factoring companies and bonding companies; p. VII-M-4 for credit unions, financial agents and foreign exchange firms; and p. VII-M-6 for insurance companies.

[139] NAFTA Annex VII(A)—Mexico, p. VII-M-7.

[140] NAFTA Annex VII(A)—Mexico, p. VII-M-5.

[141] NAFTA Annex VII(A)—Mexico, p. VII-M-12.

[142] NAFTA Annex VII(A)—Mexico, p. VII-M-10.

[143] NAFTA Annex VII(B)—Mexico, para. 2.
[144] NAFTA Annex VII(B)—Mexico, para. 5.
[145] NAFTA Annex VII(B)—Mexico, para. 6.
[146] NAFTA Annex VII(B)—Mexico, para. 7.
[147] NAFTA Annex VII(C)—Mexico, para. 4.
[148] NAFTA Annex VII(C)—Mexico, para. 2.
[149] NAFTA Annex VII(B)—Mexico, para. 8.
[150] NAFTA Annex VII(B)—Mexico, para. 9.
[151] NAFTA Annex VII(B)—Mexico, para. 12.
[152] NAFTA Annex VII(B)—Mexico, para. 13.
[153] All types of insurance services are to be considered as one type of service, but life and non-life insurance operations may be conducted by a single or separate foreign financial affiliate.
[154] Not explicitly. However, Citibank is the only foreign bank with branches in Mexico. Paragraph 5 of Section B provides that the capital of foreign bank branches is excluded from the aggregate capital limits described in §8.5(5)(a)(i).
[155] NAFTA Annex VII(A)—United States, p. VII-U-1.
[156] NAFTA Annex VII(A)—United States, p. VII-U-2.
[157] NAFTA Annex VII(A)—United States, p. VII-U-4.
[158] NAFTA Annex VII(A)—United States, p. VII-U-5.
[159] NAFTA Annex VII(A)—United States, p. VII-U-6.
[160] NAFTA Annex VII(A)—United States, p. VII-U-7.
[161] NAFTA Annex VII(A)—United States, p. VII-U-8.
[162] NAFTA Annex VII(A)—United States, p. VII-U-9.
[163] NAFTA Annex VII(A)—United States, p. VII-U-10.
[164] NAFTA Annex VII(A)—United States, p. VII-U-11.
[165] NAFTA Annex VII(A)—United States, p. VII-U-12.
[166] Discussed in §8.2(2)(e)(ii).
[167] This description of the Interstate Branching Act is based on *Clinton Signs Interstate Bank Branching Bill and says all he needs now is GATT*, BNA Washington Insider, September 30, 1994 (see The Daily Report for Executives, 30 September 1994, A21) and on the *Conference Report on H.R. 3841*, 103rd Congress 2nd Session, 140 Cong. Rec. H 6625, Vol. 140 No. 104, August 2, 1994.

CHAPTER 9

GOVERNMENT PROCUREMENT, COMPETITION POLICY AND MONOPOLIES, TEMPORARY ENTRY AND INTELLECTUAL PROPERTY

9.1 GOVERNMENT PROCUREMENT

Governments affect trade by setting the rules under which goods and services are traded. Governments also affect trade through the practices that they follow in procuring goods and services for their own consumption and by controlling the activities of state enterprises in producing and trading in goods and providing services. NAFTA Chapter Ten (Government Procurement) sets out rules respecting the practices followed by the governments of the NAFTA countries in procuring goods and services for their own consumption. NAFTA 1502 (Monopolies and State Enterprises), discussed in §9.2(2), covers the activities of state enterprises.

Governments are significant consumers of goods and services. The Canadian Government has estimated that the government procurement markets of the three NAFTA countries have a combined value of about $1 trillion (US).[1] Discriminatory government procurement practices can be effective barriers to trade. For political reasons governments are always under pressure to favour locally produced goods and locally provided services over those produced or provided by foreigners. Discriminatory government procurement requirements can result from policies designed to create opportunities for small businesses or disadvantaged groups. Governments also use their procurement practices to encourage local employment through requiring, through "offsets", that a certain amount of the work necessary to complete a contract be performed locally.

The drafters of the original GATT set out rules in GATT Article XVII covering the activities of state trading enterprises but did not establish disciplines respecting the procurement activities of governments for their own consumption. In fact, "laws, regulations or regulations governing the procurement by governmental purposes" are expressly excluded under GATT Article III:8 from the general GATT national treatment requirements. However, the trade distorting effects of government procurement practices were addressed in the Tokyo Round of GATT negotiations. The result was the *Agreement on Government Procurement* which first came into effect on January 1, 1981, and was amended on November 20, 1986 (the "1980 GATT Government Procurement Code" or "1980 Code"[2]).

(1) Government Procurement Practices of the NAFTA Countries

The governments of all three NAFTA countries follow discriminatory procurement practices. In the United States, discriminatory federal procurement practices are mandated by the Buy American Act.[3] This legislation establishes a general requirement that, with some exceptions, only domestic end products[4] be acquired for public use. Buy American requirements are waived to the extent necessary to comply with international agreements.[5] In Canada, discriminatory practices are not mandated by legislation or regulation but are applied in practice. With procurements not covered by international obligations, price premiums are allowed for Canadian content and foreign-based suppliers are not invited to bid if sufficient competition exists among Canadian suppliers.[6] Mexican procurement practices generally impose a 50% local content requirement and procuring authorities have considerable discretion in determining whether to include or exclude foreign competition.[7]

(2) The 1980 GATT Government Procurement Code

The 1980 GATT Government Procurement Code covers procurement of products and incidental service contracts whose value does not exceed the value of the product. Otherwise the 1980 Code does not cover government procurement of services. The procurements covered by the 1980 Code include only those with a value exceeding 130,000 SDR (the "Code threshold", which at the time of writing is $223,000 or $186,000 (US)).[8] The obligations imposed by the 1980 Code apply only to procurements by the federal government entities specifically listed for each signatory country in Code Annex II. For the procurements to which the 1980 Code applies, the 1980 Code requires member countries to treat products and suppliers of other member countries no less favourably than their own except for the imposition of customs charges. The rules of origin that a member country applies in its ordinary trade must be applied. Locally established suppliers with foreign affiliations must be treated no less favourably as regards government procurement than other locally established suppliers. Article V of the 1980 Code sets out rules governing tendering procedures which are designed to give foreign suppliers a reasonable opportunity to participate in the tendering process. Article VI of the 1980 Code requires that signatory countries publish laws, regulations, judicial decisions and government procurement procedures. Government entities must inform unsuccessful tenderers within seven days of the award of a contract and, if requested, must give reasons and disclose the identity, characteristics and relative advantages of the successful tenderer. The 1980 Code sets out exceptions respecting essential security interests and non-arbitrary and non-discriminatory measures relating to public morals, health, safety, intellectual property and products of the handicapped, philanthropic institutions and prisons.

While the lists of government entities set out in Annex I of the 1980 Code are lengthy, the portion of government procurement activities covered by the 1980 Code is relatively small. Services, other than incidental service contracts, are not included and the essential security exception effectively excludes defence procurement. The 1980 Code does not cover provincial, state or local government procurement.

(3) Provisions of the FTA

FTA Chapter Thirteen had the effect of creating two sets of government procurement rules as between Canada and the United States. The FTA incorporated the 1980 GATT Government Procurement Code so that its provisions continued to apply as between Canada and the United States for procurements of products with threshold limits exceeding the Code threshold ("Code Procurements"). The FTA created a separate set of procedures that applied only to procurements of products with a value of less than the 1980 Code threshold and in excess of $25,000 (US) or its Canadian dollar equivalent[9] ("FTA Procurements"). The requirements respecting FTA procurements applied to the same government entities as set out in the 1980 Code. The FTA Procurements were subject to the "expanded procedural obligations" set out in FTA 1305. These procedures contain rudimentary disciplines such as equal access to pre-solicitation information, equal opportunity to compete in the pre-notification phase, equal opportunity to respond to the requirements of the procuring entity in the tendering and bidding phase, using decision criteria in the qualification of potential suppliers, evaluation of bids and awarding contracts that meet certain prescribed criteria, providing reasonable access to information and providing transparency in the procurement process. All of these had more elaborate counterparts in the 1980 Code. However, the FTA expanded procedural obligations also set out bid challenge procedures in FTA Annex 1305.1 which do not have a counterpart in the 1980 Code. As with the other expanded procedural obligations, the bid challenge procedures applied only to FTA Procurements and not Code Procurements. The FTA expanded procedural obligations set out a special rule of origin for FTA procurements.[10] This approach was at variance with the Code requirement that signatory countries use the rules of origin that apply in the ordinary course of trade. The expanded procedural obligations referred only to goods and not to services.

(4) The Uruguay Round

As noted in §1.4(1), one of the Plurilateral Agreements set out in Annex 4 of the WTO Agreement is the *Agreement on Government Procurement* ("1994 GATT Government Procurement" or "1994 Code").[11] When it becomes effective in 1996,[12] the 1994 GATT Government Procurement Code will supersede the 1980 Code. Canada and the United States are signatories to the 1994 Code but Mexico is not.

NAFTA Chapter Ten is largely based on the 1994 GATT Government Procurement Code. Like NAFTA Chapter Ten, the 1994 Code covers procurements of services and construction services as well as procurements of goods. There are five annexes to the 1994 Code for each member country. Annex 1 lists central government entities covered by the Code. Annex 2 covers sub-central government entities and Annex 3 covers other entities. Annex 4 lists services covered and Annex 5 lists construction services covered. The thresholds for each member country for each category of procurement are specified in the Annexes in SDRs. For each of Canada and the United States, the thresholds are 130,000 SDRs[13] for goods and services and 5,000,000 SDRs[14] for construction services.

As between Canada and the United States, both NAFTA Chapter Ten and the 1994 Code will apply. Unlike FTA Chapter Thirteen and the 1980 Code, which covered mutually exclusive procurements, the procurements covered by NAFTA Chapter Ten and the 1994 Code overlap significantly.

(5) Provisions of NAFTA

The NAFTA provisions covering government procurement are set out in NAFTA Chapter Ten. Unlike FTA Chapter Thirteen, NAFTA Chapter Ten creates a single set of rules that apply to all procurements within the scope of the Chapter. Unlike the FTA, NAFTA does not incorporate the 1980 Code. The only reference made to the 1980 Code in the NAFTA text is in NAFTA 1024(4) in respect of the negotiations provided for in Code Article IX:6(b) which contemplates expansion of Code coverage to include service contracts. As between Canada and the United States, the rule in NAFTA 103 applies and NAFTA Chapter Ten takes precedence over the 1980 Code. NAFTA Chapter Ten makes no reference, either directly or indirectly, to the 1994 GATT Government Procurement Code. Therefore, as between the United States and Canada the considerations discussed in §1.6(6)(b) apply in determining which of NAFTA Chapter Ten and the 1994 Code prevails.

NAFTA Chapter Ten establishes a basic principle of non-discrimination respecting the procurements covered by NAFTA Chapter Ten as among goods, services and suppliers of other NAFTA countries. These obligations are supplemented by standards that must be applied by the NAFTA countries in respect of the procurements to which NAFTA Chapter Ten applies.

(6) Scope and Coverage of NAFTA Chapter Ten

NAFTA Chapter Ten applies to measures maintained by NAFTA countries relating to procurement by specified federal government entities and enterprises of specified goods or services or construction services where the estimated value of the contract exceeds specified thresholds.[15] Procurement includes procurement by purchase, lease or rental, with or without an option to buy, but does not include non-contractual agreements or government assistance,[16] or the acquisition of fiscal agency or depository services, liquidation and management services for regulated financial institutions or sale and distribution services for government debt. The obligations of Mexico under NAFTA Chapter Ten are subject to transitional provisions set out in Annex 1001.2a, and the obligations of all three NAFTA countries are subject to the General Notes set out in Annex 1001.2b which lists, for each NAFTA country, procurements to which NAFTA Chapter Ten does not apply. The obligations imposed by NAFTA Chapter Ten do not apply to procurements at the provincial or state government levels, although, as discussed in §9.1(17), negotiations with provincial and state governments for possible future inclusion of their entities and enterprises is contemplated.

(a) Specified federal government entities and enterprises

The federal government entities and the government enterprises whose procurements are covered by NAFTA Chapter Ten are listed in Annex 1001.1a-1 and Annex 1001.1a-2, respectively. The entities and enterprises listed in these annexes are collectively defined in NAFTA 1025 as "entities".[17]

(i) Annex 1001.1a-1: federal government entities

Annex 1001.1a-1 lists the federal government entities whose procurements are covered by NAFTA Chapter Ten. The list of Canada includes almost all of the entities listed in the corresponding 1980 Code and FTA Annexes and there are a significant number of additions including, most notably, the Department of Communications, the Department of Fisheries and Oceans,[18] the Department of Forestry, the Department of Transport, the Department of Veterans Affairs, the Veterans Land and Administration, Canadian Radio-television and Telecommunications Commission, the Federal Court of Canada, Investment Canada and the Procurement Review Board.[19] The list of the United States includes almost all of the entities listed in the corresponding 1980 Code and FTA Annexes[20] and three new entities, namely, the Department of Transportation,[21] the Department of Energy (excluding national security procurements made under the Atomic Energy Act and oil purchases related to the Strategic Petroleum Reserve) and the Office of Thrift Supervision. The list of Mexico, which includes a lengthy list of federal government departments, cannot be compared with any predecessor list because Mexico is not a signatory to the 1980 Code. Annex 1 of each of Canada and the United States to the 1994 Code list the same entities and the U.S. list includes a number of additional entities.

(ii) Annex 1001.1a-2: government enterprises

Annex 1001.1a-2 lists the government enterprises whose procurements are covered by NAFTA Chapter Ten. The list for Canada includes the National Capital Commission and Defence Construction (1951) Ltd., both of which were on the FTA list. The list also includes Canada Post Corporation,[22] the St. Lawrence Seaway Authority, the Royal Canadian Mint,[23] Canadian National Railway Company,[24] Via Rail Canada Inc., Canadian Museum of Civilization, Canadian Museum of Nature, National Gallery of Canada and the National Museum of Science and Technology. Annex 3 of Canada to the 1994 Code includes the same entities. The list of the United States is comprised of the Tennessee Valley Authority, the Bonneville Power Administration, the Western Area Power Administration, the Southeastern Power Association, the Southwestern Power Association, the Alaska Power Association and the St. Lawrence Seaway Development Corporation. Annex 3 of the United States to the 1994 Code includes the same entities. With the exception of the St. Lawrence Seaway Development Corporation, procurements by these enterprises will apply to Canada only when NAFTA Chapter Ten applies to procurements by Canadian provincial (excluding local) hydro utilities. The list of Mexico includes thirty-six government enterprises including, most significantly, PEMEX and CFE. Mexico's obligations respecting PEMEX and CFE are subject to the transition provisions described in §9.1(6)(d) and the exclusions in the General Notes described in §9.1(6)(e)(ii).

(b) Specified goods, services and construction services

The goods, services and construction services whose procurement by the entities described above is covered by NAFTA Chapter Ten are specified in Annex 1001.1b-1, Annex 1001.1b-2 and Annex 1001.1b-3, respectively.

(i) Annex 1001.1b-1: goods

Annex 1001.1b-1 provides that NAFTA Chapter Ten applies to procurements by the listed entities of all goods except those purchased by the Canadian Department of National Defence and the Royal Canadian Mounted Police, the Mexican Secretaria de la Defensa Nacional and Secretaria de Marina, and the U.S. Department of Defense. For these entities, the obligations of NAFTA Chapter Ten apply to the goods listed in Section B of Annex 1001.1b-1. The goods on the list, which are identified by Federal Supply Classification ("FSC") codes, are all non-military items. The list in Section B is carried forward from the FTA and the 1980 Code and is set out in Annex 1 of each of Canada and the United States to the 1994 Code. Procurements of goods on this list are also subject to the essential security exception in NAFTA 1018(1) discussed in §9.1(13). Annex 1001.1b-1 also provides that NAFTA Chapter Ten does not apply to certain goods, identified by FSC code, purchased by the U.S. Department of Defense. This provision corresponds to the FTA and 1980 Code Annexes and is set out in Annex 1 of the United States to the 1994 Code.[25] The effect of Annex 1001.1b-1 is to carry forward the same limitations which applied under the FTA and which continue to apply under the 1980 Code to procurement of military and related goods.

(ii) Annex 1001.1b-2: services

Annex 1001.1b-2 provides that NAFTA Chapter Ten applies to procurements of all services by the listed entities and enterprises except for construction services (which are covered by Annex 1001.1b-3) and the services listed in the schedule of exclusions for each NAFTA country in Section B of Annex 1001.1b-2. The schedule for Mexico set out in Section B is incomplete. Until Mexico completes its schedule of exclusions, which must be done by no later than July 1, 1995, the obligations of NAFTA Chapter Ten as they relate to Mexico apply only to the services listed in Appendix 1001.1b-2-A. Once Mexico has completed its schedule of exclusions, each NAFTA country may, after consultations with the other NAFTA countries, revise its schedule of exclusions.

To determine the status of a particular service being procured by a Canadian or American specified entity or enterprise, reference should be made to the schedules of exclusion in Section B of Annex 1001.1b-2 of the original NAFTA text until the process of revision referred to in the preceding paragraph is complete. After that time, reference should be made to the revised Canadian or American schedules of exclusions resulting from that process. If the service is not listed on the schedule of exclusions, it is covered. To determine the status of a particular service being procured by a Mexican specified entity or enterprise, reference should be made to the temporary schedule in Appendix 1001.1b-2-A of the original NAFTA text. Unless the service is on the list, it is not covered. Once Mexico has completed its Section B schedule of exclusions and the revision process is complete, reference should be made to the Mexican schedule of exclusions. If the service is not listed on the schedule of exclusions, it is covered.

Appendix 1001.1b-2-B provides for the NAFTA countries to work on the development of a common classification system for services.

Annex 4 of Canada to the 1994 Code lists services to be covered while Annex 4 of the United States to the 1994 Code lists exclusions.

(iii) Annex 1001.1b-3: construction services

Annex 1001.1b-3 provides that NAFTA Chapter Ten applies to procurements by the listed entities of all construction services set out in Appendix

1001.1b-3-A except those listed in Section B. Appendix 1001.1b-3-A sets out a single list of construction services based on United Nations Central Product Classification (CPC) Division 51 that applies to each NAFTA country. Section B excludes dredging for each of Canada and the United States and construction contracts tendered by the Canadian Department of Transport.[26] There are no Section B exclusions for Mexico in this Annex.

Annex 5 of Canada and the United States to the 1994 Code include all services covered by Division 51 with the exception in the case of Canada only of dredging contracts and contracts tendered by the Department of Transport.

(c) Threshold values

For NAFTA Chapter Ten to apply, the estimated value of the contract to be awarded must be equal to or exceed the thresholds set out in NAFTA 1001(1)(c). The thresholds for procurements of goods or services or a combination of them by federal government entities is $50,000 (US) and by government enterprises is $250,000 (US). The thresholds for procurements of construction services by federal government entities is $6.5 million (US) and by government enterprises is $8.0 million (US).

(i) Annex 1001.1c: indexation and currency conversion

Annex 1001.1c provides for indexation of the thresholds with an indexation formula based on the U.S. Producer Price Index and adjustments taking place every two years. Paragraphs 3 and 4 of Annex 1001.1c set out the conversion formula for converting U.S. currency into Canadian and Mexican currency, respectively. Conversion into Canadian currency for each two-year period commencing January 1, 1994, January 1, 1996, and so on is fixed at the average of weekly values of the official Bank of Canada conversion rate for the two-year period ending the previous September 30th. The Mexican conversion rate is the Bank of Mexico conversion rate on each December 1st for the following January 1st to June 30th period and on each June 1st for the following July 1st to December 31st period.

(ii) Annex 1001.2c: preservation of FTA threshold between Canada and the United States

Annex 1001.2c provides that as between Canada and the United States, the FTA threshold of $25,000 (US) applies to goods contracts with incidental services entered into by the government entities listed in Annex 1001.1a-1. The currency conversion provisions of Annex 1001.1c apply but the indexation provisions do not.[27] This lower threshold does not apply to procurements by the government enterprises listed in Annex 1001.1a-2.

(iii) Valuation of contracts

NAFTA 1001(4) sets out the basic principle that no NAFTA country may structure procurement contracts to avoid the obligations of NAFTA Chapter Ten. An example would be breaking a contract into a series of smaller contracts, each beneath the applicable threshold.[28] The rules for valuing contracts are set out in NAFTA 1002. Values are to be estimated at the time of the publication of the notice of the invitation to participate. All forms of remuneration must be taken into account. NAFTA 1002(5) sets out rules covering contracts awarded in separate parts and NAFTA 1002(6) covers contracts for lease or rental. If the tender documentation requires option clauses, NAFTA 1002(7) requires that these optional purchases be taken into account. The NAFTA provisions on valuation of contracts closely follow those set out in Article II of the 1994 Code.

(d) Annex 1001.2a: the transitional provisions for Mexico

Annex 1001.2a permits Mexico to set aside from the obligations of NAFTA Chapter Ten specified percentages of the total value of procurement contracts above the applicable thresholds for goods, services and construction services procured by each of PEMEX and CFE. There is also a set-aside provision with the same percentages that applies to construction services excluding those procured by PEMEX and CFE. The specified percentages are 50% for 1994, 45% for each of 1995 and 1996, 40% for each of 1997 and 1998, 35% for each of 1999 and 2000, 30% for each of 2001 and 2002, and 0% thereafter. Procurement contracts financed by loans from regional and multilateral financial institutions are not included in these calculations and are not covered by NAFTA Chapter Ten. Procurement contracts set aside by PEMEX or CFE in a year under a single class (FSC or other agreed classification) may not exceed 10% of the total permitted for that year to be set aside. PEMEX and CFE must also make reasonable efforts after December 31, 1998, to ensure that the total value of procurement contracts set aside by PEMEX or CFE in a year does not exceed 50% of PEMEX or CFE procurement contracts in that class. There are permanent set-aside provisions in the General Notes for Mexico discussed in §9.1(6)(e)(ii). There is also a general statement of recognition by the NAFTA countries that Mexico may encounter transition difficulties.

Until January 1, 2002, NAFTA Chapter Ten does not apply to procurement by certain entities and enterprises of drugs not currently patented in Mexico or whose patents have expired.[29]

There are also transitional provisions respecting Mexico's obligations under NAFTA 1012 (Time Limits for Tendering and Delivery, discussed in §9.1(11)(d)), NAFTA 1019 (Provision of Information, discussed in §9.1(14)) and NAFTA 1020 (Technical Cooperation, discussed in §9.1(15)).

(e) Annex 1001.2b: the general notes — procurements to which NAFTA Chapter Ten does not apply

Annex 1001.2b, entitled "General Notes", sets out in a separate schedule for each NAFTA country, procurements to which NAFTA Chapter Ten does not apply.

(i) Schedules of Canada and the United States

The schedules for Canada and the United States exclude set-asides for small and minority businesses and procurement of transportation services that form part of or are incidental to a procurement contract. To ensure that the FTA threshold set out in Annex 1001.2c does not apply to Mexico, both schedules provide that the MFN obligation in NAFTA 1003, discussed in §9.1(8), does not apply to procurements covered by this annex. The Canadian schedule provides that national security exceptions include oil purchases related to strategic reserve requirements and procurements made in safeguarding nuclear materials or technology. As noted in §9.1(6)(a)(i), the United States achieved the same effect in Annex 1001.1a-1 by the limitations placed on its NAFTA Chapter Ten obligations respecting the U.S. Department of Energy. The Canadian schedule also excludes: shipbuilding and repair; urban rail and transportation equipment; communications, detection and coherent radiation equipment; and procurements by the Departments of Transport, Communications and Fisheries and Oceans of automatic data processing equipment, software supplies and support equipment, office machines, text processing machines, visible record equipment and special industry machinery.

(ii) Schedule of Mexico

The most significant feature of the Mexican schedule to the General Notes is that it provides for permanent set-asides. The total value of contracts set aside that may be allocated by all entities other than PEMEX and CFE is the Mexican peso equivalent[30] of $1.0 billion (US) per year until December 31, 2002, and $1.2 billion (US) per year thereafter.[31] Following January 1, 2003 (the date that the transitional set-asides in Annex 1001.2a described in §9.1(6)(d) expire), PEMEX and CFE may set aside contracts with an aggregate value not exceeding the Mexican peso equivalent of $300 million (US). These amounts are subject to adjustment for cumulative inflation beginning January 1, 1995, on a formula based on the implicit U.S. GDP price deflator. The total value of contracts under a single class (FSC or other mutually agreed classification) set aside in a year may not exceed 10% of the total value of contracts permitted to be set aside for that year, and no entity may set aside contracts in a year with a value exceeding 20% of the total value of contracts that may be set aside in that year. If Mexico exceeds the total value of contracts permitted to be set aside or under the transition provisions in Annex 1001.2a described in §9.1(6)(d), Mexico will consult with the other NAFTA countries with a view to providing additional procurement opportunities in the following year. However, the other NAFTA countries maintain their rights under the dispute settlement procedures in NAFTA Chapter Twenty. Notwithstanding the foregoing, set-asides respecting procurement contracts for biologicals and drugs patented in Mexico are not permitted.

As under the Canadian and U.S. schedules, NAFTA Chapter Ten does not apply to the procurement of transportation services which are part of or incidental to a procurement contract.

NAFTA Chapter Ten does not apply to procurements made with a view to commercial resale in government-owned retail stores[32] or pursuant to loans from regional or multilateral financial institutions to the extent that such institutions impose different procedures (other than content requirements) or to procurements by one Mexican entity from another. Entities may impose local content requirements in respect of certain construction, supply or installation projects described in paragraph 6 of the schedule. Paragraph 10 provides that nothing in NAFTA Chapter Ten shall be construed as requiring PEMEX to enter into risk-sharing contracts. As discussed in §7.10(1)(a)(i), these are contracts that permit the contracting party to receive a share of the profits from the project or venture.

(7) Goods and Suppliers of Other NAFTA Countries

NAFTA Chapter Ten confers benefits on goods of other NAFTA countries and suppliers of other NAFTA countries of goods, services or construction services falling within the scope of the Chapter as just described.

(a) Goods of other NAFTA countries and rules of origin

Goods of other NAFTA countries are "goods of another Party" as defined in NAFTA 1025. NAFTA 1025 defines "goods of another Party" as "goods originating in the territory of another Party, determined in accordance with Article 1004". Following the approach set out in both the 1980 Code and the 1994 Code, NAFTA 1004 provides that a NAFTA country shall not apply rules of origin for goods imported from another NAFTA country that are different from or inconsistent with those that it applies in the ordinary course of trade. This is being applied as meaning the general rules of origin that a NAFTA country applies for MFN purposes and not the NAFTA rules of origin. Consider, for example, a good imported into the United States from Mexico. The good will be considered as "originating" in Mexico if it is originating under the "substantial transformation" rule that the U.S. applies in determining eligibility for the U.S. MFN rate.[33] If the good is not "originating" under this rule of origin, it will not be entitled to the benefits accorded by NAFTA Chapter Ten to "goods of another Party". While this approach rectifies a deficiency of the FTA in that it is consistent with the 1980 Code, it still results in one rule of origin being used for tariff preference purposes and another for government procurement purposes.

NAFTA 1004 states that the applicable rules of origin may be the Marking Rules (discussed in §3.2) if they become the rules of origin used in the normal course of trade. As of the time of writing, the United States Customs Service is proposing using the Marking Rules as country of origin rules for all merchandise imported into the United States. The notice of the proposed rules did not cover origin determinations under government procurement statutes.[34]

(b) Suppliers of other NAFTA countries and denial of benefits

A supplier of a NAFTA country is a national of that country or an enterprise constituted or organized under its laws that has provided or could provide goods or services in response to a call for tender.[35] As with investors and service providers under the NAFTA investment and services provisions discussed in §7.7(1)(b) and §7.8(1), a supplier need not be controlled by nationals of a NAFTA country to be entitled to the benefits of NAFTA Chapter Ten. However, as under the NAFTA investment and services provisions, NAFTA 1005 provides that subject to prior notification and consultation a NAFTA country may deny the benefits of NAFTA Chapter Ten to a supplier owned or controlled by persons of a non-NAFTA country that has no substantial business activities in any NAFTA country. A NAFTA country may also deny NAFTA Chapter Ten benefits to suppliers controlled by nationals of a non-NAFTA country if the NAFTA country does not maintain diplomatic relations with the non-NAFTA country or if measures adopted by that NAFTA country respecting the non-NAFTA country would be violated if the benefits were accorded to the supplier.

(8) National Treatment and Non-discrimination

NAFTA 1003 provides that, except for duties and other import charges, a NAFTA country must accord to goods of other NAFTA countries, to the suppliers of such goods and to service suppliers of other NAFTA countries treatment no less favourable than to its own goods and suppliers and those of other NAFTA countries. This non-discrimination provision does not impose a full MFN treatment obligation because goods and suppliers of non-NAFTA countries are not mentioned. Locally established suppliers[36] cannot be treated less favourably than other locally established suppliers on the basis of foreign affiliation or ownership (which can be any foreign affiliation or ownership) or discriminated against because the goods or services that they offer are those of another NAFTA country. Article III of the 1994 Code sets out similar provisions.

(9) Prohibition of Offsets

Offsets are conditions imposed or considered in the procurement process that encourage local development or improve balance of payments accounts by local content requirements, licensing of technology, investment, counter-trade or similar requirements. For example, an entity procuring equipment may require that certain subassemblies be built by local subcontractors. NAFTA 1006 requires NAFTA countries to ensure that their procuring entities do not consider, seek or impose offsets. Article XVI of the 1994 Code also prohibits offsets with an exception for developing countries.

(10) Technical Specifications

NAFTA 1007 requires NAFTA countries to ensure that their entities do not prepare, adopt or apply technical specifications[37] for the purpose of creating unnecessary obstacles to trade. Unlike its counterpart respecting standards-related measures in NAFTA 904(4), discussed in §6.6(3)(d), this provision does not contain a deeming provision for legitimate objectives. NAFTA countries must, where appropriate, ensure that technical specifications are specified in terms of performance criteria rather than design or descriptive characteristics and are based on international standards, national technical regulations, recognized national standards or building codes.[38] Technical specifications must not require a particular trademark or name, patent, specific origin or producer or supplier unless there is no other way of describing the requirements of the procurement and, if this is the case, the specification must be qualified by the words "or equivalent". Entities must not seek advice respecting the preparation of technical specifications from persons that may have a commercial interest in the procurement. Article VI of the 1994 Code sets out similar provisions.

(11) Tendering Procedures

The standards that must be applied by the NAFTA countries in respect of the tendering procedures to be followed by entities in making procurements are set out in NAFTA 1008 through to NAFTA 1016. Tendering procedures are comprised of open tendering procedures, selective tendering procedures and limited tendering procedures. Open tendering procedures are those under which all interested suppliers may submit a tender. Selective tendering procedures, which must comply with NAFTA 1011, are those under which suppliers invited by an entity may submit a tender. Limited tendering procedures, which must comply with NAFTA 1016, are procedures under which an entity contacts suppliers individually.[39] Tendering procedures must be applied in a non-discriminatory manner and meet the minimum standards described in NAFTA 1009 to NAFTA 1016, described in §9.1(11)(a) through (h). NAFTA 1008 requires that entities not provide information to any supplier in a manner that would preclude competition and suppliers must have equal access to information. Article VII of the 1994 Code contains a similar requirement respecting providing information but not the requirement respecting equal access to information.

(a) Qualification of suppliers

The procedures followed by an entity for qualifying suppliers must be consistent with the norms set out in NAFTA 1009(2). Conditions for participation must be published sufficiently in advance so suppliers have adequate time to complete qualification procedures. Conditions for participation shall be limited to those essential for the fulfilment of the contract.[40] Financial, commercial and technical capacity must be based on both a supplier's global business activity and its activity in the NAFTA country of the procuring entity. Qualification procedures are not to be misused to exclude suppliers of other NAFTA countries and suppliers of other NAFTA countries that meet the conditions for qualification must be recognized as qualified suppliers. NAFTA 1009(2) sets out rules covering various situations in which suppliers of other NAFTA countries that have not yet qualified should be permitted to complete the qualification procedure. Suppliers must be advised of decisions and, upon request, be given reasons for the rejection of an application for qualification. Each entity must use a single qualification procedure for its procurements unless a need can be demonstrated for multiple procedures and NAFTA countries must minimize the differences in qualification procedures among their entities. Article VIII of the 1994 Code sets out similar provisions.

(b) Invitation to participate

NAFTA 1010 establishes norms to be applied by entities in inviting suppliers to participate in tendering procedures for procurements covered by NAFTA Chapter Ten. Except when limited tendering procedures are permitted, invitations to participate must be published in the government publications listed in NAFTA Annex 1010.1.[41] NAFTA 1010(2) sets out the information that must be contained in the invitation to participate issued by an entity. Paragraph 6 of Article IX of the 1994 Code sets out similar provisions. NAFTA 1010(3) relaxes these requirements for the government enterprises listed in Annex 1001.1a-2 in that, subject to some minimum requirements, they only have to supply such of the information referred to in NAFTA 1010(2) as is available to them. NAFTA 1010(4) sets out rules respecting notices of planned procurements as invitations to participate and NAFTA 1010(5) permits a government enterprise listed in Annex 1001.1a-2 to use a notice regarding a qualification system as an invitation to participate provided that certain requirements are satisfied. NAFTA 1010(6) requires that in the case of selective tendering procedures, an entity that maintains a permanent list of suppliers must fulfil certain annual publishing requirements respecting the list. NAFTA 1010(7) covers amended or reissued notices of tender documentation and NAFTA 1010(8) requires that all notices under NAFTA 1010 indicate that the procurement is covered by NAFTA Chapter Ten.

(c) Selective tendering procedures

If an entity is using selective tendering procedures, NAFTA 1011(1) requires that tenders be invited from the maximum number of domestic suppliers and suppliers of other NAFTA countries consistent with the efficient operation of the procurement system. NAFTA 1011(2) provides that an entity that maintains a permanent list of qualified suppliers may select those to be invited from the list. However, subject to the efficient operation of the procurement system and to there being sufficient time to complete the qualification procedure, NAFTA 1011(3) requires entities to permit suppliers who wish to participate in a procurement to submit tenders and to consider such tenders. Comparable requirements are set out in Article X of the 1994 Code. NAFTA 1011(4) requires that an entity, upon request, promptly give reasons to a supplier who has not been invited to participate.

(d) Time limits for tendering and delivery

NAFTA 1012(1) sets out several general requirements respecting setting time limits for submitting tenders. Suppliers of other NAFTA countries must be given adequate time to prepare and submit tenders before procedures are closed. Factors to be taken into consideration include the complexity of the procurement, the extent of subcontracting anticipated and the time normally taken to transmit tenders by mail.

NAFTA 1012(2) sets out specific time limits applicable to open and selective tendering procedures. For example, NAFTA 1012(2)(a) requires that in open tendering procedures, the period for the receipt of tenders must be no less than forty days from the publication of the notice to participate or other relevant notice under NAFTA 1010.[42] Annex 1001.2a provides that this is only a best efforts obligation for Mexico until January 1, 1995. NAFTA 1012(3) permits the abridgement of these time periods in certain instances, such as that of urgency or of second or recurring contracts. NAFTA 1012(4) requires that an entity establishing a delivery date take into account the complexity of the procurement, the extent of subcontracting required, as well as several other factors. Article XI of the 1994 Code sets out similar provisions with the same time periods.

(e) Tender documentation

NAFTA 1013 sets out requirements that apply to tender documentation provided by entities to suppliers. NAFTA 1013(1) establishes the general requirement that tender documentation contain all information necessary to permit suppliers to submit responsive tenders and sets out a specific list of information requirements. NAFTA 1013(2) requires that entities forward tender documentation to suppliers upon request and respond promptly to reasonable requests for explanations. Entities must also respond to reasonable requests for information provided that the effect is not to give any supplier an advantage over its competitors. Article XII of the 1994 Code sets out similar provisions.

(f) Negotiation disciplines

NAFTA 1014 limits the ability of an entity to conduct negotiations when procuring goods, services or construction services covered by NAFTA Chapter Ten. An entity may negotiate only when it has indicated in its invitation to participate its intention to negotiate or that it appears from an evaluation of the tenders that no tender is obviously the most advantageous in terms of the evaluation criteria set out in the notices or tender documentation. Negotiations are to be used primarily to identify strengths and weaknesses in the tenders. Tenders must be kept in confidence and information cannot be given to one supplier to enable it to bring its tender up to the level of that of another supplier. NAFTA 1014(4) provides that entities cannot discriminate between suppliers and sets out a number of requirements to ensure adherence to this principle. Article XIV of the 1994 Code sets out similar provisions.

(g) Submission, receipt and opening of tenders and awarding of contracts

NAFTA 1015 sets out requirements respecting the submission, receipt and opening of tenders and awarding of contracts.

(i) Submission, receipt and opening of tenders

Tenders must normally be submitted in writing either directly or by mail. NAFTA 1015(1)(b) through to (d) set out rules respecting tenders received by telex, telegram or other means of electronic transmission. Tenders by telephone are prohibited. Procedures for giving the opportunity to suppliers to correct unintentional errors must be administered on a non-discriminatory basis. A supplier whose tender was received late solely through the fault of the entity will not be penalized. All tenders received under open and selective tendering procedures must be opened under procedures and conditions guaranteeing the regularity of the opening of tenders. Specific procedures are not prescribed. Information respecting the opening of tenders must be retained and shall be at the disposal of the competent authorities of a NAFTA country for the bid challenge procedures under NAFTA 1017, the provisions of information requirements under NAFTA 1019 or the general NAFTA dispute settlement procedures in NAFTA Chapter Twenty. Paragraphs 1 to 3 of Article XIII of the 1994 Code set out similar provisions.

(ii) Awarding contracts

NAFTA 1015(4) sets out the requirements to be followed by entities in awarding contracts. To be considered for an award, the tender must conform to the essential requirements of the notices or tender documentation and have been submitted by a supplier that meets the conditions for participation in the procurement. An entity may inquire respecting a tender with an abnormally low price. Unless contrary to the public interest, the award of a contract shall be made to the supplier determined to be fully capable of undertaking the contract whose tender is either the lowest priced or is the most advantageous in terms of the criteria set out in the notices or the tender documentation. Awards must be made in accordance with the criteria and essential requirements specified in the tender documentation. Option clauses cannot be used to circumvent NAFTA Chapter Ten. Paragraph 4 of Article XIII of the 1994 Code sets out similar provisions. NAFTA 1015(5) prohibits an entity from making the award of a contract conditional upon the supplier having previously been awarded a contract by an entity of that NAFTA country or having previous work experience in the NAFTA country in question.

(iii) Post-award information

NAFTA 1015(6) requires that, upon request, entities promptly inform suppliers on decisions on contract awards and the reasons for decisions. NAFTA 1015(7) requires entities to publish certain information respecting contracts in the publications listed in Annex 1010.1 not later than seventy-two days after the date of the award. NAFTA 1015(8) permits a NAFTA country to withhold information where disclosure would impede law enforcement or otherwise be contrary to the public interest or would prejudice the commercial interests of a particular person or prejudice fair competition between suppliers.[43] Article XVIII of the 1994 Code sets out similar provisions.

(h) Limited tendering procedures

NAFTA 1016 sets out the conditions under which an entity may use limited tendering procedures. These permitted derogations from NAFTA 1008 through NAFTA 1015 are subject to the general requirement in NAFTA 1016(1) that limited tendering procedures cannot be used to avoid maximum competition or as a means of discrimination between suppliers of other NAFTA countries or to protect domestic suppliers. NAFTA 1016(2) permits limited tendering procedures in the following instances: in the absence of tenders in response to an open or selective call or when tenders have resulted from collusion or do not meet the essential requirements of the tender documentation; where goods or services can be supplied by only one supplier and no reasonable alternative exists; extreme urgency; for additional deliveries by the original supplier intended as replacement parts or continuing services for existing supplies, services or installations where a change in supplier would compel the entity to procure non-interchangeable equipment or services, in certain circumstances involving first prototypes; for goods purchased on a commodity market; for purchases made under exceptionally advantageous circumstances such as liquidation situations; for contracts awarded to the winner of an architectural design contest so long as certain conditions are met; and for consulting services regarding matters of a confidential nature whose disclosure would compromise government confidences, cause economic disruption or be otherwise contrary to the public interest. Entities must prepare and retain a report on each contract awarded in accordance with the foregoing which can be used in dispute settlement proceedings. Article XV of the 1994 Code sets out similar provisions.[44]

(12) Bid Challenge

NAFTA 1017 carries forward and elaborates upon the bid challenge procedures established under the FTA. Each NAFTA country must allow suppliers to submit bid challenges concerning any aspect of the procurement process, which begins with an entity's decision of its procurement requirement and ends with a contract award. NAFTA countries may encourage suppliers to resolve disputes with entities before initiating bid challenges and shall ensure that entities give fair and timely consideration to complaints. A NAFTA country cannot prevent a supplier from initiating a bid challenge. The period for initiating the bid challenge can be limited to but must be not less than ten working days from the time that the basis of the complaint became known or reasonably should have been known to the supplier. A NAFTA country may require that a bid challenge be initiated only after notice of the procurement has been published or after tender documentation has been made available. If a NAFTA country imposes such a requirement, the ten-working-day period cannot run until the notice is published or the tender documentation made available.

Each NAFTA country must establish a reviewing authority that will expeditiously investigate the challenge, although the reviewing authority can be required to limit its considerations to the challenge itself. A reviewing authority may delay the awarding of a proposed contract pending resolution of a challenge except in cases of urgency or where the delay would be contrary to the public interest. The reviewing authority will issue a recommendation to resolve the challenge and entities will "normally" follow the recommendations of the reviewing authority. A NAFTA country must authorize its reviewing authority to make additional recommendations respecting any aspect of the procurement process of the entity against which the bid challenge was initiated that is identified as problematic. Findings and recommendations must be provided in writing and in a timely manner and be made available to the NAFTA countries and to interested persons. Bid challenge procedures must be specified in writing and made generally available. NAFTA countries must ensure that their entities maintain complete documentation regarding each of its procurements, including a written record of communications, for at least three years after the contract was awarded.

Article XX of the 1994 Code also sets out challenge procedures. Unlike NAFTA 1018, paragraph 6 of Article XX sets out a number of requirements respecting the composition of the review body and the procedures that it must follow in its deliberations.

(13) Exceptions

NAFTA 1018 sets out two general exceptions that apply to the obligations set out in NAFTA Chapter Ten and carry forward the exceptions set out in Article VIII of the 1980 Code. NAFTA 1018(1) provides that nothing in NAFTA Chapter Ten will prevent a NAFTA country from taking action or not disclosing information that it considers necessary for the protection of its essential security interests relating to military procurements or procurement necessary for national security or national defence. As discussed in §9.1(6)(b)(i), the procurements by the defence departments of all three NAFTA countries are expressly subject to this exception. NAFTA 1018(2) carries forward the exception that, subject to the "arbitrary or unjustifiable discrimination" and the "disguised restriction" exceptions discussed in §1.3(4), NAFTA Chapter Ten is not to be construed to prevent a NAFTA country from adopting measures necessary to protect public morals, order or safety of human, animal or plant life or health or relating to goods or services of handicapped persons or philanthropic institutions or prison labour.

(14) Provision of Information

NAFTA 1019(1) sets out provisions that supplement the general publication obligation in NAFTA 1802(1). NAFTA countries must promptly publish laws, regulations, precedential judicial decisions, administrative rulings and procedures regarding government procurement covered by NAFTA Chapter Ten. Paragraph 1 of Article XIX of the 1994 Code sets out a similar provision.

NAFTA 1019(2) requires NAFTA countries to explain, upon request, their government procurement procedures to other NAFTA countries, to ensure that entities promptly explain procedures and designate contact points. NAFTA 1019(3) entitles a NAFTA country to seek additional information respecting the award of contracts to determine whether a procurement was fairly and impartially made and, subject to consultation in instances of possible prejudice, a NAFTA country to which an inquiry is made must provide information respecting the characteristics and relative advantages of the winning tender and the contract price. NAFTA countries must also provide, upon request of other NAFTA countries, information concerning covered procurement and individual contracts awarded. However, NAFTA 1019(5) provides that a NAFTA country may not disclose confidential information which would prejudice the legitimate commercial interests of a person or prejudice competition between suppliers without the consent of the person who gave the information.[45] Presumably this obligation would override a request for information from another NAFTA country. Also, NAFTA 1019(6) provides that NAFTA countries are not obliged to disclose information that would impede law enforcement or be otherwise contrary to the public interest. Paragraphs 2 through 4 of Article XIX of the 1994 Code set out similar provisions.

In order to monitor the procurement obligations of NAFTA Chapter Ten, NAFTA 1019(7) sets out provisions imposing obligations on the NAFTA countries to collect statistics regarding various aspects of procurement and reporting to each other on an annual basis. Paragraph 5 of Article XIX of the 1994 Code sets out similar provisions.

In paragraph 8 of Annex 1001.2a, the NAFTA countries recognize that Mexico will have to undertake extensive retraining, introduce new data maintenance and reporting systems and make major adjustments to the procurement systems of some entities in order to comply with NAFTA 1019.

(15) Technical Co-operation and Small Business

NAFTA 1020 requires the NAFTA countries to provide to other NAFTA countries and suppliers information regarding training and orientation programs regarding their respective government procurement systems. Paragraph 10 of Annex 1001.2a provides that Canada and the United States furnish technical assistance to aid Mexico's transition. NAFTA 1021 provides for the establishment of a Committee on Small Business to facilitate the activities of the NAFTA countries for promoting government procurement opportunities for their small businesses.

(16) Rectification or Modification and Divestiture of Entities

NAFTA 1022 permits a NAFTA country to modify its coverage under NAFTA Chapter Ten but only after notifying the other NAFTA countries and proposing compensatory arrangements. If the compensatory arrangements are considered unsatisfactory by the other NAFTA countries, NAFTA 1022(5) provides for recourse to the NAFTA Chapter Twenty dispute settlement procedures. NAFTA 1022(3) permits a NAFTA country to make rectifications of a purely formal nature and minor amendments to its schedules in Annexes 1001.1a-1, 1001.1b-1, 1001.2a and 1001.2b so long as notification procedures are followed and no NAFTA country objects. One instance in which this will occur is in the restructuring of government departments.

NAFTA 1023 contemplates the contingency of further privatization, which is particularly relevant in the case of Mexico. If, as a result of a public share offering or privatization through other means, a government enterprise listed in Annex 1001.1a-2 ceases to fall under government control, a NAFTA country may delete it from its schedule to that annex.

(17) Further Negotiations and States and Provinces

NAFTA 1024(1) commits the governments of the three NAFTA countries to commence negotiations among themselves by December 31, 1998, to liberalize further their respective government procurement markets.

NAFTA 1024(3) requires each NAFTA country to endeavour to consult with their state and provincial governments with a view to obtaining commitments that state and provincial government entities and enterprises be subject to the NAFTA Chapter Ten disciplines.

Annex 2 of the United States to the Marrakesh text of the 1994 Code lists a number of departments and agencies of state governments. Annex 2 of Canada to this text offers to cover provincial government entities on the basis of commitments obtained from provincial governments. No provincial entities are listed.

(18) Concluding Remarks

The NAFTA government procurement provisions substantially increase the range of procurements covered over that of the 1980 Code and the FTA. The major departure of NAFTA from these earlier arrangements is the inclusion of procurements of services and construction services. The Canadian government has estimated that procurements covered by NAFTA are valued at about $78 billion (US), as compared to about $20 billion (US) covered by the 1980 Code and the FTA.[46] The NAFTA government procurement provisions are also an improvement over those of the FTA because they set out a single set of provisions that apply to all covered procurements. For example, while the bid challenge procedures under the FTA applied only to procurements below the Code threshold, the NAFTA bid challenge procedures apply to all covered procurements.

9.2 COMPETITION POLICY, MONOPOLIES AND STATE ENTERPRISES

NAFTA Chapter Fifteen sets out provisions respecting competition policy, monopolies and state enterprises.

(1) Competition Policy

Market economies do not function effectively if market forces are subverted by anti-competitive conduct. Prices signal to firms the quantities and types of goods and services to produce or provide. If prices are manipulated or quantities of goods or services supplied are determined through collusion or the unilateral actions of dominant industry players or through government action, resources will not be allocated in an optimal manner and overall welfare will be adversely affected.

Anti-competitive conduct consists of a number of practices. Anti-competitive practices include: collusion among business to fix prices or otherwise agree to limit competition; predatory pricing, where a producer sells at excessively low prices to drive competitors out of business; price discrimination, where a supplier charges different prices to different customers for goods of like quantity and quality; resale price maintenance, where a supplier influences upward the price at which its distributors sells the goods supplied; and bid-rigging, where persons submitting tenders for contracts collude in the tenders submitted.[47] Also, excessive market concentration through business mergers can create a situation in which a single enterprise dominates an industry and can manipulate quantities of goods or services supplied and the prices at which they are supplied to the detriment of consumers.

Competition policy addresses anti-competitive practices in a variety of ways. Prospective market concentration is addressed by administrative review of proposed mergers over a certain size and blocking those that will have anti-competitive results. Existing situations of excessive market concentration are addressed by curbing anti-competitive practices by enterprises that dominate industries. Some anti-competitive practices are treated as criminal offences and are attacked through prosecution. Others are reviewable, and, while not illegal per se, can be blocked by remedial orders if it is established that their results are anti-competitive. Anti-competitive practices can also be addressed through granting civil actions to those that are adversely affected by them. This approach has been followed much more extensively in the United States than in Canada and, unlike Canadian competition law, U.S. law allows for treble damages in some instances.

Approaches to competition policy vary from country to country for a variety of reasons. For example, a degree of market concentration that would be untenable in a large country such as the United States may be acceptable in smaller countries such as Canada in industries in which only large enterprises can compete effectively on a global scale. Foreign competition made possible through trade liberalization has probably had the effect of lowering the risk to smaller countries of permitting higher levels of domestic market concentration.

(a) Competition law and international trade

There are linkages between competition and trade policy. Both are directed at making markets work more efficiently and both are concerned with actions that limit competition. Trade policy addresses the anti-competitive effects of government policy that increases the price of foreign goods or restricts their availability for the purpose of sheltering domestic industries from foreign competition. Competition policy addresses the anti-competitive effects of the actions of enterprises within an industry that subvert the functioning of market forces. Trade policy and competition policy address two different aspects of the same problem.

The original GATT did not address the question of anti-competitive conduct within member countries. However, the draft Havana Charter that resulted from the Havana Conference of 1947-1948 and which was to supersede the provisional GATT contained an entire chapter on restrictive business practices.[48] As discussed in §1.4(1), the ITO never came into existence with the result that the Havana Charter and its chapter on restrictive trade practices was never accepted by the GATT contracting parties.[49] In 1960, a group of experts appointed to study alternative ways of dealing with restrictive business practices recognized that such practices and the activities of international cartels could frustrate GATT objectives but concluded that insufficient consensus for a multilateral agreement on restrictive business practices existed at that time and recommended that a process of consultation be adopted.[50] The question of restrictive business practices was not covered by any of the agreements resulting from either the Tokyo Round or the Uruguay Round and was not addressed in the FTA.

In some of the practices that it sanctions, trade policy can work at cross purposes with competition policy. As discussed in §11.4(1), while dumping may be viewed as a form of predatory pricing, what constitutes dumping in trade law is very different from what constitutes predatory pricing in competition law. The functioning of internationally sanctioned antidumping laws, particularly when undertakings from foreign producers to maintain prices above certain levels are involved, is the antithesis of what competition policy is designed to achieve.

(b) Competition and antitrust laws in the NAFTA countries

(i) Canada

Canada's competition laws are set out in the *Competition Act*.[51] The *Competition Act* establishes a number of practices as *per se* offences, such as conspiracy to limit competition unduly, bid-rigging, price discrimination, predatory pricing and resale price maintenance,[52] while a number of other practices are reviewable. This legislation is administered by the Bureau of Competition Policy and applications by the Director of Investigation and Research respecting reviewable practices such as abuse of dominant position, refusal to deal, exclusive dealing, tied selling and market restriction are adjudicated by the Competition Tribunal. The legislation sets out mandatory pre-notification requirements for larger proposed mergers. The Tribunal has the power to review mergers and, in appropriate cases, to order their dissolution. The standard applied is whether the merger will substantially prevent or lessen competition.[53] Canadian legislation provides for an efficiency defence, which can apply if it can be demonstrated that the merger will result in efficiency gains that would not be obtained without the merger and that these gains offset the lessening of competition.

(ii) United States

The principal U.S. anti-trust statutes are the Sherman Act, the Clayton Act, the Robinson-Patman Act, the Hart-Scott-Rodino Antitrust Improvements Act of 1976 and the Federal Trade Commission Act. Principles of U.S. antitrust law have also evolved in the extensive case law developed over the years in the application of these statutes.[54]

The Sherman Act[55] provides for criminal sanctions against contracts, combinations or conspiracies in restraint of trade and against monopolizing or attempting to monopolize or conspiring to monopolize any part of trade, whether within the United States or with foreign countries. The Clayton Act[56] makes unlawful practices such as price discrimination,[57] tying and exclusive arrangements[58] and mergers by stock acquisition where the effect may be to lessen competition substantially or tend to create a monopoly.[59] This legislation does not provide criminal sanctions but does establish the civil remedy of treble damages for those who are injured as the result of anything forbidden in the antitrust laws, which include the Sherman Act.[60] The Robinson-Patman Act imposes criminal sanctions against price discrimination and predatory pricing.[61] The Hart-Scott-Rodino Antitrust Improvements Act of 1976[62] sets out pre-notification requirements for mergers over a certain size.

The Federal Trade Commission Act[63] establishes the Federal Trade Commission ("FTC") and empowers it to prevent "persons, partnerships and corporations" from "using unfair methods of competition in or affecting commerce and unfair or deceptive acts or practices in or affecting commerce''.[64] This legislation includes false advertising as a deceptive practice[65] and empowers the FTC to prescribe interpretative rules and general statements of policy respecting unfair or deceptive acts or practices.[66] The FTC can order hearings and issue cease and desist orders.[67] The FTC also has broad investigative powers that enable it to seize documents and compel the attendance of witnesses.[68] The power of the FTC to initiate proceedings is concurrent with that of the Antitrust Division of the U.S. Department of Justice.[69]

(iii) Mexico

Monopolies and monopolistic practices are generally prohibited in Article 28 of the Mexican Constitution. The Mexican government enacted the Federal Economic Competition Law (Ley Federal de Competencia Economica) in December 1992[70] and it came into effect in 1993. The legislation created the Comision Federal de Competencia (the Federal Competition Commission), which has the responsibility of preventing, investigating and opposing monopolistic practices and concentrations. The legislation distinguishes between absolute monopolistic practices and relative monopolistic practices. The absolute monopolistic practices, which include agreements to manipulate prices, restrain production, divide markets and collude in bids, are analogous to the *per se* offences in Canadian and U.S. law. Acts in violation of the legislative provisions respecting these practices have no legal effect and violators are subject to sanctions. Relative monopolistic practices are analogous to reviewable practices in Canadian and U.S. law in that they are not unlawful *per se* but can be restrained if they limit competition. These practices include exclusive dealer arrangements, imposing prices and other conditions on distributors[71] and suppliers, tied selling, conditions of sale restricting use of goods or services provided by third parties and refusal to deal.[72] The legislation sets out provisions respecting mergers which require pre-notification of larger transactions and empowers the Federal Competition Commission to order the dissolution of concentrations if certain conditions are found to exist.[73]

(c) Provisions of NAFTA

The provisions of NAFTA respecting competition policy are set out in NAFTA 1501.

(i) Proscribing anti-competitive conduct

NAFTA 1501(1) requires that each NAFTA country adopt or maintain measures to proscribe anti-competitive conduct and to appropriate measures respecting such conduct. The NAFTA countries recognize that such measures will enhance the fulfilment of the objectives of NAFTA. NAFTA does not define "anti-competitive conduct" and, unlike with some other areas of law such as intellectual property, does not establish any standards that must be incorporated into each NAFTA country's domestic laws. However, this NAFTA provision has been credited with having caused Mexico to enact its current competition legislation in order that it could fulfil its obligations under this NAFTA provision.[74]

(ii) Competition law enforcement

Trade liberalization and the increased foreign competition that results weakens the ability of large firms to manipulate prices and supplies of goods and services within a single country.[75] However, the problem of anti-competitive practices pursued on an international scale becomes more acute. Practices that contravene competition and anti-trust policy increasingly involve actions in more than one country. In these cases, officials responsible for enforcing competition legislation frequently require co-operation from officials in other countries to carry out their functions effectively.

Canada and the United States are party to three bilateral arrangements that provide for co-operation between the two countries in the area of competition policy.[76] These are the *Memorandum of Understanding as to Notification, Consultation and Cooperation with Respect to the Application of National Antitrust Laws*[77] (the "MOU"), the *Treaty between the Government of Canada and the Government of the United States of America on Mutual Legal Assistance in Criminal Matters*[78] (the "Mutual Legal Assistance Treaty") and the *Treaty on Extradition between the Government of Canada and the Government of the United States of America*[79] (the "Extradition Treaty"). The MOU requires notification and consultation in a number of circumstances involving enforcement actions, such as where an investigation is likely to inquire into activity carried out wholly or partly in the other country. Exchange of information between the authorities of the two countries is subject to confidentiality safeguards in each country, which have been an impediment to enforcement co-operation.[80] The Mutual Legal Assistance Treaty provides for mutual assistance in criminal matters and the language is broad enough to cover criminal antitrust or competition offences. Each country can invoke the compulsory processes in the other for gathering and taking evidence, executing searches and seizures, serving documents and so on. The scope of this treaty is confined to criminal matters and does not cover civil or administrative procedures.[81] The Extradition Treaty has been expanded to cover criminal antitrust matters punishable by imprisonment for one year or more. Canada and the United States are also party to the *OECD Recommendation on Restrictive Business Practices*, a non-binding multilateral arrangement providing for notification and consultation between governments respecting antitrust enforcement activities involving "important interests" of another country. Mexico is not party to any of these arrangements.

Under NAFTA 1501(2), the NAFTA countries recognize the importance of co-operation and co-ordination among their authorities in competition law enforcement, and they agree to co-operate on issues of competition law enforcement policy. This includes mutual legal assistance, notification, consultation, and exchange of information relating to enforcement of competition laws and policies. NAFTA 1501(2) does not set out details as to how this co-operation is to occur.

Unlike the provision of information requirements in the NAFTA provisions respecting sanitary and phytosanitary measures, standards-related measures and government procurement, the exchange of information provision in NAFTA 1501(2) is not subject to an exception for disclosure of information that would prejudice the legitimate commercial interests of particular enterprises.[82] However, NAFTA 1501(2) is subject to the general exception in NAFTA 2105 which provides that a NAFTA country will not be required to furnish or allow access to information contrary to its laws protecting personal privacy. These laws presumably include confidentiality safeguards in competition legislation.

(iii) Dispute resolution does not apply

NAFTA 1501(3) provides that a NAFTA country may not have recourse to NAFTA dispute resolution for any matter arising under NAFTA 1501.

(iv) Working Group on Trade and Competition

NAFTA 1504 provides for the establishment of a Working Group on Trade and Competition which is to report to the Free Trade Commission by January 1, 1999, on relevant issues concerning the relationship between competition laws and policies and trade in the free trade area. There are a number of issues that will be considered by the Working Group. These include: the permitted extent of information sharing among competition and antitrust authorities consistent with confidentiality safeguards, mutual assistance in civil cases, rules respecting private rights of action, elimination of export cartel exemptions for trade among the NAFTA countries and jurisdiction and extraterritorial application of competition laws.[83] This Working Group may also consider the effect of the application of antidumping laws on competition, although the primary forum for discussing possible reforms of these laws will be the Antidumping Working Group established by the NAFTA countries in their joint announcement of December 2, 1993.

(d) Concluding remarks

The fact that dispute settlement procedures do not apply to NAFTA 1501 significantly diminishes its potential effectiveness. However, in adopting NAFTA 1501 and establishing the Working Group in NAFTA 1504, the NAFTA countries clearly acknowledge the importance of the relationship between trade and competition policy trade and have laid the groundwork for the development of a more comprehensive arrangement.

(2) Monopolies and State Enterprises

Governments influence the trade in goods and services by becoming direct participants through state enterprises or by granting a monopoly over a goods or services sector to a state-owned or privately owned enterprise. Several GATT articles set out disciplines covering monopolies and state trading enterprises. FTA 2010 set out rules governing the designation of monopolies and NAFTA 1502 carries these forward with some elaboration. NAFTA 1503 sets out rules respecting state enterprises.

(a) Monopolies, state trading enterprises and the GATT

The principal GATT provisions respecting state trading enterprises and monopolies are set out in GATT Article XVII. GATT Article II:4 applies to import monopolies and an Interpretative Note to GATT Articles XI, XII, XIII, XIV and XVIII provides that "import restrictions" and "export restrictions" used in these articles include those made effective through state trading enterprises.[84]

GATT Article XVII:1 obliges each contracting party to ensure that state enterprises or enterprises to which exclusive or special privileges[85] have been granted act, in its purchases or sales involving imports or exports, in a manner consistent with the general principles of non-discriminatory treatment prescribed by the GATT for measures affecting imports and exports by private traders. The enterprises covered by GATT Article XVII include marketing boards. The exclusive privileges need not amount to a monopoly. Such enterprises must make such purchases or sales solely in accordance with commercial considerations. This obligation, which applies only to purchases and sales, has been interpreted as imposing an MFN obligation, meaning that an enterprise cannot discriminate in its purchases of goods from or its sales of goods to other countries. The MFN obligation is a flexible one in that the Interpretative Note to GATT Article XVII provides that an enterprise can charge different prices in different markets provided that these are the result of commercial considerations. GATT Article XVII:1 does not impose a national treatment obligation.[86] However, as indicated by the GATT beer decision discussed in §5.5(4), a government can violate GATT Article III:4 by mandating a parallel marketing system in which imported goods must be sold through a state enterprise, but domestic goods may also be sold through privately owned outlets. GATT Article XVII:2 provides that the obligations imposed by GATT Article XVII do not apply to purchases by government for its own use.

GATT Article II:4 addresses the question of mark-ups that can be charged by import monopolies on products listed on a contracting party's Schedule of Concessions and covered by bound tariffs. The product cannot be afforded more protection through the monopoly than that afforded by the Schedule. In other words, an import monopoly cannot apply mark-ups to imported products that protect the domestic industry more than would be the case if the products were imported by private traders subject to the bound tariff. If the product is not covered by a concession, GATT Article XVII:4(b) obliges a contracting party to provide mark-up information upon the request of another contracting party with a substantial trade in the product concerned.

One of the understandings included in GATT 1994 referred to in §1.4(1) is the *Understanding on the Interpretation of Article XVII of the General Agreement on Tariffs and Trade 1994*. This understanding imposes notification requirements on GATT member countries in respect of their state trading enterprises[87] but does not otherwise expand the scope of this GATT provision. GATT Article XVII does not apply to services.

(b) NAFTA and the designation of monopolies

The NAFTA provisions respecting the designation of monopolies are set out in NAFTA 1502. NAFTA 1502 carries forward a similar provision set out in FTA 2010, with some modification. The genesis of FTA 2010 was that the Canadian negotiators wanted a clear statement that the FTA did not prevent the designation of monopolies. This statement appears in FTA 2010(1) and is carried forward in a somewhat different form in NAFTA 1502(1). The expression "designate", which applies only to actions taken after January 1, 1994, is defined in NAFTA 1505 broadly enough to include expanding the scope of activities of existing monopolies.

It is important to keep in mind that while a NAFTA country or a state or province may designate a monopoly, the expropriation and compensation requirements of NAFTA 1110 discussed in §7.7(7) must be fully satisfied. The obligation to compensate, particularly when enforceable through the investor/state dispute settlement procedures described in §11.3, is a significant inhibiting factor to designating a monopoly in sectors in which there is any significant private sector presence involving investors of other NAFTA countries. The purpose of creating a monopoly to provide essential services such as health or automobile insurance with a view to reducing costs through the elimination of profit and the efficiencies attainable through a single payer system can be largely frustrated if existing providers must be fully compensated for their economic loss.

NAFTA 1505 defines a monopoly as an entity that in any relevant market is designated as the sole provider or purchaser of a good or service.[88] However, an entity that has been granted an exclusive intellectual property right, such as a patent, is not a monopoly for the purpose of NAFTA 1502 solely because of that grant. NAFTA 1505 defines a government monopoly as a monopoly owned or controlled through ownership interests by the federal government of a NAFTA country or by another such monopoly. Significantly, a government monopoly does not include a monopoly owned by a state or provincial government.

(i) Designation of monopolies

NAFTA 1502(2) requires that a NAFTA country designating a monopoly provide prior written notification, where possible, to other NAFTA countries whose persons' interests will be affected. The corresponding FTA provision also required consultations prior to the designation if the other country requested them.[89] The NAFTA country designating the monopoly will endeavour to introduce conditions on the operation of the monopoly that will minimize or eliminate nullification or impairment. The concept of nullification and impairment is derived from the GATT and NAFTA 2004 which is referred to in NAFTA 1502(2)(b) is discussed in §11.24(4). The requirements of NAFTA 1502 apply to any monopoly designated by a NAFTA country, including monopolies owned by provincial or state governments.

(ii) Requirements to be observed

NAFTA 1502(3) sets out requirements that must be observed by government monopolies, which, as mentioned earlier, include only those owned by federal governments that a NAFTA country maintains or designates. The expression "maintains" means designated prior to January 1, 1994 and existing on that date.[90] Therefore both existing and future federal government monopolies are included. NAFTA 1502(3) also applies to privately owned monopolies that a NAFTA country designates, regardless of which level of government designates them. As "designates" is defined to apply only to actions taken after January 1, 1994, NAFTA 1502(3) does not apply to privately owned monopolies designated prior to that date. The requirements of NAFTA 1502(3) do not apply to monopolies owned by provincial or state governments.

NAFTA 1502(3)(a) requires that monopolies covered by NAFTA 1502(3) must act in a manner not inconsistent with NAFTA obligations in exercising any regulatory or administrative authority delegated to them in connection with the monopoly good or service, such as the power to grant import and export licences, approve commercial transactions or impose quotas, fees or charges. As an example of delegated authority, licences to import and export Canadian wheat are issued by the Canadian Wheat Board.[91] There was no corresponding requirement in FTA 2010.

NAFTA 1502(3)(c) requires that any monopoly covered by NAFTA 1502(3) provide non-discriminatory treatment to investments of investors (such as, for example, a U.S. owned subsidiary operating in Mexico) and to goods and service providers of other NAFTA countries in its purchases and sales of the monopoly good or service. The expression "non-discriminating treatment" is defined in NAFTA 1505 as meaning the better of national treatment and MFN treatment as set out in relevant NAFTA piovisions. The non-discrimination requirement in FTA 2010(3)(a) included only sales, but applied to all monopolies.

NAFTA 1502(3)(d) requires that a monopoly covered by NAFTA 1502(3) not engage in anti-competitive practices in non-monopolized markets that adversely affect investments of other NAFTA countries. Examples given are discriminatory provision of the monopoly good or service (such as charging lower prices to a non-monopoly business owned by the monopoly), cross-subsidization (using profits from the monopoly operation to lower prices in a non-monopoly operation) and predatory conduct. The corresponding provision in FTA 2010(3)(b) applied to all monopolies. NAFTA 1305 requires that monopolies designated to provide public telecommunications transport networks or services not engage in anti-competitive conduct in the provision of enhanced or value-added services. Measures to prevent such anti-competitive conduct include a requirement that competitors providing these services be allowed access to the public telecommunications public network on no less favourable terms than the monoploy itself or its affiliates. Unlike NAFTA 1502(3), the scope of NAFTA 1305 extends to monopolies owned by provincial or state governments.

NAFTA 1502(3)(b) requires that monopolies covered by NAFTA 1502(3) act solely in accordance with commercial considerations in its purchases and sales of the monopoly good or service in the relevant market. This requirement is similar to that in GATT Article XVII:1(b) except that it also applies to services. However, a monopoly can deviate from this requirement to the extent necessary to comply with the terms of its designation, so long as the terms of the designation are not inconsistent with NAFTA 1502(3)(c) or (d) described earlier. GATT Article XVII:1(b) does not contain a similar qualification. There is no corresponding provision in FTA 2010.

(iii) Concluding remarks

While NAFTA 1502 is somewhat broader in its terms than FTA 2010, it is significantly narrower in one important respect, that none of its substantive provisions apply to provincially or state-owned monopolies. NAFTA 1502 affects these monopolies only in the notification requirement and the nullification and impairment requirement of NAFTA 1502(2). However, these monopolies are subject to the provisions set out in NAFTA 1503 respecting state enterprises.

(c) State enterprises

NAFTA 1503 covers state enterprises. There was no provision in the FTA comparable to NAFTA 1503. A state enterprise with respect to Canada[92] means a Crown corporation within the meaning of the *Financial Administration Act*,[93] a Crown corporation within the meaning of any comparable provincial law or an equivalent entity incorporated under a provincial law. In the other NAFTA countries, a state enterprise is an enterprise owned or controlled through ownership interests of a NAFTA country which, presumably, includes a state.[94] In Mexico, the Compania Nacional de Subsistencias Populares (National Company for Basic Commodities) is not considered a state enterprise for the purposes of sales of maize, beans and powdered milk.[95] A state enterprise is a monopoly that is also subject to the NAFTA provisions respecting monopolies described in §9.2(2)(b).

NAFTA 1503(1) provides that nothing in NAFTA prevents a NAFTA country from designating a state enterprise. NAFTA 1503(2) covers regulatory, administrative or other authority delegated to state enterprises. Such authority must be exercised in a manner that is not inconsistent with the NAFTA country's obligations under Chapter Eleven (Investment) and Chapter Fourteen (Financial Services). The comparable provision for monopolies in NAFTA 1502(3)(a) discussed in §9.1(2)(b)(ii) requires that such delegated authority be exercised in a manner not inconsistent with all NAFTA obligations. NAFTA 1503(3) requires that state enterprises accord non-discriminatory treatment in the sale of goods and services to investments of investors of other NAFTA countries. This is a narrower obligation than the non-discrimination requirement in NAFTA 1502(3)(c) that applies to monopolies and includes purchases as well as sales and goods and service providers as well as investments of investors of other NAFTA countries. This obligation prevents a provincially or state-owned hydroelectric utility from discriminating in its sales of power to its customers but does not affect the discriminatory purchasing practices of provincially or state-owned liquor monopolies.[96]

9.3 TEMPORARY ENTRY FOR BUSINESS PERSONS

NAFTA Chapter Sixteen carries forward on a trilateral basis and with some modifications the provisions of FTA Chapter Fifteen respecting the temporary entry of business persons. These provisions are intended to facilitate business travel among the NAFTA countries as a necessary complement to the NAFTA objectives of liberalizing investment laws and reducing barriers to trade in goods and services. The temporary entry provisions prevent the frustration of these objectives through the denial of entry to persons travelling to other NAFTA countries to trade in goods or provide services or carry on investment activities.

Like FTA Chapter Fifteen, NAFTA Chapter Sixteen simplifies procedures for "temporary entry", which is defined as "entry without the intent to establish permanent residence''.[97] As under the FTA, only procedures relating to temporary entry are affected. Procedures of each NAFTA country respecting applications for permanent residence or immigrant status are unaffected.

(1) Legislation Affecting Business Travel

One objective of immigration policy as applied to non-immigrants is to avoid adversely affecting employment opportunities available to a country's own citizens and permanent residents. Accordingly, persons seeking admission to a country on a temporary basis to pursue commercial activities are usually required to obtain an employment authorization or work permit before entering or at the port of entry. In many instances the employment authorization will not be granted unless the person seeking entry or his or her prospective employer goes through a process of satisfying immigration authorities that citizens or permanent residents have been given the opportunity to apply for the position. This process is referred to as "employment validation" in Canada and "labour certification" in the United States.

A business traveller may also have to satisfy visa requirements over and above the employment authorization and employment validation or labour certification requirements just described.

The following descriptions of Canadian and U.S. requirements are those that apply generally to business persons and persons seeking temporary employment. Each country modified its procedures *vis à vis* the other to fulfil its FTA obligations and each country has special arrangements respecting the temporary entry of persons from some other countries.

(a) Canadian requirements

Canadian requirements respecting temporary entry are set out in the *Immigration Regulations*[98] and in Chapter Fifteen of the *Immigration Manual* published by Employment and Immigration Canada.[99]

(i) Visa requirements

Citizens of Mexico and citizens and permanent residents of the United States are exempt from visa requirements.[100]

(ii) Employment authorization and validation

Generally, a person seeking employment in Canada who is not a Canadian citizen or permanent resident must first obtain an employment authorization from a Canadian immigration officer.[101] "Employment" is broadly defined as "any activity for which a person receives or might reasonably be expected to receive valuable consideration".[102] Employment authorizations, if required, may be issued to U.S. citizens and permanent residents at a Canadian port of entry but Mexican citizens and permanent residents must obtain employment authorizations before arriving at a port of entry.[103] An employment authorization will not be issued if the immigration officer is of the opinion that employment opportunities for Canadian citizens or permanent residents would be adversely affected.[104] One factor to be taken into account in forming the opinion is whether a prospective employer has made reasonable efforts to train Canadian citizens or permanent residents for the position.[105]

In order to establish that the employment authorization criteria are satisfied, an employment validation must usually be obtained by a prospective employer. An employment validation will be issued only if it is determined that the admission of the foreign worker will not adversely affect domestic employment opportunities.[106] This determination and the "validation" of the job offer is made through the Canada Employment Centre where the vacancy is located.

(iii) Exemptions from employment authorization

The regulations exempt a number of categories of employment from employment authorization requirements. These include diplomats, consular officers, clergymen, performing artists, crews of foreign ships, employees of foreign news companies covering Canadian events, persons representing businesses outside Canada buying Canadian goods or services for that business or selling goods for that business to purchasers other than the general public, permanent employees of organizations outside Canada consulting with their Canadian colleagues, persons rendering emergency services, certain persons in sports-related situations and competitions, guest speakers, external thesis examiners, expert witnesses and certain other categories of entrant.[107] The exemption from employment authorization requirements means that employment validation is also not required for these categories.

(iv) Exemption from employment validation

Some categories of entrant subject to employment authorizations are exempt from the validation requirements.[108] These include some specific categories such as emergency repair personnel and entertainers and certain classes of scientists and trainers.[109] Persons entering pursuant to international agreements are exempt from validation requirements.[110] Persons whose employment is related to approved research, educational or training programs are exempt from employment validation requirements.[111]

An employment validation will not be required where the purpose of an entry is to establish a business which will employ or train Canadian citizens or permanent residents or where significant benefits will result to Canada.[112] This category includes self-employed persons coming to Canada to temporarily establish a business employing Canadian citizens or permanent residents[113] and persons entering Canada to install or service specialized machinery purchased or leased outside Canada.[114] A senior executive or manager who is transferred to Canada by a company to work at a senior position at a "permanent or continuing establishment" of the company or a related entity must obtain an employment authorization but is exempt from the validation requirement under this category.[115]

(v) Other requirements

Business visitors must comply with Canadian security and health protection regulations. Entry may be denied for health reasons or where national security or the welfare of Canadians is threatened.[116]

(b) U.S. requirements

U.S. immigration law defines an "alien" as anyone who is not a U.S. citizen or national.[117] Section 101(a)(15) of the Immigration and Nationality Act sets out various classes of non-immigrant aliens and defines as immigrants all aliens not falling within one of the non-immigrant classes.[118] U.S. law respecting temporary entry is comprised of the statutory and regulatory requirements respecting the entry of these classes of non-immigrants.[119] Each class carries with it throughout the regulations a designation corresponding to the letter of the clause in s. 101(a)(15) in which it is defined. For example, s. 101(a)(15)(B) defines as a class aliens entering the United States temporarily for business or pleasure. The regulations setting out the requirements for entry refer to these entrants as "B-1 visitors for business" and "B-2 visitors for pleasure"[120] and if a visa is required the visa will be a "B-1" or "B-2" visa.[121] The non-immigrant classes most relevant for business travellers are the temporary visitors for business class just discussed (B-1), treaty traders and treaty investors (E), temporary workers (H), intra-company transferees (L) and individuals with extraordinary ability (O).[122]

(i) Visa requirements

Canadian nationals except those in the treaty trader and treaty investor class (E) are exempt from visa requirements.[123] There are limited exceptions for Mexican nationals. A Mexican national possessing a border crossing identification card and applying for entry as a temporary entry for business or pleasure is exempt from visa requirements.[124]

(ii) Petitions and labour certification

The terminology in U.S immigration law is somewhat different from that in Canada. In the U.S. immigration laws and regulations, a petition is an application made by a prospective employer or other relevant organization for the entry of a non-immigrant into the United States. A petition that has been approved by the Immigration and Naturalization Service has the same effect as an employment authorization in Canada. Petitions for some categories must be accompanied by a labour certification issued by the Secretary of Labour. The content of the labour certification depends on the statutory or regulatory requirements applicable to the category in question. For example, a labour certification for non-agricultural temporary workers must state that qualified workers are not available and that the alien's employment will not adversely affect wages and working conditions of similarly employed U.S. workers. Labour certification is the rough equivalent of employment validation in Canada.

(iii) Temporary business visitors (B-1)

A temporary business or B-1 visitor is described in the visa requirements for this class as a person engaged in attending conventions, conferences, consultations and other legitimate commercial or professional activities but not in local employment or labour for hire.[125] For the visa to be issued, the person must intend to leave the United States and have permission to enter a foreign country at the end of the temporary stay and adequate financial arrangements must have been made to enable the person to carry out the purpose of the visit and leave the United States.[126] B-1 visitors may be admitted for up to one year and be granted six-month extensions.[127] Neither a petition nor a labour certification is required.

(iv) Traders and investors (E)

A trader or investor is described in s. 101(a)(15)(E) of the Immigration and Nationality Act as an alien entitled to enter under a treaty of commerce and navigation between the United States and the country of which he or she is a national. The purpose of the entry must be solely to carry on substantial trade,[128] principally between the United States and that country, or to develop and direct the operations of an enterprise in which the alien has invested or is investing a substantial amount of capital. These persons may be admitted for an initial period of one year and granted extensions in increments of not more than two years.[129] No petition or labour certification requirements are prescribed.

(v) Temporary workers (H)

Section 101(a)(15)(H) of the Immigration and Nationality Act divides temporary workers into three broad categories: (i) those of distinguished merit and ability (H-1); (ii) temporary workers who perform services in jobs of a non-permanent character for which qualified American workers are not available (H-2); and (iii) non-resident trainees who are in the United States for the purpose of training and not for the permanent staffing of a U.S. company (H-3).[130] For a worker to enter the United States as a temporary worker under any of these categories, the employer must file a petition with the United States Immigration and Naturalization Service.[131] Other specialized documents are required depending on the applicable subcategory. Approved H petitions are valid for a variety of periods, depending on the category.[132]

Category H-1 is broken down into registered nurses (H-1A)[133] and persons in specialty occupations (H-1B). Specialty occupations normally involve a baccalaureate or higher degree or its equivalent although there are a number of ways of qualifying.[134] A petition for an H-1B applicant must be supported by evidence that the person qualifies to perform services in the specialty occupation. The petition must be accompanied by a labour condition application showing that prevailing wage, notice and other conditions have been met.[135] Aliens classified as H1-B non-immigrants excluding those involved in Department of Defense research projects, may not exceed 65,000 in a year, and those involved in such projects may not exceed 100.[136]

Category H-2 is broken down into agricultural workers (H-2A) and non-agricultural workers (H-2B). Petitioners for H-2A agricultural workers must establish that employment is of a temporary or seasonal nature and labour certification is required.[137] The labour certification process determines whether the employment is open to U.S. workers, whether such workers are available and the adverse impact of employment of a qualified alien.[138] Petitioners for H-2B non-agricultural workers must establish that the temporary worker is not displacing U.S. workers and that the employment of the temporary worker will not adversely affect the wages and working conditions of U.S. workers.[139] A labour certification substantiating these requirements is required. If this cannot be obtained, the petitioner may file countervailing evidence to the effect that U.S. workers are not available, and this evidence will be considered.[140] Aliens classified as H-1B non-immigrants may not exceed 66,000 in a year.[141]

An H-3 trainee is a non-immigrant seeking to enter the United States to receive training in any field of endeavour, excluding physicians.[142] The petitioner must demonstrate that the proposed training is not available in the alien's home country, that the beneficiary will not be placed in a position which is in the normal operation of the business and in which U.S. citizens or residents are normally employed and that the beneficiary will not engage in productive employment other than that incidental to the training. The petition must be supported by a statement including a number of matters such as a description of the training and reasons why the training is not available in the home country.[143] No labour certification is required.

(vi) Intracompany transferees (L)

An intracompany transferee is described in s. 101(a)(15)(L) of the Immigration and Nationality Act as an alien who has been employed continuously for at least one year within the preceding three years by the same firm or an affiliate and who seeks to enter the United States to work with the same or a related employer in a managerial or executive capacity or one involving specialized knowledge.[144] A petition prepared by the employer must be submitted to the applicable local immigration service office with a statement describing the applicant's employment capacity both abroad and in the United States.[145] Labour certification tests are not required. Generally, the maximum duration is five years for persons in a specialized knowledge capacity and seven years for persons in a managerial or executive capacity.[146]

(vii) Persons with extraordinary ability

This classification covers persons who have extraordinary ability in the sciences, arts, education, business or athletics that is demonstrated by national or international acclaim and who are coming to the United States to continue work in the area of achievement.[147] A petition must be filed establishing the extraordinary ability or achievement of the person and that the work in the United States is in that area.[148] The regulations prescribe the standards that must be achieved[149] and require that the position requires the services of a person with extraordinary ability or achievement.[150] The petitioner must obtain and file an advisory opinion from a peer group or a labour or management organization with expertise in the field.[151] The maximum period for approved petitions under this category is three years.[152]

(c) Mexican requirements

The Mexican provisions respecting temporary entry are set out in the General Demography Law (*Ley General de Poblacion''*) 1974, as amended. Like Canadian and American immigration law, Mexican immigration distinguishes between immigrants and non-immigrants and sets out nine different categories of non-immigrants. The most commonly used categories for business travel are the Visitor or *Visitante* category,[153] the Members of a Board of Directors category[154] and the Distinguished Visitors category.[155]

The Visitor category is broken down into several subcategories. In each case, application is made from any Mexican Consul abroad. With the Visitors Entering Mexico Authorized to Engage in Lucrative or Non-Lucrative Activities category, no petition or approval from the Mexican Immigration Department in Mexico City is required.[156] With the Visitors Entering Mexico to Engage in Scientific, Technical, Artistic, Sporting, or Similar Activities category, the applicant must present evidence explaining the purpose of the trip and a letter from the Mexican company requesting his or her services.[157]

As the name suggests, a person to whom entry is authorized under the Members of the Board of Directors category may enter for the purpose of attending directors or shareholder meetings. The Distinguished Visitors category provides for the issuance of permits to researchers, scientists, journalists and other prominent individuals.[158]

(2) NAFTA Temporary Entry Provisions — General

Like the FTA, NAFTA simplifies procedures for temporary entry by prohibiting employment validation or labour certification requirements for all categories of "business persons" covered by NAFTA and by prohibiting employment authorization requirements in respect of the "business visitor" category discussed in §9.3(3)(b)(i).

In NAFTA 1601 and NAFTA 1602, the NAFTA countries recognize the desirability of facilitating temporary entry and agree that all measures governing temporary entry of business persons be applied and enforced expeditiously to avoid undue interference with trade and investment activities under NAFTA. NAFTA 1603(1) requires each NAFTA country to grant temporary entry to "business persons" who otherwise qualify for entry under the immigration regulations respecting public health, safety and national security standards in accordance with the provisions of NAFTA Chapter Sixteen. A "business person" is defined in NAFTA 1608 as a "citizen of a Party who is engaged in trade in goods, the provision of services or the conduct of investment activities".[159] The categories of business person and the basis upon which temporary entry will be granted to each category are set out in NAFTA Annex 1603. As under FTA 1502(5), NAFTA 1603(4) limits fees for processing applications for temporary entry to the approximate cost of the services rendered.

NAFTA 1603(2) provides that a NAFTA country may refuse to issue an immigration document authorizing employment to a business person where the temporary entry of the person might adversely affect the settlement of a labour dispute at the intended place of employment or the employment of any person involved in the dispute. While there was no corresponding provision in the FTA, NAFTA 1603(2) closely resembles an existing provision in the Canadian *Immigration Regulations*.[160] NAFTA 1603(3) requires that if a NAFTA country refuses entry on this basis, it must provide written reasons for the refusal to the person to whom entry is refused and the NAFTA country of that person.

Throughout NAFTA Chapter Sixteen the expression "existing" as between Canada and the United States means existing on January 1, 1989, and as between Mexico and each of Canada and the United States means existing on January 1, 1994.[161] The expression "existing" is used in conjunction with various immigration laws and regulations maintained by the NAFTA countries. The effect is to freeze these measures as they were at the dates specified.

(3) Categories of Business Persons

NAFTA Annex 1603 creates the same four general categories of business persons as FTA Annex 1502.1, namely, business visitors, professionals, traders and investors and intra-company transferees. However, NAFTA Annex 1603 is formatted differently from FTA Annex 1502.1 in that rather than setting out country-specific requirements for each category, NAFTA Annex 1603 sets out non-country specific standards.

(a) Requirements common to all categories

(i) No prior approval procedures or numerical restrictions

A NAFTA country may not impose prior approval procedures, petitions, labour certification tests or other procedures of similar effect (such as Canadian employment validation procedures) with respect to any of the categories of business persons described in NAFTA Annex 1603.[162] These requirements are to be distinguished from employment authorizations or work permits that are prohibited with respect to the "business visitor" category but are permitted with respect to the other categories. Numerical restrictions are also prohibited with respect to all categories,[163] subject to certain numerical limitations permitted as between the United States and Mexico respecting professionals described in §9.3(3)(b)(iv).

(ii) Visa requirements

A NAFTA country may impose a requirement that a business person seeking temporary entry obtain a visa. Except in the case of the "traders and investors" category a NAFTA country must, before imposing a visa requirement, consult with other NAFTA countries whose business persons will be affected and, respecting existing visa requirements, consult upon request with a view to removing same.[164]

(iii) Compliance with existing measures

Business persons in all categories must comply with a NAFTA country's existing immigration measures applicable to temporary entry except as modified by NAFTA Chapter Sixteen. The expression "existing" has the meaning described in §9.3(2).

(b) Description of the categories and specific requirements

(i) Business visitors

The "business visitor" category described in Section A of NAFTA Annex 1603 is a catch-all category that includes most business travellers. The category is broken down into those business visitors engaged in business activities set out in NAFTA Appendix 1603.A.1 and those not engaged in those business activities. Appendix 1603.A.1, which closely follows its counterpart in Schedule 1 to FTA Annex 1502.1, sets out seven types of activities: research and design; growth, manufacture and production; marketing; sales; distribution; after-sales service; and general service.[165] The listed activities involving land transportation include limitations directed at cabotage.[166]

A NAFTA country may not require that a person falling within the business visitor category, regardless of whether the business activity is listed, obtain an employment authorization.[167]

Business visitors engaged in business activities listed in Appendix 1603.A.1 must provide proof of Canadian, American or Mexican citizenship and documentation demonstrating that the business person will be engaged in the listed activity and describing the purpose of the entry. The person must also demonstrate that he or she is not seeking to enter the local labour market. This requirement will be satisfied if the primary source of remuneration for the activity, the principal place of business and the place that profits predominantly accrue is outside the NAFTA country being entered.[168]

Business visitors engaged in activities not listed in Appendix 1603.A.1 are not subject to these requirements. Such persons must be granted temporary entry on terms no less favourable than those set out in measures specified for each country that, in the case of Canada and the United States *vis à vis* each other, existed on January 1, 1989, and in the case of Mexico *vis à vis* the other two NAFTA countries existed on January 1, 1994. The effect for business visitors in this category is to preserve the status quo as between Canada and the United States as it existed when the FTA became effective and as between Mexico and the other two NAFTA countries as it existed when NAFTA became effective.

(ii) Traders and investors

The "traders and investors" category is described in Section B of NAFTA Annex 1603. This category is similar to the U.S. trader and investor class of non-immigrant described in §9.3(1)(b)(iv). Traders and investors are business persons seeking entry to carry on "substantial" trade in goods or services between the NAFTA country of which the business person is a citizen and the NAFTA country into which temporary entry is sought or to establish, develop, administer or provide advice or key technical service to which the business person or his or her enterprise has committed or is committing significant capital. A business person in this category must act in a capacity that is supervisory or executive or that provides specialized skills.[169] As "substantial" is not defined, its interpretation will depend on administrative discretion.

(iii) Intra-company employees

The "intra-company employee" category is described in Section C of NAFTA Annex 1603. An intra-company employee is a person employed by an enterprise who seeks to render services to that enterprise or a subsidiary or affiliate that are managerial or involve specialized knowledge. To accommodate U.S. requirements respecting its intra-company transferee class of non-immigrant described in §9.3(1)(b)(vi), a NAFTA country may require the person to have been employed continuously for a one-year period within the three-year period immediately preceding the application.[170]

(iv) Professionals

The "professional" category is described in Section D of NAFTA Annex 1603. The professions covered are listed in NAFTA Appendix 1603.D.1. This list is more extensive than its counterpart in Schedule 2 to FTA Annex 1502.1 and is more specific in that it identifies the minimum educational requirements and alternative credentials necessary to qualify for the profession. A person seeking temporary entry under this category must present proof of citizenship and documentation establishing that the person will be engaged in business activity in the listed profession and describing the purpose of the entry. The United States may maintain a numerical limit of 5,500 entries annually from Mexico under the professional category. These limits do not include renewals of temporary entry periods or a spouse or children accompanying the business person or certain other entries of professionals covered by U.S. legislation, including the H1-B category which is subject to the numerical limitation described in §9.3(1)(b)(v).[171] The United States will consider increasing the limits each year and the requirement must be terminated by January 1, 2004.[172]

(4) Provision of Information

NAFTA 1604 requires each NAFTA country to provide the other NAFTA countries with materials that will enable them to become acquainted with its measures relating to NAFTA Chapter Sixteen.[173] By January 1, 1995, each NAFTA country must publish and make available explanatory material in a consolidated form that will explain its temporary entry requirements in a manner that will enable business persons in other NAFTA countries to become familiar with them.

The NAFTA countries must collect, maintain and make available to other NAFTA countries, in accordance with domestic law, data respecting temporary entry granted under NAFTA Chapter Sixteen.[174] Domestic law would include domestic confidentiality requirements. This obligation does not apply to Mexico until January 1, 1995.[175]

(5) Establishment of Working Group

NAFTA 1605 provides for the establishment of a Temporary Entry Working Group which will meet at least annually to consider various issues relating to the operation of NAFTA Chapter Sixteen, including the waiving of labour certification tests or procedures of similar effect for spouses of business persons who have been granted temporary entry for more than one year under any of the categories of business persons described above.[176]

(6) Dispute Settlement

NAFTA 1606 carries forward limitations on initiation of the dispute settlement procedures with respect to matters arising under NAFTA Chapter Sixteen similar to those that were set out in FTA 1504. The matter must involve a pattern of practice and the business person must have exhausted available administrative remedies. These will be deemed to have been exhausted if a final determination has not been issued within one year after the institution of the proceeding so long as the delay is not attributable to the business person.

(7) Concluding Remarks

The NAFTA temporary entry provisions, like their FTA counterparts, complement the general NAFTA objectives of liberalizing trade and investment measures as among the NAFTA countries. However, the limited scope of the NAFTA temporary entry measures underscore the fact that the NAFTA countries have no intention of creating a common market along the lines of the European Union. Just as the NAFTA trade-in-goods provisions do not result in the free movement of goods, the NAFTA temporary entry provisions are clearly not intended to result in the free movement of people among the NAFTA countries.

9.4   INTELLECTUAL PROPERTY

Until recently, international agreements for the protection of intellectual property rights have been negotiated independently from trade agreements. GATT references to intellectual property rights arise in the context of exceptions to GATT obligations. For example, the exception in GATT Article XX(d)[177] for the enforcement of laws includes laws for the protection of patents, trademarks and copyrights. However, with the exception of certain geographical indications,[178] the GATT does not impose obligations on GATT members to protect intellectual property rights. Similarly, the FTA dealt minimally with intellectual property rights. As discussed in §10.1(3)(b)(iii), FTA 2006 dealt with retransmission rights to resolve an irritant between Canada and the United States that existed at that time. Aside from this, the FTA imposed no substantive obligations on either Canada or the United States respecting intellectual property rights. However, Canada and the United States agreed in FTA 2004 to co-operate in the Uruguay Round to improve protection of intellectual property.

There are clear linkages between the trade and investment liberalization objectives of NAFTA and laws protecting intellectual property rights. Cross-border investment will be inhibited if the laws of a host country do not adequately protect the intellectual property that investors from other countries bring with them or develop within the host country. The value of intellectual property rights can be destroyed by goods imported from countries that do not recognize or adequately enforce proprietary interests in intellectual property. Yet over-zealous enforcement of intellectual property rights at the border can inhibit trade and put importers at a significant disadvantage to their domestic counterparts. Also, intellectual property rights are inherently trade restrictive in that they confer rights that permit the holder to prevent other people from using the subject-matter of the right.

The need for co-operation among countries in the area of intellectual property rights has long been recognized and there are major international agreements and international organizations covering various aspects of intellectual property. However, NAFTA and the *Agreement on Trade-Related Aspects of Intellectual Property Rights* (the "TRIPS Agreement") are the first international agreements addressing intellectual property rights in the context of a trade agreement. The TRIPS Agreement, which will become effective at the same time as the other Uruguay Round agreements, was negotiated prior to NAFTA and the NAFTA intellectual property provisions are largely based on it. NAFTA and the TRIPS Agreement build on existing international agreements by requiring that effect be given to their provisions and both agreements establish their own standards in respect of the various categories of intellectual property. NAFTA and the TRIPS Agreement are precedent-setting in that failure to accord the agreed standard of protection, whether by failing to meet a NAFTA or TRIPS standard or failing to give effect to one of the enumerated international agreements, will be subject to the NAFTA or WTO dispute settlement procedures, depending on which agreement is invoked.

(1) Standards and Reciprocity

Application of the national treatment and MFN treatment non-discrimination principles are not sufficient to ensure adequate protection of intellectual property rights. A country providing the same minimal protection of intellectual property rights to its own nationals as to foreigners would be acting consistently with the national treatment principle. None the less, producers in that country could appropriate intellectual property rights held by foreigners and seriously undermine the value of those rights. To be effective, an agreement respecting intellectual property rights must go beyond establishing basic non-discrimination obligations and prescribe minimum standards of protection of intellectual property rights that each country must provide.

Reciprocity or mutual recognition is an important principle in the international treatment of intellectual property rights. A country can agree to extend the protection of its intellectual property laws to intellectual property created in other countries in exchange for similar treatment in those other countries. A country can also agree, in exchange for similar treatment, to recognize the intellectual property right of a foreign national over a competing domestic claim when the foreign claim for protection was made after the domestic claim in that country but at a prior time in the foreign country.

(2) International Intellectual Property Conventions and Organizations

The two major international intellectual property conventions are the *Paris Convention for the Protection of Industrial Property, 1967* (the "Paris Convention") and the *Berne Convention for the Protection of Literary and Artistic Works, 1971* (the "Berne Convention").[179] There are a number of other international conventions covering specialized areas of intellectual property. The conventions referred to in NAFTA and the TRIPS Agreement are the Paris Convention, the Berne Convention, the *Geneva Convention for the Producers of Phonograms Against Unauthorized Duplication of their Phonograms, 1971* (the "Geneva Convention"),[180] the *International Convention for the Protection of Performers, Producers of Phonograms and Broadcasting Organizations* (1961) (the "Rome Convention"), the *International Convention for the Protection of New Varieties of Plants, 1978* (the "UPOV Convention, 1978"), the *International Convention for the Protection of New Varieties of Plants, 1991* (the "UPOV Convention, 1991") and the *Treaty on Intellectual Property in Respect of Integrated Circuits* opened for signature on May 26, 1989 (the "Integrated Circuits Treaty"). The principal international organization dealing with intellectual property is the World Intellectual Property Organization ("WIPO").

(a) The Paris Convention

The original version of the Paris Convention was signed in 1883 and entered into force in 1884.[181] Prior to that time, the only international protection of intellectual property rights was through bilateral agreements.[182] The Paris Convention was revised in 1900, 1911, 1925, 1934, 1958 and 1967. The Paris Convention covers patents, utility models, industrial designs, trade marks, service marks, trade names, indications of source or appellations of origin, and the repression of unfair competition. The member countries of the Paris Convention constitute a Union. Article 2 provides that nationals of any country in the Union enjoy the benefits of the laws protecting intellectual property of any other country in the Union. Article 4 of the Paris Convention provides that a person who files an application for a patent, utility model, industrial design or trade mark in one Union country will have a right or priority for twelve months for patents and utility models and six months for industrial designs and trade marks for filing in other Union countries. Articles 4 and 5 cover various aspects of patents, including a provision for compulsory licensing to prevent the abuses of the exclusive rights conferred on the patent holder, such as the failure to work the patent.[183] Article 5quinquies requires that industrial designs be protected in all Union countries. Articles 6 to 9 cover various aspects of trade marks. For example, Article 6bis requires countries of the Union, where confusion is likely, to refuse or cancel the registration and prohibit the use of a trade mark which is a reproduction, imitation or translation of a trade mark that is already the trade mark of a person entitled to the benefits of the convention and that is well known. Article 6quinquies provides that a trade mark registered in its country of origin shall be accepted for filing in other countries of the Union subject to certain reservations. Article 9 provides for the seizure of goods unlawfully bearing a trade mark that is entitled to legal protection in the importing country. The Paris Convention establishes an institutional structure in the form of an Assembly.[184] However, disputes are resolved through recourse to the International Court of Justice.[185]

As of January 1, 1994, the United States and Mexico were parties to the 1967 level of the Paris Convention. Canada was a party to the 1934 level of the Paris Convention and had agreed to be bound by Articles 13 to 30 of the 1967 level.

(b) Berne Convention

The Berne Convention was originally signed in 1886 and was revised in 1908, 1928, 1948, 1967 and 1971. The Berne Convention covers "literary and artistic works", which are broadly defined to include books and various other written works; musical composition; cinematographic works; works of drawing, painting, architecture, sculpture, engraving and lithography; photographic works; works of applied art; and illustrations, maps, plans, sketches and three dimensional works relative to geography, topography, architecture and science.[186] These works are to be protected in all countries in the Union created by the Berne Convention and the protection operates to the benefit of the "author" of the work and his successors. Protection in the country of origin of a work[187] is governed by domestic law. However, authors who are not nationals of the country but entitled to the protection of the Berne Convention receive the same protection as national authors. The protection accorded by the Convention operates independently of protection of a work in its country of origin and, unlike the Paris Convention, the enjoyment and exercise of the rights is not subject to any formality.[188] Member countries can provide greater protection than that required by the Convention[189] and governments of Union countries can enter into special arrangements providing for greater protection.[190]

The basic protection required by the Berne Convention lasts for the life of the author and fifty years after the author's death.[191] Authors have the exclusive right of making and authorizing translations and authorizing reproductions of their works,[192] the public performance of their works,[193] the broadcasting or other public communication of their works,[194] the adaptations, arrangements or other alterations of their works.[195] Authors have the exclusive right of authorizing cinematographic adaptation and reproduction of their works.[196] However, without prejudice to the copyright in adapted works, cinematographic works are protected as original works.[197] The Convention sets out provisions respecting quotations and reproduction of articles by the media.[198] It is sufficient that an author's name appear on a work for the author to be entitled to commence infringement proceedings.[199] Infringing copies of works are liable to seizure.[200]

The Appendix to the Berne Convention makes certain exceptions for developing countries. These include substituting the exclusive rights respecting the translation and reproduction of works with systems of non-exclusive and non-transferable licences granted under prescribed conditions and subject to certain limitations.[201]

Like the Paris Convention, the Berne Convention establishes an institutional structure comprised of an Assembly[202] but provides for the resolution of disputes through the International Court of Justice.[203] The United States became a party to the 1971 level of the Berne Convention on March 1, 1989.[204] As of January 1, 1994, Canada was a member of the 1928 level of the Berne Convention and had agreed to be bound by Aritcles 22 to 38 of the 1967 level. As of that date, Mexico was a member of the 1967 level.

(c) Geneva Convention and the Rome Convention

The Geneva Convention was created at Geneva on October 29, 1971, and applies to producers of phonograms. A phonogram is an "exclusively aural fixation of sounds of a performance or of other sounds",[205] such as a record, a cassette tape or a compact disc, and the producer is the person or legal entity who first fixes the sounds. Copyright in phonograms or sound recordings exists independently from the copyright in the work that is recorded. While the producer of a sound recording needs the authorization of the holder of the copyright in the work being recorded, the producer will hold an independent copyright in the resulting sound recording.[206]

The Convention obliges contracting states to protect producers of phonograms who are nationals of other contracting states against making duplicates of phonograms without consent for distribution to the public or importing duplicates for such distribution.[207] If domestic law specifies the duration of protection, that duration must be at least twenty years from the end of the year in which the sounds were first fixed or the phonogram was first published.[208] The Convention limits the formalities which must be complied with to claim protection[209] and permits compulsory licensing only if certain conditions are met.[210] The Convention does not provide for any institutional structure and is silent on the subject of dispute resolution. The United States became a party to this Convention on March 10, 1974,[211] and Mexico became a party on December 21, 1973.[212] Canada is also a party to this convention.

The Geneva Convention by its terms is not to derogate from the protections accorded by other international agreements, including the Rome Convention.[213] The Rome Convention was adopted in 1961 and became effective on May 18, 1964. The Rome Convention provides protection to performers and broadcasting organizations as well as to producers of phonograms. As of the time of writing, Mexico was a party to the Rome Convention, but Canada and the United States were not.

(d) The UPOV Convention (1978) and the UPOV Convention (1991)

The original UPOV Convention was created as of 1961 and was revised in 1972, 1978 and 1991. The NAFTA text makes reference to both the UPOV Convention (1978) and the UPOV Convention (1991). These two levels of this Convention provide for the same basic rights, but there are a number of differences in detail. As with the other intellectual property conventions, the members of the UPOV Convention (1978) and the UPOV Convention (1991) constitute a Union.

The purpose of both Conventions is to protect the rights of breeders in new varieties of plants. Each Convention sets out a national treatment provision that requires that nationals and legal persons resident or having their offices registered in one member state enjoy the same rights as accorded by other member states to their own nationals.[214] The UPOV Convention (1978) applies to specified botanical genera[215] and species while the UPOV Convention (1991) applies to all genera and species.[216] In order to be entitled to protection, the variety must be new, distinguishable (1978) or distinct (1991), homogeneous (1978) or uniform (1991) and stable.[217] The right of the breeder is that certain acts in respect of a protected variety require the breeder's consent. Under the UPOV Convention (1978), these are production for purposes of commercial marketing, the offering for sale and the marketing.[218] The UPOV Convention (1991) include the further acts of conditioning for the purposes of propagation, exporting, importing and stocking.[219] Rights are applied for and a breeder who duly files in one member country has a right of priority of twelve months for filing in other member countries.[220] The minimum period of protection under the UPOV Convention (1978) is fifteen years[221] and under the UPOV Convention (1991) is twenty-five years for trees and vines and twenty years for other plants.[222] Each Convention creates an institutional structure comprised of a Council[223] but is silent on the subject of dispute resolution.

Canada signed the UPOV Convention (1978) in 1978 and ratified it in 1991.

The United States is a party to the UPOV Convention (1978). At the time of writing, Mexico was not a party to either the 1978 or the 1991 level of this Convention.

(e) Integrated Circuits Treaty

The Integrated Circuits Treaty was adopted in Washington on May 26, 1989, by a conference convened by WIPO.[224] The treaty was regarded as necessary because of the perception that layout designs of integrated circuits are not protected by patent or copyright law.[225] Article 2 of the treaty sets out definitions, including a technical definition of "integrated circuit" and "layout design (topography)". Article 3 sets out the basic obligation of each member country to provide intellectual property protection to layout designs within its territory. The layout design must be original (*i.e.*, the work of the creator's own intellectual effort) and not commonplace. Article 5 sets out national treatment obligation that extends to the persons described in §9.4(5)(a)(v).

Article 6(1) requires member countries to consider as unlawful reproducing, importing, selling or otherwise distributing protected layout designs without the authorization of the holder of the right.[226] Article 6(3) permits compulsory licensing under certain circumstances. Article 6(4) provides that member countries are not obliged to consider innocent infringement as unlawful. Article 7 provides that member countries do not have to protect a layout design until it has been commercially exploited and member countries may require registration.[227] Article 8 requires that protection last at least eight years. Article 12 provides that obligations under the Berne Convention and the Paris Convention are not affected by the treaty and Article 16(3) provides that member countries do not have to extend the treaty protection to layout designs existing when the treaty became effective.

As under other intellectual property conventions, the member countries comprise a Union[228] with an institutional structure consisting of an Assembly.[229] Disputes are settled through consultations and a panel process.[230]

(f) World Intellectual Property Organization

There are a number of international organizations that deal with the subject of intellectual property. Each of the international agreements just described has its own institutional structure. The principal international organization dealing with intellectual property matters is the World Intellectual Property Organization. WIPO, which is headquartered in Geneva, is a specialized agency of the United Nations that was established by a convention signed in 1967 that entered into force in 1970.[231] The objectives of WIPO are "to promote the protection of intellectual property throughout the world" and to "ensure administrative cooperation among the Unions".

WIPO has been criticized as having been an ineffective vehicle for improving international standards of intellectual property protection and for providing effective enforcement of standards.[232] These perceived deficiencies in the international intellectual property system were the main impetus to negotiating and concluding both the TRIPS Agreement and NAFTA Chapter Seventeen.

(3) Intellectual Property Rights in a Trade Context

The United States tabled a draft counterfeiting code towards the end of the Tokyo Round of GATT negotiations, but this code was not included in the final codes emerging from the Tokyo Round in 1979.[233] The impetus for including provisions for the protection of intellectual property rights in the Uruguay Round negotiations came largely from the private sector in the major developed countries.[234] The standards in the existing intellectual property conventions were seen as deficient and enforcement as ineffectual. By bringing the protection of intellectual property rights within the context of the GATT, disciplines would apply to more countries than ever before and enforcement of intellectual property rights could be linked to market access.

The proponents of a GATT agreement protecting intellectual property rights had three major objectives. First, the agreement would establish minimum standards of intellectual property protection based on the principles set out in the major international conventions and would require each member to provide effective remedies to enforce these standards domestically. Minimum standards coupled with effective domestic remedies would protect the holder of an intellectual property right within a country. Second, the agreement would require effective enforcement of intellectual property rights at the border, so that an intellectual property right holder could be protected from infringing imported products. Third, the disputes under the agreement would be resolved through improved GATT dispute settlement procedures with trade-related sanctions which would give member countries effective recourse against other member countries that failed to adhere to the obligations imposed by the agreement.[235]

Developing countries had a very different view of the priority that should be placed upon the protection of intellectual property rights in a trade context. There was a general perception in many developing countries that intellectual property rights were instruments that developed countries used to maintain economic control and that negotiations over intellectual property rights should be conducted through the WIPO and not the GATT.[236] However, the view of the developed countries prevailed and the objectives described previously were achieved in the TRIPS Agreement. In the Uruguay Round, Canada supported the concept of a GATT agreement protecting intellectual property rights but the Canadian approach differed in some respects from that of the United States. U.S. application of proceedings under Section 337 of the Tariff Act of 1930 against infringing imports had caused several disputes between the two countries and Canadian patent laws as applied to pharmaceutical products had been a point of contention between the two countries.

The objectives described earlier respecting the Uruguay Round were also the principal factors shaping the negotiation of NAFTA Chapter Seventeen.

(4) NAFTA and the TRIPS Agreement

The NAFTA intellectual property provisions resemble the NAFTA provisions on technical barriers to trade and sanitary and phytosanitary measures in that, like the 1994 GATT Technical Barriers Code and the GATT Sanitary and Phytosanitary Measures Agreement, the TRIPS Agreement establishes a parallel set of obligations dealing with the same subject-matter in a somewhat different manner.

As with these other Uruguay Round agreements, the considerations discussed in §1.6(6)(b) apply as between NAFTA Chapter Seventeen and the TRIPS Agreement. NAFTA makes no reference to the TRIPS Agreement or its relationship to NAFTA Chapter Seventeen. The MFN provisions in Article 4 of the TRIPS Agreement, which have no counterpart in NAFTA, exempt international agreements that entered into force before the WTO Agreement. The TRIPS Agreement does not contain any other general provisions that clarify its relationship with NAFTA Chapter Seventeen. However, the provisions in both NAFTA Chapter Seventeen and the TRIPS Agreement that more extensive protection of intellectual property rights than required may be provided so long as they are not inconsistent with the obligations imposed by the relevant agreement could be construed as meaning that the agreement requiring the higher standard is the one to be applied.[237]

NAFTA 1721 defines intellectual property rights as "copyright and related rights, trademark rights, patent rights, rights in layout designs of semiconductor integrated circuits, trade secret rights, plant breeders' rights, rights in geographic indications and industrial design rights". The TRIPS Agreement defines "intellectual property" by reference to the categories of intellectual property for which it establishes standards. These parallel the rights listed in the NAFTA definition with the exception of plant breeder rights.[238]

NAFTA 1701(1) obliges each NAFTA country to provide nationals of other NAFTA countries with adequate and effective measures to protect and enforce intellectual property rights while ensuring that such measures do not become barriers to legitimate trade. As discussed in §9.4(5)(a), the concept of "nationals" is tied to definitions in certain international agreements. NAFTA 1701(2) provides that the minimum that each NAFTA country must do to fulfil this expansive obligation is to give effect to NAFTA Chapter Seventeen and to the provisions of certain international conventions. The TRIPS Agreement requires member countries to accord to nationals of other members the treatment provided for in the TRIPS Agreement. As under NAFTA, the TRIPS Agreement ties the concept of "national" to its meaning in the international agreements to which the TRIPS Agreement refers. With the exception of the UPOV Convention (1978) and the UPOV Convention (1991), the TRIPS Agreement refers to the same international agreements as NAFTA.[239] NAFTA and the TRIPS Agreement both set out national treatment obligations and both agreements deal with the question of abusive or anti-competitive practices.

NAFTA 1705 through to NAFTA 1713 prescribe minimum standards of protection that must be in effect in each NAFTA country in respect of copyright, sound recordings, encrypted program-carrying satellite signals, trade marks, patents, layout designs of semiconductor integrated circuits, trade secrets, geographic indications and industrial designs. These provisions are discussed in §9.4(9) through to §9.4(17). Part II of the TRIPS Agreement sets out minimum standards for these same categories of intellectual property except for encrypted program-carrying satellite signals.

NAFTA 1714 through to NAFTA 1718 set out provisions respecting the enforcement of intellectual property rights that are discussed in §9.4(18). Articles 41 through to 61 of the TRIPS Agreement set out parallel provisions. As discussed in §9.4(19), NAFTA 1719 provides for co-operation and technical assistance and Article 67 of the TRIPS Agreement covers technical co-operation. NAFTA 1720 and Article 70 of the TRIPS Agreement cover the protection of existing subject-matter.

(5) Scope and Coverage of NAFTA Intellectual Property Provisions

The scope and coverage of NAFTA Chapter Seventeen is delineated by the definition of "intellectual property rights" described previously, the definition of "nationals of another Party" in NAFTA 1721 and the provisions respecting existing subject-matter.

(a) Nationals of NAFTA countries

The persons entitled to the benefits of the NAFTA Chapter are "nationals of another Party". This expression is defined in terms of persons who would be eligible for protection under the terms of specific international conventions respecting the categories of intellectual property rights covered by those conventions.

(i) Paris Convention

If the intellectual property right is a patent, utility model, industrial design, trade mark, service mark, trade name or an indication of source or appellation of origin (*i.e.*, geographic indication), a "national of another Party" is a person who would be eligible for protection under the Paris Convention. The Paris Convention applies to nationals of a member country and to nationals of other countries who are domiciled in a member country or have "real and effective commercial establishments" in a member country. A person entitled to the benefits of the Paris Convention does not have to be domiciled or have an establishment in the member country from which protection is claimed.

(ii) Berne Convention

If the intellectual property right is copyright covered by the Berne Convention,[240] a "national of another Party" is a person who would be eligible for protection under the Berne Convention. These persons are nationals of a member country or persons who have their habitual residence in a member country. Protection is also extended to an author who is not a national of a member country for a work first published in a member country. Thus, if an author in the United Kingdom wrote a book that was first published in Canada, that author would be a "national of a Party" (*i.e.*, Canada) for the purposes of that book.

(iii) Geneva Convention and the Rome Convention

If the intellectual property right is the right to protection of a phonogram covered by the Geneva Convention, a "national of another Party" is a person who would be eligible for the protection under the Geneva Convention. These persons are nationals of a member country. No provision is made for the extension of coverage to persons domiciled or resident or having an establishment in a member country. However, as the definition of "producer of phonograms" in the Geneva Convention includes legal entities, presumably the concept of "national" under this Convention includes legal entities as well as individuals.

Although NAFTA does not require that the NAFTA countries give effect to the provisions of the Rome Convention, the Rome Convention is listed among the international agreements upon which the concept of "nationals of another Party" is based. Presumably it is intended that this concept for rights in phonograms be based upon the Geneva Convention, the provisions of which must be given effect by the NAFTA countries. The reference to the Rome Convention can only have meaning in respect of the other two areas which it covers, namely, performers and broadcast organizations.

(iv) UPOV Convention (1978) and UPOV Convention (1991)

If the intellectual property right is a breeder's right to protection of a plant variety, a "national of another Party" is a person who would be eligible for protection under the UPOV Convention (1978) or the UPOV Convention (1991). These persons are nationals of a member country as well as natural persons resident and legal entities having their registered offices within a member country.[241]

(v) Integrated Circuits Treaty

If the intellectual property right is in a layout design of an integrated circuit, a "national of another Party" is a natural person who is a national of or domiciled in a member country or a legal entity which or natural persons who have real and effective establishments in another member country for the creation of layout designs or the production of integrated circuits.

(vi) Catch-all provision

NAFTA 1721 provides that if an intellectual property right is not the subject of any of these Conventions, a "national of a Party" is an individual who is a citizen or permanent resident of a NAFTA country.[242] Except for trade secrets, all the categories in the definition of "intellectual property rights" in NAFTA 1721 are subject to at least one of the foregoing Conventions.

(b) Protection of existing subject-matter

NAFTA 1720 deals with the protection of existing subject-matter and, as such, serves as a transitional provision. The provisions of NAFTA 1720 closely follow those of its counterpart in Article 70 of the TRIPS Agreement. NAFTA 1720 sets out some general principles that apply to all intellectual property rights. These will be discussed here. NAFTA 1720 also contains specific provisions relating to copyright, sound recordings and patents that will be discussed under §9.4(9), §9.4(10) and §9.4(13).

NAFTA 1720(1) establishes that NAFTA Chapter Seventeen does not give rise to obligations in respect of acts that occurred prior to January 1, 1994. Thus, past failures of NAFTA countries to protect intellectual property rights will not be caught by the obligations imposed by NAFTA. NAFTA 1720(2) requires that the NAFTA countries apply NAFTA Chapter Seventeen to all subject-matter existing on January 1, 1994, and protected on that date or that meets the NAFTA criteria for protection.[243] With one exception respecting motion pictures discussed in §9.4(9), a NAFTA country will not be required to restore protection to subject-matter that has fallen into the public domain. Applications for protection pending on January 1, 1994, may be amended to include any enhanced protection provided for in NAFTA, but the amendments may not include new matter.

NAFTA 1720(4) recognizes that specific objects embodying protected subject-matter may become infringing because of laws implementing the requirements of NAFTA Chapter Seventeen coming into effect. If significant investment has been made in such an object before January 1, 1994, a NAFTA country may limit the remedies applicable in such a situation respecting "continued performance". In other words, the right holder may be precluded from stopping the activity. However, the NAFTA country must at least provide for the payment of equitable remuneration to the right holder.

(6) Give Effect to Provisions of International Intellectual Property Conventions

NAFTA 1701(2) requires each NAFTA country to give effect to the substantive provisions of the Geneva Convention, the Berne Convention, the Paris Convention and either the UPOV Convention (1978) or the UPOV Convention (1991). NAFTA 1701(2) obliged NAFTA countries to make every effort to accede to each agreement prior to NAFTA becoming effective if they had not already done so. NAFTA 1710(1) requires that each NAFTA country protect layout designs in accordance with certain provisions of the Integrated Circuits Treaty. These provisions are discussed under the heading Layout Designs of Semiconductor Integrated Circuits in §9.4(14).

(a) Relationship of international conventions to NAFTA

NAFTA does not incorporate any of these conventions by reference and does not set out any special rule respecting inconsistencies. Therefore, the basic rule of prevalence in NAFTA 103 described in §1.6(1) applies to obligations existing under these conventions on January 1, 1994.[244] One would expect this result given the objective of both NAFTA and the TRIPS Agreements of improving on the protections accorded by the conventions.

(b) Exceptions

NAFTA Annex 1701.3 sets out several qualifications to the obligation set out in NAFTA 1701(2) as it applies to Mexico and the United States.

Mexico has until December 17, 1994,[245] to comply with the substantive provisions of the UPOV Convention (1978) or the UPOV Convention (1991) but is obliged to accept applications from plant breeders starting January 1, 1994.

NAFTA 1702(b) confers no rights and does not impose obligations on the United States respecting Article 6[bis] of the Berne Convention. Under this provision of the Berne Convention, an author has the right to claim authorship of a work and to object to acts in respect of the work (such as distortion or mutilation) that would be prejudicial to his or her honour or reputation. These "moral rights" are independent of economic rights and continue after their transfer. The incorporation of moral rights into U.S. copyright law was widely opposed by a variety of interests in the United States at the time that the Berne Convention Implementation Act 1988 was passed and this legislation does not provide for moral rights as required by Article 6[bis].[246]

(c) TRIPS Agreement and the international conventions

The TRIPS Agreement requires member countries to comply with speci-fied provisions of the Paris Convention[247] and the Berne Convention,[248] and to provide the protection to layout designs of integrated circuits in accor-dance with certain provisions of the Integrated Circuits Treaty.[249] The Geneva Convention, the UPOV Convention (1978) and the UPOV Convention (1991) are not mentioned. Unlike NAFTA, the TRIPS Agreement has a non-derogation provision in respect of existing obligations under the Paris Con-vention, the Berne Convention, the Rome Convention and the Integrated Circuits Treaty.[250]

(7) National Treatment and Most-Favoured-Nation Treatment

(a) National treatment

NAFTA 1703(1) sets out a national treatment obligation respecting the protection and enforcement of intellectual property rights that applies to "nationals of another Party". As discussed in §9.4(5)(a), the meaning of this expression and, therefore, the scope of this national treatment obliga-tion depend upon the category of intellectual property in question and the scope of the protection afforded by the corresponding convention. Article 3 of the TRIPS Agreement sets out a similar obligation that, unlike the NAFTA obligation, is expressly subject to exceptions provided for in the Paris Convention, the Berne Convention, the Rome Convention and the Integrated Circuits Treaty.

NAFTA 1703(2) provides that no NAFTA country may require copyright holders to comply with formalities or conditions in order to be accorded national treatment. NAFTA 1703(3) permits certain derogations from the national treatment obligation in procedural matters (such as requiring nationals of other NAFTA countries to appoint an agent for service) provided that the derogation is consistent with the applicable convention and certain other conditions are satisfied.[251]

(b) Most-favoured-nation treatment

Unlike the TRIPS Agreement, the NAFTA intellectual property provisions do not contain a MFN obligation. The TRIPS Agreement MFN obligation is set out in Article 4 and requires that advantages, favours, privileges and immunities granted by a member to another country be granted to all mem-ber countries.[252] Advantages, favours, privileges and immunities granted by the three NAFTA countries to each other under NAFTA Chapter Seventeen are covered by the TRIPS Agreement MFN obligation.

(8) Control of Abusive or Anti-competitive Practices

NAFTA 1704 recognizes the potential conflict between protection of intellectual property rights and the objective of competition policy of restricting anti-competitive conduct.[253] NAFTA 1704 has the effect of permitting NAFTA countries to specify licensing practices or conditions that constitute an abuse of intellectual property rights because they have an adverse effect on competition and to take appropriate measures that are consistent with NAFTA to prevent or control such practices or conditions. A corresponding provision is set out in paragraph 2 of Article 40 of the TRIPS Agreement.

Article 8 of the TRIPS Agreement permits measures consistent with the agreement to prevent practices that "unreasonably restrain trade or adversely affect the international transfer of technology".[254] Article 8 also permits measures consistent with the TRIPS Agreement necessary to "protect public health and nutrition", and to promote the public interest in sectors of vital importance to "socio-economic and technological development".[255] The "public health and nutrition" provision may apply measures designed to curb cigarette consumption by requiring generic packaging, although the scope of such application depends on the interpretation of "consistent". There is no counterpart to this provision in NAFTA.

(9) Copyright

In addition to the requirement in NAFTA 1701(2) that NAFTA countries give effect to the Berne Convention, NAFTA 1705 sets out minimum standards for the protection of copyright. The copyright provisions of the TRIPS Agreement are set out in TRIPS Agreement Articles 9 through to 13.

NAFTA 1705(1) and TRIPS Agreement Article 10 both provide that computer programs are literary works within the meaning of the Berne Convention and shall be protected as such. Compilations of data or other material, "which by reason of the selection or arrangement of their contents constitute intellectual creations"[256] shall also be protected as such, although this protection does not extend to or prejudice copyright in the data or material. The Berne Convention itself does not specifically refer to either of these categories of intellectual property.

NAFTA 1705(2) requires that each NAFTA country provide the authors of literary works within the meaning of the Berne Convention (which include the computer programs and the compilations just discussed) with the right to authorize or prohibit: the importation of unauthorized copies of the work; the first public distribution of the original and each copy of the work by sale, rental or otherwise; and the communication of the work to the public. The right to authorize or prohibit also applies to the rental of the original or copy of a computer program except when the computer program itself is not the essential object of the rental. NAFTA 1720(5) provides that the rental requirement need not be applied to originals or copies purchased prior to NAFTA becoming effective. Putting an original or copy of the program on the market does not exhaust the rental right. The TRIPS Agreement contains a similar provision respecting computer rentals,[257] but does not contain the other requirements of NAFTA 1705(2).

NAFTA 1705(3) provides for the free transfer of economic rights in copyright and for the persons acquiring such rights by transfer to exercise them. There is no comparable provision in the TRIPS Agreement. NAFTA 1705(4) and Article 13 of the TRIPS Agreement both provide that except for photographic works and works of applied art, where the duration of protection is based other than on the life of a natural person, the term of protection must be at least fifty years from the end of the calendar year in which the first authorized publication occurred or, failing that, the end of the calendar year of making.

NAFTA 1705(5) and Article 13 of the TRIPS Agreement both provide that limitations and exceptions are to be confined to special cases that do not conflict with the normal exploitation of the work or unreasonably prejudice the legitimate interests of the right holder. NAFTA 1705(6) has the effect of prohibiting the translation and reproduction licences provided for in the Appendix to the Berne Convention discussed in §9.4(2)(b). As the Appendix applies only to developing countries, this provision is obviously directed at Mexico. NAFTA Annex 1705.7 imposes certain obligations on the United States to protect motion pictures declared to be in the public domain under U.S. law.[258]

(10) Sound Recordings

In addition to the requirement in NAFTA 1701(2) that NAFTA countries give effect to the Geneva Convention, NAFTA 1706 sets out minimum standards for the protection of producers of sound recordings. The TRIPS Agreement makes no reference to the Geneva Convention but Article 14 of the TRIPS Agreement sets out standards respecting the protection of the producers of phonograms.[259]

NAFTA 1706(1) requires that each NAFTA country provide the producer of a sound recording with the right to authorize or prohibit: direct or indirect reproduction of the sound recording; importation of copies of the sound recording; the first public distribution (by sale, rental or otherwise); and commercial rental of the original and each copy of the sound recording except (in the case of commercial rental) when the contract between the producer and the authors of the recorded work provides otherwise. NAFTA 1720(5) provides that the requirement respecting commercial rentals need not be applied to originals or copies purchased prior to NAFTA becoming effective. The right to prohibit reproduction and importation goes beyond the Geneva Convention requirements in that there is no *caveat* that the reproduction or importation must be for "distribution to the public" for the protection to apply. The TRIPS Agreement contains a similar provision respecting reproduction[260] and addresses commercial rental,[261] but does not cover first distribution.

NAFTA 1706(2) requires a term of protection for sound recordings of fifty years from the calendar year of fixation. This is a significantly more stringent standard than the twenty-year term provided for in the Geneva Convention. The TRIPS Agreement provides for the same duration of protection as set out in NAFTA.

NAFTA 1706(3) requires that limitations or exceptions to the rights provided in NAFTA 1706 be confined to special cases that do not conflict with normal exploitation of the sound recording or prejudice the legitimate interests of the right holder.

Article 14 of the TRIPS Agreement also sets out standards of protection for performers respecting the fixation (*i.e.*, recording) of their performances on a phonogram. Performers can prevent the unauthorized fixation of their performances and the reproduction of such fixation.[262] The only reference in NAFTA to performers is in NAFTA 1703(1), which permits a NAFTA country to limit the application of national treatment to performers (as distinct from producers) of another NAFTA country in respect of the use of sound recordings for broadcasting or other public communication[263] to those rights accorded to its nationals in that other NAFTA country. This NAFTA limitation does not apply to producers of sound recordings.

(11) Encrypted Program-Carrying Satellite Signals

NAFTA 1707 obliges each NAFTA country to make it a criminal offence to make available devices for decoding an encrypted program-carrying satellite signal without authorization from the lawful distributor and a civil offence to receive such a signal without authorization in connection with commercial activities or further distribution. These measures are to be in effect by January 1, 1995. Encrypted program-carrying satellite signals are not included in the NAFTA definition of "intellectual property rights".

(12) Trade Marks

In addition to the requirement in NAFTA 1701(2) that NAFTA countries give effect to the Paris Convention, NAFTA 1708 sets out minimum standards for the protection of trade marks. The trade mark provisions of the TRIPS Agreement are set out in TRIPS Agreement, Articles 15 to 21.

NAFTA 1708(1) describes what a trade mark is and follows the language of the TRIPS Agreement.[264] NAFTA 1708(2) sets out the basic right of a trade mark holder to prevent persons, without consent, from using identical or similar signs in connection with goods or services for which the trade mark is registered where such use would cause confusion. Use of an identical mark is presumed to cause confusion. The corresponding TRIPS Agreement provision uses almost the same language.[265] NAFTA 1708(3) follows the TRIPS Agreement[266] in permitting a NAFTA country to make registrability depend on use but prevents a NAFTA country from refusing registration solely because intended use has not occurred within three years of the application date. NAFTA 1708 sets out the basic procedural requirements of a registration system with somewhat more detail than its TRIPS Agreement counterpart.[267]

NAFTA 1708(5) follows the TRIPS Agreement[268] in providing that the nature of goods or services to which a trade mark is to be applied will not form an obstacle to registration. The corresponding provision of the Paris Convention refers only to goods.[269] NAFTA 1708(6) extends the provisions of Article 6[bis] of the Paris Convention discussed in §9.4(2)(a) to services. The TRIPS Agreement contains a similar but differently worded provision.[270] Note that Article 6[sexies] of the Paris Convention obliges countries of the Union to protect service marks but does not oblige them to provide for the registration of such marks.

NAFTA 1708(7) provides for a minimum initial registration term of ten years and that registrations be renewable indefinitely for successive ten-year terms. The corresponding TRIPS Agreement provision provides for an initial seven-year term and that registrations be renewable indefinitely.[271] NAFTA 1708(8) provides that NAFTA countries require that a trade mark be used for registration to be maintained and that registration may, subject to some extenuating circumstances, be cancelled after two uninterrupted years of non-use. The corresponding TRIPS Agreement provision is permissive as to requiring use and the period of non-use is three years.[272] Both NAFTA 1708(9) and the TRIPS Agreement provide that use by another person under the control of the owner constitutes use of the trade mark.[273]

Both NAFTA 1708(10) and the TRIPS Agreement,[274] with somewhat different wording, provide that the use of a trade mark may not be encumbered with special requirements, such as a use that reduces the trade mark's function as an indication of source or a use with another trade mark.

NAFTA 1708(11) follows the TRIPS Agreement[275] by permitting a NAFTA country to determine the conditions of licensing and assignment of trade marks and by prohibiting compulsory licensing. This provision confirms the right of a trade mark owner to assign its trade mark with or without a transfer of the business to which it belongs.

NAFTA 1708(12) follows the TRIPS Agreement[276] in permitting limited exceptions, such as fair use of descriptive terms, so long as the legitimate interests of owners and third parties are taken into account. NAFTA 1708(13) requires NAFTA countries to prohibit the registration of words that generically describe goods or services in English, French or Spanish and to refuse to register trade marks that consist of immoral, deceptive or scandalous matter. These provisions do not have counterparts in the TRIPS Agreement.

(13) Patents

In addition to the requirement in NAFTA 1701(2) that NAFTA countries give effect to the Paris Convention, NAFTA 1708 sets out minimum standards for the protection of patents. The patent provisions of the TRIPS Agreement are set out in TRIPS Agreement, Articles 27 to 34.

(a) Subject-matter

NAFTA 1709(1) requires NAFTA countries to make patents available for any inventions, whether products or processes, in all fields of technology provided that the inventions are new, result from an inventive step and are capable of industrial application. The TRIPS Agreement contains a similar provision with some wording differences.[277] NAFTA 1709(2) follows the TRIPS Agreement[278] in permitting the exclusion from patentability of an invention if preventing the commercial exploitation of the invention is necessary to protect *ordre public* or morality or human, animal or plant life or health, or the environment. NAFTA 1709(3) also follows the TRIPS Agreement[279] in permitting the exclusion from patentability of: diagnostic, therapeutic and surgical methods for the treatment of plants and animals; plants and animals other than micro-organisms; and essentially biological processes for the production of plants and animals. Notwithstanding the exclusion of plants, NAFTA countries are required to protect plant varieties which, as noted in §9.4(2)(d), are covered by the two UPOV Conventions.

NAFTA 1709(7) provides that patents must be available and patent rights enjoyable without discrimination as to the field of technology, the NAFTA country where the invention was made or whether products are imported or locally produced. Paragraph 1 of Article 27 of the TRIPS Agreement contains a similar provision. NAFTA 1720(6) provides that this requirement, in so far as it concerns a field of technology, does not have to be applied to authorizations for use without authorization of the right holder granted by a government of a NAFTA country before the Draft Final Act Embodying the Results of the Uruguay Round of Multilateral Trade Negotiations became known, which was on December 20, 1991.[280]

(b) Basic rights

NAFTA 1709(5) sets out the basic rights conferred by a patent. If the subject-matter of a patent is a product, the patent holder may prevent other persons from making, using or selling the subject-matter of the patent without the holder's consent. If the subject-matter is a process, the holder can prevent other persons from using the process or using, selling or importing products directly obtained from the process without the holder's consent. Article 28 of the TRIPS Agreement sets out a similar provision. NAFTA 1709(6) and Article 30 of the TRIPS Agreement permit limited exceptions to the exclusive rights granted by a patent. Both NAFTA 1709(9) and paragraph 2 of Article 28 of the TRIPS Agreement require that patent holders be permitted to assign patents or transfer patents by succession and to conclude licensing contracts.

NAFTA 1709(12) provides for a term of protection of twenty years from the date of filing or seventeen years from the date of grant. The term of protection under Article 33 of the TRIPS Agreement is twenty years from the date of filing. NAFTA 1709(8) permits revocation of a patent only when grounds exist that would have justified refusing to grant the patent or the grant of a compulsory licence has not remedied the lack of exploitation of a patent. Article 32 of the TRIPS Agreement requires only that an opportunity for judicial review be made available in the event of revocation.

NAFTA 1709(11) requires that the burden of proof be placed on the defendant of proving that an allegedly infringing product was made by a process other than the patented process if the product obtained by the patented process is new or if it is likely that the allegedly infringing product was made with the patented product and the patent holder cannot determine through reasonable efforts the process actually used. Article 34 of the TRIPS Agreement contains a similar but somewhat differently worded provision.

(c) Compulsory licensing

NAFTA 1709(10) sets out provisions respecting compulsory licensing, which is the permitted use of the patent without the consent of the owner. Compulsory licensing has the legitimate purpose of countering the lack of exploitation of a patent by its holder[281] or curtailing anti-competitive acts. However, aggressive use of compulsory licensing by some governments had become a significant issue for governments of highly industrialized countries, particularly the United States, and disciplining its use was an objective of U.S. negotiators in both the NAFTA and the Uruguay Round of negotiations.

The NAFTA compulsory licensing provisions closely follow those set out in Article 31 of the TRIPS Agreement, and both agreements provide much stronger disciplines than Article 5 of the Paris Convention. Both agreements permit compulsory licensing but subject to disciplines. For compulsory licensing to be permitted, a proposed user must have made efforts to obtain authorization from the owner on reasonable commercial terms and conditions and such efforts must have failed to be successful within a reasonable period of time. The exceptions to this requirement are for national emergencies and also to remedy practices judicially determined to be anti-competitive.

The scope and duration of the use must be limited to the purpose for which it was authorized. The use shall be non-exclusive and non-assignable except as part of the enterprise or goodwill enjoying the use. The use must be primarily for the domestic market of the NAFTA country imposing the compulsory licensing. Subject to some protections, the authorized use may be terminated if the circumstances that gave rise to it have ceased to exist.

One critical condition of compulsory licensing is that the right holder be paid adequate remuneration, taking into account the economic value of the authorization. This provision prevents governments from using compulsory licensing to obtain technology or products such as pharmaceuticals at a lower price than would be the case if the right holder received full royalties for its right. The need to prevent anti-competitive practices can be taken into account in determining the amount of remuneration.

The legal validity of decisions relating to authorizations and remuneration must be subject to judicial or other independent review.

NAFTA 1720(6) provides that the requirements of NAFTA 1710 do not have to be applied to authorizations granted before the Draft Final Act Embodying the Results of the Uruguay Round of Multilateral Trade Negotiations became known which, as noted earlier, was on December 20, 1991.

(d) Pharmaceutical and agricultural chemicals

NAFTA 1709(4) sets out a special rule respecting pharmaceutical and agricultural chemicals. A NAFTA country that did not provide patent protection as of January 1, 1992, for pharmaceutical or agricultural chemicals that are naturally occurring substances described in NAFTA 1709(4)(a) or as of January 1, 1991, for other subject-matter must permit an inventor to obtain protection for such a product. The protection must be for the unexpired term of a patent for such product granted in another NAFTA country. The product cannot have been marketed in the NAFTA country required to provide the protection and the request for protection must be timely. There is a comparable provision in paragraph 8(c) of Article 70 of the TRIPS Agreement without the qualification respecting marketing or the requirement that a request be timely.

(14) Layout Designs of Semiconductor Integrated Circuits

NAFTA 1710 sets out provisions respecting layout designs of semiconductor integrated circuits. The corresponding provisions of the TRIPS Agreement are set out in Articles 35 to 38.

The Integrated Circuits Treaty is not included in the list of conventions in NAFTA 1701(2) to which effect must be given. However, NAFTA 1710(1) requires that layout designs of integrated circuits be protected in accordance with Articles 2 through 7, 12 and 16(3) of the treaty which are described in §9.4(2)(e). Article 6(3), which provides for compulsory licensing, is excluded and NAFTA 1710(5) prohibits compulsory licensing of these products. Article 35 of the TRIPS Agreement contains the same requirement with the same Articles and the same exclusion of Article 6(3). However, the TRIPS Agreement does not specifically prohibit compulsory licensing. NAFTA 1710(6) and Article 38 of the TRIPS Agreement provide for protection of ten years from the date of filing an application for registration or first commercial exploitation anywhere in the world.[282] NAFTA 1710(2) and Article 36 of the TRIPS Agreement set out provisions respecting unauthorized importing, selling and distributing similar to that in Article 6(1)[283] of the treaty described in §9.4(2)(e).

NAFTA 1710(3) prohibits a NAFTA country from considering as unlawful an act respecting an integrated circuit incorporating an unlawfully reproduced layout design when the person involved did not know or had no reasonable grounds for believing that the layout design was unlawfully produced. NAFTA 1710(4) makes certain provisions respecting stock on hand or ordered and payment of a royalty after such person receives notice that the reproduction was unlawful. Article 37 of the TRIPS Agreement contains similar provisions. Article 6(4) of the Integrated Circuits Treaty addresses the same problem but is permissive as to whether the member country treats the act as lawful or unlawful.

NAFTA 1710(9) and Annex 1710.9 provide that Mexico shall implement NAFTA 1710 by January 1, 1998, and shall make every effort to do so sooner.

(15) Trade Secrets

NAFTA 1711 sets out obligations respecting trade secrets. The corresponding provisions of the TRIPS Agreement set out in Article 39 use the term of art "undisclosed information". NAFTA 1711(1) requires NAFTA countries to provide the legal means for persons to prevent trade secrets from being disclosed to, acquired by or used by others without consent of the person lawfully in control of the information in a manner "contrary to honest commercial practice".[284] The information must be secret and have actual or potential commercial value and the person in control must have taken reasonable steps to keep it secret. This provision is based on Article 39 of the TRIPS Agreement. Duration of the protection cannot be limited so long as these conditions exist.

NAFTA 1711(5) and paragraph 3 of Article 39 of the TRIPS Agreement both require protection against disclosure of data submitted as a condition imposed by a NAFTA country for approving the marketing of pharmaceutical or agricultural chemical products.[285]

(16) Geographical Indications

Geographic indications are covered by NAFTA 1712 and by Article 22 of the TRIPS Agreement. A geographic indication is an indication identifying a good as originating in a NAFTA country or a region or locality of a NAFTA country where particular quality, reputation or other characteristic of the good is essentially attributable to its geographical origin.[286] NAFTA 1712 and Article 22 of the TRIPS Agreement contain various provisions that give the legal means to interested persons of preventing the use of various means of misrepresenting the true origin of goods so as to mislead the public as to their geographical origin.[287] This obligation extends to refusing to register or invalidating geographic indications that although correctly indicating the territory of origin none the less mislead as to geographic origin.[288] NAFTA 1712(4) and (5) set out circumstances involving long-term good faith use where these obligations to prevent use of a geographical indication do not apply. NAFTA 1712(7) permits NAFTA countries to impose a time limit in respect of any request made respecting a trade mark of five years following the adverse use becoming generally known or after the registration of the trade mark so long as the use or registration has not been in bad faith. NAFTA 1712(9) provides that geographical indications that have fallen into disuse do not have to be protected.[289]

Article 23 of the TRIPS Agreement provides additional protections for geographical indications for wines and spirits. For example, interested persons must have the right to prevent the use of a geographical indication identifying wines for wines not originating in the place indicated.[290] As discussed in §5.5(5)(b), NAFTA Annex 313 sets out specific requirements respecting certain types of spirits but does not contain any general provisions comparable to those in Article 23.

(17) Industrial Designs

NAFTA 1713 sets out requirements respecting industrial designs that closely follow the provisions of Articles 25 and 26 of the TRIPS Agreement. NAFTA countries must provide for the protection of independently created industrial designs that are new and original. Requirements to secure protection for textile designs (in terms of such matters as cost) shall not unreasonably impair a person's opportunity to seek protection. An owner of a protected design will have the right to prevent other persons from making or selling articles for commercial purposes bearing or embodying a design that is a copy or substantially a copy of the protected design. The term of protection in both NAFTA and the TRIPS Agreement is ten years. Limited exceptions are permitted subject to conditions.[291]

(18) Enforcement of Intellectual Property Rights

As discussed in §9.4(3), the proponents of a GATT agreement protecting intellectual property rights had as objectives the creation of obligations to ensure that there would be effective domestic remedies to enforce the standards established by the agreement and the means to enforce effectively intellectual property rights at the border. These objectives were achieved in Articles 42 through to 60 of the TRIPS Agreement. The corresponding NAFTA provisions are set out in NAFTA 1714 through to NAFTA 1718 and follow their TRIPS Agreement counterparts very closely.

(a) General provisions

NAFTA 1714(1) obliges NAFTA countries to ensure that the enforcement procedures set out in NAFTA 1715 through to NAFTA 1718 are available under domestic law to permit effective action to be taken against acts of infringement of the intellectual property rights protected by NAFTA Chapter Seventeen. Such enforcement procedures must be applied in a manner that avoids the creation of barriers to legitimate trade and must contain safeguards against abuse. The balance of NAFTA 1714 sets out basic standards for enforcement procedures such as requirements that procedures be fair and equitable and not unnecessarily complicated or costly and that administrative decisions be subject to judicial review.[292] NAFTA countries are not obliged to establish judicial systems for the enforcement of intellectual property rights that are distinct from their general judicial systems. Article 41 of the TRIPS Agreement sets out the same general standards with very similar wording.

(b) Civil and administrative procedures

NAFTA 1715 sets out a basic code of civil procedure for the enforcement of the intellectual property rights provided for in NAFTA Chapter Seventeen. NAFTA 1715(1) closely follows Article 42 of the TRIPS Agreement and sets out requirements respecting matters such as notice, the right to counsel and the means of identifying and protecting confidential information. NAFTA 1715(2)(a) and (b) require that judicial authorities have the power to order the production of evidence under certain conditions and to make determinations on the basis of evidence presented when an opposing party refuses access to relevant actions. Article 43 of the TRIPS Agreement sets out similar provisions.

NAFTA 1715(2)(c) requires that judicial authorities be empowered to grant injunctive relief. In the case of imported goods the order must be enforceable immediately after customs clearance. However, NAFTA countries are not obliged to provide such relief before a person knew or had reasonable grounds for knowing that the matter in question entailed the infringement of an intellectual property right.[293] Paragraph 1 of Article 44 of the TRIPS Agreement sets out similar provisions.[294]

NAFTA 1715(2)(d) requires that the judicial authorities be empowered to award damages if the infringer knew or had reasonable grounds for knowing that it was infringing. Paragraph 1 of Article 45 of the TRIPS Agreement contains a similar provision. NAFTA 1715(4) extends this right in the cases of copyrighted works and sound recordings to cases in which the infringer did not know or have reasonable grounds for knowing that it was infringing. Paragraph 2 of Article 45 of the TRIPS Agreement differs in that it permits members to authorize judicial authorities to order recovery of profits and/or payment of pre-established damages "in appropriate cases" when the infringer did not have knowledge, without reference to any particular category of intellectual property right. Both paragraph 2 of Article 45 and NAFTA 1715(2)(e) require that judicial authorities be empowered to order infringers to pay right holders' expenses, including attorney's fees. NAFTA 1715(2)(f) requires that judicial authorities be empowered to deal with situations involving abuse of enforcement procedures. Article 48 of the TRIPS Agreement sets out similar provisions.

NAFTA 1715(5) requires that NAFTA countries empower judicial authorities to dispose of infringing goods, without compensation, outside channels of commerce so that right holders will not be injured. Alternatively, unless contrary to constitutional limitations, infringing goods can be ordered destroyed. Judicial authorities must also be empowered to dispose of materials and implements used to make infringing goods. Simple removal of trade marks from counterfeit goods will not be sufficient except in exceptional cases. Article 46 of the TRIPS Agreement sets out similar provisions.

NAFTA 1715(6) and paragraph 2 of Article 48 of the TRIPS Agreement limit the right to exempt public authorities to situations involving good faith administration of law. When a NAFTA country itself is sued, NAFTA 1715(7) permits remedies to be confined to payment of adequate remuneration to the right holder.

(c) Provisional measures

NAFTA 1716 and Article 50 of the TRIPS Agreement require that right holders be provided with means of obtaining interim relief pending judicial or administrative determination of the merits of the case of the person alleging infringement. In NAFTA and TRIPS Agreement terminology, these are "provisional measures".

NAFTA 1716(1) requires that NAFTA countries provide that judicial authorities have the authority to order prompt and effective measures to prevent infringement and in particular to prevent infringing goods from entering channels of commerce. In the case of imported goods,the right to prevent such entry is to begin immediately after customs clearance. Such authority extends to measures to preserve relevant evidence. Paragraph 1 of Article 50 sets out similar provisions.

NAFTA 1716(2) provides that judicial authorities shall require that applicants for provisional measures provide evidence that the applicant is the right holder whose right is being infringed or that infringement is imminent. The applicant must establish that delay will result in irreparable harm or that evidence may be destroyed. Authorities may require that security be provided. Paragraph 3 of Article 50 of the TRIPS Agreement contains similar provisions. NAFTA 1716(4) and (5) make provision for *ex parte* relief when irreparable harm is likely or there is a demonstrable risk of evidence being destroyed. Paragraphs 2 and 4 of Article 50 of the TRIPS Agreement set out similar provisions.[295]

NAFTA 1716(6) provides that judicial authorities may revoke or cease to apply a provisional action if the applicant does not pursue its action within a reasonable time[296] and NAFTA 1716(7) provides that the defendant be compensated in such instances. Paragraphs 6 and 7 of Article 50 of the TRIPS Agreement set out similar provisions.

(d) Criminal procedures and penalties

NAFTA 1717 requires that each NAFTA country provide for criminal procedures and penalties in the case of wilful trade mark counterfeiting or copyright piracy on a commercial scale, with monetary fines, imprisonment or both sufficient to act as a deterent. Such procedures and penalties may be provided in respect of other intellectual rights where infringement is wilful and for a commercial purpose. Provision must also be made for seizure in appropriate cases. Article 61 of the TRIPS Agreement sets out similar provisions.

(e) Enforcement of intellectual property rights at the border

NAFTA 1718 and Articles 51 through to 60 of the TRIPS Agreement provide the means for intellectual property right holders to enforce their rights at the border. The right of customs administrations to suspend release of such goods is mandatory under both agreements for counterfeit trade mark goods and pirated copyright goods and may be applied to other intellectual property rights so long as NAFTA or TRIPS Agreement requirements are met. Corresponding procedures may be provided respecting the exportation of infringing goods.[297] An applicant must establish that there is a *prima facie* infringement under the laws of the importing country and supply Customs with a description of the goods sufficient for Customs to identify them. Customs must inform the applicant of the acceptance of the application and when they intend to take the action.[298] Provided that recourse to the procedures is not deterred, competent authorities may require that security be posted to protect the defendant and the authorities and to prevent abuse.[299] Provision is made for the release under certain circumstances of goods involving industrial designs, patents, integrated circuits and trade secrets upon posting of security sufficient to protect the right holder against infringement.[300]

Customs authorities must promptly inform the importer and the applicant of the suspension of release.[301] Provided that other conditions for release have been met, customs authorities must release the goods if within ten working days they have not been informed that a party other than the defendant has initiated proceedings or that a competent authority has prolonged the suspension through provisional measures.[302] Competent authorities must be empowered to order the applicant to pay compensation for wrongful detention or for goods released under the foregoing provision.[303] If proceedings are commenced, a review including a right to be heard shall take place at the defendant's request with a view to deciding whether the measures taken by customs authorities should be modified, revoked or confirmed.[304] Subject to certain conditions, rights of inspection while the goods are detained are to be granted to both the right holder and the importer.[305]

Both NAFTA and the TRIPS Agreement set out rules respecting self-initiated proceedings when competent authorities have *prima facie* evidence that an intellectual property right is being infringed. Public authorities and officials may be exempted from liability only where actions are taken or intended in good faith.[306]

Competent authorities must have the authority to destroy or dispose of infringing goods. Counterfeit goods may not be re-exported in an unaltered condition.[307]

Both NAFTA and the TRIPS Agreement permit the exclusion from the application of these provisions of small quantities of goods of a non-commercial nature in travellers' personal luggage or in small non-repetitive consignments.[308]

NAFTA Annex 1718.14 requires that Mexico comply with NAFTA 1718 by December 17, 1995,[309] and make every effort to do so sooner.

(19) Co-operation and Technical Assistance

NAFTA 1719(1) provides for the exchange of technical assistance and the promotion of co-operation among their respective competent authorities. NAFTA 1719(2) provides for co-operation in eliminating the trade in goods that infringe intellectual property rights, the establishment of federal government contact points and the exchange of information respecting the trade in infringing goods.

(20) Concluding Remarks

The effect of both NAFTA and the TRIPS Agreement is to provide comprehensive international codes of behaviour respecting the protection of intellectual property rights. Each agreement attempts to balance the protection of such rights against the potential anti-competitive and trade restricting activities that can flow from their exercise. Both agreements represent the developed industrialized country viewpoint of the importance of providing effective procedures for the international protection of intellectual property rights.

The TRIPS Agreement makes some concessions to developing countries in the transition arrangements set out in Part VI. For example, members are not obliged to implement the TRIPS Agreement until one year after the WTO Agreement comes into effect.[310] If a developing country member is obliged under the agreement to extend patent protection to areas of technology that it did not previously protect, the implementation of the provisions respecting product patents based on that technology can be postponed for five years.[311] There is a special ten-year delay provision for least-developed country members.[312] NAFTA makes minimal transitional concessions. This fact is probably as much reflective of Mexican self-perception as of the negotiating positions of its NAFTA partners.

ENDNOTES

[1] See North American Free Trade Agreement, Canadian Statement on Implementation, *Canada Gazette*, Part I, Saturday, January 1, 1994, at p. 140.

[2] These expressions refer to the code as amended on November 20, 1986.

[3] 41 U.S.C. (1988 Edition) §10a *et seq.*

[4] See 48 CFR Ch. I (10-1-93 Edition), §25.101 for the definition of "domestic end product". The definition is similar to that of "eligible goods" in FTA 1309 in FTA Chapter Thirteen (Government Procurement).

[5] See 48 CFR Ch. I (10-1-93 Edition) Subpart 25.4 that sets out rules respecting procurements covered by the 1980 Code, the Caribbean Basin Economic Recovery Act, the United States-Israel Free Trade Area Agreement, the FTA, the Agreement on Civil Aircraft and the Memorandum of Understanding between the United States of America and the European Economic Community on Government Procurement. Subpart 25.4 has been amended to replace the FTA with NAFTA as set out in the Federal Register, Vol. 59, No. 3, Wednesday, January 5, 1994, pp. 545-9.

[6] See Canada, Department of Supply and Services, Deputy Minister's Directive 609, dated March 6, 1987, to ADMs, DGs, Branch Directors, Group Directors and Section Chiefs from Georgina Wyman. The author understands that this directive was still in effect at the time of writing. The Canadian Government publication, *Government Business Opportunities*,

categorizes each proposed procurement on the basis of whether or not it is covered by the GATT, the FTA or NAFTA.

[7] Kathleen E. Troy, "NAFTA Chapter 10: Government Procurement" (paper presented at the American Conference Institute North American Free Trade Agreement Conference, March 17-18, 1994, Washington D.C.).

[8] SDR means Special Drawing Right, an international unit created by the International Monetary Fund. See *Bretton Woods and Related Agreements Act*, R.S.C. 1985, c. B-7, Sched. 1 for the text of this agreement. The Canadian dollar equivalent of 130,000 SDR for government procurement purposes was fixed on January 1, 1994, at $223,000 for a two-year period ending December 31, 1995. For the current U.S. threshold of $186,000 (US), see Federal Register, Vol. 59, No. 3, p. 546, amending 48 CFR Pt. 25. See §25.402(a)(1).

[9] The method for determining the Canadian dollar equivalent is set out in FTA 1304(2).

[10] See the definition of "eligible goods" in FTA 1309 which closely resembles the definition of "domestic end product" used in administering Buy American Act requirements. See §25.101, 48 CFR Ch. I (10-1-93 Edition).

[11] The comments on the 1994 GATT Government Procurement Code are based on the text that was signed in Marrakesh on April 15, 1994.

[12] Unlike the other Uruguay Round agreements, the 1994 GATT Government Procurement Code is not scheduled to become effective until January 1, 1996. See Article XXIV.

[13] $223,000 (Cdn) and $186,000 (US) for government procurement purposes in 1994.

[14] $8,576,923 (Cdn) and $7,153,846 (US), based on conversions of SDRs for government procurement purposes for 1994. See note 8.

[15] NAFTA 1001(1).

[16] See list of examples in NAFTA 1001(5)(a), which include such things as loans, grants, fiscal incentives, etc.

[17] The definition also includes entities listed in NAFTA Annex 1001.1a-3, which is entitled "State and Provincial Government Entities". No entities are listed. This list will only exist if and when procurement rules are negotiated with the provincial and state governments.

[18] Only the Fisheries Price Support Board was included in the FTA Annex.

[19] This list is not exhaustive. There were sixty-six separate entities listed in the FTA Annex as compared with 100 separate entities listed in NAFTA Annex 1001.1a-1. A number of the additional entities listed came into existence after the FTA was signed.

[20] The Civil Aviation Board is not included.

[21] The FTA list included the Maritime Administration of the Department of Transportation.

[22] The FTA Annex included the Department of Post Office.

[23] Does not apply to procurements of inputs used in minting anything other than Canadian legal tender.

[24] Railway operations only.

[25] The language of Annex 1001.1b-1, which closely follows that of FTA Annex 1304.3 and the 1980 Code Annex, is confusing in so far as the obligations of the United States are concerned. First, paragraph 4 provides that NAFTA Chapter Ten "generally" applies to procurements by the U.S. Department of Defense of the goods listed in Section B. The corresponding Canadian and Mexican obligations are not so qualified. Second, one questions the need for the additional exclusions of U.S. Department of Defense purchases if the intent of paragraph 4 is to restrict the scope of NAFTA Chapter Ten to U.S. Department of Defense purchases of goods listed in Section B. None of the items excluded by paragraph 5 are listed in Section B.

[26] The note at the end of Schedule B provides that "buy national" requirements on articles, supplies and materials acquired for use in construction contracts covered by Chapter Ten shall not apply to goods of Canada or Mexico. The "buy national" requirements referred to must be "buy American" requirements.

[27] This is consistent with the FTA. The currency conversion rules in paragraph 3 of Annex 1001.1c are based on the rule in FTA 1304(2). The FTA did not provide for indexation of the $25,000 (US) threshold.

[28] This contingency is specifically addressed in NAFTA 1002(4).

[29] See para. 6 of Annex 1001.2a. The federal government entities are the Secretaria de Salud (Ministry of Health), the Secretaria Defensa Nacional (Ministry of National Defence) and

the Secretaria de Marina (Ministry of the Navy). The government enterprises specified are IMSS (Mexican Social Security Institute) and the ISSSTE (the Social Security and Services Institute for Government Workers).

[30] This schedule does not set out currency conversion rules and the rules in Annex 1001.1c apply only to conversions of the thresholds in NAFTA 1001(1)(c).

[31] The rules respecting set-asides are set out in para. 3 on the Annex.

[32] Such stores would be subject to the rules in NAFTA Chapter Fifteen respecting monopolies and state enterprises, discussed in §9.2(2).

[33] See the amendments to 48 CFR Pt. 25, published in the Federal Register, Vol. 59, No. 3, Wednesday January 5, 1994, at p. 546. §25.401 is amended by adding a definition of "Mexican end product" that means an article that (a) is wholly the growth, product, or manufacture of Mexico, or (b) in the case of an article which consists in whole or in part of materials from another country or instrumentality, has been substantially transformed in Mexico into a new and different article of commerce with a name, character or use distinct from that of the article or articles from which it was transformed. There is a corresponding definition of "Canadian end product".

[34] See Federal Register, Vol. 59, No. 1, January 3, 1994, at p. 142. The notice does not cover origin determinations under government procurement statutes, "although the authorities responsible for promulgating determinations under these statutes may avail themselves of these rules if they so choose".

[35] This is the combined effect of the definition of "supplier" in NAFTA 1025 and the definitions of "person", "enterprise" and "person of a Party" in NAFTA 201.

[36] Defined in NAFTA 1025 as including a natural person resident in a NAFTA country, an enterprise organized or established under a NAFTA country's law and a branch or representative office located in a NAFTA country.

[37] See NAFTA 1025 for definition of "technical specification".

[38] NAFTA 1025 provides that "technical regulation" and "standard" have the same meanings as set out in NAFTA 915 and discussed in §6.4(2)(b) and §6.4(2)(c). These definitions are based on para. 3 of Article VII of the 1994 Code.

[39] The expressions "tendering procedures", "open tendering procedures", "selective tendering procedures" and "limited tendering procedures" are all defined in NAFTA 1025.

[40] See NAFTA 1009(2)(b). These include financial guarantees and technical qualifications.

[41] In Canada, Government Business Opportunities (GBO) and Open Bidding Service, ISM Publishing. In the United States, Commerce Business Daily (CBD). In Mexico, the Official Gazette of the Federation (Diario Oficial de la Federación). Mexico is to endeavour to establish a specialized publication for notices of procurement which, when established, will be substituted for the Diario Oficial.

[42] For the timing requirements for selective procedures without and with a permanent list of qualified suppliers, see NAFTA 1012(2)(b) and NAFTA 1012(2)(c), respectively.

[43] This limitation on the obligation to provide information is differently worded, but is similar in effect to those that apply to sanitary and phytosanitary measures in NAFTA 721(b) and to standards-related measures in NAFTA 912(b).

[44] Paragraphs 1(f) and (g) of Article XV set out additional instances relating to construction contracts.

[45] This is different from the "legitimate commercial interest" limitations in NAFTA 721(b), NAFTA 912(b) and NAFTA 1015(8)(b) in that this provision prohibits a NAFTA country from disclosing such information while the other provisions are rules of construction that prevent NAFTA from being construed to require the disclosure of such information.

[46] North American Free Trade Agreement, Canadian Statement on Implementation, *Canada Gazette*, Pt. I, January 1, 1994, at p. 141.

[47] There are other practices such as refusal to deal, exclusive dealing, tied selling and market restriction. Canadian competition legislation also covers such practices as misleading advertising and pyramid selling.

[48] For a brief discussion of this, see John H. Jackson, *World Trade and the Law of GATT* (Indianapolis, Bobbs-Merrill Co., 1969), at p. 330.

[49] There is an argument that the GATT contracting parties must observe the general principles of the Havana Charter, including those of Chapter V on restrictive business practices. See

GATT Article XXIX which requires the GATT contracting parties to observe the general principles of Chapters I to VI and Chapter IX of the Havana Charter pending its acceptance. While the Havana Charter was never accepted, GATT Article XXIX was not amended, and there is a technical argument that the "general principles" of the chapters enumerated in GATT Article XXIX should be applied. See Jackson, *ibid.*, at pp. 312-14.

[50] The group of experts was appointed in 1958. See 7th Supp. BISD 29 (1959). Their report is set out in 9th Supp. BISD 170 (1961) and the GATT decision of November 18, 1960, resulting from the report is set out in 9th Supp. BISD 28. It is evident from paragraph 3 of the report that considerable work had been done in the preceding fifteen years on the subject of international restrictive business practices.

[51] R.S.C. 1985, c. C-34, as amended. This statute replaced the earlier *Combines Investigation Act*, which had been in effect for many years. The original form of the *Combines Investigation Act* was enacted in 1889, one year before the U.S. Sherman Act.

[52] *Per se* offences also include promotional allowances, misleading advertising and pyramid selling.

[53] See s. 92 of the *Competition Act*.

[54] For example, unlike Canada, there is no specific statutory provision in U.S. law prohibiting resale price maintenance. U.S. principles respecting "vertical price fixing" are set out in case law. See R.J. Roberts, *Roberts on Competition/Antitrust: Canada and the United States*, 2nd ed. (Toronto, Butterworths, 1992) at p. 185, note 1.

[55] 15 U.S.C. §§1-7 (1988).

[56] 15 U.S.C. §§12, 13, 14-19, 20, 21 and 22-27 (1988).

[57] Section 2. See 15 U.S.C. §13 (1988).

[58] Section 3. See 15 U.S.C. §14 (1988).

[59] Section 7. See 15 U.S.C. §18 (1988).

[60] 15 U.S.C. §15(a) (1988). "Antitrust laws" are defined in 15 U.S.C. (1988) §12(a).

[61] See 15 U.S.C. §13a (1988). See Roberts, *op. cit.*, note 54, at p. 138, note 4, for a comparison of s. 3 of the Robinson-Patman Act and s. 50 of the *Competition Act*.

[62] 15 U.S.C. §18a (1988).

[63] 38 Stat. 717 (1914), as amended. For statutory provisions respecting the Federal Trade Commission, see 15 U.S.C. §§41-58 (1988).

[64] 15 U.S.C. §45(a)(2) (1988).

[65] 15 U.S.C. §§53-55 (1988).

[66] 15 U.S.C. §57a.

[67] 15 U.S.C. §§45(b)-45(l) (1988).

[68] 15 U.S.C. §§46 to 50 (1988).

[69] Phillip Areeda and Donald F. Turner, *Antitrust Law — An Analysis of Antitrust Principles and Their Application*, Vol. II (Boston, Little Brown & Co., 1978), at pp. 12-13.

[70] See Diario Oficial de la Federación, December 24, 1992.

[71] Imposing price conditions on distributors is resale price maintenance under Canadian law is a *per se* offence. As noted above, the U.S. approach to "vertical price fixing" is somewhat different.

[72] These and some other practices are set out in Article 10 of the legislation.

[73] Such as an economic agent having the power unilaterally to fix prices or substantially to restrict supply.

[74] See Calvin S. Goldman, Milos Barutciski and Douglas E. Rosenthal, "Competition Policy and NAFTA" (paper presented at the American Conference Institute North American Free Trade Agreement Conference, March 17-18, 1994, Washington D.C.), at p. 3. The authors observe that the current Mexican competition legislation was enacted shortly after the NAFTA text was finalized by the three NAFTA countries. The current Mexican competition legislation abrogated some earlier legislation dealing with competition matters.

[75] See Jackson, *op. cit.*, note 48, at p. 527, for a brief discussion of the relationship between declining trade barriers and national and international antitrust policy.

[76] The discussion of the existing arrangements between Canada and the United States that follows is based on "Competition Policy and NAFTA", *supra*, note 74. This paper contains an excellent discussion of these arrangements and the issues arising in the area of competition law enforcement co-operation and co-ordination (see pp. 8-15).

[77] March 9, 1984, supplemented by a minute dated April 27, 1985. See note 74, at p. 10.

[78] March 18, 1985, in force January 14, 1990, Canada Treaty Series 1990, No. 19. See note 74, at p. 11.

[79] Dated December 3, 1971, in force March 22, 1976, Canada Treaty Series 1976, No 3, as amended by a Protocol dated January 11, 1988, in force November 22, 1991, Canada Treaty Series 1991, No. 37. See note 74, at p. 12.

[80] *Op. cit.*, note 74, at p. 9. See, for example, s. 29 of the *Competition Act*, which prohibits disclosure of information by persons administering the legislation except to a Canadian law enforcement agency or for the administration or enforcement of the legislation.

[81] This treaty and some of the issues surrounding its application are discussed in Goldman, *et. al.*, *op. cit.*, note 74, at pp. 11-13.

[82] See NAFTA 721(b) respecting sanitary and phytosanitary measures, NAFTA 912(b) respecting standards-related measures and NAFTA 1019(5) respecting government procurement.

[83] This list of issues is taken from Goldman, *et. al.*, *op. cit.*, note 74, at pp. 18-26. This paper also discusses "positive comity", a concept in the 1991 US/EC Competition Policy Agreement, under which one country may request another to take enforcement action respecting conduct in the other country that adversely affects the interests of the first country. See pp. 20-22 for a discussion of this concept and its limitations.

[84] As discussed in §5.5(2), listing and delisting practices followed by Canadian provincial liquor monopolies have been held to contravene GATT Article XI on the basis of the Interpretative Note to GATT Article XI.

[85] The Interpretative Note to GATT Article XVII provides that these do not include measures to ensure standards of quality or efficiency in the operation of external trade. This would occur if a government prescribed quality standards for an exported good and only some enterprises were capable of meeting the standards. These also do not include privileges granted for the exploitation of national natural resources. For a discussion of this note and its derivation, see Jackson, *op. cit.*, note 48, at pp. 341-2.

[86] Jackson, *ibid.*, at pp. 346-7.

[87] Paragraph 3 of the understanding requires that notifications be made in accordance with the 1960 questionnaire set out in BISD 9S/184.

[88] Besides monopolies, NAFTA 1502 refers to government monopolies, which is defined, and privately owned monopolies, which is not.

[89] FTA 2010(2)(a)(ii).

[90] See NAFTA 1502(5).

[91] See §5.3(2)(a)(ii).

[92] See NAFTA Annex 1505, para. (a).

[93] R.S.C. 1985, c. F-11, as amended.

[94] NAFTA follows a drafting style that evidences the intention to include only federal entities by specifically referring to the federal government of a NAFTA country. See, for example, the definition of government monopoly.

[95] See NAFTA Annex 1505, para. (b). Affiliates and successors are also included.

[96] As discussed in §9.2(2)(b)(ii), provincially or state-owned monopolies are not subject to the broader non-discrimination provision set out in NAFTA 1502(3)(b). However, as discussed in §5.5(2), discriminatory listing and delisting practices have been found to contravene GATT Article XI, which is incorporated into NAFTA by NAFTA 309.

[97] NAFTA 1608.

[98] *Immigration Regulations*, SOR/78-172. For a consolidation of these regulations, see Frank N. Morrocco, Q.C., and Henry M. Goslett, eds., *The Annotated Immigration Act of Canada 1994* (Scarborough, Carswell, 1993).

[99] Chapter Sixteen of the *Immigration Manual* sets out the procedures that applied to persons seeking temporary entry under the FTA.

[100] *Immigration Regulations*, s. 13 and Sched. II. Schedule II refers to "nationals" rather than "citizens" of the United States. "National" is not defined in the *Immigration Act* or the *Immigration Regulations*. "National of the United States" is defined in 8 U.S.C. §1101(22) as a citizen of the United States or a person who, although not a citizen of the United States, owes permanent allegiance to the United States.

101 *Immigration Regulations*, SOR/78-172, s. 18(1), as amended. See the definition of "employment authorization" in s. 2(1).

102 *Immigration Act*, R.S.C. 1985, c. I-2, s. 2(1). For a consolidation, see *The Annotated Immigration Act of Canada 1994, op. cit.*, note 98.

103 See *Immigration Regulations*, s. 19(3)(a)(i) and (ii) for U.S. citizens and permanent residents. There are a number of other categories listed in s. 19(3) regarding who may obtain employment authorizations at the point of entry. The general statutory rule set out in s. 10 of the *Immigration Act* is that a person must obtain an employment authorization before arriving at the point of entry.

104 *Immigration Regulations*, SOR/78-172, s. 20(1)(a).

105 *Ibid.*, s. 20(3).

106 The *Immigration Manual*, Ch. 15, p. 2. The expression "employment validation" appears only in the *Immigration Manual* and not in the *Immigration Regulations*. The need for employment validation is inferred from provisions in the *Immigration Regulations*, such as those described above.

107 The categories are set out in the *Immigration Regulations*, s. 19(1). Each of these exempt categories is further explained in the *Immigration Manual*, Ch. 15, s. 15.04, pp. 6-13. Business visitors described in NAFTA Annex 1603.A discussed in §9.3(b)(i) are exempt from employment authorization requirements. See *Immigration Regulations*, s. 19(1)(w), which was added by SOR/93-609. The operation of the corresponding s. 19(1)(v) implementing Canada's FTA obligations was suspended by SOR/93-609.

108 See generally *Immigration Regulations*, s. 20(5) and *Immigration Manual*, Ch. 15, ss. 15.07-15.18, pp. 15-28. Section 15.07 of the *Immigration Manual* points out that exemption from validation requirements does not exempt persons from the need to establish that they are qualified for the work to which they are destined.

109 *Immigration Regulations*, s. 20(5)(a), which includes several other categories of entrant. See also *Immigration Manual*, Ch. 15, s. 15.09, p. 15.

110 *Immigration Regulations*, s. 20(5)(b). For a list of the international agreements, see *Immigration Manual*, Ch. 15, s. 15.10, pp. 16-18. The FTA was and NAFTA is such an agreement.

111 *Immigration Regulations*, s. 20(5)(d) and *Immigration Manual*, Ch. 15, s. 15.12, pp. 19-20.

112 *Immigration Regulations*, s. 20(5)(e)(i).

113 See exemption codes E01 and E03 described in *Immigration Manual*, Ch. 15, s. 15.15(4), p. 22.

114 See exemption code E10 described in *Immigration Manual*, Ch. 15, s. 15.15(4); pp. 22-23. Service work must be done pursuant to the original agreement.

115 See exemption code E15 described in *Immigration Manual*, Ch. 15, s. 15.15(4), p. 23.

116 *Immigration Act*, s. 19(1). Section 19(1) sets out the categories of persons to whom entry will be denied for health reasons and other reasons. For example, s. 19(1)(a) covers persons suffering from diseases which would endanger public health. Section 19(1)(b) includes persons incapable of supporting themselves. Section 19(1)(c) and (d) include criminals. Section 19(1)(e) and (f) cover persons who have engaged in espionage. There are several other categories.

117 8 U.S.C. §1101(3) (1988). See note 100 for a discussion of "national".

118 8 U.S.C. §1101(15) (1988).

119 The applicable regulations are set out in 8 CFR Ch. I (1-1-93 Edition), Pt. 214, *Nonimmigrant Classes*. If a visa is required, 22 CFR Ch. I (4-1-93 Edition), Pt. 41, *Visas: Documentation of Nonimmigrants under the Immigration and Nationality Act*, as amended must also be consulted.

120 8 CFR Ch. I (1-1-93 Edition) §214.2(b)(1). Section 214.2 is entitled *Special requirements for admission, extension, and maintenance of status*. Section 214.2 is broken down into paragraphs (a), (b), and so on through to (r). The letter designation of each of these paragraphs corresponds to the letter designation of the class in s. 101(a)(15) of the Immigration and Nationality Act. Thus, the special requirements for the class of temporary entrants created by s. 101(a)(15)(B) is set out in §214.2(b). There is a §214.2(s) covering NATO personnel.

121 The classification symbols for visas issued to non-immigrants are set out in 22 CFR Ch. I (4-1-93 Edition), §41.12.

122 The other classes are briefly summarized as: diplomats (A); aliens in transit (C); alien crewmen (D); foreign students (F); representatives of foreign governments to international organi-

zations (G); representatives of foreign media, based on reciprocity (I); exchange visitors (J); fiancees (K); vocational students (M); parents and children of special immigrants (N); performing athletes and entertainers (P); participants in international cultural programs (Q); religious personnel (R).

[123] See 8 CFR Ch. I (4-1-93 Edition). See §41.2(a) for the general exemption. Section 41.2(m) provides that the general exemption does not apply to treaty traders and treaty investors (E). The exemption also does not apply to the fiancees of U.S. citizens (K). See §41.2(k).

[124] 8 CFR Ch. I (4-1-93 Edition) §41.2(1) and (2). There are also exemptions for Mexican nationals employed as aircraft crew members in §41.2(3) or bearing Mexican diplomatic or official passports in §41.2(4). See §41.32 for procedures respecting issuance of border crossing identification cards.

[125] 22 CFR Ch. I (4-1-93 Edition) §41.31(b)(1). As noted previously, Canadian nationals are not subject to these visa requirements. The provisions respecting Canadians for this class under the FTA were set out in 8 CFR Ch. I (1-1-93 Edition) §214.2(4).

[126] 22 CFR Ch. I (4-1-93 Edition) §41.31(a)(1)-(3).

[127] 8 CFR Ch. I §214.2(b).

[128] Defined in 8 CFR Ch. I (1-1-93 Edition) §214.2(e)(2) as the exchange, purchase or sale of goods and/or services.

[129] 8 CFR Ch. I (1-1-93 Edition) §214.2(e)(1).

[130] 8 U.S.C. §1101(a)(15)(H) (1988) and 8 CFR Ch. I (1-1-93 Edition) §214.2(h).

[131] 8 CFR Ch. I (1-1-93 Edition) §214.2(h)(1) and §214.2(h)(2).

[132] The time periods are set out in 8 CFR Ch. I (1-1-93 Edition) §214.2(h)(9)(iii).

[133] The petition requirements for registered nurses are set out in 8 CFR Ch. I (1-1-93 Edition) §214.2(h)(3).

[134] See 8 CFR Ch. I (1-1-93 Edition) §214.2(h)(4) for the requirements respecting this category. There are special rules in §214.2(h)(4)(i)(C) dealing with fashion modelling.

[135] See 8 CFR (1-1-93 Edition) §214.2(h)(4)(B)(1) and 8 U.S.C. §1182(n)(1) (1988 Edition, Supplement V).

[136] 8 CFR Ch. I (1-1-93 Edition) §214.2(h)(8)(i)(A) and (B). See also 8 U.S.C. §1184(g)(1)(A) (1988 Supplement V), which prescribes the limitation of 65,000 for any fiscal year, beginning with the fiscal year 1992.

[137] See 8 CFR Ch. I (1-1-1993 Edition) §214.2(5) for the requirements applicable to this category.

[138] 8 CFR Ch. I (1-1-1993 Edition) §214.2(h)(5)(ii).

[139] The requirements for H-2B workers are set out in 8 CFR (1-1-93 Edition) §214.2(h)(6). See §214(h)(6)(i) for this particular requirement.

[140] 8 CFR Ch. I (1-1-93 Edition) §214.2(h)(6)(D). The evidence must also establish that the terms and conditions of employment are consistent with the nature of the occupation, activity and industry in the United States.

[141] 8 CFR Ch. I (1-1-93 Edition) §214.2(h)(8)(i)(C). See also 8 U.S.C. §1184(g)(1)(B) (1988 Edition, Supplement V), which prescribes the limitation of 66,000 for any fiscal year beginning with the fiscal year 1992.

[142] 8 CFR Ch. I (1-1-93 Edition) §214.2(h)(7).

[143] For the petition requirements, see 8 CFR Ch. I (1-1-93 Edition) §214.2(h)(7)(ii).

[144] The preceding three-year requirement is added in the regulations. See 8 CFR (1-1-93 Edition) §214.2(l)(1)(i). Section 214.2(l)(1)(ii) defines expressions such as "managerial capacity", "executive capacity", "specialized knowledge", subsidiary" and "affiliate". The visa symbols for this class are L-1 for intracompany transferees and L-2 for their spouses and children. See 22 CFR Ch. I (4-1-93 Edition) §41.12.

[145] 8 CFR (1-1-93 Edition) §214.2(l)(2) sets out the petition requirement. Section 214.2(l)(3) describes the evidence that must accompany the petition. Section 214.2(l)(4) provides for blanket petitions.

[146] 8 CFR Ch. I (1-1-93 Edition) §214.2(l)(12)(i). There are restrictions on readmission. There are also some exceptions.

[147] 8 CFR Ch. I (1-1-93 Edition) §214.2(o)(1)(ii)(A)(1). Section 214.2(o)(1)(ii)(A)(2) specifically includes extraordinary achievement in motion picture and television production.

[148] 8 CFR Ch. I (1-1-93 Edition) §214.2(o)(2)(i) and §214.2(o)(3)(i).

[149] 8 CFR Ch. I (1-1-93 Edition) §214.2(o)(3)(iv).

[150] 8 CFR Ch. I (1-1-93 Edition) §214.2(o)(3)(iii).

[151] 8 CFR Ch. I (1-1-93 Edition) §214.2(o)(5)(i)(C). The advisory opinion is not binding on the Immigration and Naturalization Service. This requirement can be dispensed with in certain cases involving the fields of art, entertainment or athletics.

[152] 8 CFR Ch. I (1-1-93 Edition) §214.2(o)(9).

[153] General Demography Law, Article 42, cl. III.

[154] General Demography Law, Article 42, cl. IV.

[155] General Demography Law, Article 42, cl. VIII.

[156] Lydia G. Tamez and Charles C. Foster, "Entry of Business Personnel into the United States and Mexico", (paper presented at the American Conference Institute North American Free Trade Agreement Conference, March 17-18, 1994, Washington, D.C.), at pp. 16-17.

[157] Ibid., at pp. 18-19.

[158] For a description of these categories, see ibid., at pp. 19-21.

[159] NAFTA 1608. The expression "citizen" in respect of Mexico means a national or citizen of Mexico according to the provisions of Articles 30 and 34, respectively, of the Mexican Constitution. See NAFTA Annex 1608. The expression "citizen" is not defined for Canada or the United States.

[160] Canadian Immigration Regulations, s. 20(1)(b)(i) and (ii). There are somewhat different U.S. provisions respecting strikes and the entry of temporary workers under class H in 8 CFR (1-1-93 Edition) §214.2(h)(17).

[161] See NAFTA 1608 and NAFTA Annex 1608.

[162] NAFTA Annex 1603: for business visitors see Section A, para. 4(a); for traders and investors, intra-company transferees and professionals, see para. 2(a) of each of Sections B, C and D, respectively.

[163] NAFTA Annex 1603: for business visitors see Section A, para. 4(b); for traders and investors, intra-company transferees and professionals, see para. 2(b) of each of Sections B, C and D, respectively.

[164] See NAFTA Annex 1603: Section A, para. 5 for business visitors, para. 3 of each of Sections C and D for intra-company transferees and professionals respectively. The corresponding requirement for the traders and investors category in para. 3 of Section B does not contain the consultation requirements.

[165] There are a few differences. For example, the General Service heading in Schedule 1 to FTA Annex 1502.1 includes computer specialists but the corresponding heading in NAFTA Appendix 1603.A.1 does not. This same heading in NAFTA Appendix 1603.A.1 includes tourism personnel and tour bus operators, while the FTA counterpart does not have a separate category for tour bus operators.

[166] See "transportation operators" under "Distribution" and "tour bus operators" under "General Service". The inclusion in NAFTA Appendix 1603.A.1 of a separate category for bus tour operators is directed at restricting cabotage rather than expanding the scope of the activities covered.

[167] NAFTA Annex 1603, Section A, paras. 1, 3.

[168] NAFTA Annex 1603, Section A, paras. 1, 2.

[169] NAFTA Annex 1603, Section B, para. 1.

[170] NAFTA Annex 1603, Section C, para. 1.

[171] See NAFTA Appendix 1603.D.4, paras. 2(c) which refers to persons in the H-1B category described in §9.3(1)(b)(v) and para. 2(d) which refers to any other provision in s. 101(a)(15) of the Immigration and Nationality Act.

[172] See generally NAFTA Annex 1603, Section D, paras. 4, 5, which are not country-specific but (in the case of para. 4) refer to NAFTA Appendix 1603.D.4. which is country-specific and identifies the restrictions as being those of the United States as against Mexico. The obligation to consider increases is in Annex 1603, Section D, para. 5(a). The time limit is in Appendix 1603.D.4, para. 3.

[173] There was a similar requirement in FTA 1502(2).

[174] There was a similar provision in FTA 1502(4).

[175] NAFTA Annex 1604.2.

[176] NAFTA 1605(2)(c).

[177] For the text, see §4.3(1).

[178] See GATT Article IX:6.

[179] The text of this convention is reproduced in David Nimmer and Melville B. Nimmer, *Nimmer on Copyright: A Treatise on the Law of Literary, Musical and Artistic Property, and the Protection of Ideas*, Vol. 6, App. 27 (New York, Matthew Bender & Co. Inc., 1993).

[180] *Ibid.*, Vol. 6, App. 29.

[181] Howard P. Knopf, "New Forms of Intellectual Property Law", 1989 Can. Intell. Prop. Rev. 247 at p. 248.

[182] Robert D. Gould, "The International Intellectual Property Organizations" (1972), 3 C.P.R. (2d) 249 at p. 250.

[183] Article 5, paras. 2-4.

[184] Articles 13 to 16 set out the basic institutional structure of the Union.

[185] Article 28.

[186] Article 2(1). Computer software is not referred to.

[187] Country of origin is covered in Article 5, para. (4).

[188] Article 5(2).

[189] Article 19.

[190] Article 20.

[191] Article 7(1). There are special provisions in Article 7 respecting cinematographic works, anonymous or pseudonymous works and photographic works.

[192] Articles 8 and 9. Article 9(3) provides that sound and visual recordings are reproductions.

[193] Article 11. This applies to authors of dramatic, dramatico-musical works and musical works.

[194] Article 11 bis and Article 11 ter.

[195] Article 12.

[196] Article 14.

[197] Article 14 bis.

[198] Articles 10 and 10bis.

[199] Article 15.

[200] Article 16.

[201] See Articles II and III respectively of the Appendix to the Berne Convention for the provisions respecting translation and reproduction. See Article IV of the Appendix for the limitations.

[202] See Articles 22 to 25 for the institutional structure.

[203] Article 33.

[204] Nimmer, *op. cit.*, note 179, at p. App-2.

[205] Article 1(a).

[206] Normand Tamaro, *The Annotated Copyright Act 1992*, (Toronto, Carswell 1992), at p. 176.

[207] Article 1.

[208] Article 4.

[209] Article 5.

[210] Article 6.

[211] Nimmer, *op. cit.*, note 179, at p. App.20-3.

[212] *Ibid.*, at p. App. 20-18.

[213] See the preamble to the Geneva Convention.

[214] UPOV Convention (1978), Article 3(1) and UPOV Convention (1991), Article 4(1).

[215] Article 4(3). A member country must apply the Convention to at least twenty-four genera or species within eight years of becoming bound.

[216] Article 3(1)(ii). There is a five-year phase-in period from the time that a member country becomes bound.

[217] UPOV Convention (1978), Article 6 and UPOV Convention (1991), Articles 5 to 9.

[218] UPOV Convention (1978), Article 5(1).

[219] UPOV Convention (1991), Article 14(1).

[220] UPOV Convention (1978), Article 12 and UPOV Convention (1991), Article 11.

[221] UPOV Convention (1978), Article 8.

[222] UPOV Convention (1991), Article 19(2).

[223] UPOV Convention (1978), Articles 15-22 and UPOV Convention (1991), Articles 25, 26.

[224] "World Intellectual Property Organization: Treaty on Intellectual Property in Respect of

Integrated Circuits" (1989), 28 I.L.M. 1477. See "Introductory Note" by Frederick M. Abbott, at p. 1477.

[225] *Ibid.*

[226] There are some exceptions in Article 6(2) to the obligations in Article 6(1).

[227] For details, see Article 7(2).

[228] Article 1.

[229] Article 9.

[230] Article 14.

[231] Knopf, *op. cit.*, note 181, at p. 249.

[232] Jacques J. Gorlin, "GATT — A view from the United States" (1989), 5 Can. Intell. Prop. Rev. 275.

[233] *Ibid.*, at p. 279.

[234] *Ibid.*, at p. 276.

[235] This summary is based on the discussion of the objectives of a GATT agreement on intellectual property that appears in Gorlin, *ibid.*, at pp. 277-9. Gorlin emphasizes on p. 278 that the establishment of minimum standards was not an exercise in harmonization.

[236] Robert H. Barrigar, "T.R.I.P.S. Negotiation under the GATT Uruguay Round" (1990), 7 Can. Intell. Prop. Rev. 8, at p. 12.

[237] NAFTA 1702 and TRIPS Agreement, Article 1, para. 1.

[238] Trade secrets in the TRIPS Agreement are referred to in Article 39 as "undisclosed information".

[239] See TRIPS Agreement, Article 1, para. 3.

[240] While the Berne Convention does not refer to computer programs, this would include computer programs because of NAFTA 1705(1)(a), which requires the NAFTA countries to protect computer programs as literary works within the meaning of the Berne Convention.

[241] UPOV Convention (1978), Article 3(1) and UPOV Convention (1991), Article 4(1).

[242] Or a "national" as defined in NAFTA Annex 201.1.

[243] This NAFTA provision refers to the obligations of NAFTA countries respecting existing works being governed solely by Article 18 of the Berne Convention. Presumably existing copyright works were intended. The corresponding TRIPS Agreement provision in para. 2 of Article 70 specifically refers to copyright obligations. Article 18 of the Berne Convention provides that the Convention applies to works that had not fallen into the public domain when the Convention became effective but does not protect works that had at that time fallen into the public domain through the expiry of the term of protection.

[244] While all these conventions existed on January 1, 1994, not all NAFTA countries had acceded to them. Arguably NAFTA 103 does not apply to obligations assumed by a NAFTA country as the result of acceding to a convention after January 1, 1994. However, as NAFTA imposes higher standards than the conventions, this hardly seems a relevant consideration.

[245] This obligation applies two years after the date of the signature of NAFTA, which was December 17, 1992.

[246] For a detailed discussion of the complex issue of moral rights and U.S. law, see Nimmer, *op. cit.*, note 179, Vol. 2, §8.21, at p. 8-278.1. The opponents included diverse entities such as IBM and the magazine publishing industry. See p. 8-279, footnote 14.

[247] TRIPS Agreement, Article 2, para. 1, which requires that members comply with Articles 1 through to 12 and Article 19 of the Paris Convention.

[248] TRIPS Agreement, Article 9, para. 1 requires that members comply with Articles 1 through to 21 of the Berne Convention.

[249] TRIPS Agreement, Article 35.

[250] TRIPS Agreement, Article 2, para. 2.

[251] See NAFTA 1703(3)(a), (b). NAFTA 1703(4) provides that the national treatment obligation does not apply to procedures provided for in agreements concluded under the auspices of the World Intellectual Property Organization.

[252] There are three exceptions: advantages accorded by members under international agreements on judicial assistance or law enforcement that are not confined to the protection of intellectual property; advantages granted under the provisions of the Berne Convention or the Rome Convention that are based on treatment accorded in another country rather than national

treatment; and advantages respecting the rights of performers, producers of phonograms and broadcasting organizations not covered by the TRIPS Agreement.

253 See §9.2(1).
254 TRIPS Agreement, Article 8, para. 2.
255 TRIPS Agreement, Article 8, para. 1.
256 This language appears in both NAFTA 1705(1)(b) and TRIPS Agreement, Article 10, para. 2.
257 TRIPS Agreement, Article 11 which also covers cinematographic works.
258 17 U.S.C. §405. This legislation sets out certain conditions under which the omission of the copyright notice required under §401 through to §403 of 17 U.S.C. from copies of works publicly distributed with the authority of the copyright owner before the effective date of the Berne Convention Implementation Act of 1988 will not forfeit protection and throw the work into the public domain. The legislation is of general application and not specific to motion pictures.
259 Paragraph 6 of Article 14 of the TRIPS Agreement qualifies certain of the standards under Article 14 by permitting members to "provide for conditions, limitations, exceptions and reservations to the extent permitted by the Rome Convention". Other than in the definition of "nationals of another Party" discussed in §9.4(5)(a)(iii), NAFTA Chapter Seventeen does not refer to the Rome Convention.
260 TRIPS Agreement, Article 14, para. 2.
261 TRIPS Agreement, Article 14, para. 4; Article 11.
262 TRIPS Agreement, Article 14, para. 1. The term of protection to performers is also fifty years from the date of fixation. See para. 5. Article 14 of the TRIPS Agreement also permits broadcasting organizations to prohibit the fixation, reproduction of the fixation and the rebroadcasting of broadcasts. NAFTA Chapter Seventeen does not cover the rights of broadcast organizations in respect of their broadcasts. However, the retransmission provision in FTA 2006 discussed in §10.1(3)(b)(iii) and §10.1(4) addresses a similar issue.
263 The expression used in NAFTA 1703(1) is "secondary uses of sound recordings", which is defined in NAFTA 1721.
264 TRIPS Agreement, Article 15, para. 1.
265 Ibid., Article 16, para. 1.
266 Ibid., Article 15, para. 3.
267 Ibid., Article 15, para. 5.
268 Ibid., Article 15, para. 4.
269 See Article 7 of the Paris Convention.
270 Ibid., Article 16, para. 2.
271 Ibid., Article 18.
272 Ibid., Article 19, para. 1.
273 Ibid., Article 19, para. 2.
274 Ibid., Article 20.
275 Ibid., Article 21.
276 Ibid., Article 17.
277 Ibid., Article 27, para. 1.
278 Ibid., Article 27, para. 2.
279 Ibid., Article 27, para. 3.
280 See the "Dunkel Draft" from the GATT Secretariat, Introduction.
281 See Article 5, para. A.2 of the Paris Convention, which permits compulsory licensing under these circumstances.
282 Unlike NAFTA, Article 38 of the TRIPS Agreement takes into account that some members may not provide for registration and also permits members to provide for protection to lapse after fifteen years.
283 Article 6(1)(ii). Article 6(1)(i) of the Integrated Circuits Treaty covers unauthorized reproduction.
284 Defined in both NAFTA 1721 and footnote 10 to Article 39 of the TRIPS Agreement as practices such as a breach of contract, breach of confidence and inducement to breach, and includes the acquisition of information by third parties who knew or were grossly negligent in failing to know that such practices were involved in acquiring the information.
285 There are some conditions set out in NAFTA 1711(5). See also NAFTA 1711(6) which pro-

hibits other persons from relying on data submitted without the consent of the person who submitted it. There is no counterpart to this in the TRIPS Agreement.

286 Defined in NAFTA 1721. See also Article 22, para. 1 of the TRIPS Agreement.

287 See NAFTA 1712(1) through to (3) and the corresponding provisions in paras. 2 through to 4 of Article 22 of the TRIPS Agreement.

288 NAFTA 1712(3) and Article 22, para. 4 of the TRIPS Agreement.

289 Article 22 of the TRIPS Agreement does not contain provisions comparable to NAFTA 1712(4) through (9).

290 *Ibid.*, Article 23, para. 1.

291 Set out in NAFTA 1713(4).

292 See NAFTA 1714(2) and (4) respectively. NAFTA 1714(3) sets out rules respecting decisions.

293 NAFTA 1715(3).

294 Paragraph 2 of Article 44 of the TRIPS Agreement provides an exception when compulsory licensing applies, and permits declaratory judgments and adequate compensation if injunctive remedies contravene a member's law. These provisions do not have counterparts in NAFTA.

295 The expression used in Article 50 is *inaudita altera parte*.

296 Or within a period not less than twenty working days or greater than thirty days in the absence of such a determination.

297 NAFTA 1718(1) and TRIPS Agreement, Article 51.

298 NAFTA 1718(2) and TRIPS Agreement, Article 52.

299 NAFTA 1718(3) and TRIPS Agreement, Article 53, para. 1.

300 NAFTA 1718(4) and TRIPS Agreement, Article 53, para. 2.

301 NAFTA 1718(5) and TRIPS Agreement, Article 54.

302 NAFTA 1718(6) and TRIPS Agreement, Article 55. This period can be extended by another ten working days in appropriate cases.

303 NAFTA 1718(9) and TRIPS Agreement, Article 56.

304 NAFTA 1718(7) and TRIPS Agreement, Article 55. NAFTA 1718(8) provides that if the suspension of release has been carried out under a provisional judicial measure, the provisions of 1716(6) described in §9.4(18)(c) apply. Article 55 of the TRIPS Agreement contains a similar provision. The cross-reference is para. 6 of Article 50.

305 NAFTA 1718(10) and TRIPS Agreement, Article 57.

306 NAFTA 1718(11) and TRIPS Agreement, Article 58. Competent authorities may seek assistance from right holders. Prompt notification is required.

307 NAFTA 1718(12) and TRIPS Agreement, Article 59.

308 NAFTA 1718(13) and TRIPS Agreement, Article 60.

309 This obligation applies three years after the date of the signature of NAFTA, which was December 17, 1992.

310 TRIPS Agreement, Article 65, para. 1. Note, however, that this provision and the other transitional provisions set out in Part VI of the TRIPS Agreement, including those in para. 4 of Article 65 and para. 1 of Article 66 described in the following sentences, do not apply with respect to patent protection for pharmaceutical and agricultural chemical products. See Article 70, para. 8.

311 TRIPS Agreement, Article 65, para. 4.

312 TRIPS Agreement, Article 66, para. 1.

CHAPTER 10

CULTURAL INDUSTRIES AND OTHER EXCEPTIONS

NAFTA Chapter Twenty-One sets out a number of exceptions to the rights and obligations created by NAFTA. As discussed in §4.3(5), NAFTA 2101 incorporates the exceptions set out in GATT Article XX. Chapter Twenty-One carries forward the FTA exception for cultural industries and sets out general exceptions respecting national security, taxation, balance of payments and disclosure of information.

10.1 CULTURAL INDUSTRIES

The Canadian negotiators entered the NAFTA negotiations with a strong mandate to preserve the exemption for cultural industries achieved in the FTA. While from a U.S. viewpoint commercial activities such as book and magazine publishing, film and video production and distribution, radio, television and cable may be businesses like other businesses, in Canada these activities are associated with national and cultural identity and are regarded as requiring special protection. This attitude is reflected in the declaration of policy in the *Broadcasting Act*,[1] which states that the Canadian broadcasting system should "serve to safeguard, enrich and strengthen the cultural, political, social and economic fabric of Canada" and "encourage the development of Canadian expression by providing a wide range of programming that reflects Canadian attitudes, opinions, ideas, values and artistic creativity".[2]

Many people in the U.S. entertainment industry treated the FTA exemption with disdain and the claim for its need with scepticism. As one U.S. commentator has expressed it: "Unfortunately, in both rhetoric and practice the Canadians have often deliberately confused commerce and culture. For the Canadians, culture is frequently invoked to mask a real commercial interest."[3]

There was concern in Canada that the FTA cultural exemption, like other FTA provisions, would be on the table in the NAFTA negotiations and there was considerable pressure from the U.S. entertainment industry to reopen the issue. However, in the end the FTA status quo was preserved. In fact, the entire FTA regime as it relates to cultural industries has been carried forward into NAFTA.

A cultural exemption was not a core Mexican demand. This may be explained in part by Mexico's cultural separation from the United States through language. Also, as discussed in §5.4, the Mexican negotiators had different priorities when it came to exemptions. The Mexicans were content to preserve certain measures relating to culture by taking the reservations under NAFTA Annexes I and II described in §7.9(3)(d)(v) and §7.9(4)(b). The result for cultural industries under NAFTA is two bilateral approaches. One set of rules applies as between Canada and each of the United States and Mexico. A second set of rules applies as between the United States and Mexico.

(1) Cultural Industries Defined

The definition of cultural industries in NAFTA closely tracks that in the FTA. The definition is as follows:

cultural industries means persons engaged in any of the following activities:
  (a) the publication, distribution, or sale of books, magazines, periodicals or newspapers in print or machine readable form but not including the sole activity of printing or typesetting any of the foregoing;
  (b) the production, distribution, sale or exhibition of film or video recordings;
  (c) the production, distribution, sale or exhibition of audio or video music recordings;
  (d) the publication, distribution or sale of music in print or machine readable form; or
  (e) radiocommunications in which the transmissions are intended for direct reception by the general public, and all radio, television and cable broadcasting undertakings and all satellite programming and broadcast network services.[4]

The sole difference between the NAFTA definition and the FTA definition[5] is the replacement of the word "enterprise" in the FTA definition with the word "persons" in the NAFTA definition. The purpose of this change was to make clear that the definition covered individuals engaged in these activities as well as business organizations.

(2) Canadian Programs

Canada has a variety of measures relating to cultural industries that affect the right of establishment and impose performance requirements as a condition of receiving advantages in the form of grants from federal and provincial funding agencies. The primary purpose of these measures is not to insulate Canadians from American cultural products but to ensure that at least some of the cultural products available to Canadians are created by Canadians and involve Canadian talent and Canadian themes. The following briefly describes certain Canadian measures affecting television, films, book publishing and magazines.

(a) Television and cable

Free television is television programming that can be received by an antenna. There are three television networks in Canada, the publicly owned Canadian Broadcasting Corporation (CBC) and privately owned CTV and Global. Most television stations in Canada are owned or affiliated with the networks. However some, like CITY in Toronto, are independent. To operate, the operator of a television station must receive a licence from the Canadian Radio-Television and Telecommunications Commission ("CRTC"). The declaration of policy in the *Broadcasting Act* includes a statement that the Canadian broadcasting system must be "effectively owned and controlled by Canadians".[6] Accordingly, a licence will not be granted unless the operator is Canadian-owned.

The declaration of policy in the *Broadcasting Act* also requires that the Canadian broadcasting system, "through its programming and the employment opportunities arising out of its operations, serve the needs and interests, and reflect the circumstances and aspirations, of Canadian men, women and children".[7] Accordingly, television stations are subject to quota requirements in their broadcasting in that a certain amount of the programming broadcast by a station must be Canadian. The rules regarding Canadian content for CRTC purposes are set forth in a public notice issued by the CRTC in April, 1984.[8] Points are awarded for particular aspects of a production being Canadian (such as the director or lead actor or actress) and the production must accumulate six points. Also, with certain exceptions at least 75% of total remuneration must be paid to Canadians and at least 75% of post-production costs must be incurred in Canada.

Cable television is delivered to subscribers through coaxial cable by a cable company. The programming may be either from free television through signals gathered by the cable company or from a cable service like TSN or CNN. Cable companies and cable services are licensed by the CRTC and must be Canadian-owned. The CRTC regulates the channels that cable companies can deliver to subscribers. For example, while Rogers Cable is permitted to carry the U.S.-operated CNN, it is not permitted to carry the U.S.-operated ESPN because it competes with Canadian-owned TSN. Cable services licensed in Canada are subject to quota requirements regarding Canadian programming similar to the free television stations.

(b) Film and video production and distribution

(i) Film production

There are no nationality-based restrictions in Canada to producing films. However, several Canadian programs clearly impose content-based performance requirements as conditions of receiving benefits. Income tax write-offs in the form of enhanced capital cost allowances are available for films that are certified by the Canadian Audio-Visual Certification Office ("CAVCO")[9] on behalf of the applicable federal government minister as a "certified production". For a film or tape to be a "certified production", it must be produced by a Canadian and earn a minimum of six units of production on a prescribed point system similar to that described above. Also, the 75% expenditure tests described above must be met.[10] Certified productions automatically qualify as Canadian for CRTC quota purposes but a production certified as Canadian under the CRTC rules will not necessarily qualify as a "certified production" for income tax benefits.

Film productions that meet CRTC content requirements command premiums because they can be used by television broadcasters and cable services in meeting Canadian quota requirements. Government funding through federal agencies such as Telefilm Canada or the National Film Board Co-Production Fund or the various provincial agencies are based on criteria which relate to nationality or content.[11]

(ii) Co-production agreements

Canada has entered into co-production agreements with over twenty-five countries including Mexico, but not the United States. Co-production agreements are individually negotiated and vary from country to country. However, a co-production agreement will describe the production media covered (such as film and television), the minimum financial and creative participation by each party, the terms of participation for third parties and procedures for entry and exit of creative and technical personnel and equipment.[12] A qualifying co-production film will be entitled to the full benefit of government incentives that are accorded to Canadian films. Co-ventures (international co-productions with countries that do not have a treaty with Canada) may none the less qualify as 100% Canadian content if certain criteria are met.[13]

(iii) Film exhibition and distribution

The major exhibitors of films in Canada are Cineplex-Odeon (partly Canadian-owned) and Famous Players (owned by Paramount, a U.S. corporation). There are no ownership restrictions on film exhibitors but Investment Canada would likely exercise its jurisdiction to prevent further erosion of Canadian ownership of the Canadian exhibition industry. There is nothing in Canada corresponding to the Mexican requirement referred to in §7.9(3)(d)(v) that a certain portion of screen time be reserved for domestically produced films. In fact, most films exhibited in Canadian theatres are produced in the United States.

Distribution of films in Canada is done principally through the U.S. majors such as Twentieth Century Fox, Tristar, Columbia and Warner. These entities acquire distribution rights to films and control distribution to exhibitors and to the video market and television. Some of the U.S. majors have Canadian subsidiaries. There are two particularly significant Canadian-owned film distributors in Canada, namely Alliance and Astral. There are no ownership restrictions in Canada respecting distributors and the proposed film distribution legislation which was contemplated in 1988 and which would have placed limitations on the ability of foreign-owned film distribution companies to operate in Canada was never passed.[14] However, Investment Canada could exercise its jurisdiction to prevent the further expansion in Canada of foreign-owned film distribution companies.

(c) Book publishing

In 1985, the Canadian government announced the so-called "Baie Comeau Book Publishing Policy" (the "Baie Comeau Policy") following the acquisition of Prentice-Hall Inc. and its Canadian subsidiary, Prentice-Hall Canada by Paramount (then Gulf & Western). The policy was designed to raise the level of Canadian ownership in publishing, which was then about 27%.[15] The Baie Comeau Policy provided that a foreign investor could only establish or acquire an interest in a Canadian book publishing or distribution business in the form of a joint venture under Canadian control. A direct or indirect acquisition of a foreign-controlled Canadian business had to be accompanied by an undertaking to divest control of the business to a Canadian at a fair market price within two years. Paramount was permitted to keep Prentice-Hall Canada but was required to sell Ginn Publishing Canada Inc., an educational publishing house that it had subsequently acquired, together with another smaller publishing house called GLC Publishing. No buyer for the companies appeared and the Canadian government, through the Canada Development Investment Company ("CDIC"), bought a controlling interest in the two companies in February, 1989.[16] This was consistent with its obligations under the FTA described in §10.1(3)(b)(ii).

In early 1992 the Canadian government decided to discontinue the Baie Comeau Policy and the concept of forced divestiture.[17] A revised book publishing policy announced in January, 1992, provides that acquisition of existing Canadian-controlled businesses by non-Canadians will not be permitted.[18] Exceptions can be made if the business is in financial distress and Canadians have been given a full and fair opportunity to purchase. Non-Canadians wishing to sell existing businesses must give Canadians a full and fair opportunity to purchase and acquisitions by non-Canadians, as well as indirect acquisitions, are subject to the "net benefit to Canada" test. The policy sets out a number of commitments that Investment Canada would typically require from a foreign investor.

In February, 1994, CDIC sold Ginn Publishing Canada Inc. to Paramount.[19] The government approved the transaction after receiving several undertakings from Paramount[20] and also approved the sale of another Canadian publishing company, Maxwell Macmillan Canada Inc., to Paramount. The Ginn transaction was widely criticized in the Canadian press as a sell-out to U.S. corporate interests. Whether the Ginn situation was unique on its own facts or represents a further shift in Canadian government policy remains to be seen.

(d) Magazines and periodicals

The Canadian government has used a combination of tax and border measures to encourage the development of the Canadian magazine industry. Section 19 of the *Income Tax Act* (Canada)[21] does not permit the deduction of outlays of expenses for advertising space in a newspaper or periodical which is not a qualified "Canadian issue" of a Canadian-controlled newspaper or periodical. Tariff code item 9958[22] prohibits the importation of special editions, including split runs and regional editions, of periodicals with advertisements directed to a market in Canada that do not appear in editions distributed in the country of origin. Split runs are issues of a periodical using substantially the same editorial content but differing in some local content and advertising. This tariff code item also prohibits the importation of issues of periodicals with more than 5% of the advertising space indicating sources of availability or terms or conditions for the sale of goods in Canada. The objective of these measures is to encourage advertisers to place advertisements in Canadian periodicals and to discourage the U.S. magazine industry from serving the Canadian market with "Canadian" editions with advertising directed at Canadian consumers but with minimal Canadian content.

These measures have encouraged the development of a domestic magazine industry which has come a long way since the 1950s when the magazine market in Canada was dominated by the Canadian editions of *Time* and *Readers Digest*. As the former Minister of Communications, Perrin Beatty, said in March, 1993: "Canada has produced a vibrant, home-grown magazine industry whose livelihood depends on Canadian advertising revenues."[23] However these measures have failed to stop split runs, which the Canadian Magazine Publishers Association views as a serious competitive threat.[24] Multinational businesses have little difficulty in achieving the benefit of a deduction for advertisements placed in U.S. magazines. Canadian editions of magazines such as *Sports Illustrated* are designed and laid out in the United States and beamed electronically to Canada for printing. As a result, they never cross the border physically and therefore are not subject to tariff code item 9958.[25] In July, 1993, the government issued new guidelines respecting the administration of the *Investment Canada Act* indicating that it would treat any new title launched in Canada by a non-Canadian publisher as a new business rather than the expansion of an existing business and therefore subject to full review.[26] These guidelines do not affect split run editions such as *Time* or *Sports Illustrated* published in Canada before the new guidelines were issued.

In 1993 the Canadian government appointed a task force to review federal measures supporting the Canadian magazine industry. The task force report, which was released in March, 1994, concluded that an increase in split-run editions would threaten the viability of the Canadian magazine industry because significant advertising revenues would be diverted from Canadian magazines.[27] The task force recommended that each issue of a split-run edition be subject to an excise tax of 80% of the amount charged for all advertising in that issue.[28] Magazines with split-run editions in circulation as of the date of the report would be exempt for the number of issues distributed in Canada in the year preceding the report. At the time of writing, the Canadian government was considering the task force's recommendations but had not acted on them.

(3) Provisions of the FTA

FTA 2005(1) provided that, subject to the exceptions discussed in §10.1(3)(b), cultural industries were exempt from the requirements of the FTA. FTA 2005(2) permitted either the United States or Canada to take "measures of equivalent commercial effect" in response to actions of the other in respect of a cultural industry that were inconsistent with the FTA but for FTA 2005(1). Exemption of cultural industries from the FTA came at the price of exposure to possible retaliation in the form of measures of equivalent commercial effect. However, the right to retaliate did not apply if the action was consistent with the FTA without having to rely upon the FTA 2005(1) exemption. The exemption applied equally to the United States and Canada, but, as noted in the U.S. Statement of Administrative Action accompanying the legislation implementing the FTA, was more likely to be exercised by Canada than by the United States.

(a) Consistency with the FTA and retaliation

Many Canadian measures relating to cultural industries were consistent with the FTA without having to rely on the FTA 2005(1) exemption. As a result of the blanket grandfathering in the FTA investment and service chapters, measures such as ownership restrictions and performance requirements which had come into effect prior to the FTA would have been unaffected by the FTA even without the FTA 2005(1) exemption. Canada's ownership requirements under the *Broadcasting Act* predated the FTA, as did its quota requirements for Canadian content requirements. The FTA services chapter and the provisions of the FTA investment chapter respecting the conduct

469

and operation of businesses applied only to "covered services". The only enterprises included in the "cultural industries" definition that provided "covered services" were "establishments primarily engaged in the wholesale dealing in books, periodicals and newspapers".[29] Canadian measures affecting the conduct and operation of businesses that were "cultural industries" but that did not provide "covered services" were not covered by the FTA. They were therefore consistent with the FTA without having to rely on the FTA 2005(1) exemption and not open to retaliation under FTA 2005(2).

The amendments to the *Investment Canada Act* made as a consequence of the FTA becoming effective retained for cultural industries the pre-FTA threshold limits for review of $5 million for direct and $50 million for indirect acquisitions. Pre-FTA thresholds were also retained for financial services, transportation services, oil and gas and uranium-mining industries. The higher thresholds did not apply to these other activities because of exclusions in the FTA investment chapter.[30] There was no provision in the FTA investment chapter that permitted the retention of the pre-FTA thresholds for cultural industries. However, there is a grandfathered provision in the *Investment Canada Act* that provides that the thresholds do not apply at all to prescribed activities that in the government's opinion are "related to Canada's cultural heritage or national identity".[31] The prescribed activities include all those under the definition of "cultural industries", except for radio, television and cable[32] which, as discussed, are subject to grandfathered ownership restrictions under the *Broadcasting Act*.

(b) Exceptions to the FTA exemption

(i) Tariff elimination

The exemption in FTA 2005(1) did not apply to tariff elimination. The elimination of tariffs on products of cultural industries has proceeded in the ordinary course.

(ii) Forced divestiture

The exemption did not apply to FTA 1607(4) which required Canada to purchase a business from an investor of the United States of America at fair open market value in circumstances in which Canada requires the divestiture of a business enterprise in a cultural industry pursuant to its review of a direct acquisition. FTA 1607(4) was directed at the Baie Comeau Policy and, as discussed in §10.1(2)(c), was applied by Canada in the case of Ginn Publishing Canada Inc. and GLC Publishing. FTA 1607(4) would apply to the forced divestiture of any cultural industry.

(iii) Retransmission rights

The exemption did not apply to FTA 2006 which protected copyright holders of television programming in respect of retransmission rights. FTA

2006(1) required that such copyright holders receive "equitable and non-discriminatory remuneration" for any retransmission to the public by cable companies of the programs where the original transmissions are carried in distant (as opposed to local) signals intended for free television.[33] At the time that the FTA was negotiated, Canadian copyright law, unlike that of the United States, did not provide for remuneration to such copyright holders. FTA 2006(2)(a) required that each country's copyright law permit the retransmission of signals not originally intended for free television (such as those produced by a cable service like EPSN) only with the authorization of the copyright holder. FTA 2006(2)(b) required that each country's copyright law permit the wilful retransmission in altered form or non-simultaneous retransmission of programs intended for free television only with the copyright holder's authorization. However, FTA 2006(3) provided that notwithstanding FTA 2006(2)(b), each country was permitted to maintain certain types of measures in effect on October 4, 1987, such as measures permitting non-simultaneous retransmission in remote areas where simultaneous reception and retransmission are not practical,[34] and to introduce measures enabling local licensees of copyrighted programs to exploit fully the commercial value of their licences.

Canada amended its copyright law to incorporate these FTA requirements.[35] Regulations were enacted to define what was meant by a local and a distant signal.[36] The legislation defines a "signal" as a signal carrying a literary, dramatic, musical or artistic work and transmitted for free reception by the public by a terrestrial (as opposed to a satellite) station.[37] The distinction between local and distant signals is highly technical, but the general idea is that a local signal is one whose "area of transmission" covers the service area of the cable retransmission system and therefore could (at least theoretically) be received on free television by a cable user in the service area, and a distant signal is one whose area of transmission does not cover the cable retransmission service area.[38] The legislation provides for the collection of royalties under the supervision of the Copyright Board[39] and the regulations set out the criteria for establishing royalties. For example, in determining royalties that are fair and equitable, the Copyright Board must take into consideration royalties paid for the retransmission of distant signals under the retransmission regime in effect in the United States.[40]

(iv) Print-in-Canada requirements

FTA 2007 required that s. 19 of the *Income Tax Act* (Canada), discussed in §10.1(2)(d), be amended to eliminate the requirement that a Canadian issue be printed and typeset in Canada. Section 19 was amended to provide that a Canadian issue could be wholly or partly typeset and printed in the United States.[41] A "Canadian issue" must still be edited in Canada by Canadian residents and published in Canada and s. 19 continues to apply. Tariff code item 9958, discussed in §10.1(2)(d), was unaffected by the FTA.

(4) Provisions of NAFTA

NAFTA Annex 2106 reads as follows:

> Notwithstanding any other provision of this Agreement, as between Canada and the United States, any measure adopted or maintained with respect to cultural industries, except as specifically provided in Article 302 (Market Access — Tariff Elimination), and any measure of equivalent commercial effect taken in response, shall be governed under this Agreement exclusively in accordance with the provisions of the *Canada — United States Free Trade Agreement*. The rights and obligations between Canada and any other Party with respect to such measures shall be identical to those applying between Canada and the United States.

NAFTA Annex 2106 has the effect, as between Canada and the United States, of incorporating into NAFTA the entirety of the FTA provisions as they affect cultural industries. While the FTA does not apply as between Canada and Mexico, the effect of the last sentence of NAFTA Annex 2106 is to apply the FTA provisions as they affect cultural industries as between Canada and Mexico. Thus the provisions of the FTA and not those of NAFTA govern measures affecting cultural industries as between Canada and each of the United States and Mexico. As between the United States and Mexico, measures affecting cultural industries will be governed by the provisions of NAFTA.

As indicated above, the NAFTA definition of "cultural industries" is slightly broader than its FTA counterpart in that individuals as well as enterprises engaged in the listed activities are included. The effect of this is ambiguous. Presumably the intent is to rectify an oversight in the FTA definition and to apply the FTA cultural industries provisions to "cultural industries" as defined in NAFTA. However, requiring that "cultural industries" within the NAFTA definition be governed exclusively by the FTA incorporates the FTA definition, which does not include individuals. Under this interpretation, measures affecting individuals engaged in the activities listed in the definition of "cultural industries" would be subject to FTA rather than NAFTA disciplines and FTA grandfathering and exclusions from coverage would apply. However, the exemption in FTA 2005(1) and the retaliation right in FTA 2005(2) arguably do not apply because "cultural industries" in FTA 2005 could be read as having its FTA meaning rather than the NAFTA meaning. This result may not be intended but there is nothing in NAFTA that replaces the FTA defined expression "cultural industries" in FTA 2005 with its NAFTA counterpart.

The sole exception in NAFTA Annex 2106 is in respect of NAFTA 302 which eliminates tariffs. In so far as goods which are the products of cultural industries (such as books, newspapers, periodicals, films, videos and sound recordings) are concerned, the elimination of tariffs will proceed in the manner prescribed in NAFTA 302 and NAFTA Annex 302.2 and entitlement to preferential tariff treatment will be determined in the manner described in Chapters 2 and 3.

The effect of requiring that cultural industries be governed exclusively by the FTA provisions is to incorporate into NAFTA not only the exemption in FTA 2005(1) and the retaliation provision in FTA 2005(2), but all the provisions of the FTA affecting cultural industries. These include the FTA trade-in-goods provisions and the FTA services and investment chapters, including the grandfathering provisions and the exclusion from the FTA definition of "covered services" of most activities carried on by cultural industries. As under the FTA, the retaliation right in FTA 2005(2) will apply only to measures affecting cultural industries that are not inconsistent with the FTA solely because of FTA 2005(1). The retaliation right will not apply to measures that are grandfathered under the FTA or are excluded by reason of not being covered services. As NAFTA Annex 2106 provides that the rights and obligations between Canada and other NAFTA countries are to be "identical" to those applying between Canada and the United States, the relevant date for grandfathering as between Canada and Mexico is the date that the FTA became effective, which was January 1, 1989.

NAFTA does not make any reference to the forced divesture requirement in FTA 1607(4), the retransmission rights provision in FTA 2006 or the print-in-Canada provision in FTA 2007. However, as all these provisions relate to cultural industries, the effect of NAFTA Annex 2106 is that these FTA provisions will continue to apply as between Canada and the United States, and will also apply as between Canada and Mexico.

The NAFTA Annex 2106 requirement that cultural industries be governed exclusively by the FTA has the effect of exempting cultural industries from NAFTA provisions that were not in the FTA. While the FTA prohibited performance requirements such as content requirements as conditions to establishing a business, NAFTA 1106(3) also prohibits such performance requirements as conditions of receiving advantages like subsidies. Telefilm Canada's Canadian content requirements for production grants would contravene NAFTA 1106(3) were it not for NAFTA Annex 2106. NAFTA Annex 2106 prevents the most-favoured-nation obligations in NAFTA 1103 and NAFTA 1203 from requiring Canada to extend the same benefits to the United States as it presently extends to other countries under its co-production agreements. Another significant effect of NAFTA Annex 2106 is that the intellectual property provisions of NAFTA Chapter Seventeen, including those respecting copyright, do not apply as between Canada and either the United States and Mexico in so far as cultural industries are concerned. The retaliation right in FTA 2005(2) will not apply to any measure respecting a cultural industry that is inconsistent with any of these NAFTA provisions.

As discussed in §7.9(3)(d)(v) and §7.9(4)(b), Mexico has taken reservations under NAFTA Annex I and both the United States and Mexico have taken reservations under NAFTA Annex II respecting a number of activities carried on by cultural industries. These reservations will be relevant to measures governing cultural industries as between the United States and Mexico. However, reservations are irrelevant as between Canada and each of the United States and Mexico because NAFTA Annex 2106 has the effect of replacing the NAFTA investment and services chapters with those of the FTA, which are based on grandfathering. Canada's reservation respecting the *Investment Canada Act* discussed in §7.9(3)(b)(i) refers to the higher thresholds not applying to "cultural businesses". However, the legitimacy of this Canadian measure under NAFTA depends not on its inclusion in this reservation but on the grandfathered provision of the *Investment Canada Act* discussed in §10.1(3)(a).

(5) Concluding Remarks

By preserving the FTA grandfathering provisions for cultural industries, NAFTA 2106 represents a departure from the general attempt under NAFTA to achieve transparency through the specific identification of non-conforming measures through reservations. The approach taken to cultural industries in NAFTA 2106 as between Canada and Mexico is particularly convoluted because the two countries will be applying between them the provisions of a treaty to which Mexico was never a party. It must be emphasized that the NAFTA 2106 operates bilaterally. While Canada has preserved the right to take measures to protect its cultural industries without regard to the obligations imposed by NAFTA, the United States and Mexico have each preserved an identical right as against Canada.

10.2 NATIONAL SECURITY

NAFTA 2102 carries forward the general national security exception in FTA 2003 which was based on the national security exception in GATT Article XXI. NAFTA 2102 provides that NAFTA will not require NAFTA countries to disclose information contrary to essential security interests or prevent NAFTA countries from taking actions considered "necessary for the protection of its essential security interests" relating to such matters as arms traffic, supplying military and security establishments and the non-proliferation of nuclear weapons, or actions taken in time of war or other emergencies. The language quoted above, which is taken from GATT Article XXI, has been criticized as being "so broad, self-judging, and ambiguous that it obviously can be abused".[42]

The scope of NAFTA 2102 is restricted in the case of energy and basic petrochemicals to the narrower national security exception in NAFTA 607 discussed in §5.4(7)(a). NAFTA 2102 is also subject to the national security exception respecting government procurement set out in NAFTA 1018 and discussed in §9.1(13).

10.3 TAXATION

(1) Taxation Measures and International Agreements

The GATT is, amongst other things, a multilateral agreement covering commodity taxation measures. The GATT contracting parties have bound themselves to maximum rates of duties that they can levy and, subject to permitted exceptions, agree to apply the same rate to the goods of each contracting party. Other commodity taxes such as value-added taxes, sales and use taxes and excise taxes are subject to specific national treatment requirements set out in GATT Article III. The principles of national treatment and MFN treatment function effectively with commodity taxes.

There are also international tax conventions covering taxes on income and capital gains. However, these tax conventions have been negotiated on a bilateral rather than a multilateral basis. The primary purpose of tax conventions covering taxes on income and capital gains is to avoid the double taxation to which taxpayers with operations in more than one country are potentially subject. Tax conventions are generally based on principles of reciprocity rather than national treatment.

Taxes on income and capital gains are applied to non-residents differently from residents for a variety of reasons. Some income tax provisions providing for differential treatment are designed to give residents an advantage over non-residents and, as such, are discriminatory. However, a fundamental reason for taxing non-residents differently from residents is because taxes on income and capital gains are difficult, if not impossible, to enforce against persons whose assets are in another country. Therefore, the principle of national treatment is difficult to apply in international conventions dealing with these types of taxes. This consideration does not apply to sales and use and value-added taxes on goods and services imported from other countries because these are imposed on domestic consumers. Collection is not an issue and a national treatment standard can be applied.

One example of differential treatment is in the case of withholding taxes. Income tax laws of many countries impose a withholding tax on income in the form of interest, dividends and royalties paid to non-residents and make the payer responsible for the payment of the tax. These rules do not apply to residents. Under a national treatment standard requiring that non-residents be treated no less favourably than residents, these payments would leave the country without being taxed and the taxing country would have no authority in the country of the recipient's residence to collect the tax that would normally apply to its own residents. A bilateral tax convention typically covers withholding taxes by setting out reciprocal obligations under which maximum rates of withholding tax are fixed and tax credits are allowed in the recipient's country of residence for the tax withheld in the other country so that the income received by the recipient will not be subject to more tax than if it had been received domestically.

(2) Provisions of NAFTA

NAFTA directly affects taxation measures such as customs duties by providing for their elimination on originating goods. The national treatment obligation respecting the trade in goods applies to other commodity taxes by requiring their non-discriminatory application. This is consistent with the international treatment of these types of taxation measures under the GATT. However, the national treatment and MFN treatment obligations set out in the NAFTA chapters respecting investment, services and financial services are not consistent with international tax conventions covering taxes on income and capital gains. The fact that international taxation issues arising from these types of taxes have been dealt with on a bilateral rather than a multilateral basis makes the MFN principle difficult to apply. The tax conventions are based on reciprocity and not national treatment, and, as discussed, enforcement problems make strict adherence to a national treatment standard unworkable for income and capital gains taxation measures.

(a) The general exception for taxation measures

NAFTA 2103 sets out general exceptions respecting taxation measures. NAFTA 2103(1) provides that nothing in NAFTA affects taxation measures except as set out in NAFTA 2103. Taxation measures exclude customs duties, which for this purpose includes antidumping and countervailing duties, importation fees and fees applied pursuant to s. 22 of the AAA.[43] This exclusion ensures that the NAFTA tariff elimination and related provisions are unaffected by the exception for taxation measures.

(b) NAFTA and tax conventions

NAFTA 2103(2) provides that nothing in NAFTA affects the rights and obligations of any NAFTA country under any tax convention[44] and that if there is an inconsistency between NAFTA and the provisions of a tax convention, the tax convention prevails. Bilateral tax conventions are in effect between each of the NAFTA countries[45] and, while covering the same general issues, are different in their specific terms and were negotiated independently from each other. NAFTA 2103(2) applies to these tax conventions and also to the tax conventions between each NAFTA country and non-NAFTA countries.

(c) Taxation measures covered by NAFTA

NAFTA 2103(3)(a) provides that the national treatment obligations respecting goods set out in NAFTA 301 (which incorporates GATT Article III and successor agreements by reference) applies to taxation measures to the same extent as GATT Article III. The taxes affected by this provision include sales taxes, excise taxes and value-added taxes such as Canada's goods and services tax ("GST") in so far as they affect goods. NAFTA 2103(3)(b) ensures that the prohibitions of export taxes in NAFTA 314 and 604 apply to taxation measures.

NAFTA 2103(4)(b) provides that the national treatment and MFN requirements in NAFTA 1102 and 1103 (Investment), NAFTA 1202 and 1203 (Cross-Border Trade in Services) and NAFTA 1405 and 1406 (Financial Services) apply to all taxation measures other than those on income, capital gains or on the taxable capital of corporations or to an asset tax imposed by Mexico described in Annex 2103.4. However, NAFTA 2103(4)(a) provides that these taxes are covered by NAFTA 1202 and NAFTA 1405 if they relate to the purchase or consumption of particular services. For example, a capital tax on banks or a tax on the premium income of insurance companies would be covered by this provision. NAFTA 2103(4)(b) also excludes taxes on estates, inheritances, gifts and generation-skipping transfers from all these NAFTA provisions. Value-added taxes such as Canada's GST are not excluded and therefore are covered by these NAFTA provisions. The application of these NAFTA provisions to the taxation measures that they do cover is subject to general grandfathering of non-conforming taxation measures existing on January 1, 1994. These NAFTA provisions also do not apply to MFN obligations in tax conventions, new taxation measures aimed at the equitable and effective imposition of taxes that do not arbitrarily discriminate or nullify and impair NAFTA benefits or to certain excise taxes on insurance premiums referred to in NAFTA Annex 2103.4.

NAFTA 2103(5) provides that the prohibition in NAFTA 1106(3), as qualified by NAFTA 1106(4) and 1106(5) and described in §7.7(4), of performance requirements as a condition of receiving advantages applies to taxation measures. The effect of this is that advantages given by way of tax concessions are subject to these disciplines. This applies to taxes on income and capital gains as well as to sales, use and value-added taxes. However, this provision is subject to the rule respecting tax conventions described in §10.2(2)(b).

If a practice contravening this provision were sanctioned by a tax convention, the tax convention would prevail.

NAFTA 2103(6) provides that the expropriation and compensation provisions of NAFTA 1110 described in §7.7(7) apply to taxation measures. However, an investor may not invoke NAFTA 1110 as the basis for a claim under the investor-state dispute settlement procedures described in §11.3 if it is determined that the taxation measure is not an expropriation. The determination is made by the taxation authorities in the country imposing the measure. If the authorities do not make a determination within six months or "fail to agree that the measure is not an expropriation", the investor may proceed with its claim. Given the "self-judging" manner of making the determination, this provision appears to permit NAFTA countries to do through confiscatory taxation what they cannot do through direct expropriation. However, NAFTA 2103(6) only limits the availability of the investor-state dispute settlement procedures and does not foreclose the application of the dispute settlement procedures in NAFTA Chapter Twenty if the NAFTA country of the investor does not agree with the determination.

(3) Concluding Remarks

Customs duties and other commodity taxes affecting goods are subject to NAFTA disciplines. Subject to general grandfathering and some other exceptions, sales and value-added taxes affecting services are covered by the NAFTA national treatment and MFN treatment requirements. Income and capital gains taxes and taxes on capital are subject to these requirements only if applied to a particular service. They are otherwise unaffected by NAFTA except for the NAFTA provisions respecting performance requirements discussed previously. Estate, inheritance and gift taxes are unaffected by NAFTA. Tax conventions prevail over NAFTA.

10.4 BALANCE OF PAYMENTS

Like both the GATT and the FTA, NAFTA 2104 sets out exceptions that apply when a country is experiencing balance-of-payments difficulties. However, the exceptions under NAFTA are more circumscribed than those in either the GATT or the FTA.

NAFTA 2104(1) provides that NAFTA will not prevent a NAFTA country from restricting transfers when it is experiencing or threatened with serious balance-of-payments difficulties. However, if a NAFTA country imposes a measure under this provision, it must submit any current exchange restrictions to the International Monetary Fund ("IMF") for review, enter into consultations with the IMF on economic adjustment measures to address the economic problems causing the difficulties and adopt or maintain policies consistent with such consultations. Article VIII(2)(a) of the "IMF Agreement"[46] provides that no member of the IMF shall impose restrictions on the making of payments and transfers for current international transactions without IMF approval. Canada, the United States and Mexico are all IMF members. Measures must avoid unnecessary damage to the interests of other NAFTA countries, not be more burdensome than necessary, be temporary and be progressively phased out as the situation improves and be applied on the better of a national treatment or MFN treatment basis. Measures protecting specific industries are permitted only if consistent with the provisions of the Article VIII(3) of IMF Agreement, which requires IMF approval of a restriction, and with the policies required as a result of the consultations with the IMF referred to above.

Restrictions on transfers other than on cross-border trade in financial services are subject to further requirements set out in NAFTA 2104(5). Restrictions on payments for current international transactions must be consistent with Article VIII(3) of the IMF Agreement. Restrictions on international capital transactions may only be imposed in conjunction with measures imposed on current international transactions and must be consistent with Article VI of the IMF Agreement. Article VI permits members to exercise controls necessary to regulate international capital movements but provides that, subject to limited exceptions, no member may exercise these controls so as to restrict payments for current transactions or unduly delay transfer of funds in settlement of commitments.[47] Restrictions on transfers covered by NAFTA 1109 (discussed in §7.7(6)) and on transfers related to trade in goods may not impede transfers from being made in a freely convertible currency at a market rate of exchange. Restrictions on transfers may not take the form of trade restrictions such as tariff surcharges, quotas, licences or similar measures. This is a departure from the balance-of-payments provisions of GATT Article XII under which such measures can be taken and from the FTA which expressly permitted restrictions undertaken pursuant to GATT Article XII.

Restrictions on transfers on cross-border trade in financial services are subject to more lenient rules set out in NAFTA 2104(6) and 2104(7). A NAFTA country may not impose more than one measure on any transfer unless it is consistent with the Article VIII(3) of IMF Agreement and the outcome of the consultations with the IMF referred to above. Once a restriction is imposed, the NAFTA country imposing the restriction must notify and consult with the other NAFTA countries to assess its balance of payments situation and the measures adopted.

10.5   DISCLOSURE OF INFORMATION

NAFTA 2105 provides that NAFTA will not be construed to require a NAFTA country to furnish or allow access to information that would impede law enforcement or be contrary to laws protecting personal privacy or the financial affairs and accounts of individual customers of financial institutions.

ENDNOTES

1 S.C. 1991, c. 11.
2 *Broadcasting Act*, s. 3(1)(*d*)(i) and (ii).
3 Jason S. Berman, "Intellectual Property Provisions of NAFTA" in *The North American Free Trade Agreement: Its Scope and Implications for North America's Lawyers, Businesses and Policymakers* (American Bar Association Section of International Law and Practice and the Division for Professional Education, 1993), pp. 6-7.
4 NAFTA 2107, "cultural industries".
5 FTA 2012, "cultural industries".
6 *Broadcasting Act*, s. 3(1)(*a*).
7 *Broadcasting Act*, s. 3(1)(*d*)(iii).
8 Canadian Radio-Television and Telecommunications Commission, Public Notice CRTC 1984-94 (April 15, 1984).
9 CAVCO is part of the Cultural Industries Directorate of the Federal Department of Communications.
10 *Income Tax Regulations*, C.R.C. 1978, c. 945, s. 1104(2) under "certified production". The units are allotted based on the individual in respect of such allotment being Canadian: director equals two units; screen writer, two units; highest paid actor, one unit; second highest paid actor, one unit; art director, one unit; director of photography, one unit; music composer, one unit; picture editor, one unit.
11 For a summary of the federal and provincial funding available and criteria for each program, see *The Guide 93* (Toronto, Canadian Film and Television Production Association, 1993) pp. 6-17.
12 *Ibid.*, p. 26.
13 *Ibid.*, p. 25.
14 See *Comprehensive Guide*, pp. 147-9 for a description of this proposed legislation and an analysis of how it would have been treated under the FTA. Intense opposition to the proposed legislation from the U.S. entertainment industry was a factor in its demise.
15 Andrew Cohen, "Corporate America beats out Canadian nationalism" *The Financial Post* (February 25, 1994) p. 15.
16 Several newspaper columnists have expressed the view that Paramount made no serious efforts to sell the companies and that the purchase price of $9.5 million was excessive. See Cohen, *ibid.*, and Val Ross, "Who's driving the bus? Publishers have a right to wonder" *The Globe and Mail* (March 2, 1994) p. C2.
17 For a lively description of the events leading to the scrapping of the Baie Comeau Policy, see Hugh Winsor, "Ginn Fizzle: The Sorry Saga of How a U.S. Giant Revealed the Tragic Flaw in Public Policy, Swallowed a Modest Textbook Publisher and Embarrassed a Fledgling Government", in *The Globe and Mail* (March 19, 1994), p. D5.
18 See "Policy Statements on the Book Publishing Industry, Notes for a press conference address by the Honourable Perrin Beatty, Minister of Communications" Toronto, Ontario, January 28, 1992, reproduced in Peter R. Hayden, Jeffery H. Burns and Susan A. Goodeve, *Foreign Investment in Canada: A Guide to the Law* (Scarborough, Prentice-Hall Canada Inc., 1992) at p. 30,053.
19 For $10.3 million. According to Andrew Cohen, in the 1989 transaction Paramount had negotiated a right to reacquire the companies if the government relaxed its policy. See Cohen, *op. cit.*, note 15.

[20] See Val Ross, "U.S. purchase of 2 publishing firms called 'beginning of end'", *The Globe and Mail* (February 19, 1994), p. C4.

[21] R.S.C. 1985, c. 1 (5th Supp.), as amended.

[22] Tariff Code item 9958 is set out in Schedule VII of the *Customs Tariff*, which covers Prohibited Goods. See also Revenue Canada Customs, Excise and Taxation Memorandum D9-1-10, which explains the provisions of tariff code item 9958.

[23] Department of Communications, News Release, "New Task Force to Review Ways to Support Canadian Magazine Industry" (March 26, 1993).

[24] Richard Silkos, "Magazine action no solution: Much ballyhooed get-tough stance only prevents more Time invasions", *The Financial Post* (July 21, 1993) p. 9. According to this article, Canadian magazines have higher editorial costs and lower circulations than popular U.S. titles.

[25] *Ibid.*

[26] The *Canada Gazette*, Part I, pp. 2381-2.

[27] *A Question of Balance: Report of the Task Force on the Canadian Magazine Industry* (the "Task Force Report") (Ottawa, Minister of Supply and Services Canada, 1994) Cat. No. Co22-137/1994, pp. 49-55.

[28] *Ibid.*, pp. 64-6. The authors of the report go to some length to argue that the proposed excise tax does not violate Canada's obligations under any of the GATT, the FTA or NAFTA. The NAFTA cultural exemption is not raised as a reason.

[29] Canadian SIC No. 5991. See FTA Annex 1408.

[30] Financial services (other than insurance services) and transportation services are excluded from the entire FTA investment chapter under FTA 1601(2). Oil, gas and uranium-mining industries are excluded from the higher threshold requirements under para. 4 of FTA Annex 1607.3.

[31] *Investment Canada Act*, s. 15(*a*).

[32] *Investment Canada Regulations*, SOR/85-611, s. 8 and Sched. IV.

[33] Free television is explained in §10.1(2)(a).

[34] FTA 2006(3)(a)(vii). Six other types of measures are listed in clauses (i) through to (vi).

[35] *Copyright Act*, R.S.C. 1985, c. C-42, ss. 28.01, 70.61 to 70.67.

[36] *Local Signal and Distant Signal Regulations*, SOR/89-254.

[37] *Copyright Act*, s. 28.01(1).

[38] See SOR/89-254, s. 2 for definition of "area of transmission" and s. 3 for the definition of "local signal". A "distant signal" is a signal that is not a local signal.

[39] *Copyright Act*, ss. 70.61-70.67.

[40] *Retransmission Royalties Criteria Regulations*, SOR/91-690.

[41] *Income Tax Act*, R.S.C. 1985, c. 1 (5th Supp.), s. 19(1)(*b*).

[42] John H. Jackson, *The World Trading System: Law and Policy of International Economic Relations* (Boston, The Massachusetts Institute of Technology, 1989) p. 204. Jackson goes on to say that because of the danger of abuse, the GATT contracting parties have been reluctant to formally invoke GATT Article XXI.

[43] See the definition of "taxes and taxation measures" in NAFTA 2107.

[44] NAFTA 2107 defines a "tax convention" as a convention for the avoidance of double taxation or other international taxation agreement or arrangement.

[45] *Canada — United States Income Tax Convention* (1980), which became law in Canada under the *Canada — United States Tax Convention Act, 1984*, S.C. 1983-84, c. 20; *Canada — Mexico Income Tax Convention* (1991), which became law in Canada under the *Canada-Mexico Income Tax Convention Act, 1991*, S.C. 1992, c. 3, Pt. III; and *Convention Between the Government of the United States of America and the Government of the United Mexican States for the Avoidance of Double Taxation and the Prevention of Fiscal Evasion with respect to Taxes on Income*, which was signed in the United States on September 18, 1992.

[46] The text of the IMF Agreement used for this discussion is set out as Schedule I to the *Bretton Woods and Related Agreements Act*, R.S.C. 1985, c. B-7.

[47] Compare this with the exception for international capital movements in FTA 2002(b)(ii), which permitted restrictions on capital movements in accordance with the 1961 *OECD Code of Liberalization of Capital Movements*. Presumably the reason for the change in NAFTA is that Mexico, while a member of the IMF, is not a member of the OECD.

481

CHAPTER 11

INSTITUTIONAL STRUCTURE, TRANSPARENCY AND DUE PROCESS, DISPUTE SETTLEMENT PROCEDURES, ANTIDUMPING AND COUNTERVAILING DUTY MATTERS

Section A of NAFTA Chapter Twenty creates the basic institutional structure of NAFTA by establishing the Free Trade Commission and the Secretariat. This simple institutional framework is supplemented by various committees and working groups created under NAFTA provisions covering specific sectors. The institutional structure of NAFTA is discussed in §11.1. The institutions created by the Environmental Co-operation Agreement and the Labour Co-operation Agreement have been discussed in §6.9(2) and §6.10(2), respectively. NAFTA Chapter Eighteen sets out transparency requirements respecting laws of NAFTA countries affecting matters covered by NAFTA and due process requirements respecting their administration. These requirements are discussed in §11.1(2).

Section B of NAFTA Chapter Twenty sets out the general NAFTA dispute settlement procedures that are modelled after their counterparts in FTA Chapter Eighteen. These provisions are modified by special requirements that apply to some sectors. The NAFTA general dispute settlement procedures are described in §11.2. The dispute settlement procedures established by the Environmental Co-operation Agreement and the Labour Co-operation Agreement have been discussed in §6.9(4) and §6.10(3), respectively. Section B of NAFTA Chapter Eleven establishes entirely new investor-state dispute settlement procedures that permit investors of NAFTA countries to submit to arbitration claims for loss or damage resulting from breaches of certain NAFTA obligations. These procedures are described in §11.3. NAFTA Chapter Nineteen carries forward, with some changes, the review procedures for antidumping and countervailing duty matters that were set out in FTA Chapter Nineteen. These procedures are described in §11.4.

11.1 INSTITUTIONAL STRUCTURE AND REQUIREMENTS RESPECTING LAWS

(1) Institutional Structure of NAFTA

Like the FTA, the formal institutional structure of NAFTA is minimal. Unlike the treaties governing the European Union, NAFTA does not create supranational institutions with powers that transcend those of the national governments of the NAFTA countries. As under the FTA, there is no permanent institution for resolving disputes. The only formal institutions created by NAFTA are the Free Trade Commission and the Secretariat. NAFTA also creates a number of committees and working groups that will carry out specified functions.

(a) The Free Trade Commission and the Secretariat

NAFTA 2001 establishes the Free Trade Commission (the "Commission"). The Commission is comprised of cabinet-level officers of the NAFTA countries or their appointees. As of the time of writing, the cabinet-level officers comprising the Commission were the Canadian Minister of International Trade, the American Trade Representative and the Mexican Secretary of SECOFI. The Commission supervises the implementation of NAFTA and will oversee its further elaboration. One such elaboration will be finalizing and updating the Uniform Regulations discussed under §3.1(2) and §3.4(1). As discussed in §11.2, the Commission plays a significant role in the resolution of disputes. The Commission also supervises the work of the various committees and working groups. The Commission may delegate responsibilities to standing committees, seek advice and generally take other actions in furtherance of its functions as may be agreed upon by the NAFTA countries. The Commission establishes its own procedures and must make decisions by consensus unless the NAFTA countries agree otherwise. The Commission convenes at least once a year.

NAFTA 2002 requires the Commission to establish and oversee a Secretariat comprised of national Sections. Each NAFTA country must establish a permanent office of its Section with a Secretary responsible for its administration and management. The Secretariat assists the Commission generally and also provides administrative assistance to panels established under both NAFTA Chapter Nineteen (discussed in §11.4) and NAFTA Chapter Twenty (discussed in §11.2).

(b) Committees and working groups

NAFTA establishes eight committees and six working groups, all of which are listed in NAFTA Annex 2001.2.

NAFTA 316 establishes a Committee on Trade in Goods which is to meet at least yearly or at the request of any NAFTA country to consider matters arising under NAFTA Chapter Three. Section 9(1) of NAFTA Annex 300-B establishes a Committee on Trade in Worn Clothing to assess the potential benefits and risks that may arise from the elimination of existing restrictions on the trade in these articles. NAFTA 706 establishes the Committee on Agricultural Trade discussed in §5.3(6)(c). NAFTA 722 establishes the Committee on Sanitary and Phytosanitary Measures discussed in §6.5(9). NAFTA 913 establishes the Committee on Standards-Related Measures described in §6.6(9). NAFTA 1021 provides for the establishment of a Committee on Small Business discussed in §9.1(15). NAFTA 1412 establishes the Financial Services Committee discussed in §8.6 and NAFTA 2022 establishes the Advisory Committee on Private Commercial Disputes discussed in §11.2(11)(b).

NAFTA 513 establishes the Working Group on Rules of Origin and the Customs Subgroup discussed in §3.4(7). NAFTA 705(6) establishes the Working Group on Agricultural Subsidies discussed in §5.3(6)(b). Annex 703.2(A)(25) establishes a bilateral Working Group comprised of American and Mexican representatives to review the operation of agricultural and grade quality standards in co-ordination with the Committee on Standards-Related Measures and Annex 703.2(B)(13) establishes a similar Working Group between Canada and Mexico. NAFTA 1504 establishes the Working Group on Trade and Competition discussed in §9.2(1)(c)(iv) and NAFTA 1605 establishes the Temporary Entry Working Group discussed in §9.3(5).

These committees and working groups should serve as useful vehicles for identifying disputes and resolving them on an informal basis or at least making constructive proposals to the Commission for their resolution. As discussed in §11.2(7), several of these bodies will serve as vehicles for the consultation stage of dispute resolution in certain types of matters. However, other than the Financial Services Committee, none of these bodies has the authority on its own to resolve disputes. The role played by the Financial Services Committee in dispute resolution is discussed in §11.3(10).

(2) Publication, Notification and Administration of Laws

Transparency is cited in NAFTA 102 with national treatment and most-favoured-nation treatment as one of the principles upon which NAFTA is based. Transparency requires that governments provide the means for people to find out what the rules are so that they can comply with them. NAFTA Chapter Eighteen sets out general transparency requirements respecting the administration by NAFTA countries of measures relating to matters covered by NAFTA. Chapter Eighteen also sets out general due process requirements that must be observed by NAFTA countries when administering these measures. Given the breadth of the activities covered by NAFTA, the requirements of Chapter Eighteen are potentially far-reaching.

(a) Publication, notification and provision of information

NAFTA 1802 requires that laws, regulations, procedures and administrative rulings of general application[1] be promptly published or made available to interested persons. To the extent possible, NAFTA countries must publish proposed measures in advance and provide an opportunity for comment. Publication in advance should always be possible except in exceptional circumstances. NAFTA 1803 requires a NAFTA country, to the maximum extent possible, to notify another NAFTA country of actual or proposed measures that might materially affect the operation of NAFTA or affect that other NAFTA country's interests under NAFTA. A NAFTA country must upon request provide other NAFTA countries with information respecting their actual or proposed measures.

As has been discussed in previous chapters, there are specific requirements in the NAFTA text that supplement the transparency requirements of NAFTA 1802 and NAFTA 1803. Listing requirements for wine and distilled spirits covered by NAFTA Annex 312.2 must be transparent.[2] The notification requirements in NAFTA 718 respecting sanitary and phytosanitary measures and in NAFTA 909 respecting standards-related measures have been discussed in §6.5(7) and §6.6(7), respectively. NAFTA 803 requires that the procedures respecting emergency action discussed in §4.7(5) be transparent. The transparency requirements in NAFTA 1019 respecting government procurement measures have been discussed in §9.1(14). The transparency requirements in NAFTA 1306 respecting access to and use of public telecommunications transport networks have been discussed in §7.11(3)(e). NAFTA 1601 cites establishment of transparent criteria as an objective of the temporary entry provisions of NAFTA Chapter Sixteen and NAFTA 1604 sets out requirements respecting the provision of information. The notification requirements respecting amendments to antidumping and countervailing duty laws are discussed in §11.4(7).

The provisions respecting financial services set out in NAFTA 1411 and discussed in §8.4(9) are expressed as being "in lieu" of the publication requirement of NAFTA 1802(2) and not "further to" it. One reason for this is because NAFTA 1411 adopts an "extent practicable" standard rather than the more definitive "extent possible" approach of NAFTA 1802(2).

(b) Administrative proceedings, review and appeal

NAFTA 1804 and NAFTA 1805 set out basic due process requirements to be applied by each NAFTA country in respect of administrative proceedings affecting matters covered by NAFTA.

NAFTA 1804 requires in administrative proceedings involving measures of general application affecting matters covered by NAFTA that persons of other NAFTA countries who are directly affected by a proceeding be given reasonable notice whenever possible. The notice must describe the proceeding, its legal authority and the issues in controversy. Such persons must be given a reasonable opportunity to present facts and arguments in support of their positions.

NAFTA 1805 requires each NAFTA country to establish or maintain judicial, quasi-judicial or administrative tribunals or procedures to review promptly and, where warranted, correct final administrative actions regarding matters covered by NAFTA. Parties to proceedings must be given the opportunity to present their positions and have the right to a decision based on the evidence and submissions of record or, if required by domestic law, the record compiled by the administrative authority. NAFTA countries must ensure that such decisions are implemented by authorities and that authorities be governed by them.

NAFTA sets out specific due process requirements respecting certain areas. As discussed in §3.4(5)(b), NAFTA 510 prescribes review and appeal requirements respecting origin determinations and advance rulings. As discussed in §4.7(5), NAFTA Annex 803.3 sets out detailed procedural requirements to be applied by the NAFTA countries in emergency action proceedings. As discussed in §9.4(18), NAFTA Chapter Seventeen sets out procedural requirements respecting the enforcement of intellectual property rights.

(c) Contact points

NAFTA 1801 requires that the NAFTA countries designate contact points to facilitate communication on matters covered by NAFTA.

11.2 CHAPTER TWENTY — GENERAL DISPUTE RESOLUTION PROCEDURES

The NAFTA general dispute settlement procedures are set out in Section B of NAFTA Chapter Twenty. Like both the GATT and the FTA, the NAFTA general dispute settlement procedures are based on consultation and, failing resolution through consultation, panel review. Panel decisions are not binding in that they do not affect the domestic law of any NAFTA country and cannot be enforced through the courts of a NAFTA country. If a NAFTA country does not bring its laws and practices into conformity with an adverse panel decision, the other affected NAFTA countries may suspend NAFTA benefits but do not have other recourse.

This system of dispute resolution is to be contrasted with the binding system of adjudication of disputes that is applied in the European Union. The European Court of Justice is a supranational institution and its rulings are binding on the national courts of European Union member countries. The European Union system is more effective from the standpoint of enforceability but the trade-off is a substantial surrender of sovereignty on the part of its members. As discussed in §1.2, the NAFTA countries did not intend through NAFTA to create a common market in the European sense and have opted for a looser and less intrusive arrangement. The consultation/panel process in NAFTA Chapter Twenty is consistent with this choice.

(1) Choice Between NAFTA Dispute Settlement and GATT Dispute Settlement

There is extensive overlap between the obligations imposed by NAFTA and those imposed by the GATT and the Uruguay Round agreements. NAFTA 301 (National Treatment) incorporates GATT Article III, NAFTA 309 (Import and Export Restrictions) incorporates GATT Article XI and NAFTA 2101(1) incorporates GATT Article XX. There are parallel provisions under NAFTA and the Multilateral Trade Agreements, discussed in §1.4(1), respecting sanitary and phytosanitary measures (Section B of NAFTA Chapter Seven and the GATT Sanitary and Phytosanitary Measures Agreement), technical barriers to trade (NAFTA Chapter Nine and the 1994 Technical Barriers Code) and intellectual property (NAFTA Chapter Seventeen and the TRIPS Agreement). As between Canada and the United States, there are also parallel provisions respecting government procurement under NAFTA Chapter Ten and the 1994 GATT Government Procurement Code. A measure that is inconsistent with NAFTA 301 will also be inconsistent with GATT Article III. A measure inconsistent with one of the Multilateral Trade Agreements just referred to could also be inconsistent with its parallel NAFTA provision.

NAFTA 2005 sets out rules respecting disputes that arise under both NAFTA on the one hand and the GATT or agreements negotiated under the GATT or any successor agreement to the GATT on the other. Like FTA 1801(3), NAFTA 2005(6) establishes the principle that dispute settlement proceedings initiated under either NAFTA or the GATT precludes initiating proceedings under the other forum. NAFTA 2005(1) provides that the choice of forum in these instances is at the discretion of the complaining NAFTA country. However, there are several limitations. NAFTA 2005(3) provides that if a responding NAFTA country claims that the action that it has taken is subject to NAFTA 104 (which provides that the environmental agreements discussed in §6.8(4) prevail over NAFTA in the event of inconsistencies) and requests resolution under NAFTA, the complaining NAFTA country can pursue its matter only through NAFTA Chapter Twenty. NAFTA 2005(4) provides that complaints respecting measures to protect human, animal or plant life or health or the environment under Section B of NAFTA Chapter Seven or NAFTA Chapter Nine may only be pursued through NAFTA Chapter Twenty if the responding NAFTA country so requests. Assuming that a complaining NAFTA country will choose GATT procedures over NAFTA

Chapter Twenty when the applicable GATT or Uruguay Round agreement provisions are more favourable to its position, the effect of giving the responding NAFTA country the choice of forum is that disputes over the application of environmental measures will likely be resolved through NAFTA Chapter Twenty rather than through GATT procedures. Upon receiving such a request, a NAFTA country will withdraw from the GATT proceedings and may commence Chapter Twenty proceedings with a request for a meeting of the Commission described in §11.2(7).[3]

Before initiating a proceeding under the GATT rules, NAFTA 2005(2) requires that a complaining NAFTA country notify a third NAFTA country of its intentions. This would be a NAFTA country not directly involved in the dispute. If that NAFTA country wants recourse under the NAFTA dispute settlement procedures, it shall inform the complaining NAFTA country and the NAFTA countries will consult with a view to agreeing to a single forum. In the absence of an agreement, the NAFTA dispute settlement procedures will "normally" be used. Thus, a third NAFTA country without direct involvement in the outcome of a matter can affect the choice of forum.

The choice of forum will govern the substantive provisions that govern the matter in dispute. Article 23 of the *Understanding on Rules and Procedures Governing the Settlement of Disputes* (the "Dispute Settlement Understanding") set out in Annex 2 of the WTO Agreement and discussed in §11.2(2)(c) requires that member countries have recourse to and abide by its rules and procedures when seeking redress under any of the agreements it covers. Thus, a NAFTA country seeking redress against another NAFTA country in respect of an intellectual property matter would have to invoke the procedures under the Dispute Settlement Understanding if it wished to have the TRIPS Agreement apply. If NAFTA Chapter Twenty procedures were invoked, NAFTA Chapter Seventeen would govern the matter in dispute.

Aside from the fact that different procedures, different time frames and different personalities are involved, the choice of forum could be critical in circumstances involving Uruguay Round agreements where parallel NAFTA and GATT obligations are not the same and the complaining NAFTA country has a stronger case under one set of obligations than under the other.

(2) Dispute Settlement Under the GATT and the WTO

(a) GATT Articles XXII and XXIII

The GATT itself does not establish formal procedures for the resolution of disputes among contracting parties. GATT Article XXII provides for consultations and negotiations among disputing parties and GATT Article XXIII authorizes a contracting party whose benefits under the GATT are being "nullified or impaired" by the actions of another contracting party to withdraw benefits if a dispute is not resolved through consultations. Disputes which have not been settled through consultation are resolved through a panel process that has evolved since the inception of the GATT. Several of the agreements resulting from the Tokyo Round of GATT negotiations also contain dispute settlement procedures.

(b) Nullification and impairment

GATT Article XXIII may be invoked if nullification or impairment of benefits results from the failure of a contracting party to carry out its GATT obligations. As discussed in §4.4(1), the non-violation nullification and impairment provision in GATT Article XXIII:1(b) also permits the procedures in GATT Article XXIII to be invoked if a measure is nullifying or impairing benefits, even if it does not conflict with a provision of the GATT. The classic example is a subsidy to a domestic industry that offsets the benefit of a tariff concession. The subsidy is not contrary to any GATT provision but the competitive advantage which the exporting country anticipated as a result of the tariff concession and for which it paid with its own tariff concessions is nullified by the subsidy. GATT Article XXIII:1(c) permits GATT Article XXIII to be invoked if the nullification or impairment is the result of the "existence of any other situation". As mentioned in §4.4(1), the approach of GATT panels to non-violation nullification and impairment has been conservative.

(c) Dispute resolution under the WTO Agreement

The Dispute Settlement Understanding establishes formal dispute settlement procedures that apply to all the multilateral and plurilateral trade agreements (the "covered agreements") included in the annexes to the WTO Agreement.[4] The Dispute Settlement Understanding does not replace GATT Articles XXII or XXIII but elaborates upon them. Similarly, the Dispute Settlement Understanding elaborates upon dispute settlement procedures provided for in the other covered agreements.[5]

The Dispute Settlement Understanding establishes the Dispute Settlement Body ("DSB") to administer these procedures and the consultation and dispute settlement procedures set out in the agreements that it covers. The provisions of the Dispute Settlement Understanding will apply only to disputes arising after the WTO Agreement comes into effect. Proceedings initiated before this time will continue under the old system.[6] The Dispute Settlement Understanding sets out rules governing requests for consultations under the covered agreements, including time limits following which a complaining party may request a panel. As under the GATT, the settlement of a dispute begins with a request for consultations. The usual time period for consultations is sixty days[7] but this period can be reduced to twenty days in urgent situations. These include, but are not confined to, situations involving perishable goods.[8]

(i) Panels

If a dispute is not resolved through consultations, the complaining party may request a panel. The function of panels is to assist the DSB in discharging its responsibilities under the Dispute Settlement Understanding. Multiple requests for the establishment of panels can be consolidated[9] and member countries with a substantial interest in the matter in dispute may make submissions to the panel as a "third party".[10] The Dispute Settlement Understanding establishes the terms of reference for panels[11] and sets out rules respecting their composition. For example, citizens of parties to a dispute or third parties making submissions cannot serve on a panel unless the parties to the dispute agree otherwise.[12] The Dispute Settlement Understanding establishes panel procedures that include a proposed timetable for a panel's work.[13] Unlike domestic courts, panels must meet in closed session. Normally parties (including third parties) will make written submissions and a first substantive meeting of the panel will take place at which the complaining party will present its case and the party complained against will be invited to express its views. Formal rebuttals will be made at a second substantive meeting of the panel. Third parties may be present during these meetings.[14] The panel considers the submissions and rebuttals and will issue a draft report to the parties to the dispute. The parties may comment in writing. The panel issues an interim report and circulates it to the parties. If no comments are received, the interim report becomes the final report and is circulated to the members.[15] Within sixty days of the circulation of the report, it will be adopted at a DSB meeting unless one of the parties chooses to appeal or the meeting chooses "by consensus" not to adopt it.[16] This is significant because the party complained against can no longer block the adoption of a report as was previously the case. The process from the time that the composition and terms of reference of the panel are settled to the issuance of the final report generally should not take more than six months and in no case is to take more than nine months.[17]

(ii) Appeal

The decision of a panel may be appealed by parties to a dispute but not by third parties. The appeal is made to the Appellate Body, a permanent institution to be established by the DSB.[18] The appeal is limited to issues of law in the panel report and legal interpretations developed by the panel.[19] The period from the establishment of a panel to the consideration of the report for adoption is generally not to take more than nine months if a panel report is not appealed or twelve months if it is appealed.[20] The drafters of the Dispute Settlement Understanding obviously intended that appeals be dealt with expeditiously.

(iii) Implementation of recommendations, compensation and suspension of concessions

If a panel or the Appellate Body concludes that a measure is inconsistent with a covered agreement, it shall recommend that the member concerned bring the measure into conformity with the agreement concerned and it may suggest ways of doing this.[21] The DSB must hold a meeting within thirty days of the adoption of the report at which the member concerned will inform the DSB of its intentions respecting the implementation of the recommendations. Members are to have a reasonable period of time within which to implement recommendations. A reasonable time is that proposed by the member if approved by the DSB or that is mutually agreed upon by the parties to the dispute or that is determined through binding arbitration within ninety days of the adoption by the DSB of the recommendations.[22] An outside period of fifteen months is suggested as a guideline. The DSB is to keep the implementation of the recommendations under surveillance.[23] If the recommendations are not implemented within a reasonable time, the Dispute Settlement Understanding permits voluntary compensation and suspension of concessions, but these are regarded as temporary and not permanent solutions.[24] Principles and procedures are set out for determining what concessions to suspend. For example, a member will first suspend concessions in the same sector as that in which the violation occurred. If this is impracticable or ineffective, concessions can be suspended in a different sector but under the same covered agreement. If this is impracticable or ineffective and the circumstances are sufficiently serious, concessions under another agreement can be suspended.[25]

(iv) Non-violation nullification and impairment

The Dispute Settlement Understanding makes special provisions for complaints based on claims of non-violation nullification and impairment under GATT Article XXIII:1(b) and (c). Essentially, less stringent results follow from a claim based on these GATT provisions. For example, if a finding of non-violation nullification and impairment is made under GATT Article XXIII:1(b), the party complained against is under no obligation to withdraw the measure and compensation may be part of a final settlement of the matter.[26] The Dispute Settlement Understanding does not provide any clarification of the meaning of "the existence of any other situation" in GATT Article XXIII:1(c).

(v) No unilateral actions

Members seeking redress in respect of any of the covered agreements must use the procedures set out in the Dispute Settlement Understanding.[27] The Dispute Settlement Understanding prohibits members from unilaterally determining that obligations under covered agreements have been violated or that benefits under such agreements have been nullified and impaired. A member must adhere to the requirements of the Dispute Settlement Understanding in order to pursue such claims.[28]

(3) Experience Under the FTA

As mentioned in §1.4(3), only five matters were resolved under the general dispute resolution procedures of FTA Chapter Eighteen.

The first case was *Re Canada's landing requirement for Pacific Coast salmon & herring*.[29] This case involved requirements imposed by the Canadian government that salmon and roe herring be off-landed at a licensed fish landing station in British Columbia. The requirement was imposed after export restrictions on these species had been removed following a GATT panel ruling that these restrictions were contrary to GATT Article XI:1.[30] The panel found that while there was some justification for the landing requirement for fishery management purposes, its application to 100% of the catch amounted to an export restriction that contravened GATT Article XI:1 and FTA 407. The opinions of the panelists were not unanimous on all issues.[31]

The next case was *Re Lobsters from Canada*.[32] This case involved a 1989 amendment to the Magnuson Fishery Conservation and Management Act prohibiting the sale or transportation of sub-sized lobsters, regardless of origin. Canada viewed the amendment as an import restriction contrary to GATT Article XI, and therefore FTA 407, and not justified under the exhaustible natural resources exception in GATT Article XX(g). The United States maintained that the amendment did not fall within GATT Article XI as it had nothing to do with imports and was governed by GATT Article III. The majority of the panel accepted the U.S. position and a minority found that GATT Article XI applied.[33]

The third case was *In the Matter of Article 304 and the Definition of Direct Cost of Processing or Direct Cost of Assembling*.[34] Unlike the other two cases which involved the application of GATT provisions, this case involved a purely FTA issue concerning the question as to whether interest expense on a loan not secured by a mortgage on real property was included in the definition of "direct cost of processing or direct cost of assembling" in FTA 304 and thus counted toward domestic value added for rules of origin purposes. The panel unanimously accepted the Canadian position that non-mortgage interest was included in the definition.

The fourth case, *Interpretation of and Canada's compliance with Article 701.3 with respect to durum wheat sales*, is discussed in §5.3(5)(a)(iii) and the last case, *In the Matter of Puerto Rico regulations on the import, distribution and sale of U.H.T. milk from Quebec*, is discussed in §6.2.

One might ask why there were so few cases during the period of time that the FTA was in effect. The dispute resolution process under the FTA was not unduly cumbersome and in fact was considerably less time consuming than its GATT counterpart.[35] There are several possible reasons. First, during the time that the FTA was in effect, the most contentious trade issues between Canada and the United States involved antidumping and countervailing duties. As discussed under §11.4(5)(b), the FTA Chapter Nineteen procedures for these matters were extensively used. Second, the most acrimonious trade disputes outside of the antidumping and countervailing duty area involved the trade in beer between the two countries. Both the United States and Canada chose to pursue their remedies through the GATT dispute settlement process. Third, the NAFTA negotiations commenced when the FTA had been in existence for barely two years. Contentious issues such as those involving the application of the FTA rules of origin to automotive goods were resolved through the process of negotiating the NAFTA. If the NAFTA negotiations had not opened what in effect became an alternative means of dispute resolution, these issues would have to have been through the panel process. Fourth, disputes over agricultural products were put on hold pending the outcome of the Uruguay Round negotiations.[36]

(4) Scope of Dispute Settlement Procedures under NAFTA Chapter Twenty

NAFTA 2004 provides that except for matters covered by Chapter Nineteen (Antidumping and Countervailing Duties) and except as otherwise provided in NAFTA, the dispute settlement procedures in NAFTA Chapter Twenty apply to all disputes respecting the interpretation or application of NAFTA. With the exception of the matters covered by NAFTA Chapter Nineteen and NAFTA 1501 (Competition Law),[37] NAFTA Chapter Twenty applies to disputes arising with respect to any matter covered by NAFTA. The investor/state dispute settlement procedures set out in Section B of NAFTA Chapter Eleven provide remedies to investors who suffer loss or damage because of a breach by a NAFTA country of its NAFTA obligations. However, the availability of these remedies does not preclude the NAFTA countries from using NAFTA Chapter Twenty to resolve disputes respecting matters covered by these remedies.[38] NAFTA 1414 sets out modifications to the NAFTA Chapter Twenty procedures when applied to disputes involving financial services that are discussed in §11.2(10)(b).

NAFTA 2004 provides that NAFTA Chapter Twenty applies if a NAFTA country considers that an actual or proposed measure of another NAFTA country is or would be inconsistent with its NAFTA obligations. NAFTA Annex 2004 also permits a NAFTA country to have recourse to NAFTA Chapter Twenty if a measure adopted by another NAFTA country that is not inconsistent with NAFTA is none the less nullifying or impairing benefits that the NAFTA country reasonably expected to receive. This provision is based on the concept of non-violation nullification and impairment set out in GATT

Article XXIII:1(b) discussed in §11.2(2)(b). NAFTA 2004 confines the application of non-violation nullification and impairment to the Trade in Goods provisions of NAFTA Chapters Three through Eight (with the express exclusion of the automotive provisions of Annex 300-A and the provisions of NAFTA Chapter Six on energy in so far as they relate to investment), NAFTA Chapter Nine (Standards-related Measures), NAFTA Chapter Twelve (Cross-Border Trade in Services) and NAFTA Chapter Seventeen (Intellectual Property). Non-violation nullification and impairment does not apply to the excluded provisions just mentioned or to NAFTA Chapters Ten (Government Procurement), Eleven (Investment), Thirteen (Telecommunications), Fourteen (Financial Services), Fifteen (Competition Law, Monopolies and State Enterprises) or Sixteen (Temporary Entry). In these areas, NAFTA Chapter Twenty proceedings may be invoked only respecting measures that are inconsistent with NAFTA obligations.

(5) Only Federal Governments have Standing

Like the procedures provided for in the Dispute Settlement Understanding, but unlike the review procedures respecting antidumping and countervailing duty matters in NAFTA Chapter Nineteen discussed in §11.4 and the investor/state dispute settlement procedures provided for in Section B of NAFTA Chapter Eleven described in §11.3, NAFTA Chapter Twenty procedures can be initiated only by the governments at the federal level. Nationals and enterprises of NAFTA countries and state and provincial governments have no standing at any stage of a NAFTA Chapter Twenty proceeding. Except for investors of a NAFTA country with standing to invoke the investor/state dispute settlement procedures, the only recourse of a national or an enterprise of a NAFTA country who is adversely affected by a measure of another NAFTA country that is inconsistent with NAFTA obligations is to persuade his, her or its government to initiate NAFTA Chapter Twenty proceedings. If a state or provincial measure is challenged as being inconsistent with NAFTA obligations, the federal government of the NAFTA country of which the state or province is a part will prepare all submissions and argue the case.

NAFTA 2021 prohibits NAFTA countries from providing for private rights of action under its domestic law against another NAFTA country on the grounds that its measures are inconsistent with NAFTA obligations.

(6) Co-operation and Consultations

NAFTA 2003 requires the NAFTA countries to make every attempt to resolve matters through co-operation and consultation. A NAFTA country commences Chapter Twenty procedures by delivering a request for consultations under NAFTA 2006(1) to the other NAFTA countries and to its own

Section of the Secretariat. The request may be made respecting any actual or proposed measure or any other matter that may affect the operation of NAFTA. A NAFTA country not directly involved in the dispute but that considers that it has a substantial interest in the outcome may participate in the consultations unless the rules established by the Commission provide otherwise. NAFTA countries participating in the consultations are required to provide sufficient information so that the effect of the measure can be examined and to avoid resolving the dispute through a means that adversely affects other NAFTA countries.

(7) Request for a Meeting of the Commission

If the dispute is not resolved within thirty days of the request for consultations, any consulting NAFTA country may request a meeting of the Commission. This period is extended to forty-five days if another NAFTA country has subsequently requested or participated in consultations respecting the same matter, and is reduced to fifteen days if perishable agricultural goods are involved.[39] A meeting of the Commission may be requested if a responding NAFTA country in an environmental dispute referred to in §11.2(1) has requested that the matter be considered under NAFTA. A meeting of the Commission may also be requested if a matter considered by the Working Group on Rules of Origin has not been resolved within the thirty-day time-frame provided in NAFTA 513(5) discussed in §3.4(7) or if consultations have been facilitated by the Committee on Sanitary and Phytosanitary Measures under NAFTA 723(3) or by the Committee on Standards-Related Measures under NAFTA 914. In these latter two instances, the NAFTA countries involved must agree that the consultations facilitated by the relevant Committee constitute consultations for the purposes of NAFTA 2006.[40]

Upon a request for a meeting, the Commission must convene within ten days and try to resolve the dispute promptly. The Commission may call on technical advisors and take other steps to assist the involved NAFTA countries to resolve the matter and may consolidate proceedings. If the matter is not resolved within thirty days after the Commission has convened, any requesting NAFTA country may request the establishment of an arbitral panel under NAFTA 2008.[41]

The requirement that the Commission act as a mediator adds an additional step to the dispute settlement process that does not appear in the Dispute Settlement Understanding. Under the Dispute Settlement Understanding, disputes proceed directly from consultations to resolution by a panel with no intervening step. Under NAFTA Chapter Twenty, disputes proceed from consultations through mediation by the Commission to resolution by a panel. The Dispute Settlement Understanding provides for a sixty-day time period from the request for consultations to the right to request a panel.[42] The corresponding time periods under NAFTA Chapter Twenty are thirty days from request for consultations to request for a meeting of the Commission, ten days for the Commission to convene and thirty days from the convening of the Commission to the right to request a panel, for a total of seventy days.[43]

Arguably an advantage in having the Commission act as a mediator is that a high level meeting respecting the dispute occurs at a relatively early stage. However, disputes can be politicized and their relative importance overblown because the Commission is comprised of cabinet-level officers and anything considered by people at this level is by definition both political and important.

(8) The Chapter Twenty Panel Process

The Commission is required to establish an arbitral panel upon the delivery of a request. A NAFTA country that is not directly involved in the dispute (*i.e.*, a "third" NAFTA country) but considers that it has a substantial interest in its outcome may join the proceeding as a complaining party. If a third NAFTA country does not join in the proceeding, it shall refrain from initiating a Chapter Twenty proceeding or a GATT proceeding on grounds substantially equivalent to those upon which the proceeding in question is based.[44] Each NAFTA country must establish and maintain a roster of up to thirty individuals, each of whom must have certain expertise,[45] be independent of and not affiliated with or take instructions from any NAFTA country and comply with the code of conduct established by the Commission.

(a) Panel selection

As under the FTA, panels are comprised of five members. Unlike the FTA, NAFTA 2011 provides for a reverse selection procedure under which each disputing NAFTA country selects panelists from rosters of other disputing NAFTA countries and not from its own. The disputing NAFTA countries must try to agree on a chair of the panel within fifteen days of the delivery of the request for a panel. If a chair is not agreed upon and there are two disputing NAFTA countries, the disputing NAFTA country selected by lot will choose the chair within five days. Each NAFTA country then has fifteen days to select two panelists who are citizens of the other disputing NAFTA country and if a selection is not made the panelists shall be selected by lot from the roster of the other disputing country.

If there are more than two disputing NAFTA countries, the NAFTA country or countries on the side of the dispute selected by lot will choose a chair within ten days. Within fifteen days of the chair being chosen, the disputing NAFTA country complained against selects one panelist who is a citizen of one complaining NAFTA country and one who is a citizen of the other NAFTA complaining country. The complaining NAFTA countries select two panelists who are citizens of the NAFTA country complained against. If the selections are not made within fifteen days, the panelists are chosen by lot using these citizenship criteria.

Panelists shall normally be chosen from the roster and a disputing NAFTA country may exercise a peremptory challenge against any person chosen who is not on the roster within fifteen days of the person being proposed. If a disputing NAFTA country believes that a panelist has violated the code of conduct, the disputing NAFTA countries will consult and if they agree, the panelist shall be removed and a new panelist selected.

(b) Procedure, third party participation, experts

Panel proceedings are to be conducted in accordance with the Model Rules of Procedure established by the Commission. There must be at least one hearing with the opportunity to provide initial and rebuttal written submissions. As with GATT panels, hearings, deliberations, the panel's initial report, submissions and communications with the panel must be confidential.

NAFTA 2012(3) sets out terms of reference that will apply unless the disputing NAFTA countries agree to other terms. If a disputing NAFTA country is arguing that a matter has nullified or impaired benefits or wishes the panel to make findings respecting adverse trade effects, the terms of reference must so state. A NAFTA country that is not a disputing NAFTA country may, upon giving written notice, attend all hearings and make oral and written submissions.[46]

A panel may seek expert advice on its own initiative or at the request of any disputing NAFTA country.[47] On the request of a disputing NAFTA country or, unless the disputing NAFTA countries disapprove, a panel may request a written report of a scientific review board on any factual issue concerning environmental, health, safety or other scientific matters raised by a disputing NAFTA country. The board must be comprised of highly qualified, independent experts. Participating NAFTA countries must have notice of and the opportunity to comment on the factual issues referred to the board and the opportunity to comment on the board's report. The panel must take the board's report and comments on it into account in its own report.

(c) Panel's initial and final reports

Reports of panels are to be based on the submissions and arguments of the disputing NAFTA countries and the advice or reports of experts or scientific review boards requested by the panel.[48] Within ninety days after the last panelist is selected, the panel shall provide an initial report to the disputing NAFTA countries with findings of fact, its determinations as to whether the measure at issue is inconsistent with NAFTA obligations or causes nullification and impairment in the sense described in §11.2(4) and its recommendations for the resolution of the dispute. Panelists may provide separate opinions on matters to which there has not been unanimous agreement,[49] but neither initial nor final reports may disclose which panelists are associated with majority and minority opinions.[50] Disputing NAFTA countries have fourteen days to submit written comments.

The panel is required to submit a final report to the disputing NAFTA countries within thirty days of the presentation of the initial report.[51] The disputing NAFTA countries will deliver the final report to the Commission, together with the report of any scientific review board and written views. The final report will be published within fifteen days of its transmission to the Commission unless the Commission decides otherwise.

The time provided for in NAFTA from the request for a panel to the presentation of the final report to the disputing NAFTA countries is 120 days, as compared to six months in the Dispute Settlement Understanding.[52] The final reports of NAFTA panels do not have to be adopted by the Commission or the disputing NAFTA countries and, unlike under the Dispute Settlement Understanding, NAFTA panel reports are not subject to appeal.

(9) Implementation, Non-Implementation and Suspension of Benefits

Once the final report of a panel is received, NAFTA 2018 requires that the NAFTA countries agree on a resolution of the dispute that shall normally conform with the panel's determinations and recommendations. The preferred means of resolution is the non-implementation or removal of non-conforming measures.[53]

If agreement on resolution of the dispute is not reached within thirty days of receipt of the final report, the complaining NAFTA country may suspend NAFTA benefits. Suspension of benefits should be in the same sector as that affected by the inconsistent measure but if the complaining NAFTA country considers this impracticable or ineffective, suspension of benefits can take place in a different sector. Special rules discussed in §11.2(10)(b) apply with suspension of benefits relating to financial services. A panel can be invoked to determine whether the level of benefits suspended by a NAFTA country has been excessive.

(10) Special Situations

(a) Emergency action

FTA 1806(1)(a) required that unresolved disputes involving emergency action be referred to binding arbitration. NAFTA 804 prohibits NAFTA countries from requesting the establishment of a panel in respect of a proposed emergency action. Presumably the reason for this provision is that NAFTA 803 and Annex 803.3 establish a comprehensive code of requirements to be followed by NAFTA countries in their emergency action proceedings.[54] NAFTA 804 would not prohibit a NAFTA country from requesting a panel if another

NAFTA country did not observe these requirements in its proceedings or implemented emergency action which did not conform to NAFTA requirements.

(b) Financial services

The FTA Chapter Eighteen dispute settlement procedures did not apply to financial services.[55] The only means of settling disputes over the FTA financial services obligations was through consultations between the Canadian Department of Finance and the U.S. Department of the Treasury.[56] The NAFTA Chapter Twenty dispute settlement procedures do apply to disputes involving the NAFTA financial services obligations but with some modifications.

NAFTA 1414(3) requires each NAFTA country to maintain a separate roster of fifteen individuals to serve as financial services panelists. These individuals must have financial services expertise. In a Chapter Twenty proceeding, normal panel selection procedures apply except that the disputing NAFTA countries may agree that the panel be comprised entirely of individuals qualified to be financial services roster members. Otherwise, panelists meeting either these qualifications or the qualifications necessary to be on the NAFTA Chapter Twenty rosters may be selected. If the NAFTA country complained against invokes the exception in NAFTA 1410 discussed in §8.4(11)(b), the chair of the panel must meet the qualifications required for financial service roster members.

NAFTA 1414(5) sets out limitations on the suspension of benefits. If a measure found inconsistent with NAFTA obligations affects only the financial services sector, benefits may only be suspended in the financial services sector. If an inconsistent measure affects a sector other than the financial services sector, benefits may not be suspended in the financial services sector. If the inconsistent measure affects the financial services sector and another sector, a NAFTA country may suspend benefits in the financial services sector that have an effect equivalent to the effect of the inconsistent measure on its financial services sector.

(c) Temporary entry

NAFTA 1606 provides that NAFTA Chapter Twenty procedures cannot be invoked respecting a refusal to grant temporary entry unless the matter involves a pattern of practice and the business person has exhausted available administrative remedies. Remedies are deemed exhausted if a final determination has not been issued within one year of proceedings being initiated where the business person has not caused the delay.

(11) Domestic Proceedings and Private Commercial Dispute Settlement

(a) Referrals of matters from judicial or administrative proceedings

NAFTA 2020 covers the situation in which an issue of interpretation of NAFTA arises in a judicial or administrative proceeding in a NAFTA country. If any NAFTA country considers that the issue of interpretation merits its intervention or if the court or tribunal solicits the views of a NAFTA country, the NAFTA country will notify the Commission which will try to agree on an appropriate response. The NAFTA country in which the proceeding is taking place will submit any agreed interpretation to the court or tribunal. If there is no agreed interpretation, any NAFTA country may submit its own views to the court or tribunal.

(b) Alternative dispute resolution

NAFTA 2022 requires the NAFTA countries to encourage arbitration and other alternative dispute resolution procedures for the settlement of international commercial disputes between private parties in the NAFTA countries. NAFTA countries must provide procedures for ensuring observance of agreements to arbitrate and for the recognition and enforcement of arbitral awards. This obligation is deemed to be fulfilled if a NAFTA country is a member of and complying with the *1958 United Nations Convention on the Recognition and Enforcement of Foreign Arbitral Awards* (the "New York Convention") or the *1975 Inter-American Convention on International Commercial Arbitration* (the "Inter-American Convention"). All three NAFTA countries are signatories to the New York Convention and Mexico is a member of the Inter-American Convention. These conventions are discussed in §11.3(4) in conjunction with investor-state dispute settlement procedures.

NAFTA 2022(4) provides that the Commission will establish an Advisory Committee on Private Commercial Disputes comprised of persons with expertise in the area. The Committee will report on matters referred to it by the Commission respecting the availability and effectiveness of procedures for the resolution of private international commercial disputes in the NAFTA countries.

(12) Concluding Remarks

While the NAFTA Chapter Twenty dispute settlement procedures are modelled after their FTA predecessors, they are more complex because of the necessity of involving three potential disputants rather than two. Further elaborations and perhaps a more permanent structure will be required if more countries accede to NAFTA. Because of the extension of NAFTA into areas not covered by the FTA, NAFTA panels will be resolving disputes involving a wider range of matters than their FTA predecessors. When the Uruguay Round

agreements come into effect, the choice of forum will become a more difficult issue than has previously been the case because of the resulting creation
of parallel but somewhat differing sets of international obligations covering
a number of areas such as sanitary and phytosanitary measures, standards-
related measures and intellectual property.

11.3   INVESTOR/STATE DISPUTE SETTLEMENT PROCEDURES

Section B of NAFTA Chapter Eleven sets out procedures for the settlement of disputes arising between NAFTA countries and investors of other
NAFTA countries respecting the obligations of NAFTA countries under Section A of Chapter Eleven (described in §7.7), NAFTA 1503(2) or NAFTA
1502(3)(a).[57] NAFTA 1503(2) and NAFTA 1502(3)(a) are the provisions
respecting the exercise by state enterprises and monopolies of regulatory,
administrative or other governmental authority discussed in §9.2(2)(c) and
§9.2(2)(b)(ii), respectively. As discussed in §8.4(2), the investor/state dispute
settlement procedures established by Section B also apply to NAFTA 1109
through NAFTA 1111, NAFTA 1113 and 1114 as incorporated into NAFTA
Chapter Fourteen (Financial Services).

(1) Who May Submit a Claim?

An investor of a NAFTA country, either on its own behalf or on behalf
of an enterprise of another NAFTA country that is a juridical person which
it owns or controls, may submit a claim that another NAFTA country or
the NAFTA country of that enterprise has breached an obligation under any
of the foregoing NAFTA provisions.[58] The investor or, if the claim is made
on behalf of an enterprise, the enterprise must have suffered loss or damage
as a result of the breach. The claim may not be made if more than three
years has elapsed from the time that the investor or the enterprise first
acquired or should have first acquired knowledge of the breach and that loss
or damage has been incurred.[59] Provision is made for consolidation of claims
arising out of the same facts by investors on behalf of enterprises and by
investors on their own behalf or by non-controlling investors in enterprises
unless one of the parties making the claim would be prejudiced.[60]

The rules permit investors to claim on behalf of enterprises that they own
or control to avoid the international law problem that could arise where the
investor did not suffer loss or damage independent from its investment.[61]
The enterprise itself, which is an "investment",[62] cannot make a claim.

(2) Initiating a Claim

NAFTA 1118 provides that the disputing parties should first attempt to settle the claim through consultation or negotiation. The use of the word "should" suggests that this step is not mandatory. The investor making the claim (the "disputing investor"[63]) must deliver to the NAFTA country against which the claim is being made (the "disputing NAFTA country"[64]) a notice of its intention to submit a claim at least ninety days before the claim is submitted to arbitration.[65] The notice must specify the name and the address of the disputing investor and, if applicable, the enterprise, the NAFTA provisions alleged to be breached, the issues and factual basis, the relief sought and the approximate amount of damages.

(3) Submitting a Claim to Arbitration

Once six months have elapsed since the events giving rise to the claim, a disputing investor may submit the claim under the *Convention on the Settlement of Investment Disputes between States and Nationals of other States* (the "ICSID Convention"), the Additional Facility Rules of the International Centre for Settlement of Investment Disputes ("ICSID") or the UNCITRAL Arbitration Rules.

The ICSID Convention can be used only if both the NAFTA country of the investor and the disputing NAFTA country are parties to the ICSID Convention. At the time of writing, only the United States is a party to this convention. This arbitration vehicle cannot be used unless either Canada or Mexico joins the ICSID Convention. NAFTA imposes no obligation on either country to do so. The Additional Facility Rules of ICSID may be used only if one of the NAFTA country of the investor and the disputing NAFTA country, but not both, are parties to the ICSID Convention. Unless and until Canada or Mexico joins the ICSID Convention, the Additional Facility Rules may be used only in disputes involving the United States or investors of the United States. Subject to these constraints, the choice of the arbitration vehicle is up to the disputing investor.

(a) ICSID Convention

As mentioned in §7.3, one of the provisions of the Model BIT provides for the resolution of disputes through the facilities of ICSID. The ICSID Convention was completed at Washington, March 18, 1965, and entered into force on October 14, 1966. ICSID operates under the aegis of the World Bank. The objective behind the creation of ICSID was to create an impartial and reliable system for disputes between direct foreign investors and host governments.[66] The host governments in question were developing countries wishing to attract investment. The need for a neutral forum arose from the fact that foreign investors did not trust the courts in host countries to be impartial and, for reasons of sovereignty and national dignity, host countries were reluctant to submit disputes to foreign courts.[67] As of 1993, 123 countries had signed the ICSID Convention and 109 countries had ratified it.[68] However, from the time that ICSID was first created until 1993, only nine cases resulted in final awards.[69]

The ICSID Convention sets out procedures for arbitration. For ICSID to have jurisdiction, both parties to a dispute must consent in writing to ICSID hearing the dispute. One party must be a contracting state and the other a national of another contracting state and the dispute must be a "legal dispute" arising out of an investment.[70] The ICSID Convention and the ICSID Arbitration Rules provide for a self-contained system for arbitration.[71] The Convention provides for a Panel of Arbitrators consisting of qualified persons.[72] Arbitrators must be of high moral character and recognized competence in the fields of law, commerce, industry or finance and be relied upon to exercise independent judgment.[73] Each contracting state may designate four persons to the panel.[74] In the absence of agreement, arbitral panels are comprised of three arbitrators, one chosen by each party and the third chosen by agreement of the parties or, failing agreement, by the Secretary General of ICSID (the "ICSID Secretary General").[75] Arbitrators may be chosen from outside the Panel of Arbitrators but must possess the same qualities.[76] The Arbitration Rules set out the procedural details. Provision is made in the ICSID Convention for the revision[77] or the annulment of awards[78] in certain instances.

The ICSID Convention provides that awards are binding on the parties and are not subject to appeal or other remedy except as provided for in the convention. A contracting state must recognize awards and enforce pecuniary obligations under an award as if it were the final judgment of a court in that state.[79]

(b) Additional Facility Rules

The Additional Facility Rules of ICSID set out a body of arbitration rules that may be used to settle disputes where the disputing parties agree. Parties need not be members of the ICSID Convention to use them. The Additional Facility Rules do not constitute a self-contained code in that if any of the rules are in conflict with an applicable provision of law from which the parties cannot derogate, the provision of law prevails.[80] States or nationals of states may commence proceedings by sending a notice to the ICSID Secretariat.[81] The rules provide for the composition and selection of arbitrators (three in the absence of a contrary agreement) and their replacement where necessary.[82] Arbitrators must possess the same qualities described in §11.3(3)(a) for arbitrators under the ICSID Convention.[83] The various procedural aspects of the arbitration are covered. For example, provision is made for pleadings, oral argument, the marshalling of evidence and the examination of witnesses and experts.[84] Unless the agreement between the parties provides otherwise, arbitral tribunals can order or recommend provisional measures. Awards, which must be written and deal with all the questions submitted, are final and binding.[85] However, a party may, within forty-five days, request correction of clerical, arithmetic or similar errors.[86] Provision is made for interpretation of the award by the tribunal if either party so requests.[87] Costs of the proceeding are determined by the tribunal unless the parties agree otherwise.[88]

(c) UNCITRAL Arbitration Rules

The UNCITRAL Arbitration Rules are the arbitration rules of the United Nations Commission on International Trade Law (UNCITRAL) that were approved by the United Nations General Assembly on December 15, 1976.[89] These rules establish a body of arbitration rules that may be used to settle disputes. The UNCITRAL Arbitration Rules are designed for use by parties to commercial agreements. Article 1 of the rules provides that where parties to a contract have agreed in writing that disputes respecting the contract be governed by the UNCITRAL Rules, the rules apply as modified by the parties. Provision is made for the appointment of arbitrators. One arbitrator can be chosen if the parties so agree; otherwise three will be chosen.[90] If three arbitrators are to be appointed, each party chooses one and the two arbitrators chosen select the third and presiding arbitrator. A mechanism is provided for choosing the third arbitrator in the absence of agreement.[91] Arbitrators may be challenged on the basis of justifiable doubt as to impartiality or independence[92] and provision is made for replacement in the case of death or resignation.[93] Articles 18 to 23 make provision for pleadings and time limits for filing of the same. Articles 24 and 25 cover evidence and hearings. Interim measures may be ordered.[94] The arbitral tribunal may appoint experts.[95] Awards are made by a majority of the arbitrators.[96] The tribunal can make interim, interlocutory or partial awards as well as final awards and awards are final and binding.[97] However, a party may, within thirty days, request a correction of errors in computation, clerical or typographical errors or errors of a similar nature.[98] Reasons shall be given unless the parties otherwise request. As under the Additional Facility Rules, provision is made for interpretation of the award by the tribunal if a party so requests.[99] The arbitral panel will fix costs.[100]

(4) Other Conventions

Section B of NAFTA Chapter Eleven also refers to the New York Convention[101] and the Inter-American Convention.[102] These conventions form part of the mechanism set out in Section B for ensuring that arbitral awards are enforceable.

(a) The New York Convention

The New York Convention[103] applies to the recognition of arbitral awards made in the territory of a state other than the state where the recognition and enforcement of the award is sought.[104] Article II of the New York Convention requires each contracting state to recognize an "agreement in writing under which parties undertake to submit to arbitration all or any differences which have arisen or may arise between them in respect of a defined legal relationship, whether contractual or not, concerning a subject matter capable of settlement by arbitration". Article III obliges contracting states to recognize arbitral awards as binding and to enforce them. Article IV provides that a party applying for recognition and enforcement supply a duly authenticated copy of the award and an original or duly certified copy of the agreement referred to in Article II. Article V sets out a limited number of circumstances in which recognition and enforcement of an arbitral award may be refused.[105] Article XI sets out provisions that apply to contracting states with federal structures.

Canada, the United States and Mexico are all signatories to the New York Convention. In Canada, federal and provincial legislation has been enacted to make the New York Convention part of domestic law.[106] The United States has also enacted legislation implementing the convention[107] and has adopted a pro-enforcement policy for arbitral awards and a narrow construction of the defences provided in Article V.[108]

(b) Inter-American Convention

The Inter-American Convention[109] was sponsored by the Organization of American States. Like Article II of the New York Convention, Article 1 of the Inter-American Convention requires an agreement among the parties to an arbitration that their differences be submitted to arbitration. Article 4 provides that an arbitral decision that is not appealable has the force of a final judicial judgment and its execution or recognition may be ordered in the same manner as decisions of national or foreign courts. Article 5 sets out grounds for refusing to recognize or enforce an award similar to those in the New York Convention. Mexico has ratified the Inter-American Convention and the United States is a signatory.

(5) Conditions Precedent to Submitting a Claim to Arbitration

A disputing investor may submit a claim to arbitration only if the investor and, if applicable, the enterprise on whose behalf a claim is made, consent to the arbitration and waive the right to commence or continue proceedings respecting the measure before any administrative tribunal or court under the law of any NAFTA country, or other dispute settlement procedures.[110] Consents and waivers must be in writing.[111] The other dispute settlement procedures do not include those under NAFTA Chapter Twenty which are not to be prejudiced by the NAFTA investor/state dispute settlement procedures and, in any event, are available only to NAFTA countries and not to individual investors.

The waiver does not apply to proceedings for injunctive, declaratory or other extraordinary relief not involving the payment of damages before an administrative tribunal or court under the law of the disputing NAFTA country. As discussed in §11.3(11), tribunals constituted under Section B of Chapter Eleven may only award damages.

As a general rule in international law, a person must exhaust local remedies before resorting to remedies afforded by international law.[112] Under Section B of NAFTA, an investor must choose between remedies provided under local law and an arbitral tribunal constituted under Section B. The general law in Canada and the United States provides local remedies for at least some breaches of NAFTA obligations, such as expropriation. However, these remedies are independent of NAFTA or the Canadian or American legislation implementing NAFTA. Unless the legislation implementing NAFTA specifically creates a domestic remedy for persons affected by a breach of a NAFTA obligation or an independent remedy already exists in the general law,[113] there is no domestic remedy in Canada or the United States and arbitration under Section B will be the only course open to an investor. For example, there is no domestic remedy in Canada that an investor may pursue for a breach by the federal government or the government of a province of a NAFTA national treatment obligation.

In Mexico, NAFTA itself gives rise to private rights of action. Accordingly, NAFTA Annex 1120.1 provides that an investor cannot allege both in an action in Mexico and in an arbitration under Section B that Mexico has breached any of the obligations covered by Section B. NAFTA Annex 1120.1 also provides that if a Mexican enterprise makes such an allegation in an action in Mexico, an investor of another NAFTA country that controls it cannot allege the breach in an arbitration under Section B.[114]

(6) Consent to Arbitration

Each NAFTA country consents in NAFTA 1122 to arbitration under the procedures set out in Section B. NAFTA 1122(2) provides that this consent, together with the written consent of the disputing investor discussed in §11.3(5), constitute the written consent required under the ICSID Convention, the agreement in writing required under the New York Convention and the agreement required under the Inter-American Convention.

(7) Constitution of Arbitral Tribunals

Tribunals are comprised of three arbitrators, with one being appointed by each of the disputing parties and the third and presiding arbitrator being appointed by agreement of the disputing parties.[115] Selection of arbitrators will be subject to the requirements of the arbitration procedure chosen by the disputing investor. However, NAFTA 1124 sets out a procedure to be followed if a tribunal is not constituted within ninety days of the date that the claim is submitted to arbitration. The ICSID Secretary General acts as the appointing authority even if the arbitration is not conducted under the ICSID Convention. At the request of a disputing party, the ICSID Secretary General chooses the arbitrators not yet chosen, provided that the presiding arbitrator be chosen from a roster of forty-five presiding arbitrators maintained by the NAFTA countries[116] or, if none is available from the roster, from the ICSID Panel of Arbitrators. The presiding arbitrator chosen by the ICSID Secretary General cannot be of the nationality of the disputing NAFTA country or of the NAFTA country of the disputing investor.

NAFTA 1125 sets out provisions respecting technical requirements regarding the appointment of arbitrators for arbitrations under the ICSID Convention or the Additional Facility Rules.

(8) Consolidation

NAFTA 1126 covers the contingency of more than one investor submitting claims arising out of the same event.[117] A disputing party may request that the ICSID Secretary General establish a tribunal and that the tribunal may assume jurisdiction over the claims if it is satisfied, after hearing the disputing parties, that the claims have a question of fact or law in common. For example, if a NAFTA country enacts a measure that a number of investors of other NAFTA countries claim amounts to a nationalization of an industry, NAFTA 1126 can be invoked by the NAFTA country itself or one of the disputing investors to consolidate separate claims made by investors into a single claim.

Despite the involvement of the ICSID Secretary General, a tribunal constituted under NAFTA 1126 must conduct its proceedings under the UNCITRAL Rules.[118] Unless and until Canada and Mexico become members of the ICSID Convention, the UNCITRAL Rules are the only rules that may be used in all combinations of disputes among investors and NAFTA countries. The panel is comprised of three arbitrators, all of whom are appointed by the ICSID Secretary General. Arbitrators are chosen from the roster of arbitrators maintained by the NAFTA countries and, failing that, the ICSID Panel of Arbitrators, and failing that (other than in the case of the presiding arbitrator), at the discretion of the ICSID Secretary General.

If the presiding arbitrator is chosen from the ICSID Panel of Arbitrators, he or she cannot be of the nationality of any NAFTA country. One of the remaining two arbitrators must be of the nationality of the disputing NAFTA country and the other of the nationality of a NAFTA country of the disputing investors.[119]

When a tribunal established under NAFTA 1126 assumes jurisdiction over a matter, a tribunal established under NAFTA 1120 ceases to have jurisdiction.[120]

(9) Involvement of Other NAFTA Countries

A disputing NAFTA country is obliged to deliver to the other NAFTA countries written notice of claims submitted to arbitration and copies of all pleadings.[121] A NAFTA country that is not a disputing NAFTA country may make submissions to a tribunal on an issue of interpretation of NAFTA.[122] A NAFTA country is entitled at its own cost to receive from a disputing NAFTA country a copy of evidence tendered and the written argument of the disputing parties.[123]

(10) Procedural Matters

Procedure is governed by the applicable body of arbitration rules except as modified by Section B. Unless the disputing parties agree otherwise, a tribunal shall hold the arbitration in a NAFTA country that is a party to the New York Convention.[124]

Issues in dispute are to be decided in accordance with NAFTA and the principles of international law.[125] This could produce some unexpected and unwelcome results in matters such as expropriation where there is, at least in Canada and the United States, extensive domestic jurisprudence. As discussed in §7.7(7)(a), there is little international jurisprudence dealing with the difficult question of where regulation crosses over into taking, particularly when matters of public interest are involved. In applying international law, an arbitral panel could grant an award completely at odds with domestic jurisprudence.

Interpretations of NAFTA provisions by the Free Trade Commission are binding on a tribunal. Specific provision is made for interpretation by the Commission when a disputing NAFTA country raises as a defence that a measure falls under a reservation or exception set out in Annexes I through to IV discussed in §7.9. If the disputing NAFTA country so requests, the tribunal will request an interpretation from the Commission. The Commission is required to submit its interpretation within sixty days and the interpretation is binding on the tribunal. This provision is significant because applicability of a reservation or exception is a likely defence to claims for arbitration. If the Commission does not issue an interpretation within sixty days (which would occur if the NAFTA countries could not agree), the tribunal may decide the issue on its own.[126]

If a NAFTA country invokes NAFTA 1410 as a defence to a claim, NAFTA 1415 requires that the tribunal refer the question of whether NAFTA 1410 is applicable to the Financial Services Committee discussed in §8.6. As discussed in §8.4(11)(b), NAFTA 1410 permits certain measures preventing or limiting transfers by financial institutions or cross-border service providers notwithstanding the obligations respecting transfers set out in NAFTA 1109 and provides that NAFTA is not to be so construed as to prevent reasonable prudential measures. The Committee will decide within sixty days whether and to what extent NAFTA 1410 provides a defence and its decision binds the tribunal. If the Committee does not make a decision within sixty days, the disputing NAFTA country or the NAFTA country of the disputing investor may request the establishment of a panel under NAFTA 2008. The panel will be constituted in the manner provided in NAFTA 1414 (discussed in §11.2(10)(b)) and will decide the issue. Its report will be transmitted to the tribunal and will be binding on the tribunal. If a panel is not requested within ten days of the expiry of the sixty-day period, the tribunal may decide the matter on its own.

A tribunal may, at the request of a disputing party or on its own initiative (unless the disputing parties disapprove) appoint experts to report in writing on factual matters concerning environmental, health, safety or other scientific matters.[127]

A tribunal can order interim measures of protection or preserve the rights of disputing parties. This can include an order to preserve evidence. However, a tribunal cannot order attachment or enjoin the application of a measure.[128]

State and provincial governments have no standing in proceedings before tribunals. If the matter in dispute involves a state or provincial measure, the recourse of the disputing investor is against the federal government of the NAFTA country of which the state or province forms a part and the federal government will be the party to the proceedings.

(11) Awards

A tribunal may award monetary damages and applicable interest. A tribunal may also order restitution of property but the award must provide that the disputing NAFTA country pay monetary damages and interest in lieu of restitution. Where a claim is made on behalf of an enterprise, the payment must be made to the enterprise. Awards are without prejudice to relief under domestic law. As discussed in §11.3(5), the waiver of the right to initiate or continue domestic proceedings does not cover claims for injunctive, declaratory or other extraordinary relief. A tribunal may not order punitive damages.[129]

Awards have no binding effect except between the disputing parties in respect of the particular case.[130] Awards under the ICSID Convention may not be enforced until 120 days has elapsed from the date of the award or until revision or annulment proceedings have been completed.[131] Other awards cannot be enforced until three months from the date of the award have elapsed without a proceeding to revise, annul or set aside the award or until a court has dismissed or allowed such an application and there is no further appeal.[132]

NAFTA countries are obliged to provide for the enforcement of awards.[133] If a disputing NAFTA country fails to abide by or comply with a final award after a request to do so from a NAFTA country whose investor was a party to the proceedings, that NAFTA country may request a panel under NAFTA 2008, discussed in §11.2(8), without having first to request a meeting of the Commission.[134] Disputing investors may seek enforcement under any of the ICSID Convention, the New York Convention or the Inter-American Convention, regardless of whether a Chapter Twenty panel has been invoked.[135]

NAFTA Annex 1137.4 sets out rules respecting the publication of awards. In cases where Canada or the United States are disputing parties, either the disputing investor or whichever of Canada or the United States is the disputing NAFTA country may publish the award. Where Mexico is the disputing NAFTA country, the applicable arbitration rules apply in respect of publication. Generally, awards under these rules may not be published or made public without the consent of the parties.[136]

Awards in respect of breaches of NAFTA obligations by state or provincial governments are the responsibility of the federal governments of which they form a part.

(12) Exclusions

Decisions of Investment Canada or the Mexican National Commission on Foreign Investment not to permit an acquisition subject to review are not subject to the dispute settlement procedures under Section B of Chapter Eleven or of Chapter Twenty.[137] A decision of a NAFTA country to prohibit or restrict the acquisition of an investment pursuant to NAFTA 2102 (National Security), discussed in §10.2, is not subject to the dispute settlement procedures under Section B of Chapter Eleven or Chapter Twenty.[138]

(13) Concluding Remarks

The investor/state dispute settlement procedures are consistent with the provisions of the Model BIT, discussed in §7.3, upon which NAFTA

Chapter Eleven is based in large part. These procedures have the merit of distancing investment disputes from the political arena. An investor who feels that it has suffered damage by reason of a measure taken by a NAFTA country can pursue its claim without having to involve its government. However, they also provide a vehicle for investors to harass governments whose policies they dislike. Whether this is bad or good depends largely on one's view of the proper role of government in society. These procedures certainly put teeth into the NAFTA obligations they cover that was not provided under the FTA. As of the time of writing, they have yet to be tested.

11.4 ANTIDUMPING AND COUNTERVAILING DUTY MATTERS

A major Canadian objective in the FTA negotiations was to achieve assurance of secure access to the U.S. market. The administration of U.S. trade remedy laws, particularly those respecting the imposition of antidumping and countervailing duties, was considered the major impediment to secure market access. While the United States considered its trade remedy laws as necessary to counteract "unfair" trading practices, Canadians viewed their application as "contingency protectionism".[139] The perceived contingency was Canadian exporters out-competing their domestic U.S. counterparts and the protectionism came in the form of antidumping or countervailing duties levied against successful Canadian products. The Canadian FTA negotiators proposed that anti-competitive pricing be dealt with under domestic competition laws rather than through antidumping laws once free trade had been fully implemented[140] and sought to negotiate a subsidies code that would clearly identify the types of subsidies that could be subject to countervailing duty actions. Neither of these objectives was achieved. FTA Chapter Nineteen was accepted by the Canadian negotiators as a transitional solution pending the negotiation of substitute procedures for dealing with antidumping and countervailing duty matters. Negotiations were commenced but were put on hold because of the NAFTA negotiations and pending the outcome of the Uruguay Round negotiations which were dealing with the same issues.

The provisions of NAFTA Chapter Nineteen closely follow the transitional provisions of FTA Chapter Nineteen except that they are intended as permanent and not as transitional. There are several possible reasons why the Canadian negotiators accepted this outcome. First, the panel review process established under FTA Chapter Nineteen functioned better than expected and protected Canadian interests in a number of significant respects. Second, the introduction of some definition of countervailable or actionable subsidies set out in the *Agreement on Subsidies and Countervailing Measures* (the "1994 Subsidies Code") partially addressed Canadian concerns in this area. Third, it was probably unrealistic to expect the U.S. Congress in

1993 to approve any regime that restrained the application of U.S. trade remedy laws more than is done by NAFTA Chapter Nineteen.

(1) Dumping and Antidumping Duties

Dumping occurs when a manufacturer, producer or exporter exports its products at a lower price than that charged in its own country or at a price that is below its cost. It is somewhat ironic that while Canadians have viewed the U.S. application of antidumping laws as "contingency protectionism", Canada was the first country to pass an antidumping law.[141] The intent of this Canadian legislation, which was enacted in 1904, was to prohibit "predatory dumping" of imported goods but the legislation itself did not require evidence of predation.[142] While antidumping laws bear a superficial resemblance to predatory pricing laws in that they are directed at the practice of selling in a particular market at low prices, they are in fact quite different. Predatory pricing is pricing below cost with the intention of driving competitors out of business. Prevention of predation by foreign producers is raised as a justification for antidumping laws.[143] However, antidumping laws do not require the establishment of predatory intent in order to justify the imposition of antidumping duties. The reasons for price differences or the motivation for selling below cost are not factors taken into account in antidumping determinations. Laws against predatory pricing are designed to enhance competitiveness and consumer welfare, while antidumping laws are designed to protect producers.

There is a strong argument to be made for the elimination of the application of antidumping laws to members of a customs union or a free trade area. Dumping as a business strategy depends on home and export markets being separated by trade barriers such as tariffs.[144] Once trade barriers are removed, price differentials become more difficult to maintain because consumers in the home market will be free to take advantage of the lower prices in the export market by re-importing the dumped goods.[145] The countries of the European Union[146] and the European Economic Area do not apply antidumping laws against each other. Antidumping laws have been eliminated in the free trade area created by the New Zealand Australia Closer Economic Relations-Trade Agreement ("CER Agreement"). The original CER Agreement entered into in 1983 permitted antidumping actions. However, as a result of the 1988 review of the CER Agreement, it was decided to accelerate the elimination of tariffs and other trade barriers, harmonize competition laws and prohibit antidumping actions. Article 4:1 of the protocol between Australia and New Zealand resulting from this review reads as follows:

> The Member States agree that antidumping measures in respect of goods originating in the territory of the other Member State are not appropriate from

the time of achievement of both free trade in goods between the Member States on 1 July 1990 and the application of their competition laws to relevant anti-competitive conduct affecting trans-Tasman trade in goods.

Article 4:2 goes on to prohibit antidumping actions following July 1, 1990.[147]

(2) Subsidies and Countervailing Duties

Government subsidies can in some circumstances enable an industry to charge lower prices for its products abroad than would otherwise be possible, with a resulting competitive advantage in the foreign market. Importing countries protect domestic industries by levying a countervailing duty to bring the price of the goods to the same level as if there had been no subsidy. The open question is what constitutes a countervailable subsidy because any government program that provides a benefit can be viewed as a subsidy. As with antidumping laws, there is considerable debate as to whether counter-vailing duty laws are justifiable. Some economists would argue that exports at subsidized prices are gifts that a foreign country is unwise enough to bestow, and that consumers should be permitted to take advantage of them. The counter-argument is that subsidized exports can cause local firms to lose market share and ultimately be driven out of business, with resulting job loss and dependence on foreign suppliers. Like antidumping laws, counter-vailing duty laws are designed to protect producers and their imposition results in higher prices to consumers.[148]

(3) GATT and GATT Agreements

GATT Article VI sets out basic requirements to be observed by GATT member countries in levying antidumping or countervailing duties. These basic requirements were amplified by the *Agreement on Implementation of Article VI of the General Agreement on Tariffs and Trade* (the "Antidumping Code") and the *Agreement on Interpretation and Application of Articles VI, XVI and XXIII of the General Agreement on Tariffs and Trade* (the "Subsidies Code") that resulted from the Tokyo Round. When the Uruguay Round agreements come into effect, the Antidumping Code will be superseded by the *Agreement on Implementation of Article VI of the General Agreement on Tariffs and Trade 1994* (the "1994 Antidumping Code") and the Subsidies Code will be superseded by the 1994 Subsidies Code.

(a) Article VI of the GATT

GATT Article VI:1 describes dumping as introducing a product into the commerce of a country at less than its "normal value". The normal value is the domestic price of the like product in the exporting country. If there is no domestic price, the normal value is the highest comparable price for a like product for export to a third country or the cost of production in the exporting country, plus an allowance for selling costs and profit. The excess of the normal value over the price at which the product is introduced into the commerce of the importing country is the "margin of dumping". GATT Article VI:2 permits member countries to offset dumping by an antidumping duty no greater than the margin of dumping.

GATT Article VI:3 provides that no countervailing duty levied against an imported product shall be greater than the estimated subsidy granted on the manufacture, production or export of the product in the country of origin or exportation. Article VI does not define the types of subsidies against which countervailing duties may be levied.

An antidumping or countervailing duty is only justified if the dumping or subsidy causes or threatens to cause material injury to an established domestic industry or materially retards the establishment of a domestic industry. The GATT does not include any procedural requirements to be observed by member countries in investigating allegations of dumping, subsidization or material injury.

(b) The Tokyo Round Codes

The absence of procedural provisions in the GATT and other perceived inadequacies in the disciplines respecting the imposition of antidumping and countervailing duties were addressed during the Tokyo Round. The result was the Antidumping Code and the Subsidies Code to which both Canada and the United States are signatories. All signatories were obliged to conform their domestic antidumping and countervailing duty laws to the requirements of the Codes.[149]

The Antidumping Code sets out rules which elaborate on the general provisions in GATT Article VI:1 and give greater definition to the concept of dumping. The Subsidies Code also sets out procedural requirements but provides no more guidance than the GATT itself as to the types of subsidies against which countervailing duties may be levied. The annex to the Subsidies Code contains an illustrative list of export subsidies, but this list relates to Part II of the Code which supplements the provisions of GATT Article XVI prohibiting export subsidies and not to the provisions respecting countervailing duties in GATT Article VI.[150]

The Antidumping Code sets out rules to be followed in determining whether or not an industry has been injured[151] and explains what constitutes a domestic industry for the purpose of this determination.[152] The Subsidies Code sets out the rules to be followed in determining injury in subsidy cases.[153] The Antidumping Code[154] and the Subsidies Code[155] establish rules for conducting investigations in dumping and subsidy cases. Investigations are normally to be initiated by a written request from the affected industry, with evidence of dumping or subsidization, injury and the causal link between them. Since subsidization cases necessarily involve the government of an exporting signatory, the Subsidies Code includes a consultative procedure to clarify the situation giving rise to the dispute and provides a vehicle for its resolution. In both antidumping and countervailing actions, the question of dumping or subsidization on the one hand and injury on the other must be considered simultaneously.[156] As discussed in §11.4(10)(a), these determinations are made by separate agencies in both Canadian and American antidumping actions.

The Antidumping Code[157] provides for the resolution of dumping cases through the acceptance of undertakings from exporters to revise prices or cease dumping. The price revision results in prices being increased sufficiently to eliminate the margin of dumping. Exporters may not be forced to give undertakings. If undertakings are given, the investigation into injury may still proceed. If it is determined that there has been no injury, the undertakings lapse. Authorities of signatories must periodically review undertakings to determine if they are still necessary. The provision for undertakings in antidumping duty law may produce a fairer result to the exporter, who at least has the option of retaining the margin of dumping through increased prices rather than having it taxed away by the importing country. However, the effect of the negotiation and acceptance of undertakings, particularly when a number of exporters are involved, runs directly contrary to the competition law objective of prohibiting price fixing arrangements. The Subsidies Code contains provisions respecting the acceptance of undertakings from governments of exporting countries or exporters in subsidy cases.[158]

The Antidumping Code and the Subsidies Code describe the manner in which antidumping duties and countervailing duties can be levied and reiterate the GATT requirements that antidumping duties must not exceed the margin of dumping and countervailing duties must not exceed the amount of the subsidy. Both the Antidumping Code and the Subsidies Code establish rules for the provisional application of antidumping and countervailing duties and both contain provisions limiting the ability of the signatories to impose antidumping and countervailing duties retroactively. Both also contain provisions for dispute settlement.

At the time that NAFTA became effective, the antidumping and countervailing duty laws of Canada and the United States followed the basic format prescribed by these Codes.[159]

(c) The Uruguay Round Codes

The 1994 Antidumping Code and the 1994 Subsidies Code will come into effect when the WTO Agreement comes into effect. The 1994 Antidumping Code makes a number of technical changes to the GATT rules respecting antidumping actions but none of the changes is major. The 1994 Subsidies Code significantly modifies countervailing duty law by introducing for the first time provisions that attempt to distinguish subsidies that are countervailable from those that are not.

(i) The 1994 Antidumping Code

The 1994 Antidumping Code carries forward the provisions of the Antidumping Code with some technical elaborations.

The 1994 Antidumping Code expressly provides that sales below cost may be treated as not being in the ordinary course of trade and disregarded in computing normal value only if they are made over an extended period of time in substantial quantities at prices that do not provide for the recovery of costs within a reasonable period of time.[160] Costs must be calculated on the basis of the records of a producer or exporter and their calculation is subject to certain requirements.[161] The rules for comparing normal values with export prices are elaborated on by adding provisions for currency conversion and weighted averages.[162]

In injury determinations, the new Code provision respecting threat of material injury lists a number of factors to be considered.[163] The content of applications for the commencement of investigations has been amplified.[164] Initiation of investigations will have to have the support of domestic producers accounting for least 25% of total production of like products[165] and publicity before commencing an investigation must be avoided.[166] Procedures are prescribed for on-the-spot investigations[167] and the use by authorities of the best information available when the interested parties do not provide information.[168]

Under the new rules, authorities will be required to calculate individual margins of dumping for each known exporter or producer unless the number of experts, producers, importers or types of products involved is so large that this is impracticable.[169] Provisional measures may not be applied sooner than sixty days from the initiation of the investigation.[170] The provisions respecting public notice of determinations and of the imposition of provisional measures have been elaborated.[171] Member countries maintaining antidumping measures must provide for prompt review of determinations and reviews of determinations by bodies independent of the authorities responsible for them. The new Code sets out more specific rules respecting the duration of antidumping duties than does the Antidumping Code.[172]

(ii) The 1994 Subsidies Code

The 1994 Subsidies Code addresses the question of which subsidies should be countervailable and which should not. A subsidy is defined as a financial contribution by government or a public body where there is a direct transfer of funds, government revenue is foregone, goods or services other than general infrastructure is provided or goods are purchased by government. In any of these instances, a benefit must be conferred for there to be a subsidy. A subsidy also exists if a government makes payments to a funding mechanism or entrusts a private body to carry out any of the foregoing.[173]

A subsidy must be "specific" to be countervailable.[174] A subsidy is specific if access to it is limited to certain enterprises.[175] However, specificity will not exist where the granting authority or enabling legislation establishes objective criteria or conditions governing eligibility, so long as eligibility is automatic and the criteria and conditions are strictly adhered to.[176] Other factors may be considered to determine whether a subsidy is specific. The use of a subsidy program by a limited number of certain enterprises or the predominant use by certain enterprises or disproportionately large amounts of subsidy to certain enterprises as well as the manner in which the discretion of the granting authority is exercised may all be taken into account.[177] Subsidies limited to certain enterprises located within a designated geographical region of the granting authority are specific.[178] Subsidies contingent upon the use of domestic over imported goods or export performance, except for those provided for in the GATT Agreement on Agriculture, are specific.[179] The GATT Agreement on Agriculture provides for certain exemptions and sets out rules respecting the imposition of countervailing duties against domestic and export subsidies that conform to the requirements of that agreement.[180]

Part IV of the 1994 Subsidies Code provides that subsidies for assistance for research activities,[181] for assistance to disadvantaged regions given pursuant to a general framework of regional development[182] or to promote the adaptation of existing facilities to new environmental requirements[183] are nonactionable even though they may be specific. Subsidies must fulfil a number of requirements to fall under any of these categories.

Part V of the 1994 Subsidies Code sets out the procedural requirements to be applied by member countries in countervailing duty actions. The requirements are based on and elaborate upon the requirements set out in the Subsidies Code. For example, the degree of support for the application by the domestic industry is prescribed.[184] The 1994 Subsidies Code sets out procedural requirements respecting the right of interested members and parties to present evidence, the treatment of confidential information and the conduct of investigations in other member countries and in the premises of firms.[185] Guidelines are established for handling situations involving government provision of equity capital, loans and loan guarantees and the provision of goods or services or purchase of goods by government.[186]

(4) Provisions of the FTA

FTA Chapter Nineteen permitted each of Canada and the United States to continue to apply its antidumping and countervailing duty laws and to amend them.[187] However, notification and consultation requirements applied to statutory amendments and such amendments were required to be consistent with the GATT, the Antidumping Code and the Subsidies Code and with the "object and purpose" of the FTA. Provision was made for panel review of amendments considered inconsistent with these norms.[188]

FTA Chapter Nineteen also established a process of binational panel review of final determinations made by Canadian and American authorities in antidumping and countervailing duty matters.[189] The objective was two-fold. The first was to provide a review body that was more impartial and less inclined to defer to the decisions of administrative authorities than domestic courts. The second was to provide a more expeditious means of obtaining determinations than that afforded by domestic appeal procedures with multiple levels of appeal. Panel review was substituted for normal judicial review procedures if any party to a proceeding so desired. Panel review procedures were subject to tight time constraints with the objective of achieving final decisions within a period of 315 days of the request for a panel.[190] Panel decisions were binding and final. However, provision was made for the establishment of a special committee to hear challenges of panel decisions if certain extraordinary circumstances applied.[191]

FTA Chapter Nineteen was to be in effect for a period of five years pending the development of a substitute system of rules in each of Canada and the United States for antidumping and countervailing duties.[192] If no system had been developed by the end of this time, the period would be extended for two more years. If the new regime was not developed by that time, either Canada or the United States had the right to cancel the FTA on six months' notice, which was a curious provision given that each country already had this right under FTA 2106.

(5) Experience Under the FTA

(a) Panel review of statutory amendments

There were no panel reviews of statutory amendments of Canadian or American antidumping or countervailing duty laws while the FTA was in effect. These provisions, which have been carried forward into NAFTA, remain untested.

(b) Panel review of final determinations

By most accounts, the panel review process for final determinations under the FTA worked well. The procedures were frequently invoked, particularly by Canada. As one commentator has observed, of the thirty panel decisions during the first four and one-half years of the FTA's existence, twenty-three were invoked by Canada.[193] Other commentators examining the first two and one-half years' experience under the FTA explain the preponderance of review of U.S. final decisions by the fact that the countervailing duty actions are much more frequent in the United States than in Canada and the cash deposit system in U.S. antidumping and countervailing duty law gives a greater incentive for challenging decisions than does Canada's system of prospective collection.[194] NAFTA panel decisions have been timely. Of fourteen cases heard between January 1989 and July 1991, only three exceeded the 315-day time limit provided for in FTA 1904.[195] The 315-day period for an FTA panel took less than half the time required for an appeal in the United States to the Court of International Trade.[196]

The composition of panels with five panelists drawn from a variety of backgrounds has been cited as a positive element and an improvement over having a single judge as is the practice before the U.S. Court of International Trade.[197] The quality of panel decisions has generally been regarded as high.[198] However, there have been some criticisms of the panel process. Conflicts of interest have arisen on a number of occasions with legal practitioners who have had to withdraw from panels after being selected.[199] The U.S. Statement of Administrative Action commented that scholars have noted the "potential within the system for disuniformity of panel decisions with each other and established U.S. law".[200] However, the scholar in question also expressed the view in the same article that panel decisions were of "high quality".[201] The dissenting U.S. member in the decision of the extraordinary challenge committee in *Certain Softwood Lumber Products from Canada* (the "Softwood Lumber case") was highly critical of the panel process, particularly over what he described as the lack of expertise of Canadian panel members in standards of judicial review in U.S. law.[202] The binational panel process has also been subjected to constitutional challenges in the United States.[203]

From a Canadian perspective, it was essential that the panel review process be seen to work effectively and to protect Canadian interests because FTA Chapter Nineteen fell significantly short of Canadian negotiating objectives. As described below,[204] the process was severely tested in *Fresh, Chilled and Frozen Pork from Canada* (the "Pork case") and was seen to have protected Canadian interests. Canadian interests were similarly protected in the recently concluded Softwood Lumber case.

(6) Provisions of NAFTA

NAFTA Chapter Nineteen, entitled "Review and Dispute Settlement in Antidumping and Countervailing Duty Matters", is based upon its counterpart in FTA Chapter Nineteen. Like FTA Chapter Nineteen, NAFTA Chapter Nineteen permits each NAFTA country to apply its antidumping and countervailing duty laws against goods imported from other NAFTA countries and to amend such laws subject to the requirements respecting statutory amendments described in §11.4(7). NAFTA Chapter Nineteen provides for panel review of statutory amendments on terms virtually identical to those in FTA Chapter Nineteen and carries forward, with a few modifications, the provisions for panel review of final determinations in antidumping and countervailing duty matters established under the FTA. NAFTA 1902(3) makes it clear that NAFTA Chapter Nineteen represents the totality of the obligations of the NAFTA countries respecting their antidumping and countervailing duty laws.

As with FTA Chapter Nineteen, the reference to "dispute resolution" in the title to NAFTA Chapter Nineteen is somewhat of a misnomer. The only "disputes" for which NAFTA Chapter Nineteen provides "dispute resolution" procedures are those for challenging whether amendments to the antidumping and countervailing duty laws of NAFTA countries conform to norms established by NAFTA Chapter Nineteen. As under the FTA, the provisions for panel review of final decisions in antidumping and countervailing duty matters create an avenue of judicial review to an internationally constituted body that serves as an alternative to the domestic judicial review procedures of each NAFTA country.

(7) Retention of and Amendments to Antidumping and Countervailing Duty Laws

Each NAFTA country reserves the right to apply its antidumping and countervailing duty law to goods imported from other NAFTA countries.[205] Antidumping and countervailing duty law includes not only relevant statutes but also legislative history, regulations, administrative practices and judicial precedents.

NAFTA countries reserve the right to change or modify antidumping or countervailing laws.[206] However, certain requirements must be satisfied in the amendment of statutes.[207] Amendments apply to goods from other NAFTA countries only if the amending statute expressly so provides. The NAFTA country enacting the amendment must notify the other NAFTA countries affected by the amendment in advance and must consult on request.

NAFTA 1902(2)(d) sets out the norms to which amendments of antidumping and countervailing duty statutes must conform. Amendments, in so far as they affect other NAFTA countries, cannot be inconsistent with the GATT or the Antidumping Code or the Subsidies Code or successor agreements. The successor agreements are the 1994 Antidumping Code and the 1994 Subsidies Code described in §11.4(3)(c). Amendments also cannot be inconsistent with the "object and purpose" of NAFTA. NAFTA 1902(2)(d)(ii) carries forward the description of object and purpose that appeared in FTA 1902(d)(ii), which is "to establish fair and predictable conditions for the progressive liberalization of trade between the Parties to this Agreement while maintaining effective and fair disciplines on unfair trade practices". This "object and purpose" is to be ascertained from the provisions, preamble and objectives of NAFTA, as well as the practices of the NAFTA countries.

The norms established by NAFTA 1902(2)(d) are minimal. The GATT obligations are significant but the NAFTA countries are bound to observe them in any event. The "object and purpose" norm is nebulous at best. One might be able to construct an interesting argument based on the resolution in the NAFTA preamble of ensuring a "predictable commercial environment for business planning and investment". However, it is difficult to see how an amendment consistent with GATT obligations could be successfully attacked as contrary to the "object and purpose" of NAFTA.

The question of the compatibility of a U.S. statutory provision with GATT requirements was raised before the FTA Chapter Nineteen panel reviewing the subsidy determinations in the Pork case. The provision in question, Section 771B of the Tariff Act, had been enacted prior to the FTA becoming effective.[208] Section 771B deems subsidies provided to producers of raw agricultural products (in this case, live swine) to be provided respecting the processed product (namely, pork) under certain conditions. The panel rejected the complainant's contention that Section 771B had to be construed in a manner consistent with the GATT. The panel did not decide the GATT issue but observed that while U.S. statutes should be construed where possible so as not to conflict with an international agreement, if reconciliation is not possible the statute prevails as U.S. law.[209] The lesson to be derived from this decision is that panels reviewing final determinations are bound to apply domestic law and will not consider whether a law that they are applying is consistent with the criteria set out in NAFTA 1902. If a NAFTA country is of the view that an amendment to another NAFTA country's antidumping or countervailing duty statutes is GATT-inconsistent, action should be taken under NAFTA 1903 described in §11.4(9).

(8) Formation of a Panel

Unlike Chapter Twenty panels, which can be trinational, Chapter Nineteen panels are always binational. This binational composition applies even if an amendment to the antidumping or countervailing duty laws of a NAFTA country or a determination in an antidumping or countervailing duty action brought in a NAFTA country affects goods of both of the other NAFTA countries. In these instances, two separate binational panels would be constituted. NAFTA Chapter Nineteen does not provide for consolidation in these or any other circumstances or for the participation in panel proceedings of NAFTA countries not directly involved in the establishment of the binational panel.

NAFTA Chapter Nineteen panels, whether for reviewing statutory amendments or final determinations, are established in accordance with the provisions of NAFTA Annex 1901.2. Each panel consists of five members chosen from a roster developed prior to the entry into force of NAFTA. Each NAFTA country was, at the time NAFTA became effective, required to choose at least twenty-five individuals for the roster on the basis of their good character, high standing and repute as well as their objectivity, reliability, sound judgment and general familiarity with international trade law. All candidates for panels are required to be citizens of NAFTA countries and no candidate may be affiliated with or take instructions from a NAFTA country. NAFTA Annex 1901.2 includes the added requirement that the roster include judges or former judges to the greatest extent practicable.[210] All panelists are subject to a code of conduct[211] established by an exchange of letters when NAFTA entered into force.

Because of the quasi-judicial functions of the panel, a majority of the members must be lawyers in good standing[212] and the chairman will be chosen from among the lawyers.[213] The reverse selection process described in §11.2(8)(a) for Chapter Twenty panels has not been adopted for Chapter Nineteen panels. As under the FTA, each involved NAFTA country has the right to choose two members of the panel.[214] Each NAFTA country is permitted four peremptory challenges disqualifying the candidates proposed by the other NAFTA country.[215] The fifth member will be chosen by agreement of both Parties.[216] Panelists are required to sign documents in the form required by each NAFTA country relating to confidentiality and, upon signing such documentation, are to be granted access to the information covered.[217] If a panelist becomes unable to fulfil his or her functions or is disqualified, the panel is suspended pending the selection of a new panelist in accordance with NAFTA Annex 1901.2.[218]

The panel will issue a written majority opinion, together with any concurring or dissenting opinions. The decision must be based on the vote of all panel members.[219]

(9) Panel Review of Statutory Amendments

NAFTA 1903 carries forward the provision in FTA 1903 providing for panel review of amendments to antidumping and countervailing duty statutes. A NAFTA country may request that a panel issue a declaratory opinion as to whether an amendment of another NAFTA country's antidumping or countervailing duty law fails to conform to the norms described in §11.4(7). A declaratory opinion may also be requested as to whether an amendment has the effect of overturning a panel decision made in connection with a final antidumping or countervailing duty determination *and* fails to conform to the required norms. It should be noted that the use of the conjunctive in this latter instance means that a declaratory opinion cannot be sought in respect of an amendment that overturns a review panel decision but is consistent with the required norms. The nebulous nature of the "object and purpose" norm might work in favour of a NAFTA country that wished to take issue with a statutory amendment enacted by another NAFTA country that had the effect of overturning a panel decision.

The procedures for making declaratory opinions are set out in NAFTA Annex 1903.2. A panel reviewing an amendment may establish its own rules of procedure (unless the NAFTA countries agree otherwise) but the rules must provide for at least one hearing before the panel with the involved NAFTA countries being entitled to make written submissions and rebuttal arguments. The panel must base its decision solely on the submissions and arguments of the NAFTA countries appearing. The initial declaratory opinion must be issued within ninety days of the selection of the panel's chairman. If the panel finds that the amendment is inconsistent with the requirements referred to above, it may recommend appropriate modifications. Panelists may present separate opinions where unanimity has not been reached. This initial opinion will become final unless written objections are presented to the panel by a disputing NAFTA country within fourteen days. The panel then has thirty days to conduct any further examination it deems appropriate and to reconsider its opinion. The final declaratory opinion, together with any dissents or concurrences, will be published unless the involved NAFTA countries agree otherwise.

If the panel recommends modifications, the NAFTA countries shall attempt to reach a mutually satisfactory solution within ninety days of the issuance of the final panel decision. If the solution involves the passage of corrective legislation, the legislation must be enacted within nine months. If the corrective legislation is not enacted or consultations fail to result in agreement, the NAFTA country which requested the panel may take comparable legislative or executive action, or terminate NAFTA on sixty days' written notice.

Like FTA 1903, the panel process provided for in NAFTA 1903 may only be invoked by the federal governments of NAFTA countries.

(10) Panel Review of Final Determinations

Like its FTA counterpart, NAFTA 1904(1) requires the NAFTA countries to replace judicial review of final antidumping and countervailing duty determinations with panel review. The expression "final determination", as defined in NAFTA 1911 by reference to NAFTA Annex 1911, is a list of specific orders and determinations under the *Special Import Measures Act* ("SIMA")[220] in the case of Canada and the Tariff Act of 1930 in the case of the United States and of certain final resolutions under Mexican antidumping and countervailing duty law. The provisions of NAFTA 1904 apply only to goods that the competent investigating authority of an importing NAFTA country in applying that country's antidumping or countervailing duty laws to a particular case determines are goods of another NAFTA country. These are defined as domestic products as understood in the GATT, which need not be "originating goods" under the NAFTA Rules of Origin.[221]

(a) Canadian and American antidumping and countervailing duty procedures

The legislation currently in effect governing antidumping and countervailing duty cases in each of Canada and the United States follows the basic procedures outlined in the Antidumping Code and the Subsidies Codes. The relevant Canadian legislation is SIMA and the corresponding U.S. legislation is Title VII of the Tariff Act of 1930.[222] In Canada, functions respecting the determination of dumping or subsidization are performed by the Deputy Minister of National Revenue for Customs and Excise (the "Deputy Minister"). The corresponding administrative functions in the United States are performed by the International Trade Administration of the United States Department of Commerce ("Commerce"). In Canada, functions respecting the determination of material injury are performed by the Canadian International Trade Tribunal (the "CITT"). The corresponding functions in the United States are performed by the United States International Trade Commission (the "ITC").

(i) Initiating investigations and preliminary determinations

The Deputy Minister in Canada or Commerce in the United States may on his or her or its own initiative or in response to a complaint (Canada)[223] or petition (United States)[224] initiate an investigation if (as required under the GATT) there is evidence that dumping or subsidizing of goods is causing or likely to cause material injury to an established domestic industry or is retarding the establishment of a domestic industry.

In the United States, the ITC makes a preliminary determination as to whether there is a reasonable indication of material injury within forty-five days of the filing of the petition or receiving notice from Commerce that an investigation has been initiated.[225] In Canada, there is no preliminary determination of material injury. The Deputy Minister in Canada or Commerce in the United States makes a preliminary determination as to whether there has been dumping or subsidization.[226] In Canada, the preliminary determination must be made within ninety days of the initiation of the investigation. In the United States, the corresponding time period for countervailing duty actions is eighty-five days and for antidumping actions is 160 days[227] from the filing of the petition or the initiation of the investigation, but in neither case before the ITC has made a preliminary determination on injury. Provisional duties may be levied in each country on the basis of affirmative preliminary determinations.[228] In Canada, once the Deputy Minister has made an affirmative preliminary determination of dumping or subsidization, the CITT is notified and commences its material injury inquiry.[229]

(ii) Final determinations of dumping, subsidization and injury

If the preliminary determinations are affirmative, the Deputy Minister in Canada or Commerce in the United States proceeds to a final determination as to whether dumping or subsidization has occurred. In Canada, the final determination is made under SIMA, s. 41 and the required time limit is within ninety days of the preliminary determination. In the United States, the final determination under the Tariff Act of 1930 is made under Section 705[230] in countervailing duty actions and Section 735[231] in antidumping actions. The required time limit is within seventy-five days of the preliminary determination of subsidization or dumping.[232]

In Canada, following the affirmative preliminary determination of dumping or subsidization, the CITT continues with its material injury inquiry and under SIMA, s. 43(1) is required to make an order or finding as to material injury within 120 days of the date that it received notice of the preliminary determination of dumping or subsidization. The CITT also determines to what goods, exporter and country the order or finding applies.[233] In the United States, upon an affirmative final determination of dumping or subsidization, the Tariff Act of 1930 requires that the ITC proceed under Section 705[234] in a countervailing duty action and Section 735[235] in an antidumping action to make a final determination as to material injury.

(iii) Assessing duties

In Canada, if affirmative final determinations have been made by the Deputy Minister and the CITT, the Deputy Minister causes a customs appraiser to determine the normal value and export price of goods released before the final determination by the CITT.[236] Determinations are also made respecting the normal value and export price or amount of subsidy on goods imported after the CITT's final determination that are of the same description as the goods covered by the Tribunal's order or finding.[237] These determinations are made so that antidumping or countervailing duties can be assessed. After paying the duty, the importer may request that the appraiser redetermine the duty or the appraiser may redetermine the duty on his own.[238] SIMA, s. 59, permits the Deputy Minister to review the determinations or redeterminations by appraisers and requires him or her to do so if requested by the importer, and in either case to make redeterminations. The question of which of two or more persons is the importer of goods may be referred by the Deputy Minister to the CITT and the CITT may make an order or finding.[239] SIMA, s. 91(3) provides that the CITT may reconsider such orders or findings under certain circumstances.

In the United States, when affirmative final determinations of dumping or subsidization and of material injury have been made, Commerce publishes an antidumping or countervailing duty order which directs customs officers to assess the appropriate duty on the class of goods prescribed in the order.[240]

(iv) Subsequent review

In Canada, the CITT may review any order or finding made by it on its own initiative or at the request of the Deputy Minister or an interested person or government.[241] SIMA s. 76(4) provides that the CITT may as a consequence of such review rescind its order or finding or continue it.[242] SIMA, s. 76(3) requires that the CITT not initiate a review unless the person or government satisfies the CITT that a review is warranted.

In the United States, Section 751[243] of the Tariff Act of 1930 requires that antidumping or countervailing duty orders be reviewed by Commerce at least annually after the first year if a request for a review is received. Upon receiving such a request, Commerce will review and determine the amount of any net subsidy in a countervailing duty matter or antidumping duty in an antidumping duty matter.[244] Section 751(b)[245] of the Tariff Act of 1930 provides for review by the ITC of certain final affirmative determinations including those respecting subsidization, dumping or injury in the event of changed circumstances to determine if such circumstances warrant the revocation of an antidumping or countervailing duty order.

(v) Undertakings

As contemplated in the Antidumping Code and Subsidies Code, the legislation in each of Canada and the United States provides that undertakings (Canada)[246] or agreements (United States)[247] to eliminate the dumping or subsidy may be accepted from exporters or governments of exporting countries. The acceptance of an undertaking or agreement suspends the investigation, although an interested party may request that the investigation continue.[248] In Canada, such a request terminates the undertaking and the investigation continues.[249] In the United States, if such a request is made, the agreement remains in force and the investigation continues.[250] In the United States, any interested party may also request a review of the suspension of the investigation and if such a request is made, the ITC will determine whether the agreement completely eliminates the injury. If the ITC finds that the agreement will not completely eliminate injury, the investigation resumes.[251] Each NAFTA country's legislation provides for periodic review of undertakings[252] or agreements.[253] Under SIMA, s. 53(1), the Deputy Minister must review an undertaking within three years of accepting it or before the expiry of any renewal period. If the Deputy Minister is satisfied that the undertaking continues to serve its purpose and that it need not be terminated because of changed circumstances, the undertaking may be renewed for up to three years. In Canada, a change in circumstances may result in the Deputy Minister terminating an undertaking and resuming an investigation.[254] In the United

States, a change in circumstances may result in the review of a determination by the ITC that an agreement eliminates injury under Section 751(b)[255] of the Tariff Act of 1930. The legislation of each NAFTA country also contains provisions respecting the violation of undertakings or agreements.[256]

(b) Mexican antidumping and countervailing duty procedures

(i) Prior to NAFTA

Unlike Canada and the United States, Mexican experience with antidumping and countervailing duty matters is relatively brief. The authority to take action against unfair trade practices flows from Article 131 of the Mexican Constitution. The Foreign Trade Act Implementing Article 131 of the Constitution of the United Mexican States[257] (the "Foreign Trade Law"), enacted on January 13, 1986,[258] established rules respecting antidumping and countervailing duty matters. The Foreign Trade Law is supplemented by the Regulation Covering Unfair Practices of International Commerce (the "Foreign Trade Regulations").[259] The first antidumping petition was filed in October, 1986.[260] Since then, the number of antidumping petitions has escalated, with thirty-seven in 1992 alone. The increased number of cases is attributed to trade liberalization, with producers relying increasingly on contingent protection as trade barriers fall.[261] Mexico has been much less active in pursuing countervailing duty matters.

In 1985, Mexico entered into a bilateral subsidies agreement with the United States.[262] The United States agreed to extend to Mexico the benefit of the injury test in countervailing duty cases even though Mexico was not a GATT member or a signatory of the Subsidies Code.[263] Mexico, in return, agreed to discipline export subsidies and that preferential pricing to domestic industries, particularly in the petroleum sector, would be countervailable.[264] Mexico acceded to the GATT in 1986 and ratified the Antidumping Code in 1987.[265] However, Mexico did not accede to the Subsidies Code.[266]

Antidumping and countervailing duty matters are administered by SECOFI and dumping, subsidy and injury investigations are undertaken by an office of SECOFI.[267] Actions are commenced by a petition, although SECOFI can also initiate proceedings on its own initiative.[268] The petitioner must represent at least 25% of Mexican producers of identical or similar goods.[269] If the petition is incomplete, the petitioner must complete it within a certain time frame or the case is dropped.[270]

Before NAFTA became effective, SECOFI was required to issue a provisional resolution (*i.e.*, determination) within five working days of the petition being filed and could at this stage impose a compensatory duty.[271] The expression "resolution" in Mexican antidumping and countervailing duty law corresponds to the expression "determination" used in Canadian and American antidumping and countervailing duty law. In practice, at least in dumping cases, SECOFI took about two and one-half months to issue a provisional resolution[272] and ceased issuing affirmative provisional resolutions without first hearing the foreign producer or exporter.[273] The provisional resolution is then reviewed and the review can result in its being confirmed, modified or revoked.[274] SECOFI then proceeds to a final resolution or determination. At any time up to the final determination, a "conciliatory hearing" can be requested and a settlement can be proposed.[275] Once an investigation is commenced, an office of SECOFI proceeds to make an injury determination.

Before NAFTA became effective, there was no procedure for periodic review of antidumping or countervailing duties to determine whether the conditions giving rise to them continue to exist. However, a foreign producer or exporter could request a declaration that an unfair trade practice has ceased to exist.[276] Provision was made in 1988 for review of final determinations.[277]

Mexico's antidumping and countervailing regime before NAFTA became effective was criticized on a number of counts. The law was vague in a number of material respects, time limits were not adhered to by administrative authorities and on some occasions lack of notice to foreign exporters and producers was a significant problem.[278]

(ii) Changes required by NAFTA

NAFTA Annex 1904.15 sets out amendments to domestic antidumping and countervailing duty laws that each NAFTA country must bring into effect. The Schedule for Mexico sets out a lengthy list of required amendments.[279] For example, the possibility of imposing duties within five days must be eliminated. The "provisional resolution" must now be termed as the "initial resolution" and the resolution arising from the review of what is now the "initial resolution" has become the "provisional resolution". Written notice of the initiation of an investigation must be provided to interested parties and the notice must be published in the Diario Oficial. Provisional duties cannot be imposed before a preliminary determination.[280] Immediate access to binational panels for review of final determinations must be provided without having to exhaust administrative appeal procedures. Explicit and adequate timetables must be provided for determinations and for the submission of questionnaires, evidence and comments by interested parties, as well as the opportunity to present facts and arguments. The amendments set out various disclosure and access to information requirements. The administrative authorities must maintain an administrative record and final determinations must be based solely on that record. Recommendations of advisory bodies[281] must be placed in that record and made available to parties to the proceeding. Final determinations must be accompanied by detailed reasons so that interested parties can make an informed decision as to whether to seek review. A right to annual review of dumping margins and countervailing duty rates must be provided. As noted in §11.1(2)(b), NAFTA countries must provide for review of final administrative actions regarding matters covered by NAFTA.

(c) Final determinations subject to panel review

The final determinations in antidumping and countervailing duty matters subject to panel review are listed for each NAFTA country in three separate subparagraphs in NAFTA Annex 911 under *final determination*.

(i) Canadian final determinations

The Canadian final determinations subject to panel review are listed under subparagraph (a). Clause (i) refers to an order or finding by the CITT arising from its inquiry as to material injury under SIMA, s. 43(1), described in §11.4(10)(a)(ii). Clause (ii) refers to an order by the CITT arising from a review of its own prior order or finding of material injury under SIMA, s. 76(4), described in §11.4(10)(a)(iv). Clause (iii) refers to a final determination of the Deputy Minister as to whether there has been dumping or subsidization under SIMA, s. 41, described in §11.4(10)(a)(ii). Clause (iv) refers to a decision of the Deputy Minister arising from his redetermination of the determination or redetermination of a customs appraiser under SIMA, s. 59, described in §11.4(10)(a)(iii). Clause (v) refers to a decision by the CITT under SIMA, s. 76(3), described in §11.4(10)(a)(iv) not to review an order or finding of material injury. Clause (vi) refers to a reconsideration by the CITT of a decision as to which of two or more persons is an importer under SIMA, s. 91(3), described in §11.4(10)(a)(iii). Clause (vii) refers to a decision of the Deputy Minister arising from the periodic review of undertakings under SIMA, s. 53(1), described in §11.4(10)(a)(v).

The decisions of the CITT referred to in clauses (i), (ii), (v) and (vi) are all subject to judicial review by the Federal Court of Appeal.[282] The decision of the Deputy Minister referred to in clause (iv) is subject to review by the CITT and an appeal from the CITT to the Federal Court of Appeal may be made on a question of law only.[283] The decisions of the Deputy Minister referred to in clauses (iii) and (vii) are reviewable by the Federal Court of Appeal.[284]

(ii) U.S. final determinations

The U.S. final determinations subject to panel review are listed under subparagraph (b). The affirmative and negative decisions referred to in clauses (i) and (ii) are final determinations made by Commerce as to the occurrence of subsidization or dumping and the ITC as to material injury under Sections 705 and 735 of the Tariff Act of 1930, described in §11.4(10)(a)(ii). Clause (iii) refers to Commerce's review of antidumping and countervailing duty orders under Section 751 of the Tariff Act of 1930, described in

§11.4(10)(a)(iv). Clause (iv) refers to determinations of the ITC under Section 751(b) of the Tariff Act of 1930, described in §11.4(10)(a)(iv) and §11.4(10)(a)(v) not to review a determination based on changed circumstances. Clause (v) refers to a determination by Commerce as to whether a particular type of merchandise is within a class or kind subject to an existing finding of dumping or antidumping or countervailing duty order. Each of these determinations is subject to judicial review by the United States Court of International Trade.

(iii) Mexican final determinations

The Mexican final determinations subject to panel review are listed under subparagraph (c). Clause (i) refers to a final resolution (*i.e.*, determination) by SECOFI respecting dumping, subsidization or injury. Clause (ii) refers to a final resolution in an annual application for review of antidumping or countervailing duty rates created by the amendments required by NAFTA Annex 1904.15, described in §11.4(10)(b)(ii). Clause (iii) refers to a final resolution by SECOFI as to whether a particular type of merchandise is within the class or kind of merchandise described in an existing antidumping or countervailing duty resolution.

(d) Initiating review by a panel

A NAFTA country may request that a panel review any of the final determinations referred to in §11.4(10)(c) to determine whether it was in accordance with the antidumping and countervailing duty law of the importing NAFTA country.[285] The jurisdiction of a panel is unequivocally restricted to applying the antidumping or countervailing duty laws of the importing NAFTA country. The antidumping and countervailing duty law of the importing NAFTA country consists of the relevant statutes, legislative history, regulations, administrative practice and judicial precedents to the extent that a court of the importing NAFTA country would have relied on them.[286] The review is to be based on the administrative record which, unless otherwise agreed by the NAFTA countries and other persons appearing before the panel, consists of all documentary or other information presented to or obtained by the investigating authority including governmental memoranda and records of *ex parte* proceedings, the final determination including reasons, transcripts and records of conferences and hearings, and all published notices in the official journal of the importing NAFTA country.[287]

Panel review is available only for the final determinations referred to above. Other determinations made in the course of an antidumping or countervailing duty matter (such as preliminary findings of dumping, subsidization or material injury or the imposition of provisional duties) are not subject to panel review.

(e) Request for a panel

A NAFTA country must request panel review of a final determination on the request of any person entitled to commence judicial review procedures of that determination under the applicable domestic law.[288] A request for panel review may also be made by a NAFTA country on its own initiative.

The request must be made in writing to the importing NAFTA country within thirty days of publication of the final determination.[289] An importing NAFTA country must inform a NAFTA country whose goods are affected by a final determination that is not published and the request for a panel may be made within thirty days of receipt of notice of the determination. If provisional remedies have been imposed, the exporting NAFTA country may notify the importing NAFTA country of its intention to request a panel and the process of establishing the panel shall begin at that time. Failure to make a timely request will preclude panel review.[290] If no panel request is made in respect of a final determination, domestic judicial review may proceed and any revised final determination arising from the judicial review is not subject to binational panel review.[291] However, once a NAFTA country has requested panel review, the final determination may not be reviewed by any domestic court.[292]

(f) Standard of review

(i) Standard of review respecting Canadian final determinations

The standard of review to be applied by a panel in the case of Canadian final determinations is that set out in s. 18.1(4) of the *Federal Court Act*,[293] which provides the following grounds for review by the Federal Court of Appeal of Tribunal decisions: acting without jurisdiction, acting beyond its jurisdiction or refusing to exercise jurisdiction; failing to observe a principle of natural justice; erring in law in making a decision or order; basing a decision on an erroneous finding of fact made in a perverse or capricious manner or without regard for the evidence presented; acting or failing to act by reason of fraud or perjured evidence; and acting in any other way contrary to law. The standard of review in the FTA for Canadian antidumping and countervailing duty matters was as set out in s. 28(1) of the *Federal Court Act*, which at the time that the FTA became effective contained the first three but not the last two requirements just described.[294]

The scope of the standard of review under the FTA for Canadian final determinations was discussed at length by the panel in *Certain Beer from the United States*.[295] In the discussion respecting error in law, the panel observed that "the jurisdiction of a court on appeal is much broader than the jurisdiction of a court on judicial review".[296] The panel discussed Canadian court decisions holding that "curial deference" should be given to decisions of bodies having expertise unless their interpretation is "not reasonable or is clearly wrong".[297] The panel concluded that if there is more than one reasonable interpretation of a statute, "a reviewing body should not substitute its judgment for that of the administrative agency so long as the agency adopts one of the possible 'reasonable' interpretations".[298]

(ii) Standard of review in U.S. final determinations

For U.S. final determinations, the standard of review is that applied by the United States Court of International Trade. The standard of review respecting a final determination of the ITC not to review a determination by reason of changed circumstances under Section 751(b) of the Tariff Act of 1930, discussed in §11.4(10)(c)(ii) is that the decision is arbitrary, capricious, an abuse of discretion or otherwise not in accordance with law.[299] The standard of review for the other U.S. final determinations subject to panel review is that the decision is "unsupported by substantial evidence on the record or otherwise not in accordance with law".[300]

The "substantial evidence" standard has been considered by the various panels reviewing U.S. final determinations under FTA 1904. For example, the panel in *Replacement Parts for Self-Contained Bituminous Paving Equipment from Canada*[301] cited U.S. jurisprudence to the effect that "substantial evidence" is "such evidence as a reasonable mind might accept as adequate to support a conclusion".[302] The panel also cited a U.S. Supreme Court decision to the effect that a reviewing court "may not substitute its own construction of a statutory provision for a reasonable interpretation made by the . . . agency" and concluded that deference to Commerce's "interpretation and implementation of antidumping laws is grounded in express congressional intent".[303] This standard is similar to that for Canada expressed by the panel in *Certain Beer from the United States* described above.

(iii) Standard of review for Mexican final determinations

The standard of review for Mexico is that set out in Article 238 of the Federal Fiscal Code (*Codigo Fiscal de la Federacion*) or successor statutes, based solely on the administrative record. Under this provision, an administrative determination is illegal on the basis of: lack of competence of the administrator issuing the decision or conducting the proceeding; omission of formal legal requirements; procedural defects in the proceeding; incorrect or misunderstood facts or improper issuance or enforcement of the decisions; or an exercise of discretionary authority inconsistent with the objectives of the law granting the authority.[304] As noted in §11.4(10)(b)(ii), one of the amendments to Mexican antidumping and countervailing duty listed in NAFTA Annex 1904.15 requires that a record be maintained and final determinations be based solely on that record.

(g) Procedure before panels and panel decisions

The authority that issued the final determination under review has the right to appear before the panel and to be represented by counsel. In addition, any other person who would have been allowed to participate in a domestic court review may appear and be represented by counsel.[305]

(i) Rules of procedure

NAFTA 1904(14) required the NAFTA countries to establish rules of procedure by January 1, 1994, based on judicial rules of appellate procedure so that final panel decisions shall be made within 315 days of a request for a panel.[306] These rules, which have been established,[307] govern the content and service of panel requests, transmission of the administrative record, protection of confidential information, participation by private persons, the filing, service, form and content of briefs, the limitation of review to alleged errors and the conduct of hearings, conferences, rehearings and timing. The statement of general intent in section 2 of the rules establishes their purpose as securing a "just, speedy and inexpensive review of final determinations" within the 315-day time frame established under NAFTA 1904(14). As under the FTA, this time frame provides for thirty days for filing the complaint, thirty days for filing the designated or certified administrative record with the panel, sixty days for the complainant to file its complainant brief, sixty days for the respondent to file its brief, fifteen days for the filing of reply briefs, fifteen to thirty days for the panel to convene and hear oral argument, and ninety days for the panel's written decision.

(ii) Uphold or remand

The panel may uphold a final determination or remand (*i.e.*, refer)[308] it back to the competent investigating authority for action consistent with its decision. The panel must establish as brief a time as is reasonable for compliance, taking into account the complexity of the issues and nature of the action, but must in no event take more time than it was permitted for making the final determination. An investigating authority shall give notice of the action that it has taken on a remand by filing a Determination on Remand with the responsible Secretariat. A participant in the proceedings may challenge the action taken by filing a written submission within a prescribed time period.[309] If the action taken by the investigating authority in response to the remand must be reviewed, the same panel shall do so and issue its "final decision" within ninety days.[310]

Actions taken in respect of remands by FTA panels have been challenged on several occasions, most notably in the Pork case. The panel considering the subsidy determination affirmed two of Commerce's countervailability determinations and remanded five others.[311] The findings remanded related to matters such as the specificity of certain programs and the use by Commerce of "best information available". The panel gave Commerce sixty days to comply. Commerce requested a further seventy-five-day extension and the panel denied the request, citing as one reason the "tight review timetable" imposed by the FTA.[312] The action taken by Commerce was challenged. The panel upheld one of the specificity findings but remanded two determinations back to Commerce for further action. Commerce in the end followed the panel's position.[313] The series of panel reviews and remands in the matter of the injury determination in the Pork case was protracted and acrimonious. In its first review, the panel found no material injury and remanded the matter back to the ITC.[314] The ITC issued a decision on remand with another injury finding, although on different grounds. In its second review, the panel pointed out that the use of the words "final decision" in FTA 1904(8), which are carried forward in NAFTA 1904(8), meant that the panel at this stage had to express its view with "as much finality as possible".[315] The panel proceeded to do this by remanding the injury decision to the ITC and issuing specific instructions as to how the ITC was to proceed.[316] The ITC characterized the panel's decision as a "counterintuitive, counterfactual, and illogical, but legally binding conclusion" and followed the panel's instructions.[317] In this dispute between a panel and an investigating agency, the panel prevailed.

(h) Extraordinary challenge procedures

As under the FTA, panel decisions are binding on the NAFTA countries involved.[318] This means that, unlike with Chapter Twenty panel decisions, NAFTA countries are obliged to give effect to Chapter Nineteen panel decisions respecting the particular matter in question under their domestic law. NAFTA countries are prohibited from providing for the appeal of panel decisions to the domestic courts.[319] Like the FTA, NAFTA does not provide for routine appeal procedures from decisions of binational panels. This is consistent with the general objective of providing expeditious procedures for settling antidumping and countervailing duty matters. However, NAFTA carries forward the FTA provisions for extraordinary challenge. Unlike the panel review process, the extraordinary challenge procedure may only be invoked by a NAFTA country and not by other persons, even though they may have had an interest in the outcome of the review.

(i) Grounds for challenge

The grounds for challenge are set out in NAFTA 1904(13) and the procedures are set out in NAFTA Annex 1904.13. A NAFTA country may avail itself of the extraordinary challenge procedures if it alleges within a "reasonable time" that one of the actions listed in NAFTA 1904(13)(a) has "materially affected the panel's decision and threatens the integrity of the binational panel review process".[320] The actions listed are: a member of the panel was guilty of gross misconduct, bias, a serious conflict of interest, or otherwise materially violated the rules of conduct; the panel seriously departed from a fundamental rule of procedure; or the panel manifestly exceeded its powers, authority or jurisdiction set out in NAFTA 1904.[321] The NAFTA language follows that of the FTA except that NAFTA adds as an example of manifestly exceeding powers a failure to apply the appropriate standard of review. The action must both seriously affect the panel's decision and threaten the integrity of the panel review process.[322] The Rules of Procedure established by the NAFTA countries for extraordinary challenge committees allow thirty days from the Notice of Final Panel Action or thirty days after a NAFTA country finds out about a panelist's misconduct if that occurs after the Notice of Final Panel Action for requesting an extraordinary challenge committee ("ECC").[323]

(ii) Extraordinary challenge procedure

The extraordinary challenge procedure is set out in NAFTA Annex 1904.13. An ECC is to be established within fifteen days of a request under NAFTA 1904(13). The ECC is comprised of three members selected from a roster of fifteen judges or former judges of a federal judicial court of the United States or Mexico or of a court of superior jurisdiction of Canada.[324] Each involved NAFTA country elects one member from the roster and then choose by lot which of them selects the third member. An ECC must make a decision within ninety days of its appointment. The corresponding FTA period was thirty days. ECC decisions are binding on the NAFTA countries involved respecting the particular matter in question. If an ECC finds that one of the grounds for challenge exists, the panel decision will be vacated (in which case a new panel is selected) or remanded back for action not inconsistent with the ECC's decision. Proceedings of ECCs are governed by the Rules of Procedure referred to in §11.4(10)(h)(i).

(iii) Extraordinary challenge experience under the FTA

The FTA extraordinary challenge procedure received its first test when the United States challenged the second panel review in the Pork case, discussed in §11.4(10)(g)(ii), on the grounds that the panel had "seriously departed from a fundamental rule of procedure or manifestly exceeded its powers, authority or jurisdiction" in five different respects.[325] The ECC reviewed the legislative history of the extraordinary challenge procedure and concluded that it was intended as a review mechanism for "aberrant panel decisions" and that it was to be available only in extraordinary circumstances.[326] The ECC cited the three-pronged test that had to be satisfied to sustain an extraordinary challenge, namely that (1) the panel or panel member had to be guilty of an action, described in §11.4(10)(h)(i), and that action had to (2) affect materially the panel's decision and (3) threaten the integrity of the panel process. The ECC cited strong descriptive terms such as "gross", "serious", "fundamental", "materially", "manifestly" and "threatens" used in FTA 1904(13), the thirty-day time period for decisions and the fact that only governments and not participants could invoke the ECC proceeding as further indications of the limited circumstances in which extraordinary challenges can be sustained. In one of the grounds for the challenge, the United States alleged that the panel had improperly considered non-record evidence. The ECC held that if the panel had relied solely on such evidence there would have been grounds for challenge. However, the panel had not relied solely on such evidence and its use of such evidence did not satisfy the second and third prong of the three-pronged test. The United States challenged the rule of finality adopted by the panel. The ECC held that the language of the FTA required expedition and efficiency. The United States also challenged the standard of review applied by the panel and the ECC held that the correct standard had been applied.[327] The ECC dismissed the request for the extraordinary challenge.

There were two more extraordinary challenges under the FTA, both by the United States. In *Live Swine from Canada* (the "Swine case"), the United States challenged a panel's decisions, both in the first instance and upon review of a remand decision, of a determination by Commerce of subsidization.[328] The panel dismissed the request for challenge and in so doing confirmed the view of the role of the ECC expressed by the earlier panel. The ECC quoted the U.S. FTA Statement of Administrative Action to the effect that the three-pronged test provided narrow grounds for extraordinary challenges and that extraordinary challenges were not meant to function as routine appeals. In the Softwood Lumber case, the United States challenged a panel decision on the basis that the panel manifestly exceeded its power, authority and jurisdiction by failing to apply the appropriate standard of review and that two Canadian panelists had broken the rules of conduct by failing to disclose information revealing an appearance of partiality or bias and, with regard to one panelist, a serious conflict of interest. The ECC dismissed the challenge. However, unlike other ECC decisions, the ECC members split on national lines with the U.S. member, as mentioned in §11.4(5), issuing a dissenting opinion expressed in the strongest possible terms.[329]

(iv) Extraordinary challenges under NAFTA

As noted above, NAFTA added the example of "failing to apply the appropriate standard of review" to the action of manifestly exceeding powers. Both the U.S. Statement of Administrative Action respecting NAFTA and the Canadian Statement of Implementation characterized this change as making explicit what was implicit in FTA 1904(13)(a)(iii).[330] The ECC in the Swine case had made the same observation in respect of the NAFTA text. The U.S.

Statement of Administrative Action then goes on at some length to discuss the importance of correct application of the standard of review and implies that the panels in the Pork and Swine cases whose decisions were subject to extraordinary challenge had not applied the correct standard of review. The statement says that if the extraordinary challenge procedure did not correct the "misapplication of law" in these sorts of circumstances, the Administration could correct the problem through legislation, having regard to NAFTA 1902.[331] The Canadian Statement of Implementation states that the amendment does not expand the scope of an extraordinary challenge proceeding and correctly points out that the three-pronged test remains.[332] The fact that the three-pronged test has survived intact preserves the "extraordinary" nature of the extraordinary challenge procedure. Even if the addition of the standard of review example does broaden the concept of manifestly exceeding powers, the other two prongs of the test (panel's decision materially affected and integrity of the panel review process threatened) still must be satisfied for a successful extraordinary challenge.

NAFTA has also extended the thirty-day period for decisions to ninety days. The ECC in the Pork case cited the thirty-day time frame as one of the indications that the extraordinary challenge procedure was not intended as a routine appeal procedure. According to the Canadian Statement of Administrative Action, the time period was extended because the decisions of the ECCs in the Pork and Swine cases had taken approximately seventy days and the ninety-day period was to provide a more realistic time frame.[333]

(11) Safeguarding the Panel Review System

NAFTA 1905 sets out procedures for safeguarding the panel review system that had no counterpart in the FTA. A NAFTA country that alleges that the domestic law of another NAFTA country prevents the establishment of a panel or prevents a panel from rendering a final decision or prevents the implementation of a panel decision or denies it binding force or results in a failure to provide an opportunity for review of a final determination by a panel or court independent of the competent investigating authorities may request consultations.[334] The consultations must begin within fifteen days of the request[335] and if the matter is not resolved within forty-five days, the complaining NAFTA country may request the establishment of a special committee.[336] The special committee must be established within fifteen days of the request.[337] The special committee consists of three members, chosen from the roster and selected in accordance with the procedures for extraordinary challenges.[338]

If the special committee makes an affirmative finding respecting any of the grounds described above, consultations must begin within ten days with a view to resolution of the matter within sixty days.[339] If the matter is not resolved within sixty days or the NAFTA country complained against has not demonstrated to the special committee that it has corrected the problem, the complaining NAFTA country may suspend the operation of NAFTA 1904 with respect to the other NAFTA country and may also suspend such NAFTA benefits as may be appropriate.[340] The other NAFTA country may also suspend the operation of NAFTA 1904 respecting the complaining NAFTA country but may not suspend other benefits.[341] The NAFTA country complained against may request that the special committee reconvene to determine whether the suspension of benefits is manifestly excessive or whether the NAFTA country has corrected the problem. The special committee has forty-five days to make its decision and if it decides that the problem has been corrected, all suspensions are terminated.[342] NAFTA 1905(11) and (12) set out rules respecting panel or ECC proceedings in progress at the time an affirmative finding is made or NAFTA 1904 is suspended and NAFTA 1905(13) and (14) set out certain provisions respecting the running of time periods.[343]

The U.S. Statement of Administrative Action characterizes the safeguard procedure as an improvement because the only course of action under the FTA in such circumstances would have been to abrogate the entire FTA.[344] It would seem to the author that if a circumstance described above had existed under the FTA, the normal dispute resolution procedures under FTA Chapter Eighteen would have applied,[345] leading ultimately in the event of an affirmative finding to the suspension of benefits. NAFTA 1905 in effect establishes a special dispute settlement procedure that constitutes an exception to the general dispute settlement procedures set out in NAFTA Chapter Twenty.

(12) Consultations

NAFTA 1907(1) requires the NAFTA countries to consult annually or on request respecting problems that may arise respecting the implementation of Chapter Nineteen.

NAFTA 1907(2) requires the NAFTA countries to consult on developing more effective rules and disciplines concerning the use of government subsidies and a substitute system of rules for dealing with unfair transborder pricing and government subsidization. Unlike FTA 1906, this provision is not subject to any time limit. The Canadian Government that was elected on October 25, 1993, expressed dissatisfaction with the absence of a clearer commitment on the part of the NAFTA countries to establish a substitute system of rules in antidumping matters. In response to these concerns, the NAFTA countries have established a working group to consider substitute rules in antidumping matters.

NAFTA 1907(3) requires that the competent investigating authorities of the NAFTA countries consult annually or on request. This provision sets out a number of matters in the context of these consultations that are desirable in the administration of antidumping and countervailing duty laws relating to providing and publishing various notices, providing reasonable access to information, providing the opportunity to present facts and arguments, protecting confidential information and preparing administrative records and written reasons for final determinations. These matters are merely described as desirable, and this provision does not establish standards.

(13) Special Secretariat Provisions, Code of Conduct, Public Information

NAFTA 1908 requires that each NAFTA country establish a division within its section of its Secretariat described in §11.1(1)(a) to facilitate the operation of NAFTA Chapter Nineteen. This article sets out various duties to be performed by the Secretaries of the Secretariat in relation to the functioning of NAFTA Chapter Nineteen.

NAFTA 1909 obliged the NAFTA countries to establish the code for panelists and members of committees established under NAFTA 1903, NAFTA 1904 and NAFTA 1905 by the time that NAFTA became effective.

NAFTA 1910 requires that, on the request of another NAFTA country, a competent investigating authority provide copies of all public information submitted to it for the purposes of an antidumping or countervailing duty action involving goods of that other NAFTA country.

(14) Concluding Remarks

NAFTA Chapter Nineteen carries forward the regime established by FTA Chapter Nineteen virtually intact. From a Canadian perspective, this is positive because the FTA Chapter Nineteen panel review process protected Canadian interests. The discontinuance of the process of developing an alternative approach to subsidies must be viewed with mixed feelings. A precise understanding as to the circumstances in which subsidies may be subject to countervailing duties would be desirable from the standpoint of predictability. However, the process of arriving at such an understanding would involve a detailed analysis of every conceivable type of subsidy and could result in severe limitations on policy options open to government. Canada is probably just as well if not better off with the general parameters that will be established when the 1994 Subsidies Code becomes effective and with the panel review process as constituted under NAFTA. The feelings are less mixed respecting developing an alternative approach to antidumping laws. As discussed in §11.4(1), antidumping laws make little sense in a free trade area once transition periods for duty elimination are over. Hopefully, the working group referred to in §11.4(12) will produce some positive results. At least this working group will not have its mandate complicated by having also to consider the more politically charged area of subsidies.

Mexico is a relative newcomer to antidumping and countervailing duty matters and Mexican law in this area is new and not well developed. There will be U.S. criticism of the attempts of Mexican panelists to apply U.S. concepts of standard of review and pressure in Congress for amendments to antidumping and countervailing duty law to correct perceived misapplications of U.S. law. Canadian and American panelists may have difficulties in coming to grips with and applying Mexican law. However, panel decisions could play a significant role in the evolution of Mexican law and practice in this area over time.

ENDNOTES

[1] These rulings do not include rulings that apply to particular persons, goods, services, acts or practices. See NAFTA 1806.

[2] NAFTA Annex 312.2, para. 3(a)(ii). See also FTA 802(1)(b).

[3] NAFTA 2005(5).

[4] See Article 1, para. 1 and Appendix 1 of the Dispute Settlement Understanding. The list in Appendix 1 includes all the WTO Agreements mentioned in §1.4(1) and the Dispute Settlement Understanding itself.

[5] Appendix 2 of the Dispute Settlement Understanding lists the dispute settlement provisions of a number of the covered agreements.

[6] Dispute Settlement Understanding, Article 3, para. 11.

[7] Article 4, para. 7.

[8] Article 4, para. 8.

[9] Article 9.

[10] Article 10.

[11] Article 7, para. 1. The parties to a dispute may agree to terms of reference other than those set out in this provision.

[12] *Ibid.*, Article 8, para. 3. Article 8 sets out the rules respecting the composition of panels.

[13] Article 12 and the Working Procedures in Appendix 3. The timetable is set out in para. 12 of Appendix 3 and can be changed if "unforeseen developments" occur.

[14] Appendix 3, paras. 6, 9 and 10.

[15] Article 15.

[16] Article 16.

[17] Article 12, para. 8. In urgent situations including those involving perishable goods, the panel is to aim for three months. Paragraph 9 provides that if these time periods are to be exceeded, the panel must inform the DSB with written reasons for the delay and that in no case may the time exceed nine months.

[18] See generally Article 17, which covers Appellate Review.

[19] Article 17, para. 6.

[20] Article 20.

[21] Article 19, para. 1.

[22] Article 21, para. 3.

[23] Article 21, para. 6.

[24] Article 22, para. 1.

[25] Article 22, para. 3.

[26] Article 26, paras. 1(b) and (d).

[27] Article 23, para. 1.

[28] Article 23.

29 (1989), 2 T.C.T. 7162 (Can.-U.S. Trade Comm. Panel).
30 *Canada — Measures affecting exports of unprocessed herring & salmon* adopted March 22, 1988, BISD 35S/255.
31 *Supra*, note 29, at p. 7179, footnotes 29, 31 and 32.
32 (1990), 3 T.C.T. 8182 (Can.-U.S. Free Trade Panel).
33 The minority were unable to draw a conclusion that the measure was aimed primarily at conservation. See paragraph 11.3.3 of the report. For a highly critical analysis of the majority decision in this case, see Ted L. McDorman, "Dissecting the Free Trade Agreement Lobster Panel Decision" (1991), 18 C.B.L.J. 445.
34 (1992), 5 T.C.T. 8118.
35 Gary N. Horlick and Amanda DeBusk, "Dispute Resolution Under NAFTA: Building on the FTA, GATT and ICSID" (1993), 10 *Journal of International Arbitration* 51 at p. 66. The authors point out that the deadlines for NAFTA Chapter Twenty panels are the same as those for FTA Chapter Eighteen panels and the time frame for GATT panels is more than twice as long.
36 Most notably over ice cream and yoghurt. The Uruguay Round negotiations did not resolve agricultural issues between Canada and the United States.
37 See §9.2(1)(c)(iii).
38 NAFTA 1115 expressly provides that Section B of Chapter Eleven does not prejudice the rights and obligations of the NAFTA countries under Chapter Twenty.
39 NAFTA 2007(1). NAFTA Chapter Twenty reduces time periods for situations involving perishable agricultural goods. As noted in §11.2(2)(c), the Dispute Settlement Understanding reduces time periods for urgent situations that can include those involving perishable goods but can include others as well.
40 See NAFTA 723(5) and 914(3).
41 NAFTA 2008(1)(a). In the event of a consolidation, NAFTA 2008(1)(b) provides that the thirty-day period may run from the time that the Commission has convened in respect of the matter most recently referred to it. NAFTA 2008(1)(c) permits the consulting NAFTA countries to agree to another time period.
42 As discussed in §11.2(2)(c), the period is twenty days in cases of urgency.
43 Eighty-five days if the forty-five-day period in NAFTA 2007(1)(b) applies (*i.e.*, another NAFTA country has subsequently requested consultations) or fifty-five days if the fifteen-day period for perishable goods in NAFTA 2007(1)(c) applies.
44 NAFTA 2008(4). This provision is qualified by the word "normally", which suggests that there are some circumstances in which these constraints would not apply.
45 See NAFTA 2009(2)(a).
46 NAFTA 2013.
47 NAFTA 2014.
48 NAFTA 2016. The disputing NAFTA countries can "otherwise agree".
49 NAFTA 2016(3).
50 NAFTA 2017(2).
51 NAFTA 2017(1). The disputing NAFTA countries can "otherwise agree".
52 Dispute Settlement Understanding, Article 12, para. 8. The time is reduced to three months in urgent cases.
53 NAFTA 2018(2).
54 Discussed in §4.7(5).
55 FTA 1701(1).
56 FTA 1704(2).
57 NAFTA 1116(1) and NAFTA 1117(1).
58 NAFTA 1116 for claims by investors, NAFTA 1117 for claims by investors on behalf of enterprises.
59 NAFTA 1116(2) for claims by investors, NAFTA 1117(2) for claims on behalf of enterprises.
60 NAFTA 1117(3).
61 Daniel M. Price, "An Overview of the NAFTA Investment Chapter: Substantive Rules and Investor-State Dispute Settlement" (1993), 27 *The International Lawyer* 727 at p. 732. The case cited is *Barcelona Traction Case* (Belgium v. Spain). See note 15 in this article.
62 See the discussion of "investment" in §7.7(1)(a).

[63] This expression is defined in NAFTA 1139.

[64] The expression used in the NAFTA text and defined in NAFTA 1139 is "disputing Party".

[65] NAFTA 1119.

[66] W. Michael Reisman, "The Breakdown of the Control Mechanism in ICSID Arbitration" (1989), *Duke Law Journal* 739 at p. 750.

[67] *Ibid.*, at p. 751.

[68] John A. Westburg, "Hague Tribunal and ICSID Case Law: An Increasingly Important Source of Rules for Resolving International Investment Issues" (1994), 17 *Middle East Executive Reports* 8. See note 10.

[69] *Ibid.* See note 8.

[70] ICSID Convention, Article 25(1). Note that a "national of another contracting state" is a natural or juridical person having a nationality of a contracting state other than the contracting state that is the party to the dispute. See Article 25(2).

[71] See Georges R. Delaume, "Experience with ICSID", in *International Arbitration between Private Parties and Governments* (New York, Practising Law Institute, 1986) 221 at p. 235. For the Arbitration Rules, see ICSID Basic Documents (Washington, D.C., International Centre for the Settlement of Investment Disputes, 1985), at p. 39.

[72] ICSID Convention, Article 12.

[73] ICSID Convention, Article 14.

[74] ICSID Convention, Article 13(1).

[75] ICSID Convention Articles 37 and 38.

[76] ICSID Convention, Article 40.

[77] ICSID Convention, Article 51.

[78] Article 52. See Reisman, *op. cit.*, note 66, for a detailed discussion of the annulment provision in the context of the case of *Kloeckner v. United Republic of Cameroon*, pp. 785 *et seq.* Until this 1983 case, the annulment provision had been untested.

[79] ICSID Convention, Articles 53 and 54. In the case of federal states, the courts are federal courts. See, however, Anne Joyce, "Arbitration: United States Court Recognition of ICSID Arbitral Award — Liberian Eastern Timber Corp. v. Republic of Liberia" (1988), 29 Harv. Int'l. L.J. 135. In this case, the plaintiff was successful in obtaining a judgment in a U.S. court against Liberia but Liberia successfully resisted execution of the award against Liberian assets in the Untied States on the basis of sovereign immunity. Article 55 of the ICSID Convention provides that nothing in Article 54 derogates from sovereign immunity laws. This result would not have followed if the award had been against the United States. See 22 U.S.C. (1988) §1650a for U.S. legislative provisions respecting ICSID awards. However, this result could follow if the award was against another NAFTA country that was a member of the ICSID Convention in respect of that NAFTA country's assets in the United States.

[80] See International Centre for the Settlement of Investment Disputes, *Additional Facility for the Administration of Conciliation, Arbitration and Fact Finding* (Washington, D.C., ICSID, 1979). See Schedule C entitled Arbitration (Additional Facility) Rules (hereafter "Additional Facility Rules"), Article 1.

[81] Additional Facility Rules, Articles 2 and 3.

[82] Additional Facility Rules, Chapter III (Articles 6 to 18).

[83] Additional Facility Rules, Article 9.

[84] Additional Facility Rules, Articles 38 to 43.

[85] Additional Facility Rules, Article 53.

[86] Additional Facility Rules, Article 58.

[87] Additional Facility Rules, Article 56.

[88] Additional Facility Rules, Article 59.

[89] NAFTA 1139. For the text of these rules, see *The 1989 Guide to International Arbitration and Arbitrators* (Dobbs Ferry, N.Y., Transnational Juris Publications Inc., 1989).

[90] UNCITRAL Rules, Article 5.

[91] UNCITRAL Rules, Article 7.

[92] UNCITRAL Rules, Articles 9 to 12.

[93] UNCITRAL Rules Article 13.

[94] UNCITRAL Rules, Article 26.

[95] UNCITRAL Rules, Article 27.

[96] UNCITRAL Rules, Article 31.

[97] UNCITRAL Rules, Article 32.

[98] UNCITRAL Rules, Article 36.

[99] UNCITRAL Rules, Article 35.

[100] UNCITRAL Rules, Articles 38 to 40. Article 40 provides that costs will, in principle, be borne by the unsuccessful party.

[101] Done at New York, June 10, 1958. See NAFTA 1139.

[102] Done at Panama, January 30, 1975.

[103] For text, see G.M. Wilner, ed., *Domke on Commercial Arbitration (The Law of Practice of Commercial Arbitration)*, rev. ed. (New York, Clark Boardman Callaghan, 1993 cum. supp.), Vol. 2.

[104] New York Convention, Article I.

[105] These are: incapacity of parties or invalidity of the agreement; failure to receive proper notice; award being outside the terms of submission of the arbitration; arbitral panel being improperly constituted; matter not being capable of settlement by arbitration; recognition or enforcement contrary to public policy.

[106] William C. Graham, "The Internationalization of Commercial Arbitration in Canada: A Preliminary Reaction" (1987-88), 13 C.B.L.J. 2 at p. 3. At the time that this article was written, the one exception was Quebec. For details of the legislation, see note 6 in this article.

[107] See 9 U.S.C. (1988) §201.

[108] Joseph T. McLaughlin, "Enforcement of Arbitral Awards under the New York Convention: Practice in U.S. Courts" in *International Commercial Arbitration: Recent Developments, 1988-9* (New York, Practising Law Institute, 1989), at p. 278.

[109] For the text, see Wilner, *op. cit.*, note 103, at p. 37.

[110] See NAFTA 1121(1) respecting claims by disputing investors under NAFTA 1116 (*i.e.*, on their own behalf) and NAFTA 1121(2) for claims by disputing investors under NAFTA 1117 (*i.e.*, on behalf of enterprises).

[111] NAFTA 1121(3).

[112] See Restatement of the Law Second, Foreign Relations Law of the United States, Part IV, Chapter 6, §206, p. 610. See §209, p. 620 for waiver of exhaustion.

[113] As noted in §11.2(5), NAFTA 2021 prohibits NAFTA countries from providing private rights of action.

[114] This explanation is set out in the U.S. Statement of Administrative Action, p. 146. As stated there, the provision avoids subjecting the Mexican government to "double exposure". The author assumes that NAFTA can give rise to private rights of action in Mexico because treaties in Mexico, unlike those in Canada and the Untied States, are self-executing.

[115] Note that this procedure does not apply to consolidation tribunals discussed in §11.3(8).

[116] NAFTA 1124(4) provides for this roster.

[117] See U.S. Statement of Administrative Action, p. 146.

[118] NAFTA 1126(1).

[119] See NAFTA 1126(5).

[120] NAFTA 1126(6).

[121] NAFTA 1127.

[122] NAFTA 1128.

[123] NAFTA 1129.

[124] NAFTA 1130.

[125] NAFTA 1131(1).

[126] NAFTA 1132.

[127] NAFTA 1133.

[128] NAFTA 1134.

[129] The provisions respecting final awards are set out in NAFTA 1135.

[130] NAFTA 1136(1).

[131] NAFTA 1136(3)(a). As noted in §11.3(3)(a), Article 51 of the ICSID Convention provides for revision and Article 52 provides for annulment.

[132] NAFTA 1136(3)(b). The reference to an application being allowed presumably addresses a situation in which an award is revised or set aside in part. If it were set aside in its entirety, there would be nothing to enforce. As discussed in §11.3(4)(a) and §11.3(4)(b), Article V

of the New York Convention and Article 5 of the Inter-American Convention provide for the refusal of recognition and execution of an award in certain instances.

[133] NAFTA 1136(4).

[134] NAFTA 1136(5).

[135] NAFTA 1136(6). NAFTA 1136(7) provides that claims submitted to arbitration are considered to arise from a commercial relationship or transaction. This is to meet the technical requirements of Article I of the New York Convention and Article 1 of the Inter-American Convention.

[136] ICSID Convention, Article 48(5). UNCITRAL Convention, Article 32(5).

[137] NAFTA Annex 1138.2. For discussions of Canadian and Mexican investment screening, see §7.9(3)(b)(i) and (ii).

[138] NAFTA 1138. This provision does not prejudice rights respecting other actions taken under NAFTA 2102.

[139] According to William Merkin, this expression was coined by Rodney Grey. See William S. Merkin, "The Challenge of the F.T.A. — Chapter Nineteen" (1991), 17 Can.-U.S. L.J. 19.

[140] Jonathan T. Fried, "The Challenge of the F.T.A. — Chapter Nineteen" (1991), 17 Can.-U.S. L.J. 11 at p. 15.

[141] Susan Hutton and Michael Trebilcock, "An Empirical Study of the Application of Canadian Anti-Dumping laws: A Search for Normative Rationales" (1990), 24 *Journal of World Trade* 123 at p. 123.

[142] Calvin S. Goldman, "Competition, Anti-dumping, and the Canada-U.S. Trade Negotiations" (1987), Can.-U.S. L.J. 95.

[143] See Hutton and Trebilcock, *op. cit.*, note 141, at pp. 126-30. The authors of this article examine predation as a justification for the imposition of antidumping duties in thirty Canadian antidumping cases decided between October 30, 1984 and February 3, 1989. They concluded that none of these thirty instances of imposition of antidumping duties could be justified "on the grounds of a serious concern over predatory pricing". See p. 130.

[144] See Goldman, *op. cit.*, note 142, at pp. 97-8.

[145] This is more feasible in a customs union than in a free trade area where origin requirements must be satisfied if preferential duty treatment is to apply.

[146] Goldman, *op. cit.*, note 142, at p. 98.

[147] See Paul Harris and Stephen Levine, eds. with Margaret Clark, John Martin and Elizabeth McLeay, *The New Zealand Politics Source Book* (Palmerston North, New Zealand, The Dunmore Press Ltd., 1993), at p. 408.

[148] For a discussion of these issues by two Canadian economists, see James D. Gaisford and Donald L. McLachlan, "Domestic Subsidies and Countervail: The Treacherous Ground of the Level Playing Field" (1990), 24 *Journal of World Trade* 55.

[149] Subsidies Code, Pt. VII, Article 19(5), and Antidumping Code, Pt. III, Article 16(6).

[150] Part I of the Subsidies Code elaborates on Article VI of the GATT while Part II of the Subsidies Code elaborates on Article XVI of the GATT. As with Articles VI and XVI of the GATT, Parts I and II of the Subsidies Code are independent of one another.

[151] Antidumping Code, Article 3.

[152] Antidumping Code, Article 4.

[153] Subsidies Code, Article 2.

[154] Article 5.

[155] Article 2.

[156] Antidumping Code, Article 5, para. 2. Subsidies Code, Article 2, para. 4.

[157] Article 7.

[158] Subsidies Code, Article 4:5.

[159] The material injury requirement of the Subsidies Code as incorporated into U.S. countervailing duty law applies only to signatories of the Code and does not have universal application. See E.R. Easton, "Countervailing Duty Investigations" in C.J. Johnston, Jr., ed., *Law and Practice of United States Regulation of International Trade* (New York, Oceana Publications Inc., 1987), Paper No. 2, p. 5.

[160] 1994 Antidumping Code, Article 2.2.1. The comparison is made with per unit fixed and variable costs of production plus administrative, selling and general costs.

[161] 1994 Antidumping Code, Articles 2.2.1.1. and 2.2.2.

162 1994 Antidumping Code, Articles 2.4.1 and 2.4.2. The provision in the Antidumping Code for comparing export prices with normal values is set out in Article 2.6.
163 1994 Antidumping Code, Article 3.7. Compare these provisions with Article 3.6 in the Antidumping Code.
164 1994 Antidumping Code, Article 5.2. The corresponding provision in the Antidumping Code is Article 5.1.
165 1994 Antidumping Code, Article 5.4.
166 1994 Antidumping Code, Article 5.5.
167 1994 Antidumping Code, Article 6.7 and Annex I.
168 1994 Antidumping Code, Article 6.8 and Annex II.
169 1994 Antidumping Code, Article 6.10.
170 1994 Antidumping Code, Article 7.3.
171 1994 Antidumping Code, Articles 12.1.1 and 12.2.1.
172 1994 Antidumping Code, Article 11.
173 1994 Subsidies Code, Article 1.1.
174 1994 Subsidies Code, Article 1.2.
175 1994 Subsidies Code, Article 2.1(a).
176 1994 Subsidies Code, Article 2.1(b).
177 1994 Subsidies Code, Article 2.1(c).
178 1994 Subsidies Code, Article 2.2.
179 See Article 2.3 of the 1994 Subsidies Code which provides that subsidies falling under Article 3 are specific. Article 3 of the 1994 Subsidies Code prohibits these subsidies.
180 GATT Agreement on Agriculture, Article 13. The GATT Agreement on Agriculture is cross-referenced in Article 10 of the 1994 Subsidies Code, meaning that the right to impose countervailing duties on these types of subsidies is subject to those provisions.
181 1994 Subsidies Code, Article 8.2(a).
182 1994 Subsidies Code, Article 8.2(b).
183 1994 Subsidies Code, Article 8.2(c).
184 1994 Subsidies Code, Article 11.4. An investigation cannot be initiated unless producers of at least 25% of total production of like product expressly support it.
185 1994 Subsidies Code, Article 12.
186 1994 Subsidies Code, Article 14. None of these is considered to confer a benefit if done on commercial terms.
187 FTA 1902(1) and (2).
188 FTA 1903 and FTA Annex 1903.2.
189 FTA 1904.
190 FTA 1904(14).
191 FTA 1904(13) and FTA Annex 1904.13.
192 FTA 1906.
193 Homer E. Moyer Jr., "Chapter 19 of the NAFTA: Binational Panels as the Trade Courts of Last Resort" (1993), 27 *The International Lawyer* 707 at pp. 709-10.
194 Gary N. Horlick and Amanda DeBusk, "Dispute Resolution Panels of the U.S.-Canada Free Trade Agreement: The First Two and One-Half Years" (1992), 37 McGill L.J. 574 at p. 577.
195 *Ibid.*, at p. 595.
196 *Ibid.*, at p. 581. See also Moyer Jr., *op. cit.*, note 193, at p. 717.
197 See Moyer Jr., *op. cit.*, note 193, at pp. 713-16. See also Andreas F. Lowenfeld, "The Free Trade Agreement Meets its First Challenge: Dispute Settlement and the Pork Case" (1992), 37 McGill L.J. 607, where he observes that the Pork case was a big and complicated case that received more thorough consideration than "it could have received from a single overworked judge in the U.S. Court of International Trade". In Canada, appeals to the Federal Court of Appeal are heard by not fewer than three judges. See *Federal Court Act*, R.S.C. 1985, c. F-7, s. 16.
198 See Horlick and DeBusk, *op. cit.*, note 194, at p. 583. See also Moyer Jr., *ibid.*, at p. 722.
199 Moyer Jr., *ibid.*, at p. 715, cites four different occasions when this has occurred. The extraordinary challenge in *Certain Softwood Lumber Products from Canada* was based in part on alleged conflicts of interest.

[200] U.S. Statement of Administrative Action, p. 195.

[201] Professor Andreas F. Lowenfeld, quoted in Horlick and DeBusk, *op. cit.*, note 194, at p. 583. The publication quoted from was Andreas F. Lowenfeld, "Binational Dispute Settlement Under Chapters 18 and 19 of the Canada-United States Free Trade Agreement: An Interim Appraisal" (report prepared for the consideration of the Administrative Conference of the United States, December 1990).

[202] *Certain Softwood Lumber Products from Canada*, [1994] F.D.A.D. No. 8. See the Dissenting Opinion of United States Circuit Judge (Ret.) Malcolm Wilkey, under VI Failure of the Substitute Appellate Review System, at p. 130.

[203] Moyer Jr., *op. cit.*, note 193, at pp. 710-13. The case was *National Council for Indus Defense v. United States*. As Mr. Moyer correctly predicted in note 31 on p. 713, the case was dismissed on procedural grounds and the merits were not considered. See 827 F. Supp. 794. Just prior to the publication of this book, a constitutional challenge was initiated by the U.S. softwood lumber industry following the dismissal of the extraordinary challenge in the Softwood Lumber case. The basis for the constitutional challenge is that the substitution of binational panel review for judicial review by U.S. courts constitutes a denial of due process guaranteed by the U.S. Constitution.

[204] See §11.4(10)(g)(ii) and §11.4(10)(h)(iii).

[205] NAFTA 1902(1).

[206] NAFTA 1902(2).

[207] These are set out in NAFTA 1902(2)(a)-(d).

[208] 19 U.S.C. (1988) §1677-2.

[209] *Fresh, Chilled, and Frozen Pork from Canada* (1990), 3 T.C.T. 8308 at p. 8317.

[210] Paragraph 1 of FTA Annex 1901.2 provided that judges were not considered to be affiliated with an FTA member country. NAFTA 1901.2 does not say this but presumably this is intended.

[211] NAFTA Annex 1901.2, para. 6. A panelist may be removed for violation of the code of conduct after consultation and agreement of both countries. Paragraph 10 provides that a panelist may engage in other business so long as it does not interfere with the panelist's duties. However, para. 11 prohibits a panelist from appearing as counsel before another panel.

[212] NAFTA Annex 1901.2, para. 2.

[213] NAFTA Annex 1901.2, para. 4. If the majority of the panel members cannot agree on a chairman, the chairman shall be chosen by lot from among the lawyers.

[214] NAFTA Annex 1901.2, para. 2. Panelists are normally chosen from a NAFTA country's roster. If a panelist is not chosen from the roster (which could occur if those on the roster were unavailable, whether through conflict of interest or otherwise), the panelist or panelists chosen must meet the criteria in para. 1 described above.

[215] See NAFTA Annex 1901.2, para. 2 for the time limits imposed on this process.

[216] NAFTA Annex 1901.2, para. 3. If the NAFTA countries party to the dispute cannot agree on a fifth member, the fifth member shall be chosen by lot from the entire roster excluding those who have been eliminated by peremptory challenges. Therefore, even if disagreements do occur, the entire selection process takes a maximum of sixty-one days.

[217] NAFTA Annex 1901.2, paras. 7, 8. Paragraph 8 requires each NAFTA country to provide for sanctions for breach of confidentiality requirements. Failure to sign disqualifies a candidate as a panelist.

[218] NAFTA Annex 1901.2, para. 9.

[219] NAFTA Annex 1901.2, para. 5.

[220] R.S.C. 1985, c. S-15.

[221] See definition in NAFTA 1911, which corresponds to that in FTA 1911. See discussion in §4.1 of the definition of "goods of a Party" in NAFTA 201. The definition of "goods of a Party" in NAFTA 1911 is the same except that it does not refer to originating goods or contemplate other agreements of NAFTA countries (such as the agreement to use the Marking Rules in some instances) as to what constitutes a "good of a Party".

[222] 19 U.S.C. §§1671-1677g (1982 and Supp. III, 1985). The Trade Agreement Act of 1979, Pub. L. No. 96-39, 93 Stat. 144 (codified in various sections of 12, 19 and 29 U.S.C.) enacted the requirements of the Antidumping Code and the Subsidies Code in the United States and brought antidumping and countervailing duty law under one title, Title VII. The anti-

dumping and countervailing duties sections were broadened and clarified by the Trade and Tariff Act of 1984, Pub. L. No. 98-573, §§601-626, 98 Stat. 2948, 3024-43.

[223] See SIMA, ss. 31-34 for the rules governing complaints.

[224] 19 U.S.C. (1988). See §1671a (countervailing duties) and §1673a (antidumping duties). §§1671, 1671a, 1671b, 1671c, 1671d, 1671e, 1671f, 1671g and 1671h set out the procedural requirements in countervailing duty cases and §§1673, 1673a, 1673b, 1673c, 1673d, 1673e, 1673f and 1673g set out the procedural requirements respecting antidumping duty cases.

[225] 19 U.S.C. (1988), §1671b(a) for countervailing cases and 1673b(a) for antidumping cases.

[226] For Canada, see SIMA, s. 38(1) for both antidumping and countervailing duty cases. For the United States, see 19 U.S.C. (1988), §1671b(b) for countervailing duty cases and §1673b(b) for antidumping cases.

[227] This is 120 days for "short cycle merchandise". See 19 U.S.C. (1988), §1673b(1)(B).

[228] For Canada, see SIMA, s. 8 for both antidumping and countervailing duty cases. Importers may pay the provisional duties or post security. For the United States, see 19 U.S.C. (1988), §1671b(d) for countervailing duty cases and §1673b(d) for antidumping cases. Commerce will order the posting of a cash deposit, bond or other security equal to the estimated net subsidy (countervailing duty cases) or estimated average excess of the foreign market value over the United States price *i.e.*, margin of dumping (antidumping duty cases).

[229] See SIMA, ss. 38(3), 42.

[230] Section 705 is codified in 19 U.S.C. (1988) as §1671d. See §1671d(a).

[231] Section 735 is codified in 19 U.S.C. (1988) as §1673d. See §1673d(a).

[232] In antidumping cases, this period can be extended to 135 days at the request of the affected exporters. See 19 U.S.C. (1988) §1673d(a)(2).

[233] SIMA, s. 42.

[234] The specific code reference is 19 U.S.C. (1988) §1671d(b).

[235] The specific code reference is 19 U.S.C. (1988) §1673d(b).

[236] SIMA, s. 55.

[237] SIMA, s. 56.

[238] SIMA, ss. 56, 57.

[239] SIMA, ss. 89, 90.

[240] 19 U.S.C. (1988), §1671e(a) in countervailing duty actions and §1673e(a) in antidumping duty actions.

[241] SIMA, s. 76(2).

[242] SIMA, s. 76(4).

[243] Codified as 19 U.S.C. (1988) §1675.

[244] 19 U.S.C. §1675(a).

[245] Codified as 19 U.S.C. (1988) §1675(b).

[246] See SIMA, ss. 49-54 for rules on undertakings.

[247] See 19 U.S.C. §§1671c(b) to (j) and 1673c(b) to (j) for rules respecting agreements in countervailing duty matters and in antidumping matters, respectively.

[248] For Canada, see SIMA, s. 51(1). For the United States, see 19 U.S.C. (1988) §1671c(g) for countervailing duty matters and 1673c(g) for antidumping duty matters.

[249] SIMA, s. 51(2).

[250] 19 U.S.C. §1671c(f)(3) in countervailing duty matters and 1673c(f)(3) in antidumping matters.

[251] 19 U.S.C. §1671c(h) in countervailing duty matters and §1673c(h) in antidumping duty matters.

[252] SIMA, s. 53(1).

[253] 19 U.S.C. §1675(a).

[254] SIMA, s. 52(1).

[255] Codified as 19 U.S.C. (1988) §1675(b).

[256] For Canada, see SIMA, s. 51(1)(a). For the United States, see 19 U.S.C. (1988) §1671c(i) for countervailing duty actions and §1673c(i) for antidumping duty matters.

[257] Ley Reglamentaria del Articulo 131 de la Constitucion Politica de los Estados Unidos Mexicanos en Materia de Comercio Exterior.

[258] Peter F. McLaughlin, "Mexico's Antidumping and Countervailing Duty Laws: Amenable to a Free Trade Agreement?" (1992), 23 *Law and Policy in International Business* 1009 at p. 1013, note 30.

259 Reglamento Contra Practicas Desleales del Commercio International, Diario Oficial, November 25, 1986.

260 Eduardo Andere, "The Mexican Antidumping Regime: Regulatory Framework, Policies and Practice" (1993), 27 *Journal of World Trade* 5.

261 *Ibid.*, at p. 6.

262 McLaughlin, *op. cit.*, note 258, at pp. 1016-17. The agreement is called the Understanding between the United States and Mexico Regarding Subsidies and Countervailing Duties.

263 *Ibid.*, at p. 1017.

264 *Ibid.*, at p. 1018.

265 Andere, *op. cit.*, note 260, at p. 18.

266 McLaughlin, *op. cit.*, note 258, at p. 1019.

267 The Office of International Trade Practices, or *Direccion General*, was established in January, 1991 and has been reorganized since then. See Andere, *op. cit.*, note 260, at pp. 7, 12. Another body, the Commission for Foreign Tariffs and Controls (La Comission de Aranceles y Controles de Comercio Exterior) plays a consulting role. The other government department involved is the General Customs Office of the Department of Finance and Public Credit (Secretaria de Hacienda y Credito Publico), which must assess and collect the duties. See p. 13.

268 Andere, *ibid.*, at p. 14. This article states that self-initiation has occurred only once in a dumping case involving steel from the EEC. However, according to Mclaughlin, *op. cit.*, note 258, at p. 1027, nearly half of seventy-five petitions during the first five years of the Foreign Trade Law were initiated by SECOFI.

269 McLaughlin, *ibid.*, at p. 1024.

270 Andere, *op. cit.*, note 260, at p. 14.

271 McLaughlin, *op. cit.*, note 258, at p. 1026.

272 Andere, *op. cit.*, note 260, at p. 8. According to this article, written in 1993, SECOFI no longer imposes duties in the provisional determination. The practice has been to impose provisional duties only upon review of the provisional determination. See p. 17.

273 *Ibid.*, at p. 16.

274 *Ibid.*, at p. 18. This review process is supposed to occur in thirty working days but, according to this article, has taken on average a little less than five months in antidumping cases since 1990. This article also states that the practice has been to impose provisional duties only upon review of the provisional resolution. See p. 17.

275 See *ibid.*, at p. 19 for a discussion of this process.

276 *Ibid.*, at p. 22.

277 *Ibid. The review is conducted by SECOFI. See p. 27.*

278 See, for example, the discussion of the Cone Mills case in McLaughlin, *op. cit.*, note 258, at pp. 1028-34.

279 The Schedules for Canada and the United States are also lengthy but the amendments are mainly technical.

280 See Schedule of Mexico, para. (d). Presumably a "preliminary determination" referred to in para. (d) is a "provisional resolution" redefined as just described.

281 Such as the Commission for Foreign Tariffs and Controls.

282 SIMA, s. 76, subject to Part I.1 of SIMA which carries forward the provisions for NAFTA panel review. An order or finding of the CITT under s. 91(3) is reviewable by the Federal Court of Appeal under SIMA, s. 96.1(1)(g).

283 SIMA, s. 62.

284 See SIMA, s. 96.1(1)(a) and (c) respectively.

285 NAFTA 1904(2).

286 NAFTA 1904(2).

287 NAFTA 1911, definition of "administrative record". The official journals are the *Canada Gazette* for Canada, the Federal Register for the United States and the *Diario Oficial de la Federacion* for Mexico.

288 NAFTA 1904(5).

289 NAFTA 1904(4).

290 NAFTA 1904(4).

291 NAFTA 1904(12).

292 NAFTA 1904(11).

293 R.S.C. 1985, c. F-7. Section 18.1(4) was added by S.C. 1990, c. 8, s. 5. Section 18.1(4) sets out the grounds upon which the Trial Division of the Federal Court may grant relief upon judicial review of decisions of federal boards, commissions or tribunals. These standards apply to judicial review by the Federal Court of Appeal, including review of decisions of the CITT. See ss. 28(1)(e) and 28(2) of the *Federal Court Act*, R.S.C. 1985, c. F-7.

294 See s. 28(1), not as amended for the text of s. 28(1) in effect when the FTA became effective.

295 (1992), 5 T.C.T. 8199. This case involved a panel review of an injury finding made by the CITT in a dumping action respecting beer imported from the United States into Canada for consumption in British Columbia. The panel affirmed the CITT's finding that an isolated market for beer existed in British Columbia and that a concentration of dumped beer originating in the United States existed in British Columbia. The panel remanded to the CITT for a determination as to whether the dumping of beer, rather than the presence of dumped beer, caused material injury.

296 *Supra*, at p. 8206.

297 *Supra*.

298 *Supra*, at pp. 8206-7. The case cited is *Canadian Pacific Ltd. v. Canadian Transport Commission* (1987), 79 N.R. 13 (F.C.A.) at pp. 16-17. The panel distinguished between the standard of judicial review of decisions of administrative bodies that should apply when a privative clause is in effect and those in which there is no privative clause. A privative clause is a statutory provision limiting review of a decision. In *National Corn Growers Assn. v. Canada (Canadian Import Tribunal)* (1990), 74 D.L.R. (4th) 449, [1990] 2 S.C.R. 1324, 114 N.R. 81, 45 Admin. L.R. 161, the Supreme Court of Canada held that because of the privative clause that was then in SIMA, s. 76, the error of law would have to be "patently unreasonable" for the decision of the Canadian Import Tribunal (the predecessor of the CITT) to be overturned. Notwithstanding that the privative provision in SIMA s. 76 was still in effect at the time that the CITT made its injury finding in the Beer case, the panel found that the "final determination of the Investigating Authority in these proceedings is not prohibited by a privative clause". See *Certain Beer from the United States* (1992), 5 T.C.T. 8199 at p. 8206. Presumably this was because the privative provision in SIMA s. 76 was at that time expressly subject to Part II of the SIMA which provided for binational panel review as required under the FTA. Therefore, the restricted scope of judicial review under privative clauses would not apply to binational panel review. SIMA, s. 76 was amended when NAFTA came into effect to delete the privative provision.

299 Section 516A(b)(i)(A) of the Tariff Act of 1930, as amended, codified as 19 U.S.C. (1988) §1516a(b)(1)(A).

300 Section 516A(b)(1)(B)of the Tariff Act of 1930 as amended, codified as 19 U.S.C. (1988) §1516a(b)(1)(B).

301 (1991), 4 T.C.T. 7045 at p. 8088. This case involved a review of a finding of dumping by Commerce. The panel remanded Commerce's determinations regarding the inclusion in its margin of dumping calculations of certain parts of allegedly non-Canadian origin and otherwise confirmed Commerce's determination.

302 *Supra*, at p. 7051.

303 *Supra*, at p. 7052. The Supreme Court decision cited is *Chevron U.S.A. v. Natural Resources Defense Council*, 467 U.S. 837, 844 (1984).

304 This description is taken from Gary N. Horlick and F. Amanda De Busk, "Dispute Resolution under NAFTA—Building on the U.S. Canada FTA, GATT and ICSID" (1993), 10 *Journal of International Arbitration* 51 at p. 58.

305 NAFTA 1904(7).

306 NAFTA 1904(14).

307 In Canada, the Rules of Procedure for Article 1904 Binational Panel Reviews (the *Article 1904 Panel Rules) Canada Gazette*, Part I, Ottawa, February 12, 1994, p. 1012.

308 The expression "remand" is defined in NAFTA 1911 as "a referral back for a determination not inconsistent with the panel or committee decision".

309 *Article 1904 Panel Rules, op. cit.*, note 307, Rule 75. This rule sets out the procedures for panel review of actions taken by investigating authorities on remand.

310 NAFTA 1904(8).

[311] *Fresh, Chilled, and Frozen Pork from Canada.* The first decision is reported at (1990), 3 T.C.T. 8308 and the second decision is reported at (1991), 4 T.C.T. 7026.

[312] (1991), 4 T.C.T. 7026, at p. 7029.

[313] Lowenfeld, *op. cit.*, note 197. This article contains an excellent summary of the progression of the subsidy and injury branches of the Pork case through the successive reviews and remands.

[314] *Fresh, Chilled, or Frozen Pork from Canada*, (1990), 3 T.C.T. 8276.

[315] (1991), 4 T.C.T. at p. 7017. See Lowenfeld, *op. cit.*, note 197, at p. 613 who interprets the panel as concluding that the FTA "did not contemplate or permit successive remands".

[316] These are set out in the panel's decision in (1991), 4 T.C.T. at p. 7026.

[317] Lowenfeld, *op. cit.*, note 19, at p. 616.

[318] NAFTA 1904(9).

[319] FTA 1904(11).

[320] NAFTA 1904(13)(b).

[321] NAFTA 1904(13)(a).

[322] NAFTA 1904(13)(b).

[323] Rules of Procedure for Article 1904 Extraordinary Challenge Committees (the *Extraordinary Challenge Committee Rules*), *Canada Gazette*, Part I, February 12, 1994, p. 1062, Rule 38. Rule 38(3) establishes an outside time period of two years in respect of misconduct. The requirement to establish rules of procedure is set out in paragraph 2 of NAFTA Annex 1904.13.

[324] The jurisdiction of "federal courts" in Canada is narrow. However, judges of "superior" courts in each province are appointed by the federal government.

[325] The decision of the ECC is reported in (1991), 4 T.C.T. 7037 at p. 7042.

[326] *Supra*, at p. 7040.

[327] *Supra*, at pp. 7043-4 for these three grounds. The other two grounds were that the panel had created a due process principle independent of U.S. law and that the panel reweighed evidence in a manner contrary to U.S. law.

[328] [1993] F.T.A.D. No. 4.

[329] *Certain Softwood Products from Canada*, [1994] F.T.A.D. No.8. All three members issued separate opinions.

[330] See U.S. Statement of Administrative Action, p. 195 and the Canadian Statement of Implementation, *Canada Gazette*, Part I, January 1, 1994, at p. 204.

[331] U.S. Statement of Administrative Action, p. 196.

[332] Canadian Statement of Implementation, *op. cit.*, note 330, at p. 204.

[333] *Ibid.*

[334] NAFTA 1905(1).

[335] NAFTA 1905(1).

[336] NAFTA 1905(2).

[337] NAFTA 1905(3).

[338] NAFTA 1905(3) and (4).

[339] NAFTA 1905(7).

[340] NAFTA 1905(8).

[341] NAFTA 1905(9).

[342] NAFTA 1905(10).

[343] For example, if a special committee makes an affirmative finding, NAFTA 1905(11)(a) provides that a panel or ECC review of a final redetermination of the complaining NAFTA country requested by the NAFTA country against which the finding is made after consultations began but not more than 150 days before the affirmative finding will be stayed. If the operation of NAFTA 1904 is suspended, NAFTA 1905(12)(a) provides that if either NAFTA country or any party to a panel proceeding so requests, the matter will be irrevocably referred to the domestic courts. There are a number of permutations and combinations set out in NAFTA 1905(11) through to (14) respecting matters in progress and the running of time periods that would have to be worked through if NAFTA 1905 is ever invoked. See pp. 205-6 of the Canadian Statement on Implementation, *op. cit.*, note 330, for a helpful description of these NAFTA provisions.

[344] U.S. Statement of Administrative Action, p. 198.

[345] FTA 1801(1) provided that except "for the matters covered by ... Chapter Nineteen... the provisions of this Chapter shall apply with respect to the avoidance or settlement of all disputes regarding the interpretation or application of this Agreement". FTA Chapter Nineteen did not cover disputes arising out of actions of Canada or the United States that would frustrate the panel review process. Therefore, such disputes would have been covered by FTA Chapter Eighteen.

CHAPTER 12

FINAL PROVISIONS AND CONCLUSION

12.1 FINAL PROVISIONS, NOTES, GUIDES TO INTERPRETATION

NAFTA Chapter Twenty-Two, entitled "Final Provisions", provides for amendment, entry into force, accession and withdrawal.[1]

(1) Entry into Force and Amendment

NAFTA 2203 provides that NAFTA enter into force on January 1, 1994. As discussed in §1.1, NAFTA became effective on that date. NAFTA 2202 provides that the NAFTA countries may agree on modifications of or additions to NAFTA and that an agreed modification or addition constitutes an integral part of NAFTA when approved in accordance with the applicable legal procedures in each NAFTA country. Modifications of or additions to NAFTA are therefore subject to full approval procedures which, in the United States, entails Congressional approval. Given the expenditure of political capital required for a U.S. President to obtain Congressional approval of any trade measure, modifications of or additions to NAFTA will likely be infrequent.

(2) Accession

Unlike the FTA, NAFTA 2204(1) expressly provides for accession to NAFTA by any country or any group of countries. An accession is subject to such terms and conditions that may be agreed upon between an acceding country or group of countries and the Free Trade Commission. This provision has the effect of requiring that the NAFTA countries negotiate collectively with an acceding country or group of countries. It is probable that any accession arrangement will have separate bilateral arrangements just as NAFTA does. These will comprise a part of the conditions of accession and will require the agreement of the Commission. As discussed in §11.1(1)(a), decisions of the Commission are made by consensus. The practical effect of this is that a single NAFTA country can block an accession.

NAFTA was structured with accession in mind. Trilaterally agreed principles are set out in the body of each chapter. Special provisions affecting particular NAFTA countries or situations are set out in annexes to the chapters

553

and the country-specific reservations to the NAFTA investment, services and financial services obligations are set out in Annexes I through to VII. The core trilateral obligations in each NAFTA chapter will form the basis of any agreement with an acceding country or group of countries. As in the existing NAFTA text, special situations or bilateral arrangements with acceding countries will be covered in separate annexes. Reservations of acceding countries to the investment, services and financial services obligations will fall within the framework of Annexes I through to VII.

NAFTA 2204(2) provides that NAFTA will not apply between a NAFTA country and an acceding country if the NAFTA country does not consent. Theoretically, a circumstance could arise in which one NAFTA country refuses to consent to an accession and the others consent. Arguably in such a circumstance NAFTA would apply between the acceding country and the consenting NAFTA countries and would continue to apply among the NAFTA countries but would not apply between the acceding country and the non-consenting NAFTA country. Given that all decisions of the Commission must be by consensus, it is virtually impossible for this circumstance to occur. A NAFTA country would have to consent through the Commission to the terms and conditions of the accession but not consent to the accession itself. Terms and conditions will have to be negotiated in any accession. At a minimum, an acceding country will have to negotiate a schedule for tariff elimination because NAFTA 302(2) requires that customs duties be eliminated in accordance with a schedule for each NAFTA country. The schedule for tariff elimination resulting from such negotiations will comprise a term or condition of accession and the consensus of the NAFTA countries would be required for the Commission to agree to it. In any accession, there will be much more to negotiate than a schedule for tariff elimination.

The NAFTA accession provision is not specific as to region. Theoretically, a country in any part of the world could join. However, the most probable candidates for accession are nations in Central and South America.

(3) Ancillary Materials

(a) Notes

At the end of the NAFTA text under the heading "Notes" are forty-seven notes containing points of clarification on various NAFTA provisions. The notes do not form part of the NAFTA text but are treated as trilaterally agreed upon authoritative guides to interpretation. Before drawing conclusions as to the meaning of any NAFTA provision, one should check for notes that modify or clarify the NAFTA provision under consideration. Notes 22 through to 27 cover various provisions of NAFTA Chapter Four (Rules of Origin) and all of these have been carried forward into the Uniform Regulations.

(b) Uniform Regulations

The Uniform Regulations negotiated and implemented by the three NAFTA countries in respect of NAFTA Chapter Four (Rules of Origin) and NAFTA Chapter Five (Customs Procedures) have been discussed in Chapter 3. The Uniform Regulations do not form part of the NAFTA text but their establishment and implementation are clearly contemplated by NAFTA 511. As a matter of national law, the Uniform Regulations have been carried forward into the law of each NAFTA country. As a matter of international law, the Uniform Regulations constitute an agreed interpretation of the NAFTA text and, as such, are binding on the NAFTA countries. However, the Uniform Regulations must fit within the parameters of the NAFTA text. An amendment to the Uniform Regulations that went beyond interpreting the NAFTA text or setting out the details of its application and applied different principles would be open to challenge. While it is unlikely that a trilaterally agreed upon amendment would be challenged by a government of a NAFTA country, the issue could be raised by a domestic challenge to the regulation implementing the amendment as being *ultra vires*.[2]

(c) U.S. Statement of Administrative Action and Canadian Statement of Implementation

The U.S. Statement of Administrative Action and the Canadian Statement of Implementation each provide useful insights into both the NAFTA text itself and its interpretation by the governments of these NAFTA countries. Each document is a unilateral interpretation of the NAFTA text and neither constitutes a formally agreed upon interpretation of the NAFTA text. As to whether an interpretation of either of these documents could be considered binding on other NAFTA countries through "tacit acceptance" is a complex question, the answer to which depends on the categorization of each of these documents under principles of international law, the opportunity that was afforded for consultations before each document was finalized and the extent to which other NAFTA countries raised objections to interpretations.[3]

The domestic status of the U.S. Statement of Administrative Action is quite different from that of the Canadian Statement of Implementation. The U.S. Statement of Administrative Action fulfils a formal statutory requirement in the U.S. process for approving trade agreements. Before a trade agreement can become effective, the President must submit to the House of Representatives and the Senate the text of the agreement, a draft of the implementing bill and "a statement of any administrative action proposed to implement such agreement, and an explanation as to how the implementing bill and the proposed administrative action change or affect existing law".[4] The U.S. Statement of Administrative Action is the Administration's explanation of the trade agreement and of the legislation required to implement it. As such, it forms part of the legislative history of the implementing legislation and will serve as an authoritative guide to its interpretation by U.S. domestic courts. This is because Congressional approval is based at least to some extent on the explanations set out in the U.S. Statement of Administrative Action. The Canadian Statement of Implementation does not fulfil any statutory requirement. The Canadian Statement of Implementation could influence the domestic interpretation of Canadian legislation implementing NAFTA in that it is an official statement as to the meaning of the NAFTA text and the Canadian implementing legislation must be interpreted consistently with the NAFTA text.[5] However, the Canadian Statement of Implementation did not influence Parliament's decision to approve the Canadian implementing legislation because it was released long after the legislation was enacted. Therefore, the Canadian Statement of Implementation is less likely to have authoritative domestic impact than its U.S. counterpart.[6]

12.2 MODEL FOR THE AMERICAS

NAFTA has created the largest free trade area in the world[7] and is the most important preferential trading relationship in the western hemisphere. NAFTA is a factor that must be taken into consideration by governments of other countries in the western hemisphere, whether from the standpoint of considering accession or as a model for structuring relationships with neighbouring countries. NAFTA has already served as the model for the bilateral agreement signed by Mexico with Costa Rica[8] and for the Group of Three (G-3) agreement among Mexico, Columbia and Venezuela.[9] With NAFTA as the dominant trading relationship in the hemisphere, the negotiators of other bilateral and multilateral regional relationships will use NAFTA as a reference point. There are two reasons for this. First, the solutions to issues devised by the NAFTA negotiators serve as useful precedents. Second, those negotiating such relationships will have to take into account the possibility of future accession to NAFTA and the fact that negotiating accession will be easier for countries that are parties to relationships that resemble NAFTA.

(1) NAFTA as a Model

If NAFTA is to serve as a model for hemispheric trade and investment liberalization, what sort of model is it? The objective of NAFTA is to liberalize rules respecting the movement of goods, services, capital and people among NAFTA countries. This objective is accomplished through the removal of specific trade barriers such as tariffs, the establishment of principles of non-discrimination and the creation of minimum standards. The MFN treatment principle of non-discrimination which is at the heart of GATT obligations plays a significant role in NAFTA. However, the predominant non-discrimination principle upon which NAFTA is based is national treatment.

NAFTA concerns the movement of goods, services, capital and people among the NAFTA countries but not in the all encompassing manner of the European Union. Capital already moves relatively freely among NAFTA countries and the NAFTA investment provisions, despite numerous reservations, will facilitate the movement of capital in the form of direct foreign investment. Trade in services and financial services will be facilitated by the NAFTA non-discrimination obligations and liberalization commitments, but greater freedom of movement, at least with financial services, could have been achieved through more reliance on principles of reciprocity. The trade in goods will be facilitated by tariff elimination and the phasing out of various non-tariff barriers, but the free movement of goods that is feasible in the European Union is not feasible in NAFTA as currently structured. NAFTA deals with the liberalization of the rules respecting the movement of people in the limited context of temporary entry for business persons and professionals and does not facilitate the movement of people among NAFTA countries beyond this limited scope.

NAFTA is a multi-faceted model. Besides creating a free trade area, NAFTA is an investment treaty, an agreement on trade in services, a financial services agreement, an intellectual property convention, a standards code and a government procurement code. The NAFTA model is based on a number of antecedents, including the FTA, the original GATT, the U.S. Model BIT and several of the Uruguay Round agreements.

(a) NAFTA as a free trade area

NAFTA establishes a classic free trade area under GATT Article XXIV:5(b), with tariffs being eliminated among the member countries but with each NAFTA country maintaining its own tariff policy against non-NAFTA countries. The tariff elimination rules, the rules of origin and the elimination of drawback all follow from the creation of a free trade area. NAFTA has the weaknesses of a free trade area, the most significant being the preoccupation with the origin of goods that a free trade area necessitates. Creating a free trade area as opposed to a customs union has the undesirable effect of substituting one border measure (a tariff) with another (the need to prove origin) and will achieve its trade liberalizing objective only if proving origin is less onerous than paying the duty. NAFTA contains the germ of a solution to the origin problem in the approach taken to automatic data processing equipment described in §2.7(1). The harmonization of external tariffs and the elimination of the necessity of establishing origin on a sector-by-sector basis could produce the same free movement of goods in the sectors affected that is possible in a customs union.

(b) NAFTA as an extension of GATT

As discussed in Chapter 4, the NAFTA national treatment obligations and the obligations respecting import and export controls carry forward, with some modifications and special provisions covering specific sectors, the corresponding obligations in the GATT. The NAFTA model in these areas is a modified GATT model and the relevant jurisprudence to interpreting these NAFTA provisions is the jurisprudence that has evolved under the GATT.

(c) NAFTA sectoral models

The special sectoral provisions described in Chapter 5 present a variety of models for addressing trade issues in different goods sectors.

(i) Automotive goods

The NAFTA provisions respecting automotive goods in NAFTA Annex 300-A described in §5.1 are primarily directed at the dismantling of the Mexican Automotive Decree. Far from creating a system of managed trade, the NAFTA automotive provisions provide a model for phasing out a major import substitution program.

(ii) Textile and apparel goods

The same cannot be said for the textile and apparel provisions in NAFTA Annex 300-B. The tariff preference level provisions described in §5.2(2)(d) provide one of the few models of managed trade that exists in NAFTA. NAFTA Annex 300-B also presents a model of bilateralism within the multilateral NAFTA in that the rules of origin that apply for some textile and apparel goods traded between the United States and Mexico differ from the NAFTA rules of origin that generally apply. NAFTA Annex 300-B also provides a model for dealing with the transition from the world of the MFA to that of the GATT. By the time that any new countries accede to NAFTA and assuming that the WTO Agreement becomes effective some time in 1995, the transition under the GATT Textile Agreement should be at least partially complete and it should not be necessary to negotiate special provisions in an accession other than to accelerate the timetable provided in the GATT Textile Agreement.

(iii) Agricultural goods

The least attractive model presented by NAFTA is in its provisions respecting agricultural goods. The creation of three separate bilateral arrangements is contrary to the multilateral approach taken throughout most of NAFTA. The single positive note from a trade liberalization standpoint is the bilateral arrangement between the United States and Mexico. This arrangement begins by adopting the approach of the GATT Agricultural Agreement of tariffying non-tariff barriers but, unlike the GATT Agricultural Agreement, continues that approach to its logical conclusion by reducing all of the over-quota tariff rates to zero over varying periods of time. The end result is free trade between these two NAFTA countries following lengthy and protective phase-in periods for sensitive goods.

(iv) Energy goods

As between the United States and Canada, the NAFTA energy provisions are little more than a reiteration of the modified GATT-based export control regime that NAFTA applies to all goods, coupled with some specific understandings that for the most part are carried over from the FTA. As between Mexico and its NAFTA partners, NAFTA represents an accommodation to political sensitivities of a particular NAFTA country. As with Canada and cultural industries, an exemption for energy was critical for approval of NAFTA by Mexico. The interesting question is how much Mexico had to concede in other sectors in order to obtain this exemption.

(v) Wine and distilled spirits

The NAFTA provisions provide for the phasing out of certain discriminatory practices in this highly regulated sector. These provisions will be of interest to Latin American countries such as Chile and Argentina that have well-established wine industries and significant markets for their products in both Canada and the United States.

(d) NAFTA as an investment treaty

Besides creating a free trade area within the GATT framework, NAFTA is an investment treaty based on the principles of the U.S. Model BIT discussed in §7.3. These provisions incorporate GATT-like non-discrimination principles but go well beyond national treatment and MFN treatment in that they establish norms respecting such matters as expropriation and compensation, performance requirements and transfers. In establishing these norms, the NAFTA investment treaty is a national-treatment-plus model. The Model BIT was designed as a bilateral treaty to protect the direct foreign investment of investors of a single capital exporting country into a single capital importing country. NAFTA applies this model on a trilateral basis in circumstances in which two of the member countries are capital exporting countries, each with significant direct foreign investment in the other.

The NAFTA investment provisions are trade liberalizing in that they remove an element of the risk in investing from one NAFTA country into another. Unlike tariff elimination, which in a free trade area comes at the expense of the additional border measure of establishing origin and the surrender of the right to duty drawback, the benefits of having a country that is a target of foreign direct investment being bound by NAFTA investment disciplines comes without cost to the investor. However, both tariff elimination and investment disciplines constrain government policy, the former quantitatively in revenues foregone from the tariffs eliminated and the latter qualitatively in limiting available policy options.

(e) The NAFTA services and financial services model

The NAFTA services provisions are derived from the FTA and constitute an agreement on trade in services based on GATT non-discrimination principles of national treatment and MFN treatment and incorporate a code of principles respecting licensing and certification.

The NAFTA financial services provisions incorporate elements of both the NAFTA investment provisions and the NAFTA services provisions. Rather than the exchange-of-concessions model presented by the FTA, the NAFTA financial services provisions present a model based on MFN and national treatment non-discrimination principles, albeit somewhat modified in the case of national treatment. As discussed in §8.7, the NAFTA financial services provisions do not provide a model for dealing with home versus host country supervisory issues that are addressed in some international arrangements dealing with financial services. The reservations in Sections B and C of Mexico's schedule to NAFTA Annex VII discussed in §8.5(5) present a model for the partial liberalization of a previously closed financial services sector.

(f) The parallel obligations model — standards, intellectual property protection and government procurement

The NAFTA negotiators intended from the beginning that NAFTA establish norms respecting standards, intellectual property protection and government procurement. At the time that NAFTA was being negotiated, the Uruguay Round agreements covering these areas (the 1994 GATT Technical Barriers Agreement, the GATT Sanitary and Phytosanitary Measures Agreement, the TRIPS Agreement and the 1994 Government Procurement Code) existed in draft form but were not finalized. The NAFTA negotiators used the draft agreements as precedents. If the WTO Agreement had been in effect when NAFTA was negotiated, the NAFTA negotiators could have incorporated these Uruguay Round agreements by reference and negotiated modifications or extended obligations.[10] The NAFTA negotiators could have incorporated these Uruguay Round agreements prospectively but incorporating agreements before they are finalized has its complications[11] and the NAFTA negotiators had no assurance at the time that the WTO Agreement would ever come into effect. The effect, however, of establishing self-contained NAFTA codes in these areas that will also be covered by the Uruguay Round agreements is that when the WTO Agreement becomes effective, each NAFTA country will have two parallel sets of obligations covering the same subject-matter but which differ in a number of respects.[12]

(g) NAFTA as a model of transparency and due process

As discussed in §11.1(2), any country complying with NAFTA requirements must ensure transparency in both the enactment and administration of a wide range of measures and must comply with substantive procedural requirements in such areas as customs laws, laws respecting the enforcement of intellectual property rights, laws respecting safeguard actions and antidumping and countervailing duty laws.

(h) The NAFTA antidumping and countervailing duty model

NAFTA carries forward the FTA model of panel review process for statutory amendments and final determinations without the FTA commitment to work out a better system. As absolute protection in the form of tariffs and quotas are phased out, contingent protection will be increasingly demanded by businesses threatened by imports. As discussed in §11.4(10)(b)(i), this has been the Mexican experience in recent years in antidumping and this form of contingent protection continues to be popular in both the United States and Canada. As trade barriers fall and import competition increases, authorities and businesses in other western hemisphere countries will doubtless discover the attractions of pursuing antidumping actions. The creative but limited approach provided by NAFTA is an inadequate long-term model for dealing with these issues. The CER Agreement, as amended in 1988 and discussed in §11.4(1), provides a better model by prohibiting antidumping actions and working towards harmonizing competition laws.

(i) NAFTA, the environment and labour

(i) The NAFTA text and the environment

The NAFTA drafters addressed environmental issues primarily through attempting to minimize, through exceptions and clarifications, the adverse impact of NAFTA trade disciplines on the ability of governments of NAFTA countries to enact and enforce environmental measures to protect their domestic environments. Global environmental issues were addressed through the provision discussed in §6.8(4) that several international environmental conventions prevail over NAFTA but not through general principles. Except for the minimal obligation imposed by NAFTA 1114, NAFTA does not address the pollution haven question discussed in §6.8(2).

(ii) The Environmental Cooperation Agreement

It became apparent during the approval process for NAFTA, particularly in the United States, that environmental groups have linked trade with environmental issues and will no longer react passively to proposed new trade agreements, particularly when developing countries are involved. The Environmental Cooperation Agreement resulting from the intervention of environmental groups addresses the pollution haven question from an enforcement perspective and results in the imposition of monetary sanctions on offending NAFTA countries. The Environmental Cooperation Agreement may not be the environmentalists' ideal solution but it does provide a model for approaching the pollution haven question and avoids creating yet another contingency protection regime which is the risk of the countervailing duty approach advocated by some.

(iii) The Labour Cooperation Agreement

Labour groups will continue to press labour issues in trade negotiations between developed and developing countries. The limited scope of the Labour Cooperation Agreement may not be the first choice of labour advocates for dealing with the perceived "unfair" advantage that developing countries may have through low wages and substandard labour standards. However, the extent, if any, to which developed countries should be dictating labour standards to developing countries is far from settled. The norms imposed by the Labour Cooperation Agreement, while falling well short of the aspirations of organized labour in the United States and Canada of creating a social charter, would probably be considered as unduly intrusive by many developing countries. The Labour Cooperation Agreement at least provides a working model for addressing these issues.

(2) Multilateralism for the Hemisphere?

When the Government of Mexico decided to initiate the negotiation of a free trade agreement with the United States, the Government of Canada was faced with the choice of standing by while the United States and Mexico negotiated a bilateral free trade agreement or requesting that it be included in the negotiations. The Canadian government perceived the development of a "hub-and-spoke" approach to free trade in the Americas, with the United States the hub and Canada, Mexico and other countries each as spokes as being contrary to its interests.[13] The United States as the hub, with preferred access to the markets of each of the "spoke" countries, would become the country of choice for investment. The United States and Mexico accepted Canada's participation and as a result, these three countries embarked on a multilateral as opposed to a bilateral approach to trade and investment relations with each other.

Given the evident desire in many western hemisphere countries to break down trade and investment barriers, is the extension of the multilateral NAFTA model throughout the hemisphere the best approach to follow? While a number of countries have expressed an interest in acceding to NAFTA, the future evolution of NAFTA is still an open question. There are already a number of existing trading arrangements among various western hemisphere countries, some of which are bilateral and a number of which are multilateral. The Latin American Free Trade Association ("LAFTA") came into existence in 1960 and was superseded in 1980 by the Latin American Integration Association ("LAIA", or "ALADI" to use the Spanish acronym). Argentina, Bolivia, Brazil, Chile, Columbia, Ecuador, Mexico, Paraguay, Peru, Uruguay and Venezuela were all signatories to the treaty creating ALADI.[14] The Andean Pact was formed in 1969 among Bolivia, Chile, Columbia, Ecuador and Peru as a regional integration agreement.[15] The Central American Common Market among the five Central American countries (Guatemala, El Salvador, Honduras, Nicaragua and Costa Rica) was created in 1961.[16] The Caribbean Community (CARICOM) was created in 1973 and is comprised of various Caribbean countries.[17] The Southern Cone Common Market (MERCOSUR) was created in 1991 among Argentina, Brazil, Paraguay and Uruguay with the objective of creating a free trade area among these countries by December 31, 1994.[18] In addition to the free trade agreement with Costa Rica and the G-3 agreement with Columbia and Venezuela discussed above, Mexico has entered into a free trade arrangement with Chile and is negotiating bilateral trade agreements with each of Honduras, El Salvador, Guatemala and Nicaragua.

There are obvious advantages to a single multilateral approach to trade liberalization as opposed to a proliferation of separate bilateral and multilateral arrangements. As a simple example, consider the position of a producer in Mexico who produces goods for export to the United States (a NAFTA country) and to Costa Rica (a country with a bilateral trade agreement with Mexico). Suppose that the specific rule of origin in both NAFTA and the Mexico/Costa Rica agreement provides for a change in tariff classification. For goods exported to the United States to benefit from tariff elimination, the producer may use Canadian, American or Mexican inputs that do not satisfy the required change but not Costa Rican inputs. For goods exported to Costa Rica, the producer may use Mexican or Costa Rican inputs that do not satisfy the required change but not Canadian or American inputs. Harmonizing the rules of origin between the two agreements does not help because the inputs considered as originating in applying the harmonized rule under each agreement will be different. If Costa Rica acceded to NAFTA, the producer could use the most advantageous combination of Canadian,

American, Mexican and Costa Rican inputs for goods exported to any of the United States, Costa Rica or Canada. With multiple overlapping arrangements, producers wishing to benefit from trade liberalization will have to satisfy multiple requirements for multiple markets. Rather than invoking the "hub and spoke" metaphor to describe the proliferation of trade arrangements being entered into throughout Latin America, a former senior U.S. trade negotiator recently described the end result of such a process as "spaghetti".[19]

The multilateral NAFTA model may expand throughout the western hemisphere. However, if this does occur it will take time. Despite its deficiencies, some in Latin America hold the view that ALADI, with its Latin American roots and its absence of U.S. domination, would be a more appropriate vehicle for trade liberalization among Latin American countries than NAFTA. The NAFTA countries themselves require breathing space to adjust to the new NAFTA rules and Mexico in particular will need time to establish the legal and procedural mechanisms necessary to fulfil its NAFTA obligations. The terms of NAFTA may contemplate accession but in a number of its structural aspects, NAFTA is not well suited to accommodating more members. The panel selection process in NAFTA Chapter Twenty is designed for three member countries and would require modification to accommodate four or five or more members. Amending the Uniform Regulations to respond to changing circumstances is going to be difficult enough with only three member countries. With four or five or more countries, amendments could be virtually impossible with the present *ad hoc* approach that NAFTA now provides. With respect to antidumping and countervailing duty matters, the United States was critical of the manner in which Canadian panelists under the FTA with similar common law backgrounds and no linguistic impediments applied U.S. principles of judicial review to final determinations of U.S. administrative agencies. This problem will become more acute with the different legal backgrounds of Mexicans sitting on binational panels and could result in severe strains on the process with persons from a number of countries judging the application of U.S. law in these matters. NAFTA will need substantial institutional modification if it is to serve as an effective multilateral vehicle for more than three countries.

A single co-ordinated approach to trade and investment liberalization in the western hemisphere would clearly be preferable to the creation of a patchwork quilt of overlapping but disconnected arrangements and NAFTA is probably the most suitable vehicle for achieving that objective. However, Latin American countries will have to be convinced that this approach is in their best interests. In the meantime, the three existing NAFTA countries should concentrate on resolving the problems in implementation that will inevitably arise and making NAFTA function effectively so that its benefits will be realized by all three NAFTA countries and the benefits of accession will be readily apparent to other countries.

12.3   CONSIDERATIONS FOR COUNTRIES CONTEMPLATING ACCESSION

Negotiators for countries considering acceding to NAFTA will have to be thoroughly familiar with the provisions of NAFTA and analyze their effect on policies that are considered essential to the national interest of their respective countries.

The starting point for analyzing the potential effect of NAFTA on policy options is to separate NAFTA provisions that have or will have matching GATT or WTO Agreement provisions from those that do not. For example, the NAFTA intellectual property provisions impose substantial constraints upon what a government can and cannot do in its intellectual property laws. However, governments of countries that are signatories of the WTO Agreement will be subject to many of the same constraints once the TRIPS Agreement becomes effective. The differences between the disciplines imposed by the TRIPS Agreement and those imposed by NAFTA Chapter Seventeen are matters of detail and not of broad principle. The same applies to sanitary and phytosanitary measures and standards-related measures. As discussed in Chapter 4, NAFTA incorporates a number of GATT provisions, in some cases (such as national treatment) without modification and in other cases (such as export controls) with modifications. In analyzing the impact of these provisions, the focus should be on the effect of the modifications. For example, the GATT prohibits export restrictions subject to a number of exceptions. NAFTA carries forward the same prohibition and the same exceptions but, as discussed in §4.3, disciplines the use of some of the exceptions. The analysis of the impact of the NAFTA export regime on policy options should focus on the impact of these disciplines. The analysis will be affected by exceptions to GATT obligations set out in an acceding country's protocol of accession to the GATT or exceptions from the strict application of GATT or WTO Agreement obligations that apply because an acceding country is a developing country. These exceptions will all be on the table in the negotiation of any NAFTA accession, as will eligibility for GSP treatment.

NAFTA clearly limits the policy options open to government. Tariff elimination means not only loss of revenue but also surrendering the option of protecting sensitive industries through tariffs from competitors in other NAFTA countries. An acceding country will have little choice but to consent to the elimination of tariffs on virtually all goods. Sensitive sectors can be protected in the short term through long tariff phase-out periods. In the long term, an acceding country will have to rely on safeguard remedies, which are subject to NAFTA disciplines and which come at a price, or antidumping or countervailing duties imposed within the GATT framework if it wishes to impose extraordinary duties. Duty drawback and duty deferral programs will have to be eliminated eventually. However, as has occurred in the case of Mexico, the elimination of these programs can be deferred for a relatively long period of time.

An acceding country will probably have little success in renegotiating the NAFTA rules of origin. An acceding country should analyze the effect of each specific rule on the goods that it produces. If a rule is regarded as problematic, an acceding country should negotiate a long phase-out period for tariffs on the goods affected. There is precedent for negotiating country specific rules of origin in NAFTA Annex 300-B for some textile and apparel goods traded between the United States and Mexico. However, the multiple origin rules for different countries would make the rules of origin more difficult to work with than they presently are and would defeat the benefits of the multilateral approach that NAFTA offers. Acceding countries should bear in mind that stringent rules of origin do not necessarily protect domestic industries because stringent rules can be satisfied with inputs originating in other member countries. Negotiating skills might be better expended elsewhere than trying to re-invent the NAFTA rules of origin. The one exception is in areas in which the existing NAFTA countries disagree on how the rules are to be applied. These situations will be fluid in an accession negotiation where existing NAFTA countries will be using the negotiations as a means for resolving their dispute.

Import restrictions and performance requirements maintained by an acceding country will all be open for negotiation in a NAFTA accession. An acceding country will be under considerable pressure to phase-out and eventually eliminate import substitution programs such as the Mexican Automotive Decree. It should be kept in mind, however, that the obligations imposed by the GATT TRIMS Agreement will necessitate substantial modifications if not the entire elimination of import substitution programs.[20]

Agriculture will be a particularly sensitive area for acceding countries. NAFTA Chapter Seven establishes a precedent for separate bilateral arrangements. If the Canada-Mexico model is followed, an acceding country would be able to shield its agricultural sector from NAFTA obligations. However, the Canada-U.S. and the Canada-Mexico agricultural arrangements are the result of particular circumstances surrounding several trade disputes that existed between Canada and the United States at the time that the NAFTA negotiations took place. The agricultural model most likely to be placed on the table in an accession negotiation is the U.S.-Mexico model which results in free trade in agricultural goods after a lengthy phase-in period. Assuming that the GATT Agricultural Agreement becomes effective as scheduled, the first step of the U.S.-Mexico model, namely, the tariffication of non-tariff barriers, will already have been completed.

The NAFTA investment, services and financial services obligations place substantial constraints on government policy and, in the case of the investment obligations, are backed up by the investor/state dispute settlement procedures described in §11.3. An acceding NAFTA country will likely find the basic obligations set out in NAFTA Chapters Eleven, Twelve and Fourteen virtually non-negotiable and will have to work within the system of reservations established in NAFTA Annexes I through to VII. Each reservation will have to be negotiated and will likely come at a price. Negotiators for acceding countries should carefully review the system of reservations established by NAFTA and the models for liberalization that have been established in various sectors. For example, an acceding country that has concerns about liberalizing its financial services sector should pay particular attention to the reservations taken and liberalization commitments negotiated by Mexico in its Schedule to NAFTA Annex VII.

Acceding countries will have to pay particular attention to the NAFTA government procurement provisions. While these provisions reflect for the most part the provisions of the 1994 GATT Government Procurement Code, none of the countries of Central or South America are signatories to this plurilateral agreement and none will be bound by it when it becomes effective. The NAFTA government procurement obligations are comprehensive and should be studied carefully by the negotiators for any country considering accession.

There is precedent in NAFTA for special exemptions for sensitive sectors. Mexico's energy sector is largely exempt from NAFTA disciplines. NAFTA disciplines do not apply as between Canada and the other NAFTA countries in so far as cultural industries are concerned. However, exemptions come at a price. Exemption of one sensitive sector will come at the price of shortened tariff elimination periods or accelerated liberalization commitments in other sectors.

Acceding countries should also carefully examine the Environmental Cooperation Agreement and the Labour Cooperation Agreement. These agreements were not just peculiar to Mexico. With each accession negotiation, there will be pressure from American and Canadian environmental and labour groups to expand the scope of these agreements. Pressure in the U.S. can be particularly effective because Congressional approval of an accession can never be taken for granted.

12.4 CONCLUSION

Canadians who were involved with the negotiation of the FTA probably did not suspect at the time that it would be in effect for five short years and be superseded by a much more comprehensive arrangement including Mexico. It took a measure of courage and foresight for the Mulroney government to join the NAFTA negotiations. The government was in the process of implementing its exceedingly unpopular goods and services tax and did not need nor want another free trade debate. The Chrétien government had the wisdom to bury its party's opposition to the FTA and proclaim into force the implementing legislation that the Mulroney government had passed. Canada preserved the preferred access to the U.S. market that it had achieved through the FTA. Canada also gained access to Mexico, a market that had previously been closed in large part to Canadian goods, at little cost to itself. Had Canada not joined NAFTA, Canadian producers would have been competing with Mexican producers for the U.S. market without the potential upside that access to the Mexican market offers.

NAFTA is a major foreign policy achievement for the United States and unequivocally beneficial to U.S. interests. Besides exchanging the elimination of low U.S. barriers to trade for high Mexican ones, NAFTA imposes a whole range of policy requirements on NAFTA countries that are congenial to U.S. interests. While some obligations to which Mexico has bound itself in NAFTA, such as those respecting intellectual property and standards, would have applied eventually under the Uruguay Round agreements, others, most notably the investment provisions, are NAFTA creations with U.S. roots. If NAFTA expands through accession, acceptance of these norms through binding treaty commitments with the United States could spread throughout the western hemisphere. The United States also preserved its antidumping and countervailing duty laws and procedures subject only to panel review.

Mexico has potentially the most to gain from NAFTA but also has the most to lose. Pre-NAFTA barriers to trade were much higher than those of either the United States or Canada. Industries such as auto parts were sheltered from import competition by import restrictions and from domestic competition from foreign firms by investment controls. NAFTA will eliminate import controls for virtually all industries and investment controls for most industries. Mexico is counting on NAFTA attracting significant direct foreign investment from the United States, Canada and other countries to offset the dislocation that will result during the period of adjustment. NAFTA is not the solution to Mexico's economic problems but is hopefully part of the solution.

The successful completion of NAFTA had a critical role in the conclusion of the Uruguay Round. NAFTA was signed when the Uruguay Round negotiations were in deadlock and was approved when the Uruguay Round negotiators were standing at the brink. The collapse of NAFTA could have precipitated the collapse of the Uruguay Round. It is unlikely that the collapse of the Uruguay Round would have simply meant a return to the *status quo ante*. Far from being rhetoric, the resolution in the NAFTA preamble that NAFTA provide a "catalyst to broader international cooperation" has real meaning.

Like any major international agreement, NAFTA represents a series of compromises among the negotiators and concessions to special interests. Compromises frequently result in needless complexity and the compromise solution often makes little sense other than as a means of obtaining agreement.[21] Concessions to special interests undermine the credibility of principles. NAFTA has its share of both compromise solutions and concessions. However, despite these, NAFTA establishes clear principles of non-discrimination that will break down barriers among its member countries. NAFTA also establishes minimum standards and principles of transparency and due process that will discipline government action and should assist in creating a more predictable business climate throughout its member countries. The FTA was a bilateral arrangement between Canada and the United States without broader ramifications. NAFTA is a potent regional force that will affect countries throughout the western hemisphere.

ENDNOTES

[1] In addition, NAFTA 2201 provides that the NAFTA annexes constitute an integral part of NAFTA and NAFTA 2206 provides that the English, French and Spanish texts of NAFTA are equally authentic.

[2] The U.S. North American Free Trade Implementation Act, H.R. 3450, 103rd Congress, 1st Session (1993), carries the text of NAFTA Chapter Four, with some modifications, into U.S. law. See section 202. A regulation carrying forward a trilaterally agreed upon amendment to the Uniform Regulations that was clearly inconsistent with the paraphrased NAFTA text set out in section 202 would be inconsistent with U.S. statute law and open to challenge as *ultra vires*. An example would be an amendment that changed a tariff shift requirement or dropped a regional value content requirement from a specific rule of origin. If the regulation was declared *ultra vires* by a domestic U.S. court and the governments of the other NAFTA countries did not agree to drop the amendment, the matter would ultimately be considered by a Chapter Twenty panel.

[3] For a discussion of the difficult subject of reservations and interpretative declarations, see Dr. Frank Horn, *Reservations and Interpretative Declarations to Multilateral Treaties* (The Hague, T.M.C. Asser Instituut, 1988).

[4] 19 U.S.C. (1988) §2112(e)(2)(A).

[5] *North American Free Trade Agreement Implementation Act*, S.C. 1993, c. 44, s. 3.

[6] The Canadian government did not issue a statement of implementation respecting the FTA.

[7] As discussed in §1.4(2), the European Union is a customs union and not a free trade area.

[8] The free trade agreement between Mexico and Costa Rica was signed on April 5, 1994, and is scheduled to take effect on January 1, 1995.

[9] The G-3 free trade agreement was signed on June 13, 1994, and is scheduled to take effect on January 1, 1995.

[10] This approach was adopted in FTA Chapter Thirteen (Government Procurement). The 1980 GATT Government Procurement Code was incorporated by reference and the provisions of FTA Chapter Thirteen covered procurements below the thresholds covered by the 1980 Code. If the 1980 Code thresholds were lowered, procurements above the new thresholds would have ceased being covered by the FTA provisions and would henceforth have fallen under the 1980 Code provisions.

[11] As Canada and the United States are finding with the provision in NAFTA 309, incorporating a provision equivalent to GATT Article XI in a successor agreement. See §5.3(7)(a).

[12] As discussed in §9.1(4), the 1994 GATT Government Procurement Code is a plurilateral (as opposed to multilateral) agreement to which Mexico is not a party. Therefore, unlike

Canada and the United States, Mexico will not be subject to a set of obligations parallel to those in NAFTA Chapter Ten when the 1994 GATT Government Procurement Code becomes effective.

[13] See Ronald J. Wonnacott, "Hemispheric Trade Liberalization: Is NAFTA on the Right Track" (Toronto, C.D. Howe Institute Commentary, No. 49, June 1993) for an analysis of the hub-and-spoke model.

[14] The treaty creating LAIA was signed in Montevideo on August 12, 1980. See Giovanni Peraza, "Latin America and Caribbean Institutions of Integration and Zones of Free Trade" (Occasional Papers in International Trade Law and Policy, No. 22, Centre for Trade Policy and Law, August 1991, Ottawa), at p. 22.

[15] *Ibid.*, at pp. 25-9. Chile withdrew in 1976.

[16] *Ibid.*, at pp. 29-31. Honduras ratified the treaty in 1962 and Costa Rica in 1963. For various historical reasons, Panama is not considered part of "Central America".

[17] *Ibid.*, at pp. 32-6.

[18] *Ibid.*, at pp. 37-8.

[19] Juluis Katz, Address (Empire Club, Toronto, May 2, 1994).

[20] See the Illustrative List of TRIMS that are inconsistent with the obligation of national treatment set out in the annex to the TRIMS Agreement.

[21] The rules of origin for automotive goods are a case in point.

GLOSSARY

AAA — *Agricultural Adjustment Act* (United States)
ALADI — Latin American Integration Association
Antidumping Code — *Agreement on Implementation of Article VI of the General Agreement on Tariffs and Trade* (Tokyo Round)
APTA — *Automotive Products Trade Act* (United States)
Auto Pact — *Agreement Concerning Automotive Products between the Government of Canada and the Government of the United States*
Automotive Decree — *Decree for Development and Modernization of the Automotive Industry* (Mexico)
Autotransportation Decree — *Decree for Development and Modernization of the Autotransportation Vehicle Manufacturing Industry* (Mexico)
Baie Comeau Policy — Baie Comeau Book Publishing Policy
Basle Committee — Committee on Banking Regulations and Supervisory Practices
BCCI — Bank of Credit and Commerce
Berne Convention — *Berne Convention for the Protection of Literary and Artistic Works, 1971*
BHCs — bank holding companies
Bilateral Agreement — Bilateral restraint agreement between the United States and Mexico
BITs — bilateral investment treaties
CAFE Rules — Corporate Average Fuel Economy regulations, established under the authority of the *Energy Policy and Conservation Act of 1975*, 42 U.S.C. §6201 *et seq.*
CARICOM — Caribbean Community
CAVCO — Canadian Audio-Visual Certification Office
CBCA — *Canada Business Corporations Act*
CDC — Canadian Dairy Commission
CDIC — Canada Development Investment Company
CER Agreement — *New Zealand Australia Closer Economic Relations-Trade Agreement*
CFE — Comisión Federal de Electricidad, the Mexican electric utility
CITT — Canadian International Trade Tribunal
Classification — Specific and General Regulation for the Direct Foreign

Investment based on the Mexican Classification of Economic Activities and Products

CMAP — Clasificación Mexicana de Actividades y Productos

Code Procurement — a procurement under the FTA to which the provisions of the 1980 Government Procurement Code apply because the value of the procurement exceeds the Code threshold

Code threshold — the monetary threshold for procurements of 130,000 SDR, above which the provisions of the 1980 Government Procurement Code apply

Commerce — International Trade Administration of the United States Department of Commerce

Commission — The Free Trade Commission established by NAFTA 2001 (see §11.1(1)(a))

Comprehensive Guide — Jon R. Johnson and Joel S. Schachter, *The Free Trade Agreement: A Comprehensive Guide* (Aurora, Canada Law Book Inc., 1988)

CPC — Central Product Classification

CPUC — California Public Utilities Commission

CRTC — Canadian Radio-Television and Telecommunications Commission

CVC — Customs Valuation Code, being the *Agreement on Implementation of Article VII of the General Agreement on Tariffs and Trade* (Tokyo Round)

CWB — Canadian Wheat Board

Deputy Minister — Deputy Minister of National Revenue for Customs and Excise (Canada)

Dispute Settlement Understanding — *Understanding on Rules and Procedures Governing the Settlement of Disputes* (Uruguay Round)

DSB — Dispute Settlement Body

Dunkel Draft or Dunkel Text — the text of the drafts of the Uruguay Round agreements released December 20, 1991 (see §1.4(1) and note 9 to Chapter 1)

EC — European Community or European Communities, now known as the European Union

EC Alcoholic Beverages Agreement — *Agreement between Canada and the European Economic Community concerning Trade and Commerce in Alcoholic Beverages*

ECC — Extraordinary Challenge Committee

ECE — Evaluation Committee of Experts

EEP — Export Enhancement Program

EIPA — *Export and Import Permits Act* (Canada)

Enhancement Act — *Foreign Bank Supervision Enhancement Act of 1991* (United States)

Environmental Cooperation Agreement — *North American Agreement on Environmental Cooperation*

ERA — Economic Regulatory Administration

EU — European Union

Exon Florio — Exon Florio Amendment

Extradition Treaty — *Treaty on Extradition between the Government of Canada and the Government of the United States of America*

FCNs — Friendship, Commerce and Navigation treaties

FERC — Federal Energy Regulatory Commission

Financial Services Commission — The Financial Services Committee established by NAFTA 1412 (see §8.6)

FIPAs — Foreign Investment Protection Agreements

Foreign Trade Law — Foreign Trade Act Implementing Article 131 of the Constitution of the United Mexican States

Foreign Trade Regulations — Regulation Covering Unfair Practices of International Commerce

FSC — Federal Supply Classification

FTA — Free Trade Agreement between Canada and the United States

FTA Procurement — a procurement under the FTA to which the FTA government procurement provisions applied because the value of the procurement was below the Code threshold but exceeded $25,000 (US) or its Canadian dollar equivalent

FTA Schedules — Schedules of Canada and the United States set out in FTA Annex 401.2

FTC — Federal Trade Commission

FTZ — foreign trade zone

GAAP — generally accepted accounting principles

GATS — *General Agreement on Trade in Services* (Uruguay Round)

GATT — *General Agreement on Tariffs and Trade*

GATT Agricultural Agreement — *Agreement on Agriculture* (Uruguay Round)

GATT Safeguard Agreement — *Agreement on Safeguards* (Uruguay Round)

GATT Sanitary and Phytosanitary Measures Agreement — *Agreement on the Application of Sanitary and Phytosanitary Measures* (Uruguay Round)

GATT Textile Agreement — *Agreement on Textiles and Clothing* (Uruguay Round)

GATT Textile Annex — Annex to the GATT Textile Agreement

GATT TRIMS Agreement — *Agreement on Trade-Related Investment Measures* (Uruguay Round)

GDP — Gross Domestic Product

Geneva Convention — *Geneva Convention for the Producers of Phonograms Against Unauthorized Duplication of their Phonograms, 1971*

GPT — General Preferential Tariff under the Canadian Customs Tariff

GSP — Generalized System of Preferences
GST — Canadian goods and services tax
G-3 Agreement — an agreement creating a free trade area entered into in 1994 by Mexico, Columbia and Venezuela
Harmonized System or HS — Harmonized commodity Description and Coding System
HTSUS — Harmonized Tariff System of the United States
IBA — *International Banking Act of 1978* (United States)
ICA — *Investment Canada Act*
ICSID — International Centre for the Settlement of Investment Disputes
ICSID Convention — *Convention on the Settlement of Investment Disputes between States and Nationals of other States*
IEA — International Energy Agency
IEP — *Agreement on an International Energy Program*
IMF Agreement — *Articles of Agreement of the International Monetary Fund*
in-quota quantity — the annual quantity of imports under a tariff rate quota, below which goods enter duty free or at a lower duty
in-quota tariff rate — the rate of duty that applies to goods entered within the in-quota quantity under a tariff rate quota
Integrated Circuits Treaty — *Treaty on Intellectual Property in Respect of Integrated Circuits*
Inter-American Convention — *Inter-American Convention on International Commercial Arbitration, 1975*
Interstate Banking Act — Riegle-Neal Interstate Banking and Branching Efficiency Act of 1994
ITC — United States International Trade Commission
ITO — International Trade Organization
Labour Cooperation Agreement — North American Agreement on Labour Cooperation
LAFTA — Latin American Free Trade Association
LAIA — Latin American Integration Association (the Spanish acronym is ALADI)
LCBO — Liquor Control Board of Ontario
LTA — Long Term Arrangement Regarding Cotton Textiles
maquiladora — Mexican in-bond manufacturing plans (see §2.3(1)(b)(i))
Marking Rules — the rules for determining whether a good is a "good of a Party" established under NAFTA Annex 311 (see §3.2(3))
MERCOSUR — Southern Cone Common Market
Mexican Investment Regulation — Regulation of the Law to Promote Mexican Investment and to Regulate Foreign Investment
Mexican Protocol — Protocol for the Accession of Mexico to the General Agreement on Tariffs and Trade
MFN — most-favoured-nation

MJDS — Multijurisdictional Disclosure System

Model BIT — Prototype BIT developed by the USTR

MOU — *Memorandum of Understanding as to Notification, Consultation and Cooperation with Respect to the Application of National Antitrust Laws*

MSQ — market sharing quota (a national production quota set by the CDC for Canadian milk production)

Multifibre Arrangement — *Arrangement Regarding International Trade in Textiles*

Multilateral Trade Agreements — the agreements in Annexes 1A, 1B and 1C of the WTO Agreement (see §1.4(1))

Mutual Legal Assistance Treaty — *Treaty between the Government of Canada and the Government of the United States of America on Mutual Legal Assistance in Criminal Matters*

NAFTA — North American Free Trade Agreement

NAFTA country — any of Canada, the United States or Mexico. The NAFTA text uses the expression "Party"

NAFTA Schedules — Schedule of Canada, a Schedule of the United States and Schedule of Mexico set out in NAFTA Annex 302.2

NAO — National Administrative Office

National Commission — National Commission on Foreign Investment

NEB — National Energy Board

NEP — National Energy Policy

New York Convention — *United Nations Convention on the Recognition and Enforcement of Foreign Arbitral Awards*, 1958

OAPEC — Organization of Arab Oil Exporting Countries

OECD — Organization for Economic Cooperation and Development

OSFI — Office of the Superintendent of Financial Institutions (Canada)

over-quota tariff rate — the rate of duty that applies to goods entered under a tariff rate quota once imports exceed the in-quota quantity

Paris Convention — *Paris Convention for the Protection of Industrial Property, 1967*

PEMEX or Pemex — Petroleos Mexicanos, the Mexican state petroleum company

Plurilateral Agreements — the agreements in Annex 4 of the WTO Agreement (see §1.4(1))

Pork case — *Fresh, Chilled and Frozen Pork from Canada* (see §11.4(5)(b))

PRC — Peoples Republic of China

Provincial Statement — *Provincial Statement of Intentions with Respect to Sales of Alcoholic Beverages by Provincial Marketing Agencies*

Protocol — *Protocol of Provisional Application* of the GATT

Rome Convention — *International Convention for the Protection of Performers, Producers of Phonograms and Broadcasting Organizations (1961)*

SDR — special drawing right, an international monetary unit created by the IMF Agreement (see §9.1(2))

SECOFI — Secretaría de Comercio y Fomonto Industrial (Mexican Secretariat of Commerce and Industrial Development)

Second Restatement — Restatement of the Law Second, Foreign Relations Law of the United States

SIC — Standard Industrial Classification

SIMA — *Special Import Measures Act* (Canada)

SL — Specific Limit

SME — square metre equivalent

Softwood Lumber case — *Certain Softwood Lumber Products from Canada* (see §11.4(5)(b))

STA — short term arrangement

Subsidies Code — *Agreement on the Interpretation and Application of Articles VI, XVI and XXIII of the General Agreement on Tariffs and Trade* (Tokyo Round)

Swine case — *Live Swine from Canada* (see §11.4(10)(h)(iii))

SYE — square yard equivalent

Tariff rate quota — a border measure that establishes an annual quantity of imports and provides that imports up to that quantity enter duty free or at a lower rate of duty and imports over that quantity enter at a higher rate of duty

Task Force Report — A Question of Balance: Report of the Task Force on the Canadian Magazine Industry

Third Restatement — Restatement of the Law Third, Foreign Relations Law of the United States

TMB — Textiles Monitoring Body

TPLs — tariff preference levels (see §5.3(2)(d))

TRIMS — trade-related investment measures

TRIPS Agreement — *Agreement on Trade-Related Aspects of Intellectual Property Rights* (Uruguay Round)

TRQs — tariff rate quotas (see §5.3(2)(d))

UNCITRAL — United Nations Commission on International Trade Law

UNCITRAL Arbitration Rules — Arbitration rules of the United Nations Commission on International Trade Law

UPOV Convention, 1978 — *International Convention for the Protection of New Varieties of Plants, 1978*

UPOV Convention, 1991 — *International Convention for the Protection of New Varieties of Plants, 1991*

Uruguay Round agreements — The WTO Agreement together with all the Multilateral Trade Agreements and Plurilateral Agreements listed in §1.4(1), the Dispute Settlement Understanding and the Trade Policy Review Mechanism, referred to collectively

UST — United States Tariff in the Canadian Customs Tariff

USTR — United States Trade Representative

VANp — Assembler's national value added from suppliers (Automotive Decree)

VANt — Assembler's total national value added (Automotive Decree)

VNM — Value of non-originating materials

WGTA — *Western Grain Transportation Act* (Canada)

WIPO — World Intellectual Property Organization

WTO — World Trade Organization

WTO Agreement — *Agreement Establishing the World Trade Organization* (Uruguay Round)

1980 Technical Barriers Agreement — *Agreement on Technical Barriers to Trade* (Tokyo Round)

1980 GATT Government Procurement Code or 1980 Code — *Agreement on Government Procurement* (Tokyo Round)

1994 Antidumping Code — *Agreement on Implementation of Article VI of the General Agreement on Tariffs and Trade 1994* (Uruguay Round)

1994 GATT Government Procurement or 1994 Code — *Agreement on Government Procurement* (Uruguay Round)

1994 GATT Technical Barriers Agreement — *Agreement on Technical Barriers to Trade* (Uruguay Round)

1994 Subsidies Code — *Agreement on Subsidies and Countervailing Measures* (Uruguay Round)

INDEX

AGRICULTURAL PRODUCTS — *Continued*
NAFTA provisions re — *Continued*
  country of origin — *Continued*
    changes to rules re, 183
    qualifying goods, 178
    tariff elimination, for, 178
  generally, 177
  trilateral or common bilateral provisions —
    changes to rules of origin, 183-4
    committee on agricultural trade, 183
    domestic support, 182
    export subsidies, 183
    grading and marketing standards, 184
    qualifying goods, 183
    voluntary restraint agreements, 184
orange juice, 197
peanuts and peanut products, 193
poultry and egg goods, 189
sugar and sugar-containing products, 193-7
tariff rate quotas —
  GATT agreements and, 185-6
  generally, 184-5
  safeguard provisions, 186-7
tariffication, 173-4
U.S. market restrictions —
  Agricultural Adjustment Act, 176
  Meat Import Act, 177
water. *See* WATER

AIR SERVICES. *See* RESERVATIONS, transportation

ALCOHOLIC BEVERAGES
discriminatory practices —
  Canada —
    listings, 213
    mark-ups, 213
    points of sale, 214
  U.S., 214
FTA provisions and, 215-16
GATT, complaints under re, 216
generally, 212
NAFTA provisions —
  beer, 218
  distinctive products, 217

PROFESSIONAL SERVICES
reservations re, 322-3

RESERVATIONS
energy and petrochemical goods —
  Canada, 314
  Mexico —
    cross-border services, 314
    electricity, 313
    generally, 203
    hydrocarbons, 311-13
    nuclear energy, 314
  U.S., 314-15
financial services. *See* FINANCIAL SERVICES, NAFTA provisions
foreigners exclusion clause, defined, 300-301
general structure of, 298-90
maritime activities —
  Canada, 321
  fisheries, 320
  Mexico, 321
  U.S., 320
NAFTA annexes —
  Annex I —
    Canadian reservations —
      corporate statutes, 304
      miscellaneous, 304-5
      state enterprises, 304
    generally, 300-301
    investment screening —
      Investment Canada Act, 301
      Mexican investment law, 302
      U.S. Exon Florio amendment, 302-3
    Mexican reservations —
      construction, 305
      duty deferral programs, 305
      entertainment and media, 306
      land ownership, 306
      mining, 305
      miscellaneous, 307
    U.S. reservations, 307
  Annex II —
    generally, 308
    sectors affected by, 309